Financial Geography

T0291222

Financial Geography is the only geographical reader explaining the intricacies of high finance from a global perspective at the turn of the millennium. It is a comprehensive presentation of institutional backgrounds, markets, products, actors and locations, a non-technical primer for future bankers and financial analysts, a keystone in the basic education of future executives.

This truly internationally focused book is as enjoyable to read as it is informative. All students and academics involved with economic geography as well as professionals in the banking and finance industries will find *Financial Geography* to be an indispensable book for their bookshelves.

Risto Laulajainen is Professor Emeritus at the Gothenburg School of Economics and Commercial Law, Sweden.

Routledge international studies in money and banking

Financial Geography
A banker's view

Risto Laulajainen

Routledge
Taylor & Francis Group

LONDON AND NEW YORK

First published 2003
by Routledge
2 Park Square, Milton Park, Abingdon, Oxfordshire OX14 4RN

Simultaneously published in the USA and Canada
by Routledge
711 Third Avenue, New York, NY 10017

First issued in paperback 2015

Routledge is an imprint of the Taylor and Francis Group, an informa business

British Library Cataloguing in Publication Data
A catalogue record for this book is available from the British Library

Library of Congress Cataloging in Publication Data
Laulajainen, Risto.
   Financial geography : a banker's view / Risto Laulajainen
      p. cm. — (Routledge international studies in money and
   banking ; 25)
   Includes bibliographical references and index.
   1. Capital market. 2. International finance. 3. International
business enterprises. 4. Financial institutions. 5. Foreign exchange
rates. I. Title. II. Series.

   HG4523.L38 2003
   332'.042–dc21   2003043206

ISBN 13: 978-1-138-81113-3 (pbk)
ISBN 13: 978-0-415-27870-6 (hbk)

Contents

Figures

Tables

Preface

The first edition of *Financial Geography* was printed in March 1998 as part of a series from the Department of Human and Economic Geography, Gothenburg School of Economics and Commercial Law, Sweden, and was intended for undergraduates. It was subsequently translated into Chinese and published by the Communist Press, Beijing. It is deeply gratifying that another recognized publisher with corresponding distribution capabilities has now included this edition in its series. The current edition has been partially rewritten to reflect the change in the financial world. Material published in languages other than English has been extensively sourced, to give balance to the narration.

The aim of this book is to provide the reader with a general treatise on international finance. Domestic issues are taken up only when they profoundly influence international affairs. This worldwide approach places heavy requirements on data and the effort would have been positively impossible without the groundwork laid by international organizations, business companies and financial journalists. The numerous publications of the Bank for International Settlements (BIS), Berne, the equally numerous trade magazines of Euromoney Institutional Investor Plc, London, the penetrating analyses of the Schweizerische Rückversicherung (Swiss Re), Zürich and the worldwide news reach of the *Financial Times* have been the key pillars on which the effort has been built; all the more so because most sources were made available free of charge or at heavily discounted academic rates. Several other organizations also provided the same level of assistance and acknowledgement is made when appropriate.

The author's roots are in economic geography and business administration, whereas this book also covers banking and national statistics, institutional funds and payment systems, among others. The going was at times quite rough and without the advice and support from Jesper Wormstrup at BIS, Rainer Köhler at IMF, Guido Boller at Schweizerische Nationalbank, Christian Schmidt at Swiss Re, and Denis J. Peters at Euroclear, in particular, the manuscript might never have seen the light of day.

The wealth of numerical material notwithstanding, the book is not a reference volume. Financial markets change too rapidly for that. There is also a limit on how well one person can follow the field all over the world. Therefore, the aim has been constrained to provide a framework and outline proportions, nothing more.

Much information is given in thematic maps (Figures). The advantage of maps over tables is that they give a holistic idea at a glance. Maps are the language of geography in the same way as Greek symbols and formulas are the hallmark of mathematics, notes of music, and miniature models of architecture. The extensive use of graphical representation emphasizes the need to stay faithful to one's roots. Basic familiarity with place names and their localization is assumed.

The economic support of the Foundation for Economic Research in West Sweden is gratefully acknowledged.

Risto Laulajainen
Professor Emeritus
Hovås, 31 December 2002

1   Introduction

Durant le même temps les problèmes bancaires de chaque jour se classaient d'eux mêmes dans une perspective géographique.

Jean Labasse (1955: 1), about his early banking years

Finances in geography

The scope

Financial instruments are fundamentally promises. This can be easily seen by considering the money which we use in our daily life. It contains an implicit promise. A $100 note is understood to be good for buying goods and services worth that much. It is formally backed by a certain amount of gold, or treasury bills and bonds, or the government's declaration that it is a legal tender. But at closer look, gold does not have too many practical uses, treasury paper is only another type of promise, and government fiat is good only as long as the government has the power to enforce it. Promises are fluid. They can (and hopefully will) be kept, but they can also be broken. The breach can be open, as when the government declares that it will delay interest payment and amortization of its debt. Or it can be disguised, as when it covers a budget deficit by using the printing press and thereby debases the money, with which it later redeems its paper. And still, government the government generally considered a good risk, a baseline from which other risks are calculated. When we know this and realize that a financial system is actually a pile of promises, although organized, we also understand that it can occasionally collapse if left unattended. To call it a house of cards may be too extreme, but it certainly resembles more a bamboo structure than a concrete construction.

Promises are immaterial. They have no physical weight and an amount of $1bn can be transferred as easily as of $1,000. That has created an idea that the friction of distance does not matter, or it matters very little. And when it matters, it is primarily because of the human administrative framework where everything must take place. The importance of that framework is obvious. But it does not follow that if the framework did not exist there would be no friction and that would be, as one provocative author expressed it, 'the end of geography'. There would be enough friction even thereafter. The most fundamental is the daily rhythm which means that working hours move geographically from east to west with the sun and financial activity with it. The rhythm cannot be rationalized away and its modification is possible only to a degree and at considerable cost – exchange late-hour trading, for example. Another reason is that people's informational radius is constrained and their ability to digest information possibly even more so. Each kilometre added to the radius means that there will be a disproportional increase in information volume, a simple geometric truth in a uniform landscape. Then there is the cultural dimension, the way things are done 'here', made visible in people's behavioural preferences. It is not easy to convince a German entrepreneur that s/he should disclose internal information for the doubtful benefit of getting the firm listed at an exchange and making it vulnerable to a hostile takeover; or that a Japanese public servant should take away his/her benevolent hand from the company and leave it unprotected to the storms of market forces. When things are so, it is better to accept the facts and admit that geography, indeed, matters. This book will show how in more detail.

Specifically, this book is a general presentation of international financial markets from a geographical angle. For shortness and convenience it is titled *Financial Geography*. The focus is on the financial community, not on welfare economics. To emphasize this, the subtitle, *A Banker's View* is added. The book is intended as a primer for people looking for a career in international business. The career need not be in banking and finances. Rather, the idea is that international finance is an integral part of the education of a modern executive. The liberalization and deregulation of financial systems have made the financial world more volatile and influential than ever before since the Second World War. This also makes it imperative for a future manager and executive in manufacturing, retailing and non-financial services to be familiar with financial basics. That package is traditionally offered by specialized financial classes and the tradition will certainly prevail in the foreseeable future. This dominance does not mean, however, that other disciplines have nothing to contribute.

Mathematics has been a prime example of such a contribution with the creation of modern portfolio theory and the spreading of derivatives trading. Political science puts the daily hurdles and technological advances into a wider context, reflected in country credit ratings, for example. General economics advises on how political priorities can be conciliated with economic realities. Commercial law lays the foundations of regulatory frameworks. Social anthropology sheds light on the selection mechanism of business partners and the cultural clashes arising from mergers and acquisitions. And because everything takes place in a two-dimensional, limited space called the globe, geographers believe that they also have something to contribute.

Financial writing is not commonplace in economic geography. Most geographers are interested in tangible things, and money, in the modern sense, is very intangible. The intangibility easily gives the impression that the friction of distance, the core of geography, will be marginal at best. And when the friction of distance is lost, the discipline also loses most of its foundations. This opinion implicitly assumes that the financial landscape is homogeneous. If it were homogeneous, the logic might hold, but the real financial landscape is not homogeneous at all. It is extremely heterogeneous and full of anomalies. This feature creates flows which otherwise would not exist, and it creates the need to explain.

This book is aimed at the simplest descriptive and explanatory level. It unravels where the financial resources are, describes the actors moving them around, and explains what the underlying infrastructure looks like. It maps markets, their organization, location and clustering into finance centres. The mechanics and terminology of the financial world are explained in some detail for those who are unfamiliar with them. The angle is international and global. National topics are of interest only when they are reflected in the international arena.

Although descriptive, the book is not easy reading. It is full of facts, often detailed facts. Details simply are important. When a $500m issue is placed in thirty minutes, some detail cannot be overlooked. Two per cent reserve requirement at the central bank or 30 per cent withholding tax can have devastating effect. Insisting that a large trade be made public immediately rather than after ninety minutes in a quote-driven exchange means that market makers start deserting the place. The money is in the small print. Details are also an indirect warning against simplistic explanations. The number of banks is a typical case: it is used frequently and very indiscriminately in academic writing as an indicator of a finance centre.

The somewhat monotonous figures easily confuse. That comes from the nature of the topic: it is a description of an entire industry and the comparatively few rich countries operate in a number of guises. But the purpose is not simply to offer a wealth of facts; these get rapidly outdated. This book also helps the reader to look in the right direction for additional information and guidance, and it puts details into a context, gives them perspective and establishes a benchmark against which specialized studies can be projected.

Still more fundamentally, the book promotes geography as a scientific discipline in financial writing. The geographical angle can be conveniently summarized in three slogans:

- spatial differences,
- processes in space,
- spatial interaction.

The setting is familiar, the applications less so. Between-country differences in minimum reserve requirements, assets under management and equity ownership obviously come under the first heading. The expansion and contraction of bank networks, or screen-based continuous auction systems at exchanges and the acceptance of mutual investment funds in various countries typify processes in space. Observed and inferred financial flows between countries, the operation of payment systems, and exchanges offering broadly similar contracts jointly or in competition over extensive areas are all examples of spatial interaction.

Financial markets comprise money, credit and capital markets (Figure 1.1). Financial instruments with maturities of twelve months and less belong to money markets, while longer maturities split into credit and capital markets. These longer maturities often lead to physical investment. Money markets have got their name from the need of banks to balance books each day by trading short-term financial instruments against cash, and the efforts of the central bank to regulate the monetary stock through the sale and purchase of short-term bills. Credit markets need the intermediation of banks, that is, they are loan markets. Capital markets may benefit from temporary intermediation but basically the contact is direct, between borrowers and lenders. The traditional products are bonds and shares, i.e. securities, which are issued in the primary market and traded in the secondary market. Nowadays they are paralleled by derivatives, which are originally instruments for risk management but which in certain circumstances can substitute securities.

Previous work

Reviewing previous financial research with geographical interest is like travelling an ocean in a row boat. One sees a vast area of water, more from the wave crest than the valley, but one knows that only a very tiny part is

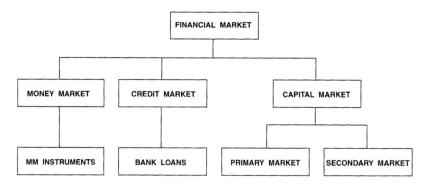

Figure 1.1 Financial markets.

Source: Die Zürcher Börse, *eine Einführung in den Börsenhandel*, 1997: 14. Copyright © 1997 of Zürcher Börse; used with permission.

within the horizon. Then there is the sky, high and equally without boundaries, with ample space for thoughts to rove and fantasy to gallop. It is where the conceptualizers thrive. This vastness should now be compressed on a few pages into a comprehensive account where everybody who happens to open this volume will find his/her work amply quoted. Such an achievement is impossible and, rather than trying to be comprehensive, this review is selective. From among a very limited array of familiar sources those are quoted which seem relevant for this study and its approach. A conscious effort has been made to ensure that the various aspects would receive a balanced treatment, a feature which need not exist within the available material. There is also another policy, to comment on work which is not published in English. Although English is the undisputed *lingua franca* of financial writing of our time, everything is not available in it and there is innovative work in other cultures, too.

A natural starting point is to consider existing reviews about financial writing in geography. Three widely known treatises are available: Corbridge and Thrift (1994), Leyshon (1995; 1997) and Martin (1999). Corbridge and Thrift outline how geopolitics have shaped the financial world, whereas Martin describes the birth of a new subdiscipline. Leyshon adopts a more philosophical attitude which may give a better background for a thoroughly empirical and practical book. The account was published in two parts with a lengthy interval.

In the first part, Leyshon (1995) focuses on political economy approaches and divides the field into geopolitics, geoeconomics and financial exclusion. The geopolitical part penetrates the smokescreens of liberal, egalitarian, socialist, or whatever ideas are routinely used to hide the underlying power politics. It helps in understanding the current financial system and gives hints about its sustainability. Since systemic shifts carry with them grave risks, while also offering unusual opportunities, the prognostic abilities of geopolitics should not be underestimated. Geoeconomics is a step closer to the operational level. The geopolitical situation is accepted and attention turned to investment portfolios, credit flows, preferred currencies and cultural surroundings constraining and shaping basic economic forces. These are topics extensively discussed by economists and financial analysts. Their inclusion in geography may be controversial, although in line with the approach of this book. The final part, financial exclusion, is more familiar ground. It states basically that poor people and poor countries cannot expect financial services on a commercial basis, or at least they are priced higher than otherwise. Where a limited savings generating capability nevertheless exists, grassroot activity leads to self-help in the shape of credit cooperatives and similar. Historically, they are the reborn savings banks and agricultural credit cooperatives, which in some quarters may have lost their roots and become part of the establishment.

The second part (Leyshon 1997) is about multiple monies, monetary networks and finance centres. The section on multiple monies is largely a historical and socioanthropological account of the many shapes which money has taken and the uses to which it has been put. Monetary networks have a heavy philosophical tilt. Although certain geographical properties are quoted, such as the territory in which specific monetary forms may be used, social and anthropological views, again, get the upper hand. The last part about finance centres is more tangible. The perspective continues to be social and cultural, but there is no denying that the persistence of these centres relies heavily on social factors. Then there is the need to build trust, best established through face-to-face contact, which in turn benefits from co-location in the same centre. This is an example of 'monetary' networks and specifically an actor-based one. Central bankers, meeting regularly at the Bank for International Settlements (BIS) to discuss common regulatory issues, would have been another example.

The prevailing political scene and philosophy is quite fundamental for the financial world and, by extension, financial writing. It is worthwhile, therefore, to be acquainted with it in broad outline. This has been the theme of Helleiner (1993; 1995) and Leyshon and Thrift (1992; 1995a) who, in four admirable articles, map the world after the Second World War, as well as partially covering the interwar period. Helleiner identifies five characteristics for financial dominance: leading creditor controlled by public institutions, banks dominating international markets, prime cities occupying the top slots of financial hierarchy and the national currency playing a global role. The global scene and Japan's role therein are described with emphasis on euromarkets, the attempts to constrain them and the triumph of rampant financial liberalism in the 1980s. The conflicting interests and power relations of the three major players, the USA, the EU and Japan, are sharply illustrated. Leyshon and Thrift focus on Europe and see its integration as a solution to the collapse of Bretton Woods, a system which either ignored or was unable to control capital formation at multinational corporations. Nor was it constructed to withstand the eroding effect of US monetary expansion because all currencies were ultimately tied to the dollar. The solution to the developing crisis was to create the EMU which also dethroned the deutschmark as the local benchmark currency. That takes us to the role of money as a measure of value, storage of wealth and vehicle of exchange, so elegantly discussed by Cohen (1998), gratifyingly from a geographical perspective. There the issues are the territorial reach of a currency, its possible sharing of sovereignty, its place in the global monetary hierarchy and the gain or loss of power emanating therefrom.

These high-level presentations can then be sharpened by specialized studies, such as Ackrill and Hannah (2001), Chernow (1990), Gall *et al.* (1995), Karyotis (1999), King (1991), Kynaston (2001), Reid (1988), Robins (1987) and Rogge (1997), to mention only a few. Their actual theme is a bank or a city, not the political background, but they show the interconnection between the operational level and the high politics.

The political game as such would not have created today's global finances without novel thinking and novel technology. Corresponding accounts are legion and the following are mentioned only to give a taste of the soup. Häusler (2002) looks at how banks have got disintermediated since the mid-1980s, and how they responded by diversifying offerings and expanding geographically. The diversification was greatly facilitated by scientific advances about portfolio theory, market efficiency, risk transformation through derivatives and so on, combined with the revolutionary enhancement of computing capabilities (Huang and Litzenberger 1998). Spatial expansion was speeded up through the development of communication technology, well observed in geographical writing (Code 1991; Hepworth 1991; Kellerman 2002; Langdale 1985). The technology is needed for the distribution of information, trading and the subsequent transfer of money and securities. Trading itself is difficult to observe from the outside but the deals can be registered without too much effort. They have remained in the realm of financial economists because most of the relevant questions have a pronounced time dimension. Where geographers could have made a serious contribution, but have not, is in payment and settlement systems. They are numerous, specialized to a degree, contain a substantial systemic risk and are full of time–space geography. (Davis *et al.* 1986; Fry *et al.* 1999; Geiger 1995; Giddy *et al.* 1993; Heller 1995; Johnson *et al.* 1998; Laulajainen and Johansson 2000; Lührig and Spremann 1995; Vital 1995)

An immensely popular monograph published a decade ago raised the issue of whether advances in communication technology and the dismantling of regulatory boundaries have made geography, i.e., distance, redundant as an explanatory paradigm (O'Brien 1992). It was a very good question and has catalysed much research. The foremost query then is, what kind and how much regulation? No exhaustive answer can be given but must involve the specific customs of the particular country, including the formal legal system, regulation based on it for banking, currency, exchanges, accounting and so on, and customs of the trade. This framework, and its efficient enforcement, has relevance far beyond financial dealings and may be a condition for economic development at large (de Soto 2001). A lucid introduction with good historical grip is provided by Economides *et al.* (1986), although at too general a level for practical needs. That shortcoming is amply remedied by the six volumes of international law authored by Wood (Stoakes 1995). The legal systems of the world are divided from financial perspective into seven main groups, six with origins in Europe and Islam's *sharia* as the 'outlier'. The criteria used are security (collateral), insolvency setoff, recognition of trust, notification of debt assignment, veil of incorporation and corporate rehabilitation. The litmus test is their status at bankruptcy (Wood 1995a; 1995b). This is assuring academically but even related legal systems are, in practice, incommensurable. The USA and UK offer a prime example (Stoakes

1999a; 1999b). Euroland may have come furthest in conciliating and con-solidating different systems but even it has a long way to go.

Administrative rulings based on existing law logically lag behind the law-making itself (Blumer 1996; Laulajainen 2000; Mikdashi 1998). To speed matters up, interested parties have created their own codes of conduct. The codification of bank capital adequacy under the auspices of the Bank for International Settlements has been epoque-making. It was preceded by accounting rules, supported by professional associations, and sanctioned and promoted by the authorities. International codification is still half-way, which is a constant nuisance to practitioners (Banque de France 2000: 122; Berton 1999; Frankel and Lee 1996; Vortmüller 2001; Waters 1996). Accounting rules are hardly commented on in geographical literature, although they are a keystone of all financial markets. They are reflected in the valuation of companies and their credit ratings, carried further to the international scene when investors compare investment objects in different countries (Laulajainen 1999). Company ratings are constrained by country ratings and here the geographical angle comes prominently to the fore (Chambers 1997; Huhne 1996). The geographical profession has been more interested in describing the structure of inter-national service companies, particularly in accounting and law. (Beaver-stock 1996; Daniels *et al.* 1989; Warf and Wije 1991)

When we approach the financial markets proper, their structure becomes relevant. It is common knowledge that the US and UK financial markets were structured around securities markets some five decades earlier than markets in Europe and Japan. Satisfied with this observation, geographical research has contented itself in discussing the general pros and cons, but not bothered about measurement – with one exception. Yasenovsky (2000a; 2000b; 2000c) has, in three seminal articles, done exactly this. He sees the banking, or financial, culture as an expression of the general development of the country, its habits and traditions (central-ization, authoritarianism), moral values (the protection of the small man, for example), globalization (securitization), spread of innovations, histor-ical development (usury rules, for example), and banking legislation (Glass–Steagall, for example). From this he develops a typology based on the role of the central bank, the system's openness, competitiveness, inno-vativeness and volatility. The main types are: Anglo-American, with its commercial/investment bank dichotomy; German, with its universal banks; Latin American; Asian conglomerate system; Offshore; and Islamic. When countries are allocated between the types, India and New Zealand end up in the Anglo-American group, whereas Argentina and Australia fall in the German one. China, Japan and Korea form the Asian group and the Latin group comprises only Brazil and Mexico. In other words, there are numerous countries which are not handled at all. The classifica-tion of countries by bond markets is a natural extension, although by dif-ferent criteria: type of issuer (government, banks, corporations), maturity range, and various other characteristics, a strikingly professional set. The typology derived is simple (using our own terminology): Anglo-American with Japan and France, the Continent with Canada and Australia, emerging economies, and laggards.

Market structure takes us to banking studies in general. Since banks are the primary financial intermediaries, they have been extensively discussed, at both the macro and micro levels. At the macro or country level, banking structure is important because it influences international competitiveness. It is discussed in a vast array of academic treatises, some partially outdated but offering evolutionary perspective (Ali 1996; Bicker 1996; Edwards and Fischer 1994; Gardener and Molyneux 1993; Hayes and Hubbard 1990; Kaufman 1992; Kilgus and Hirszowicz 1992; Klebaner 1990; Lévy-Leboyer 1995; Robins 1987). A timely alternative for them are the Yearbooks and Country Supplements published by the *Euromoney* magazine and supported by banking data in the International Financial Statistics by IMF (mostly domestic; Grubel 1989) and the Quarterly Reviews by BIS (international; Wooldridge 2002). Domestic banking is typically an areal activity and data about it apply to the country as a whole. International banking, by contrast, is concentrated in the largest cities and small offshore territories allowing the tie-up of country data with a particular city, except in the very largest countries (O'hUallacháin 1994; de Prati 1998; Vortmüller 2001).

Two aspects of banking have distinct geographical features: office networks and their expansion abroad. Both have been popular topics among economists and geographers alike, and have in practice often merged (Brealey and Kaplanis 1994; Choi *et al.* 1986; 2002; Dahm and Green 1995; Goldberg and Johnson 1990; Goldberg and Saunders 1980; 1981; Haga 1997; 1999; 2002; ter Hart and Piersma 1990; Hultman and McGee 1990; Reed 1981; Tickell 1994; Wright and Liesch 1995; Yamori 1998). For economists, it has been the traditional FDI while geographers have searched for a hierarchical structure and then used banks and banking as indicators of a finance centre. Economists, faithful to their aggregate tradition, have normally handled the question from the angle of commercial banks alone, overlooking the special needs of investment and private banks, the numerical minority. Nor have they paid much numerical attention to the stages in which entry to a market normally takes place (Heinkel and Levi 1992; Tickell 1994). Expansion by cross-border merger is a specialized sector, difficult in the sense that administrative and cultural factors in the shape of varying accounting rules, ownership structures and relative bank sizes need to be accounted for (Buch and DeLong 2002). Haga (2002) may have gone furthest in the handling of global structures in office networks.

At the micro level, the clustering of bank headquarters into the largest cities is well established (for example, Ahnström 1973; Goodwin 1965; Semple 1973). The strength of foreign relations reflects headquarter locations (O'hUallacháin 1994). Regional centre hierarchies have been identified with the help of bank offices and their functions (Jöns and Klagge 1997; Klimanov and Lavrov 1995; Labasse 1955; 1974). Geographical bias is possible in large countries. The application of regulatory constraints reflects cultural and historical pasts, and influences through them the areal expansion of office networks followed by restructuring (Lord 1987; 1992; Lord and Lynds 1984).

When it comes to bank operations, such as lending, advising in mergers and acquisitions (M&A), underwriting, trading and custodianship, geographical writing is mostly from a more recent time. Asset management is an exception, to be discussed below. Custodianship is practically virgin territory. Its difficulty originates from the many activities which must be conciliated: technical, in transferring and storing data; legal, in wrangling with authorities; financial, in giving customer guarantees; and economic, in finding acceptable outsourcing solutions. Geographers have touched the last of these, although more in the form of back-office operations in general than in a financial context (Dicken 1998: 396–398). Work on cross-border lending appears to belong to the economist's fiefdom (for example, Alworth and Andresen 1992; de Brouwer 2001; Haindl 1991; McCauley *et al.* 2002). Of course, the field is inherently economic and, in addition, plagued by the shortage of O/D flow data. Outflows and inflows may be known, but their interaction is not. Turner (1991) provides a useful overview on available possibilities whereas Martin (1994) describes a vignette about the 1980s with a particular emphasis on euromarkets. But one swallow does not make a summer and the relative neglect by geographers is unfortunate because static data about deposits, loans, customers and maturities has, by now, worldwide coverage and often also a respectable time perspective (Martin 1994). Warf and Cox (1996) come closest to the topic in analysing the spatial outcome of the US savings bank crisis. That was a domestic, not international, affair but was repeated in many other countries with more devastating results. Cross-border M&A is explained by Green and Meyer (1997) but from a general angle, not the role of bankers in facilitating the deals. Budd (1999) gives a professional overview on the trading of equities, derivatives and currencies, nicely completed by cases concerning interest swaps by Australian banks (Agnes 2000), M&A advising, loan syndication and equity trading in/from Frankfurt versus London (Grote *et al.* 2002), and forex dealing in Singapore (Langdale 2001). Yet, it is the economists who have identified distance decay and other geographical biases in investment and trading, primarily of equity but also of money in the form of discount rates (Calomiris and Schweikart 1991; Grinblatt and Keloharju 2001; Hau 2001a; 2001b; Sarkissian and Schill 2001). Databases for such analyses are seldom available in published form but at least exchanges have been generous in making detailed data available on request. The topic is hot in Europe, where the consolidation of exchanges is looming, yet very little has been written about it by geographers (Laulajainen 2001; Power 2001). From a wider perspective, the transfer of trading from the exchange floor to the screen has meant that, given administrative consent, the activity has got detached from its physical location (Budd 1999; Committee on the Global Financial System 2001). The comprehensive discussion by Lee (1998) offers a good starting point to the field.

Banking networks contain the most conspicuous elements of spatial theory for financial dealings found by the author (Bernet 1995; Spremann 1995). The key word is 'topology', the science of relations in space. In banking, topology is about the location of units and their tie-up into a system. The key issues are the location of the operative centre, the number and location of distribution units, the split between production and distribution activities, the identification of production functions to be centralized and of distribution functions to be dispersed. Because banks have many activities, there is no single answer, nor need the solutions be compatible with each other.

Production in banking is about information and communication. Its management comprises of planning, steering and control, and the goals are costs, quality, flexibility and security. Production topology revolves around production depth and outsourcing, the latter involving security aspects and becoming easily irreversible when competencies are lost. The three conventional types are: the island model, where every geographical unit has complete production functions, centralized information excluded; the factory model, where all operational functions are centralized; and the service centre model, where operational functions are outsourced and only planning remains. Direct production costs decline in this order, whereas transaction and agency costs increase. The factory model is potentially inflexible. The correct choice depends on competition, available technology and its price, and quality of available staff. As an example, Swiss Bank Corporation was organized regionally until the end of 1993, customer service after the island model and other production functions moving towards the factory model (Zimmermann 1998). The 1994 reorganization then introduced customer segments at home, and risk and product segments abroad. Outsourcing has always been part of operations, in the shape of correspondent banking and custodianship for example, but has gained pace with the escalating cost of information technology. These are important questions with great geographical potential and the interested reader should consult Ehlern (1997) for further applications.

The location of funds is a widely discussed geographical topic. The overall questions are: which kind of fund and how are the fundamentals? That is, do income levels and fiscal policies make funds possible and attractive? Some countries encourage the emergence of funds, and particularly private funds, but many countries do not. It may be a purely ideological question; pension funds with beneficiary contributions are tantamount to social inequality, along with the necessity governments feel to finance budget deficits with the help of high-interest, low-tax treasury paper which vacuum clean available savings. Insurance funds are a corollary of insurance because of the time lag between the payment of premiums and damages. But there is also a grey zone because life policies often contain a savings element and offer an alternative to pension funds. Finding the locations where conditions are propitious for the existence of funds, pension, investment and insurance, is a task as much for economics and political science as geography (Bachmann 1976; Clark 1998; 2000; 2003). That is the macro, country level. At the micro level, several studies from the USA testify that investment funds can be found all over the country, although they thrive best in large cities (Graves 1998; Green 1993; Green and Meyer 1992). The popularity of various types of fund has changed but there has been no dramatic geographical shift in the locational pattern.

Pension, investment and insurance funds are collectively known as 'institutional investors'. When the beneficiaries are small investors, the funds are subject to strict rules in their investing, about maturity, geography, object and concentration, in the way banks are in terms of lending. But when the circle of beneficiaries become small, rules are relaxed, and when funds are domiciled offshore there may be practically no rules at all, the realm of hedge funds and private bankers. The basic asset allocation philosophies have been analysed in numerous studies (Blattner *et al.* 1996; de Brouwer 2001; Ehlern 1997; Schierenbeck 1998; Tsatsaronis 2000). Distance decay and geographical bias have been identified, guided by currency domains and information asymmetries (Ahearne *et al.* 2002; Clark and Wójcik 2002; Cohen 1998; Green 1993; Kerr Christoffersen and Sarkissian 2001; Portes and Rey 2001).

Research on banking networks, commented upon above, has normally the identification of a finance centre hierarchy as its objective. There is no doubt that banks are an important, perhaps the most important, formal element in the birth of a finance centre. But to them must be added securities houses, exchanges, fund managers, insurance companies and a host of support services such as accountants, lawyers, information vendors, printers and so on. It is logical to rank the centres by the number of bank headquarters, foreign offices, banking and insurance assets, exchange market capitalizations and trading volumes, and seek reasons for their relative advance and retreat. But the final step, consolidating these data into one ranking index, has proved problematic (Blattner *et al.* 1996; Blumer 1996; Covill 1999; Dahm and Green 1995; Daniels 1993; Davis 1990; Davis and Latter 1989; Goldberg *et al.* 1988; Häuser *et al.* 1990; Labasse 1974; Lee and Schmidt-Marwede 1993; Leyshon and Thrift 1992; Peet 1992; Reed 1981; Sassen 1991: 168–191; Scholtens 1992; Thrift 1987; Thrift and Leyshon 1994). Surveys, asking respondents to rank centres by given criteria, to be collapsed into comprehensive scores by centre, give more promise but are difficult to administer (e.g. Abraham *et al.* 1993; Binde-mann 1999). Therefore, the hierarchy or at least ranking is often found with the help of bank offices or using one's judgement. Case studies about major finance centres and their comparisons are then a valuable data source, and they can originate from trade press as well as the academic world (e.g. Bank of England 1999: 10–16; Barber 2002; Budd 1999; Cobham 1992; Currie 2000; Fairlamb 1999; Häuser *et al.* 1990; Handley 1998; ter Hart and Piersma 1990; Holtfrerich 1999; Rahul 2001; Shirreff 1999; Simon 2000; Wong and Leahy 2001). Countries where two compara-tively equal centres are struggling for supremacy, Australia, Canada and Spain, make exciting real-life laboratories (Code 1991; Kerr 1965; O'Brien 1992; Porteous 1995; 1999).

The major finance centres are flanked by subsidiary, some might say parasitic, centres which thrive on the spillover finance of nearby main hubs and attract business through low taxes, lenient regulation and strict secrecy. Because many are islands or political enclaves, they often go under the label 'offshore'. There is hardly a true centre hierarchy and the explanation is excessive specialization, the result of scale economies in a narrow sector and smallness of labour pool unable to support a range of financial services. Numerous excellent overall presentations are available (Crisell 1995; Hampton 1994; 1996; Hudson 1999; Johns and LeMarchant 1993; Park and Zwick 1985; Roberts 1994) as well as a wealth of case studies (such as Cobb 2001; Crisell 2002; Peagam 1989; Roberts 1995; Sele 1995; Ungefehr 1987–1990; Warf 2002). To genuine offshore centres can be added the offshore sections of major onshore centres, some formal, others informal. Euromarkets are the largest and most colourful informal sector and attract much commentary (for example, Chernow 1990; Haindl 1991; Hampton 1996; Rogge 1997; Sele 1995).

Insurance is part of the financial world because of its fund-generating ability and, more marginally, because conventional insurance lacks the ability to fully cover the risks it intends to and must in emergency come to financial markets to fill the gap. In other words, insurance is not a central theme of this book but rather a world of its own. That does not mean, however, that it should be ignored by geographers writing about finances to the extent as has been the case. Among geographical treatises known to the author, van Rietbergen's (1999) groundbreaking monograph about Euro-pean insurance stands head and shoulders above other contributions. It can be rounded out by an insight into *takaful*, the Islamic variant (Rakiya 1999: 6–10). Then there are scattered articles (Leyshon and Thrift 1995b; Palm 1971; van Rietbergen 1994). And yet, insurance is full of geography, best understood by browsing the issues of *sigma*™, the popularizing research series of the Swiss Reinsurance Company. Particularly property and casualty insurance, dealing with earthquakes, windstorms, avalanches, marine safety, crop failures and traffic accidents unites the two halves of geography: eco-nomic and physical; a unison about which much is talked but little done.

The bulk of geographical writing about finance and money consists of sectoral contributions. These take a comparatively narrow segment and penetrate it at varying depth. Most writing is of article length which sets its restrictions. The field at large has become popular only since the late 1980s. Before that, geographical contributions used to come from economists and were often connected with foreign trade. There were good reasons for such a state of affairs, such as the shortage of in-depth information about many segments. Financial statistics were normally available by country or, in large countries, by state/province. Internationally, the situation was better, although not good. Reference has already been made in this chapter to the shortage of flow data, but the available origin and destination data were also quite rudimentary before the early 1970s. It was only after exchange controls were dismantled, rates started fluctuating, and financial markets in general were liberated that there was any great need to collect and publish large amounts of data. Nor was there much academic incentive to discuss a heavily regulated and seemingly static industry. Euromarkets were still too new and esoteric to arouse much interest. Moreover, they were heavily localized in London and therefore probably unknown to many geographers. Stated simply, the field is still too new for the emergence of comprehensive geographical treatises.

Against this background it is all the more noteworthy that the discipline can produce a scholar who was decades ahead of his time, Jean Labasse. His professional life started with a bank job in Lyon, which gave insight into practical banking, access to normally confidential local databases and permitted a successful survey of momentous size. The result was a PhD thesis in 1955 about the financial geography of the Lyon region. It describes the development of banking networks, the trade areas of bank offices, the financial links of urban centres, the varying administrative shapes of banking, banks in the urban morphology, their dependence on and support of the regional economy, its monetary stock, financial cycles, deposit-generating capacity and bank lending. The monograph paved the way for two parallel careers in Paris, as president of a large private bank and a university professor in urban planning.

The former job catalysed in 1974 a comprehensive volume covering most of the financial field, nationally and internationally. The expansion of banking networks, urban financial morphology, the national and international hierarchies of finance centres, regional payment balances, deposit generating capabilities and financial spheres of major cities are familiar themes from the earlier work, but are now elaborated with the help of numerous cases from all over France, many foreign countries and even globally. There is a rare discussion of global financial markets with eurodollar flows, the intermediary role of finance centres, including those offshore, exchanges, foreign investment, and cross-border bank claims. It was an amazing scholarly achievement and, as can be expected from a bank president, a very solid, professional treatise about a world preceding ours.

The decades which have elapsed have, understandably, rendered much of the detail as outdated. More recent and voluminous cross-border data have become available and modern structures have come to replace those known to Labasse. But principles do not change so easily, and much of the groundwork laid by him is intact. This fact, in combination with the depth and wide coverage of his monographs, still makes them very worthwhile reading for a serious student of financial geography.

Fortunately enough, the tradition has not been allowed to die, although the very considerable time lag may have created that impression. Linge and Schamp (1993) give a short but essentially comprehensive overview of global finances in the 1980s. Lucia's (1999) contribution has the same approach but, being of book size, offers much more detail. The treatment is systematic and analytical with an ambition for geographical synthesis. In the tradition of Labasse (1974), the principles are illumin-ated by numerous examples from Italy.

Setting the scene

Alternative approaches

Labasse's work essentially triggered off this book, although there were also other stimulants. Among them was the class looking at London as an international finance centre which the author occasionally delivered to second-year undergraduates. It could not be based directly on Labasse, as many facts had to be updated to the late 1980s/early 1990s and elabo-rated, so that students could relate the underlying philosophy of inter-national finance to their field trip to London. The angle was pronouncedly British and inevitably the author's curiosity was aroused to see what Americans and Japanese thought about similar issues. This linked well with his ongoing corporate studies where acquisitions and mergers played an important role.

Within academia, monetary economics and financial matters in general had enhanced their status and student headcount by leaps and bounds. Then came a flood of media exposure about financial achievements and failures during the vibrant 1980s. Exciting as these developments were, they often left a layperson in the dark. The terminology was unfamiliar, the monetary amounts unusual in their size and fluidity, and alleged threats of catastrophic risks looming beyond the horizon created an atmo-sphere of insecurity. Symptomatic was the student who, after the fall of Barings Bank, came to ask whether the global financial system was now about to collapse. There was obviously a basic educational need. Here also was an opportunity to take geography to a realm which was less well explored than the traditional ones: resources, manufacturing, retailing and transportation. The stage was thus set for writing a book.

Alternative approaches were available. The book could be a research monograph (Porteous 1995), focus on a particular segment such as banking (Bicker 1996; Gardener and Molyneux 1993; Klebaner 1990), exchanges (Diamond and Kollar 1989), fund management (Kay *et al.* 1994), or it could be an overall presentation (Bennett 1980; Cobham 1992; Labasse 1974). It could penetrate the financial system of a single country (Edwards and Fisher 1994; Lucia 1999; Robins 1987) or take an international or even global angle (Labasse 1974). It could content itself with a temporal cross section or take a longitudinal view. It could pick up details from the operational level or stay among central bankers and finance ministers. Each approach could be motivated by some criterion, fresh angle, scholarly excellence, practical need, data availability, scope of effort and so on.

The first decision was to have a global outlook. That is what the financial world is today: global, or at least international. Back in 1980, few investors, institutional or private, cared to put more than 5 per cent of their money into foreign securities. Today, 15 per cent is quite usual, and in many, small wealthy countries it is 30 per cent and more. Forecasts are unanimous that this share will increase. Of course, there are national barriers and idiosyncrasies at work recommending that even a global study should not leave the national markets out of sight. Global finances are also fascinating, much more so than national ones, because of their size and variety. This was an important aspect when launching a project that would last for a prolonged period of time. The romance should not fade away during the years of hard work.

The global view represents the geographical dimension. It is paralleled by the functional dimension, the disaggregation of the market by segment. When the purpose is holistic understanding, and the choice is a global rather than a national focus, it is natural that many rather than one or a few segments should be included. This is also motivated by the numerous links which tie them together: derivatives cannot exist without the underlying cash market. Companies issue equity when their price/earnings ratio is high and bonds when interest rates are low. Banks prefer fee-earning business when regulators enforce higher capital ratios for conventional lending. And so on.

Choosing a global and holistic angle inevitably leads to a certain shallowness in treatment. It is impossible to be well informed about everything that goes on all over the world. And the change is rapid. Details which were valid when the book was started have become outdated before it was finished. The solution has been to take a general approach to the latest facts and preferably to see facts as expressions of general trends which run at different speeds and in different phases in various parts of the world. It is also difficult to generalize on a worldwide scale. Things may look similar but have different driving forces. Or problems have got solutions which are essentially different but which cannot be ranked without very fundamental assumptions about the future. Pension systems based on funded monies or out-of-pocket contributions are a typical example. Many times there are no rational explanations, just habits and traditions. Why is the Anglo-American financial system market-based but the Continental system bank-based, for example?

The sheer size of the effort has led to a rather static study. It means that the second task of geography, the study of spatial processes, is mostly ruled out. This is deplorable, but the inclusion of a time dimension would have easily doubled the volume of the book. That was beyond practical possibilities. There are occasional references to the past and some speculation about events to come, but that is not the main theme of the study. The main theme is an overall description and explanation of the world as it was recently and as it is today.

The treatment moves primarily on the operative, i.e. executive, and higher levels but excludes the moulding of financial policies by central bankers and politicians. The daily routine is overlooked unless it contributes essentially to the higher levels. Exchange trading systems are a practical example. The operative level is what the young people, for whom this book is written, target in the first place. It is about the way markets function and how financial institutions are run, and is believed to be a comparative novelty in geography. The higher levels, the geographical, institutional and regulatory environments, are more familiar ground and necessary for the sake of perspective. The chosen emphasis has guided the data sources used.

Data mountain

The most relevant, accessible and up-to-date information about the operative level is available in trade magazines and academic journals targeting applications rather than theoretical issues. Foremost among them are *Euromoney* and the *Financial Times*, which have been screened for relevant material since 1987. Their Special Surveys, in particular, offered a wealth of information in compressed space. Within the insurance sector, *sigma*™ has constituted the keystone since 1987. It is actually a company (Swiss Re) publication but fully comparable with a high-quality academic series. These basic sources were complemented by the latest issues of *The Banker, Corporate Finance, Global Investor, Global Reinsurance, Institutional Investor* and *Reactions*. Geographical journals occasionally contain financial articles, as explained above. July/August 2002 was adopted as the approximate deadline for integrating new information.

The said publications are written for practising executives, managers and officers. They discuss topics which are important and current, although sometimes slightly speculative. In addition to the executive and analyst view, they contain volumes of hard-to-get numerical data. Important financial segments, such as fund management and global custody, are covered only by private data vendors, and their statistics are routinely quoted in the said journals. Many of the original statistics were also access-ible on a complimentary basis.

A shortcoming is that topics are not necessarily covered regularly. Those not subject to stress and offering no 'scoops' are ignored for more newsworthy material. Typical is the attention paid recently to global custody and banking secrecy, while syndicated bank lending has been in comparative shadow. Another, although latent, weakness, is that most of these journals are edited in Europe and necessarily reflect the European view. Of course, Europe is awash with money and full of variation. It is close and familiar, and therefore easy to understand. Were it not so, geog-raphy would have lost its significance. But Europe is only one-third to one-quarter of the financial world and myopia is a deadly sin. Other continents are definitely not overlooked but topics which are important to Europeans get a disproportionate amount of space. For the sake of balance, it would have been valuable to be able to also follow the *Wall Street Journal, Nihon Keizai Shimbun* and *The American Banker*, for example. Available resources, time and money, did not permit this.

Sources offering background information for executive decisions came mainly from supranational organizations, central banks and organized exchanges. The best data about international banking and international fixed income are probably available from the Bank for International Set-tlements (BIS), a cooperative forum for the central banks of practically all the countries and territories which really matter in international finance. One practical conclusion has been the discontinuation of OECD's *Finan-cial Market Trends* and the transfer of its financial statistics to BIS publica-tions as from 1996. In addition to quarterly statistics about bank claims, debt, equity and OTC derivatives, BIS conducts periodic and *ad hoc* surveys, among which the three-yearly derivatives and foreign exchange survey is renowned.

International Financial Statistics by the International Monetary Fund (IMF) has excellent geographical coverage and contains reasonably detailed statistics about the balance sheets of financial institutions, where foreign assets and domestic deposits are also given separately. The time lag between the publishing time and the latest data, up to several years, can be a weakness. The World Bank and its subsidiary, the International Finance Corporation (IFC), are more oriented towards developing than industrialized countries, and their financial publications are predomin-antly about emerging markets.

Financial, banking and insurance statistics of individual countries often contain geographical breakdowns of selected topics. Interesting insights can be gained, for example, into the use of Bermuda by US reinsurers and the intermediary role of Swiss banks. The limitation of these sources is that they cannot be consolidated across borders but remain national in scope because the selected topics, geographical breakdowns and compil-ation principles tend to vary by country. There can be a substantial errors and omissions line, making it impossible to join the ends without seams, a problem familiar from international trade statistics.

Occasionally one is confronted by flow data of securities which are compiled by private interests. Investment banks such as Schroeder Salomon Smith Barney and Morgan Stanley are known to have worked along these lines, but the results are available only for customers. They also prepare analyses and updates about equity and bond markets, recent issuance and the maturity profile of outstandings, and calculate stock indices. Some of these publications are filed by libraries.

The best coverage of equities is normally available from stock exchanges. The issuance of equity is difficult, even impossible, without listing on an organized stock exchange and the bulk of trading is conducted there. Many exchanges also list private bonds to give them better credibility and may trade them in quantities exceeding those of equities. The Federation of Stock Exchanges (FIBV) has started compiling these data and made them available on its website. Derivatives exchanges release corresponding information, also to be compiled by the FIBV in the near future. The largest exchanges publish *Fact Books*, sometimes a source of geographically detailed information. So far things are excellent. Problems arise when exchanges are compared, because their instruments and statistical compilation principles differ, and activities overlap to some extent. This might constitute a serious problem in an analysis but can be largely overlooked here.

Then there are commercial directories strictly for reference purposes, about banks, asset managers, foreign exchange dealers, brokers, custodians, etc. They vary tremendously in comprehensiveness, quality and price. Their primary strength is the ability to offer a rapid overview. It can be extremely informative to browse the *Dow Jones Telerate Bank Register*, or *Banker's Almanac*, or *Evandale's Directory of World Underwriters*, or *Nelson's Directory of Investment Managers*. One rapidly gets the 'feel' about the magnitude of the field and its parts. But it can be dangerous to start an analysis from these sources without a prior understanding of the topical industry.

One way to gain that understanding is to make use of standard textbooks (Czinkota *et al.* 1994; Daniels and Radebaugh 1995; Giddy 1994; Hanink 1994; Mishkin and Eakins 1999; Ross *et al.* 2000). They explain the terminology, outline the general setting and have no need for journalistic dramatizing, which occasionally plagues academic writing. We hope to be able to join this league.

Organizing the book

For presentational purposes, the field must be organized, and in a book that means a number of chapters and subchapters. This implies that the narration is one-dimensional, that it has a logical beginning and a logical end. To an extent this also holds here. Environment, undoubtedly, is the topic to start with but where the end pole should be put is less clear. The exact path is also judgemental because complete conciliation of the possible angles – actor's, functional and instrumental – is impossible. Issuance and trading, for example, concern several financial instruments and are conducted by many actors. Topics branch into several directions and overlap each other. Banks locate comfortably adjacent to institutional investors, because both are institutions and have partially overlapping activities. Since both are important actors, their placing in a chapter about financial markets also appears natural. But banking is a very wide topic, and a case can be made for giving it a separate chapter. Derivatives are a reasonably coherent group but organizationally divided between exchanges and over-the-counter (OTC). Forex dealings can be seen from the actor's, that is, the bank's, angle but also as a part of financial markets. Exchanges are part of financial markets but, because of their formal organization and transparency, are preferably discussed in a chapter of their own. Payment is a particularly thorny issue, because it is an integral part of every financial transaction whether at exchanges or OTC, and consequently fits in almost everywhere.

It is rather arbitrary in which sequence these particular topics are taken up and to what extent they are kept together or disaggregated between chapters and subchapters. So, what will follow is one alternative of many. Whatever the solution, a certain repetition of the same topic in different contexts is unavoidable. Actor, functional and instrumental angles mix and blend into a web where it is more convenient to repeat some matters rather than make constant reference to other parts of the book.

Contrary to many introductory book chapters, we not only outline the field to be entered but also comment on the factual contents, 'results'. It is believed that this will facilitate the digestion of the main text, which is alien territory to many economic geographers.

Playground

The main body of the book is divided into six chapters. Chapter 1 paints a picture of the financial environment, the 'playground'. Financial assets, like all property, reflect accumulated savings, but financial assets differ from property in general by their abstract character and comparatively good liquidity. Liquidity is a valuable characteristic, because the owner is not hopelessly tied to a particular form of wealth but can normally escape by selling out. This positive feature must be juxtaposed with the susceptibility of financial assets to inflation, unless they happen to represent real values, which they sometimes do. In inflationary times people's willingness to possess financial assets is consequently less than otherwise.

The ability to accumulate savings and thereby financial assets varies greatly between countries and regions. The rift between the rich 'North' and poor 'South' has become proverbial. Its reasons are subject to some controversy. Social and international peace are clearly necessary conditions for widespread prosperity. Educational standards are important. Sound legal framework and vigorous enforcement are conducive. Some cultures appear to further wealth creation more than others. Members of Protestant churches often congratulate themselves on their good work ethics and thriftiness. But things do not stay still, and these qualifications may become diluted in some quarters while they emerge elsewhere. Wealth distribution can have a bearing. Societies which place great importance on the economic equality of their citizens seem to be less generative than those where individual initiative is allowed free rein. It is probably impossible to draw unambiguous causal links from these general ideas to the actual financial wealth of nations. It is equally impossible to be specific about the split of national wealth between financial and real assets, particularly as many financial assets reflect underlying real values. What is possible is to give an estimate of the size and type of financial assets in a country. This sets the stage.

Some economies save more than they can comfortably invest, while others must borrow from these surplus countries to meet part of their investment needs and sometimes consumption as well. There are thus sources and sinks, and flows from the former to the latter. Some flows purport physical investment, the renowned FDI, others portfolio investment, and the rest are flows between financial institutions, mostly of short duration. In line with the book's geographical mission, the possibility of describing the origins, destinations and character of the flows is investigated, a task inherently more difficult than the mapping of international trade flows, for example.

The financial world has become heavily institutionalized. Gone are the days when a narrow layer of wealthy individuals was the main source of capital for bonds and equities, when Lloyd's with its Names dominated maritime insurance, and when a bank account was the privilege of few. Two great wars, the power of organized labour and awakened social consciousness brought with them progressive taxation and the more equal distribution of national wealth. Public saving was enforced in the budget. Private saving in homes and pensions was encouraged by tax breaks. Investment funds unshackled captive bank clients and opened up to them the lucrative opportunities enjoyed by the mightiest of capitalists. The era of the institutional investor dawned. But their importance varies greatly between countries. Some encourage the funding of pension monies and small savings, while others resist it. Growing economies do not see problems in meeting future obligations from current earnings. Leftist ideology sees private pensions as counter-egalitarian, while rightist people detest compulsory ones. Investment funds are seen by many as vehicles prone to fraud and reckless speculation, and oppose them in the name of public interest and particularly the interest of the small investor.

Worry about the honesty and safety of financial markets has led to many types of regulation. Central banks are responsible for the soundness of money and the banking system. Financial markets at large are supervised by the appropriate ministry, the Ministry of Finance (Treasury), which usually delegates the operational work to special agencies. These can practise hands-on supervision or rely on the self-regulation of market practitioners. Regulatory stringency varies from free-wheeling offshore centres to tightly regulated Asia Pacific economies.

A particular form of regulation is accounting standards. Originally there was only the entrepreneurial self-interest to be aware of the standing and profitability of the firm for which its owners were fully responsible with all their property. When financial markets developed, the need to protect the interests of lenders and shareholders became important. Sound accounting practice was codified into law, and public companies were decreed to publish their accounts at least once a year. This was fine within a national economy, but when investment flows became international, interpretation became a problem. There are many ways to produce acceptable accounts, but once one alternative is chosen, comparability with others will suffer. International standardization is under way, but progress is slow and tedious.

Uniform accounting standards permit comparisons between companies and borrowers. This is welcomed by all investors, but professional investors like fund managers, making investment and divestment decisions daily and wanting to diversify their portfolios over a large number of script, find it impossible to analyse each potential security in detail. The choice of the most appropriate instruments becomes mechanical but also more rational, less personalized. The task is greatly facilitated if somebody has already done the groundwork in a consistent way. It is here that rating agencies come into play. Their ratings form the basis for lending and issuance, the availability and price of financial resources. Their networks encircle the globe, although the mesh is denser in established than in emerging markets.

Statutory regulation and accounting law are just two pieces of the legal system at large. If these two pieces vary across nations, the whole system is still more prone to do so. Some consolation is given by the fact that the origins are generally in Europe and thereby constrained by the Continent's legal heritage. This is divided into case law as practised in England and codified law as practised on the Continent, where, in addition, the tradition of Roman law differs from that of Germanic law. Nations wishing to join the mainstream of global finance have no choice but to adapt to the prevailing legal system. Chance has often decided which variant has been selected. The core of commercial law is the rule set regulating bankruptcies, defining the rights of creditors and protecting third parties in good faith. Another important structure is the concept of trust because of its ability to separate ownership from benefaction and the ensuing need to store and manage wealth. The variation in detail is great, and neither geographical proximity nor cultural kinship guarantees the similarity of principles.

Markets

The chapter about financial markets is the core of the book. Functionally, markets are divided into primary and secondary, i.e. issuance and trading, and organizationally into over-the-counter and organized exchanges (Figure 1.1). Issuance is tantamount to raising new capital, either equity capital or debt. It is the primary activity. The issue must be priced and sold (placed), an activity usually handled by financial intermediaries like banks and securities houses. Equity is issued for the remaining life of the company, while debt normally has a defined maturity. Some investors prefer to hold their purchase until maturity, while others sell it when circumstances change. This creates the secondary market or trading in the issue. Because nobody can be quite sure whether s/he is able to hold the issue until maturity, the existence of a secondary market will make the original purchase less risky and therefore more attractive. Logically, sophisticated authorities and regulators try to facilitate the emergence of secondary markets and supervise their smooth functioning.

Neither issuance nor trading need be tied to a specific location. Then the activity is said to take place over-the-counter (OTC) and much of it, indeed, follows this course. The advantages are relative freedom from rules and supervision and, therefore, lower cost and more flexibility. But there are disadvantages. The contracts take many forms and are therefore not as easily tradable (negotiable) as the standardized contracts available at exchanges. In other words, their liquidity is less. There is also the risk that the counterparty will fail to fulfil the contract. More fundamentally, the issuer of the security may itself be a poor bet, unable to service its debt, or pay dividends, or it may be ridden with corruption. In the OTC market, the investor or trader must evaluate these aspects, while an organized exchange sets conditions for listing and exercises control over honest trading. Its clearing house habitually also comes between sellers and buyers as a counterparty. In broad outline, equities, many private bonds and derivatives are listed at exchanges, but only equities are traded at them more or less exclusively. Derivatives and private bonds are split between exchanges and OTC, while public bonds are predominantly OTC.

The conventional financial instruments include bank loans, bonds, equity and derivatives. To them can be added the forex spot market. Bank loan is the traditional instrument, although ceding ground to securities. The reason is simple enough, securities are cheaper than bank loans when the borrower has a good credit rating. Banks' lending portfolios consequently shift towards the retail end of the market. But globally the picture is full of variation. There are banking-oriented countries and there are securities-oriented countries. Asia Pacific and the European Continent typify the first group while the English-speaking world belongs to the second one. The second group has a tendency to consider the first one underdeveloped. The first group pays in kind and finds the second one exposed to speculative disturbances. Both opinions have some substance, but fundamentally it is as much the result of varying cultural heritage and historical starting positions than anything else. Over and above the standard customer lending, one finds interbank business, which is mostly short-term but internationally important.

The bond market includes here traditional bonds and the more recent medium-term notes (MTN). MTNs differ from standard bonds by their average shorter maturity and, more importantly, in that they are normally tailored to suit the needs of investors rather than borrowers. Bond markets are mostly domestic, and the dominant issuer is usually the central government. Small sovereigns with large borrowing needs but limited domestic capital markets also come to the international market. Relatively speaking, however, the international market is the realm of banks with excellent credit standing. International issuance can take place in the country where the issue will be placed, in its currency and subject to its rules. But the issue can also be managed from a major finance centre and denominated in any convertible currency which is acceptable to the borrower and the market. The start was made in Europe with US dollars, which gave the name 'euro(dollar) market'. The label also includes appropriate bank loans and has become a generic name.

Equity differs from bonds by being issued only by business companies. A profitable, growing company normally seeks listing at a stock exchange, the topic of a separate chapter. Listing facilitates equity issues and probably raises the company's market value. Very large companies seek listing in several countries. The depth and intensity of equity markets varies by country. Reference was made above to 'cultural' factors, which all too often boil down to hard financial facts. In many countries with undeveloped equity investment, trading is expensive, insider control lax, minority protection weak and the free float small. After these shortcomings have been corrected, some time is needed to get the message home to investors.

Investment in equity is risky because company destinies fluctuate with the vagaries of economy, customer preferences and competitive action. Bonds are safer because most have fixed interest. But fixed interest changes shape when it is related to the bond's market price rather than its nominal value. The interest becomes yield and this fluctuates with the benchmark interest rate of the economy, and with the foreign exchange rate when the denomination is in foreign currency. Fortunately, an investor can hedge against the fluctuation with the help of derivatives. That is, there are speculators, often banks, who are willing to accept the risk against a fee. They promise to buy or sell something in the future (future/forward), or they grant a corresponding possibility (option). One can also exchange the payment flows of existing obligations (swap). As derivatives do not give ownership until exercised, they avoid some taxes. They entail less administrative work than equities and bonds, which gives lower trading fees. And a contract is bought for a modest down payment (gearing or leverage), which also encourages their use. It is still more attractive when the underlying instruments like equities can be replaced by an index which reflects their movements. Therefore, derivatives are welcomed by investors who wish to change their exposure often, rapidly and at low cost. The speed makes derivatives react more rapidly at times to market news and change in sentiment than the underlying securities.

The intensive fluctuation of exchange rates since the early 1970s opened the way for derivative contracts in forex. Established exchanges were slow to grasp the opportunity and banks took the lead keeping the market at large off exchange floors. The same applies to spot forex, which has always been in the hands of banks. Although the market lacks an exact location on the local scale, it is heavily concentrated internationally, organizationally and currencywise. The top five banks handle almost one-half of all forex trading and most of the deals are made in a handful of global finance centres. The US dollar, euro and yen are the dominant currencies. The dollar is also an important reserve currency and has, in addition, replaced, either by law or in practice, the national currency in several financially weak countries.

If forex is the glue which holds international markets together, the texture must still be equipped with systems for payment and delivery. The speed of the actual transmission is hardly an issue, it is a matter of seconds or minutes. The problems are in administrative routines, incompatible legal systems and the differences in office hours between time zones, leading to settlement lags counted in days. Since many transactions are large, the ensuing exposures have prompted intense development towards more efficient and robust clearing and settlement systems.

Exchanges

Much of the financial activity takes place in informal markets, over-the-counter. They can be very efficient in plain trading when the instrument is strictly standardized. The forex spot market is a typical case. Issuance is irrelevant, being the domain of central banks. One dollar note is as good as another (fungible), so the heterogeneity of the trading object does not play a role. When delivery is versus payment, there is no credit risk. The only element of uncertainty is the price of dollar in other currencies. When the market is concentrated and professional, consisting of banks and business companies, intermediation is minimal and trading inexpensive. The other end of the OTC spectrum is a financial product tailored to meet the specific needs of the customer. Then the attraction is not cost, liquidity or risk but in the qualitative aspects of the product. Somewhere in the middle of the spectrum we find organized exchanges.

The most obvious change which an organized exchange brings to the free-wheeling OTC market is that it gives a place and time where and when to trade. This has the very great advantage that demand and supply are concentrated, which in turn means that buyers and sellers have a better chance to find a counterparty and, presumably, get a better price more rapidly than otherwise. This phenomenon, loosely called liquidity, is the historical explanation of practically all exchanges, some of which can go back centuries. The external conditions could be most rudimentary and the obvious trading method was verbal communication, probably rather loud in the general bedlam, the open outcry of our times. The repeated gathering of many like-minded people furthered the dissemination of general market information, functioned as an informal credit rating agency and performed rudimentary supervision, all functions to be found at modern exchanges. Although the beginnings were often spontaneous, the need for regulation, creditworthiness and efficient price finding soon enforced a formal organization. Exchanges became exclusive clubs for members to trade, either on their own account or for customers against a commission.

Exchanges deal in objects whose quality is easy to standardize, called 'commodities'. Metals and many agricultural products fit the bill, and so do financials when suitably structured. It is helpful if the object can be easily stored and delivered, although physical delivery can be replaced by cash settlement. This holds for physical as well as financial commodities. The commoditization of financials does not yet mean that they are necessarily traded at exchanges – equity, if of sufficiently high quality, usually is, while bonds often are not. The simplest explanation is that rated bonds with a fixed interest are much easier to evaluate than shares and have less need for exchanges as a trading forum. Equities and bonds are the traditional financials, listed and traded at stock exchanges. They have been complemented during the past quarter of a century by futures and options, originally traded at separate derivatives exchanges. The reason for two sets of exchange was largely cultural. Early derivatives exchanges only added financials to agricultural and livestock products, while stock exchanges traded mostly spot and looked askance at the speculative element involved in derivatives.

The central task of an exchange is price finding. The historical method of open outcry on the trading floor has been largely replaced by electronic, screen-based trading because of its lower trading cost. It has numerous variations, but the basic distinction is between auction or order-driven markets and dealer or quote-driven markets. Which one is better depends on circumstances. The geographically important question, however, is to what extent electronic trading will sever the link between an exchange and its location. The evidence so far is inconclusive.

Liquidity is the magic word of an exchange. Good liquidity attracts trading and new listings, poor liquidity repels them. The result is a concentration of activity, first nationally and then internationally. Most exchanges get the majority of their business from domestic products. Logically, then, big countries have big exchanges, or usually one dominant exchange where both product categories, securities and derivatives, coexist as divisions. The exact size depends on the country's financial structure and tradition at large. There are countries where fair-sized companies are, as a rule, listed at exchanges, where trading is lively, and equity ownership widespread. And there are countries which are the exact opposite, where the financial life circulates around banks rather than exchanges. There, exchanges live in the comfortable certainty that sooner or later listed companies will expand the free float of their shares and state-owned and closely-held companies will seek listing. Where the opposite holds, expansion depends on the growth of domestic economy and the internationalization of stock ownership.

An exchange's internationalization has several aspects: its attractiveness for foreign investors and listings; the launching of products which are also competitive abroad; the extension of business hours to cover other time zones; and the forging of links with foreign exchanges. The attractiveness for foreign investors has aspects familiar from domestic dealings: the possibility of diversifying securities portfolios, price/earning ratios, trading costs, disclosure rules, taxation and so on. More foreign listings mean increased listing fees and trading and settlement commissions. Foreign companies, in turn, expect enhanced investor interest and a higher share price. To facilitate listing they have often repackaged their script into so-called depository receipts. Some world-class stock exchanges have been reasonably successful in attracting foreign companies and may in due course out-compete smaller national exchanges into oblivion. At derivatives exchanges, where company listings are no issue and where international interest in the underlying securities is widespread, competing products and links to other time zones have been tried out extensively, with varying results.

Banking

Markets are the collective concept for the opposing forces of buyers and sellers and, as such, are rather intangible. Their physical expression are formal exchanges, one half of the story. The other half are financial intermediaries, or simply banks. The person on the street knows banks as places to deposit and borrow money, have a cheque account, make payments and, less often, buy travel exchange and store valuables. Deposit taking and lending are, indeed, the most generally accepted characteristics of a bank all over the world. Payment, forex and custodian services are recognized but neither considered essential nor necessarily available at every office. This says indirectly that many things happen behind the opaque glass wall which separates the customer service area from the inner sanctum. It also suggests that banks have very varied product offerings, which ostensibly differentiate their competitive position, customers and geographical reach.

These products are typical of a retail bank servicing the general public and small companies. But they are not sufficient for a wholesale bank targeting large corporations and institutional investors who need help in issuing debt and equity, advice when merging with other companies, acquiring them, or defending themselves against unwelcome bids. They have assets which not only need the safety of a bank vault but also active management. These services, and the wholesale business in general, have a better chance to cross borders than the retail end of banking.

Since few organizations can excel simultaneously all over the scene, they specialize. Some are renowned for their ability to organize and place new issues, others prosper as merger and acquisition specialists, reliable asset managers, skilful forex traders or efficient custodians. The product roster may have a connection with an initial and fairly random advantage, or it may be a judicious response to a shifting environment, competition and ultimately profitability. Regional specialization, by contrast, tends to have more deterministic elements, geographical and cultural closeness, for example.

Culture and the historical past have moulded the organizational shape of banking. It is not just the split into retail and wholesale business, there are also other dimensions. A distinction is often made between securities-oriented and banking-oriented financial cultures. The invisible hand of market forces governs the former with banks acting as moderators, while in the latter banks assume the leading role, working either directly or through securities markets. The reasons for the difference are open to speculation, while the structure of the banking system may be traced to people's democratic traditions and their religious doctrines. Certain mores have been codified in the formal law, while others are embedded in the web of customs and are a part of good banking practice. Custom and law also discriminate between products. Some are in high demand, others languish and some are forbidden. The result is a varied global banking map.

Cross-border banking takes many forms. It may consist of simple correspondence connections, in the way agents further international trade. It may lead to the opening of representative offices and branches, then establishing subsidiaries in foreign countries, to negotiate deals, serve existing customers, solicit new ones, and benefit from a more remunerative and open environment. Foreign entry may also give access to skills and personal networks which are unavailable at home. The crucial questions are whether foreign entries should be restricted to the wholesale services, or whether it is preferable to go truly native and have a retail banking network also. The network need not be outrageously profitable as such, but it gives a source of funds which is both stable and in local currency. These are important advantages because wholesale funds, often available in sufficient volume only in the interbank market, are subject to rapid shifts in volume, interest rates and exchange rates. But retailing in an alien country is difficult and, in practice, cross-border banking is dominated by interbank flows.

Insurance

Insurance is a relative outlier in this book. It is not traditionally considered part of financial markets, although this view is changing. Premiums collected but not yet paid as claims need to be invested somewhere, and financial markets offer a flexible and usually profitable alternative. The capital available for insurance companies interacts with financial markets at large. When inadequacies are identified, like in the US catastrophe insurance, it is consoling to learn that the shortage falls within the daily variation of the national capital market. It is not the lack of money but rather how it can be attracted to provide insurance cover. At the retail end, banks have started selling simple insurance products at their tellers, the bancassurance.

Insurance is a typical 'rich man's industry' with a clear positive correlation between per capita income and per capita premiums. Over and above that comes a multitude of cultural and taxation-induced features. Because premiums must be invested, insurance is discouraged where religion sees interest on investment as immoral. Strong family ties act as a deterrent, since substituting insurance for family care is easily seen as a subtle form of negligence. Society at large may offer a basic safety, which makes insurance uninteresting. At the other end of the scale are societies which encourage insurance with an inbuilt savings element as a form of private pension planning. Tax breaks are the standard instrument to that end.

The great bulk of insurance is national, although insurers may be foreign-owned. National markets result from heavy regulation and local idiosyncrasies, which make it difficult for a foreigner to achieve synergies across markets. Regulation is eased only when domestic capacity is found insufficient or when the capacity to export insurance services exists. To give a feeling for various national settings, three important and internationally open markets are taken up as case studies: London, the USA and Bermuda.

London is the established international insurance centre, building on a 300-year tradition and the country's pre-First World War status as the international creditor and the home of the global trading currency. This exceptional perspective still gives London a competitive advantage as an organizer of international insurance, and particularly reinsurance, catastrophe, marine and aviation insurance. The risk capital is less British than it used to be, however, and the city is preferably an outpost for a multitude of foreign insurance companies, large and small, which want presence in a world-class hub.

The US market is, first and foremost, characterized by its size. But it is also characterized by its fragmentation, because the Constitution leaves insurance to state legislators. The result is fifty separate markets rather than one. Another curse is the heavy cross-subsidization of politically sensitive insurance objects as an entry ticket to attractive segments. When domestic companies decline, foreigners have an opportunity to step in their place. Another opportunity is catastrophe insurance. Domestic companies are reluctant to provide sufficient cover because of the heavy regional concentration of risks. Foreigners also used to insure health risks and professional malpractice, but the dramatically escalating damages granted by US courts have driven insurers, domestic as well as foreign, offshore.

The most renowned of the offshore insurance centres is Bermuda, a self-governing British dependency, which has capitalized on stifling US legislation and turmoil in London. In the mid-1980s, Bermuda caught London in international premium income and for a while threatened to replace it as the top international insurance centre. The island's barriers of comparative isolation and limited human resources were too high, however, and Bermudan companies have now established subsidiaries in London, to be where the action is.

A special segment of the Bermudan saga, and the internationalization of insurance at large, is that of captive insurers. They handle in-house insurance for companies and professional bodies in segments which are poorly served by commercial insurers. Most captives are located in low-tax territories with lenient regulation, although some US states, and Vermont in particular, have also succeeded in carving out a market niche.

Finance centres

Finally, it is time to start tying loose ends together. This happens in a chapter about finance centres. The topic is familiar to urban geographers wanting to rank centres or classify them into a global hierarchy. When functions assumed to reflect a city's rank, such as retailing, wholesaling, administration, retail banking, education and similar have been exhausted, and cities like New York and Los Angeles still cannot be differentiated into separate classes, it is customary to fall back on high-order financial functions. Bank headquarters with global charters and various exchanges are typical indicators.

While these suit as indicators, they tell little or nothing about fundamentals, the prerequisites and processes which raise one centre to prominence but are missing at another one. The issue is very fluid. It was long thought that a strong national economy and a healthy current account surplus were indispensable for a major finance centre. Most commentators probably had eighteenth-century Amsterdam and nineteenth-century London in mind. But then New York and Tokyo gained these characteristics for a while without, however, dominating the global financial scene in proportion to their inherent strength. There were obviously other forces at work, too. Regulation was among the key factors. It was originally scheduled for domestic needs and, although amended, was unable to cope with international issues. It had to be loosened and partially dismantled. London, which had lost the traditional advantages, also regulated the domestic market but allowed the international one a long leash. That was blatant free-riding, because the international sector was based on currencies from countries with far more stringent regulation and therefore vulnerable to London's competition. In the process, London could build on its still existing skill base and the network of the former Empire. It was helped by the globalization of financial dealings, which split the globe into three time zones, each of which needed a financial hub.

New York, London and Tokyo became the time zone hubs, but besides them a large number of national centres have been able to survive, often protected by legislation and administrative practice. Europe is a case in point. Another explanation is the uneven commoditization of financial products. A freely convertible currency or government bond of a major country is for all practical purposes a commodity which can be traded with equal ease anywhere, and trading, logically, gravitates towards the largest centres with best liquidity. Equities, by contrast, are closely linked with decisions made at corporate headquarters, which means that the best information is available locally. This gives national intermediaries and markets a competitive advantage and protects them.

The question is topical in Europe because of the monetary integration. London, Frankfurt and Paris are the main competitors, politically about taxation and the powers of the central bank, and commercially through their underlying economies, financial policies and financial skills. The competitive situation in Europe is well-structured with London in the top slot, whereas it is more opaque in Asia Pacific. Tokyo's fundamental supremacy is unquestioned for the time being, but it has been slow in exploiting available possibilities. This has opened the door for competing regional centres, Hongkong and Singapore in particular.

Hongkong and Singapore are actually examples of offshore finance centres, previously called tax havens. While any activity beyond domestic borders is formally offshore, a true offshore centre is something else. Its fundamental role is intermediation, the collection and redistribution of financial resources. In a way it is a bank, although in a territorial rather than a corporate sense. It can fill this role with a minimum of underlying national economy and a currency which is practically unknown beyond its borders. Many are, indeed, small islands or archipelagos. Their strength is a flexible and speedy administration, light regulation and an advantageous tax regime, all scaled to the needs of the international financial community. When skilled labour and modern infrastructure are also available, the territory has the potential to develop into a true management centre. When they are lacking, it will survive as a booking centre, 'mail box'. The foremost offshore centres compete with small countries in the size of their bank assets, funds under management, insurance premiums, exchange trading volume and similar. This product scope is possible only in the largest of them, however. The usual situation is specialization, into wholesale banking, private banking, bond issuance, fund management, reinsurance, captive insurance and so on.

Offshore centres fulfil a subsidiary role to national and global hubs. This puts good communications with the 'parent' at a premium and leads to clustering, islands and small principalities swarming around their larger neighbours. The phenomenon is well developed in Western Europe and the Caribbean but less so in Asia Pacific. There, tolerance towards such arrangements is less, less monies have been on the lookout for a safe haven and the political stability may have appeared shakier than in the Atlantic arena.

Now the stage has been set and we can proceed to a detailed discussion of the various topics.

2 Playground

Assets

Keeping track of magnitudes

This chapter provides the monetary and institutional background against which the subsequent chapters will be projected. A background is needed because the world to be unfolded is unfamiliar to most geographers. It is unfamiliar in concept and perhaps logic. It is certainly unfamiliar in size. A student surviving on an annual budget of $8,000 or a run-of-the-mill academic making $80,000 a year may have some difficulty in grasping the difference between $1bn and $2bn, or still worse, between $1bn and $1tr (bn = 10^9; tr = 10^{12}). To sense the difference it is useful to have a mental picture about the relations between million, billion and trillion. And to be able to be precise, expressions like 'sand grains on the beach' are not acceptable.

An exact image of one million, well-known to everybody, is a square metre of paper divided into minuscule one-square-millimetre rectangles. The total number, of course, is one million. That one million is a very large figure is rapidly revealed when one starts piercing the minuscule squares with a needle. The job is likely to take a month or so. One million will be the smallest monetary unit in this book. There will also be percentages and basis points (bp, 1/100th of a per cent), but they denote fractions not volumes. When we move to the billion size class, we take the square metre one thousand times. The image becomes a one-kilometre-long strip of one-square-metre paper sheets each filled with one million minuscule squares. Most volume figures in this book are in billions. The largest class is in terms of trillions. Now, the one-kilometre strip must be taken one thousand times, which makes the total area one-square-kilometre (about 0.39 square miles). For the sake of comparison, Hyde Park in London is about 2.6 sq. km and Central Park in New York about 3.4 sq. km. One trillion is already so large a figure that even in the world of finance only the largest countries and global markets have need of it. For example, the US financial assets were roughly $37tr, and the capitalization of global stock markets was of the same order at the end of the year 2000. An experienced reader does not mix them with $37bn, which was the size of Chilean pension assets, but a newcomer gets easily confused.

When volumes are recorded in other currencies than US dollars, extra caution is necessary. This applies first and foremost to yen, which fluctuated in the early 1990s, the period of some statistical information used here, within the range of 100–150 yen to a dollar. The conversion is not difficult but when one reads rapidly some noughts may disappear and unwelcome mistakes arise. Therefore, currencies are converted into US dollars if at all practicable. That is no panacea, of course, because the dollar has appreciated against most other currencies since the mid-1980s until early 2002.

Financial markets can exist only where the money is. 'Money' here means accumulated savings which are not already invested in fixed assets, unless their ownership is easily transferable in small standardized lots like shares and bonds. The first indicators of saving which we might look at when operating on a global scale are 'Gross Fixed Capital Formation' or 'Net Saving' (Table 2.1). The former is reasonably insensitive to short-term economic fortunes but does not account for the wear and tear of machinery, homes and infrastructure. The latter is more volatile and is preferably averaged over several years. Basically, however, both are annual rather than accumulated.

Two things stand out. The so-called Western countries trail Japan and other East Asia in their ability to generate savings. Their economies,

Table 2.1 Savings in selected economic regions, 2000

Country/region	Gross fixed capital formation		Net saving	
	$bn	(% of GDP)	$bn	(% of GDP)
United States	1,718	17	555	6
Argentina, Brazil and Chile	177	19	–	–
Euroland	1,266	21	463	8
Rest West Europe	427	18	153	7
Japan	1,233	26	47[1]	8[1]
Korea and Mexico	254	25	145	14
'South' Asia[2]	278	25	–	–
Hongkong, Singapore and Taiwan	137	36	–	–
China	390	36	–	–
Total	5,880	21.4	–	–

Sources: *IFS*, March 2002, Country tables; *National Accounts of OECD Countries*, Vol. 1, 1989–2000, Tables 1 and 4; *China Statistical Yearbook 2001*: Table 3 11; *Industry of Free China*, June 2001: Table A.5.

Notes
1 Year 1999.
2 'South' Asia includes India, Indonesia, Iran, Malaysia and Thailand.

reflecting savings already accumulated, are so large, however, that this compensates the modest saving propensity to a degree. Developing countries in general, omitted from the table, are a comparatively marginal force because of their low saving propensity and small economies. The weakness of these figures is that they lack the cumulative effect. Nor do they differentiate between the various shapes in which financial resources exist.

Accumulated savings, also called assets, are the basis of financial markets. Assets are an abstract concept which has a real-world counterpart in property. All property need not be based on savings, however, like a homestead given for free by the government, although most are. A large proportion of savings is invested in housing, probably more than in industrial plants. To the extent that homes are not mortgaged, these savings are lost to the financial world. Some savings go to agriculture in the form of land upgrading and reclamation. They also are largely lost to the world of finances. A similar fate may wait for savings which are invested in plant equipment. If the plant is family-owned, the chances are fair that the only outside capital employed is working capital. The company does not issue shares or bonds and its only link with financial markets is through the bank credit line. The family members naturally have private bank accounts, a part of their savings may be with life insurance policies and they have monies in investment funds, which promise a better return than bank deposits or government bonds. All are parts of the financial system. These examples state an important principle. Only assets which are in an easily transferable, and ideally in a non-material form, are part of the financial markets, the topic of this book.

Statistics to make the idea tangible are not directly available but must be compiled from various sources. The ensuing compilation is adequate for educational purposes but is of questionable analytical value. The reasons will become obvious as this chapter proceeds.

A straightforward database would be tax declarations. They would indicate the actual location of the owner, whether a physical or a legal person, and they would also minimize the danger of double counting. As the world is, however, zero-tax jurisdictions, tax evasion, tax exemptions and definitional inconsistencies make the idea impractical and recourse is made to more indirect sources. The main geographical disadvantage is that the jurisdiction where the census is taken need not correspond to the owner's domicile or the location where the actual management takes place. The actual data used here is of end-December 2000 or covers the year 2000. It has been collected mostly from countries with about $50bn or more of Gross Domestic Product (GDP) in 2000 or, occasionally, 1999 (*IFS* 2002). This simplification has saved resources without affecting the conclusions drawn.

Three asset classes

The compilation integrates three broad quantities, called here for simplicity, equity, debt and bank deposits. Equity is measured by its market value on the stock exchange. Unlisted companies escape the measurement. Equity belongs to company liabilities (towards its shareholders) and is found at the right-hand side of the balance sheet. So does corporate debt. Debt (bonds, notes, bills) issued by other entities like central and local governments, building societies and banks follow the same or similar accounting principles as corporate script. So do deposits at banks. Like debt, they belong to external liabilities and neatly round out the system. The seemingly attractive alternative of using bank assets or claims instead of deposits leads to double counting, because loans are made possible by deposits, bank bonds and equity.

This simple scheme is subject to numerous qualifications when put into practice, as real life is always more complicated than theoretical constructions. There are grey areas, which can be handled in different ways with equal justification, and there are very real measurement difficulties. Some originate from the deficiency of data and some from the inherently unstable nature of the phenomena they try to measure.

Equity   Equity or market capitalization at stock exchanges is in theory a very simple concept. Company capitalization, or market value, is derived by multiplying the number of outstanding shares by their price. The exchange-wide figure comes by totalling over all listed companies and the worldwide figure by totalling over all exchanges. But some underlying data are only partial and subject to, at times, heavy fluctuation.

Corporate price histories normally apply to marginal deals. When somebody wants to buy a controlling stake or even the whole company, there is a surcharge, perhaps 15–100 per cent depending on circumstances. Alternatively, the bulk of shares may not be for sale at all. They are owned by the founding family or business associates; what remains is called free float and it is by no means unusual that it is only one-quarter of all shares. Restrictions of ownership by certain type of investors, foreigners in particular, can also have a distortionary effect. In short, a company's market capitalization includes a substantial calculatory element.

Add to this the fluctuation caused by economic cycles and, in international comparisons, exchange rates. The year-end 1996 world equity market capitalization was 15 per cent higher than the 1993/1994 figure. It resulted primarily from higher share prices and only secondly from the privatization of state-owned companies. For a three-year period, this is moderate. More drastic was the 14 per cent slump during 2001, comparable to the halving of the Tokyo SE during 1989–1992, or the rise of the New York SE Composite Index from 98 to 122 in 1985. Outright alarming was the 33 per cent fall of the Hang Seng Index in Hongkong during 17–29 October 1997, or the 22 per cent fall of the Dow Jones Industrial

Index on 19 October 1987. Stock market rises normally last for lengthy periods but a negative correction can be dramatic. Emerging markets are still more volatile. Cycles in the Russian stock market were of the order of 60 per cent in the mid-1990s.

Capitalization figures may comprise different universes. Many exchanges quote both shares and bonds, shares usually, but not always, dominating. There are also closed-end investment funds which are formally public limited companies but, as the name implies, exist only for investment in other companies' shares. The figures used here comprise only shares and warrants (rights to buy shares at a later date), and exclude investment funds. At large exchanges, specific statistics are normally available, at small ones this need not be the case.

Multiple corporate listings are a potential source of inaccuracy, because there is a tendency for exchanges to include all the outstanding shares of a listed company in its market value. This is the case in India, for example. Fortunately, the share prices are about the same everywhere because of arbitrage. Internationally, double counting can be avoided by recording only the domestic shares. The split into domestic and foreign shares is always available when foreign shares play a significant role. The weakness of this solution is that truly international exchanges, such as London SE, New York SE and Nasdaq, are deprived of some of their importance. Shell and Unilever, groups with double nationality, allocate their constituent companies between Amsterdam SE and London SE according to their domiciles.

Domestically, possible double counting is sometimes cleaned up by the exchanges themselves. This is the case in Germany. Exchanges may also prohibit domestic multiple listing, or are so specialized that no problem arises. This is the case with the USA. When such built-in checks do not exist, the best solution is to record only the dominant stock exchange. Companies with a listing only at regional exchanges are then excluded, but the effect on the country total is likely to be modest. The question becomes more delicate when regional identities are strong and when regional exchanges roughly equal the conventional main exchange. Such a situation exists, for example, in Brazil, Japan and Spain. A negative bias is probably introduced by accounting only for the dominant exchange.

The figures used here have been taken from the website of the International Federation of Stock Exchanges (FIBV). The organization is located in Paris and its figures need not tally with those routinely quoted in the English-language media, used also in the first edition of this book. In particular, Paris Bourse (Euronext Paris) overtakes Deutsche Börse and closes some of the gap to London SE. Different accounting systems can partially explain this (see Chapter 4).

Debt Debt is used here as a generic concept including all loan certificates irrespective of maturity, issued in large numbers and of standardized denominations. The terminology is not well established, but the main categories might be called bills, notes and bonds. Bills have a maturity of less than one year, notes between one and ten years and bonds five years and over. The terminology varies by country. Bills are also called money market instruments. As bonds dominate debt, these two terms will occasionally be used as synonyms.

Most debt is not listed at organized exchanges but is issued over-the-counter (OTC); and, even when listed, they still may be traded OTC. That makes most debt prices less transparent than equity prices. Many bond issues are also privately placed. The placement price may be known but, as there is no public marketplace, subsequent price information is fragmentary. It is also usual that such bonds are kept until maturity. Older bonds, whether government or corporate, and bonds by smaller sovereign issuers may be fairly illiquid, making their prices arbitrary. In the reasonably liquid eurobond market, there are only forty-to-fifty issues which are actively traded at a time.

That was the bad news. The good news is that debt prices fluctuate much less than equity prices because two factors causing instability are absent: uncertainty about earnings and dividends and the question of corporate control. Bonds issued by defaulting sovereigns and corporations are, of course, an exception. It is not only the Third World; Channel Tunnel bonds were trading at year-end 1995 at one-third of their nominal value. The practical solution for calculating bond market value, then, is to use the nominal (par) value. Geographically, debt is recorded like shares, by the issuer's domicile.

Probably the most comprehensive data set is collected by the Bank for International Settlements (BIS). The data on outstandings (issued but not yet matured nor redeemed) are fairly complete while that of trading covers only international business. Domestic trading is too dispersed by holder, dealer and geography to be amenable to comprehensive presentation.

Deposits Bank deposits here include all demand and time deposits at deposit money banks and other banking institutions within the country, irrespective of who owns the bank office. Deposits by residents are detailed in International Financial Statistics (IFS) country tables and deposits by non-residents in the *BIS Quarterly Report*. The BIS data also covers offshore centres and separates deposits in offshore dependencies (colonies) from those of the mother country. Statistics on the Euroland can be aggregated from country statistics but then data on non-residents applies to national and not Euroland boundaries. The solution is to use ready Euroland aggregates without non-residents, a maximum error of about 15 per cent.

Deposits by public bodies and interbank activity are excluded. The former solution is illogical because public holdings of equity and debt are included, but only because they cannot be separated. The public sector often dominates the economy of developing countries but these seldom meet the GDP criteria used here. The interbank segment, central banks included, belongs to the grey area. It is important because it is so large. Almost three-quarters of all cross-border deposits are interbank, and domestic figures can be of comparable magnitude. But the figures also create an inflated picture because they are short-term. To put it very simply, when a non-bank customer makes a deposit, it may be lent to another bank for three months, re-lent further to a third bank for one month and so on. The original deposit multiplies itself many-fold within a year if it stays within the interbank market. Therefore the exclusion.

The coverage of the source depends on national practice. Cooperative banks, postal savings banks, mutual funds, credit associations and building societies often resemble deposit banks in certain respects but not in others. Their relative importance varies by country, and there is no guarantee that they have been included in a consistent way. Comparisons with banking statistics published by the USA, Japan and Germany show discrepancies with IFS which can only be explained by definitional differences. As the comparison can be very laborious, it will not be developed further. Two amendments are made, however, because of their practical importance. The Japanese domestic banking statistics are substituted for the IFS figures, which roughly doubles the deposit stock, and the US bank and thrifty deposits are rounded out by time deposits at money market funds, which increases the total by one half (*IFS* 2001; *Japan Statistical Yearbook* 2001).

The differentiation between domestic and cross-border assets is problematic. It surfaces with deposits because their statistics are reasonably detailed. In the context of securities it mostly remains hidden. Domestic companies can be identified and usually also domestic issuers of debt, but it is impossible to identify their owners on a global scale. Equity ownership is known if owners care to register themselves, which is not always the case, and the registers are made public. Debt ownership remains partially disguised because of many bearer issues, that is, ownership is tied to the holding of the physical script and remains anonymous. Therefore, much of what has been done above is illogical and its only justification is that there has been no alternative.

The financial assets worldwide can be estimated at $98tr (Table 2.2). It is a very large figure, more than three times the global GDP, about $30tr (*UN Statistical Yearbook* 1998: 133). When it is assumed, for the sake of example, that the global economy saves annually 6 per cent of its output, then it would take about twenty years to arrive to that figure (Table 2.1). On the other hand, company market values normally exceed their substance values, the difference being called 'goodwill' by accountants, and from that angle $98tr is too high a figure. But it can also be considered too low. It does not cover all countries. Deposits at many non-bank financial institutions escape the net. The calculatory market value of gold is omitted, $1.3tr for above-ground stocks or $450bn for bar and coin hoarding (Klapwijk *et al.* 2002, Table 1, Figure 47). A case can be made for accounting for the derivative instruments in some way. There are actors

Table 2.2 World financial assets, end December 2000

Class	$bn
Bank deposits (non-banks)	29,541
Domestic	27,471
Cross-border	2,070
Securities	68,012
Equity	31,894
Debt	36,118
Total	97,553

Sources: *IFS*, March 2002, Country tables; *BIS QR* June 2001: Tables 3B, 15A–B, 16A; www.fibv.com: Tables 1.3.B, VB.

Notes
Domestic bank deposits only in countries of about $50bn or more of GDP. Equity in 2001 $26,611bn.

who prefer to conceal their wealth. There is little we can do about these shortcomings and, therefore, we take the above estimate and round it slightly upwards to $100tr, a figure easy to remember.

Structurally, global financial assets split 30/70 between bank deposits and securities. That reflects the stock market boom culminating in 2000 and the established trend from banking towards securitization. It is possible to see a development sequence from bank deposits and other short-term assets to bonds and further to equities. At the same time, we should note that exchanges and active capital markets are very much an Anglo-American institution and play a more subdued role in other cultures. Several reasons are apparent. Many investors perceive bank deposits and bonds as safer than equity. Illiquid and corrupt stock exchanges may be the origin of such a perception. Bonds can be beyond the small investor's reach altogether because of large nominal values. Mutual funds need legislation and supervision which may not exist. Companies may avoid bonds because the issuance is heavily regulated and possibly taxed. Companies may also be too small and unknown to raise capital by issuing them. Family control may preclude equity. The end result is that companies and individuals alike rely on banks for much of their borrowing.

Colourful geography

The USA and Japan overshadow every other country financially. The third pole, Europe, is fragmented into numerous countries. Transforming and emerging economies have very modest financial assets, sometimes in dramatic contradiction with their real economies. These circumstances make it virtually impossible to produce a legible figure based on countries. The solution is to cluster nearby and financially similar countries into groups and adopt an approximate lower limit of $300bn (Figure 2.1).

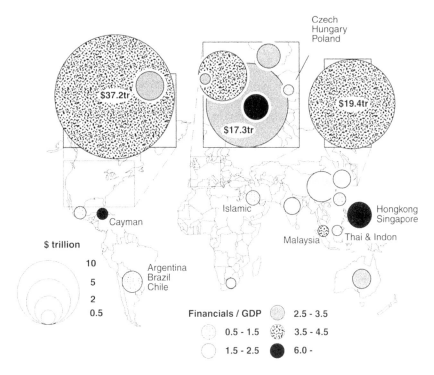

Figure 2.1 Financial asset intensity, 2000.

Sources: see Table 2.2.

The most obvious case for clustering is the European Monetary Union (EMU or Euroland). Its members still show considerable individuality but the gradual integration of its financial policy recommends clustering. The largest members, down to the Netherlands, locate in size approximately between the UK and Canada. Adjacent clusters are Scandinavia, which does not belong to EMU, and the transition economies of the Czech Republic, Hungary and Poland (Eastern Europe). Thereafter the UK, Switzerland and Ireland are the only noteworthy 'independents'. In Asia, the entrepôt cities of Hongkong and Singapore, dominated by the Chinese ethnic group and having a similar colonial past, are clustered (Entrepôts). That past, their emigrant mentalities, and trading and industrial occupations give them a similar outlook. Thailand and Indonesia are kept separate from Malaysia where the Chinese element is much stronger and the influence of Singapore more keenly felt. Among the Islamic countries only those in the Middle East (Egypt to Pakistan) are put into a cluster (many below $50bn GDP). Maghreb is not very important financially and Turkey is more akin to Europe than the Islamic world. In South America, Argentina, Brazil and Chile (ABC) form a cluster with Brazil as its dominant member. Australia,

Canada, China, India, Korea, Mexico and South Africa are too separate geographically to recommend clustering and sufficiently large to be legible cartographically. Among pure offshore centres, only the Cayman Islands are important enough to warrant a marker.

The relativity of the figures should be emphasized. A good measure is the comparison of the assets of Islamic countries in Figure 2.1, some $500bn, and the estimated size of Arab assets invested abroad, $350bn–$600bn private monies and another $600bn royal family assets (Allen 1996; Dudley 1997: 97–98). In the same vein, the market value of precious metals in private Indian hands, a substitute of bank deposits, can be guesstimated at $70bn (author's estimate based on Klapwijk *et al.* 2002: Table 2, Figure 47) when the formal financial sector is $700bn. Russians are believed to have $40bn as dollar notes when the formal sector is about $100bn (Thornhill 1999).

Financial assets do not necessarily correspond to conventional perceptions on national economic power. There are countries and territories with hugely oversized assets and those which are their direct opposite. Financial assets are just one aspect of economic might, no panacea, and certainly not a part of an international beauty contest. A standard indicator of relative financial size ('intensity') is to compare assets with GDP (Figure 2.1). The former is a stock variable and the latter a flow variable. It might appear preferable to replace the stock variable with a flow variable, possibly based on trading values and loan turnovers. Such data, however, are not always available.

Financial intensity is largest in countries and territories loosely known as financial centres. In our classification, Switzerland and the Entrepôts belong to this category with intensities exceeding 6.0. Both benefit from substantial deposits by non-residents, a certain sign of a financial turning table. Within the Euroland, Luxembourg and the Netherlands would also qualify. Luxembourg's intensity exceeds 20, thanks to its deposit base by residents and non-residents alike, while the Netherlands stays at 5.2. The Netherlands is not generally perceived as a finance centre and it is actually a combination of various financial services which makes it exceptional. The Cayman Islands with its minuscule GDP is an outlier even in this category. The UK, USA, Japan and Malaysia form the next category. The first two are wealthy and permeated by a financial-friendly culture, the former also hosting London, a world-class finance city. Japan's intensity rests essentially on the liberal interpretation of its deposits. If only the deposits given in the IFS are considered, the total assets would be one-quarter smaller and financial intensity about the same as the Euroland's. Malaysia appears to be out of context, and its intensity is also close to the lower class limit. The remaining countries/clusters make up a coherent pattern, moderate financial intensity in the industrialized countries, particularly with British roots, and a decline when one moves towards the subtropics and tropics.

So much for the size of the markets. But there is also their structure: the split between equity, debt and deposits (Figure 2.2). Each asset class has it adherents. Offshore centres are practically all-deposit, for obvious reasons. Asia Pacific and the Islamic world also lean heavily on bank deposits. Islam rejects fixed interest, which makes debt morally suspect and equity dubious. Japan is a special case because of the generous inclusion of deposits from all possible sources. Certain types of deposits there also enjoy interest rates which compare favourably with riskier investments.

The dearth of debt in most of the Asia Pacific is conspicuous. The population's traditional self-reliance has kept government debt low and only Japan and Korea have tried to issue themselves out of economic difficulties. Private issuance has been handicapped by the vast masses of low-income population and weakness of institutional investors. Japanese authorities also worry about excessive corporate borrowing and closely monitor their debt. Large debt is typical for welfare economies where generous social benefits strain the economy's capacity to provide them. Scandinavia and much of the Euroland struggle with debt shares of 40 per cent and over. The USA also has a lot of debt but there the structure is different. Public debt is issued to finance infrastructure projects and it originates from all administrative levels, federal, state and municipal, and not

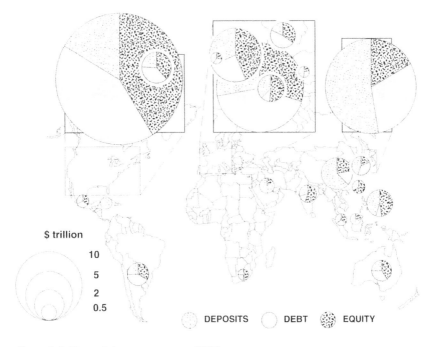

Figure 2.2 Financial asset structure, 2000.

Sources: see Table 2.2.

only the highest one as is the case in Europe. Much debt is issued by corporations who find it more tax-efficient than equity.

Equity characterizes countries with developed financial markets. And where the markets are developed, their regulation and investor protection receive serious attention, encouraging equity type of saving. This is the principle to which shadings can be added. Price variation, much higher in equities than debt, plays a role. Japan's boisterous past in the mid-1980s is still regretted. Equally fundamental, although it applies to all securities, is that the location where the script is registered need not coincide with the domicile of owners. Finland, here part of the Euroland basket, is a case in point because of Nokia's foreign owners. Switzerland and South Africa are similar cases. Much of the equity listed in Hongkong is actually Chinese. In India, extensive multiple listing distorts the picture. The US equity market prospers because pension funds and mutual funds need investment objects and drive up share prices. This institutional factor is at work also in the UK and the Netherlands.

There is, thus, regularity, although the geographical logic is less easy to detect. It is worth an attempt, however. Specifically, the twenty-one observations are grouped with the help of cluster analysis. Offshore centres are an obvious group and not included. The three segments of deposits, debt and equity are the underlying variables, and their respective percentages out of the total are the entries. Distances between observations are measured by squared Euclidean distances and the hierarchical centroid method is used for grouping. Several other distance measures and grouping methods were also tried. The results broadly coincided with those given here (Figure 2.3).

Superficially, most groups correspond with intuitive expectations. The opinion rests on the implicit acceptance of a suitable number of groups. With twenty-one observations, five groups appear meaningful. With oversimplified titles these are: West (7), Empire (4), Transform (4), Turntable (3) and Embryonic (3). The West consists of two subgroups. The USA and Scandinavia are an unexpected pair for anybody who is not a Scandinavian. At closer look, the USA was practically the only destination for emigrants and its culture is widely imitated today. The larger subgroup covers most of the Continent and important overseas countries with European culture, whether of Anglo-American or Latin variant. A balanced sectoral structure appears to link the UK with the ethnically alien parts of its former Empire around the Indian Ocean into one group. If balance is the criterion, Ireland (Eire) should be part of that group rather than the next one, an obvious shortcoming of the centroid method used. Japan, Korea, Eire and Eastern Europe have each a large deposit and small equity sector, typical for transforming economies. Japanese and Koreans may not like their countries being classified as such, but the idea has substance. The transformation is from a strictly guided financial system to a market oriented one. The Turntable consists of three acknowledged finance

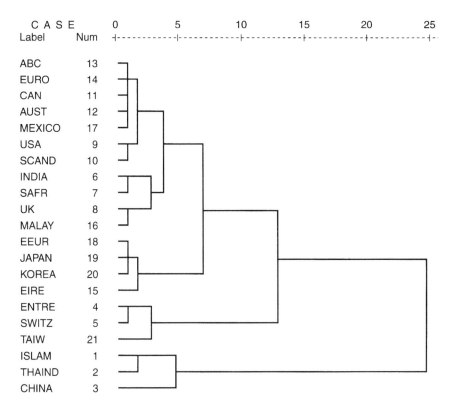

Figure 2.3 Financial taxonomy, 2000.
Sources: see Table 2.2.

centres and Taiwan. The common denominator is a parenthetical debt sector and the group is differentiated from the Transform by a large equity sector. Taiwan, of course, is no finance centre, a fact well documented by its low financial intensity. The Embryonic group is characterized by a dominant deposit sector. In reality, it also includes countries and enclaves with a respectable equity sector such as Kuwait, Lebanon, Oman and Shanghai, engulfed by their neighbours and disguised by a rudimentary statistical base. This group is quite apart from the rest.

Monetary flows

The propensity of capital formation varies between countries and regions (Table 2.1). So does the need for capital. Supply and demand seldom balance regionally, and certainly not at short notice. The banking system is there to allocate the surpluses between deficit regions. That can be done directly by accepting deposits and granting loans, or indirectly by bringing lenders and borrowers together as happens at issuance. Both ways require that the bank is aware of the opportunities and has either the necessary funds or the connections. Short of funds, it can go to the inter-bank market and borrow there. That is also the place to lend surpluses. Whatever the technicalities, the smoothing of surpluses and deficits gives rise to monetary flows.

Their origins and destination thus reflect the supply and demand of finance capital, its price (interest rate) and the form in which it is avail-able: direct or portfolio investment; loans, bond or equity investment. Capital, and private capital in particular, flows from surplus to deficit regions, the gap between supply and demand being indicated by the respective domestic interest rates. These are often tied to international benchmarks thought to reflect the market at large, so-and-so many basis points above/below LIBOR (London InterBank Offered Rate) or the Fed Rate (Federal Funds Rate) at which the US central bank lends to the banking system.

> LIBOR is the average rate at which eight-to-sixteen (depending on the currency) internationally active, high-quality London banks lend to each other. The survey is conducted each banking day at about 11 am. With the coming of euro, LIBOR now has a Continental competitor, EURIBOR. Its panel consists of fifty-seven banks all over the Euroland. The quality of the panel members is more variable than in London and the range of their quotations correspondingly wider. (Anon. 1998; Bank of England 1998: 40)

As the balance of supply and demand changes, the interest rate will follow suit. The rate also reflects risk. There is risk attached to any project in itself. Oil drilling in the Barents Sea is riskier than construction of a new toll bridge. Another risk is linked with the debtor, its cashflow and indebtedness. The US government is a safer risk than a new fast food company. Project and debtor risks are easier to evaluate at home than abroad, which means that money is cheaper for domestic lending and investing. On top of that comes exchange risks in cross-border operations. Borrowing in a country with an appreciating currency can become very expensive in domestic currency, and is likely to be compensated for by a lower interest rate. The length of maturity matters, since long maturities are more risky than short ones.

Consistent imbalances on current and capital accounts, and plain inter-est rate differentials suggest that countries can be classified into capital exporters and importers. The split is useful to a degree, but for explaining quarterly, monthly, weekly and daily financial markets it is too coarse. The markets are too differentiated and the interest and exchange rates too mercurial for a simple explanation. The long-term outlook may attract syndicated loans, while 'hot' money moves in response to temporary opportunities and threats. Industrial structures vary by country, and when companies internationalize, opposite financial flows will arise. Japanese banks recapitalize their foreign subsidiaries after a crunch in interbank credit availability, while foreign banks are building up their subsidiaries in Japan to benefit from its deregulation. Fluctuation in the domestic deposit-taking of banks is balanced in the international interbank market. The availability and price of financial instruments vary by country and invite cross-border operations. For example, German investors save in Luxembourg to avoid taxes at home but are happy when the Luxembourgeois intermediary invests their monies in familiar German securities. Institutional investors diversify their portfolios and trim them continuously for higher profitability and less risk. Speculative money moves around. For example, professional investors borrow cheaply in Japan and lend the monies elsewhere, accepting the exchange rate risk (carry trade). Currency trades may be rerouted through third-country finance centres to avoid the prying eye of the central bank, which prides itself on the convertibility of its currency but does not like attacks on the exchange rate, and interferes to defend it. The picture is very varied, and simply labelling a country a capital exporter or importer can be badly misleading.

The complexity calls for simplification. The simplest case geographically is when outflows and inflows are recorded by region/country but the other end of the flow is left undefined. The situation can be made tangible by an imaginary pool or black box which first collects the outflows and then distributes them as inflows (Figure 2.4).

Consolidating the outflows and inflows into a complete flow matrix is less usual. The labour input is much larger and it simply is not possible to fully record the destination of all outflows or the origin of all inflows. The sometimes substantial 'errors and omissions' element in national accounts testifies to this. The issuance of bearer securities, eurobonds included, is just one aspect of the problem; offshore centres are another. Difficulties notwithstanding, proprietary estimates are occasionally published, this time by an investment bank (Figure 2.5). It is noteworthy that the figure republished here displays equities which have a better chance of being registered than bonds. Registration is needed if shareholder rights are going to be exercised, and trading mostly takes place at exchanges which are subject to regulator and media scrutiny. The figure is also noteworthy in displaying gross flows. It is easy to visualize the distortion if gross flows were replaced by net ones.

That risk may be worth taking, however, when the number of origins and destinations grows. Otherwise the figure would become too clogged and foreclose oversight. It may also be easier to offer explanation when the figure is streamlined. Our example is from the interbank market of developed countries during the first quarter of 2000 (Figure 2.6). The activity was unusually lively, the interbank assets increasing fivefold compared to non-bank loans. The frenzy is thought to have originated by the

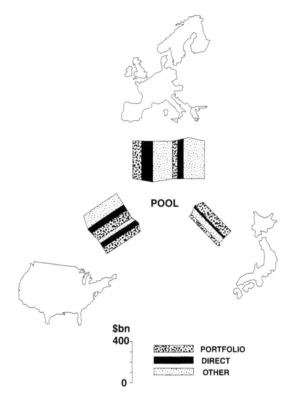

Figure 2.4 Major capital flow origins and destinations, 1994.

Source: *BIS AR* 1994/1995: 129.

needs of mobile phone operators in Europe. Governments auctioned UMTS licences and because many operators lacked the funds to participate they turned to their bankers, who sourced the interbank market. The basic pattern was that funds were raised in New York and Hongkong, passed on to Zurich and Tokyo, and pooled in London, though not necessarily in that order. Euroland banks drew heavily on them. Some fund raising involved winding-down of short-term inter-office claims offshore, US funds in the Bahamas and Japanese in Hongkong and Singapore. The latter were monies lent to Japanese companies but channelled via overseas branches (Gadanecz and von Kleist 2000: 14). This exciting account does not find full substantiation in the figure. For example, there is no flow from the USA to the UK, nor one from Singapore to Japan. Obviously there were many other forces who partially disguised the causal chain of the telecom operators.

But sometimes the main force is powerful enough to bury all secondary forces under it. The vigour of the US economy and its booming stock exchanges was such a force for European investors and catalysed the

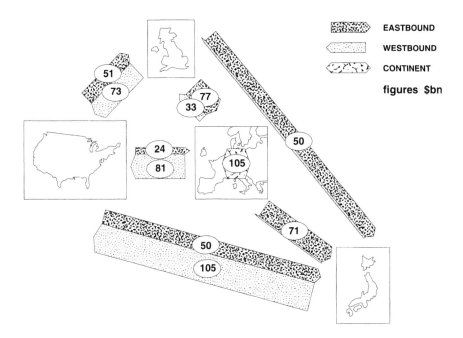

Figure 2.5 Major equity flows, 1988.

Source: Evans, Garry, 'Riches in the store': 72. *Euromoney*, September, 1989: 71–74. Copyright © 1989 of Euromoney Institutional Investor plc, England; used with permission.

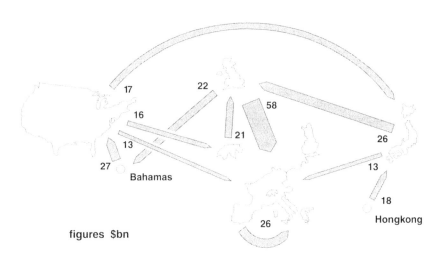

Figure 2.6 Major interbank net flows, Q1 2000.

Source: Gadanecz, Blaise and von Kleist, Karsten, 'The international banking market', Graph II.1.1. *BIS QR*, Aug. 2000: 13–19. Copyright © 2000 of the Bank for International Settlements, Basle; used with permission.

purchase of equity stakes. The desirability of having a solid foothold in the market called for acquisitions. The ensuing flows were not balanced by opposite deals because the European economy was sluggish and Americans were already well established there. Japan, the third pole, was in the midst of a recession and unable to participate. In contrary, foreigners were, for the first time since the 1920s, able to make substantial investments in the country. Americans made use of the opportunity. Japanese exports, however, maintained competitiveness and the current account remained positive. Its investors, burned earlier by ill-judged foreign acquisitions and real estate deals, preferred debt. These economic fundamentals were sufficiently sustained to leave their imprint on the portfolio flows, and through them, exchange rates (Figure 2.7).

Equity and debt are kept separate in the figure and both are cumulative net flows. The flows go from left to right, 'Japan/USA' meaning that the positive flow is from Japan to USA, while the negative flow goes in the opposite direction. The exchange rates are inverted, when necessary, so that a rising positive flow is paralleled by a declining rate index (Dec. 1997 = 100). When flows for both equity and debt are positive, debt is

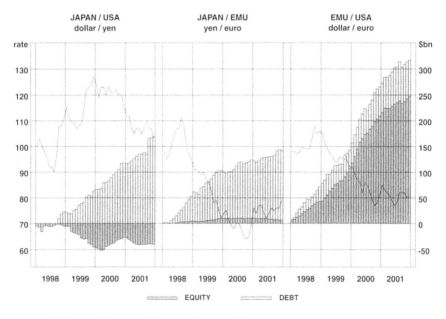

Figure 2.7 Cumulative portfolio net flows, 1998–2001.

Source: *BIS AR* 2001/2002, Graph V.4. Copyright © 2001 of the Bank for International Settlements, Basle; used with permission.

Notes
Left-hand scale for exchange rate index. Right-hand scale for flow. Flows relabelled and converted so that a positive flow is from a left region to a right region. Negative flow goes in the opposite direction. Underlying exchange rates inverted, when necessary, so that a rising positive flow is paralleled by a declining index (Dec. 1997 = 100).

piled upon equity. When their signs differ, the net effect must be gauged visually. The aggregate flow from Japan to USA and EMU has been mostly for debt, and from EMU to USA it has been for equity. The plausible reasons were given above. Factors underlying exchange rates are numerous and layered but here the effect of portfolio flows is very explicit. After the cumulative flow had gained momentum at the end of 1998 or 1999, a steep downward trend in exchange rate index developed. It slowed and was partially reversed in 2001 when the equity boom faltered and portfolio flows levelled off.

Institutional investors

Big and powerful

While the principles of lending and investing are clear and simple, there can be some difficulty in making the practical decision, about the object, the amount, the rate, the maturity and so on. The banker is there as s/he has always been, mostly as a deposit taker, lender and custodian but increasingly also as a fund manager, perhaps in the shape of a private banker. This is the trend. The traditional private investor is yielding ground and being replaced by the institutional investor, personified by the professional fund manager. From that angle this subchapter could just as well be integrated with the banking chapter. The reason this has not been done is that the institutional investor is more than just an additional actor in the financial scene. It is as much a herald of broad societal forces which arrive and gain ground at different times and different intensities in various countries. Therefore, institutional investing can be considered part of the general background or infrastructure, as the case may be.

The funds can be of substantial size. Some are freestanding, others consolidated into umbrella organizations, or have brokerage as their main business. The United Bank of Switzerland (UBS) occupies the number one slot, with $1,533bn of managed assets at year-end 2001, followed by Fidelity Investments with $1,038bn. Fidelity is the largest US asset management company with over 300 funds and some 15 per cent of the daily turnover in US equities. Fidelity Magellan, its largest fund, exceeded all international equity issuance in the mid-1990s, too much for efficient management. Magellan's transactions moved markets, and picking small promising stocks was meaningless for it, because these did not affect the overall performance. The largest Asian manager is Kampo, the Japanese insurance giant, with $770bn, whereas the small Netherlands can boast ING Group with $468bn, including one-quarter of all Dutch pension assets. The brokers Merril Lynch and Nomura handle three times more customer monies than is under management proper. (Authers 1997; Brice 1995; Corrigan and Harris 1997; Denton 1995; Evans 1997; Graham 1997b; Zlotnick 1996; www.watsonwyatt.com 2001)

Size brings with it considerable power. When placing large issues, there are only about 150 organizations, some say 200–300, which really matter, and at new equity issues a core group of twenty to twenty-five giant funds and management companies are rising into dominance. Many are specialized to some extent, which means that actors in narrower market segments are still fewer. The market gets increasingly individualistic, behavioural features become stronger, and the dominance of economists in explaining things will get hollowed out. Behavioural scientists already contribute essentially to explaining short-term market dynamics. Fundamentalists are giving way to chartists. (Ensor 1996; Graham and Martinson 1997; Lee 1993: 30; 1994: 89; O'Barr and Conley 1992; Shirreff 1996a)

It is one thing to have substantial financial assets at one's disposal and another to be an important international player. Many fund managers are cautious when it comes to making cross-border investments. There are also legal limits to the maximum share which can be invested abroad, the percentage applying at the time when the investment is made. The limits vary considerably between countries, and type of fund and investment. Pension and insurance funds are more tightly controlled than investment funds, the laudable purpose being that when it is time to pay retirement monies and insurance claims, often to the proverbial 'small man', the necessary means really are available. Small countries awash with funds tend, for obvious reasons, to take a liberal attitude. For the sake of example, in the mid-1990s, the foreign share in Hongkong exceeded 50 per cent, in Belgium and Ireland it was 35 per cent, and in the UK close to 30 per cent. France, Germany and Japan, by contrast, were below the 10 per cent mark. No wonder, Japanese pension funds and life insurers had made currency losses to the tune of $250bn–$400bn (¥37tr) during 1985–1994. In a way they were compelled to take this particular risk because low domestic interest rates made it impossible to honour policies with generous guaranteed rates of return. The losses catalysed a retreat back home, which led to a halving of the said rate, from 6 to 3 per cent (Anon. 1995: 38; Dawkins 1996a). In cross-border investment the name of the game is congruency, assets are invested in the country where the risks are. With the coming of the EMU the geographical horizon has been correspondingly extended, making most of Europe congruent.

Historically, the legal limits have seldom become operative, although the situation may well change in the future, there being a clear trend towards cross-border investment. The rationale is that investment income can be raised, its fluctuation decreased and risk lowered (possibly excluding foreign exchange risk) by spreading investment over more markets. The development has far-reaching operational consequences. Internationalizing funds do more research in-house, value anonymity, try to find a direct counterpart for transactions, but still demand more from intermediaries and exchanges, require unbundling of services and more active corporate governance (Biltoft 1996: 30). Only large, solid organizations are able to respond to this challenge.

But matters are seldom black or white. The EU was intended to become a common market for pension funds and EMU should have given it a special boost. Such a vision necessitates joint rules applicable everywhere and freedom to sell pensions from other member countries without local legal presence, the single passport principle. In reality, the vision has remained just that, a vision. There are no joint rules and companies must set up a separate pension scheme for each country, which raises costs by 0.4 per cent of assets. To that come separate tax regimes. The difficulty is in regulation. Can the matter be left to the funds, assuming that they will act prudently and report frequently? Or should policing be by a strict rule book? The UK, the Netherlands, Belgium, Ireland and Sweden, that is, the Maritime Europe, prefer the first alternative, and the rest mostly the second one. It is true that the prudent person rule has fared twice as well during the past fifteen years but that has also been a period of a rising stock market and it is there that most of the prudent assets have been invested. With the stock market in the doldrums, the argument has lost some of its validity. (Hargreaves 2001; Targett and Gimbel 2002; Tassel and Guerrera 2002)

Restrictiveness in cross-border investment is one way to avoid risk, currency and regulatory risk in particular. But internationalization can also be seen as a diversification strategy when foreign markets do not correlate, or correlate negatively, with the domestic one. The same principle can be extended to various asset classes. Stable, or at least predictable, income is important to insurers whose payments can be estimated and timed with great accuracy. Bonds, and particularly those issued by governments and blue chip multinationals, come close to this ideal. The income is fixed and the credit risk is low. Bond prices do fluctuate, but the fluctuation is much less than can be expected of shares. In return, shares usually give a better protection against inflation and offer more opportunity for capital gain. The former is important when the obligations are in the distant future and related to prices and wages. Life insurance with a savings component is a case in point. Real estate has properties similar to shares, while mortgages are halfway between bonds and shares. The shortcoming of mortgages from a fund manager's point-of-view is that the credit risk is more difficult to gauge and the debtors are likely to be numerous, which means increased administration.

Three investor categories

Funds have various missions. Some pay pensions after retirement, others settle insurance claims after death or accident and still others try to maximize investment income and capital gain by shrewd placement. A special category is the trust, a property management vehicle where ownership and benefaction have been separated from each other. Trusts constitute an important institutional group in the English-speaking world and are substituted by foundations on the Continent. Many are located in low-tax offshore centres and shrouded in secrecy. The information available about them is too fragmentary to permit numerical discussion.

Pension funds hold assets from which people get paid after retirement. The payment stream consists of a combination of investment income and capital rundown. Because pensions are linked with salaries and wages, it is important that fund assets are invested in a way that reflects people's earnings. Equities are an obvious alternative and an important asset class in countries where funded pensions are the rule. These have been widely accepted in some countries but not in others (Figure 2.4). The Netherlands, the UK, Switzerland and Denmark are among the most faithful adherents and the USA is tilting towards the same mould. The principle of funded pensions is also visible in Asia, although there it is enforced by governments and the lending has, until now, been primarily to them. The Central Provident Fund in Singapore and the Employee Provident Fund in Malaysia are well-known examples.

Most Continental countries follow the pay-as-you-go philosophy and have only modest or no pension funds. The practice has undeniable merits in times of rapid economic growth and large inflation. But in more settled times, unfunded pension obligations easily become a financial burden. At worst, they exceed the GDP as is the case in Japan, France and Germany (*sigma* 8/1998). The reason can be ideological as well as economic; important labour unions in France oppose the funded system and have retarded its development. Only civil servants and self-employed individuals can have a complementary system. The policy is reflected in the Paris Bourse, currently Euronext Paris, where private pension funds represent just 10 per cent of trading against 60 per cent in London (Jack 1996). The German government follows the pay-as-you-go principle and companies top-up these pensions for their long-term employees. The company funds are mostly book entries, however, because it is tax-efficient to invest the money internally rather than make it available to financial markets at large. Italy has a similar system, although for severance payments rather than pensions. Employees made redundant get one month's salary for each year worked, the funds staying within the company until needed. The practice is ideal for evaluating the investment risk, but the income is likely to suffer. For example, British pension funds, known for active management, derive about 80 per cent of their income from investment and only 20 per cent from contributions, while the split in a typical Continental fund is 60/40. (Dugan 1990: 120; Edwards and Fischer 1994: 55–56; Fisher 1996; Lee 1996; *sigma* 6/1997)

The current level of pensions is unsustainable by the pay-as-you-go system alone and a systemic change to funded pensions is in the making. It will give a boost for fund management, although the effects for net saving may be negligible. The less well-to-do may not have the means to insure themselves and the wealthy will take private insurance only if they trust that the government will not fiddle their money and impose special taxes once it has been collected. The Argentinian experience is thought-provoking.

> When the government could not borrow from abroad any more it started exerting pressure on private pension funds. These had to lend $3.5bn to the government, swap $40bn of dollar-denominated bonds for lower-interest government paper and transfer $2.3bn of assets to the central bank to be used for the purchase of more government paper. When the government defaulted in December 2001 on $141bn of debt, the funds had 70 per cent of their assets in public sector securities which stopped paying both interest and capital. (Catán 2002)

This was an unusually brash act of confiscation and unlikely to be often repeated. The more likely but equally devastating avenue will be that an increasing percentage of funds will be channelled to societally desirable but low-yielding purposes. The equation has important unknowns, and only time will tell.

The above account also outlines the essentials of funds managed by insurance companies. Excluding public *insurance assets*, the split between life and non-life assets is roughly 80/20, against gross premiums 62/38 (*sigma* 6/2001, Table I; *Institutional Investors Statistical Yearbook 2001*). The explanation, naturally, is the substantial savings element in many life policies. Therefore, countries where life insurance is important have insurance assets which are oversized in relation to their economies, and the other way round. The UK, the Netherlands and South Africa, in particular, but also Japan, belong to the former group, with Austria, Italy and Spain in the latter one.

Pension and most insurance funds face the requirement of paying their beneficiaries a secure income stream at times fairly well known in advance. This urges for caution when choosing investment strategy. *Investment funds*, by contrast, are set up for the specific purpose of enhancing investment income which need not be available at preset times. As a result, they can be more venturesome and flexible in action and the range of supervision is wider. Some, like the US mutual funds, can be very strict as to the setup of managers and retrieval of funds, while others are extremely liberal. This is the case when the money is raised privately and in large amounts, the idea being that professionals do not need the same degree of protection as the small investor. The large investor finds investment funds useful because they offer solid expertise with modest (and presumably cheaper) administrative effort and facilitate diversification, thereby lowering risk. The small investor is attracted by their ability to give

proper diversification and access to markets where the minimum investment is oversize – money markets and many bond markets, for example.
Investment objects are varied. Some funds specialize by industry, like
biotechnology and electronics, others by geography, like Latin America
and China, still others by the level of development, like emerging markets.
For those investors who find such specialization uncomfortably risky,
money market rates too low and who do not want to have the trouble of
allocating their monies between funds themselves, superfunds, also called
funds of funds, will do the job on their behalf.

Organizationally, investment funds fall into two broad categories, open-
ended (US mutual, Japan investment trust, Euroland Ucit, France Sicav)
and closed (unit). The former accepts investment any time and can also
be left whenever desired. The fund adjusts simply by buying and selling
assets. While maximally flexible and therefore attractive, it does not allow
the user to retrieve possible capital gain when leaving. The gain remains
with the fund and is distributed, if at all, as higher interest payment.
Closed funds are actually limited companies. They raise money through
share issues, many are quoted on stock exchanges, their share price fluctuates like that of any other company and permits the shareholder–investor
to pocket possible capital gain when leaving.

Hedge funds are the ultimate high-profit, high-risk end of investment
funds. The name comes from the cautious investment strategy of their originator but the actual behaviour has undergone a complete metamorphosis. Hedge funds strive for absolute profits rather than beating industry
average or some other benchmark. Their profit/risk profile arises from the
willingness to take leveraged, unhedged market positions. Sustained returns
around 30 per cent have been recorded, but also similar losses. On average,
their record surpasses that of mutual funds. They invest in anything which
moves rapidly, the separation of the pound sterling from the European Currency 'snake' in September 1992 belonging to their palmy days. They are
for large investors (minimum $1m) and often domiciled offshore to mini-
mize regulation, although managed from the onshore company. It has been
widely believed that the concept is a US speciality but in reality Swiss funds
appear to have a 30 per cent share, quite in line with the country's importance as a fund management centre. There is no reliable information about
their size and guesstimates from the millennium shift span a range of
$200bn–$650bn. Be that as it may, the real power of hedge funds originates
from their ability to leverage, to the staggering amount of $2tr–$3tr, and
attract imitators, banks in particular. Banks are only too happy to cooperate
because that helps them to imitate the funds and make a buck for themselves as well. The currency crisis in Southeast Asia in summer 1997 is a
recent example. Recalling that central bank currency reserves in the region
are typically of the order $25bn–$40bn, the struggle was between unequals.
(de Brouwer 2001: 4–10, 25; Celarier 1995; 1998; Coggan 1995; Covill 1996:
100; Hall 2002; Marshall 2002; Tsatsaronis 2000)

Overall picture

Institutional investors have become an indispensable vehicle for private and collective saving. They invest mostly in debt and equity. Real estate is an alternative when the maturing of obligations can be estimated reliably. Bank deposits carry too low an interest to be attractive. Precious metals and commodities are normally outruled. What remain are securities. Without institutional investors, securities markets would be considerably smaller. Therefore, it is useful to compare the size of institutional assets with the securities sector (Table 2.3). Both are stock variables which makes the comparison also theoretically valid. The ratio is called institutional intensity. Its numerical value is 57 per cent. Since the total securities market was $3tr larger end-1999 than end-2000, 55 per cent may be more accurate. That is within measurement error. For example, hedge funds are almost certainly not included, nor are trusts, and investment funds also operate in derivatives markets. The percentage is about the same as six years earlier. That leaves much financial wealth in the hands of comparatively few very rich individuals.

When the entries are put on a map using the same geographical breakdown as previously, a broadly similar intensity picture emerges (Figure 2.8). Countries with the Anglo-American financial culture rank highest and the rest of the industrial world follows. Then there are shadings. South Africa and Korea compare with the USA and UK because people save in life policies. Pensions also play an important role in Scandinavia, although the monies are divided between pension funds, life insurance companies and government stand-in funds which smooth out fluctuations in the pay-as-you-go system. Euroland naturally hides much variation within it.

These explanations become more tangible when the institutional asset pie is divided by segment (Figure 2.9). The division is approximate because the substance of the segments cannot be defined unambiguously.

Table 2.3 Relative size of institutional investors, 1999/2000

Assets (1999)	$tr	Securities (2000)	$tr
Pension	14.2	Equity	31.1
Insurance	12.3	Debt	36.1
Investment	11.9		
Total	38.4	Total	67.2

Sources: see Table 2.2. European Insurance in Figures 2001: 80; Industry of Free China, July 2001: Tables 23–24; *Institutional Investors Statistical Yearbook* 2001: 21–23; *Investment Company Institute Fact Book* 2001: 100; McGregor 2001; Mercer 2000; Mulligan 2001; Nossel 2001; Shakir 1999.

Note
Various sources give different estimates. The highest one is normally selected, a policy which appears to give correct proportions.

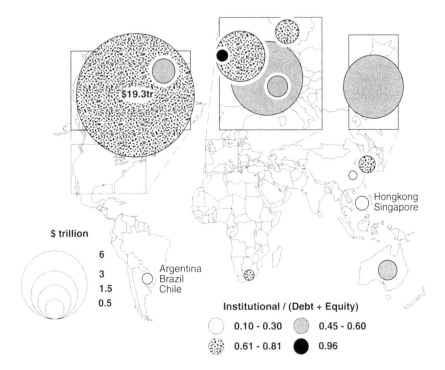

Figure 2.8 Institutional financial asset intensity, 1999/2000.

Sources: see Table 2.3.

The ERISA (Employee Retirement Security Act) pension system in the USA is a case in point:

> ERISA offers two alternative payouts: defined benefit and defined contribution. The former gives a fixed amount and the latter an amount varying with the value of investments. Technically, any asset manager is capable of handling both cases. Yet, a pension fund is more likely to be selected for defined benefit and an investment fund for defined contribution.

Life policies with a large savings element are a similar borderline case. Such overlap notwithstanding, Figure 2.9 tells something. For example, it gives a dramatic image of the unimportance of pensions in the financial systems of Asia Pacific, Japan excluded, and Latin America, not to speak of the Islamic world. One could almost use the same words about the Euroland, the difference being that pensions well exist but have only a modest impact on funded assets. That gap is partially filled by mutual funds, pre-EMU as post-EMU. Interestingly again, these are relatively absent in the UK, Scandinavia, Switzerland, Japan and the Netherlands

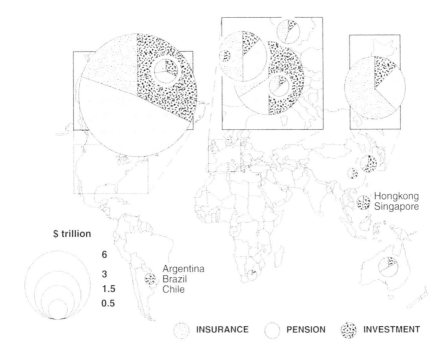

$ trillion

6
3
1.5
0.5

Argentina
Brazil
Chile

Hongkong
Singapore

INSURANCE   PENSION   INVESTMENT

Figure 2.9 Institutional financial asset structure, 1999.
Sources: see Table 2.3.

(not shown). One can speculate about the reasons – investment opportunities elsewhere (offshore, trusts), late start compared with competing segments, discrimination by the tax collector and so on.

As explained earlier, pension funds, insurance companies and mutual funds have quite rigid investment guidelines, while private and offshore investment funds enjoy greater freedom. It follows that the latter are more important international players than their absolute size alone would suggest. This partially explains why the USA weighs so heavily as a source of international finance capital.

Gatekeepers

The institutional dimension is not only apparent with fund managers. It is also manifest in the many actors whose common task it is to protect, guide and evaluate the financial industry. Without them financial markets could hardly exist, and their consent and support is indispensable for anyone wishing to operate in them. Therefore, these actors are appropriately called 'gatekeepers'. We discuss three groups: regulators, raters and accountants. Regulators are public servants who lean on the legislative power of a sovereign state and the international agencies which it has created. The operational side of their work is called 'supervision'. They protect the system and its actors from systemic failures, unscrupulous, felonious behaviour and excessive risk taking. Rating agencies operate on a commercial basis. They evaluate the creditworthiness of organizations who issue securities, and thereby facilitate investment decisions. Accountants are also commercial operators. They follow generally accepted standards and lay the numerical foundations for both regulating and rating.

There is also a fourth group of gatekeepers, the judiciary and lawyers, a blend of public and private interests. Their work takes place within distinct legal systems with strict rules and long traditions. Therefore, a separate subchapter is dedicated to legal issues.

Regulators

Financial markets are there for the optimal allocation of scarce resources. For this to happen, markets must be safe and just. Safety then means that the markets are reasonably protected from fraud and reckless business practice; justness that all participants have, in principle, the same opportunities and risks. Regulation is a means to achieve these goals. Its intended effects are thus beneficial. But it also has costs, direct costs arising from the regulatory apparatus itself and indirect costs because the apparatus has a tendency to distort the normal operation of markets. A particular form of market distortion is merit regulation, practised in countries with strong paternalistic traditions. Regulators are not only intent on supervising safety and the smooth functioning of the market but also promoting and directing it by administrative guidance. Minimum and maximum interest rates, issuance queues and the requirement to invest in government debt are typical measures. But even in countries where merit regulation is not practised, it has proved impossible to create rules so neutral that they would have no undesirable side effects. It follows that there is some ideal optimum where the marginal benefits and costs are in balance.

The first regulating layer consists of legislators, who leave the practical administration to ministries, central banks and other regulators. Some, like SEC (US stock exchanges), CFTC (US futures exchanges), Federal Accounting Standards Board (US) and FSA (UK securities), are statutory. Others, like American Accounting Association, BIS (international banking) and ISMA (international securities trading), are voluntary but still influential. Their rule books and administrative guidance can make or break a market, as the examples of London and Tokyo demonstrate.

Historically, regulation has had two targets, institutions and markets. The foremost institution interesting regulators has been the banking system, and the safety of depositors has been a key purpose. This has obvious populist undertones, because most deposits are small in relation to the size of a bank, and the number of people at risk is therefore large. Systemic stability is the other goal. The main instrument has been the capital/asset ratio (capital adequacy), the idea being that the bank's equity provides a cushion against credit and other losses. Less obvious is that almost any practicable equity will be insufficient if the bank loses the confidence of its peers. It cannot operate if no other bank wants to do business with it, in the interbank market, for example. Minimum reserves deposited at a central bank and deposit insurance follow the same philosophy. The former also constrains the amount of credit a bank can give and thereby monitors the monetary system. The deposit may, but need not, be interest bearing, although at such a low rate that it is unattractive to the bank. Strict minimum reserve requirements have pushed much banking business abroad. Another important regulatory lever is the diversification of the loan portfolio, for example, by decreeing the maximum percentage that can be lent to a single customer. Less usual are formal rules about the quality of credit, although it may ultimately be the most important aspect of all.

Banking regulators tend to focus on credit risk. But there are many other types of risk: price movement (market risk), poor liquidity, political action (country risk), interpretation of law, unforeseen taxation practice or badly managed operations. These have received less or no regulatory attention. Some of them actually better fit the securities slot where the primary concern is about fraud, malpractice and negligence rather than lack of capital:

> Illuminating about the many-fold types of risk is the UK case where the House of Lords decreed that swaps are more akin to gambling than insurance and therefore outside the contractual powers of local authorities. The ruling invalidated at a stroke a large number of deals between 130 local authorities and nearly eighty banks, and threatened the latter with market losses of $1.1bn. The legal motivation was that swaps are based on notional rather than actual amounts. The underlying reason may have been purely political, however. Some counties had made disastrous losses in swap deals and it was opportune to let them off the hook. (Moore 1991)

Regulators need tangible objects for their action. Institutions are welcome for the purpose, and markets correspondingly embarrassing. When markets are everywhere and yet nowhere, when they lack an identifiable location, they are difficult to regulate. One possible way is to register market practitioners and subject them to appropriate minimum qualifications. Besides definitional ambiguities, this approach may have difficulty in monitoring activities when practitioners are numerous and geographically dispersed. Investment advisors are an excellent example. The regulatory task is much easier when the participants are few and have exact locations. Exchanges, securities houses and funds are obvious targets, and this brings us back to the regulation of institutions.

Most regulation is domestic and never extends beyond the national boundaries. Its roots are in the familiar legal system, business practice and cultural tradition. Once implemented, regulation creates rigidities and vested interests, which make change difficult. Cultural diversity combined with rigidity is important, because it creates systematic differences in the international marketplace. Countries with low capital/assets ratios, for example, offer their banks an important competitive advantage. Those with lenient regulation attract international finance, because costs are lower and the scope for profits correspondingly larger. Understandably, these jurisdictions also foster unscrupulous practice, and the ensuing scandals have an unfortunate tendency to spill over national boundaries. This is one reason why national regulators strive for international cooperation and a common set of rules. The other reason is the perception that market efficiency is thereby furthered.

International regulation is most advanced in the banking sector where the Bank for International Settlements (BIS) in Basle functions as an informal clearing house for the central banks of its member countries, offers a discussion forum for their governors, and initiates and coordinates efforts to strengthen the stability of the international banking system. Its fifty central bank members represent all the financially important countries although the extent of their reporting may vary. Minimum capital adequacy rules, regulatory responsibility for internationally active banks and the upgrading of settlement and payment systems belong to its core achievements. Capital adequacy and regulatory responsibility are taken up here, while settlement and payment are postponed to Chapter 3.

The BIS capital adequacy rules originate from 1988 and were amended in 1997 to account also for trading risk. They have been endorsed by national central banks, which are responsible for their enforcement. Importantly, their governments have not committed themselves, which makes the rules 'gentlemen's agreements' only. The purpose is to make sure that the global banking system is properly capitalized, and that competitive relations are not unduly distorted ('a level playing field'). The agreement covers only internationally active banks. Others and non-bank financial intermediaries such as funds, insurance companies, credit associations and building societies are not included. The rules are designed to protect against credit risk, and their benchmark is gross rather than net exposure, which would be much more difficult to implement. The actual marks were tailored after US and UK interests; they were a bit lax for well-capitalized Germans and not too demanding for French and Japanese (Brady 1990; Leyshon and Thrift 1997).

The basic rule is that a bank's capital must be at least 8 per cent of its assets, which are weighted according to their assumed credit risk. Eight per cent is a comparatively high figure. Top international banks estimate that they would manage well with 5 per cent and it is by no means unheard of that respected European banks have managed with 3.5 per cent at home. In Asia Pacific, domestic regulators insist on 17–19 per cent because of riskier and less diversified environments. That is the clue: riskiness. Banks' own capital in the USA was 55 per cent in 1840, 25 per cent in 1890, but only 6 per cent in the 1980s. The explanation is the ability to diversify better and the existence of a proper central bank, the lender of last resort (*BIS AR* 1997/1999: 120; Mikdashi 1998: 166–167, 318).

The 8 per cent cited above is divided into three tiers, Tier One and Two for banking risk and Tier Three for trading risk. Tier One must be at least 4 per cent, and it consists of paid-up capital, perpetual preferred stock, disclosed reserves and minority interests. Preferred stock is a concession to Americans, who use it extensively. Elsewhere it is rare and, excluding the UK and some other English-speaking countries, unknown in legislation. Tier Two consists of hidden reserves, subordinated capital, loan reserves and similar. However, at most 45 per cent of the hidden reserves can be accounted for. Tier Three consists of short-term, subordinated, unsecured and fully paid capital. These rules give rise to little controversy. It is certainly cheaper to raise Tier Two than Tier One capital, but preferences are not for cheap solutions everywhere. German banks are very much in favour of Tier One, and their domestic customers appreciate it. The proper handling of assets is much more difficult (Brady 1990; Gallatin 1992; Osborn and Evans 1988; Stewart 1997).

The main principle is that all tangible assets, including those off the balance sheet, are included. Goodwill does not qualify as an asset, which is understandable but will discourage bank acquisitions. The real challenge is the proper weighting of asset classes, and the unavoidable shortcoming is that safe and risky assets are lumped together on the basis of some external characteristic. As can be expected, sovereign debt gets the highest rating, a 0 per cent risk if the country belongs to the OECD. Commercial paper also has a 0 per cent weight, while underwriting facilities and mortgages score 50 per cent. Interbank loans within the OECD are weighted at 20 per cent, actually too low but adopted to keep the interbank market liquid. When a loan of over one year is made to a non-OECD bank, however, the weighting is 100 per cent. This is also the weighting for private sector corporations and asset-backed securities, irrespective of their credit rating. These are minimum requirements, which national regulators can adjust upwards if they so choose. Some do, very much to the chagrin of their banks (Gallatin 1992; Osborn and Evans 1988).

The principles are sound, but their application can lead to undesirable and utterly ludicrous results. A multinational with the highest credit rating carries a risk weight five times higher than a shaky bank. The bank gets its loan, but only for a short time to prevent it from turning sour. The multinational bypasses the banking system entirely and issues bonds in the capital market. Lending to governments is also attractive, although these may finance budgetary deficits rather than productive investments.

Activity which needs little assets, like brokerage and corporate finance, gains in attraction. Multinational banks with equity in one currency but assets in twenty may face unexpected problems when exchange rates fluctuate. These examples should suffice. Neutral standardization is impossible in a diverse and changing world. Nor is it possible to rank countries with respect to BIS capital ratios. If anything general can be said, it is to identify the high ratios common in the Middle East, contrasted with banks in industrialized countries. This reflects the rudimentary state of the Arab interbank market, among others (Gallatin 1992; Osborn and Evans 1988).

Trading risk, the realm of Tier Three capital, applies only to banks engaging in such activity. As practically all internationally active banks do, the concept has relevance here. Trading risk is extremely difficult to define, measure and, therefore, also regulate. The difficulty originates from market volatility, the pace of securities inventory turnover, changing environment, the uniqueness of stress periods – no single period is like the others, and the fact that many markets simply discontinue functioning during extreme stress. In the most tangible terms, there will be no liquidity and all trading will grind to a halt (Clow 1998; Lee 1992; McDonough 1993; Waters 1992). One possibility of solving the regulatory impasse is to let banks evaluate trading risk by their proprietary risk management models. The Value at Risk (VAR) indicator developed by JP Morgan was the breakthrough and is accepted by regulators like SEC. VAR gives the risk across an entire portfolio in a single figure. This is multiplied by 12.5, and the product is added to the conventional credit risk to obtain a comprehensive figure. Unfortunately, VAR has serious shortcomings. It uses predetermined statistical distributions, calculates frequencies rather than dollars and does not account for illiquidity (Gapper 1995; Iskander 1996; Massey 1997; Mikdashi 1998: 112).

Current discussion revolves around operational risk, such as the collapse of a bank's accounting system or hiccups in a national payment system. A 30 per cent rise in regulatory capital has been suggested and vehemently opposed. No rapid action is in sight because nobody has succeeded in developing a comprehensive measure in the first place.

Overall regulatory responsibility for banks on foreign soil revolves around their liquidity (ability to meet obligations on time) and solvency (assets exceed liabilities) on the one hand and their legal form on the other, whether branch or subsidiary. A subsidiary is a separate legal entity with its own board of directors and share capital. That capital forms the ceiling of the parent's legal responsibility. A branch, in contrast, is in every respect subordinated to the parent company which is responsible for its entire share capital. On the other hand, the host country regulator has far less insight into a branch than an incorporated subsidiary and there are countries who insist that banking must be practised through subsidiaries and not branches. These facts have moulded the Basel Agreement of 1975, subsequently amended so that regulation takes place on a consolidated basis. For example, a bank cannot have its domicile and main activity in separate countries.

Liquidity is always the responsibility of the host country. This is practical because liquidity is a temporary issue and essential for the smooth functioning of the banking system. Solvency, in contrast, is a fundamental question and best left to the regulator of the subsidiary's home country. It is only to be hoped that the home country has the ability and willingness to do its job properly. At worst, internationally active banks may in reality have no lender of last resource. Therefore the host will limit the exposure, for example by refusing the participation in local payment systems (Mikdashi 1998: 274–281; Scott 1992).

Another important regulatory body is the European Union's Financial Services Commission. Its directives are law, not agreements, and they address harmonization as much as prudential behaviour. The principle is that authorization in one EU country gives licence to operate in all of them, subject to the operational rules of each host country. That hopefully puts pressure on the harmonization of national licensing and supervisory practice. Anticipating profound incompatibilities, the Commission also gives host country authorities the right to invoke the 'greater good' concept and reject an application. The principles apply to banking, securities, mutual funds (Ucits) and the insurance of large risks. Although directives have been issued, they are not necessarily implemented everywhere, and it may well take four or five years before a single market in an intended financial service will actually emerge. Pan-European marketing in particular becomes possible only after the tax systems have been integrated (Coggan 1996; Moir 1996).

It is more difficult to give a proper review of *national regulation*, because it varies so much from country to country. In some countries, regulation has been left to the market practitioners (self-regulation), while in others it is in the hands of authorities. The former alternative, in its most liberal form, can be equated with the rules of an association when the possibility of conducting business is tied to its membership. The latter alternative is based on law or formal international agreement. The details vary. The overall guidance normally rests with one or more ministries, while application and even rule making are left to specialized bodies. The central bank and the Ministry of Finance (Treasury) have been the natural regulators of the banking system and capital markets, but the new trend is towards a super-regulator, responsible for all financial segments. The rationale is that the segments are becoming so intertwined with each other that supervision by segment is no longer efficient. Scandinavian countries, the UK and Japan have taken practical measures. In countries with an embryonic financial system, the central bank has often assumed the role of super-regulator. Elsewhere, specialized authorities are still the rule. An overview of the largest countries will give an idea of the field, although the slogan 'bigger is better' does not apply here.

The USA is a cauldron of conflicting interests and political compromise, a legacy of its large size and federal structure. The top regulatory echelon is the President and Congress, the former because of his/her nominative powers and the latter because of its legislative and controlling (hearings) role. There are four important federal regulators: the Comptroller of the Currency, the Federal Reserve Board of Governors ('the Fed'), the Securities and Exchange Commission (SEC) and the Commodity Futures Trading Commission (CFTC). The Comptroller is in charge of federally chartered banks; the Fed of bank holding companies within the federal system and state chartered banks volunteering to its supervision; SEC of equities, bonds, stock options, and investment and mutual funds; CFTC of futures. Pension funds are the realm of the Department of Labor. The interests of so many authorities are at times difficult to reconcile, particularly when financial instruments and operational modes increasingly overlap. The system originates from 1934 and is gradually being overhauled.

The most noteworthy features of banking regulation used to be the separation of commercial and investment banking, restrictions placed on the opening of branches and the separation of banking and insurance. These restrictions practically disappeared during the 1990s but left as legacy the large number of comparatively small banks, which take time to rationalize, and the separate regulators for banking and securities business, a division unlikely to disappear in the near future.

The core areas of SEC and CFTC appear at first sight to offer little potential for an overlap. Securities, that is, equities and debt, have little in common with commodity futures, and equity (but not index) options are defined as securities by law. So it was also in the beginning. Equities were issued and traded on stock exchanges, mostly in New York, while agricultural exchanges in Chicago were the prime location of futures. Debt has mostly been traded OTC, but it links better with equities than futures. The regulatory problem arose when the Chicago exchanges extended the idea of futures to foreign exchange, interest rates and stock indices. Interest rates applied primarily to debt, and stock indices were a natural extension of equities themselves. Both now came under the CFTC umbrella, because it was the regulator of futures exchanges.

The opposition from New York came too late. It has proved impossible to transfer the disputed contracts from CFTC to SEC, or to merge the two regulators. That would probably have led to the submerging of Chicago into the New York market. Swaps, a major derivatives instrument, became the decisive bone of contention. Corporations wanted tailor-made, that is, OTC, swaps for their portfolios. The Chicago exchanges wanted swaps to be defined as futures, because all futures in the USA must be traded on exchanges. The attack targeted top-tier investment banks, i.e. the New York establishment, which were Chicago's biggest customers and often members of its exchanges. To avoid the Congress interfering, all finally supported legislation which exempted swaps from futures regulation. The law stipulates that swaps are tailor-made (OTC), held to maturity, not supported by a clearing organization, concluded in direct line of business and not marketed to the public. The victory had an important geographical outcome. Banks' swap teams, which had been moved to London in December 1987, when faced with a draft proposal, were repatriated. (Durr 1990; Hargreaves 1989; Harverson 1994; Herzel and Shepro 1990; Morse 1992)

SEC and CFTC do not interfere directly with the markets they oversee. The control is through rulings, and these can be challenged in the law courts. Much of the daily routine is delegated to exchanges and trade organizations. SEC is more prone to hands-on supervision and consequently has the higher profile of the two. The markets it oversees also used to be much larger and possibly more exposed to sharp practice. The principal areas of enforcement are insider trading, market manipulation, issuance, change of corporate control and disclosure. Disclosure is central to the whole system, and market participants are expected to form their own opinion on the basis of data released by corporations and issuers. The quality and equal availability of these data then becomes the centrepiece of enforcement.

Regulatory resources are not overly impressive. The Fed and Comptroller of Currency had, in the mid-1990s, jointly about 7,000 people, of which one-half were supervisors for the field work. SEC's total staff numbered 2,300, and only 300 of them were inspectors in the field (Blumer 1996: 115–118; Bush 1990). This can be compared with 10,000 banks (declining rapidly), 16,500 registered investment advisers and 500,000 securities industry employees. Financial criminality is always difficult to disclose and prove. Loans have no recognized market and customer individuality is great. Computer scans are routinely made to detect price aberrations at exchanges. But proving illegal concert action in a company takeover, or an insider tip before an equity issue, needs cooperation from within. Soliciting it, once a lead has been identified, is greatly facilitated by the legal system, which makes plea bargaining, confession of small crimes against immunity from prosecution for larger ones, attractive. Some legal ambiguity combined with draconian investigative powers, originally aimed at Mafia-type crime, also help, because they give regulators and judiciary negotiation leverage. The penalty for serious crime can be twenty years in jail, plus fines, plus triple damages for the illegal gain.

The regulatory power does not end at the US border. Indirectly, it encompasses the whole globe because of the attraction which the US capital market and exchanges exercise on foreigners. It sets disclosure standards for foreign issuers and withholds approval for the trading of foreign financial products when it finds their domestic surveillance lax and their authorities reluctant or unable to share information. For example, it has only been possible to trade the German equity index derivatives legally in the USA since the early 1990s.

The UK system has similarities with the US one but also differs from it in important respects. The very undercurrent is different. The British style is less outgoing and confrontational than the US practice and, although the earlier regulation 'by a quiet nod', exercised by the Bank of England has given way to more formal procedures, something of the low-key tradition still remains.

Regulation used to be divided mainly between three authorities: the Bank of England, supervising deposit-taking banks; the Department of Trade and Industry (DTI), having insurers under its wings; and the Treasury, bossing over the Securities and Investment Board. SIB, in turn, delegated matters to three self-regulatory organizations (SROs), of which the Securities and Futures Authority, supervising exchanges, was the most important. Market participants were habitually given much responsibility and were able to mould matters after practical needs. It became apparent, however, that fragmented supervision was out-of-step with the blurring of boundaries between financial institutions. Some spectacular failures speeded the establishment of a super-regulator, the Financial Services Authority (FSA), according to the Scandinavian example (Graham 1997a; House 1997).

The FSA organizes under the Treasury and consolidates the regulatory roles of the Bank of England, DTI, and SIB with its SROs. Its responsibility is the institutional structure and legislation, and its mandate covers banks of all colours and denominations, insurance companies, financial markets, Lloyd's insurance market included, and settlement systems. It can fine without upper limit but its decisions can be challenged at an independent tribunal. The sheer size of the FSA and the disparate parts from which it has been created has raised doubts about its ability to implement the new philosophy. And the vast powers have aroused concern; will it be accountable and pro-competition? It is too early to tell since there is no track record yet. The total staff is 2,000 with a modest 175 enforcing the rulings. The requirement, laid down by law, that the FSA's activity must be cost-effective is certainly innovative. (Dickson 2000; Mackintosh 2001)

The formal structure of the *Japanese* model used to be a close copy of the US system, but in spirit it was much closer to the old-time British way. Now also the formal setup is tilting towards the British FSA. The financial system, commodities excluded, used to be the realm of the Ministry of Finance (MoF). Its Banking Bureau supervised the large banks, and the Securities Bureau had securities issuance and trading, including derivatives, under its wing. Small banks were to be the realm of local governments. Then the system came under intense stress. There was a mountain of bad loans from real estate speculation, concentrated in major cities. Securities houses had bribed important customers. Inspectors had been wined and dined by the financial community. Losses had been concealed by creative accounting, partially in offshore centres. International markets responded with a 40–90 bp blanket premium charged for Japanese financial institutions. The outcry was tremendous and some spectacular failures were allowed to take place. Finally, the large (city) banks, brokers and foreigners were transferred from the MoF to a new Financial Supervisory Agency (FSA) with wide powers; it can suspend a bank from business and close down a broker. Nor has it hesitated to use the whip, and organizations found guilty of serious or repeated breaking of rules have been fined and banned from the specific business for several months. (Abrahams and Tett 1997; Rafferty 2000; Tett 1998)

In general, there has been cautious liberalization along the US lines. Banking is no longer compartmentalized, nor is securities business separated from it. Licences for new branches are more easily available. Disclosure is important, as in the USA, but it is more a matter of form rather than substance. There are rule books supported by self-regulatory organizations, and a lenient insider legislation has been in force since 1989. The detail is overwhelming and has contributed to the weak international showing of the country's financial muscle. The core of the system is not in its letter but its practice, however. A law typically sets the target but leaves the means open. There may also be a reservation that, in certain circumstances, authorities have the right to intervene. These features are the foundation of administrative guidelines (*gyosei shido*). For example, stronger actors are pressurized to support weaker competitors in a crisis. One might say that what is forbidden in principle can still be subject to exemption, and what is legitimate in principle can still be temporarily forbidden by an administrative ruling. In other words, there is scope for negotiation. Fundamentally, that resembles the British practice of judgemental regulation which is generally praised for its flexibility. The really disturbing thing may not be the rulings but the difficulty in soliciting them in advance. (Dawkins 1996b; Reading 1998; Shirreff 1994; Tett 1997)

Germany has generally been considered a laggard in financial regulation and supervision. The image is incorrect in banking which is traditionally held in high esteem. It has been more appropriate in securities markets which remained a regulatory backwater ten to fifteen years longer than in the UK, and were considered by the German public as a place for the wheeler-dealer and unscrupulous. Unprofessional practice and petty regulation about securities markets was also rife, the latter reportedly to enforce interest-free reserves at the central bank (Evans 1992). That discouraged private equity ownership, supported bond issuance by banks, delayed the international issuance and trading of German script, and pushed it abroad. The approval of domestic bond issues by the Bundesbank was only abolished in 1990, and the law equating derivatives markets with gambling was changed the same year. Insider trading was criminalized, and the supervision of exchanges transferred from state commissioners to a federal supervisor as late as 1995. But still the takeover code protecting minority shareholders is only voluntary.

The Bundesbank has overseen banking directly, and securities and derivatives through the state (*Länder*) central banks, the securities watchdog lacking proper infrastructure. The solution has been natural, since universal banks dominate securities markets. Now, Germany will also join the 'bankwagon' and establish a consolidated super-regulator, the Federal Financial Supervisory Agency. To placate the financial community, the old structure is not dismantled, however, but topped by this superstructure. Its powers and resources will be broadly comparable with those in other countries, with authority to fine up to €1.5m for market manipulation and delaying of information, and a staff of 1,000 (Simonian 2001; Williamson 2001; 2002).

This short review of national regulation displays the major philosophies, from decentralized and largely independent agencies to a centralized, hands-on system led by a ministry, central bank or a super-regulator. Where superficial similarity exists in the form of insider legislation and formal rule books, the detail and application can be worlds apart. And still the discussion has been at a very general level. Nothing has been said about the percentages and multipliers which are an integral part of any regulatory structure. Much of the cutting edge is actually in such detail and, when they and exemptions from general rules are overlooked, important information is also left unused. For example, the British pragmatism and flexibility which has helped to make London a global finance centre does not come to the fore here. The review shows, nevertheless, that international financial markets are not quite as rational and effective as they are readily perceived to be. It means that well-informed and skilful operators will find market imperfections which they can exploit, entirely legally, for maximum profit.

A related question is whether regulatory systems are sufficiently powerful and skilled for the job they are supposed to do. An indicator hinted at above is the number of regulatory staff and severity of penalties. Another is the number and size of major market disruptions. They need not entail criminal action but are the outcome of unbridled market forces or gross managerial incompetence. Examples abound: the October 1987 stock market crash at major exchanges; the derivatives speculation by Barings Bank at the Singapore Stock Exchange, which wiped out the bank's equity; the near collapse of the Long-Term Capital Management (LTCM), an unregulated hedge fund with an estimated leverage of 150–200 and $1tr of off-the-balance-sheet notional principal; and the actual collapse of Enron, an unregulated commodities trader (Anon. 2002; Evans 2002; Gapper and Denton 1996; Lambert 1988; Plender 1998; Putnam 1998; Shirreff 1998). Two of the examples are from heavily-regulated exchanges, and general indicators, if not the inner details, were widely visible to anybody who wanted to see. They still happened. The two others were in the regulatory margin. LTCM was not regulated but the banks which lent to it were. Enron was not regulated either, the type of business it conducted being exempted by CFTC; whether justly or not is an open question. Do observe, though, that there was no criminal action, which would offer much more devastating stories. Were the regulators too weak or just incompetent and careless? It is the same type of question which can be raised about the police. How much more in resources and executive power should it be given to enable it to stamp out all violent crime? Crime is there for everybody to see, so the answer should be as obvious as it is for bridling market forces and educating managers about their fiduciary duties.

It is not possible to address financial regulation without also commenting on *money laundering* and the measures taken to combat it. Laundering is a big issue; the IMF guesstimates the annual volume at 2–5 per cent of global GDP (Catán 1999; Willman 2001). Most originates from drug trading but also smuggling, general racketeering and embezzlement of public funds, aid monies included. Large-scale criminal organizations follow standard business principles and are very professional. Because drug sales are retail, one must be able to handle large amounts of cash in small denominations. It cannot be stored in the basement but must be integrated in the banking system. Because onshore banks may be required to inform authorities about cash deposits above a certain limit, several people are needed to make a large number of comparatively small regular deposits to numerous geographically scattered accounts (smurfing). Disguising such activity during long periods is difficult and it is better to have a parallel legal business which generates large amounts of cash. Restaurants, hotels, cinemas, petrol stations, corner stores, supermarkets and similar are ideal for the purpose. Foreign trade is also popular. Shipping papers go through a bank which pays and cashes money against them. The physical inspection of the merchandise is conducted by customs officials who are not necessarily well informed about the true value of the goods they are clearing. The surplus value is laundered money.

At the wholesale end it is better to access financial markets directly. Offshore centres are a possibility although the days when one could walk in a bank with a suitcase full of $100 notes are mostly over. The safeguards can go to unexpected lengths, even in offshore centres. The LGT Bank in Liechtenstein, owned by a royal foundation, did not at the time accept clients from Latin America. Nor did some older Liechtenstein lawyers deal with them. Some US banks pulled out of the Colón Free Trade Zone in Panama because of suspicions that the zone was used for money laundering. (Evans 1991; Fidler 1996)

It may be more efficient to contact an intermediary in some large finance centre and arrange a fake transaction. For example, a speculative position is taken in one market and an offsetting position in another. The loss is paid by dirty money while the gain is clean money. Over-the-counter markets are preferred because formal exchanges use sophisticated computer algorithms which are capable of discovering dubious trading. For example, the opposing trades cannot add to zero and originate from the same broker. Therefore, the deal is repeated several times in different markets with varying amounts. Scale economies in the form of numerous simultaneous deals are an obvious advantage. If the paper trail can be broken, it will essentially hamper possible investigation by authorities later on. Of course, intermediaries take their fees and it is estimated that the total cut comes up to 30 per cent of the monies. (Catán 1999; Hall 1999; Schwander-Auckenthaler 1995; Willman 2001)

The possibilities to combat money laundering are made difficult by the sad fact that the underlying criminal activity rests on a sound economic rationale. There is a strong demand which cannot be met by legal means or, if it can (alcohol, tobacco), at a price which far exceeds production and distribution costs. That makes illegal activity very lucrative, a gross profit margin of 300 per cent has been estimated, and able to resist severe shocks. Drug trade were profitable even when three-quarters of the merchandise were confiscated. The actual share may be 10 per cent or less. Because physical measures are inefficient, authorities try to curb the money flow, and to succeed they need the cooperation of the financial community. It always seems to boil down to the same basic rule: know your customer. When an unknown person tries to conduct a suspect transaction, for example, open an account without proper identification, the bank should alert authorities. It puts a heavy responsibility on the clerk at the teller, and also on the manager in the nearby booth, because declined business is lost business and probably a lost customer also. Once the customer relation has been established, it requires a well-nigh divine clairvoyance to separate dirty deals from clean ones. And once a lead has been identified, it would be tremendously helpful to have the legitimation to penetrate banking secrecy and trust arrangements even abroad, and to have a strong legal infrastructure at home to pursue the case. The first requirement is increasingly being fulfilled, the other is lagging. Even the USA, renowned for its tough legislation and draconian enforcement, has dragged its feet on this score. (Beard 2002; Catán and Burns 1999; Fidler and Burns 1997; Hamilton Fazey 1998; Willman 2001)

Raters

Rating agencies evaluate the creditworthiness of borrowers, their ability to pay in time and in full. Borrowers include commercial entities like retailers, manufacturers, insurers, banks, securities houses and building associations. They also include public authorities, sovereigns ('countries') and supranationals like the World Bank. Rating helps lenders to evaluate the credit risk and is also used by authorities in their regulatory work. It does not deal with currency exposure, interest rate risk, debt liquidity or country risk (except for country ratings). It is particularly valuable when the borrowers are too numerous to be known individually by lenders. It is no coincidence, then, that the practice started in the USA and is gaining in importance with the internationalization of financial markets.

Few regular borrowers escape rating. It is simply not rational, because an unrated borrower is almost certain to pay a higher interest rate than if it were rated. In the USA, practically all bonds are rated, while in the euromarkets the figure is 60 per cent for long-term bonds. The French used to have difficulty in euromarkets because few issuers had ratings, among other things (Humphreys 1992). In Latin America, bond issuance is often made dependent on a minimum rating. Japan used to follow the same practice.

An interest rate for virtually riskless lending, the Fed Rate, LIBOR, or government bonds, is taken as a basis to which a risk premium is added. Occasionally the premium may also be negative. It broadly reflects the rating given by leading rating agencies and has real significance. When the average rate is about 6 per cent for bonds with the highest creditworthiness, it is 7.5 per cent for the lowest investment grade, and a hefty 21 per cent for organizations on the verge of default (see Figure 2.10). At the company level, however, a range of 1–2 per cent for identically rated firms is quite possible. Because rating affects the price of borrowed funds, rating agencies have real power and a downgrading (transition risk) can have serious consequences:

> Indosuez is a French investment bank with extensive swap (see p. 136) operations. Interest swaps are sensitive to the parties' credit rating because these remain responsible towards a third party. Fitch IBCA downgraded Indosuez from AA to A− which led to the decline of its swap business. When also the parent's, Compagnie de Suez, short-term debt got downgraded to A2, Indosuez lost its implicit guarantee. As a result, business in general deteriorated rapidly and enforced the sale of Indosuez. (Shirreff 1996b)

The basic split is between investment grade and speculative grade (high-risk or 'junk'). The split has significance beyond the interest rate alone. Many lenders are not allowed, either by law or their own bylaws, to deal with borrowers below investment grade, and often the practical limit is set higher than the minimum. The purpose, of course, is to protect the beneficiaries of the lending entity from any misjudged or unscrupulous behaviour from its officers. Pension funds and insurance companies, in particular, have strict standards. Occasionally such restrictions can be evaded by leaving the script unrated. Investment in speculative grade debt is not only risky, it is also labour intensive. The script has poor liquidity and is often held to maturity. Credit analysis becomes important and the labour input is claimed to be eightfold compared with investment grade paper. But the poor image of junk bonds, as conveyed by the mass media, is not entirely justified. Before their appearance, unrated midsize companies in the USA had no access to the bond market and relied exclusively on expensive bank loans. Foreign borrowers often pay more than domestic ones. This can be motivated by the larger effort to retrieve payment in case of eventual default. (Ensor 1998)

The dominant rating agencies are Moody's Investment Services (est. 1909), Standard & Poor's (est. 1916/1922), Fitch IBCA (est. 1978) in banking, and A.M. Best (est. 1899) in insurance. Only IBCA has non-US roots. The dominance of the US agencies naturally incites criticism abroad. Usual is the claim that their outlook is too American, and that unwritten cultural rules of good business practice and public responsibility towards depositors, employees and customers cannot be derived from financial information. The response is that these values are, indeed, accounted for. For example, companies with government ownership or guarantee, even implicit as may be the case with banks, get a better rating than otherwise. A still more convincing argument in favour of the US agencies is the financial weight of their country. If the really heavy lenders are there, then it is only natural that their value system is accommodated. Still, the majors face some competition from national agencies in the UK, France, Germany, various Southeast Asian countries and so on. For example, three local rating agencies focus on midsize German companies, often world champions in their narrow segments, on the pretext that large international agencies may be unfamiliar with local tax and regulation (Althaus 1999).

Most ratings are done on a voluntary basis, that is, the borrower makes contact and asks to be rated. But Moody's also does unsolicited rating – and publishes the results, much to the chagrin of the objects, who usually feel that they have scored worse than appropriate. The rating process begins by scrutinizing relevant corporate material placed at the agency's disposal and making plant and store visits; it continues with the evaluation of the environment in which the company operates, including authorities, competition, localities and so on; and is finished by a look at the management and their qualifications. It goes without saying that the environmental and managerial aspects introduce a heavy subjective element. The results are compiled in a report of thirty to fifty pages in length and subjected to an expert panel of anywhere between four and ten persons, who make the rating. The rating and the report are then submitted to the organization, which can appeal, at least in theory. It can also ask that the result should not be made public, a request which may be honoured depending on the country and rating agency. The fee will be $15,000–$30,000 for a bond issue of $200m, or perhaps a lump sum of $100,000. Unsolicited ratings are based mainly on published material. Supported by lively demand, the agencies have grown fabulously. S&P, for example, rates about 38,000 organizations in eighty-six countries covering $11tr of debt (Brown 1996; Jacquin et Pouzin 1995; Vittori 1992; White 2001: Table 1).

Ratings are done about short-term and long-term debt and about various asset classes, also issued by organizations domiciled in different countries. It goes without saying that the scales are only conditionally comparable and to emphasize this fact different notation may be used. It is the same with ratings given by different agencies about the same objects. Considering the many subjective judgements involved and procedural differences not discussed here, that is hardly astonishing. If there is systematic difference it is between small and large agencies, the latter being more thrifty in their scoring. Differences of opinion are most pronounced in the case of poor credit risks, which is also logical. The apparent similarity of notation should, therefore, not deceive (Table 2.4).

Ratings should have the ability to forecast defaults. In the aggregate, this is the case. Ratings done at the time of issuance and collected over lengthy periods indicate unambiguously three facts. First, a high rating implies considerably less risk than a low rating (Figure 2.10). Second, the risk grows with time, even for highly rated paper. Third, the risk depends on a business cycle. The first observation holds by definition, while the second one can be explained by changes in environment and corporate inability to adapt rapidly enough. The third aspect puts the agency in a dilemma, should ratings follow the cycle or remain approximately static, in which case the cyclicity would become apparent in fluctuating default probability.

Curves like the one in Figure 2.10 cover thousands of issues, and inevitably hide gaffes, too. Infamous is the floundering of Orange County, CA in December 1994, rated AA at the time of the default. No less unflattering was the 1997 financial crisis in Asia Pacific which had long been in the making but was not reflected in ratings. Inability to interpret or misplaced respect for local sensitivities (Irvine 1998)?

Table 2.4 Rating scales of long-term debt, simplified

Grade	Symbol		Verbal
	Moody's	*S&P*	
Investment	Aaa	AAA	Superior
	Aa	AA	Excellent
	A	A	Good
	Baa	BBB	Adequate
Speculative	Ba	BB	Questionable
	B	B	Poor
	Caa	CCC	Very poor
	Ca	C	Extremely poor
	D	D	Default

Sources: Jacquin and Pouzin 1995; Swiss Re, *sigma* No. 7/1995.

Note
The verbal characteristic is a compromise between Moody's and S&P.

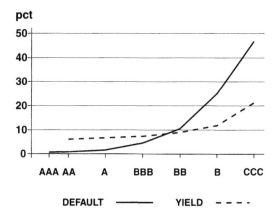

Figure 2.10 Risk and reward, US corporate issuers, 31 December 2001.

Sources: Brady and Bos 2002: Table 2; Standard & Poor's Risk Solutions 2002; both courtesy of Standard & Poor's. *Financial Times*, 2 January 2002: 20.

Note
Credit indices (OAS) added to treasuries yield; for investment grade (AAA to BBB) ten-year maturity and for speculative grade (BB to CCC) five-year maturity.

The environmental effect becomes tangible with country ratings. They reflect here the default risk of government bonds denominated in foreign currencies (Figure 2.11). Foreign currency increases the risk, because the option to pay up by printing more money does not exist. Logically, denomination in local currency gives a rating 1–5 notches (plus or minus) higher. The EMU has been given a single rating by the major agencies. Moody's considers euro as a domestic currency, while S&P and Fitch IBCA use foreign currency ratings. Governments keep their normal ratings for their individual debts (Beers and Cavanaugh 1997; Currie 1997).

The main impression unfolding from Figure 2.11 is the steep grading of countries. Basically, only established industrial countries enjoy good ratings, sustained budgetary deficits and large national debts notwithstanding. Some explanation can be found in their tax collection ability; the screw can always be turned a few turns tighter. The interconnectedness of their economies also matters. A default by one important country would have uncomfortable consequences for the rest, and this encourages mutual assistance. An overall explanation is that things are much worse in the multitude of countries with a speculative rating or none at all. Some are unable to issue bonds internationally and must rely on project loans, by banks and direct investors, and development aid. But one should observe that being a developing country does not automatically mean a speculative rating. Botswana and UAE, supported by export revenue from diamonds and crude oil, respectively, and spiced with a dose of responsible economic administration, are investment grade.

Figure 2.11 Sovereign risk, foreign-currency bonds, 29 November 2001.

Source: Moody's Investor Service 2001.

Note
Government bonds denominated in foreign currencies.

Another type of risk is that the government puts up exchange controls which do not allow the repatriation of private bank deposits (Truglia *et al.* 1995). This risk is clearly larger than the one connected with government bonds, because any sovereign is reluctant to jeopardize its future borrowing ability by defaulting on its own script (Cantor and Packer 1995, Table 2). Making a bank or a private firm the scapegoat through exchange controls is more convenient. The difference between government bonds and bank deposits appears sufficiently important in developing countries to warrant separate ratings, while industrialized countries manage with a single rating.

It follows that an organization normally cannot get a better rating than its home country. It may have assets abroad which can be sequestrated in extreme cases, but that does not help the rating.

> Reliance Industries, the Indian petrochemicals company and an unquestionable blue chip, cannot get investment grade rating because of its home country. It pays roughly 100 bp more for its borrowing than a similar US company. (Miller 1997: 114)

The only exception is for countries where the dollar has largely replaced the national currency. (*BIS QR* Aug. 1997: 20)

Accountants

A borrower's financial health is the basis of its credit rating. The appropriate indicators are substantially influenced by the accounting standards followed. These are national, which makes international comparisons potentially hazardous. Among the most important sources of vagueness are the handling of goodwill (purchase price over book value) at acquisitions, the valuation of assets, pension obligations, and off-balance-sheet items like guarantees given, and special purpose vehicles (SPVs) used for cleansing the balance sheet.

It is commonplace that the price paid for companies in unfriendly acquisitions is 15 per cent higher than their market value, and the surcharge can go up to 100 per cent. That surcharge is usually too large to be written off at the end of the fiscal year but is capitalized as goodwill, instead, and written off during a longer period, sometimes indefinitely. It is easy to understand the effect that the choice of the amortization period can have on profit and assets.

The valuation of assets is a many-faceted question. Physical assets is the simple case, valued at either the purchase or repurchase (market) price from which eventual wear and tear is subtracted. Inflation means that the repurchase price is higher and should consequently give a fair idea of the value of the item. Of course, a possible forced sale is unlikely to command anything like fair value. Financial assets are more mercurial, and many analysts see the best solution to be in 'marking them to market', that is, recording them at the current price. The result is heavy fluctuation in asset value and earnings which probably disturbs normal business. Therefore, and to reduce taxes, hidden reserves are created in good times by postponing revenues and exaggerating expenses. Most securities can be marked to market but bank loans cannot because they have no ready market. It is known, however, that, as a group, their value cannot rise but could well decline. The technique is to make writedowns and reservations which are believed to reflect the true value of non-performing ('bad') and suspect loans. Judgement is thereby substituted for 'objective' measurement. In Asia, there may be rules about the largest permitted annual percentage.

Pension obligations are important in so far that there is great variation in the retirement systems between countries. Where the pay-as-you-go philosophy dominates, the issue is marginal. But where the emphasis is on funded pensions with a substantial employer contribution, it is important to know whether pension obligations are fully funded or not. If the fund is not on the balance sheet, there should at least be a note about its existence and financial status.

Banks routinely give various guarantees to their customers against a fee. These are disclosed off the balance sheet, but the practice became general only in the 1990s. Potentially more dangerous are obligations connected with derivatives, that is, futures, options and swaps. The problem is not so much derivatives as such but the fact that much of the activity is highly leveraged, promises to buy and sell are backed by a narrow capital base, and that options contain a very large loss potential. Since derivatives are more volatile than the underlying securities, their notional amounts often large, and the contracts numerous, it is quite impossible to come to grips with the attached risks through conventional accounting practice such as unaudited quarterly balance sheets. Although the obligations are disclosed, the recorded situation is already outdated. It is more a question of regulatory supervision and corporate risk management than conventional accounting.

Since there are no hard logical rules to handle the outlined situations, national legislators have resorted to *ad hoc* solutions. These differ sufficiently to constitute a nuisance for the international finance market. An attempt at unification is the International Accounting Standards promoted by IASC, a European organization. Many German, French and Swiss companies have started issuing financial statements in compliance with them, the London Stock Exchange accepts them as a basis of listing and, by 2005, they should apply to all companies listed in the EU. They also get backing from China and Arab countries (Banque de France 2000: 122; Kelly 1997; Waters 1996). A competitive position vis-à-vis US exchanges has thereby been created. There, the International Accounting Standards are considered too vague and therefore unacceptable. For example, the Continental practice of creating undisclosed reserves is anathema to Americans. Should the IASC tighten its rules, however, not only the US but also Japanese and Canadian markets would probably be opened. But that has been too much for France and Germany to swallow, and the question has remained in limbo. It is partly a matter of national pride but also of differing tax systems and accounting philosophies. The US system focuses on the cash-generating ability of capital, while the Continental European approach gives a better idea of a company's worth in eventual liquidation, both logical outcomes of financial systems oriented towards capital markets and bank loans, respectively.

Then there are purely practical aspects. A large multinational company is listed at several exchanges in various countries, each with its listing requirements. Nestlé operates normally under the IAS regime. If it wants to get listed at an American exchange it must comply with the Generally Accepted Accounting Principles (GAAP), which is the US standard for financial reporting. The parallel set of rules, the Standard Accounting Principles (SAP), is for government use and does not apply here. Nestlé must consider whether it is worth the expense to produce two sets of figures for each of its 800 subsidiaries, the one following GAAP for Americans and the other following IAS for the rest of the world (Waller

1996). The difference between the GAAP and IAS, or various European standards, is by no means a cosmetic one. IASC accepts the revaluation of fixed assets but GAAP forbids it. IASC allows infinite amortization of intangible assets while GAAP limits it to twenty years. IASC accepts pooling of interests at merger, GAAP does not (Berton 1999). The net effect can be dramatic. Daimler-Benz, in its June 1993 half-year report, announced an after-tax profit of $155m according to the German rules but an $875m loss according to the GAAP (Waters 1996).

Legal issues

A comparative study about the core accounting principles in key financial countries, suitable for cartographic presentation, would be most welcome. While such a study may not yet exist, the legal profession has prepared its version of the same topic (Wood 1997). Indeed, the international comparison of legal systems has considerable seniority over that of accounting principles, and what is outlined in this section is only the highest peak of the proverbial iceberg.

The starting point is the opinion that insolvency law is the foundation of commercial and financial law. It has several dimensions, among which the scope of security, insolvency set-off and divided ownership cover important areas. Should insolvency lead unconditionally to bankruptcy or should the insolvent be given an opportunity for reconstruction? Are creditors allowed to net out credit exposures in case of insolvency or should the solvent counterpart join the other creditors? Are securities under custody secured against bankruptcy proceedings should the custodian default, considering that a third party may be unable to see the difference between apparent and beneficial owner? Questions like these are legion, and the solutions which they have received in various countries are not easy to reconcile. It is a widespread idea among non-professionals and one easily conveyed in overall presentations that the split into common law countries and those following a civil code clears the worst snags, whereafter culturally close, and usually neighbouring, countries can be safely grouped together (Economides *et al.* 1986).

This idea does not correspond with reality, which is far more complex. The dichotomy of common law versus civil code has lost much of its former significance since the essentials of commercial life have been codified into coherent laws almost everywhere, and because past verdicts by higher courts cannot be easily overlooked anywhere. Geographical closeness need not have much significance. France and England face each other across the Channel but are diametrically opposite in most aspects, while German influence is significant in China, Japan and Korea (Stoakes 1995). The Dutch recently succeeded in exporting their legal system to Russia, reportedly because it had just been updated. Cultural closeness fares somewhat better, although it is a fluid issue and particularly so when it comes to details (Wood 1997). One accepts readily that Scandinavia and Germany have similar legal systems, and after some thought the former Austrian Empire comes alive in Austria, Hungary, the Czech Republic, Slovakia, the former Yugoslavia and Italy. Old colonial connections, as usual, are alive and well. But there are also unexpected breaks. One would expect Iran to follow the *sharia* law in the way of Saudi Arabia instead of the traditional Franco-Latin sphere in which it can actually be found. Ireland follows England, while Scotland does not, grouping as it does with the Channel Islands and Québec. This is the broad canvas and, unfortunately, it is too varied in detail for a black-and-white cartographic presentation. Instead, the status of trust is displayed. Trust is cartographically uncomplicated, and its role as a financial structure is undisputable.

Trust is a legal vehicle for disconnecting benefaction from ownership. It is established through a deed in which the ownership of property is transferred to a trustee, while the net revenue goes to a separate beneficiary. The trustee can give the practical management further to a third person. This is the traditional concept purporting to preserve family wealth for further generations. In the financial world at large, the modified concept (no ownership transfer) has other applications. Settlement systems handle very large amounts of other people's money every day. The routine administration of a security portfolio is often handed over to a custodian, and particularly so if the portfolio happens to be abroad. Should the trustee, custodian or settlement organization go into receivership, it is important that the trust property can be claimed from the estate. And should it have been wrongfully dispossessed, it can hopefully be traced (recovered) to the owner. The chances for these matters to succeed are considerably enhanced when there is specific legislation to fall back on. And that varies a great deal all over the world with consequences for the location of financial activity (Figure 2.12). For example, it is not by mere chance that US and British banks are in the forefront of global custodianship, and Euroclear located in Belgium only after the country had created trust for securities (Stoakes 1995).

The legal mess around Lloyd's, the insurance market's, attempt to recover insurance claims from its US members (Names) serves as an example of the desirability of unifying legal principles and procedures internationally:

> Lloyd's solicited a great number of US members during the 1980s. The members were obliged to back Lloyd's policies with their whole property and had agreed that possible disputes should be solved according to English law. Many policies subsequently incurred heavy losses, allegedly because of incompetent underwriting and negligent supervision by Lloyd's. Several members consequently refused to honour their obligations and sued Lloyd's at US courts. Their procedural argument was that English law cannot overrule US law in the USA and that a waiver to that effect is unconstitutional.

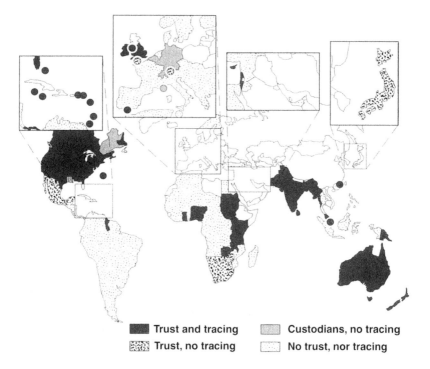

Figure 2.12 Divided ownership (trust) by jurisdiction, mid-1990s.

Source: Wood, Philip R., Map 10. Allen & Overy Global Law Maps: *World Financial Law*, 3rd edn, September 1997, Philip R. Wood, Allen & Overy, London. Copyright © 1997 of Allen & Overy, London; used with permission.

Note
The original figure has been simplified.

The first obstacle facing unification is the difficulty in mobilizing an influential pressure group to promote the new construction. The warmest adherents are those who recognize the familiar features of their national law in it; the rest remain lukewarm. The other problem is that even the best law creates a mere superstructure which must be filled with practical experience. Such experience can come only from intensive use, and it takes time. Therefore, it may be as well to adopt an already functioning legal system for international use.

English (not British!) law is an obvious candidate (Blanden 1990). It is basically case law, which has greatly facilitated the grafting into it of cases which have very little to do with England directly. Centuries of global trade and a 200-year history of commercial law are reflected in considerable sophistication and a momentous wealth of cases. The prevalence of English as a commercial language and the role of London as a finance centre bring the customers. Most eurobonds, for example, are subject to

English law. But English law is not without competition. The main challenge comes from the USA and specifically from the state of New York
(Rice 1995). The central role of its investment banks in placing bond and
equity offerings, raising project finance, and arranging mergers, takeovers
and privatizations creates a demand for legal services. These are based on
New York rather than English law. Inroads have been recorded particularly in Continental Europe and Asia. Fortunately for English law firms,
Americans make far too much money at home to be particularly keen to
expand abroad (Eaglesham 1999).

Some do, however. Baker & McKenzie is the most internationalized US
law firm and its locational pattern compares well with that of Clifford
Chance, the largest British law firm. The labour forces are in the same size
brackets and both embrace the better part of the globe, having started
internationalization after the Second World War (Figure 2.13). Baker &
McKenzie opened its first foreign office in Caracas in 1955 while Clifford
Chance started international expansion in 1962 with an office in Paris.
Clifford Chance is more focused, having a very strong presence in Europe
and other offices primarily in the USA and Asia Pacific. That looks very
British, irrespective of gaps in Australia, Canada and South Africa. One
half of the locations are quite recent, from the 1990s. The US bridgehead
was established in 1987 to distribute securities there.

Baker & McKenzie has spread its beans much more evenly, following
domestic customers to every corner of the world. Although the headquarters are in Chicago, the labour force in Europe is larger than at home. It is
strong in Latin America, as can be expected, and also outguns its rival in
Asia Pacific and the Middle East. The expansion has not been as mercurial
as by Clifford Chance, but rather at a rate of one or two offices a year.
There has been speculation about the merging of American and British
law firms across the Atlantic, thereby creating global champions in the way
it has been done in accounting. In view of our examples, there may be no
real need. The global presence is already there.

The practical significance of selecting an appropriate law is illuminated
at bond defaults. Bonds are loan notes issued in large numbers at identical denominations and conditions. They have no inbuilt mechanism for
negotiation between the issuer and bond holders. International bonds,
and eurobonds in particular, are often bearer paper which makes it
almost impossible to address all holders. That would be highly desirable if
it becomes necessary to reschedule the loan, to prolong the payback
period, for example. Yet, the New York law requires that rescheduling
necessitates consent by all bond holders, a practical impossibility. Therefore, an offer to exchange old bonds for new ones is made. Some holders
are certain to refuse and try to extract full payment by various tricks, free-
riding on the back of the consenting majority. The English law, by contrast, allows the introduction of a majority clause (*quorum* requirement) in
the loan conditions, which states that rescheduling can be made by a

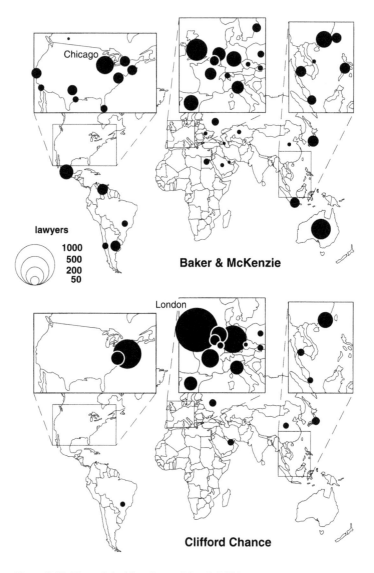

Figure 2.13 Two global law firms, March 2002.

Sources: www.bakermckenzie.com; www.cliffordchance.com.

Notes
Clerical staff omitted. USA and Canada by city, the rest by country.

supermajority of, say, 75 per cent of those attending the topical meeting (Stoakes 1999a; 1999b).

All serious international actors will one day face an American counterpart, simply because the country is so dominant in many financial markets (Figures 2.1 and 3.2). One need only recall that the dollar is the dominant reserve currency and the use of these reserves goes through US banks in New York. In other words, foreign banks have accounts with their correspondents and these monies can be frozen by court decree, for example. The local law will apply and any clause which says that it does not is null and void (antiwaiver provision; cf. Lloyd's above). When abroad, Americans naturally also prefer their own legal system there. Because the system differs in some important aspects from systems in other countries, one is well advised to be familiar with them.

The USA is a litigious country. The American Bar Association estimates that one in three US professionals is sued sometime during her/his career and that 94 per cent of all the world's lawsuits are filed there. This is made possible by a few simple features: both parties, including the winning one, pay their own costs in a civil (as opposed to criminal) case. A plaintiff's lawyers normally work on a contingency fee basis; if the case is lost there is no fee, if it is won the lawyer gets a 30–60 per cent share of the damages. Juries are made up of laymen who may not be up to the required level of understanding for complicated cases which could last for several months. The judge is entitled to treble the damages actually suffered. The damages are often judgemental and the amounts sentenced can be astronomical by European standards. It is possible to raise a class action which covers all similar cases without additional lawsuits taking place. Reference can later be made to this single judgement. US states have wide legal powers and lawyers are well aware where a particular case has the best chances to succeed.

Contingency fees and very high damages have made litigation into a business. It is estimated that even when only 5 per cent of cases are lost, it is still rational for the defendant to pay up. Indeed, 95 per cent of all cases are settled out of court. The most explosive cases are related to work injuries like asbestosis and environmental issues. They may be marginal for financial intermediaries themselves but not their customers. A property owner is responsible for cleaning contaminated real estate irrespective of tort, and the obligation is extended to everybody who has contributed to its contamination, for example the trucking company which carried out the transportation years ago. The stakes are heavily against the defendant and many companies have been forced into bankruptcy-like reorganization ('Chapter 11') by suffocating damages (Burt and Rice 1997; Stoakes 1996; Tomkins 1998).

The shortcomings of the system are widely acknowledged. Its defence is mostly ideological. A small litigant can challenge a mighty corporation and win if the case is righteous. The generous damages are a kind of substitute for shortcomings in social security. For a foreigner that gives cold comfort. His strategy is to keep out of the trouble's way. If the business is retail, there should be liability insurance for triple damages. Mediation and arbitration should be tried first and litigation left for absolutely outrageous cases (Burt and Rice 1997). The same applies in wholesale business but there it may be possible to select the locus of court in advance. Serious consideration should then be given to the State of Delaware. It has specialized in corporate law which is seen in economic and not moral terms. The law is revised continuously by committees of lawyers and amendments are delivered to the legislature in final form. There is a trial court and the Supreme Court can issue preliminary oral opinion. Lawyers' fees are related to the benefit and not hours worked. It is a rapid and efficient system (Herzel and Shepro 1988).

Conclusion

This chapter has laid the foundations. It has explained the concept of financial assets and estimated their size by asset class: equity, debt and bank deposit, a staggering total of $100tr. It has unfolded the geographical pattern and compared it with the underlying economy to derive a financial intensity index. It has clustered the twenty-one areal units into five logical groups using the shares of asset classes as criteria. That is the static picture. To it has been added dynamic elements with the help of financial flows. They range from simple outflows and inflows at major economic poles to net and gross flow matrices between numerous origins and destinations, some short term, others long term. In some cases it has been possible to give tentative explanations about reasons and observe effects in financial indicators.

The financial system has changed in one generation from a population of wealthy individuals to a universe dominated by a small group of professionals, managing the nation's collective savings. They are the sharp edge of institutional investors, that is, pension funds, insurance companies and investment funds which are the backbone of modern securities markets and hold over one-half of their assets. The democratization of finances has made institutional investments everybody's interest and a lever for political influence and power. It has become more important than ever before that the market mechanism is perceived to function justly and efficiently. Means to that end is a vast array of rules and norms, and an army of professionals, inspectors, supervisors and regulators who apply and enforce them. The judiciary, the legal and accounting professions, credit rating agencies and the public administrative apparatus itself, all contribute to that goal. To give life to the framework, it has been spiced with numerous examples. They should give a feeling about the spirit of the game and the complexity of practical life. In the chapters to follow, detail and focus is added, first by unfolding the broad canvas of financial markets and thereafter turning attention to actors and places.

3 Markets

All possible markets

Financial markets offer an efficient mechanism to channel savings for tangible investments. This is the credit and capital market and its outlook is long term. It is complemented and paralleled by the money market which is interbank and short term, down to overnight money. There the purpose is to trim the banks' balance sheets, provide interbank credit and tune the amount of money in circulation. This chapter is mostly about credit and capital markets.

Financial assets are activated by investment decisions, public and private, commercial and non-commercial. Some investments are made to gain operational control of the underlying physical assets and are called 'direct investments'. Others are made for the sake of investment income only and are portfolio investments. Since the stake needed for control varies, the difference between direct and portfolio investment is vague. Debt and loans are typical portfolio investments, while equity can be of both types. But it is not only the split between direct and portfolio. The picture is much more varied and the availability of financial assets is also conditioned by the borrower's qualifications.

Consider non-underwritten facilities. They are a credit line without a formal commitment by the bank (thus, non-underwritten), intended for a very general use and available when needed. Commercial paper, a short-term unsecured promissory note much used by corporations as working capital, is a typical example. But being unsecured, facilities are not available to every borrower. Bonds have similar features. The purpose can be given in general terms but the actual issuance necessitates investor acceptance. Bank loans are more strict. Bankers ask for an acceptable collateral and like to know the purpose for which they lend. The similarity to bonds is that neither one can normally be redeemed (paid) before maturity (eurobonds can). Dissimilarities dominate, however. Loans are seldom granted for periods exceeding fifteen-to-eighteen years, while bonds can have maturities of thirty years and beyond. There can be a considerable difference in the time needed for arranging a loan compared with a bond issue, although which one takes less time varies by circumstances. When not all the money is needed upfront, loans are safer because nobody can forecast the reception of successive bond issues. Logically, up to one-half of syndicated credits can be standby (Gardener and Molyneux 1993: 139). Syndication is popular in international loans and used to enhance their size and distribute risk. The syndicate evaluates the borrower's creditworthiness and negotiates loan conditions, an unstructured and opaque situation. Bank lending is more expensive than bond issuance, which reflects the lower (or no) credit rating needed. High-risk (junk) bonds have shattered this old rule, however. In case of default, it is easier to negotiate restructuring with a handful of bankers than an anonymous multitude of bondholders.

Listed equity has some commonalities with bonds. The company's financial standing is well-known and the share price widely available. As it is mostly growth companies who issue new equity, optimistic expectations will push the price up. Equity prices are often volatile which makes the timing of an issue more important than otherwise. Uncertainty also means that the discount from market price is larger and fees are higher than with bonds. Pricing will be further complicated when the issue is Initial Public Offer (IPO) and advice is sought with banks or securities houses. New equity dilutes ownership and control, and shareholders are more opinionated than bondholders. The great attraction is that equity is disposable indefinitely and its dividend can be passed in troubled times. Another advantage is tradability, which includes narrow spread (ask–bid price) and liquidity (ability to place a large lot without moving the price).

New loans and the issuance of debt and shares constitute the primary market. It is followed by trading, i.e. the secondary market. The existence of a secondary market is important because it allows the investor to sell at any time for a fair price. That enhances interest in the script and boosts its issuance price. The split into primary and secondary markets is relevant for some financial instruments but not others. Equity and debt have both. Loans have a primary market but the secondary market is weakly developed. It can be created for mortgages and consumer credit by repackaging them to debt instruments, so-called asset-backed securities (ABS). These securities are standardized and therefore saleable. The operation can be done internally or a subsidiary, a special purpose vehicle (SPV), can be established for the purpose. The advantage of this arrangement is that the credits disappear from the bank's balance sheet and free regulatory capital. Should the credits default and the SPV falls into receivership the bank remains responsible. Therefore, the commitment must be mentioned off the balance sheet. Standard loans are too customized to be readily saleable or swappable, although even this is beginning to change (*BIS AR* 1996/1997: 120, 127; Luce 1997). In derivatives, the distinction between primary and secondary is less clear. Contracts are written when they are needed, one by one. If this takes place at an exchange, they can be sold repeatedly until exercised or they expire. If it is OTC, a position is cancelled by an opposite contract.

Trading takes place at organized exchanges or outside them, OTC. There is no sharp boundary between the two. OTC is a screen and phone market, but so are many exchanges. Equity tends to be traded at exchanges, however, and bonds OTC. The apparent reason is that bonds, as a group, are less homogenous than equities and call for individual treatment. Trading at an organized exchange necessitates listing and adherence to its rules, which makes an exchange a safer place to deal than OTC. The counterparty risk is largely eliminated because a clearing house guarantees each trade and collects a percentage margin to ensure fulfilment when trading is at credit. The instruments are standardized for ease of trading and this gives better liquidity and price transparency, at least for small trades. Exchanges have also become increasingly the realm of small funds and individuals, while large players operate mainly OTC. The weak side of exchanges is administrative overhead which makes them expensive. They are discussed in detail in Chapter 4.

It is possible to display the cross-border lending by banks and the international issuance of securities for a lengthy period (Figure 3.1). The activity does not include interbank operations, i.e. it is 'real' business. Lenders and borrowers are residents of different countries and the issues are also intended for investors who are not residents of the country of placement. Where the script then ends when trading begins is often shrouded in mystery. The time series originates from OECD until 1995 and thereafter from BIS. There is a clear discontinuity in 1995/1996, best discovered by comparing both data sets in 1996, with BIS data having a better coverage. The terminology changes too, OECD's non-underwritten facilities being replaced by BIS's money market instruments. For our purposes such differences are not so important. A visual overview is sufficient and it tells that roughly one-half of the international primary market has originated from the banking system and one-half from securities. The split has varied between 40/60 and 60/40 depending on the relative health of the said systems, but the average is about 50/50. Some other ratios may be more trendy. Money market instruments have clearly gained ground at the expense of syndicated credits. They are attractive because they are flexible and the growing awareness of the creditworthiness of giant corporations has overcome prejudices against their unsecured debt. Cross-border equities have also gained acceptance, although their share is only 3–7 per cent out of the total market, or 7–17 per cent of bond issues. At some domestic markets equity issues have in the past accounted for 20–25 per cent out of gross bond issues (Turner 1991: 54).

The temporal picture is rounded out by geography (Figure 3.2). It comprises securities, that is, equities, debt and exchange-traded derivatives disaggregated by country or region. The comparison is between 1990 and 2000, both healthy years for the topical instruments, although with

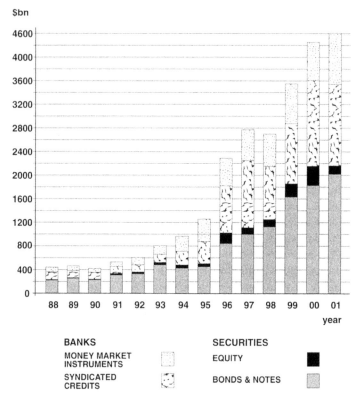

Figure 3.1 Cross-border gross lending and issuance, 1988–2001.

Source: OECD various issues, Table 1, 1988–1995; *BIS QR* various issues, 1996–2001.

Notes
There is a break in the series 1995/1996. BIS terminology is accepted.

geographical shadings. The emphasis is on proportions. The US dominance becomes dramatically apparent. That is the reason why the country is given so much attention in this book, not only in the strict international context but also domestically. Its domestic habits and activities have a strong bearing internationally. Beyond that, the proportions have not changed much. There are only three features worth commenting on. The Japanese equity market has contracted dramatically, while the debt has grown. The market's buoyancy rested on booming exports and an expansive monetary policy. Low interest rates supported an equity market where prices related to earnings (p/e) were three times higher than in the USA or Europe and made the Tokyo Stock Exchange the largest in the world. When interest rates were raised, the bubble burst and three annual GDPs worth of paper wealth was destroyed. The exchange was reduced to a 'normal' size by 2000, far behind its homologue in New York. The gap was

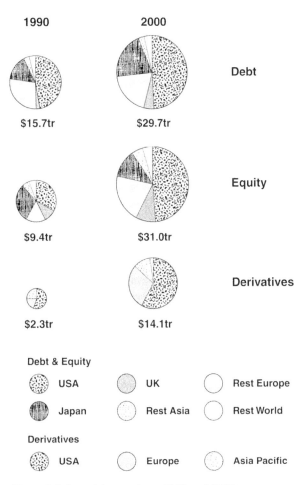

Figure 3.2 Securities markets, 1990 and 2000.

Source: Swiss Re, *sigma* No. 7/2001: Figures 2–4. Copyright © 2001 of Swiss Reinsurance Company, Zurich; used with permission.

Notes
Outstandings, domestic market capitalization, open interest at exchanges. The total in 2000 is 25 per cent less than estimated in Table 2.2.

then filled with government debt issued in the vain hope that it would stimulate domestic economy and turn it into growth again. The share of European debt has declined and it is not only a consequence of the growth in Japan. The European welfare economies had overextended themselves and many were approaching the limit where their public debt was no longer saleable. A retrenchment took place and the debt is now slowly declining. Finally, Europeans have started using derivatives and taking market share from Asians. This is part of a learning process, with the origin in the USA.

All financial markets have three dimensions: the creation of new credit, the trading of existing credit and the volume of accumulated credit. The terminology can vary depending on context. The creation of new credit by banks is called 'lending' or 'new loans', while the same process with bonds and equity is issuance. Statistically, both can be either net or gross, with paid loans, redeemed bonds and bought shares either being netted against new issues or not. The difference between announced and completed issues is obvious. Sadly enough, these details are not always spelled out, which leaves the non-professional in doubt. Bank loans outstanding are the same as bank claims. Bonds are also outstanding and derivatives have notional outstandings, except when they are traded at organized exchanges where contracts outstanding are called 'open interest'. The vacillating terminology is largely accidental, as many markets have developed semi-independently of each other, creating confusion and demanding alertness. Equally important is a feeling about the relationship of the three dimensions, which can vary a good deal between the markets.

Table 3.1 consolidates the facts, the primary market (gross issuance), its accumulated stock (outstandings) and the secondary market (trading). Consistent comprehensive data is normally available about cross-border markets. Domestic data is less standardized and may be available only from domestic sources. Domestic lending is carried out by all kind of financial intermediaries, and also to public bodies. The inclusion of

Table 3.1 Capital and money markets, 2000

		Issuance $bn	Trading $bn	Outstanding $bn	Iss/Out (%)	Trd/Out (%)
Loans	Cross-border	1,460	neg.	8,333	18	n.a.
	Domestic		neg.	37,175		n.a.
Debt	International	2,635		6,385	41	
	Money market	860	n.a.	334	257	n.a.
	Notes and bonds	1,775		6,051	29	
	Domestic			29,733		
Equity	Total	896	59,044	31,894	3	185
	International	316	5,527			
Derivatives	Exchanges	n.a.	383,773	14,302	n.a.	2,683
	OTC	n.a.	346,750	95,199	n.a.	364
Forex	Spot	n.a.	130,096	n.a.	n.a.	n.a.

Sources: *BIS QR* June 2001: Tables 3A, 10, 15A–B, 16A, 18, 19, 23A; Aug. 2000, March 2001: Tables 14A–B; *BIS F* 2001: Tables C2, E9; *IFS* March 2002, Country Tables; www.fibv.com: Tables 1.3.B, 1.4.B, 1.8.B, VB.

Notes
Announced issues gross. Cross-border lending only syndicated loans. Cross-border loans outstanding include but domestic loans exclude interbank lending. Fragmentary evidence in IFS suggests that the average interbank share is 10 per cent domestically. Derivatives outstandings at notional value. Derivatives OTC and forex spot trading in 2001, 250 days assumed. n.a. = not applicable; neg. = negligible.

public bodies is responsible for the large discrepancy with deposit data (Table 2.2). Both approaches are 'correct'. They only have different angles. When data is too fragmentary, cells are left blank. Cells which cannot be filled in a meaningful way are labelled accordingly. Figures on issuance are gross because that is what market analysts need. The terms of new and renewed loans and issues reflect the current state of the market, which differs from the state when the original deal was made. Renewals also mean fee income, and the competitive pattern of the financial community will be put to a new test at each issue. Net figures would be the other possibility but they make sense for economists who follow the national economy in aggregate. Two intensity indicators, relating market activity to outstandings, are calculated. Their inverses give an idea of average maturity and average turnover (velocity), respectively.

In the language of systems analysis, outstandings is a stock variable displaying the state of affairs at a moment of time, while issuance and trading are flow variables displaying activity during a time period. Both types of variables are dramatically larger than the underlying 'real' world. It is customary to give the global exports as a yardstick. It was $6.3tr in 2000, a mere 6.3 per cent of the financial assets and still less of equity trading, not to speak of major interbank payments flows, roughly $1,400tr in 1999, or the $1.2tr of daily foreign exchange trading in April 2001. The scale of the activity easily raises negative comments about a casino economy and fears about the destabilizing potential of financial markets. Such nightmare scenarios are largely unfounded. The professional knows that most of the activity originates from portfolio trimming by institutional investors and the balancing of books by bankers. Bankers follow safety rules set by regulators and the accounting community, and get punished if they do not. Institutional investors also have guidelines to follow, to beat an equity index or outperform peers, for example. It is risky to wait for the stabilization of constantly changing markets, and expensive to implement large corrections when they have become necessary. It is much better to adjust the portfolio continuously and this leads to very large trading figures. Of course, not all trading originates from trimming. There is also a hedging element, the desire to insulate core activity from market oscillation. For this counterparts are needed, speculators who have the insight and courage to take an opposite view of the market's development and shoulder the risk against a fee.

Bank lending – where it all started

Banking is discussed in three contexts. Chapter 5 describes the institutional setting, operational detail and country specifics. Banking is also a core element of finance centres, onshore and offshore, the topic of Chapter 7. This subchapter gives only a short overview with focus on the international market. The domestic market constitutes the bedrock, of course. Out of total claims on non-banks, $39tr at year-end 2000, a paltry 5 per cent were cross-border. There the industry structure comes into play. It is reasonable to assume, for example, that savings banks opt for domestic lending, while commercial banks have the organization to benefit from foreign opportunities as well. Their internationalizing customers need trade finance which is their forte. When margins at home get narrow, cross-border lending becomes attractive. Foreign offices are opened. The ongoing concentration of banking has an inbuilt international element and the interbank share will grow with it.

The discussion can, in principle, be conducted from the lender's as well as the borrower's angle. The purpose is to give an idea about relative magnitudes and the share of cross-border business. To that end, both aspects are pretty much the same. We select the lender's angle which for data reasons is more practicable domestically; monetary institutions are the lenders, but who are the borrowers? For the same practical reason the borrower's (issuer's) angle is taken when discussing debt and equity. The lending data comprises both public and private borrowers. The geographical aggregation is first the same as in Chapter 2, whereafter countries/territories are used.

> Because much data is compiled by BIS, a note of its terminology is appropriate. The lender's angle is called 'loans' (claims) and borrower's angle called 'deposits'. External (cross-border) operations are conducted by non-residents. 'Local operations' are conducted by residents but in foreign currency. The aggregate of these two is 'international operations'.

Figure 3.3 displays banking intensity by comparing non-bank claims with GDP. Interbank claims are not considered because domestic information about them is fragmentary. It is believed, however, that the worldwide figure is easily one-quarter out of non-bank claims, or roughly $9tr. Unfortunately, some important countries have not released data and among the rest the share varies heavily, say, 2–50 per cent (*IFS*). In cross-border lending, the interbank volume is three times non-bank, or $6.3tr, again with large variation by country. The total worldwide bank lending thus approaches $55tr of which $39tr is non-bank, or 'real' business. It is this non-bank share which is given in the intensity figure.

Five distinct groups emerge: high- and low-intensity finance centres, high- and low-intensity banking countries and emerging/transforming countries. Finance centres have intensities exceeding 2.1. Foremost are 'recognized' centres among which only the Cayman Islands and Luxembourg are large enough to be shown but which comprise the Bahamas and Bahrain as well. Countries/territories also having noteworthy real economies such as Hongkong, Singapore, Switzerland and Ireland belong to the lower-intensity group. Japan is a special case because one-half of its

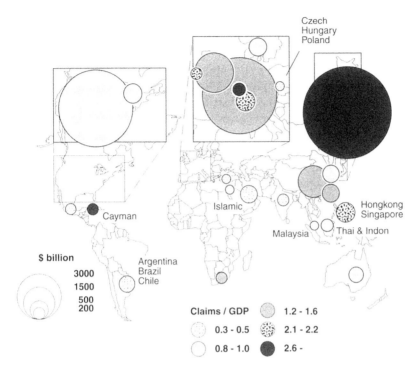

Figure 3.3 Banking intensity, December 2000.

Sources: *BIS QR* June 2001: Table 3B; IFS, March 2002.

Note
Domestic lending to non-banks/GDP.

lending goes through financial institutions which are not classified as deposit-taking banks. The Post Office is the foremost among them but there are others. Were these institutions excluded here, Japan would belong to the same high-intensity banking group as Euroland. The other members are the UK, South Africa, China and Taiwan. The mantra is that countries with Anglo-American financial culture are oriented towards securities and Continental countries towards banking. But the UK does not fit this perception. Its position in the high-intensity group is very solid, impossibly based on the external banking business of the Channel Islands. Can it be so that London's role as a global banking centre blurs the country's domestic, 'true' character? Not necessarily, and the structural figures in Chapter 2 support this opinion (Figures 2.2 and 2.3). South Africa, reflecting its mixed heritage and Dutch legal tradition (Figure 2.12), does not belong to the low-intensity banking group either. The low-intensity banking group has eight members and is thereby the largest and also most widely spread. The Anglo-American connection is undoubtedly there, although the following in Asia Pacific may better indicate the area's ascendancy from the emerging group. The emerging/transition countries are in their namesake group. But the ABC countries' location there raises eyebrows. Have their frequent financial troubles destroyed people's trust in the banking system and led to the creation of parallel economies?

Although the *cross-border* share of non-bank lending is a modest 5 per cent worldwide, its geographical distribution is of interest because the segment differentiates finance centres from the rest, and offshore centres from onshore centres. True offshore centres have a negligible domestic deposit base and practically everything is cross-border, which is not the case with onshore centres.

It is occasionally difficult to differentiate between domestic and cross-border. The UK dependencies of Bermuda, the Cayman Islands and the British Virgin Islands are given separately from the mother country in BIS statistics, whereas the equally important territories of the Channel Islands and the Isle of Man are not. In IFS they all are part of the UK. The effort to sort things out here would be too large and the outcome would hardly affect the conclusions. And then there is the functional offshore within onshore.

> To better compete with offshore centres, the USA and Japan have created within their borders international banking facilities. These facilities are financial free zones, where intermediaries escape many of the host country taxes and avoid the full weight of its regulation. There is a minimum limit for transfers, which preserves the facilities for wholesale banking. In concert with many offshore centres, all dealings must be cross-border. In the USA, their share out of non-bank cross-border deposits is about 20 per cent and of all deposits about 40 per cent. Japan does not disclose recent figures.

Such statistical ambiguities notwithstanding, the message is very simple (Figure 3.4). Cross-border activity is a noteworthy part of bank lending in the finance centres singled out above. The Cayman Islands are practically 100 per cent cross-border, in the Bahamas and Bahrain (not shown) the share is close to 90 per cent. Luxembourg and Singapore are at the 40 per cent mark. The third group consists of Ireland, Hongkong, the UK and Switzerland which locate in the 23–15 per cent range. Euroland and Scandinavia narrowly manage the 5 per cent mark, probably because of their Pan-European business. The internationalization of US banks does not become apparent at all. There are only few commercial banks seriously engaged in international business, many prefer to source local deposits for local lending, and investment banks have their main activity elsewhere than in the interest rate business. Another explanation can be sought in the exclusion of interbank lending, our next target.

This time the country groupings are disbanded and discussion is by

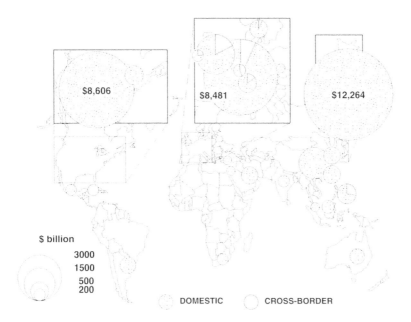

Figure 3.4 Lending to non-banks, December 2000.

Sources: *BIS QR* June 2001: Table 3B; *IFS* March 2002.

Note
Minimum cross-border share shown 5 per cent.

country/territory, except for Scandinavia. The reason is the comparatively great variation of the non-bank share out of all cross-border lending. Equally important is the need to compare the absolute volumes. There the weight of finance centres, offshore and onshore, is fully revealed (Figure 3.5).

Offshore, that is, the Cayman Islands, the Bahamas and Bahrain have one-eighth of total lending, and onshore, that is, Switzerland, Hongkong, Singapore, Luxembourg and Ireland have another two-eighths. The total share is one-third. Switzerland compares favourably with Japan and Germany, and only the UK and USA overtake it by a clear margin. It is also a matter of semantics whether the UK, with a share of one-fifth, should be considered a finance centre or not. In simple terms: cross-border lending is finance centre business, hardly a revolutionary observation. The relative volumes by the USA and Japan are modest and although much of their external banking can be found in offshore/onshore finance centres, it is crystal clear that their cross-border lending does not correspond to their inherent potentials.

It was anticipated that the status of a finance centre would be reflected in the split between interbank and non-bank business. For example, one

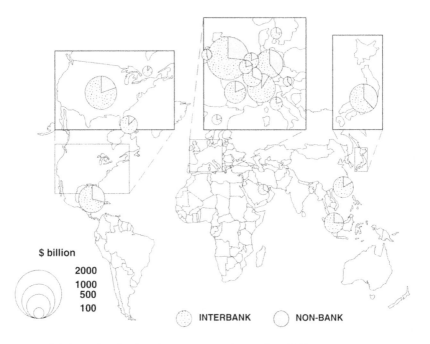

Figure 3.5 Cross-border lending structure, December 2000.

Sources: *BIS QR* June 2001: Tables 3A–B.

Note
Scandinavia has not been disaggregated into countries.

could hypothesize that interbank lending would take place onshore where bank headquarters are, whereas non-bank business would be booked off-shore. Judged against facts, this hypothesis appears far too simple and must at least acknowledge the delegation of power to offshore sub-sidiaries. If any order can be seen in the countrywise split, it is the substantial non-bank share in Germany, Austria and Japan, all recognized manufacturers with substantial foreign interests. Luxembourg can be seen as an extension of the German (and Belgian) banking system with a similar lending structure. To them can be added Bahrain which finances manufacturing and trade in the Gulf area. But such explanations are speculative because they overlook Ireland and the Cayman Islands. There must be several simultaneous factors of varying force, leading to a different picture at some other time.

The discussion has been from the lender's angle, but there is no radical difference between borrowing and lending, at least in a longer time perspective. What goes in must also come out, although the statistics used here suggest one-third more non-bank lending than what deposits would allow (Table 2.2). The inclusion or not of public bodies certainly matters. But that is not the point. The point is whether there is systematic geographical variation in the non-bank ratio claims/deposits (C/D). There, indeed, is, although the underlying data is too unreliable to stimulate cartographic presentation. Suffice it to say that the C/D is substantially below 1.0 in typical offshore, about 1.0 in the two entrepôt cities, Luxembourg and transforming economies, and well above 1.0 elsewhere, Switzerland included.

Constrained to cross-border data but including also interbank activity, lending is about one-tenth smaller than borrowing. Geographical variation is less and its structure simpler than above. Finance centres are about 1.0 C/D, and most of the rest below 1.0. Switzerland is then classified as a finance centre and the UK allocated to the rest. Taiwan, Japan and Finland clearly exceed 1.0. Such figures are little amenable to conclusions.

The discussion has revolved around the financially important countries. That is natural because they count. Information about them is more detailed, and small actors are difficult to handle cartographically. But the total picture is much more varied than the major actors alone suggest. Syndicated credit facilities announced during one year comprise a larger and more representative sample of the global pattern because developing countries are more likely to be capital importers than exporters (Figure 3.6). These data are not comparable with those already discussed,

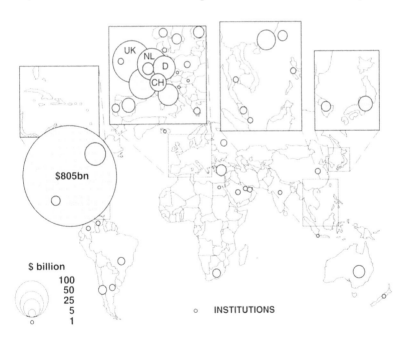

Figure 3.6 International syndicated credit facilities, December 2000.

Source: *BIS QR* June 2001: Table 10; Bank of England 2001.

Notes
Announced facilities, registered by borrower's nationality.

however, being issuance rather than outstandings and arranged by borrower's nationality rather than residence. They simply offer a different
perspective.

Developed industrial countries in North America and Europe dominate. That is interesting because they have well functioning financial
markets and large banks. One might think that each country is capable of
handling most of its borrowing internally. This is a qualified truth. There
are structural and temporal imbalances, risk needs to be distributed
among several lenders and actors may prefer local borrowing because of
currency risk. This being the case, the rank of the USA as the largest international borrower is natural. The country is a net importer of capital, and
possibly the only surprise is the volume of its needs. In contrast, Japan,
being the world's major net exporter of capital, is a very small borrower.
Interesting is the difference in volume between Hongkong and Singapore.
They are about the same as locations of cross-border lenders (Figure 3.5)
but now Hongkong outranks Singapore. It is a gateway to southern China
with brisk demand for capital. Singapore, in contrast, must suffer from the
aftermath of the Southeast Asian currency crisis 1997/1998. Latin
America has apparently regained creditworthiness after defaults in the
1980s, which excluded the Continent from the international loan market
for a decade.

Debt – safe and plentiful

Domestic and international debt

This subchapter is mostly about bonds, although it also includes money
market instruments. Bond issuance competes directly with bank lending.
At least internationally, bonds need a higher credit rating and allow lower
costs, issuing cost and interest rate, than bank loans. The amounts raised
by private rather than public issuers, however, tend to be smaller, and the
issuing terms leave less scope for individualized solutions. The difference
is similar to that of exchange-traded and OTC derivative instruments. For
corporations, $1bn may be the approximate upper limit, on the same level
as a world-class industrial project. Deutsche Telecom's and Telecom
Italia's $10bn–$13bn issues in 1996 and 1999, respectively, are among the
largest corporate offers, on a par with supranationals and sovereigns, or
mega-size acquisitions. For retail distribution, name recognition of the
issuer is crucial (Covill 1996; Luce 1999b).

As previously, a rapid overview is given about the debt instruments in
relation to GDP (Figure 3.7). Applying the same geographical aggregation
as in Chapter 2, the USA rises head and shoulders above all the others,
with an intensity of 1.7. It is a high figure for a country of that size and has
been achieved by the combined efforts of all kinds of issuers, public and
private. The rest of the developed industrial world appears to form a

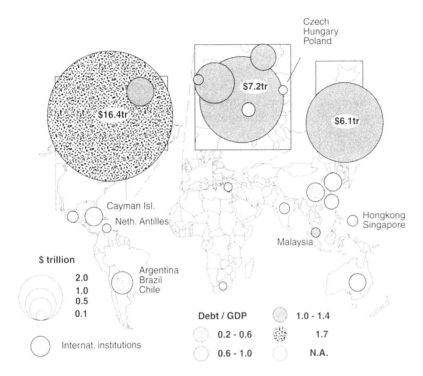

Figure 3.7 Debt intensity, December 2000.

Source: *BIS QR* June 2001: Tables 11 and 16A.

Note
By issuer's residence.

coherent block when it actually is very heterogeneous. There are countries
such as the Netherlands, Denmark and Belgium with intensities in the
range 2.3–1.6, not to speak of Luxembourg which has 3.7. The much criticized spendthrifts of Italy, Japan and Sweden have intensities close to 1.3
only. At the lower end are the oil-rich Norway, Spain and Portugal in the
range 0.8–0.6. Such diversity cannot have a single explanation. Suffice it to
say at this stage that heavy government spending, be it for welfare purposes or a growth injection for the economy, has so far not succeeded in
raising the intensity above 1.3. There are also other reasons. A territory's
role as a launching pad for international issues is one of them, but can be
easily identified only in pure offshore centres such as the Cayman Islands
and the Netherlands Antilles. Interestingly, then, Switzerland does not
seem to fit this role and a straightforward explanation is that it is a taxation regime which discourages international issuance. It is also well served
by its banks.

When we move towards the Equator and beyond, the picture changes.

There is the odd case of Malaysia, which appears to fit better into Europe than Southeast Asia, and there is Australia, which links better with Asia Pacific than the industrialized north. The overall situation in Asia Pacific (Japan excluded), the Indian subcontinent, South Africa and Latin America, however, is that debt markets are not only small but also undeveloped in relation to the economies. This is seen as a grave obstacle for economic development because savings are not properly mobilized. The banking system alone cannot shoulder the task because it is geared more towards short-term than long-term lending. Companies avoid bonds and the ensuing public disclosure. The regulatory constraints for issuance can also be very stiff, virtually enforcing bank intermediation (*BIS AR* 1996/1997: 101; *QR* Aug. 1997: 9). Balanced or surplus budgets notwithstanding, several Asian governments have started issuing bonds to educate investors and to offer a benchmark against which private issues can be launched (Dalla *et al.* 1995). Whatever the script's origin it needs buyers and then the existence of institutional investors, perhaps the government's own pension fund, is welcome. If there are no institutional investors worth mentioning, issuance relies on banks and private investors. The former can be pressurized to purchase but the latter are capricious, shunning paper which is illiquid and which they doubt will lose value in inflation. Latin America probably suffers from its frequent inflationary periods, although its record of servicing bonds is better than of bank loans.

> Argentina's central bank was established in 1935 and the currency has since depreciated against the dollar by a factor of 6,000bn (Catán 2002). Inflation in Brazil was so rampant in the 1980s that the IMF discontinued publishing the currency's exchange rate for a couple of months (*IFS* March 1989). The largest contract of the Brazilian derivatives exchange BM&F is the one-day interbank deposit future.

Similar experience in Europe after the great wars of the past century has essentially contributed to its banking culture. Banks can and do go bust but when storm clouds gather one can at least try to recover savings therefrom. With illiquid government bonds, nothing can be done.

Debt is recorded here mainly by the issuer's residence. All issues are not intended for investors in the country of residence, however. More than that, the issuer often prefers to issue in some other location because it can then access a larger investor base and get a better price, or place larger issues, or avoid red tape at home. This creates the split into domestic and *international issues* (Figure 3.8). The compilation by the issuer's residence makes sense for credit raters and forex dealers, however. Large external debt needs corresponding exports and a positive current account, or the country's credit rating will suffer with consequences for the companies domiciled there. The currency will strengthen when the money flows in, but when loan servicing begins the

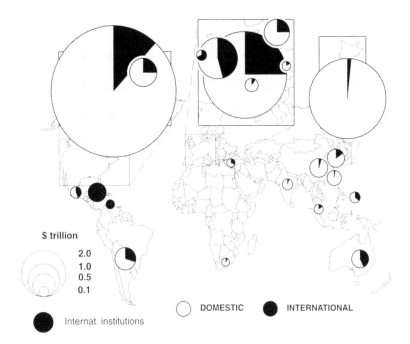

Figure 3.8 Debt structure, December 2000.

Source: *BIS QR* June 2001: Tables 11 and 16A.

Notes
By issuer's residence. International (cross-border) debt includes money market instruments, notes and bonds.

effect will be the opposite. Our interest is partially elsewhere, namely the country's role in the international financial system. For that purpose, the compilation principle is not optimal. An issue launched in the USA by a Swiss bank is registered in Switzerland. That is acceptable. We are aware of the Swiss banks' role as international intermediaries and that perception now gets support. But when a Swedish bank goes to the London market for the same purpose we have second thoughts. Sweden is no international finance centre while London is. But the transaction does not get registered in London as we might like it. Unless, of course, the Swedish bank uses a subsidiary domiciled in the UK. Keeping this ambiguity in mind, we can look at the topical figure. Its message has many aspects.

The largest international shares, actually 100 per cent, are in the offshore centres of the Cayman Islands and the Netherlands Antilles. Their banks are mostly owned by foreigners – by large onshore banks, for example. But the domicile is offshore and the issuance gets registered there. The explanation for Ireland's and the UK's large shares must be similar. An international share of about 25 per cent appears standard in Euroland, Scandinavia, Canada and the ABC countries. But in reality,

Euroland is about as heterogeneous as previously, the share varying from 60 per cent in the Netherlands to 9 per cent in Italy. Such figures have all kind of explanations. Italians save in government bonds because the terms are very lucrative. The need for foreign debt is correspondingly less. The country's banks are comparatively small and not well equipped to source international capital markets. The Netherlands is the direct opposite, with two world-class banks and a host of foreign holding companies. Heavily debted small countries are compelled to source the international market because their governments have needs too large to be met at home. But for the international market their issues, ironically, may be too small and therefore have poor liquidity. The remedy has been to replace old, small issues by new, large ones, or issue at longer intervals. Large countries, even when indebted, have a better chance to find domestic investors, simply because the inflow of funds to the market is more continuous. Asian countries with little appetite for debt are particularly cautious with international debt.

The role of finance centres can also be investigated from another angle. Data on international debt issuance is classified and published both by the issuer's residence and its nationality. For example, a German bank can issue from Germany or through a subsidiary in the Cayman Islands. By the nationality principle both issues are German, but by the residence principle the second issue is Caymanese (subsidiary domiciled there) and only the first one is German. The issuance ratio residence/nationality then discloses whether a country takes part of its business abroad, or gets it therefrom. More precisely, that can be assumed to hold in most cases but not always, because lost and won business can balance each other out. We accept the assumption and calculate the ratios. To get the maximum number of observations and better cartographic legibility, no attention is paid to the absolute sizes (Figure 3.9). It follows that some very small issues are also displayed and that rounding error possibly distorts some ratios.

The foremost offshore centres in the Caribbean, and Bermuda further afield, become immediately noticeable. They are followed by most onshore centres elsewhere: Luxembourg, the Netherlands, the UK and Ireland in Europe, and Singapore and Hongkong in Asia Pacific. This is as it should be. But then there are Argentina and Australia, for which no explanation can be given. The middle-of-the road countries are less interesting, except that so many of them use the finance centres as launching pads for their issues. The interesting cases are those with comparatively little domestic issuance: Switzerland, Japan, Spain and Portugal. The onerous issuing conditions in Switzerland and Japan are well known. Assumedly the same applies in the Iberian Peninsula. Anecdotal evidence thus gets substantiated by worldwide hard facts. What remains anecdotal, however, is who issues where. It appears logical that everybody uses centres nearby: Americans use the Caribbean; Europeans use Luxembourg, the UK and the

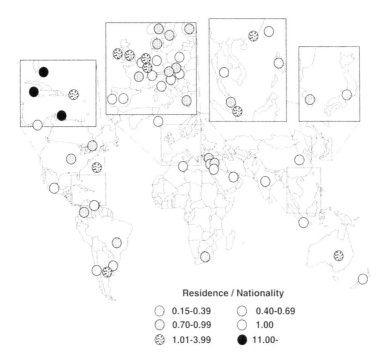

Figure 3.9 International debt issuance by residence and nationality, 2000.
Source: *BIS QR* Aug. 2000 and March 2001: Tables 14 and 15.

Netherlands; and Asians use the two entrepôt cities – but not exclusively. The massive Japanese presence in the Cayman Islands is well known; everybody comes to the London eurobond market; and it would be very sange if Europeans abstained from the Caribbean cays.

The international debt market splits into foreign and euro. Foreign bonds are issued in another country than the issuer's own and denominated in that country's currency. Some have colourful names after the country of placement: yankees (USA), samurais (Japan), dragons (Asia outside Japan), bulls (UK). The purpose is that the script stays abroad and does not drift back to the issuer's country, which it often does. To counteract the flowback and protect domestic markets, American and Japanese authorities used to decree a seasoning period, forty days in the mid-1990s, during which resale was not allowed. It was often a pure rearguard action and the rules are being phased out. The placing of foreign debt follows the rules of the country of placement and can best be discussed in the domestic context. Yankees and samurais, the largest segments, continue to be hampered by regulatory structures which are onerous compared with eurobonds.

Eurobonds are also issued in another country than the borrower's own but nominated in a third country's currency (*BIS QR* Feb. 1997: 21). This is the standard definition, although some experts also include script in domestic currency placed largely with international investors (Rose 1994: 28). Given this conceptual disarray, the estimate of $3tr–$4.5tr outstandings is just that, an estimate (Luce 1999d). The bonds are bearer paper, exempt from withholding tax and can be redeemed whenever desired, a considerable handicap (*BIS QR* Feb. 1997: Stewart 1997). The euromarket is supported by an efficient infrastructure, and its large size contributes to liquidity, which is what most investors, increasingly international in outlook, want. London captures about three-quarters of issuance and trading.

Euromarkets were born in the 1960s because US authorities maintained an interest rate ceiling on domestic dollar deposits, taxed foreign issuance and lending and, finally, prohibited FDI. Eurodollar deposits paved the way and eurobonds followed in the 1970s. Barriers notwithstanding, US banks could have dollar accounts abroad and the issuance of dollar denominated bonds overseas was also allowed. Had these been refused, the market would have probably withered away, since dollar liabilities, whether bank loans or bonds, must be paid by dollars and the ultimate source of dollars is the USA. Specifically, interbank dollar payments are settled through demand deposits with banks in New York. The necessary lever was thus available but the negative consequences were also clear; US banks would have been elbowed out of Europe, Singapore and Japan. Euromarkets enhanced the attractiveness of the dollar, helped the USA to maintain its financial hegemony, and were consequently in the national interest. They were allowed to live. In a longer time perspective, they promoted financial reform worldwide and that, too, was in the US interest (Chernow 1990: 545; Hampton 1996: 5–58, 79; Helleiner 1995: 323, 328–329; Sele 1995: 59–60).

> A central bank's ability to call the shots is excellently illustrated in Switzerland. Only a few eurobond issues have been denominated in Swiss francs, the attractive investor base notwithstanding. The immediate reason is an apparently innocent rule: only a bank domiciled in Switzerland is eligible as lead manager of Swiss franc issues. The stated purpose is to protect domestic underwriters from the adverse effects of the turnover tax which burdens securities issuance and trading in the country. At the same time, the rule prevents a large amount of debt floating outside the central bank's control. The national economy is not overly large and is potentially susceptible to destabilizing forces from the outside (Birchler and Rich 1994: 403, 406; *Guide to Switzerland* 1996: 9).
>
> Monetary authorities can also favour eurobonds. That was the stand of the German authorities in the 1960s, who saw the euromarket as a means of easing the upward pressure on the mark. And to discourage the purchase of German domestic bonds by foreigners, they

put a withholding tax on them. At best, a withholding tax is cumbersome, since it must be reclaimed from systems which only too often are inefficient and obsolete. At worst, it is disastrous if the topical countries do not have a double-taxation treaty. Unexpected gaps in the treaty network may turn up. As late as in the 1980s, Germany still did not have such treaties with Japan, Saudi Arabia or Taiwan, all important global investors (Anon. 1993: 27; Koenig 1988: 50).

Eurobonds have, in the meantime, received a serious challenger from euroMTNs, an intellectual offshoot of the US medium-term notes (MTN). The market is in the ascendancy, having passed its US counterpart in early 1995 with outstandings at $500m (Clifton 1996). There are two reasons for MTN's popularity: issuing costs have declined close to the bond levels and the issues are normally tailored to the need of a specific investor. Maturities, for example, vary between nine months and thirty years. In other words, the initiative comes from the lender and not the borrower, as is normal in bond and equity issuance. This has led to a great multitude of comparatively small, say, $2m–$10m issues, which can be placed within an hour or two and settled in two-to-three days. Placing is private, which means that the market lacks transparency. Listing at a stock exchange would be of little help as there is very little trading. It simply is not in the lender's interest that others will benefit from the market niche s/he has discovered. The tough SEC requirements and legal costs prevent the two MTN markets on both sides of the Atlantic from merging.

Many of the factors which originally gave birth to the euromarkets have ceased to exist or have lost their former importance. Controls of interest rate, foreign exchange and bond issuance are things of the past, or almost. Tax evasion is losing importance, the eurobond's bearer form notwithstanding, because of the coming of institutional investors. The interest rate gap, which used to favour euromarkets to the detriment of domestic ones, has all but closed, while arbitrage, through offshore vehicles and derivatives, has smoothed out price differences. Arbitration is important, since it has put the eurobond market at the centre of world financial trends where innovations take root first. The practical ten-year ceiling of maturities excludes important borrower segments, however. Competition has pressed the issuing fees so low that underwriters consider eurobond issuance as a loss leader for generating revenue from attached trading, forex and derivatives. What remains is the exemption from withholding tax but even there pressure by the European Union and US taxman is mounting (*BIS AR* 1995/1996: 151; *BIS QR* Feb. 1997: 22–25; Froud 1996: 40).

Oblique hints have been made about the character of issuers, governments, banks. It is also possible to display the data from that angle (Figure 3.10). The display is by the issuer's nationality and not residence and is therefore not strictly comparable with the previous one. The disag-

gregation is threefold; public bodies, financial institutions and corporations. Financial institutions dominate almost everywhere. Supranationals
such as the World Bank, Asian Development Bank and European Investment Bank contribute, but the bulk consists of ordinary banks. The share
is about three-quarters in most of the industrialized world, two-thirds in
Asia Pacific and only in Canada and Latin America is it below one-quarter.
Once again, the heterogeneity of Euroland must be emphasized. Financial
intermediaries dominate the core countries, 94 per cent in Germany,
for example. But the fringe is different: 9 per cent in Greece and 20 per
cent in Finland. Norway, part of Scandinavia, is also exceptional with its
2 per cent.

General explanations can be offered. The reluctance of the largest sovereigns to come to the international market was mentioned above and it
enhances the relative weight of private issuers. These want to avoid restrictions and controls at home, seek finance for operations in a particular
country, or just to make use of profitable opportunities. Typical domestic
hurdles are minimum credit ratings of the issue, maximum issue
sizes, issuance queues, time-consuming registration routines, excessive
commission fees and withholding taxes. Japanese banks, for example,
used to go to Hongkong and London for this specific purpose. Such regu-

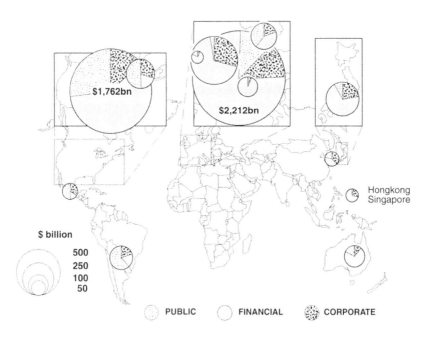

Figure 3.10 International debt structure, December 2000.

Source: *BIS QR* June 2001: Tables 12A–12D.

Note
By issuer's nationality.

lations are on the way out but, where they still exist, they raise costs. Commercial banking is organized to raise funds internationally and it is rational to make use of this capacity. Multinational corporations have the same capability but at the end of the day they conduct most of their financial operations through banks. This is the aggregate explanation. At the country level, a host of idiosyncrasies plays in, though these are not relevant for this general discussion.

The lengthy discussion about international debt may have disguised the fact that *domestic bond* markets are about 90 per cent of the global total. There the public sector is king (Figure 3.11), in sharp contrast to the international market. In most countries, public sector is the same as the national government. Reasons for its heavy involvement have been discussed above (pp. 101–102). Excepting countries with a federal structure, subnational entities have too narrow a financial base to be able to issue debt even in the domestic market. Their taxing power may be restricted or subject to overt and hidden constraints by the state. This raises doubts about their ability to service the debt. Their needs are usually too modest to allow issue sizes which would attract institutional investors. If private investors are the main target group, liquidity will be low because individuals tend to hold the paper to maturity, making the

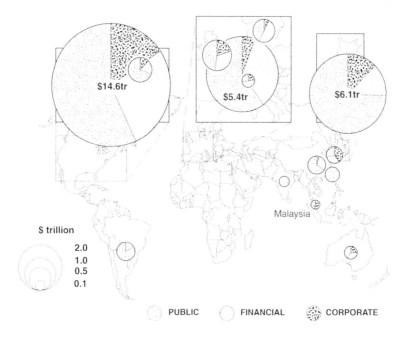

Figure 3.11 Domestic debt structure, December 2000.

Source: *BIS QR* June 2001: Tables 16A–16B; *Industry of Free China* 2001: Table 24.

Note
By issuer's residence.

issue still less interesting to other investor groups. US states and munici-palities, Canadian provinces and some German *länder*, enjoying a proper legal framework, wide taxing powers and exemption from federal taxes, are sustained issuers. German *länder* are also backed by the federal government should they become illiquid. The pack has recently been joined by Ilê de France and Spanish Andalucia and Catalunya. Chinese CITICS, supported by provincial governments, have made a foray but with mixed results. Large municipalities, capital cities for example, are good borrowers as long as the high-income elites remain within their boundaries. This is no longer the case in the USA and the credit ratings have declined accordingly. (Harding and Marshall 2002; Laulajainen 1999; Parsons 2001)

The split between the financial and corporate sectors has its own reasons. The US financial sector is swelled by asset-backed securities which are very popular there. It is not only private intermediaries who use the technique; government sponsored agencies are also involved and consti-tute part of the financial sector.

'Fannie Mae', 'Freddie Mac', 'Sallie Mae' and similar, are government agencies for issuing bonds backed by mortgages (house loans) and study loans originated by private financial and educational institutions. A mortgage cannot exceed 80 per cent of house value. The scheme is intended to free capital because the sales revenue from bonds is used for granting new loans. The agencies' combined market share of all mortgage financing is more than 50 per cent with $2.5tr in outstand-ings.

European financial intermediaries have for long had ABS of their own, although under different names. The most renowned example is the German *pfandbriefe*, issued by banks and with outstandings exceeding government paper by 50 per cent. The idea of *pfandbriefe* is similar to US government agencies and it has been accepted, with local modifications, in several European countries.

Banks purchase (originally public sector) loans and mortgages: put them into a pool and issue bonds against it. The pool is responsible for every single issue and total issuance cannot exceed 60 per cent of the pool, which is supervised by a trustee. The issuing bank keeps the script on its balance sheet and remains responsible for it. These safe-guards make *pfandbriefe* equally safe as treasuries and warrant the name 'baby *bunds*' rather than 'mortgage bonds'. *pfandbriefe* can be issued only to match new lending which easily leads to small issues and illiquidity. The problem has been addressed by increasing the issue size and appointing market makers. A straight issue of at least DM1bn (€650m) and three market makers is called 'Jumbo'. (Anon.

1996; 1997b: 6; Currie 1997: 107; Herges 2001; Moore 1996; Moritz 1995)

Corporate debt appears unimportant in Europe, Switzerland and the UK excepted. Reality is more complicated although the basic tenor is undoubtedly that. The reason and the result of this are open to conjecture. Continental Europe has its banking culture which means that companies in general are not rated. This is changing but not overnight. It was relatively late when interest expenses became tax deductible in the UK and Germany (and Japan), for example, in sharp contrast to the USA (Dalla *et al.* 1995: 129). Investors are conservative, readily accepting only A-rated paper, while Americans accept all kind of paper when the interest rate is right.

> American readiness for risk taking gave birth to 'junk' bonds, i.e. bonds below investment grade. They have gained notoriety when defaulting en masse but have also been a welcome vehicle for small companies whose only alternative were expensive bank loans, and value-hungry investors when interest rate levels decline.

The outcome is that there is a credit gap for B-rated European companies and, logically, less outstanding corporate debt. This reasoning can be extended to commercial paper as well, and particularly because it is unsecured.

Japanese companies issue at home as much as Americans do, although rating there is still more rare than in Europe. That has not been necessary because of the *keiretsu* system; associated banks, insurers and employees buy the paper. The difference between the USA and Japan is rather in the financial sector which is very narrow in Japan. Indeed, one half of bank issuance takes place abroad (Figure 3.10). There, Japanese issuers, those able to source the international capital market, have faced a dilemma. The domestic interest rate has been extremely low but issuance cost three times higher than at euromarkets. Upon that has come a heavily fluctuating yen making foreign borrowing extremely risky (Terazono 1995).

> At the root of the high cost was the trust bank fee. An issuer of secured bonds had to nominate a trust bank to administer the collateral and shoulder the issuer's obligation in case of default. That nullified the issuer's implied credit rating, good news for weaker companies while blue chips turned to euromarkets. A favoured technique was to issue eurobonds denominated in dollars and swap them for yen.

On top of the risk and high cost came a multitude of petty regulation.

Things are changing, however. Non-investment-grade companies can issue bonds, local securities firms increasingly price bonds according to credit ratings, shelf registration is possible, the ratio of maximum debt to company's net worth has been raised from two to three, and so on (Ogino 1992: 210–212; Olivier 1996: 92).

Domestic bonds are issued in the borrower's country and denominated in its currency. Logically, their bulk is purchased by domestic investors. But the possibility of a better yield at unchanged risk, more liberal regulation, and heightened familiarity with hedging techniques have bolstered foreign ownership. Nowadays the figures for government bonds are 10–20 per cent in France, the UK, the USA, and 30–40 per cent in Japan and Germany (Gordon-Walker 1995: 57, 59; *Guide to Japanese Government Bonds* 1999: 11; Mooyart 1998). US treasury bonds are the most widespread foreign instrument (Figure 3.12). It is not simply the case of Japan financing the US deficit but, rather, that the paper enjoys wide international recognition. The equation has several variables: the belief that the US government does not default, the vision that the dollar will appreciate rather than depreciate, and the understanding that politics will not jeopardize the servicing of the debt. Logically, countries with close political and commercial ties with the USA are important investors.

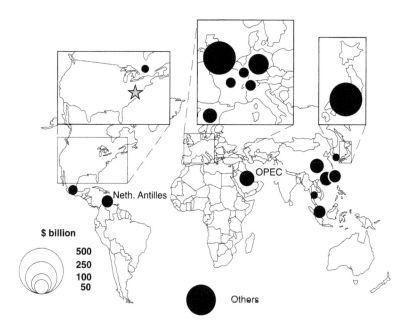

Figure 3.12 Foreign holders of US treasuries, June 1998.

Source: Lowenstein 1998: 26.

Issuance and trading

Private issuance is quite similar to equities. The main techniques are auction and syndication. What is not placed immediately will be on tap, i.e. sold when a buyer appears. Auction is usual at domestic markets while underwriting syndicate is popular in the euromarkets (Dalla *et al.* 1995: 121). A syndicate has three overlapping phases, management, underwriting and placement (selling). Management comprises the negotiation of issuance terms, allocation of the issue between underwriters, and back-office administration. Underwriting is a guarantee that the whole issue will be placed at the agreed price. The effort is coordinated by the lead manager, a bank or securities house, who invites additional members to the underwriting syndicate when needed. Everything goes in a great hurry and those invited may have an hour or so to respond. The lead manager is usually from the same country as the currency of denomination, reflecting the ability to place the issue (Figure 3.13). Dollar issues, however, are an exception, since various nationalities have the topical ability. The other possibility, to follow the issuer's nationality, belongs to syndicated loans (*BIS QR* Aug. 1997: 27–29).

Correct pricing is the key question; sufficiently low that everything can be placed but not too low because of loss of revenue. To gauge what the

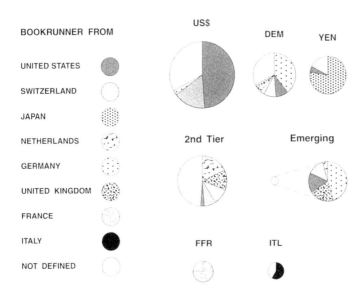

Figure 3.13 Euro- and global bonds by currency, the ten largest bookrunners, April 1995 to March 1996.

Source: *Euromoney* 1996, May: 110, 112.

Note
In large issues there can be several syndicates which are coordinated by a bookrunner, probably one of the lead managers.

market can bear, when-issued trading is used in the US and UK domestic markets. A price range with other details is disclosed about ten days before auction and prospective investors will indicate their order sizes and price ideas upon which the final auction price (bids are for quantities) will be decided (Dalla *et al.* 1995: 121; de Prati 1998: 171). Allocation has long been by the pot method which has by now also come to Europe. Orders are split into retention and pot, perhaps 50/50. The retention is allocated to syndicate members in proportion to the orders they have solicited, while the lead managers decide how the pot is divided between the syndicate and the investors. Access to the co-managers' customer lists gives the lead manager opportunity to bully investors to designate himself falsely as originator and get the fees. In USA, where important players are 30–40 and well-known, such tactics are likely to fail, but in Europe regional fiefdoms get disclosed and competitive advantage lost. The issuer benefits by seeing who has distribution power. The same transparency is achieved when investors place their orders through the Internet. The World Bank offered $1.7bn of its $5bn issue through the Internet in 2000 and achieved a 20 per cent acceptance in the middle and retail market (Goodhart 2000; Lee 1999c; Walker 2000).

When issues are large and investors few, it may be advisable to arrange presentations where the top brass of the issuer can be questioned. This 'roadshow' moves from city to city and may circle the globe. When retail sales are also topical, which is common in Japan and Switzerland, the branch network of retail banks becomes indispensable, and the underwriting syndicate is enlarged into a selling syndicate with numerous members. Each participant is entitled to a percentage fee, which becomes progressively smaller the further down one comes in the hierarchy. The idea is that the issuance terms negotiated by the management group will be followed by each member of the selling syndicate, and that selling begins simultaneously on the offering day at an agreed price. This may not be the case in practice, and disciplining the disparate group can be a major task for the lead manager. Therefore, and to gain time, with smaller issues the potential lead manager may buy the whole issue and place it alone ('bought deal'). When the terms of an issue are attractive and the market is buoyant, the placement may be done within thirty minutes, while two days is highly satisfactory when retail investors are the target (Lewis 1989b: 56, 60). The virtue of speed is twofold: capital is freed rapidly and the possibility that the market will move against the issue is smaller. Of course, the market can also move in favour of the issue, but as the purpose of underwriting is to earn fees rather than speculate by taking market positions, this possibility is usually not considered. When the issue starts trading in the secondary market, the lead manager is generally expected to quote ask–bid prices, make market in it, at least during the first year.

The placing becomes more demanding when the issue is offered in several countries simultaneously. Particularly when the countries are in different parts of the world, the buzz phrase 'global bond' is used. The purpose of a global issue is savings in interest, 10–20 bp, and better liquidity. The response can be very revealing about the depth and sophistication of regional markets. Maturity is a good indicator, and a case makes the matter tangible.

> The Malaysian state-owned oil and gas company Petronas launched a global bond in late 1996. The plan was for two $500m tranches of five and ten years' maturity. Since demand was lively the issue size was augmented twice. First, the planned tranches were increased to $600m each and a $300m thirty-year tranche was added. It is unusual that a new maturity tranche arises out of the marketing effort. Second, the ten-year tranche was increased further to $800m and the thirty-year tranche to $500m, almost doubling the planned size. Maturity and regional demand correlated, testifying for the relative depth and sophistication of markets. The five-year tranche was popular in Asia and Europe, the ten-year tranche in Europe and the USA, and the thirty-year tranche almost exclusively in the USA. (MB 1996)

With large issues it is almost unavoidable to denominate in dollars and tap the US market. To facilitate that, global bonds are exempted from US seasoning requirements and withholding tax, and enjoy provisions for easy cross-market trading and clearing. Institutional investors can be approached through private placements which need no registration, while placement at retail customers brings with it the normal disclosure and registration hurdles. In practice, only the World Bank, some sovereigns and the largest multinationals have been able to raise capital by global issues (*BIS QR* Nov. 1996: 43; Chesler-Marsh 1992; Dyer 1993).

The normal vehicle for foreign companies to issue in the USA is yankee bonds. Most in demand are triple As and triple Bs. The former have liquidity and can be used in swaps, the latter give performance. The attractions of the US market are many. It can normally absorb larger issues than eurobonds, say, $2bn, or $20bn–$50bn a year. It is dominated by institutional investors and is, therefore, more reliable than a retail market. Maturities can be very long if so desired; twenty-to-thirty years is quite normal and there is a demand for 100-year maturities (century bonds). (Corrigan and Iskander 1997; Lee 1999b; Sharpe 1996)

> Century bonds are issued when interest rates are low and the premium over treasuries is small. They are essentially preferred equity and professional investors see them as trading vehicles.

Name recognition is not essential, as investors depend on credit rating, which can be lower than in euromarkets. The main drawbacks for foreigners are the preparation of the registration document, which may disclose more than desirable and involves much work, and the GAAP accounting rules, which involve still more work.

The drawbacks have scared foreigners away to other markets and prompted the SEC to ease regulation (Table 3.2). Since 1990 it has been possible for foreign companies, under rule 144a, to issue debt (and equity) without registration at SEC and compliance with GAAP, when the paper is sold to Qualified Institutional Buyers (QIB), who number roughly 3,000 in total. These manage at least $100m of assets and are considered sufficiently sophisticated to look after themselves. They can trade the security freely among themselves, and after a two-year seasoning period it can be offered to the general public. Parallel to the 144a market, it is also possible to make private placements which need no registration but have no secondary market either. Bearer bonds are outlawed because of tax fraud (Adams, J. 1997: 28; Froud 1996; Urry 1996).

The growing prosperity of Asia Pacific region, combined with its gargantuan appetite for investment, has stimulated efforts to create a bond market suited to its particular needs. The first effort, dragon bonds, priced, listed and distributed in the region, withered away from lack of interest. The new effort, coined as 'euro-asian bonds', a kind of global bond, is priced in the region, listed there in addition to Europe, and distributed with a view to, but not exclusively, the regional market (Horwood 1997). Eurobond, launched and priced in London, arrives in Asia Pacific some twelve hours later, if at all, since attractive issues are already picked off in Europe and North America. A euro-asian, by contrast, is launched during the Asia Pacific morning hours, which gives local investors at least a five-hour time window before London comes to the market. They can also stay at their desks until late in the evening to see how the issue performs. If it does well, many sell in a rising market, leaving perhaps only 30 per cent in the time zone, to central banks, funds, insurance companies and cash-rich corporations, but seldom retail investors. The euro-

Table 3.2 Placing a bond issue

Feature	Yankee private	Rule 144a	Yankee public	Euro	Global
SEC registration	No	No	Yes	No	Yes
Rating	No	Two	Two	No	Yes
Timing (months)	3	2	4	2	4
Cost	Low	Moder.	High	Low	High
Distribution	Moder.	Moder.	Wide	Wide	Wide
Currency	US$	US$	US$	Range	Range
Size, US$m	200	200	300	200	1,000
Maturity (max. years)	30	30	100	10	10
Liquidity	Low	Moder.	Good	Moder.	Good

Source: de Prati, Christian F., *Chinese Issuers in International Capital Markets*: Table 12. Haupt, Berne, 1998. Copyright © 1998 by Verlag Paul Haupt, Berne, Switzerland; modified with permission.

asian is still in an experimental stage but, given the region's growth record and the permanency of time zones, it has potential to develop into a major segment of 'euro' bonds.

For *government bonds* issued at home the process is somewhat different. As many governments are regular and large issuers, it would be impractical to arrange a syndicate for each issue and pay the necessary fees. Therefore, monetary authorities nominate large banks and securities houses as primary dealers and issue exclusively through them. The numbers vary widely, from about forty in the USA and Germany to over 1,700 in Japan. Foreigners play a significant role. A primary dealer undertakes to make a realistic bid for each offering (or most of them), either in an auction or as a syndicate member, and subsequently to make secondary market in the script. The compensation varies and may include, except for the right to bid, proprietary information by the central bank, the exclusive right to deal through inter-dealer broker (IDB) screens, and the use of the repo market (see p. 121).

> IDBs allow dealers to trade anonymously with each other. Defections of syndicate members, for example, take place through IDBs, who place themselves between the seller and buyer.

The attraction of government paper (treasuries, t-bonds) is enhanced and the borrowing cost indirectly lowered when issuance is regular and covers the whole maturity spectrum. On top of that come characteristics enhancing liquidity (see p. 121). Regular issuance allows institutional investors with stable cash flows, like pension funds and many insurance companies, to plan their investment strategy with greater precision. Coverage of the whole maturity spectrum facilitates the trimming of portfolios. The need for that may originate from unexpected payment obligations, changes in the income stream, or a changed economic outlook. The government itself may also wish to take advantage of changed perspectives. The standard situation is that bond yields are higher at long than short maturities because of the larger risk, although the principle is by no means set in stone (Figure 3.14). The flip side of regular issuance is that the borrowing needs and market conditions may not warrant the activity.

Attractivity is further stimulated if issuance terms can be kept unchanged over lengthy periods – a year, for example (everything is relative). This creates benchmark issues with fungible (interchangeable) tranches, gauging the current interest rate and identifying zero credit risk – assumed to exist with government paper. Benchmarks are widely sought, command lower interest rates, add to liquidity and form the basis of derivatives. Ten-year government bonds constitute the benchmark in many countries. Benchmarks are important not only for issuance but also for marking a bond portfolio to market, that is, finding its current market value. Since bonds often trade OTC and many are fairly illiquid, a position

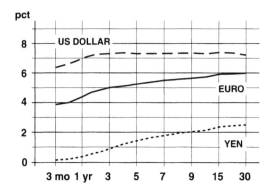

Figure 3.14 Yield curves of interest rate swaps, March 2000.

Source: *BIS AR* 2000/2001: Graph VI.4. Copyright © 2001 of the Bank for International Settlements, Basle; used with permission.

Note
Yield is related to the market price whereas interest rate is related to the nominal value.

without reference prices or benchmarks can deteriorate without anybody observing it (King 1994: 185).

It has been an established truth since the 1970s that government bonds offer the ideal benchmark. They have zero risk, sufficient depth (immunity to squeezes) and react to economic stimuli in a logical way. These features also make treasuries a preferred collateral (security) for repos and an underlying instrument for derivative contracts. With the decline or disappearance of budget deficits, their ready availability is no more guaranteed, however. Pricing is related to the most recent, on-the-run, issue which is most liquid. These have become smaller and less frequent but the need to realize collateral and find deliverable paper when derivatives mature is unchanged. The result is increased and erratic price volatility, hardly a desirable characteristic for a benchmark. The search for a substitute has led to the use of swap curves, the difference between the fixed and floating interest rate curves. Swaps have very large volume, excellent liquidity and are free of credit, tax and accounting effects, that is, they offer better comparability than government bonds. The curves in Figure 3.14 are not for bonds but their swaps. Swaps are not the only possible substitute, however. The US government agencies have recently tailored their issuance programme with a view to gaining benchmark status. But numerous as their issues are, they are probably too small, $2bn–$5bn, to become a real surrogate treasury. Also, their government guarantee is only implicit. Bonds issued by large corporations were used up to the 1960s and may regain some of their former status. (Bank of England 2001: 21–22, 26–29; Bedford 1998a; Clow 2000; McCauley 2001; Simpkin 1999; Smalhout 1999; 2001; Wooldridge 2001)

The situation in Euroland is further complicated by the coexistence of independent treasuries, all of which issue government debt. Their national economies vary in health and their governments follow budgetary policies of varying stringency. It follows that the paper's creditworthiness varies by the issuer, irrespective of Euroland's overall AAA rating. What the rating is actually worth remains to be seen because European central banks are constrained in their capacity to create money and thereby act as lenders of last resort (Lee 1999b). Before the coming of the euro, the differences in creditworthiness were much larger and the best paper issued in sufficient volume, the German ten-year bond (*bund*), was widely accepted as the Pan-European benchmark. After the euro, it maintained the status although the denomination was not in deutschmarks any more. More than that, issuers outside Euroland also started using it as collateral and derivatives deliverable. That was more than the issuing programme could bear, large issue sizes notwithstanding. Pricing became erratic and squeezes developed, leading to its partial substitution by the swap curve (van Duyn 2001b; Politi 2002).

The *secondary market* is still largely OTC, i.e. displaying indicative prices on screens and striking deals on the phone. This applies domestically as well as internationally. Automated screen trading has got a firm foothold, however. Worldwide, there are over 300 bond trading systems, one-third of them in the USA, mostly single-product and on the sell side, still a far cry from an integrated network. But the technology has only been available since the late 1990s. In particular the open architecture, which has made it possible to have several trading services on one screen, has contributed to commercial application. Largest strides have been made with government bonds because the volume of outstandings is so large. It started with US and Italian treasuries and has spread to other countries and issuers, supranationals, government agencies and even corporations, and is now in the process of spreading to derivatives and the money market. In Europe, the leading system is EuroMTS with 25 per cent of European government bond trading. To get listed, an issue must be at least €3bn and the issuer's total outstandings €10bn. There must be at least five market makers quoting continuously firm two-way prices, and the minimum trade size is €5m (Banque de France 2000: 92; Committee on the Global Financial System 2001: 21; van Duyn 2001a; Galati and Tsatsaronis 2001; Luce 1999c; Peterson 2000). Although seldom traded at organized exchanges, bonds, and particularly corporate bonds, may be listed there. The reason is that many institutional investors can buy only listed bonds. Unlisted bonds are considered too risky and exposed to outright fraud. Luxembourg, London, New York, Tokyo and Osaka are usual listing locations.

A fundamental characteristic of the secondary market is its liquidity. Good liquidity means that large trades can be completed at any time without moving the price. A 'large' trade might here mean $100m, a perfectly realistic amount for a Japanese pension fund wishing to trim its portfolio. An important reason for illiquidity is that many issues are far too small for such trades. The average size of an outstanding international bond, about $100m, is clearly insufficient. A World Bank issue of $1.5bn might marginally qualify but such issues are not too numerous. The euromarket, in spite of its size, is only conditionally liquid. The corporate eurobond market in particular should not be compared with US treasuries but with US domestic corporate bonds. At the end of 1991, only 10 per cent of eurobond issues had more than ten market makers, and 25 per cent had more than five. At emerging markets, brady bonds with $140bn outstanding, one half of the market, have become popular, because their liquidity and long maturity give profit potential from improving sovereign credit (*BIS QR* Nov. 1996: 17–19; Hagger 1992a: 81; Shale 1987: 114, 1992: 50).

> A brady bond is rescheduled sovereign debt packaged into twenty-year bonds. The principal is backed by a US treasury zero-coupon note. The market consists basically of twenty benchmark bonds and is, in normal times, very liquid (Ghaffari 1998).

The much larger domestic markets offer better liquidity. Average bond and note issues by the major Treasuries are located within the $1bn to $9bn range and are still dwarfed by the $20bn mega issues released by the US, Japanese and German treasuries. Trading is intensive, with the annual value often twice the outstandings and the average holding period declining with the size of the issue, say, from six months to one month. The attraction of US treasury bonds, in particular, is their awesome trading value, $175bn on an average day in late 1995 with corresponding liquidity (Benzie 1992: Table 6; Gordon-Walker 1995: 57).

Although the size of an issue is a key dimension of liquidity, on top of that comes the location where trading takes place.

> In the late 1980s, it was difficult to get quotes in Frankfurt for German *bunds* in excess of DM20m, while in London DM50–DM100m was a standard block size. The difference was connected with the size of the market rather than the issue and, on that score, differences can be great. The daily trading value of US treasuries was in those days some $100bn in New York but $400m in London, and only before the New York trading hours. Not surprisingly, New York's ask–bid spread (indicator of liquidity) was one-half of London's. The advantage which kept London 'alive' was its earlier time zone, as two-to-three hours can be gained by coming to London at noon GMT (7 am EST) rather than waiting for the opening of New York (Crabbe 1988: 37; Koenig 1988: 48).

There is also a time dimension, a kind of learning effect.

> The prevailing philosophy in Germany in the 1970s was that a good investor keeps the paper until maturity. Trading was accepted only with the arrival of foreign banks. By 1985, it was possible to deal in DM1m lots at a spread of 50 bp. Three years later, the trade size had grown to DM10m, and the spread had declined to 10–20 bp (Osborn 1988; von Ribbentrop 1990).

The tradability of less liquid issues can be upgraded by offering lending and borrowing facilities. Somebody, the owner or an outside custodian, has to safekeep the script, to have them in custody. Rather than just guarding securities which are not actively traded at the moment, the custodian can lend them to any needy and trustworthy partner against a fee and collateral agreed to by the owner, who gets free custody and 60–70 per cent of the fee. Borrowers are money brokers, securities houses and traders who have short sold a lot (sold non-owned securities for future delivery) but have been unable to buy it before the deadline. Aware of the borrowing possibility, they have made the deal. Without that possibility they might have abstained – with lower liquidity as a result. Obviously, there are limits to how large a percentage of an inventory can be lent (5–10 per cent), and the relatively high fee, perhaps one per cent, also limits the practice. Stock lending is well-established in the USA but alien to many other national legislations. Questions about capital gains tax, dividends payable when stock is on loan and the length of lending chains can be thorny. Only three links per chain are allowed in London, for example. Off-limit areas remain. In Asia Pacific, the activity is legally possible only in Japan, Hongkong, Singapore, Malaysia and Thailand.

Government bonds are the preferred instrument of repo (repurchase) transactions.

> At repo, market bonds are sold back to the government against a promise to repurchase them at a later date at an agreed price. Essentially the deal is a collateralized loan by the government and a cheaper way of obtaining short-term funds than non-collateralized interbank loans.

The activity started in the USA and has spread from there to other countries (Figure 3.15). The effect is the same as with lending facilities: enhanced liquidity. (*BIS QR* Nov. 1996: 22; Blanden 1992; Graham 1996; Warner 1994b)

Finding the correct security for delivery in sufficient quantity is more complicated than a layperson would anticipate. For obvious reasons, trading is concentrated on benchmark issues. Derivative contracts of

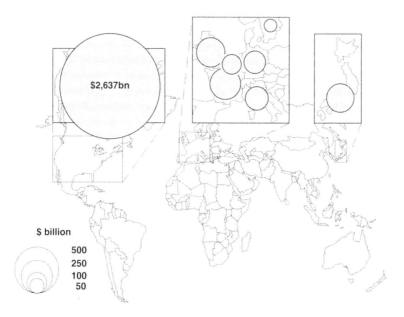

Figure 3.15 Repo market in selected countries, December 2000.
Source: *BIS QR* Sept. 2001: Table 1 (page 58).

organized exchanges are even created around benchmarks, real or fictive, to facilitate trading. The *bund* three-month call future offers an example. It purports the purchase of a ten-year 6 per cent €100,000 German federal bond in three months' time. Since most ten-year bonds have already been in circulation for some time, all federal bonds with a residual maturity of eight-and-a-half to ten years are considered acceptable for delivery. They are interchangeable, fungible, for this purpose. Since they trade at different prices, a set of conversion factors is applied to arrive at the correct delivery. Even so, some issues are cheaper to deliver (CTD) than others and these, naturally, are delivered if at all possible. Since supply is limited, squeezes may develop (Breedon 1996: 14; Simpkin 1999; www.eurexchange.com 2002). The basket of *bund* deliverables is comparatively homogeneous, though, and contrasts favourably with US thirty-year t-bonds which are fifteen years and up, or the UK long gilt which is ten-to-fifteen years.

Trading in domestic markets is subject to national *regulations*. By contrast, eurobonds thrive in a seemingly unregulated state. This perception is not quite correct. Although eurobonds are 'stateless' and traded OTC, it does not mean that the market is unregulated. Capital adequacy rules must be followed and liquidity is supervised by the host country authorities (Haindl 1991: 33, 188). Other regulation originates from the market itself. From a historical perspective, this was also the case with today's organized exchanges which relied exclusively on self-regulation until gross misbehaviour combined with the spreading of share ownership to wider layers of the society compelled authorities to introduce external surveillance and regulation. Euromarkets still exist in the self-regulatory era, primarily because the actors are professionals and presumably capable of looking after themselves without the need of public protection, so important for the small investor.

The foremost self-regulating organization is the ISMA (International Securities Markets Association), currently active in forty-one countries. Its reporting dealers are prepared to make market for a selection of bonds in agreed trade sizes and report their published prices and the size of completed trades each business day. The reports constitute an important database about market behaviour. In return, reporting members get access to the IDB screens.

Equity – the adventurous alternative

Why so adventurous?

As indicated previously, bond and equity markets have a number of similarities. Both split into primary and secondary markets. The issuing methods for private script are broadly similar. The market intermediaries are the same. Trading takes place in parallel in the same fora. The same investors have them in their portfolios and move in and out of them as prices, interest rates and earnings prospects change.

Then there are differences. Equity (shares) is more risky than bonds. A bond may become practically valueless, but the prospect of it appreciating much beyond the nominal value is remote. The reason, of course, is the interest rate which is a fixed percentage of the nominal value or, when floating, still follows the prevailing rate. Equity, by contrast, does not have this limitation. The basic logic is as follows. Each share represents, as its name suggests, a fixed share out of the total net assets of the company and is entitled to that share of its earnings. When earnings grow, a higher dividend per share becomes timely. This makes the share more valuable and its price will increase. If some of the earnings are not distributed, the company's net assets also grow and each share becomes more valuable in accounting terms (book value). Its price will reflect this, and probably disproportionately so, because of the expectations of continued growth. The share appreciates in value. When expectations are rampant, the appreciation can be substantial; a doubling of share price within a year is not uncommon. Such things are rare with bonds and mostly affect script which trades much below its nominal value – some brady bonds, for example (Greenbaum and Thakor 1995: 647). Of course, all expectations are not realized and the downhill can be as steep as the uphill with bankruptcy as an end station. The varying expectations are reflected in the price/earnings (p/e) ratio, and its fluctuation within the approximate range of seven to seventy is telling enough. Potential rewards are sufficiently large to invite sharp practice, and it is particularly in equity markets where insider crime can be a problem.

How large the market (price) risk can be is dramatically revealed by comparing three major equity price indices at various times in October 1987 when the market was in free fall, and again in 1993, which can be characterized as a normal year (Figure 3.16). The time periods from one to fifteen days broadly reflect the time needed for settlement at major exchanges at the topical time, the so-called 'settlement lag'. Under normal market conditions, it was about five days in New York, three days in Tokyo and up to two weeks in London. From that point of view, Tokyo was in October 1987 a 'safe' place, while London was extremely 'dangerous'. Tokyo's safety also depended on price support measures initiated by the authorities. Six years later, the tables were turned and Tokyo was facing the consequences of an unprecedented speculation bubble which had burst.

It follows that investors who value safety more than income prefer bonds to equity. Retail investors, as a group, are known for their cautious instinct, an instinct which the regulator tries to encourage in institutional investors. A standard rule concerns the maximum amount of assets which

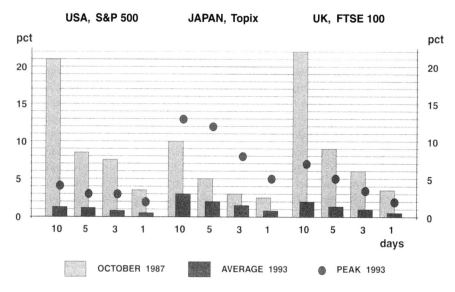

Figure 3.16 Market risk at settlement.

Source: *BIS AR* 1993/1994: 183. Copyright © 1994 of the Bank for International Settlements, Basle; used with permission.

Note
The fifteen-day period is not shown.

can be invested in equities. The exact percentage varies tremendously between countries and investor groups, but 15 per cent should be acceptable in most cases, and doubling that is quite possible. There is actually a trend towards higher percentages, well visible in countries with developed pension funds. In the UK, for example, equities made up 25 per cent of pension assets thirty years ago, against 70 per cent today. And Japanese trust banks have not needed to invest over 50 per cent of their assets in fixed-income securities since April 1996 (Brady 1993; Olivier 1996: 96).

The trend appears defensible. Growing demographic dependency ratios put pressure on pension funds for maintaining benefit levels, and that can only be achieved by investing in higher yielding paper than government bonds. The privatization of state-owned companies contributed towards this purpose. Modern portfolio theory has shown how risk can be controlled and yield increased by appropriate diversification; it has also given the numerical tools of implementing this insight. Volatile and unpredictable assets have suddenly become useful. The internationalization of equity markets has dramatically increased the practical possibilities.

The response varies according to country and region. British institutions are little constrained by restrictions of cross-border investment, in direct contrast to their peers on the Continent. The Erisa legislation in the USA, emphasizing the performance of the entire portfolio, has made the cross-border diversification of pension funds meaningful there, and 20–30 per cent of European privatizations were earmarked for US investors. But in practice the Americans are largely absorbed in domestic needs, and the share of foreign assets (not only equities) tends to hover around the 10 per cent mark. Large investors in small countries are pushed abroad by constraints at home. For example, in Switzerland the number of shares that can be registered for one shareholder is often limited by company bylaws. (Blume *et al.* 1993: 107; Humphreys 1992: 77; Riley 1997; Waters 1997)

Greater market risk is not the only drawback equity has in comparison with bonds. The income is also less predictable. It may be higher on average, but varies between accounting periods. Predictable income, however, is desirable for investors who have similar commitments, although of such a short maturity that inflationary pressures are unimportant. Motor insurance insurers are a typical example.

Operationally, the fluctuation of equity price and dividend is cumbersome, because the market must be monitored more closely than the bond market, and that becomes expensive. Corporate individuality contributes to this. Of course, bond issuers also show individual features, but as the bulk of outstanding bonds originates from a few major issuers, or just one (the government), the effect is not felt as intensely. It follows that price finding for equities is more difficult, and is an important reason why equities are predominantly traded at organized and therefore expensive exchanges, while bonds do well in the OTC market.

Placing an issue

The primary market for equities does not differ radically from that of corporate bonds. The differences are more in emphasis than substance. Flotations tend to peak after the publication of audited results. At most companies this happens in March or April, with the result that flotations cluster in May or June. The traditional underwriting syndicate, outlined for bond markets, continues to be important when an issue is small or directed at retail investors (Sharpe 1995b). But otherwise it is on the retreat. The long time-lag, up to two weeks, between pricing and distribution leads to a market risk, which the syndicate tries to avoid. Book building, tailored to institutional investors, achieves this.

Book building originates from the USA and has been accepted in Europe for privatizations and other large IPOs (initial public offering). It is resisted for secondary offerings, because current investors may have pre-emptive rights to buy the new script and believe it might not be honoured in the process. The essence, however, is to get a firm idea of the demand at various prices and thereby lessen the market risk of the syndicate. This happens by soliciting non-binding orders from prospective customers. The soliciting lasts several weeks and intensifies towards the end of the period. All orders are tagged with customer identification, put into a common pool and screened. The purpose is to place the issue at stable investors rather than arbitrageurs, who buy for short-term profit. The issuer may also have an opinion for or against a particular investor or investor group, which can now be excluded. In countries where bearer shares are the rule, France and the Netherlands for example, the issue is probably of wider interest in that it also reveals the identity of shareholders. Duplicate orders, solicited by different syndicate members, are halved. When the demand is known, the issue is priced and the lead manager allocates it among the syndicate. S/he also decides how the issuing fee is split among the members.

The power of the lead manager is great, and in keenly priced issues there is a temptation to use it for one's own advantage, not only in allocation and fee splitting but also elsewhere. The lead manager gets to know the customers of his or her co-managers, but not the other way round. This information can be misused in subsequent issues and the secondary market. S/he has the option to ring-fence the issue, i.e. define sales regions and decide who is allowed to sell in which region. Investors like that because there will be fewer sales calls for the same issue. But ring-fencing bars co-managers from entering new markets. It may also thwart sales efforts in general, because a co-manager cannot inform his or her customers on how the whole issue is selling. S/he knows only his or her own region. Ring-fencing has undeniable anticompetitive features, and it may soon be history.

It is customary to emphasize the need to diversify investor portfolios.

Similar tendencies exist on the issuing side as well. Current privatizations have been too large to be placed domestically alone. This is particularly true in small countries like Denmark and Portugal. Amounts raised are routinely $3bn, and the first tranche of Deutsche Telecom chalked a hefty $13.2bn. The placing must be international if not global. The USA is almost certainly involved, and so is the UK. This can be explained by the size of their funds, their need to perform, which discourages investment in bonds, and the international outlook of their managers. As one authority put it: 'The stock is either placed in the UK and US, or it is not placed' (Corrigan 1995).

In practice, it is quite difficult to organize a true global placing because local conditions vary so much, but they must still be observed. Europeans have realized this long ago when trying to sell their equity in the USA. The first hurdle used to be different accounting standards and more strict disclosure rules. Adaptation to the standards would have required the Europeans to revamp their domestic accounting or running two systems in parallel. Disclosure rules asked for more than what many Europeans were willing to reveal, and recently they have been joined by companies from the emerging markets. Nor were they prepared for the intense interest in company affairs which is typical of US investors. The issuance process is already hiding snags. SEC does not allow advertising before issuance except for what is printed in the prospectus. But what exactly counts as advertising is difficult to define. To be on the safe side, lawyers advise against articles and interviews in the media. That, however, is contrary to foreign practice, and stock exchanges abroad may claim that publicity for new fund raising is in the interest of existing shareholders. Since the foreign trade press is read in the USA, that creates real problems (Lee 1997b).

Conflicting accounting standards and disclosure rules could be handled by changing the law – once interest in European stock had grown sufficiently to make it worthwhile in the shape of rule 144a (Table 3.2). But this option is not available for an issuer who wants to access the general public and have the shares traded at an organized exchange. It can be a consumer goods company seeking a stronger name recognition. Or perhaps the company believes that listing gives it a wider share ownership. Or it may have a US subsidiary and wants to attract executive talent through stock options. It may also use its shares as payment for acquisitions. It can be big money. When Deutsche Bank, in its internationalizing drive, bought Bankers Trust in the USA, it had to pay a 10 per cent surcharge, or $1bn, because its shares were not listed on NYSE and could not be used as payment (Harnischfeger 2000). The difficulty is that US exchanges normally trade in lots of 100 shares and have rules about the nominal value and other details. Applying these rules to some foreign shares makes them virtually untradable, for example, because their nominal value may be around $5,000 and market value ten times higher (cf. Peyer 1996: 368–370).

To avoid such impasses, the foreign shares are replaced by receipts issued by a recognized and respected custodian. The repackaging is indirectly paid by investors as the receipts are more expensive to use than the underlying shares. The receipts tally with US exchange rules and are readily tradable. They are purchased and sold in dollars. Their dividends are in dollars, and they are settled through the Depositary Trust Corporation, which avoids the complexities of a foreign system. This metamorphosis also involves another and most important aspect. The receipts are classified as US securities in the sense that regulatory investment restrictions do not apply to them (Corrigan 1997a; Patel 1992). The actual shares are kept at a depositary, probably abroad. The custodian handles the usual groundwork such as keeping shareholder records, informing them about corporate matters and paying dividends. This role is usually shouldered by a bank in New York. Because the receipts were originally issued for the US market, they have become known as 'American Depositary Receipts' (ADRs).

A closer look shows that the ADR issuance is layered in three levels. The lowest, level 1, is for shares traded in foreign secondary markets. Level 2 is for existing shares listed at one of three US stock exchanges, NYSE, Nasdaq or Amex (see Chapter 4). The highest, level 3, is for new issues at these exchanges. The layering is parallel to rule 144a, which would locate between levels 1 and 2. Since US listing is a seal of legitimacy for many American investors, these companies can expect analyst attention, higher share price and a wider shareholder base. In return, they must comply with full SEC surveillance including regular filings. Level 1 escapes this, but trades only OTC and probably relies on name recognition for success. Nestlé and Bayer, for example, belong to this group (Adams, J. 1997: 31; Berton 1999; Corrigan 1997b; Wheatley 1997).

Today, there are DRs for other regions too, with appropriate titles, and even Global DRs. For example, during January–September 1996, GDRs accounted for about one-quarter of all DRs issued. As the principle is unchanged, the flourishing terminology may appear a pure marketing gimmick. Far from it. The GDR investor base is wider than ADR's, Europeans typically taking up 80 per cent although US sales are possible under rule 144a. Being listed in London or Luxembourg, GDRs are cheaper than ADRs. They are a vehicle for bypassing foreign ownership limits, for example, in India, South Korea and Taiwan, and trade at a 20–100 per cent premium to the underlying shares. For Russia's foremost blue chip, Gazprom, the ADR premium is fourfold. Depositary receipts also smooth matters considerably in countries where the infrastructure, such as settlement and central share depository, is weak or non-existent. This is the case in many emerging markets, and it is particularly important because script there is only likely to be kept for short periods. (Featherstone 1997: 136; Field 1996: 87; Higgins 1996: 32; Lapper 1995; 1996; Lee 1997a: 64)

Such are the markets as seen through the glasses of an institutional investor. In a way, this is correct, because the retail end has shrunk steeply in relative terms, at least in countries with a long tradition of equity saving like the USA and UK (Figure 4.1). It is more convenient, less risky, and possibly also more profitable to invest in mutual funds where professional managers are constantly on the lookout for best value. But there still are situations when retail investors are important – privatizations, for example. In the privatizations of British Telecom and British Gas, they took about two-thirds of the issues. Deutsche Telecom's first tranche was expected to succeed or fail on the strength of retailer demand and in the second tranche in 2000 their allocation was about 70 per cent. But there are also cynics. They point to incentives routinely given to retail investors. If a deal is saleable, they claim, incentives are not necessary and therefore essentially political, to promote people's capitalism or smooth nationalist sentiment when the crown jewels are sold. Normal incentives are 3–6 per cent price cuts, payment by instalment, free shares for buyers who hold their purchases for at least twelve-to-thirty-six months, and even twelve-month price guarantees in the secondary market (Middelman 1995).

It appears to work, but all that is domestic. Internationally, no issuer name, no intermediary and no method can guarantee the success of an issue. What then, if a failure appears imminent? In the US, the issue is simply withdrawn, and there will be few comments. In Europe, the same thing is seen in a much harsher light and considered a minor disaster (Sharpe 1995a).

Index – purpose and structure

Trading in equity and the ensuing settlement is labour intensive, i.e. expensive. Trades can be subject to turnover tax and settlement takes time. Equity (stock) indices are a convenient way to gain exposure to a market without the cost, time delay and other problems of trading in the underlying script. They are promoted by various information vendors and exchanges. Since an index gives no ownership of the underlying equity, it escapes tax and avoids the elaborate registration procedure linked with ownership. Exchanges and brokers also charge lower fees for index than equity trading. The inflow of money into some funds has become too large to be placed in individual equities alone. An index fund is the logical solution. By the early 1990s US institutional investors already had 20 per cent of their domestic monies in index funds, while, for managed funds in London, it was 15 per cent (Anon. 1989: 30; Blume *et al.* 1993: 91; Waters 1993). Every country with a stock exchange has at least one domestic index. Dow Jones, S&P 500 and NYSE Composite in the USA, FTSE 100 in the UK, DAX in Germany, CAC 40 in France, Nikkei 225 in Japan and Hang Seng in Hongkong are well known examples. For international investing, MCSI dominates in the USA and has won a wide following in Euroland while FTSE has it adherents in the UK.

An equity index is intended to reflect the composition of the listed equities and follow their movements. To achieve this, a representative sample of companies is selected, weighted by their respective market capitalizations on a certain day (basis) and averaged. Price movements are accounted for by adjusting the weights. In small countries a handful of equities dominate the market, while in large ones with a long tradition of equity ownership, hundreds of companies are needed for the same share of market capitalization. The FT Actuaries World Indices in 1987 reflect the selection principles.

> The indices are based on 2,400 equities in twenty-three countries and comprise about 15 per cent of the more than 15,000 listed companies worldwide, with well over 70 per cent of market capitalization at main stock exchanges. The main purpose is to provide a benchmark for international fund managers. Therefore, only equities which can be owned by foreigners are included. For example, registered shares of Swiss companies and Swedish bank shares are excluded on this ground. Companies where at least 75 per cent of capital is controlled by dominant shareholders are excluded. The index tries to capture at least 70 per cent of domestic capitalization in each country involved. The largest companies are the ones most likely to be included, but a sample of all companies of at least $100m market capitalization is included as well. This pattern has one exception, the USA, which is so large that only 600 companies are included to keep the index manageable. (Lambert 1987)
>
> Dow Jones Industrial, the most quoted index in the DJ family, is an anachronism in this world. It is the average unweighted price of thirty equities. When a company is deemed to have lost its charter it is replaced by another one. The index was created in 1876 and, from the original twelve companies, one, General Electric, was left in 2002. The other eleven had been merged, broken up in antitrust action, removed from the index, evolved to something else, or in one case simply dissolved.

It appears very simple but in practice all kind of complications arise. The number of equities and the cover targeted is a very fundamental decision. S&P 500 includes 500 companies, not particularly much for a country with approximately 8,300 listed companies at its major exchanges. The existence of the Russel 2000 index, created for small companies (small caps), testifies to that. Superficially, the more numerous the companies, the better. On closer inspection, the intended purpose will put limits to such ambition. The idea with stock index is that it creates a benchmark against which a portfolio can be compared. Numerous equities in a portfolio mean more administrative work, expensive adjustment, declining free float and increasing cross-ownership. Overall restructuring of a global equity portfolio with hundreds of companies may cost, in commissions, taxes and market impact, 1.5–3 per cent of its value, i.e. its annual yield (Willoughby 1997). Equities (and countries) correlate with each other and it may be sufficient to have only 100 of them. Free float can be a real problem. It changes, it cannot be defined exactly and no reliable information may be available. Then one creates a shortcut and includes total capitalization, or uses best judgement.

> After its first flotation, Deutsche Telekom's free float was below 20 per cent, yet DJStoxx weighted its market capitalization at 100 per cent, MSCI at 80 per cent, DAX at 40 per cent and only FT/S&P at 20 per cent (Bedford 1998b; Mathias 1999).

National indices get problems with internationalizing companies.

> When Daimler-Benz acquired Chrysler in the USA, the merged company, incorporated in Stuttgart, was excluded from S&P 500. It would have appeared logical to exclude BP-Amoco, Shell and Unilever as well because all are incorporated abroad. That did not happen because investors wanted to have them in the index. Apparently the cultural distance to Daimler-Benz was too far, made tangible by the German-style top management structure (Authers and Burt 1997; Bream 1998; Wright 2000).

Exclusion from an index means that investors committed to following that index must sell, and the other way around. The share price will inevitably move, perhaps 5–15 per cent. Investors will lose money irrespective of direction because they are compelled to sell/buy at an inopportune time to maintain the share's correct weight in their portfolios. It is still more problematic when a merged company gets so large that its weight in the index exceeds the investor's diversification limit.

> Vodafone/Mannesmann and Glaxo Wellcome/SmithKline Beecham mergers raised their weights in the FTSE 100 index to 18 per cent and 31.5 per cent, respectively, far too high for prudent portfolio diversification (Lee 1999a; Luce 1999d; Mathias 1999; Targett 2000).

Attractive companies can be excluded because the countries where they are incorporated are found to be too risky. Country criteria might be the availability of reliable information, liquidity, honest custody, effective settlement, relevant legislation, impartial judiciary and free transferability of capital. They may be problematic in many emerging and transitional economies.

Slow settlement in India could be traced back to the dominant Mumbai (Bombay) Stock Exchange which was controlled by brokers. Frustrated by its unwillingness to modernize the market regulator authorized financial institutions to open a competing exchange. The screen-based National Stock Exchange started equity trading in November 1994 and compelled BSE to adopt electronic trading early in 1995. NSE also introduced weekly settlement cycles, started India's first clearing corporation in April 1996, which guarantees trades from counterparty risk, and launched the first share depository in December 1996 (Tassell 1997).

Many Russian companies are still their own registrars, an inherently unhealthy situation. Data availability was so poor that no index was calculated in the first place until 1996 (Anon. 1997a; Thornhill 1997). China is only now implementing modern financial legislation and internationally valid accounting (Harding 1998; Vortmüller 2001: 214–216). Where stock certificates have not been dematerialized (as computer entries), forgery is a very real possibility. Foreigners face an upper limit of permitted equity ownership, say 20 per cent, in many Asian countries; the practice was commonplace in Europe a decade or two ago.

An investor can select an index for a particular exchange, country, world region, or the whole world. Subindices for various industries are also available, gold in South Africa, automobiles in Germany, chemicals in Switzerland and so on. When making the selection, the underlying capitalization must be large enough for the resources to be invested. This is no problem in large markets but may be in small ones (Figure 3.17).

Indices are discussed in the context of equity because they matter most there. But there are bond indices as well, such as Lehman Brothers' aggregate index and Salomon Smith Barney's broad investment grade index in the USA. Both are also used in Europe and face competition by iBoxx, launched by Deutsche Börse and seven banks. They are less well known than equity indices and no derivatives contract is based on them. Debt yields fluctuate less than equity prices and bond prices are far less transparent because of fragmented trading and many illiquid issues. There is also the problem that too much debt by the same issuer downgrades its attractiveness. If nobody wants it, inclusion in an index is meaningless (Butler 2001; van Duyn 2000; Luce 1998).

Derivatives – risking the family silver?

What they are

Derivatives include futures, forward rate agreements ('forwards' or 'FRAs'), options and swaps. Stock indices are also a kind of derivative,

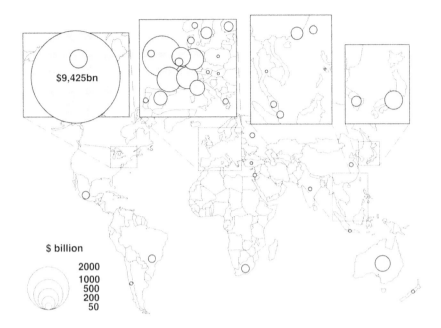

Figure 3.17 Country weights of the FTSE All-World Index, 31 May 2002.

Source: Courtesy of Nomura International plc, London.

Note
Includes all securities at exchanges and OTC.

although not necessarily classified as such. Maturities vary between a day
and a decade. Both futures and forwards are promises to buy or sell the
underlying instrument at maturity. The difference between them is that
futures contracts are standardized in their structure and traded at organized exchanges, whereas forwards are tailored to customer need and are
traded only OTC. They are less liquid than futures when trades remain
small, but when the amounts climb to $500m and beyond, they may be the
only alternative. Options give the right to buy or sell the underlying instrument at a certain price and time, or during an agreed period. They give
protection in the form of a price limit like futures/forwards but allow, in
addition, the option holder to reap the fruits of a favourable price development. Logically, they are comparatively expensive products. Standardized options are traded at exchanges, unstandardized at OTC. Swaps are
agreements to barter the payment streams of the underlying instruments
or/and the instruments themselves. As the barter objects may be of
unequal value, sidepayments are possible. Swaps are difficult to standardize and therefore OTC.

The boundaries between the classes are not sharp, as many instruments
are partial substitutes or can be constructed from each other. For

example, approximate options and swaps can be constructed from futures and forwards, although at a cost of a larger administrative effort. The outline is also rudimentary in so far that OTC derivatives can be constructed to almost any complexity. The complexity is partly driven by customer demand, but also by the intense competition which rages between financial intermediaries and which is reflected in rapidly eroding margins and ready imitation of competitors' products. Although OTC and exchange contracts are not fungible, there is still interaction between the two markets, as the sellers of OTC products often hedge their net exposures at exchanges. These hedges are not perfect but they reduce the risk.

The original use of derivatives was for hedging, protecting oneself against price change. Commodity exchanges offered simple hedges in the shape of futures and options. When financial markets were liberalized and became more volatile, the hedging concept was developed further and applied to financial instruments. Foreign exchange (forex) derivatives came in the 1970s, interest rate and currency swaps in the early 1980s and equity derivatives in the late 1980s. Credit derivatives followed in the 1990s. The increasingly sophisticated applications were made possible and promoted by advances in portfolio theory; computer-based modelling, communication and trading; enhanced risk awareness; and off-balance-sheet accounting. With the help of derivatives it is possible to change a portfolio's risk profile, shift its exposure between markets and currencies, unbundle different types of risk such as counterparty, interest rate and forex risk, and get a higher return at unchanged risk. Derivatives are speedy, convenient and low-cost. The low cost comes from leveraged deals, lower trading fees, absence of custody costs, turnover and capital gains taxes. Cost savings of 90 per cent can easily be achieved. In emerging markets, derivatives are used to circumvent restrictive ownership rules, difficult settlement and custody, and currency controls. (Hargreaves 1988: 35; Harverson 1992b; Jeanneau 1995: 29, 36; King 1994: 181; Ostrovsky 1999; Zimmermann 1998: 19–25)

For hedging to be possible, there must be speculators who are willing to accept the risk against a fee. Writing derivative contracts is inherently risky because of the leverage, and because the best customers, multinationals and fund managers, operate in large amounts. Servicing them requires solid capitalization, but once it is available the large size also permits internal netting of portfolios, continuous risk management and the spreading of fixed costs over large portfolios. Market concentration is high and five US banks – JP Morgan, Bankers Trust, Chase (with Chemical), Bank of America and Citicorp – accounted for 90 per cent of the global business in the early 1990s (Bennet 1993; Corrigan and Harverson 1992).

The wisdom of derivatives has often been questioned by laypeople. Aggregate benefits and losses obviously outbalance each other, which makes the activity look more like a casino rather than a serious and useful pursuit. The rationale exists at the individual, not aggregate, level: derivatives remove constraints which market participants find cumbersome and replace them with new and less burdensome ones. They redistribute risk.

Scope

The usual instruments underlying derivatives ('underlyings') are deposits, bonds, equity indices and foreign exchange ('forex'). Derivatives of individual equities are less common and may be even forbidden. The deposit or bond derivative is called 'interest rate', because the nominally fixed rate translates into a variable rate ('yield') when the price moves. The geography of forex derivatives will be postponed to the next subchapter (pp. 140–145), where the underlying spot ('cash') market is also discussed. This subchapter deals only with the non-geographical aspects. The complete classification with four underlying instruments, three derivatives and two markets, exchange and OTC, becomes a twenty-four-cell cube. Activity, however, is heavily concentrated in some of the cells only (Figure 3.18). The large figures and historical growth record easily create the image of an unbridled octopus threatening the stability of the world financial system, a fear which is completely unfounded. The disproportional

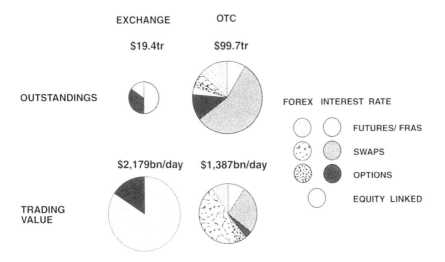

Figure 3.18 Derivatives outstandings and daily trading value, 31 March 2001 and April 2001, respectively.

Source: *BIS F* 2001: Tables C2 and C6; *QR* June 2001: Table 23A.

Notes
Reported figures only; OTC adjusted for local and cross-border inter-dealer double counting. 'OTC forex swaps in outstandings' are currency swaps (change of payment streams and finally of principals) and in 'Trading' they are foreign exchange swaps (simultaneous purchase and sale with different value dates), split between futures and options at exchanges as during Q1.

growth of derivatives in relation to cash markets also appears to be a thing of the past.

The usual indicators of derivative activity are trading value ('turnover'), volume and notional amount outstanding. Outstandings (open interest at exchanges) refer to the value of the underlying instrument. The figures are not strictly comparable, however. There are gaps in OTC reporting while exchange data have not been adjusted properly for double counting. The method of unwinding a contract is different, doubling the amount outstanding in OTC, but netting it out at organized exchanges (*BIS AR* 1995/1996: 159). The size difference between the exchange and OTC markets is, nevertheless, very real. Outstandings at exchanges are only 20 per cent of OTC outstandings, while the trading value is 50 per cent larger (Figure 3.18). More lively trading is natural for standardized contracts while the lack of swaps at exchanges has a bearing for outstandings. Swaps are difficult to standardize because they are so specific as to counterparts and circumstances. Large market actors also make too much money in OTC to be interested in supporting exchange products (Oakley 2001).

The popularity of swaps may come as a surprise. And still they have contributed to the globalization of markets in a very important way; in certain years, 80 per cent of eurobond issues are swapped to the desired currency (Rose 1994: 32). But why swap in the first place? Would it not be better to hit right from the outset? A simple answer is that markets, and expectations about them, change and recommend measures to be taken, but that all expectations do not point in the same direction. Then it makes sense to swap payment streams while the underlying liability towards the original lender remains unchanged. There are also more specific explanations. For example, fixed rate debt calls for a higher credit risk premium than floating debt. A higher rated borrower may access the fixed rate market and swap with a lower rated borrower to a floating rate. The deal is attractive when the swap spread is wide. Alternatively, a European borrower may have obligations in US dollars, but because its credit standing is better at home it prefers to borrow there at a lower rate. Thereafter it swaps the payment obligations with a US counterpart, who gets money cheaper at home than in Europe.

> The deal between the European Investment Bank and Tennessee Valley Authority is a textbook case. The organizations simultaneously launched two ten-year global bonds, DM1.5bn and $1bn, and swapped the proceeds, thereby cutting off several basis points from the interest rate. (Lee and Irvine 1996)

Since an international swap involves at least two currencies, it gives birth to forex deals as a sideline. Swap is widely used as a hedging instrument because of its excellent liquidity along the whole yield curve. For example, central banks use swaps in adjusting the maturity of their liabilities and swaps are the primary hedging instrument of US government agencies (Laitner 2001).

The geographical discussion here is focused on the OTC interest rates, while forex is postponed to the next subchapter (pp. 140–145) and exchanges to Chapter 4. The equity segment is small and can be over-looked here. It is reasonable to expect that the pattern of derivative instruments broadly corresponds to the size of underlying financial markets. This holds well for interest rate products. They are important in the USA, UK, Ireland and Euroland where much lending is located and debt issued (Figure 3.19). The extent of cross-border activity comes as a surprise and illustrates the internationalization of debt markets, at least in the North Atlantic part of the world (Figure 3.20). The share is particularly large in Euroland which is still a collection of intertwined national markets. It is natural that market opinion is less unidirectional there, the need to hedge is larger and opportunities to arbitrage more numerous than in the USA, for example. The UK is an intermediate case between Euroland and the USA. This is unexpected, recalling London's role as an international

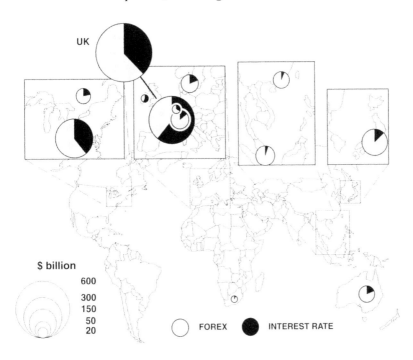

Figure 3.19 OTC derivatives, daily trading value, April 2001.

Source: *BIS F* 2001: Tables E32–E35.

Notes
Reported figures only; adjusted for local (but not cross-border) inter-dealer double counting. Luxembourg is taken as separate from Euroland.

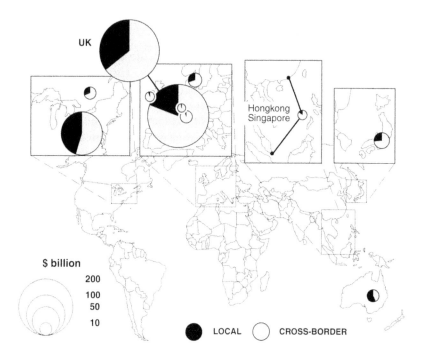

Figure 3.20 OTC interest rate derivatives, daily trading value, April 2001.

Source: *BIS F* 2001: Tables E32–E35.

Notes
Reported figures only; adjusted for local (but not cross-border) inter-dealer double counting. Luxembourg is taken as separate from Euroland.

finance centre and the very large cross-border share of other finance
centres. Is London already so large that basically international deals can
be conducted there 'internally' and therefore end under the local label?

Risky or not?

The perception of the extreme riskiness of derivatives necessitates a short
treatment. Gross market value has become popular as a derivative risk
indicator. It gives the replacement cost of a contract should the counterpart default. It cannot be compiled from standard surveys but must be calculated separately. Its weakness is that, in a period of major stress, the
market upon which the contract is projected may itself be in a state of
turmoil. Gross market value divided by outstandings may be preferable
because it gives the relative risk. The ratio still includes the said weakness
but puts matters into perspective. An overall figure of 3 per cent emerged
from the BIS survey, a far cry from the impressive notional outstandings.

Where the risks are high, as in forex swaps and equity index products, the explanation is in market volatility or long maturities (Figure 3.21).

In practice, many mutual obligations can be netted out, whereafter the magnitude of the remaining risk is similar to that in banks' loan books. The important thing, however, is not so much the size of exposure as the mix of counterparties and the share of unusual or seasoned products. In addition, netting reduces the capital needed to support the business, by up to 50 per cent. The weakness of netting is that it is recognized unconditionally only in US law. BIS has given it unofficial approval, but that is of doubtful value as long as national bankruptcy laws do not accommodate it. The legal ambiguity notwithstanding, some organizations offer the service globally, although the response has been more wary than expected (Bennet 1993; Harverson 1992a; Lee 1992).

Multilateral netting would obviously be more attractive. Its implementation faces two problems. The first is the variability of OTC contracts, particularly of long-term contracts, which makes their valuation difficult. Models can do the job, but to get everybody to agree with specific models will not be easy. The other problem is the necessary central clearing house, which would introduce margins and make operations more expensive. In the USA, it would probably lead to the regulation of OTC contracts, an unpalatable vision.

When netting is impractical, risk can be reduced by requiring a collateral. Collateral was offered in the late 1980s by lower-rated US securities houses which had difficulty in competing with higher-rated banks. When banks also lost their high credit ratings, collateral became common. It has been characterized as the last throw when an existing player tries to stay in the game. From the investor angle, collateral is a prudent way to protect

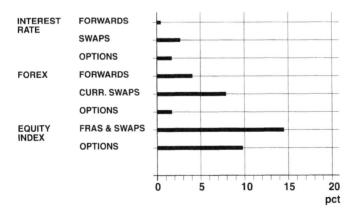

Figure 3.21 Relative risk by OTC derivatives segment, April 2001.

Source: *BIS F* 2001: Table C6.

Note
Adjusted for double counting.

oneself, particularly at long maturities, and institutional investors may be forced to require it because of their bylaws. They are in good company, since the World Bank asks its counterparts for US government securities as collateral (Bennet 1993; Lee 1995).

The real difficulty in managing derivative risk, however, is market dynamics. When a dealer can be in or out of money several times and to varying degrees during the lifetime of a contract, when quotes change twenty times a minute for a major currency, and when a profitable port-folio can become worthless in minutes, balance sheet information is entirely inadequate, being outdated even before it has been prepared. Therefore, there is no substitute for senior management walking around the trading floor, talking to traders, and asking what is going on (Chesler-Marsh 1992; Kodres 1996: 23; Lee 1992; McDonough 1993).

Foreign exchange – the global glue

Overview

Foreign exchange markets are the glue which keeps the world economy together. The spot market is very large, about \$130tr in annual trading value or twenty-one times the global exports of goods. The derivatives market is almost twice its size. Most of the trading is simply the balancing of positions, however. Spreads are very narrow and balancing con-sequently inexpensive. Customer trades thus have a substantial multiplier effect. Much depends on the OTC practice of closing or modifying a posi-tion by writing a new contract rather than cancelling the old one. Deals between currencies for which keen quotes are difficult to obtain are made via the dollar, which automatically doubles the figures (Brady 1991; Thomas 1995). Flexibility in the face of fluctuating exchange rates encourages derivatives of short maturity, which leads to frequent renewals. These examples may suffice. Rampant speculation, which stimulates many a layperson's fantasy, gets scaled down to its proper size. It certainly exists; the fleecing of the British taxpayer in 1992 when the Bank of England used £11bn of its reserves to defend the pound and enriched traders by £3bn has gone down in monetary history. But the coup needs sustained imbalance; a deficit in payment balance exceeding 3.5 per cent of GDP has been suggested, and political stubbornness to succeed. The lack of formal regulation facilitates speculation but also outright sharp practice, such as action-based and word-based price manipulation, criminalized in other markets (de Brouwer 2001: 7, 158–159; Currie 2000; Howell 1997).

Forex is the best example of a global marketplace with twenty-four-hour trading. It is an OTC market, far too liquid and customer-oriented to be dislodged by organized exchanges which have only 1 per cent market share. Since the wholesale market is dominated by a handful of banks in the largest finance centres, its implied dispersion is illusory. The market is overseen by central banks, which interfere in the event of menacing interruptions. The generally short duration of exposures is also helpful. About 30 per cent of trades are spot while 40 per cent of forwards and 70 per cent of swaps have maximum maturities of seven days. On the other hand, trades are large and occasionally very large. The normal minimum in interbank trading is $10m, and individual orders from hedge funds are known to have approached $3bn. Such amounts comfortably exceed the equity of all but the 150 largest banks in the world and constitute a real risk. The logical solution is to create a clearing house to net exposures. (Bennet 1994; *BIS F* 2001, Tables E9, E12–E13; Lewis 1989a; Pouzin 1995)

Spot forex has been a telephone market for most of the post-Second World War period. Traders received orders, made offers and concluded trades on the phone. There was no central marketplace, no clearing house and no Big Board (NYSE) to display the current price at a glance. Customer–dealer and direct interbank trades were not disclosed to the market. What market transparency there was arose from brokered interbank trades, some 40 per cent of the total. The lack of transparency played into the hands of the big actors, custodians included, who stayed informed because of the constant flow of inquiries and orders, a typical bank making 3,000–4,000 trades within twenty-four hours. These became the indicators for price change. The 'metro business', trades below $5m, provided liquidity. But trading was expensive because human labour is expensive. Efforts were made to automate the marketplace and electronic trading was the solution, nowadays with an attached artificial voice for those who think that it raises both attention and ambience. It came to dominate interbank and inter-dealer trading. (Blitz 1993; Derrick 2002; Ito and Folkerts-Landau 1996: 125; Kodres 1996: 22; Nairn 2001)

Automation is no panacea, however. It takes more time to look at the screen and use the keyboard than to listen for a price and shout 'done' on the exchange floor. During hectic activity the screen easily becomes 'dead', since nobody has time to key trades into the computer. An announced buy/sell price on the screen is risky because the unknown counterpart can hit either side. Trading systems tend to be proprietary and tie the user to a particular bank, with no guarantee about best execution, the very task of a fund manager. The system operator also learns the sensitive credit limits of counterparts. Still, the advantages are so great that 90 per cent of broking, and particularly the main currency pairs, are automated in London. The critical mass for making the system profitable is fifty banks, which implies very considerable scale economies. (Adams, R. 1997; Blitz 1993; Cooke 1996: 90; Galati 2001; Murphy 1989; Salmon 1996: 155)

Reuters launched the first dealing system in 1981 and, with its 17,000 dealer terminals, accounted a decade later for one-half of the global business. Competitors, Telerate (Dow Jones) and Quotron (Citicorp), which entered the market eight years later, were unable to catch up. Minex (absorbed by EBS in 1995) in Japan was more successful but only at home.

Then Reuters made a mistake; it became over-ambitious. The banking market was reasonably saturated and had little growth, while 30–40 per cent of spot dealing went through brokers who used the phone ('voice broking'). Reuters wanted to penetrate this segment, too, and decided to upgrade its systems further. A virtual monopoly was in the making, and the banks were expected to foot the bill. Rather than complying, they revolted and launched, in cooperation with Quotron, a system of their own, EBS (Electronic Broking Service), in 1993. Initially, ten large banks in Europe participated and, by May 1995, the number of branches had doubled, mostly by non-owners. Two years later, EBS had overtaken Reuters and pushed it to the retail and pound markets. (Adams, R. 1997; Anon. 1992; Cooke 1996; Gawith 1995a; 1995c; Kuper 1997a; 1997b; Laurie 1990; RB 1993)

Currencies and counterparts

The forex market is dominated by three currencies: the dollar, euro and yen (Figure 3.22). These three are the counterpart in 75 per cent of all trades, and the dollar's share alone is 45 per cent. The dollar's high percentage results in superior liquidity and keen prices. Therefore, even when the original transaction does not involve the dollar at all, it still may be advantageous to go through it. This creates a self-reinforcing circle but also a segmented market, the dollar deals and the rest, called 'currency crosses'. The coming of Euroland has led to considerable rationalization. The aggregate 38 per cent share of the legacy currencies six years previously has shrunk to the euro's 19 per cent (*BIS F* 1996, Table 1–G). Considering that many expected the euro to partially replace the dollar as a reserve currency, this is a low share. The sluggishness of the European

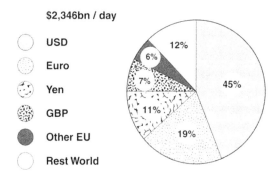

Figure 3.22 Forex trading by currency, daily average, April 2001.

Source: *BIS F* 2001: Table E1.

Notes
Every trade counted twice. Only reported trades. Net of local and cross-border inter-dealer double counting.

economy and the political uncertainties underlying the euro have largely deprived it of that role. The yen's share is also more modest than necessary but that is the result of an active policy. A role as an international reserve currency would mean partial loss of control, and more extensive invoicing in yen might damage international competitiveness (Dawkins 1996).

The three dominant currencies are the centrepiece of most action and parties to all the really important currency pairs, also involving four other countries: Australia, Canada, Switzerland and the UK (Figure 3.23). Compared with the pattern six years earlier, there is very little change. Impressive as these nine flows (40 per cent of all trading) are, there is very little money in them. Spot deals, and particularly those broked electronically, are so keenly priced that they are meaningful for dealers only as spinners of attached business, derivatives in particular. The action is in the difficult crosses between the exotic currencies of the transforming and developing economies. Formally, the currencies may float freely, but intervention without forewarning is always looming. Almost by definition, these markets are small. The combined market share of the twenty leading exotics is about 3 per cent of the global total. When mature currencies react to international events, exotics turn to local news. They cannot be traded offshore, deals must be directed through local banks, forwards are limited in size and duration, price finding may take a week and settlement is slow. Logically, the spreads are ten-to-fifteen times wider than in the leading currencies and offer a good opportunity for those with skill and

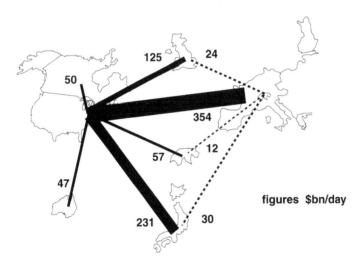

Figure 3.23 Forex trading by main currency pair, daily average, April 2001.

Source: *BIS F* 2001: Tables E2 and E3.

Notes
Only reported trades. Net of local and cross-border inter-dealer double counting.

patience. Leading currency banks like Citicorp and Standard Chartered estimate that one-half of their forex profit comes from exotics. (*BIS AR* 1996/1997: 91; Gawith 1996a; 1996b; Hagger 1992b)

It is reasonable to assume that a currency has its trading base at home, i.e. that most trades have the one counterpart within the national boundaries. As a broad generalization, the assumption holds, although there are important exceptions (Figure 3.24). The assumption has a natural corollary, namely, that most trades, irrespective of currency, are booked in countries with the leading currencies. The corollary is incorrect. A leading currency need not attract trading in other currencies, or the other way round.

London is the prime example. The pound sterling has a market share of only 7 per cent, but 31 per cent of the global forex trading value is in London, making it the largest hub in the world. In fact, it is larger than New York and Tokyo combined, which rank next by the strength of their national currencies. This ranking has remained unchanged since 1986,

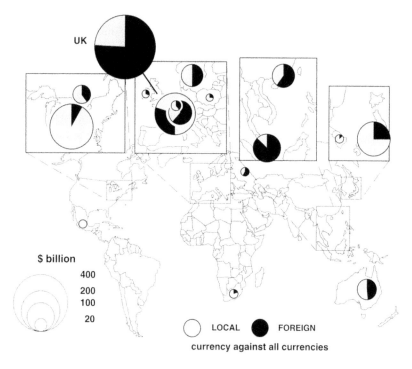

Figure 3.24 Forex trading by currency and country, daily average, April 2001.

Source: *BIS F* 2001: Tables E4 and E7.

Notes
Spots, forwards and foreign exchange swaps. Because trading value is identified by location, each deal is counted twice. Only reported trades. Net of local (but not cross-border) interdealer double counting.

when the surveys were started, and London has actually increased its leadership. Most noteworthy, the largest dollar market is not in New York, as the currency pairs would suggest, but in London, and in yen trades, London is a solid number two. It also surpasses the aggregated Euroland in euro deals. It is conveniently located within the global time zones, lightly regulated and enjoys the advantage of tradition.

Singapore and Hongkong clearly trail Tokyo, although only in yen and dollar deals. Their trading values have the same structure, with the dollar as the core currency. Singapore has gained market share and is seen by many to be on the road to becoming Asia's forex hub. Currently it outranks Hongkong except in the minor reporting currencies, not detailed by the BIS. The success has created controversy, neighbours accusing Singapore of speculation (Gawith 1995b; Kynge 1997). In Europe, Switzerland has some of the same flair as these two entrepôt cities. It is situated between the large neighbours Germany, France and Italy and has a structure similar to theirs.

Reserve and parallel currency

The use of a currency as an international payment instrument implies that actors have it hoarded somewhere, to smooth imbalances between inflows and outflows. Basically, the actors are central banks and that 'somewhere' is an account at the central bank issuing the currency. In practice, banks and their customers can intervene. A company can have a currency account at its bank which in turn has a currency account at the domestic central bank or at a correspondent bank abroad. The correspondent, naturally, has an account at its own central bank. For practical reasons most currency reserves can be found on these accounts. The existence of an account at a central bank does not yet make that country's currency a recognized reserve currency. It is also necessary that the account holders want to use the currency for that purpose, the more numerous they are the better. The central bank must also be prepared to create money when the account holders so wish. These circumstances are instrumental for the currency's liquidity, not only monetary liquidity but also political liquidity. If foreigners doubt that the host government will deny access to their central bank accounts – freeze their assets – they will find another reserve currency. It probably helps if the currency keeps its value – is strong – although that alone is not sufficient. The Swiss franc is strong but not a true reserve currency (Cohen 1998: 96–97; Luce 1999b).

The distribution of currency reserves between countries is rather different than the standard pattern of financial assets (Figure 3.25). Asia Pacific dominates, Europe follows and North America lags. Considered by country, the transforming and developing world compares well with the industrialized world. The explanation cannot be the need to smooth

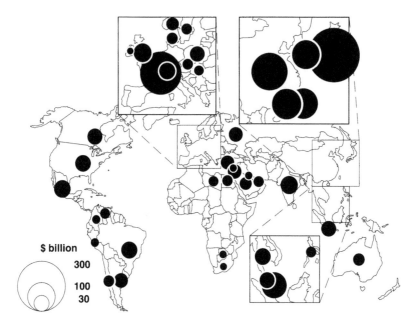

Figure 3.25 Foreign exchange reserves, December 2000.

Sources: *IFS*, Country Tables, 2002; www.taamn.org/Taiwan%20Statistics.htm.

Notes
Special Drawing Rights of IFM not included.

imbalances in international payments alone. The reserves are also there to defend the currency against speculative attacks. The currency crisis which rocked, but not necessarily unseated, Southeast Asia in 1997/1998 comes first to mind. Thailand may have faced the worst gale, using $20bn of its $37bn reserves to defend the baht in May 1997. The experience raised the issue of an Asian currency union, or at least a pledge of concerted action by China, Japan and Korea if one of their currencies were subjected to attack. Their aggregated reserves, some $600bn without Hongkong, are impressive but so are the resources which hedge funds can mobilize. The best defence, of course, is a balanced economic policy.

Another explanation for the unconventional distribution is that the dollar and euro are reserve currencies themselves with shares of 60 per cent and (a guesstimated) 25 per cent respectively (*BIS AR* 2001: Table V.1). This is visible particularly in the US reserves, about the same size as Thailand's. Its government can use the printing press and ride out a storm that way. It would be more difficult in Euroland with its bickering governments and a formal inflationary target written into the charter of the ECB; but it can be done. Japan chose not to let its yen become a reserve currency and has scaled, perhaps even overscaled, foreign exchange reserves accordingly. And should the need arise, it can sell some of its foreign assets; US treasuries, for example. There is also a third explanation for the handsome reserves of the transforming and emerging countries, namely, that there are not so many attractive investment opportunities available and cash-in-hand gives flexibility.

The structure of the reserves follows economic ties. Excluding the reserve currency originators themselves, Europe is a blend of the dollar and the euro while the rest of the world clearly prefers the dollar. The strength of the link varies and is strongest where the national currency is pegged to the reserve currency. When the peg has legal status, the arrangement is called 'currency board'. It means that a national central bank can print money only in relation to its reserves in the reference currency. That contributes to stability and constrains inflationary policy but also the central bank's ability to change interest rate and act as a lender of last resort. The control slides over to foreigners. Currency pegs and boards best suit small, open economies trading mostly with a much larger economy. Small Latin countries, small transforming economies in Europe, Hongkong and Brunei are among them. Argentina experimented with a diluted variant of the concept with only one-third of the dollar reserves required by a full currency board for government bond issuance (Caplen 1998; Montagnon 1998).

A currency board is not the final stage of abandoning control. It is when a foreign currency becomes a parallel currency in a country, when it is accepted as readily as, or more readily than, the national currency in transactions. It may even gain the status of a legal tender, meaning that transactions affected by it are enforceable in courts. The dollar has (had) that status, at least in Argentina, Ecuador, El Salvador and Panama, and the deutschmark in Bosnia, Kosovo and Montenegro. Much of the parallel currency assets are in private hands as cash, stashed in a bank vault, old shoe box, under the mattress and so on. Figures can only be rough estimates but the amounts are significant (Table 3.3). Information about their location is still more fragmentary and only the largest concentrations are known: dollars in Russia ($40bn–$60bn) and Argentina ($25bn–$40bn), deutschmarks in former Yugoslavia and Turkey, and HKdollars in southern China (Catán 2002; Porter and Judson 1996; Thornhill 1999).

One can ask about the meaningfulness of allowing one's currency to circulate abroad and to be used as a reserve currency. It can be used as a political lever, for example by threatening its availability in a political crisis.

> In an effort to oust Panama's president from office in March 1988, the USA froze Panamanian assets in US banks and stopped dollar transfers to Panama, which used the dollar as a parallel and practically only legal tender. Panama was compelled to all but close the shop (Cohen 1998: 45; Warf 2002).

Table 3.3 Currency in circulation abroad, late 1990s

Currency	$bn	(%)
Cash		
USdollar	250	65
Deutschmark	60	40
Yen	370	10
HK dollar	7	25
Total	687	
Currency deposits at home and abroad		
industrial countries	1,282	
Central bank gold reserves	260	

Sources: *BIS QR* Sept. 2001: Table 1; Cohen 1998: 109–111; Hope and Wright 2001; Klapwijk *et al.* 2002: Table 1, Figure 47; Warner 1994a.

Note
Hongkong out of monetary base, others out of notes printed.

It is a source of national pride. The US Fed thinks that the use of the dollar as an international currency is a proof of faith in the US government. But more than anything else, it is a question of earning seignorage, estimated variously at 0.5–4 per cent out of GDP, depending on circumstances (Cohen 1998: 40–41, 54; Covill 1999).

> For notes, seignorage is the difference between their nominal value and the printing cost. For account money, it is the interest earned on the funds so created.

The downside is that the money created and the notes printed may one day return home without any counter performance, and this danger is present all the time. The Japanese think that the effort is not worth the trouble.

Pay up – in time

It is not sufficient that actual trading functions without friction. Deals cannot be completed without a reliable infrastructure. Its exact limits are judgemental. Phone and computer networks are the technical devices, possibly too sophisticated for laypeople to discuss from that angle. But the central role of modern electronic equipment in trading and administration, combined with its high cost, should be recognized. The cost has already left its footprint. Banks have been compelled to outsource important but computer-intensive functions to specialized competitors. Exchanges and their users have invested so heavily in proprietary trading systems that they have been unable to cooperate lest they merge with other exchanges, thereby delaying necessary rationalization. From among the vast array of infrastructure segments, three are chosen for discussion: clearing and settlement (c&s) systems, payment systems and messaging.

Cleared and settled

OTC derivatives trading is perceived as extremely risky by a casual observer, because the notional amounts are so large. As we know now, the actual risks from the actor's viewpoint are comparable with normal credit risks. It is much more likely that the ensuing settlement which follows the deals, and the payment flows impose larger risks. The problems are typically OTC because organized exchanges have their clearing houses which step in as a counterpart between buyers and sellers and assume the counterparty risk. Clearing houses have a certain ability to absorb losses and a ready mechanism to distribute them among exchange members.

The major OTC segments are bonds, derivatives and spot forex. Their risk profiles differ in so far that bonds and derivatives always involve the delivery of script against payment while spot forex may not involve a non-financial balance at all. Consequently, the exposure in spot forex tends to be of shorter duration than in the other two. This is countered by the size of forex transactions, absolutely and in relation to the actor's own capital and cash flow. Some \$400bn–\$500bn are transferred on an average day, single payments of \$200m–\$500m are commonplace, and aggregate exposures, up to three-to-four working days, at times exceed the capital of the bank involved. Such transfers are handled by large-value or wholesale systems, which are dominant internationally and, therefore, come under the scope of our topic (*BIS S* 1996: 11; Kodres 1996: 23).

The administration of a deal begins by verifying the identity of the buyer and seller; is followed by validating and matching the trade, that is, controlling that the two versions of the same trade coincide; followed by clearing, that is, calculating the exact mutual obligations (like accrued interest) of the counterparties and locking them in; and is finished by settlement, that is, the final delivery of the script against (versus) payment, preferably by book entry and simultaneously (DVP). There the payment system comes into the picture. If the securities are registered, the registrar (a central depositary or an authorized bank) will make the necessary entries. Originally, settlement and payment systems were separate, but organizations providing the one service have started offering the other as well, and the dividing line has become blurred. There is also a connection between the settlement technique and the necessary funds to make the system work.

As the description implies, the various steps are often done in batches and possibly at different locations. A fair amount of manual work may be involved. That sounds strange but is a fact of life even in the USA where recent surveys indicate that one-quarter of equity allocations at issuance are communicated verbally and one-quarter by fax or other paper-based methods. That becomes expensive because human labour is expensive and prone to errors which lead to settlement failures. In cross-border institutional trades, failure rates exceeding 20 per cent are reported. The batch process with manual input is also slow, which increases market risk. Automated, seamless, electronic transfer of information in real time is the obvious remedy with the settlement lag compressed to one or even zero days (T + 1, T + 0). The approach is coined as 'Straight Through Processing' (STP) and it is already reality in technically advanced firms and for many types of securities transactions. The introduction of file transfer and IP (information protocol) network technologies have eliminated manual intervention for an increasing number of trades through to settlement. The requirements are high: real-time DVP, dematerialization of securities, finality of payment, electronic links to foreign depositories and electronic investor information. The cost is high and will delay and prevent adoption in small markets. Even the USA hesitates to make an investment equal to one-half of the securities industry's annual pretax profit but which would also comprise all market actors of any significance. Custodians are pleased about any delay because STP might destroy their livelihood. (Brown 2001; Kutler 2000; Rutter 1999; Warms and Penney 2001)

The simplest situation in conceptual terms is when each trade is settled as soon as it is reported to the system. For this to happen, it is necessary that the seller has the script or can borrow it, the buyer has the money or corresponding credit, and the payment order is final, irrevocable. This is called 'Real-Time Gross Settlement' (RTGS), and it is very much recommended by central banks because it minimizes systemic risk (domino effect of a default). But RTGS has weaknesses. There must be ample funds available all of the time. When this is not the case, the central bank and a range of commercial banks must provide the credit unless settlement is allowed to grind to a halt, because recipient banks cannot honour their commitments until they get paid themselves. The number of payments is large, each of them necessitates a confirmation, and many transactions involve a chain of payments. Currently about one-half of the major industrialized countries have at least one RTGS system for their domestic use, and more countries are joining the pack (Bank of England 1996: 2, 9; Ito and Folkerts-Landau 1996: 131; Large 1996a: 26).

The large number of messages and the amount of funds needed have led to the netting of mutual interbank obligations before payment. Netting is either bilateral (pairwise) or multilateral (net–net). Multilateral netting leads to a clearing house type of arrangement, where each counterparty makes or receives only one payment per currency every day. Netting cannot be done in real time because offsetting obligations take time to accumulate. Usually it takes place at the end of a business day. How large the savings are varies from case to case. Balanced mutual obligations and the inclusion of all-important counterparts clearly give the largest savings. A 50 per cent cut in payments is possible in bilateral netting, while in multilateral netting the percentage is over 70 for twenty participants and up to 95 per cent beyond that (*BIS AR* 1993/1994: 176; Ito and Folkerts-Landau 1996: 134).

Netting thus produces great savings but has its own weaknesses. Since there is a time lag, securities and forex face market risk and the whole transaction bears settlement risk. This latter risk is disaggregated into credit, liquidity, systemic and temporal components (Bartko 1991). From the geographical angle, the temporal component is interesting, as it has come to mean the risk which arises from the different opening hours of various settlement and payment systems. The topic has particular relevance in cross-border transactions between time zones (Figure 3.26, p. 157). For example, the period when Tokyo, London and New York have the same calendar day is only ten hours (Anon. 1993: 18–19).

The temporal risk has materialized only once.

> The German private bank Bankhaus Herstatt was closed by the German authorities on 26 June 1974 because of insolvency. At closure, 3.30 pm local time, it had received payment in marks for dollar deals and sent a payment order to the USA for the dollar leg, to be carried out through the settlement and payment system Chips (see p. 155). Learning of the closure, Herstatt's US correspondent suspended the order. It was able to do this since Chips' settlement begins only at 4.30 pm EST (10.30 pm German time). This left $620m forex deals uncompleted. The ensuing disorder in Chips lasted for three days, during which normal activity declined by 40 per cent. The temporal component of settlement risk has thereafter been coined as 'Herstatt risk'. (*BIS AR* 1993/1994: 186; *BIS S* 1996: 6)

The episode has left a lasting impression on the minds of bankers and catalysed, among others, the extension of the Fedwire (p. 155) operating time by six hours. This has created a two-and-a-half-hour overlap with Japan and covers the whole of the European business day. Simultaneously, an anomaly has arisen in California, where the next settlement day now starts at 9.30 pm (Ito and Folkerts-Landau 1996: 132; Shirreff 1996: 72).

Cross-border netting, and particularly the multilateral variant, also suffers from the legal uncertainty of its agreements and practices. The uncertainty originates from national bankruptcy laws, which give different answers to concepts like the validity of netting when a counterparty goes bankrupt and the control of collateral which the members must put up. A legal opinion would be most helpful, but none is available since there are no precedents (Ito and Folkerts-Landau 1996: 136; Kodres 1996: 25).

Equally troublesome is that many, if not most, important actors are only lukewarm about cross-border multilateral netting. Large banks with high credit ratings dislike the clearing house, because it gives all deals the same rating and thereby erases their competitive advantage. Central banks are reluctant to link domestic payment systems, because they would end up as guarantors of the netting system's liquidity without any clear guidelines about how much responsibility each of them should shoulder. Where forex constitutes a large share of interbank payments, a multicurrency settlement mechanism could have a major impact on domestic settlement and money markets, their liquidity and inflationary pressure, for example. The problems would be accentuated where money markets are shallow. Money markets are an integral element of settlement because they can be sourced for short-term funds should the need arise. (*BIS S* 1996: 26; Ito and Folkerts-Landau 1996: 132; Kodres 1996: 24; Shirreff 1996: 67)

Most clearing and settlement (c&s) systems are national. The bulk of their operations is domestic but they also handle transactions which have the other counterpart abroad. Organizations which specialize in cross-border clearing and settlement are rare and only two have gained prominence: Euroclear and Cedel (current Clearstream) (Table 3.4). Both are located in Europe and were created with eurobonds. Originally, the trades were cleared in New York and payment was made against physical delivery. That was cumbersome and led to severe abuses (Dickenson 1999).

To help matters Morgan Guaranty, part of JP Morgan since 1959, established Euroclear in Brussels in 1968. Securities were kept in custody, in their countries of issuance and elsewhere, while clearing and settlement were conducted in Brussels as book entries. The idea was an immense success and led within two years to the establishment of a competing organization, Cedel. Two more years and Morgan Guaranty sold Euroclear to its users, to prevent customers establishing additional competitors.

Table 3.4 Selected settlement systems, 1999

Country	System	Security	Settlem. lag, min.	Particip. no.	Transactions mill.	$tr
France	RELIT	G, E, O	T + 0	339	25.5	5.5
Germany	Clearstream	G, E, O	T + 0	322	73.2	15.3
Japan	JGB, immat.	G	T + 3	377	1.0	54.2
Switzerland	SECOM	G, E, O	T + 3	359	11.7	2.6
UK	CREST	G, E, O	T + 1	22,949	43.2	15.3
USA	Fedwire	G	T	9,936	13.4	179.5
	DTC	E, O	T + 3	527	189.0	94.0
Multinational	Euroclear	E, O	T + 0	1,996	15.7	46.5
Memory item	Swift	G, E, O	n.a.	6,797	1,058.8	n.a.

Sources: *BIS Statistics on Payment Systems in the Group of Ten Countries*, March 2001: Tables 12, 14 and 15; private communication with Euroclear. Copyright © 2001 of Bank for International Settlements, Berne, Switzerland; used with permission.

Notes
The table does not necessarily list all settlement systems used in a country.
G = government, E = equity, O = other, n.a. = not applicable.

It remained Euroclear's operator and banker, however, which gave a healthy, stable cash flow and contributed to the bank's triple-A rating. The rating was most welcome, as Morgan Guaranty guaranteed all security loans made by Euroclear. The JP Morgan connection was also welcome, because the US broker community, which plays a key role in international finance, used Morgan credit extensions to increase settlement efficiency (Edwards 1994: 35; Kerr 1995).

As eurobonds gained acceptance and expanded their geographical coverage Euroclear followed suit and became the dominant cross-border settlement organization in the world, with 70 per cent of all primary issues in the euromarkets. Some 30 per cent of its clients are in Asia, and of them one-quarter are in Japan. Euroclear has representative offices in Tokyo, Singapore and Hongkong to deal with settlement problems during Asian daylight hours, which gives a five-hour window to get things fixed before Europe opens. A twenty-four-hour real-time settlement service is forthcoming, likely to pre-empt the looming Asiaclear backed by HSBC, which was intended to service that time zone alone (Irvine 1997: 136).

Cedel's development was more straightforward, since it was established as a joint venture by its users with a maximum stake of 5 per cent. The organization was located in Luxembourg, has a francophone flavour and a traditional customer base in Europe. To facilitate expansion in the USA, SEC granted it an exemption to clear and settle US securities, the first non-US organization ever, followed by Euroclear. It also got a banking licence in 1994, which cut owners' capital needs from 100 to 20 per cent. But it missed the early start by two years and remained the smaller of the two organizations. When Euroclear started developing real-time settlement, Cedel was compelled to abstain because many clients could not accommodate it. The relative sizes, which appeared fairly constant, even aroused speculation about Cedel's ability to survive; it seemed an unlikely vision because of the ensuing monopoly by Euroclear. Cedel was expected to benefit from JP Morgan's entry into the securities business as a principal, since this put Morgan into direct competition with its broker clients (Cowan 1996b; Morris 1996).

The two organizations were rather similar in their locational choice, scope, pricing and operational efficiency. Neither were located in a major finance centre, plagued by withholding taxes and restrictions in securities lending, but went to nearby jurisdictions willing to grant exemptions from standard rules. They both handled about 90,000 securities, domestic bonds accounted for 70 per cent of the trading value, the failure rate was about 3 per cent, they had operational links to national settlement systems all over the world, and a link ('bridge') connected the two organizations with several transfers during a twenty-four-hour period. The difference was that Euroclear became dominant in repo business and was, in general, associated with fixed income, while Cedel had an equity image. (*BIS QR* Nov. 1996: 24; Cowan 1996a; Davis 1990: 7; Kerr 1995; Wendlandt 2000)

All that is history. Deutscher Kassenverein, the c&s unit of the German exchange (DB) merged with Cedel and became Clearstream. This allowed DB to concentrate operations in Frankfurt where German equities, by law, must be settled. The united ownership of the exchange and its c&s unit is coined the 'silo' model and gives a lever over customers, in pricing for example. That contrasts with the horizontal philosophy where c&s units are user-owned, the Euroclear way. Euroclear has merged with five local settlement systems in France, the Netherlands, Belgium, Ireland and the UK. It has also assumed the operating and banking roles of JP Morgan through a Euroclear Bank in 2000. It has remained independent and would obviously like to be the Pan-European settlement organization. But in the fluid European scene, everything is possible. The most likely suitor is Euronext, made up of the Paris, Brussels, Amsterdam and Lisbon exchanges, with an 80 per cent owned clearing unit, Clearnet. Euronext already has a 3 per cent stake in Euroclear, a legacy of past times, and it also has, through its subsidiary, Liffe, a 17 per cent stake in London Clearing House (LCH) which clears many repo trades, the Swiss–British joint venture Virt-x, and London Stock Exchange equity trades. LSE equities are settled by Crest, which was overtaken by Euroclear in 2002. At the same time, Crest and the Swiss unit SegaInterSettle (SIS) have formed an alliance and claim to handle half of Europe's domestic transactions, although they have very little cross-border business. The Swiss already had cooperated with both Frankfurt (Eurex) and London (Virt-x), so there appears to be a snowball effect. It can also be seen as a countermove against Clearnet and LCH, the different product lines notwithstanding. All that is reasonably complicated, typical for a transitory phase. A thorough overhaul of the European c&s landscape is long overdue considering that Americans handle their business, twice the size of the European one, at half the cost. (Boland 2000; Dalla-Costa 2002; Luce 1999a; Marshall 2000; Skorecki 2002a; 2002b; Vogt and Symons 2001)

Cooperation is also practised elsewhere. There is a longstanding link between Chicago Mercantile Exchange (CME) and Singapore Exchange for clearing eurodollar and euroyen futures. Dealmakers can select either one of the clearing houses. Alternatively they can clear at home whereafter the clearing houses become counterparties to each other (Hills and Young 1998).

Domestic settlement and payment systems exist in some form in all developed countries and in emerging markets as well. Their relative efficiency is relevant to global investors and fund managers. A performance index can be derived by multiplying the percentage of failed trades, average trade size, cycle length and a key national interest rate. This information is available from custodians. Exchange-based and OTC products can be differentiated at need. But comparisons across systems are fraught with pitfalls.

Cash settlement is much simpler than one involving securities. The number of securities handled plays a role. Central control of the stock is crucial for a short settlement cycle. It can be achieved by immobilization, when the script exists in physical form but is held in a central depositary, or dematerialization, when ownership exists only as a computer entry. Both possibilities create resistance when introduced, particularly among retail investors who, however, seldom put their stock up for sale. In the time perspective, the index reflects a gradual shift from retail to institutional business, leading to larger trades, the upgrading of settlement systems with shortened settlement cycles and a lower share of failed trades as a result. But it also reflects occasional bursts in trading activity, during which the cycle lengthens and the fail rate increases, not to speak of the fluctuation of interest rates with its own, independent logic.

Payments made

Payment systems are closely related to settlement and the two are often used as synonyms. At closer look, they partially overlap, depending on the character of the deal. If the payment is made for physical goods there is no settlement in the financial sense of the word. If it is made for foreign currency, the two payments are either part of two separate batches to be settled by netting or they are dealt with by RTGS. In both cases the ideal is that the counterparts pay and are paid simultaneously, payment-versus-payment (PVP). If the payment is made for securities the money is handled by a conventional payment system while the probably immobilized or dematerialized securities will stay put at the depository and only change the owner. Again, the ideal is that both parts of the deal are implemented simultaneously, delivery-versus-payment (DVP). In view of all of this, the hierarchical order of settlement and payment is a matter of judgement. Because there is so much common ground, only complementary features are taken up. As in settlement, it is customary to differentiate between retail and wholesale systems, although some systems accept both types of business. The emphasis here is on wholesale systems (Table 3.5).

The systems are either netting, or RTGS, or a combination. Netting systems have less participants than RTGS because fewer participants means a higher credit rating and lower default risk. Non-members must use members as correspondents and act through them. Many systems are specialized to an extent. On the payments side, Target connects Euroland via its central banks into one single system and is indispensable for liquidity management. Fedwire is a government-owned system for securities and money market instruments also accessible for foreign banks, whereas Chips has an international focus with major New York banks as owners. One-half of all forex traffic goes through it and the rest are international loans and eurodollar placements (*BIS S* 1996: 4). The dominant system in the UK is Chaps which has a sterling part for domestic traffic and a euro part to connect it with Euroland via Target. SIC is an all-round system: retail, wholesale, domestic and international, with 80 per cent of traffic

Table 3.5 Selected interbank funds transfer systems, 1999

Country	System	Type	Participants direct	Transactions mill.	$tr
European Union	Target	RTGS	4,261	42.3	240.6
France	PNS	Net/RTGS	25	5.2	25.6
Germany	EAF	Net	68	12.1	41.6
Japan	BOJ-NET	RTGS	409	4.8	302.8
	Feycs	Net/RTGS	47	10.0	62.4
Switzerland	SIC	RTGS	291	141.7	28.8
UK	Chaps Sterling	RTGS	14	19.8	72.3
USA	Chips	Net	77	57.3	297.9
	Fedwire	RTGS	9,994	102.8	343.4
Multinational	CLS (note)	Net	39	7.5	75

Source: *BIS Statistics on Payment Systems in the Group of Ten Countries, March 2001*: Tables 10a–b; www.cls-bank.com. Copyright © 2001 of Bank for International Settlements, Berne, Switzerland; used with permission.

Notes
The systems are simplified. CLS Bank annualized by the eighth operational week in 2002, perhaps one-third to one-half of the final level.

originating from forex trades. Feycs in Japan is for forex trades and BOJ for the rest. The French and German systems are owned by banks and have both domestic and international traffic. The bulk of international traffic, particularly the largest and time-critical payments, however, goes through Target.

Normally market actors can freely select the system they want to use. For example, the European Banking Association launched its own netting system about the same time as the European Central Bank got Target on-stream. Financial intermediaries have several criteria when making the choice, such as the fees charged, the amount of funds tied in the system, the speed of the system, the latest time when payment orders can be given for next-day delivery, the latest time when they can be cancelled and the ability to follow the passage of the order through the system. Netting tends to lower transaction costs because less funds are tied than in RTGS but cannot compete in execution speed because netting takes place once or twice a day. But RTGS systems can also show differences in this respect. Fedway usually executes in ten seconds and, at most in minutes; some national European systems manage in twenty seconds but Target gives thirty minutes as the maximum time limit.

The time when a payment order cannot be cancelled any more and becomes irrevocable also marks the beginning of the credit risk. The risk continues until the payment has gained finality. Broadly speaking, that happens when the consignee has received it. We have to say 'broadly speaking', because here the national laws play in. Many countries in Europe and Latin America turn the clock back to 0.00 at insolvency and declare all transactions during that day null and void. In a payment system context, however, the law has been amended so that the actual local time applies. The time span between irrevocability and finality has been surprisingly long, days, and particularly so in intercontinental payments which cross many time zones (Figure 3.26). Most of the time was spent within inefficient domestic systems, bank routines included, but these have since been upgraded.

National systems normally handle the national currency and, at most, a few trading currencies, and net, if at all, bilaterally. This simplifies operations but also leads to a great number of bilateral connections and raises costs, and risk, in that way. It is comparatively simple technically to establish a hub where payment flows are netted multilaterally, but the legal and competitive aspects mentioned above have delayed proper implementation. Echo, Multinet and Group 20 were the early birds, differentiated by

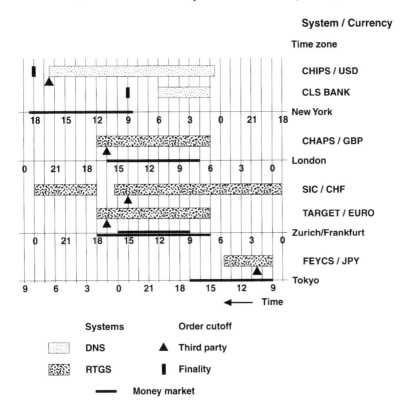

Figure 3.26 Operating hours of some major payment systems, December 1999.

Sources: *BIS AR* 1993/1994: 185; *Statistics on Payment Systems in the Group of Ten Countries* 1996: 129–131; private communication. Copyright © 1994 of the Bank for International Settlements, Basle; used with permission.

Note
Time scale runs from east to west following the sun.

the size and nationality of participants. Echo consisted of European banks, often of midsize only. Multinet was a Canadian group with a US inkling but was too small to carry on alone and subsequently merged with Echo. Group 20 was the largest of them, continued to grow and has become operational under the Continuous Linkage Settlement (CLS) Bank logo. It comprises more than seventy large banks with tier-1 capital exceeding $1bn and minimum credit rating BBB+, irrespective of geographical origin. Each participant has an account at CLSBank and uses it as a correspondent bank. All settlement currencies are swappable (fungible) and all major currencies can be used, with some minor ones in the pipeline, which will raise the percentage out of total worldwide payments traffic to 80 per cent. An absolute requirement is that their domestic payment systems have an overlapping time window with CLSBank. The bank was conceived in London and the holding company is still there but the operational unit has been located in New York and is regulated by the Fed. The location is a weakness in many eyes because of the US penchant of freezing the assets of politically recalcitrant countries. (Graham 1997; Oakley 2002; Shirreff 1996; 1998; Willoughby 1998)

Security is a key issue for all electronic payment systems. It is partly a question of authentication, the ability to prove that the sender and receiver really are who they say they are. This is achieved with the help of passwords, issued separately for each bilateral link. Since the passwords must be changed frequently, the number of participants remains limited. The other half of security is encryption, the coding of messages to make them unreadable for outsiders, and their subsequent decoding by the receiver. The fairly standard content of the messages greatly facilitates criminal decryption and imposes great demands on the encryption code. The US military had, for a long time, the top technology based on a 56-bit key. European central banks were given permission to use it for their own network but banks at large had to develop their own, less secure systems. After the development of a new standard Rijndael, based on a 128-bit key, the computing time to break the code has risen 47×10^{20}-fold necessitating the linkup of hundreds if not thousands of computers to do the job, clearly beyond the capacity of individual hackers. Still better, the new standard can be run on mainframes, desktops and smart cards alike. The Internet has started to use it. (Bilefsky 2000; Cooke 1995; Querée 1997; Sharpe 1998)

Parallel to formal payment systems, also informal ones do exist. They rely on trust. A broker buys currency in one country and the partner delivers another currency in another country. There is no formal documentation, maybe a slip of coded paper or just a phone call, and accounts may remain open for months or years. Amounts up to $1m are transferred. Judging from their names, *hawala* and *fei chien*, such systems thrive in Asia. Their origins are in exchange controls and administrative mess, and most transactions serve otherwise legitimate trade. The aggregate amounts can be substantial, the annual 'hawala' business being estimated in Pakistan as $1.5bn–$2bn or one-tenth of the country's banking system (Miller 1999).

Messages sent

The payment orders must be sent to banks, settlement organizations and consignees. The messages go through public and private IP networks but their content and form need to be administered for better efficiency and lower cost. The information must be accurate, complete and in a standardized form which is easy to handle. The basic case is that every organization has its own information system. Large international banks are a prime example. But even they must interact with other systems and, without standardization, complications will arise. The percentage of failed cross-border institutional trades (p. 149) gives an inkling of what can be expected. Proprietary systems are also comparatively expensive although this is partially compensated by higher security. The benefits of cooperation are sufficiently large, however, to make a worldwide organization, Swift (Society for Worldwide Interbank Financial Telecommunication) viable.

The start was made in Europe where international communication was intensive but where countries and their banks were small compared with internationally active American and Japanese ones. It made sense to cooperate. Swift became operational in 1977 with banks as the only members. Non-banks were allowed to join ten years later and fund managers in 1992. The emphasis is on messaging, whether of straight payments, securities, treasury operations or trade finance. Messaging is flanked by two netting services, the bilateral netting of forex, money market instruments and derivatives (Accord) and the multilateral netting of payments (Ecu). Importantly, messaging is for information only and needs a linkup with Accord, Ecu or some other settlement system to arrive at the transfer of funds between accounts. (Bank of England 1996: 2, 15; Large 1996b: 13; Laurie 1991: VI)

The organization has gradually been accepted in other Continents which do not have anything comparable to show (Figure 3.27). Large American banks prefer their internal networks and give only the restposts to Swift. Japanese are traditionalists, use paper and have only a few entry nodes to Swift. The character-based writing naturally contributes. As an interbank message system Swift has a very strong position. Its interfaces are electronic, it is inexpensive and it passes cost savings on to its members. The only serious threat is perceived to come from the Internet and then only when it can guarantee security.

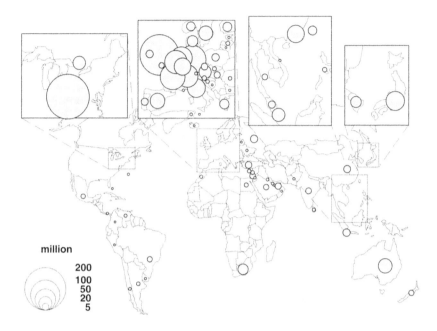

Figure 3.27 Swift, messages sent, 2000.

Source: *Annual Report* 2000: 46.

Conclusion

This chapter constitutes, together with Chapter 5, the core of this book. Here are the markets, there are the actors. The markets have been disaggregated into bank lending, debt, equities, derivatives and forex. Debt has received a comparatively detailed treatment while equities are largely postponed to the chapter about exchanges (Chapter 4). This chapter has also been a convenient place to comment upon the role of forex as a reserve and parallel currency. The core infrastructure elements of clearing and settlement, payment systems, and messaging have been discussed. There, time zones, perhaps the most fundamental geographical element of finance, come into focus. The emphasis has been on wholesale operations and their international aspects in particular.

Functionally, the securities markets, and bonds and equities in particular, have been divided into primary (issuing) and secondary (trading). In debt, the split into public and private has also been made. The actual market practice is often about the same whichever the taxonomic cell. This is particularly true in issuance and only when it is frequent does a differentiating feature, primary dealers of government debt, appear. The secondary markets differ in so far that bonds trade primarily OTC and equities at organized exchanges. Bonds are too heterogeneous to fit comfortably in the standardized exchange routines and, by staying OTC, they probably save in transaction cost. The dividing line is less clear in derivatives where OTC and exchanges co-exist in futures and options but not swaps which, again, are too heterogeneous for exchanges. The derivative instruments are based on deposits (interest rate), debt (interest rate), equities (indices) and forex.

Geographically, the markets have been divided into domestic and cross-border. The spatial aggregation varies depending on circumstances. Country, the country groups used in Chapter 2, or some intermediate form, have all been used. Euroland has usually been kept together, mostly for cartographic reasons, and its constituencies commented in the text. Luxembourg, however, has often been regarded as separate because of its 'offshore' character. Indeed, the geographical content of this chapter gives much if not most of the numerical base for evaluating the finance centres in Chapter 7.

4   Exchanges

Genesis

Clubs or public institutions

Chapter 3 painted the broad canvas and described OTC markets. Here
the focus is on formal markets organized into exchanges, the other end of
the spectrum. Their birth, when it is organic and not administered by
authorities, is rather stereotypical. A group of traders get into the habit of
coming together in a place and at a time to do business and exchange
information. The concentration in space and time makes it easier to find a
counterpart, and the familiar faces make it possible to separate
respectable from unscrupulous individuals. The place offers some shelter
against weather, like a buttonwood tree, and possibly also refreshments,
like a coffee house. The possibility of making money attracts all kinds of
unwanted elements, however, and at some point in time their presence
becomes sufficiently disturbing to prompt the creation of an organized
club able to select its members, and the transfer of activity into private
premises closed to outsiders.

These moves have a natural corollary, the creation of a rule set to
create an orderly and fair market. The set includes rules about the way
offers to sell and buy ('asks' and 'bids') are announced to the other
members, the proper way of accepting them, the way of consummating a
trade (delivery and payment), the way of safeguarding against defaults, by
other members and the trading public, and the way of penalizing misfits.
The rule set, applicable to members, continues to be the core of a formal
exchange, while the physical premises have lost much importance with the
coming of modern information technology. It is no longer necessary to
trade face-to-face on a trading floor to achieve the full benefits of a centralized market, maximum information, maximum liquidity, best price
and immediacy. The same effect can also be achieved by computer screens
linked into a more or less automated trading system. The location of the
screens is immaterial as long as there is one trading system rather than
several. If there are several, the harmful effects can still be minimized by

allowing arbitrage between the systems. This risk of fragmented trading does not only apply to locations, it also functions over time. Therefore, exchanges with a low trading volume restrict trading hours or accumulate trading, and with it liquidity, into an auction.

If enhanced liquidity, information, immediacy, price and security are arguments for a centralized market in the form of an organized exchange, the indispensable rule set also constrains activity. Liquidity means that trading is lively, but lively trading leaves little room for individual negotiation, which is the hallmark of the OTC market. To facilitate trading, exchanges standardize the instruments if at all practicable. Many instruments are standardized by nature, government bonds, for example, which were the dominant instrument of early exchanges. The default risk did not vary much between issues, which differed mostly by their yield and maturity. Company shares had more variable yields and credit risks but there were only a few types of share per company. When shares had low nominal values, they were aggregated into lots of suitable size. At commodity exchanges, the quality of merchandise also had to be standardized, making the trading instruments somewhat abstract. Therefore, when the age of derivatives arrived, commodity exchanges had the skill to create instruments which did not have a strict physical equivalent.

Standardization did not stop at the instruments but was extended to incoming orders (market, limit, stop loss, day, etc.). This aspect gained in importance with the differentiation of the client base. Wealthy individuals and financial intermediaries were followed by the small retail investor, to be in turn overtaken by institutional investors. Their relative importance varies from country to country and affects the organization of exchanges (Figure 4.1). An exchange seeing the small investor as its primary client base is organized to handle a large number of small orders in an inexpensive and transparent routine. The New York Stock Exchange (NYSE) offers an example of this strategy. Where institutional investors dominate,

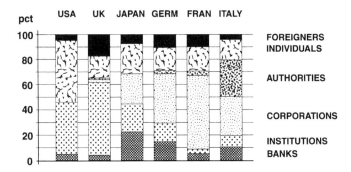

Figure 4.1 Equity ownership in some countries, early 1990s.
Source: OECD 1995: 17.

utmost transparency is not desirable, while the possibility of some negotiation is. The London Stock Exchange (LSE), after its reorganization in 1986, was scaled largely according to their needs. As both exchanges, nevertheless, service both types of customer, they must compromise. The need for compromise is all the more pressing, as exchanges exercise a substantial monopolistic power, and as their fair and smooth operation is considered to be in the public interest. This opens the gates to external regulation, which becomes expensive and repels large customers to the OTC market.

Members and revenues

Most major exchanges have come about organically, from the practical trading needs of individuals or, more recently, financial intermediaries. Legally, they tend to be associations whose members own the premises, intellectual property such as the contracts traded and computer software and, most importantly, have the necessary trading rights. The details vary tremendously. In the mid-1990s, the Tokyo Stock Exchange (TSE), although large by any other standard, had only 124 members. The rationale offered was the limited space available on the trading floor. A similar argument was encountered at the London International Financial Futures Exchange (Liffe). One seat was allocated to each floor trader and a tight rein had to be kept on their number to prevent congestion at the trading pits. Large American exchanges, by contrast, count their members in hundreds, if not thousands. The explanation is 'locals', a member category which is less usual elsewhere.

> Locals are individuals who trade for their own account and do not accept customer orders. With limited capital resources they must content themselves with small trades but compensate this by a multitude of trades of very short-term price movements. This gives trading continuity and a feeling of liquidity. For survival, 25 per cent of a local's trades must be winners, at most 15 per cent can be losers and 60 per cent can be scratches (breakevens). Locals resist screen trading because of the high upfront cost of the screens and the lower skill level, or simply different skills, needed.

Their importance is not in the volume of trading but the number of trades, perhaps one half of the total. It means in practice that most of the time there is a fresh quote available. Volume comes from financial intermediaries, i.e. banks, securities houses and large brokerages, and institutional investors where they are allowed to be members. Exchange management and the state can also be members. (Khan and Ireland 1993: 52–53; Lee 1998a; Massimb and Phelps 1994: 40)

Heterogeneous membership poses administrative problems for an exchange. Being a member of an association, a local tends to have the same voting power as a large intermediary, and as a group locals can, by force of their large numbers, outvote the latter. At NYSE, where membership is vested in individuals and through them in the firms for which they work, the largest brokerage house, Merrill Lynch, has only 2 per cent of votes, although it has about 20 per cent of the business. The headcount may also better reflect past than current business, a dilemma of rapidly developing exchanges like the CBOT, where agricultural members are in full control although generating only 20 per cent of trades. Broadly speaking, at US exchanges, locals and floor brokers have the majority of votes while elsewhere the political power is in the hands of the institutional market. (Blume *et al.* 1993: 48; Lee 1998a: 30; Morse 1992b; Osborn 1989: 45)

It is not so much the number of votes but the volume of business which the institutionals bring. The two big Swiss banks do more than half of all trades at their domestic exchange, SWX, or its London-based joint venture, Virt-x. The four largest securities houses used to handle over one-half of trading at TSE directly, and 70 per cent indirectly when affiliates were included. In Germany, banks as owners and users largely control exchanges. One chief executive of an LSE member firm is quoted as saying: 'It would only take us and four other major players to put our prices directly into Reuter and the Stock Exchange could not survive. The whole market would fragment' (Wolman 1988).

The fact, nevertheless, is that power is shifting from exchange members towards institutional investors. (Barber 2000; Dalla-Costa 2002; Gapper 1996a; Hayes and Hubbard 1990: 274, 277; Rodger 1994)

Another characteristic commonly found in associations is their reluctance to accept new members, particularly from new member pools, thereby possibly working against their own long-term interests. It is all the easier where the exchange is the only sensible place to deal or even has a legal monopoly.

Because membership gives access to physical and intellectual property and offers an income stream, it usually has a price. The price is related to the size of the exchange and the current state of the market, whether buoyant or depressed, i.e. the possibilities of making money. Membership at a good regional exchange such as the Philadelphia Stock Exchange, Shanghai Stock Exchange and Deutsche Börse (DB) locates within the $100,000–$150,000 range. LSE is graded according to the size of the firm but is amazingly inexpensive on entry, maximally £10,000 ($16,000), and thereafter £50,000 ($80,000) a year. At other world-class exchanges like NYSE, TSE and CME a seat can exceed $2m but slump close to $100,000 when times are difficult. Leasing is also possible, perhaps at 15 per cent of the purchase price. But no rule is without an exception. The Paris Bourse used to allocate rather than sell memberships and did not charge any entry fee either.

This world is fading away. Monopolies have been deregulated in many quarters. All the important exchanges in Europe and many in Asia Pacific have been transformed into corporate form (demutualized), and the process has also started in America. The new corporations have even been listed on these very exchanges or their affiliates. The reason is competition by electronic communication networks (ECNs), which the old membership structure cannot fight effectively. It is not suited for rapid decision making and has difficulty in raising the capital for building sophisticated electronic trading systems, which have become technically feasible and economically attractive. A corporation can issue shares and it is more creditworthy as a borrower than a motley group of exchange members. Demutualization has also been a way to promote rationalization, facilitating exchange mergers, for example. But, at the same time, exchanges have become vulnerable because now they can be acquired against the will of incumbent management (Butler 1999; Luce 1999a).

Irrespective of whether an exchange is an association or a corporation, it needs income. Historically, the main sources have been fees for transactions, company listings, clearing and settlement services; company news; price and quote data; and memberships (Lee 1998a: 51). Membership fees are not available at demutualized exchanges, nor company news at derivatives exchanges. Listing and settlement fees, obviously, are important competitive tools for attracting business. Some services are essential, others can be outsourced and automation has been instrumental in that. This raises the question of indispensable core services and the fringe, which is more exposed to competition.

Unfortunately for the exchanges, there seem to be few core services which cannot be also offered by other organizations. Opinions diverge about specifics. Issuance appears safe because it gives the quality stamp of the exchange (see p. 170). Trading is exposed to competition by ECNs but these normally rely on price data from exchanges. Information vendors such as Bloomberg and Reuters try to intermediate by purchasing digital data, reorganizing it and selling further. Delaying tactics are efficient. Data streams half a minute late are worthless for arbitrage or derivatives trading. Severing the link between trading and the sale of market information underlines the fact that the traditional exchange has lost its former monopolistic position. The distinction between it and OTC has become blurred. Settlement and clearing appear comparatively safe but this opinion overlooks the services offered by independent organizations such as Euroclear and their scale economies. It is also well to recall that LSE has shed its settlement and information services, which still accounted for two-thirds of the annual budget in 1992. (Cooke 1994: 26; Lee 1998a: 111; Waters 1993b)

One can generalize and claim that when an income stream is outsourced or lost to competitors, a corresponding expense item also disappears from the profit and loss account. There is an important expense item, however, for which this philosophy does not hold. It is the enforcement of statutory regulation and trading standards. Of course, surveillance can be used as a sales argument but the effect is difficult to measure. The service is needed first and foremost to protect unsophisticated retail customers while institutional investors and financial intermediaries are more capable of looking after themselves – more, but not fully capable. Collusion by traders, although widely suspected, can be impossible to prove without penetrating the actual ring itself, as happened in the Chicago derivative exchanges. Exposure by an academic study followed by phone bugging, as happened with some Nasdaq dealers, is also exceptional. The job is preferably done by painstakingly tracking a myriad of transactions to detect suspect price movements and trading patterns, particularly by insiders. At LSE a generic algorithm completed with fuzzy logic, able to discover clusters consisting of several accounts, is used for the task. From among 80,000 transactions a day, it alerts the exchange each month to some 860 suspects, of which 10 per cent turn out to be insider cases. (Hargreaves 1989; Moran 1996; Urry 1995; Waters 1996)

Products and organizations

The financial instruments listed and traded at exchanges are 'stocks', that is, shares (equities) and bonds on the one hand, and derivatives on the other. The derivatives are normally futures, options and indices, directly or indirectly based on shares, bonds and deposits. As their names imply, stock exchanges are the place for stocks while derivatives exchanges handle derivatives. Reality, however, is less clearcut. Many stock exchanges offer share indices and options, a natural accessory to equities themselves. But few have made a go of them. When the time of launching derivatives was there, from the mid-1970s to the mid-1980s, resistance, even contempt, was widespread:

> 'this was not the sort of activity we want in the City...', the founders of Liffe learned in 1980 when they tried to interest LSE in financial futures (Lapper 1996).

At NYSE, the CEO took the initiative about options but was likewise rejected. In Germany and Japan, financial futures were forbidden by law until 1985. The speculative element was too pronounced and the whole trading culture too alien to organizations which appeared to be doing quite well, thank you. Vested interests outside stock exchanges may have fared better. Currency (forex) trading was the realm of a handful of money-centre (large) banks and has remained so. (Abken 1991: 14; Blume *et al.* 1993: 234)

> When the CEO of CME suggested establishing a joint venture for currency futures the idea was regarded as 'too ridiculous to discuss' (Blume *et al.* 1993: 80).

It was a question of mentality, and the futures mentality and talent were in Chicago.

Existing derivatives exchanges, usually commodity-based, stepped into the gap, or new specialized exchanges were established. When stock exchanges finally moved, they encountered well-established contracts which could not be dislodged. Trading volume remained low, and finally the activity was discontinued or sold to competitors. This happened in London, where LSE's subsidiary, LTOM, was overtaken by Liffe in 1992, and in New York, where NYSE's options business was sold to CBOE in 1997. It has also gone in the opposite direction: stock exchanges acquiring derivatives exchanges or merging with them. That happened in Hongkong and Singapore in 2000, and would have happened in Sydney were it not for monopolistic worries. Deutsche Terminbörse (DTB) became a division of DB in 1997 and Euronext purchased Liffe in 2001. There has been a parallel geographical development and it is accelerating. For example, the six regional stock exchanges in Australia merged into Australian Stock Exchange in 1987; those in Frankfurt, Düsseldorf and Munich merged into Deutsche Börse in 1993; those in Zurich, Geneva and Basle merged into Swiss Exchange (SWX) in 1995; DTB merged with Soffex into Eurex in mid-1998; Nasdaq in the USA overtook both Amex (American Exchange) in New York and the Philadelphia Stock Exchange in the same year; and the Paris, Brussels and Amsterdam stock exchanges merged into Euronext, incorporated under Dutch law, in 2001, and this rapidly acquired the Lisbon Stock Exchange.

Although many, maybe most, stock exchanges list both shares and bonds, the great bulk of bonds, and government bonds in particular, is, in most countries, traded OTC or on ECNs, while *shares* remain at exchanges. Two explanations are routinely offered. The first claims that equities (like financial options and futures) have an important retail clientele, and that this is better served by a centralized and regulated trading forum than a multitude of free-wheeling traders. The second is based on the characteristics of equities compared to bonds: they are comparatively few and homogeneous, they have a variable rather than fixed interest, they offer the possibility of a large capital gain or loss and they are the vehicle for gaining control over wealth much larger than themselves. Therefore, the argument runs, they are far more difficult to rate correctly than bonds and should be traded in a transparent and strictly controlled environment. Both explanations have merit, although the retail clientele group is losing importance relative to wholesale customers.

The relative importance of listed shares and bonds at exchanges which carry them both naturally varies. In 2000, bond trading was very lively in Johannesburg, considerable in Scandinavia and noteworthy in London and Frankfurt, both in absolute figures and in comparison with equities. The relative attractiveness of equity and bond markets in general is important for such ratios, as is the free float of equity available and trading practices, such as the internal netting by brokers. It is difficult to generalize, except that OTC trading of equity is marginal, and that stock exchanges seem to be most valued as places for trading it. The practical conclusion here is that stock exchanges will be discussed as listing and trading fora for equity, and their bond operations will be largely over-looked.

From an exchange's angle, stocks are easy products in so far as their dimensions are given by the issuer. The exchange naturally has an opinion about the issuer itself, and it may advise on the nominal value of its script, but that is generally as far as it goes. This is the cash market. *Derivatives* are different. They are not given from the outside but must be created by the exchange itself to meet a practical need. We recall the need of institutional investors to track the performance of the equity market and the desire of all types of investor to hedge against uncertainty while making the most of forthcoming opportunities. The tracking unmistakingly points towards indices, whether for equities, debt, or some segment of them. The hedging equally points towards futures, which are binding commitments, and options, which provide an opportunity but are not binding. Options can be of futures, indices or the underlying stocks.

Experience shows that a national market needs three key products: one equity index contract and two interest rate contracts, one for three-month bills and one for ten-year bonds. One of the three is likely to gain a healthy volume, while the other two remain viable. Only where cash markets are very large can other bond maturities or several equity indices survive. A supplementary interest rate contract is positioned close enough to the flagship contract on the yield curve so that competitors, usually from abroad, cannot interfere. Where close substitutes, nevertheless, survive, it is because of arbitrage or investor preference for the home market (Jeanneau 1996: 42; Raybould 1994: 2–3).

Whether tracking or hedging, the need to use derivatives depends on the volatility of the underlying instruments, and they in turn on external economic and political developments beyond the influence of the exchange. What the exchange can do is to select the most heavily traded and volatile stocks as the underlying building blocks. It follows that the derivatives market and the cash market locate in the same time zone. Satellite markets in other time zones do exist, but their volumes cannot compare with the primary zone, save during exceptional market turbulence. A large trading volume implies good liquidity, and this becomes crucial when a derivative contract needs to be exercised. Usually this contract is a future or an option, seldom an index comprising tens and hundreds of companies. When the underlying instrument is a bond, its homogeneity and low probability of default are also relevant. Purely technical aspects play a role, such as the size of the contract, currency of denomination, other possible exercise currencies, expiry date, trading hours, minimum price change (tick), maximum daily fluctuation and so on. The trend is towards long-term and flexible, i.e. complicated variants. (*BIS AR* 1995/1996: 157; Jeanneau 1996: 40; Raybould 1994: 2–3)

It is difficult to launch a successful contract at the first try, and it is not at all unusual for exchanges to tune and relaunch existing contracts. The important thing is to be first in the market, because pioneer contracts have a far better chance of succeeding than imitations. Recalling that the golden era of new derivatives contracts was from the mid-1970s to the mid-1980s, and that the USA led the pack, it is not surprising that most of the volume at US exchanges is from contracts at least fifteen years old. The initial advantage also applies internationally. Well-known was Liffe's 70 per cent market share of the *bund* derivative, thanks to a two-year lead vis-à-vis DTB's competing contract. By contrast, DTB's *bobl* (five-year bond) derivative never had a direct competitor. The *bund* trading eventually returned home but only because Liffe did not gauge the competitive advantage of screen-based trading over open outcry early enough. The partial transfer of the Nikkei 225 index contract from Osaka to Singapore was another case, although this was triggered by the regulator rather than the exchange. As new launches are made all of the time, most of them necessarily misfire, failing to reach breakeven volume. Some claim that the outcome is visible within three months, although evidence from Liffe suggests that even a year's trading is still inconclusive. The exact volume varies considerably. In Europe a good contract trades 3,000–5,000 a day, while in the USA the figure is 20,000–30,000. The corresponding open interest would be 20,000 and 100,000, respectively. (Corkish *et al.* 1997: 15; Gordon-Walker 1996; Laulajainen 2001; Raybould 1994: 7, 15; *Tradeus* 1994: 13)

Listing hurdles

An important income source at the stock exchanges is the fees which companies pay for the privilege of getting their stock listed and traded on an exchange. Derivatives exchanges do not have this possibility as the contracts are their own property. By accepting a listing, the exchange sends a 'fit-and-proper' signal to the investing and trading community, an act similar to accepting a new member, although from another pool of applicants. It is also a similar balancing act. It is important to have new members and new listings, but they must live up to the standards of the exchange. Therefore, exchanges routinely announce minimum listing requirements. Those applied by NYSE are typical although demanding (Table 4.1).

There are several noteworthy aspects. First, non-US companies face more demanding criteria than US ones. Large companies are easier to follow and less likely to flounder, at least without warning. As foreigners are more difficult to follow and understand, it is prudent to have a safety

Table 4.1 Some listing requirements at NYSE and Nasdaq, early 2002

Criterion	NYSE non-US	US	Nasdaq standard 3
Round-lot holders	5,000	2,000	400
Public shares (free float)	2.5m	1.1m	1.1m
Market value of free float	$100m	$100m	$20m
Operat. cash flow, three years	$100m	$25m	n.a.
Pretax earnings, three years	$100m	$6.5m	n.a.
most recent two years	$25m	$2.5m	n.a.
Market makers	n.a.	n.a.	4

Sources: www.nyse.com; www.nasdaq.com.

Notes
Global free float. Last three years aggregate. n.a. = not applicable.

margin. Logically, eligible companies numbered in the mid-1990s about 2,300 abroad against 2,950 in the USA (Grasso 1995). The absolute figures have changed but not the relations. There is a corollary to the size criteria. US companies are likely to have the bulk of their shares traded in the USA, foreigners are not. Having identical criteria would mean that the liquidity of foreign shares at NYSE would be much less. Demanding criteria balance this weakness to an extent. Listed foreign firms must naturally follow GAAP or concile IAS to GAAP in footnotes.

The requirements for the number of shareholders and the number of publicly held shares are there to ensure a reasonable liquidity, and prevent a small group of owners from holding the market to ransom. If there is a block of closely held shares which never come to the market, they are consequently excluded. The market value excludes small companies, which would radically add to the administrative burden but contribute comparatively little to activity. Of the approximately 11,000 publicly held companies in the USA, about 8,000 were too small for the NYSE. Tangible assets (no goodwill) and pretax income exclude corporate shells and fakes. So does the requirement of operating history. The company pays a fee, related to the number of shares, for getting listed. It is quite expensive: $500,000 and above for a world-class company.

Nasdaq (National Securities Dealers' Automated Quotation System) is the most ready US alternative for companies which do not qualify for NYSE or do not want to list there. The unwillingness may have been connected with the difficulty of delisting, for which NYSE required two-thirds majority at a general meeting with less than 10 per cent opposing. This rule was changed in late 1997, however, to a majority of the board of directors and the audit committee. Nasdaq is a market rather than an exchange (application pending), but because it competes, even head-on, with NYSE, it is routinely used as a point of reference. The listing requirements are lower, even substantially lower, than at NYSE. This allows the listing of many more companies, 4,700 against about 2,900 at year-end 2000, which compensates for their smaller size to some extent. New companies with growth potential, high-techs for example, and foreigners have found Nasdaq an attractive and affordable market. It was thought that these new companies would move to NYSE when they matured but that has not always happened, and about 20 per cent of Nasdaq companies actually meet NYSE listing requirements. The relationship is somewhat similar to that between the Tokyo and Osaka Stock Exchanges. TSE is the dominant one, while OSE tries to attract Asian companies by asset and profit requirements which are 10 per cent of Tokyo's (Anon. 1997a; Corrigan 1997; Terazono 1996).

NYSE and Nasdaq provide the general framework used all over the world. Only the details differ. It is usual, for example, to have the main national stock exchange segmented (main board, official market, first section, small caps and so on) according to the size and trading volume of companies, and to give the free float as a percentage rather than the number of shares. A section may be designed for venture capital and has no profitability or trading record criteria. Nasdaq has been the copied but, excluding some excesses, the idea has been slow to gain momentum in conservative Europe. World-class exchanges do not necessarily outpace their smaller brethren in listing stringency. In Singapore, for example, the requirements are more demanding than at NYSE, and the scrutiny is particularly keen for companies from China, Taiwan and Korea. Hongkong also has a critical attitude towards foreign stocks (Shale 1993a: 44; Shirreff 1997b: 63–64).

Getting the company listed is half of the game. The other half is maintaining it. Share price is the over-riding criterion. If the price gets too low, the company is given some time to upgrade, and if that fails it is delisted. In the USA, a price of $1 or less for thirty subsequent days is sufficient and the grace period to fix matters is ninety days. There is also a fee for maintaining the listing, perhaps one half of the initial fee. In addition to that come costs associated with regulation and disclosure. French firms claim a 30 per cent increase in annual legal and auditing costs when listing in the USA, and about 40 per cent of companies actually listed there have faced at least one lawsuit by investors. When the company is listed at several exchanges, costs rapidly escalate. Listing in the fragmented Europe amount to $1m per year, a strong argument for having a Pan-European stock exchange. More relevant than the absolute cost is the cost related to trading, however. Trading reflects the interest in the company, probably raises the share price and bodes well for eventual issues. Then the picture gets more colour. Listing costs per 1,000 shares traded were, in the mid-1990s, $1–$6 at US exchanges, $6–$10 in Europe, and 'much more than that' in Tokyo where translation costs weigh heavily. (Baker and Waters 1995; Evans 1994; Labate 2000; Labate and van Duyn 2001; Minder 2001)

Trading techniques

Getting started

Transaction cost is an essential element in an exchange's ability to compete and survive. This and other competitive topics are taken up in the next subchapter, but because many are related to the way trading is done, familiarity with the main techniques will be helpful. There are fifty-odd automated trade execution systems alone when all the details are accounted for (Domowitz 1993). Fortunately the important features can be considered separately and allow simple splits. The introduction is best served with the use of two examples, one from LSE and the other from NYSE. Although both are stock exchanges, the principles apply equally well to derivatives exchanges. For simplicity, many details will be overlooked.

The *London Stock Exchange* offers five trading systems. Which system a stock is traded on depends on the stock's liquidity, the type of stock and the geographical location of its issuer. The most liquid domestic and some international equities with the largest volumes belong to Sets. The mid-cap UK equities and the most liquid new company (AIM) equities are traded on Seaq. Seats Plus is the platform for the least liquid domestic stock. Liquid equities from transforming and emerging countries are allocated to the IOB (International Order Book) and less liquid ones to SeaqI ('I' for 'international'). Sets and IOB use central order book and the rest market making, which is the older system. Trade execution on Sets and the IOB is electronic, whereas only price quoting and trade reporting is electronic for Seaq and SeaqI. Seats Plus uses a hybrid system.

The core of market making is a mainframe computer containing the volumes and prices of firm offers to sell ('asks') and buy ('bids'). The offers are keyed in through dealers' terminals connected with the mainframe and are displayed on the trading screens. The screens are also available for investors and brokers who follow the market through them. An investor can contact a dealer directly or go through a broker. Each listed security has at least two competing dealers, market makers, who continuously display a sell and buy price and are committed to deal in them in displayed minimum volumes. The commitment means that a market maker must have the money to buy and the script to sell, i.e. they must invest capital in the business. The reward comes from commission and the difference between ask and bid (spread). They can also borrow stock from the settlement system or some custodian and deal anonymously through inter-dealer brokers (IDBs), both privileges accessible only to market makers.

Anybody wishing to trade must phone a market maker. The only way they can refuse to deal the displayed volume at the displayed price is to ignore the phone. But there is scope for negotiation, to sell less cheaply or buy more dearly, or deal a larger volume than displayed. The chance to negotiate a better price grows with the size of the trade, and the really big ones are negotiated 'upstairs' (see also NYSE, below). Once the trade has been agreed on, the price and volume are keyed into the system and displayed in due course to the market at large.

The qualification 'due course' appears innocent but is in reality full of passion – and money. It is particularly the buy trades which a market maker makes for his or her own account which are sensitive. Other market makers know that s/he lacks the capital to keep the lot in his or her books for any length of time, and even if the capital exists, s/he will run the risk that the market will move against him or her. Therefore, the market maker is committed to dispose the position as soon as possible. If now the size of the trade and the price paid for it become widely known, our market maker is at the mercy of colleagues. Therefore the display of a large trade is delayed, the exact time depending on the size of the trade and being subject to change when necessary.

> When the Kuwait Investment Office wanted to sell 3 per cent (out of its 9.3 per cent holding) of British Petroleum stock the merchant bank Schroeders was asked to select from among three bidders the one who would handle the sale at the indicated price. Bids were to be submitted within an hour, and within twenty minutes Schroeders had its seven top equity executives on both sides of the Atlantic at a conference waiting for the bids. The going price at LSE was 744p, too high for rapid placement. Then the bids came in: 705, 710, 710.5, and within ninety minutes the decision was made. Goldman Sachs got 170 million shares worth $2bn for placement. It was 6.10 pm London time, one hour before NYSE would close ADR trading. Goldman Sachs kept quiet for two hours, to limit price risk in New York. At 8 pm London time it let its 500 salespeople loose. Customers were contacted at their homes and orders were taken like in book-building. The shares were placed that night, equivalent to one month's BP trading in London but only one day's oil company trading in New York. By 9.00 am New York time, the placement was made public. (Lee 1997)

Market making was a good technique in a time when trades were small and commissions fixed because it guarantees liquidity, albeit modest. But investors became larger and so did the trades which led to the squeezing of commissions and spreads. By the mid-1990s, commissions had become so low and spreads so narrow that the capital employed for making markets in the largest and most liquid stocks gave only 1.0–1.5 per cent in interest. Small companies, which were also comparatively illiquid, were not affected so much and their market making has staying power. Nasdaq, operating in an environment where institutional customers play a less dominant role than in London, is a good example. But the largest companies could be traded profitably only in a system where customers provided price ideas in the form of limit orders and traders did not commit too much capital. (Hennessy 2001: 196; www.londonstockexchange.com 2002)

The new trading system, Sets, which became operative in October 1997, is based on an electronic central limit order book (LSE 1996; 1997) (Figure 4.2). An order is keyed into the order book directly or through a broker. The identity of the order originator is not disclosed but otherwise the book is open to all subscribers of the LSE screen. The lowest ask and highest bid are matched in time sequence, executed and the trade is displayed immediately. Specifically, the execution price and volume are available to all participants, but not even the trading parties will learn their mutual identities, i.e. there is a central counterparty. This is the standard way of trading. But there is also a non-standard way, 'worked principal agreement', which is for very large orders. The difference is that the order need not be keyed in as received but can be broken into pieces for execution during the course of the day. The execution may well comprise opposing trades to conceal what is going on and involve the trader's own risk capital, exactly as in the market making system.

Sets reduced trading cost by 60 per cent and prevented a large-scale transfer of trading to Tradepoint, an ECN. In this respect its launch was

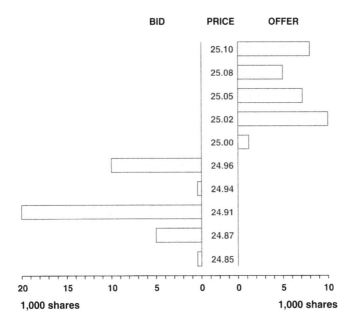

Figure 4.2 Hypothetical limit-order book.

Source: author.

absolutely necessary. It has also brought with it better liquidity, narrower spreads and increased market transparency. Transparency is welcome in reasonable doses and fundamental to the very existence of exchanges. But excessive transparency will harm very large orders. These are likely to move prices, and when the reason becomes known, competitive activity will intensify the movement. When all opaqueness is regulated away, large orders start avoiding the exchange, thereby downgrading its liquidity and the information it provides. Overall, Sets with its almost 200 equities has passed in four years the 65 per cent mark of trading value, still some way off the anticipated 75–85 per cent. (Gemmill 1998; Graham 1997a; 1997b; Minto 1997; www.londonstockexchange.com 2002)

The *New York Stock Exchange* follows a pattern rather different from the old LSE system. Trading is conducted on the trading floor, which is divided between groups of shares. Each group has its specific trading location, 'post' (in the UK, 'pit') where interested traders, the 'crowd', will meet. The crowd, basically, trades with itself and gets guidance from the prices displayed at the post. These used to be about completed trades but that has changed. The change is intimately connected with the role of the 'specialist', a dealer assigned to each equity to facilitate its trading, to buy or sell for his or her own account when nobody else does and thereby dampen price fluctuation. This proprietary trading amounts to 10–15 per cent of the total volume, depending on the way it is counted. The main perk for the service used to be access to all the orders which came to the post, while a trader got informed only about the orders which arrived from his or her own company. Today, that perk has been lost by making the specialist's display book available at a computer terminal. It is too early to say what that means to the profession but a gloomy view is that specialists will disappear or get degraded to market making at best. Such a development may, indeed, be possible judging from their limited capital base and the growing size of dealers and brokerages. (Abken 1991: 7; Hasbrouck *et al.* 1993; Metzger 1994: 34; NYSE 1996: 19, 2002a: 17; Sollmann 2001)

> Merrill Lynch, the largest brokerage, has an equity of about $9bn, or seven times the combined capital of all NYSE specialists. Worse than that, the specialist capital has not kept pace with the value of trading. Although consolidation has taken place among them, the power has shifted to 'upstairs' where block trades are arranged. Actor roles have also become mixed. Banks own specialists and brokerages own institutional funds, much trading is proprietary and not for customers. (Willoughby 1998)

Two-thirds of orders, generally smaller ones, are routed by the electronic delivery system SuperDot to the specialist's display book, and the rest by the BBSS order management system to floor broker terminals.

Orders below 2,100 shares are executed automatically while above that the execution takes place at the post, by internal crossing in the specialist's display book if a matching order is available and by open outcry otherwise. Large 'block' orders (at least 10,000 shares or $200,000 value) are taken to the post by a floor broker who may key them into the display book, but is more likely to use execution strategies intended to minimize market impact. This means that these orders are executed piecewise at a range of prices, and they may also have been negotiated in advance, 'upstairs', before taking them to the floor for execution. About 15 per cent of the order volume takes this route. But to the floor they must, because it is the place where all trading takes place. The traditional trading technique is open outcry and it is still used at the specialist's post. Ask and bid prices are shouted to the crowd in standardized, concise terms, perhaps followed by hand signals, and answered in kind. It is then up to the counterpart to indicate the volume he or she is willing to trade. (Carroll *et al.* 2000; Massimb and Phelps 1994: 40; Metzger 1994: 55; NYSE 1996: 8, 2002a: 23, 2002b; Sofianos and Werner 1997: 3–4)

Analysing the alternatives

This cursory discussion shows that there are two fundamentally different approaches and a number of conflicting alternatives. The most fundamental difference is whether the market is based on quotes originated by *dealers* or on orders handled in an *auction*. This gives the labels 'quote-driven' or 'dealer market' and 'order-driven' or 'auction market'. The old LSE was the former and NYSE is the latter, although modified by specialist action.

The strong side of a dealer market is that, except for times of extreme market turbulence ('fast market'), there is always somebody willing to trade at the displayed price. This, however, is really important for thinly traded securities only. More than that, the volume to which the price applies may be quite small, although at LSE it was larger than at Nasdaq, which has the same system (Huang and Stoll 1992: 52). Dealing is also expensive, because market making requires capital and this is compensated by wider spreads.

Auction takes place in batches or continuously. Batches are used at small exchanges where the order flow is too small for continuous active trading. It is also usual to match available orders when an exchange opens, easily one-fifth of a day's trading. The matching is actually a pure batch auction and is also conducted at NYSE, which is a continuous market during the rest of the day.

Both at LSE and NYSE, market participants, locals excepted, trade in double capacity, for customers and for their own account. This is not always allowed and when it is, care must be taken that dealers do not give priority to their own trades. LSE market makers can also deal at other exchanges and OTC in securities listed at LSE any time they want. At NYSE this is possible only during off-hours. The obvious rationale is to keep the market concentrated and thereby preserve maximum liquidity.

The possibility to negotiate a price at a dealer market does not imply that an auction market cannot upgrade the displayed historical price. Quite the contrary. At NYSE, for example, an average improvement of $2–$3 per 100 shares has been recorded for small trades (Blume *et al.* 1993: 222). The important point is rather that large orders benefit from negotiation ('upstairs') also at auction markets. Derivatives exchanges which need exact prices for the pricing of their own products do not like negotiated deals whether 'upstairs' or on the phone, nor do they like two-way quotes. But least of all do they like delays and blackouts in price disclosure.

The corollary of an 'upstairs' block trade is the matching of sell and buy orders outside the exchange. Internal matching ('crossing') by an intermediary is the simplest and most rapid alternative and therefore very common. It may also be the only alternative when customers want immediate and certain execution. Lower transaction cost is an additional bonus (Postelnicu 2002). The value of crosses by a large intermediary can exceed the trading at a large European exchange. Because conflicts of interest are obvious, crosses are usually regulated and sometimes completely banned.

Market transparency comprises the incoming order flow and the prices and volumes of executed trades. Its selective use is part of the market power which exchanges exercise when they try to attract customers and maximize income. In plain English, different participants are offered different information packages. Traditionally, a customer has a screen displaying prices of current trades but not bid–ask prices, which are available only to dealers and brokers, to whom he or she must go when wanting to trade. The order flow can be disclosed on automated systems but traders tend to shun complete transparency and the exchange probably complies with their wishes. Executed trades are less sensitive, or their publication is too essential to be avoided, and then price is disclosed more readily than volume. Information about the counterparts is the most sensitive part and usually withheld except possibly for the participants themselves (Khan and Ireland 1993: 14).

The US equity market has strict reporting requirements. The prices and volumes of all trades must be reported within ninety seconds to the Consolidated Tape Association (tape) and Consolidated Quotation Service, which are available to all US professionals. Programme trades must be displayed immediately, however.

A programme trade is a simultaneous, or almost, trade of at least fifteen stocks with a value of at least $15m.

This rule helped in pushing some 10 per cent of trading abroad, primarily to London (SeaqI, see below) but also Tokyo. The mechanics are that off-hour trades are reported to the exchange but not to the tape, so that the market at large misses them. Nasdaq International, the twenty-four-hour market, had a longer reporting period during the London trading hours to enable competition with SeaqI, but at the end of the European session, the ninety-second US rule came back into operation. (Abken 1991: 11; Cooke 1994: 27; MacIntyre 1991: 51; Metzger 1994: 22–24)

London was also varied in its reporting, although in another way. In the domestic section, a large trade had to be published within ninety minutes, while in the SeaqI there was no obligation to disclose anything. There was a transparent period after the deregulation in October 1986, but it led, among other things, to large losses for market makers and was abandoned. Exactly because of its relative secretiveness, London has been able to attract foreign equities. It is NYSE's main rival for overseas listings, and large trades have come not only from New York but also Paris, where the reporting period is much shorter. Paris does not care because it prefers to protect the retail investor. (Cohen 1994; Harverson 1992; Pagano and Roell 1990: 69; Waters 1992a)

The final and very visible difference between LSE and NYSE is that the former is basically screen-based, while the latter relies on open outcry. Since the trend is towards screen-based trading, it is taken as the basis of discussion.

It is generally acknowledged that efficiency is better in an electronic market, the only meaningful possibility when trading volumes are small. Most of the reasons are related to labour, a fixed cost item. A floor trader is more expensive than a screen trader, since floor trading skills are more scarce and more support personnel are needed. A screen trader can, by contrast, follow several screens in slowly-moving markets. The screen is easier to regulate and can easily add new instruments and users. There is evidence that its use gives narrower spread. It has no out-trades (non-matching trades) which is important, because even under normal conditions some 15 per cent of deals done by phone are subsequently disputed in some way. The percentage by open outcry cannot possibly be less. The physical limits of effective floor trading also matter. The largest pits at Liffe accommodated sixty-five people and were considered saturated, while Eurex had 350 people comfortably trading the same derivative contract at a time. It is true that a crowd in Chicago can reach 600 but the question is whether the crowd is not disintegrating into several subcrowds. The emergence of exclusive and strictly off-limits trading rings within the crowd in the late 1980s would suggest this. (Anon. 1997b; Campbell 1989a; Khan and Ireland 1993: 30, 56–61; Massimb and Phelps 1994: 46–48; Waters 1993a)

When trading volumes become large, opinions diverge. The partisans of open outcry emphasize the wealth of information which trading in a crowd offers. Who trades with whom? In how large volumes? Under heavy pressure? How much short trading? How does the crowd react? What are the latest rumours? All this is part of market intelligence and most of it is lost on the screen. Immediacy, the execution time, is also stressed and particularly so in futures where lightning speed is essential. It takes longer to key in orders than shout them. In fast-moving markets and with large volumes, that matters. But in the long term, developing technology has worked against human capacity and now offers liquidity comparable with open outcry. (Campbell and Hargreaves 1990; Iskander 1997; Lapper 1995a; Morse 1997a)

Making the choice

The first contest is between dealer and auction markets, intertwined with the role of screen trading. Among stock exchanges, auction is undoubtedly the preferred trading technique and only Nasdaq still adheres exclusively to market making. At derivatives exchanges, the techniques mix and the main reason appears to be the larger complexity of products. Options, in particular, require complicated multilateral reasoning and took a long time to standardize (and automate). But, ultimately, the scale also appears to have tilted in favour of auctions there.

The next question concerns the ranking of open outcry ('with floor') and screen trading. Screen is much cheaper than floor; ratios of 1:4 and 1:2 appear in the literature. It is easier to regulate against insider crime because a complete trading history is available. It is also easier to control traders at the screen than on the floor and although the collapse of Barings Bank cannot be traced back to floor trading as such, it nevertheless appears to have influenced the decision when the eventual switch to electronic trading was deliberated.

> A trader at the Singapore office of Barings Securities, a subsidiary of the bank, hid loss-making derivative trades in a special account between August 1992 and February 1995. To correct things he increased bets so that finally he became the market. All this was possible because he was simultaneously in charge of trading and the back office, a cardinal sin, and because his superiors did not understand the technical side of his work (Gapper and Denton 1996).
>
> This happened in distant Singapore but at Liffe in London, locals could make and lose as much money in a day as a bank. Folklore has it that one individual lost £10m ($16m) in three hours but, in the heat of the moment, continued trading although technically bankrupt. He duly got a six month jail sentence to cool off (Evans 2001).

But screen is vulnerable to front running because own and customer screens are next to each other. It will squeeze out locals and, with them, much liquidity, no matter how superficial. Screen is also susceptible to typing errors. (Clow 1998; Fisher 1997b; Luce 1999b; Maguire 1998)

> When making the IPO of Dentsu at TSE, a desk assistant at USB Warburg keyed in a sell order of 610,000 shares at ¥16, instead of sixteen shares at ¥610,000 ($4,700). In two minutes 65,000 shares, or almost one half of the IPO, had been sold. Attempts to reverse the trade may cost $50m–$100m (Cockerill 2002).

It is attractive to speculate that, because the screen is more competitive at low trading volumes, it would have penetrated small exchanges first. There is some evidence for this thesis. Soffex, the Swiss options exchange which opened in 1988, was the first fully electronic derivatives exchange in the world. Stockholm SE introduced electronic trading in 1989. But these two were not the general rule and probably the initial investment was too large for many a small exchange. Where open outcry and screen have existed in parallel, the screen was initially relegated to the smaller contracts and late hours when trading was slow. CME and Matif cooperated with Reuters around the Globex system, Liffe developed its APT video game, and CBOT a very similar Aurora (subsequently Project A). They all facilitated extended trading hours, which essentially means entry into other time zones. Their contribution to the total volume was modest, however, at 2–6 per cent. (*BIS QR* Feb. 1997: 29; Rogge 1997; Zimmermann 1998: 23)

Older derivatives exchanges have been more committed to open outcry than newer ones. The Chicago exchanges in particular have resisted the screen. The political clout of locals who see their livelihood threatened has been decisive. The power of CFTC to grant and refuse authorization for new exchanges should not be forgotten either. The resistance was similar at Liffe but its location in the midst of competitive exchanges made it more vulnerable. Also its largest contract was based on the German *bund*. When Germans (and Swiss) introduced the cost-efficient Xetra system, trading moved to Frankfurt. Liffe's very existence was threatened and locals' resistance crumbled in the melée. Screen trading has also made inroads in Chicago, less at CME and more at CBOT where the modified Xetra is used for trading the ten-year treasury note futures contract, the exchange's second largest, parallel with the floor. Screen has increased its share to over 50 per cent. Also at Matif in Paris, screen trading was delayed by the locals and it was the plight of Liffe which triggered off the change in 1998. At DTB locals did not have much influence and the best way to get the dispersed German exchanges to cooperate was to give them a level playing field unconnected with geography – and that meant screen. (Bowe 2002; Iskander

1997; Khan and Ireland 1993: 31; Laulajainen 2001; Luce 1997: 13; Shirreff 1998b)

Among the large stock exchanges, only NYSE has open outcry and even there the electronic order routing system SuperDot has taken some activity away from the floor. LSE was the first major exchange to close its floor and go over to screen trading in 1986. It first relied on the phone and then turned to automated matching by Sets in 1997. TSE followed suit in 1999. Only 6 per cent of the volume was traded on the floor, which proved too expensive to run and was closed (Tett 1998).

Overcoming distance

The contest between open outcry and screen is still something of a sideshow for formal exchanges. Much more alarming is the fact that deregulation has allowed trading and membership from a distance. The start was made by Nasdaq in the USA. It was established in 1971 to thwart SEC's attempt to regulate OTC and, within a decade, had become a serious competitor for NYSE. Soffex was first in Europe but it, like Nasdaq, was a national organization. Cross-border trading came later, with Nasdaq in London in the 1980s and with the EU's Investment Services Directive on the Continent in 1996, which allowed remote membership. Stockholm SE was the trail blazer and NatWest Securities started trading from London under Swedish rules and regulations. Others followed suit; Eurex has also opened access points in the USA (Figure 4.3). Remote member-

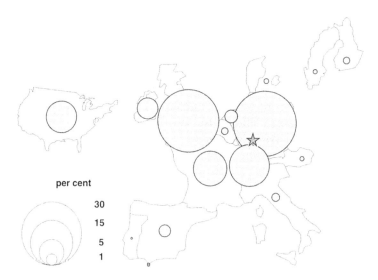

per cent

30
15
5
1

Figure 4.3 Eurex trading value by country, 2000.

Source: www.eurexchange.com, Monthly statistics, Derivatives market, December 2000: Table 1.3.

ship means that large intermediaries can concentrate activity in a single trading room and cut costs. Local offices are needed only for corporate finance, advisory business and research on domestic companies. Companies, in their turn, can avoid multiple listings within a Continent. (Cohen 1995b; Covill 1996: 60; Luce and Boland 1999)

In fact, what really distinguishes screen trading at exchanges from OTC, including ECNs, is regulation. It is much more strict at exchanges. Otherwise, screen eliminates the distinction between investors and exchange members as soon as both are given access to the same information flow. ECNs are normally pure matching (crossing) systems with hit rates between 5 and 35 per cent, and depend on the cash market's price information. Their strength is low cost and total anonymity which exchange order books seldom offer because broker–customer relationships are known. The American regulator has also allowed ECNs to become regulated exchanges if they so wish. Some of the largest ones, Archipelago, Instinet and Island, have applied. The ruling was a punishment for Nasdaq for certain market abuses. Overall, ECNs have taken market share from exchanges and Nasdaq in particular: 30 per cent of the trading volume of Nasdaq-listed shares and 5 per cent of NYSE-listed ones is at ECNs. Such figures apply in the USA but not Europe. Although the electronic order book at European exchanges may be too transparent, it is inexpensive and deprives ECNs of profitability. Their challenge may apply more to the bilateral OTC market than exchanges and, in the long run, ECNs may replace OTC altogether. Of course, exchanges have been forced to adapt, by extending delivery months and developing more flexible OTC-type products, for example. The use of collateral for swaps is increasing and somebody has to manage it. Exchange clearing houses have this expertise and sell it to OTC. (Baker 2000; Carroll *et al.* 2000; Cooke 1994: 26–27; Currie 2001; Davey 1995; Morse 1992a; 1995c; Ross *et al.* 1996)

The discussion of electronic trading systems, cross-border trading and remote membership easily creates the impression that distance has lost most of its significance. It has not. Time zones are here to stay, people need rest at night, and double or triple trading teams and settlement crews become expensive. But within time zones, does it really matter? There is sound evidence that it does. Investors in general prefer assets which are close to them and which they understand. Academic wisdom about the need to diversify portfolios by looking for asset pools which correlate negatively with existing portfolio has limited validity in practice. Geographical proximity, common language, cultural and colonial ties, and similar industrial structure matter more. People simply prefer new markets which correlate positively with existing ones. It is not only a question of cross-border investment. The same principle also applies nationally (Figure 4.4). That is the investor angle. Traders do not fare any better. Those located abroad underperform their domestic peers whether

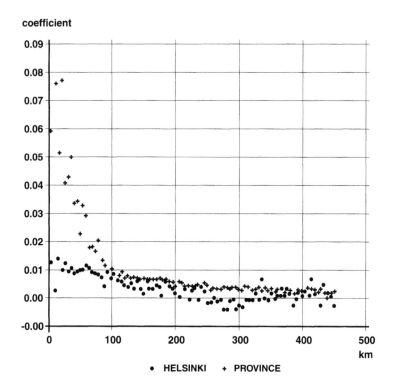

Figure 4.4 Distance discourages investment, Helsinki Stock Exchange, 1 January 1997.

Source: Grinblatt, Mark and Keloharju, Matti, 'How distance, language, and culture influence stockholdings and trades', Figure 1. *The Journal of Finance* 2001, 56 (3): 1053–1073. Copyright © 2001 of *The Journal of Finance*, used with permission.

Notes
Household shareholders. Institutional shareholder curves show more variation.

measured per day, week or quarter. They trade less, which makes the underperformance more difficult to discover but it is there, nevertheless. There is nothing mystical about the observation. The ability to gather, screen and evaluate information declines with increasing distance, physical and cultural, and leads to underperformance. Put another way, a circle's area increases in second power when its radius in increased, and so does the volume of available information. (Grinblatt and Keloharju 2001; Hau 2001a; 2001b; Sarkissian and Schill 2001)

Performance criteria

Many exchanges live on their tradition, they are the dominant national institutions, and companies and investors have always come to them and received service in their own language in a familiar and reassuring style. Remaining regulations in many countries still give national exchanges a strong, monopolistic position. This cosy situation is changing, however. Deregulation is the song of the day, most barriers to international capital flows have been removed, and there are tentative attempts to streamline tax regimes. Tradition alone does not suffice any more. An exchange must offer real benefits to its users. These benefits come under two broad headings: liquidity and cost. The cost of being listed was discussed above (pp. 171–172). Here, it is about the transaction cost.

Liquidity and the rest

Liquidity, up to now, has been used in a fairly loose fashion, the possibility to buy or sell without affecting the price. It is measured by the difference between ask and bid prices, the so-called 'spread', most relevant for small trades. Liquidity in this narrow sense must be completed by three other dimensions: depth, immediacy and resilience. Depth indicates the way the spread widens when the order becomes larger. Immediacy tells how soon a price can be found at which it is possible to trade. Resiliency is the extent to which the transaction price departs and returns to equilibrium price. In conclusion, in a perfectly liquid market, it is possible to buy and sell an infinite volume without delay at the same price. One often meets in literature the qualification that a trade will be made at 'the best price'. It is important to note that best price is not necessarily the visible quote but rather a balance of immediacy, speed of execution, minimal market impact and anonymity. (Lee 1998a: 50–51; Nickson 2000: 42)

At first sight, the use of spread as a measure of liquidity appears strange. If one has decided to purchase something, why worry about selling it? The answer is twofold. Many market participants, and dealers in particular, make a living by selling what they have just bought (a 'round trip'). To make a profit, a dealer must wait until the market has risen so much that it exceeds the spread plus trading cost. A narrow spread makes this happen sooner. Participants who hold the script will also find a narrow spread useful when they estimate the calculatory profit of their purchase ('mark it to market') at the end of the accounting period. So, the reasoning also applies to them. At dealer markets, the quotations can be taken from trading screens and, at continuous auction markets, from the order flow, specifically to limit orders (with firm price). It is only in call auction, used during opening sessions and at small exchanges, that the spread does not exist.

The use of spread as an indicator of market depth has some pitfalls. If it is abnormally wide, one can suspect insider trading or some other kind of market manipulation. Nasdaq came under SEC's scrutiny in 1994 when an academic study concluded that spreads in most shares were twice as wide as necessary. One authority claims that, wherever excessive spreads exist, at most 40 per cent can be accounted for by insider trading. But a wide spread can also be a function of market transparency. Where the identity of market participants is disclosed or can be guessed, spreads are wider than otherwise (Pagano and Roell 1990: 112; Waters 1996).

Spreads are product-specific and true liquidity tends to be concentrated into comparatively few stocks (Figure 4.5). A marketwide average may, therefore, be badly misleading. As an illustration, LSE's SeaqI had, in the late 1980s, 1 per cent spreads for blue chips and 10 per cent for very thinly traded equity. To alert investors to the risk, stock exchanges routinely segment their shares into heavily and thinly traded script. Therefore, it is appropriate to include only the largest and most frequently traded stocks in an international comparison. One possible set is LSE 1.44 per cent, NYSE 0.32 per cent and Paris Bourse 0.30 per cent; and a later set is LSE 0.6 per cent and Continental exchanges 0.15–0.2 per cent, i.e. the relations are constant. But there is still a pitfall. The negotiating element made the old London market much deeper in reality than on screen. There is also a circular element. Simply moving a share from a thinly traded segment to a heavily traded one can narrow its spread. When the German Exchanges launched an index for seventy mid-size companies (70 MDAX), their spreads were on average halved. (Brady 1989: 123–124, 128–129, 131; Cohen 1995a; DTB AR 1995: 23; Graham 1997b: 17)

At dealer markets additional variance arises because dealers often quote different spreads. In such a case, the analyst might replace spread by touch, which compares the best outstanding quotes ('over-dealers') on either side of the market.

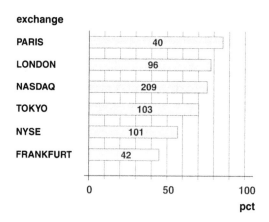

Figure 4.5 Share of equity trading value of the top 5 per cent of companies, 2000.

Source: www.fibv.com, Table I.7.1.

Note
The number of companies constituting the 5 per cent is indicated.

The size of the trade naturally affects the spread. Whether it is narrow for small trades and wide for large ones, or the other way round, is a contested issue. There is no doubt that average trade sizes differ between exchanges, for example £5,800 in Paris against more than £200,000 in London in the early 1990s. Trading intensity plays a role. International companies at LSE (SeaqI) saw their spreads roughly doubling between 1990–1994, when European trading moved wholesale back to the Continent. The widening, when a share's home market is closed, is well known (Figure 4.6). This makes off-hour trading risky. Events may cause market makers to disappear, and when the home market opens next day prices may be far away from the closing price. (Cooke 1996: 25; Lee 1993: 45; MacIntyre 1992: 23–25; Pagano and Roell 1990: 77)

A similar functional relation exists between a derivatives contract and its underlying instrument ('basis risk'). When Chicago is open, the t-bond cash market has one-tick spread, and when it closes the spread widens fivefold. It is important to note this particular relation. The futures market is the reference point and the cash market follows it. That happens when the futures contract is more liquid than the corresponding cash market. And it is more liquid because the trading cost is lower. The German *bund* is another example. (Anon. 1991a: 35; Corrigan and Harverson 1992; Osborn 1989: 43)

Poor depth imposes a market cost. When execution moves the price, sales revenue is less or purchase outlay more than at the starting point. The old Frankfurt market was exceptionally shallow for its size. One large order could push the price up by 5 per cent. This, indeed, is the theoretically correct way of measurement and is applied by NYSE, for example. The

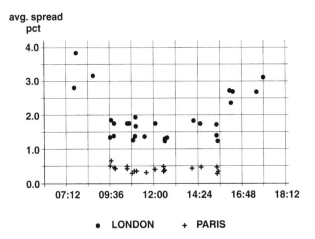

Figure 4.6 The spread of French equities quoted in London and Paris, 3–13 July 1989.

Source: Pagano, Marco and Roell, Ailsa, 'Trading systems in European stock exchanges: current performance and policy options', Figure 5; *Economic Policy* 1990, 10: 65–115. Copyright © 1990 of the *Economic Policy*; used with permission.

exact indicator is the price change between trade clusters of at least 3,000 shares. The average change was 91 per cent of time at most $1/8 when the minimum change (tick) was $1/16 (before decimalization). At derivatives exchanges open interest, that is, the number of contracts which have not been cancelled by opposite contracts at the end of the day, can also be used. The indicator reflects traders' willingness to leave themselves exposed overnight. It is more usual to measure market depth by the ask–bid spread, however. (Khan and Ireland 1993: 6, 33; NYSE 1996: 20)

Poor immediacy also exposes the investor to market risk. When the order is waiting for execution the market has time to move, and it may move against the investor. Of course, the opposite move will be to his or her benefit, but this speculative element is overlooked in the reasoning. It is possible to give estimates about the time needed to execute a market order at particular exchanges for various financial instruments in specific market conditions. It is also possible to make historical calculations about the variation of these instruments and with their help put a price tag on immediacy. No empirical figures are available, but it is obvious that such calculations do exist.

Immediacy and market depth are partially contradictory to each other. Immediate execution must accept the prevailing market depth with ensuing spread, whereas splitting and postponing the deal may help matters. Investors following passive strategies, or balancing their port-folios, can make use of this possibility (Cooke 1994: 28).

As can be expected, liquidity has direct competitive effects. The excellent liquidity and depth of NYSE and TSE is reflected in the sparseness of American and Japanese listings, respectively, on other stock exchanges, whereas the relative illiquidity of European exchanges discourages US and Japanese investors from operating there (Bromhead 1990).

Transaction costs

Trading costs include commissions and fees and taxes. In addition to these come market impact and settlement costs. Such divisions are some-what academic, however. In practice, the dividing line between commis-sion and spread, for example, need not be sharp, and particularly not when intermediaries act in a dual capacity.

Both commissions and taxes have been drifting downwards for a long time. The process started in May 1975 at NYSE, which decreed against fixed commissions by its members. This increased competition on LSE, which followed suit in October 1986. Then Tokyo among the central time zone centres started feeling the heat and, in turn, phased out fixed com-missions, although only for OTC transactions exceeding ¥1bn. Complete liberalization followed later. In each case, the average commission came down by about one-half, it went up for small deals but radically down for large ones. Locals were adversely affected because they have a large number of small transactions, while institutional investors are often charged no commission in anticipation of other paid business. Trading volumes naturally went up, about doubling in the immediate aftermath (Figure 4.7). (Hayes and Hubbard 1990: 109; Lapper 1997a; MacIntyre 1992: 19; Pagano and Roell 1990: 67–68; Waters 1991)

Cyclical components may be imposed on such trends. Commission rates in Chicago, for example, are lowered during a bull market and raised back during a bear market. The same has applied to derivatives margins which are a kind of transaction cost. CME raised the initial margin from 5 to 15 per cent in late 1987 to counter accusations of rampant speculation and market destabilization. Half-a-year later, the initial margin for hedge users was lowered back to below 5 per cent (Evans 1988: 109; Hargreaves 1988; Lindsey and Schaede 1992: 50).

Derivatives trading is conducted at credit. When a trader enters a contract (not option) s/he pays an initial margin. If the market goes against the contract the clearing house collects variation margin to prevent the trader from abandoning the contract. The trader probably has a margin account at a broker. When this account falls below a specified minimum, so-called 'maintenance margin', the broker makes a margin call. Such calls can become a serious drain of liquidity in extreme conditions. In the 1987 stock market crash, margin calls and settlements jumped from $1bn to $4bn in certain key derivatives markets. (*BIS AR* 1993/1994: 188–189; Kuprianov 1993a: 192–193)

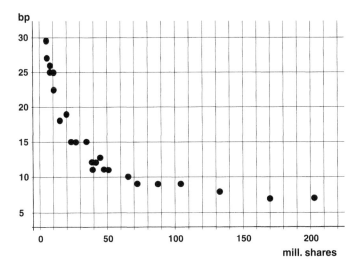

Figure 4.7 NYSE trading volume as a function of commissions.

Source: Swiss Re, *sigma* No. 7/2001: Figure 17. Copyright © 2002 of Swiss Reinsurance Company, Zürich; used with permission.

Taxes show similar competitive features. They tend to favour foreign investors and securities and discriminate against small investors and domestic shares, which are considered captive, midcaps in particular. At the Paris Bourse, foreigners did not pay stamp duty on the main market, where they accounted for one-third of investors and half of trading (Jack 1996a). But all domestics are not captive and this complicates matters. The doubling of the Swedish turnover tax on shares to 2 per cent in July 1986 raised transaction costs three to fivefold compared to London or New York and resulted in 85 per cent of the free float of blue chips being traded abroad. When the Swiss stamp tax on proprietary trading was abolished in April 1994, trading rapidly moved from OTC to the exchange floor and back home from London (Taylor 1988; Zurich Stock Exchange 1995: 4). Dealers are offered privileges. Market makers, or recognized intermediaries of Sets at LSE, are exempt from the 0.5 per cent stamp duty for customer (principal) trades. To catalyse rationalization, the government promised to abolish the stamp duty on all share dealings once settlement was automated. The automation is there but the duty remains. Also, members at London derivatives exchanges are exempt for principal trades (Corrigan 1992; Graham 1996; Waters 1991).

Equities tend to be more heavily taxed than bonds almost everywhere. The result is reduced liquidity. The reasons may be ideological; bonds are often issued by public bodies, while equities belong to the capitalistic establishment. But it is equally plausible that bonds are given preferential treatment because they are a prime investment vehicle of pension funds and insurance companies, which are frequent traders. Derivatives are usually lightly taxed because they do not give ownership. In Switzerland, their exempt status was motivated by the lack of derivatives legislation. One could not tax something that did not exist (Anon. 1991b: 26).

This variety makes comparisons between exchanges difficult. It is always possible to rank them, but the preceding lines have shown the limits of such efforts (Figure 4.8). Still, some details are conspicuous. The US commissions are low by any standard and the Canadians compare favourably. This is connected with the consolidation of the brokerage industry, in sharp contrast to Europe, and the enforcement of anti-trust legislation (Harrington 1996). These facts are contrasted by the large market impact, understandable in the relatively shallow Canadian market but strange at NYSE. In Asia Pacific protective barriers are largely intact and the costs are thereafter. Turnover taxes have become rare at major exchanges and are therefore not displayed.

An executed deal needs to be cleared and settled, that is, the seller's and buyer's versions of the transaction are compared, conciliated if different, payment is made, the security delivered and possibly registered, depending on the system. This sounds very simple, and simple it is when the deal is made in an automated system and the partners can deliver and pay immediately. Only too often this is, however, not the case. The part-

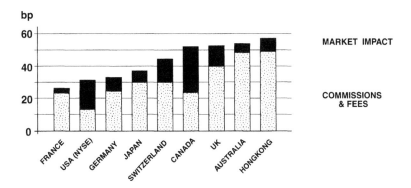

Figure 4.8 Exchange-based equity trading costs in some major countries, 1997.
Source: Willoughby 1998 (original Elkins Mc. Sharp Co.): 118.

ners may be short of script because of shortselling, or because some earlier deals have misfired. Stock lending becomes expensive and is not permitted everywhere. When trading is not automated, phone discussions can be misheard and deals keyed erroneously into the settlement system. Trading can explode to heights never seen before and clog the system. These are not merely academic possibilities; there is plenty of historical evidence available.

At NYSE, 25–40 per cent of all brokers' deliveries of stocks to banks (registrars) were rejected in 1968 because trade recording was inadequate. This happened at a time when settlement was manual, and the experience triggered off the development of automated order routing and settlement. Electronic transfers between NYSE brokers became possible the following year and three-quarters of the workload disappeared. By the end of 1975, the service had also been extended to other parties (Blume *et al.* 1993: 117, 124–125). But the problems were in no way solved because deregulation raised trading volumes. When the next upsurge came, in October 1987, over 40 per cent of all international equity trades failed because of settlement gremlins. Failure did not necessarily mean that an intended trade had to be unwound but, rather, that it was delayed or needed arbitrage. The figure also comprised only international trades, which may have been 10–15 per cent out of the total. After the backlog of unsettled trades had subsided, the system was upgraded to a level three-and-a-half times the highest historical daily peak. The current daily fail rate under normal conditions is less than 0.2 per cent. London has faced similar difficulties, with around 15 per cent of all deals made by phone are subsequently disputed in some way. (*The Exchange* Jan. 1996: 7; NYSE 2002: 25; Shale 1987: 58; Waters 1993a)

The practical importance of an efficient settlement system is considerable when markets move fast, say, 10 per cent before trades settle

(Figure 3.16). This is the market risk ('forward replacement cost'), and it can only be reduced by shortening the settlement cycle. The counterparty risk, of non-delivery and non-payment, is assumed by the exchange's clearing house when one exists. This is a major argument for using an exchange rather than OTC in the first place.

A short settlement cycle is possible only when the stock is immobilized or dematerialized. Both possibilities are equal for the settlement cycle and both create resistance. Tax avoiders prefer bearer stock, which is in physical form and seldom registered. But tax avoidance alone cannot explain the adherence of the Continental countries to bearer shares. There is also a cultural factor involved, a reluctance to give outsiders an insight into one's financial sphere. It is not a purely Continental idiosyncrasy either. National Securities Clearing Corporation (NSCC) in the USA processes 'only' 90 per cent of equity trades on NYSE, Amex and Nasdaq with book entries at the Depositary Trust Company, which leaves 5–10 per cent for paper-based systems. Crest in the UK offers the same options although without a central registrar, a concession to the major banks (Gapper 1996b; Jack *et al.* 1993; MacIntyre 1991: 52). Retail investors seem to have emotional motives for having a paper certificate. Their settlement is about twice as expensive as for paperless script, but that is rather immaterial because the stock is seldom put up for sale.

Paperless settlement (and trading) is the dominant mode, in many less important markets also. It is carried either continuously or in batches. In a typical batch system a day's trades are taken to settlement in the evening ('rolling settlement') and the process is ready on the third business day at the latest (Table 3.4). Continuous settlement with one-day or same-day service is available, for example, at NSCC in the USA and at Euroclear Bank which is the international settlement system in Belgium, France and Switzerland. This is on a level with Germany, where settlement takes twenty-four hours, if started early in the day, and in no case more than forty-eight hours. Italy is also well advanced. Its central depositary, Monte Titoli, handles 85 per cent of the float, and only 2.5–3 per cent of trades fail to settle in time, a far cry from the old days when it could take up to 6 months to get a trade fully processed. (Paris Bourse 1996: 24–25; Shale 1987: 58; Sington 1990: 291; Waller 1993)

It is virtually impossible to consolidate the exchange performance criteria into an overall index. Different user groups also have varying preferences. Retail investors generally appreciate safety and round-the-clock availability. Cost is not the prime consideration, because they are infrequent customers. They are probably aware of general price trends, but their time perspective is weeks and years rather than minutes and days. Institutional investors look for price, liquidity, anonymity and settlement. Being well informed about price movements, they generally feel that liquidity is more important than transparency, although they may be unaware of its true cost (Cohen 1994: Nickson 2000: 42).

Major exchanges

Understanding the figures

The roles played by organized exchanges at home vary greatly. They can be the linchpin of equity investment, as is the case in the Anglo-American financial culture. They can be the playground for a handful of powerful actors, as is often the case in Continental Europe. Or they can be places for wild speculation and insider trading, which plague many emerging markets. Do keep in mind, then, that the same troubles have once characterized today's established exchanges.

Most exchanges have a primarily domestic role. Where the domestic economy is large and financial markets sophisticated, exchanges are also large, and the other way round. How their size should be measured best is open to discussion. The number of listed companies is one possibility, that of listed issues (several issues by company) another. Investment funds may also be listed, because unit funds are technically companies. As company size varies, the number of outstanding shares is a possibility, usually weighted by price, which amounts to market capitalization. Capitalization divided by GDP, an intensity measure, gives an indication of the exchange's importance to the national economy. A weakness of market capitalization is that the free float of many listed companies may be restricted to, say, 25 per cent of total equity, and that market prices apply only for marginal stakes. Then trading volume (number of shares) or trading value can be used as a substitute indicator. It is attractive to compare trading value with market capitalization to get an indicator for velocity (or turnover).

Although domestic economy usually dictates an exchange's size, many have some international exposure. A few have risen to international and even global prominence because of the country's capital market (which attracts borrowers) or the size and soundness of its economy (which attracts investors). In the first case, the exchange can show numerous foreign listings with attached trading, and in the second case, lively trading by foreigners. A substantial share of foreign exchange members and a widespread distribution of its terminals can be expected. This calls for measuring the extent and force of an exchange's influence and making comparisons.

Putting these simple ideas into reliable numerical shape can be amazingly difficult, although great strides have been made by the Federation of Stock Exchanges in streamlining available statistics. For example, a clear distinction is now made between equity and bonds, and between domestic and foreign equity. Investment funds are excluded from market capitalization. Similar effort is underway with derivatives exchanges. But many question marks remain (*Market Statistics* 1995).

Probably the most difficult one originates from the two parallel trade reporting systems, Trading System View (TSV) and Regulated Environment View (REV). The former includes all transactions passed through a central trading system or executed on the floor. The latter includes all transactions executed by members whether at home or abroad. Gross discrepancies occasionally emerge when data compiled by competing exchanges, stock and derivative, are compared. Usually, but not always, an exchange exclusively follows one or the other reporting system (Figure 4.9).

> Seaq International claimed in the mid-1990s a 52 per cent share in French equity transactions. Paris Bourse commissioned a special study on the topic which arrived at 8 per cent. The Swiss claimed that trades in their securities were counted twice or even three times at LSE. The Bank of England has raised doubts about the way Matif in Paris records its euro notional futures contract which, reportedly, took 25–40 per cent of the market from the *bund* future at Eurex in 1999/2000. The probable explanation is the downsizing of contracts. (Bank of England 2000: 36–37; *Euromoney*, Sept. 1996: 130; Jack 1997; Jeanneau 2000)

The aggregation of regional and subsidiary exchanges has a corresponding effect. Germans have consistently displayed nationwide figures

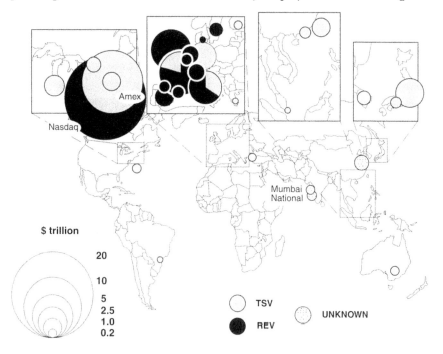

Figure 4.9 Reporting system at some stock exchanges, 2000.

Source: www.fibv.com: Table I.4.B.

because all the exchanges are parts of the same legal entity, Deutsche Börse. They do not disguise, however, that about 85 per cent of all trading takes place in Frankfurt. The Swiss followed similar practice, with two-thirds of trading done in Zurich, before going all-electronic when the question became irrelevant. Euronext, the recent merger of the Paris, Brussels, Amsterdam and Lisbon exchanges, also prefers aggregate figures although does not conceal the location-specific ones.

When a country has several exchanges it is usual that the largest companies are listed at all of them and that each exchange includes them in full in its market capitalization. Considerable double-counting arises. The solution, imperfect but used nevertheless, is to look only at the largest exchange where most of trading takes place. The USA is an exception here because the largest exchanges – NYSE, Nasdaq and Amex – do not list each other's companies.

Trading is generally assumed to be homogeneous; all trades are equally important. That is a moot point. Some transactions are for customers, while others are between dealers. The former are undoubtedly 'real' business, while the latter may be just a case of balancing the books. Still, they easily exceed 20 per cent of all trades, and reporting systems generally cannot distinguish between the two. The problem is particularly acute in a dealer market like Nasdaq, or the old LSE, where the investor always has a dealer as counterpart. The market looks liquid but may deceive institutional investors, who use liquidity as a yardstick when allocating funds. When damages are required they are routinely related to the trading volume. The different structures come dramatically to light when companies are transferred from Nasdaq to NYSE with a 50 per cent median drop in trading volume. By contrast, when the transfers were from the small Amex to NYSE, there were 12–18 per cent median increases. (Atkins and Dyl 1997; Gould and Kleidon 1994; Littmann 1991; NYSE 2002: 17; Smith and Sofianos 1997)

It is generally assumed that trading statistics refer to listed securities only. It happens occasionally, however, that unlisted domestic securities, stock lending and repos are included in trading statistics.

Some exchanges count every transaction twice (sell and buy), while most do it only once. When deals go through exchange members, the difference is immaterial because all trades are reported in full and can be halved when necessary. But when outsiders, who may have no reporting obligation towards the exchange, trade in their own capacity, ambiguities appear. They are compounded when floor and screen are used in parallel, because the two do not necessarily follow the same reporting rules. Computerization, naturally, helps because all deals are registered automatically.

Derivatives exchanges differ from stock exchanges. The concept of market capitalization is irrelevant and can be replaced by the aggregate notional value of underlying contracts. Open interest is another indicator but preferably used in the context of exchange liquidity rather than its size. The number of contracts traded is a frequently used volume indicator but suffers from the varying contract size: contracts with short maturities tend to be larger than those with long maturities. The reason is risk. It increases with the length of maturity, and the way to control risk is to use smaller contracts. The total of notional values traded might then appear preferable, but this is not necessarily the case, because short contracts are renewed more frequently than long ones and distort measurement in that way. Contract prices might be the theoretically optimal alternative but it is cumbersome because futures and options are priced differently and the statistics may not be available (Jeanneau 1995; 2000; 2001).

It all boils down to the number of contracts (volume). From this information exceptionally small contracts and contracts of individual shares are excluded. This particularly affects the Chicago Board of Options Exchange (CBOE), Amex and Korean Stock Exchange. The solution does not give full comparability but is a step to that direction (*BIS QR* 2002, March: 37; *Contract Specifications* 1996: 1).

Market capitalizations, trading volumes and values are subject to change: trends, cycles and random effect. Their force and timing varies from exchange to exchange. Emerging markets, in particular, are subject to pronounced shifts. Therefore, cross-section observations can only give general indications. On the other hand, changing definitions and compilation principles make time series data notoriously inconsistent (Anon. 2001; Jeanneau 2000; Pagano and Roell 1990: 111).

The discussion will be in three parts. The first one looks at stock exchanges, the second at derivatives exchanges and the third at their competition in geographical space.

Stock exchanges

Stock exchanges are places for listing and trading equities and bonds, and occasionally their indices and options. Equities usually dominate and here the focus is also on them. Three aspects are taken up: market capitalization, trading value and turnover or velocity.

Market capitalization is given for the largest national exchange only, the USA and India excepted, to avoid double counting (Figure 4.10). In the USA, the largest exchanges – NYSE, Nasdaq and Amex – do not list each other's equity, with SEC's consent. In India they do, but because the competition between the Mumbai and the National Exchange is so keen and double counting so obvious, both are displayed. All figures are for domestic equity and the reporting principles have no bearing. The size of free float, instead, may have. Its small size in many Continental and Asian exchanges is well known but whether that inflates or downsizes market capitalization is, in many cases, subject to conjecture.

The size of NYSE is overwhelming, comfortably exceeding all of Europe. Aggregated, the North American exchanges exceed the rest of

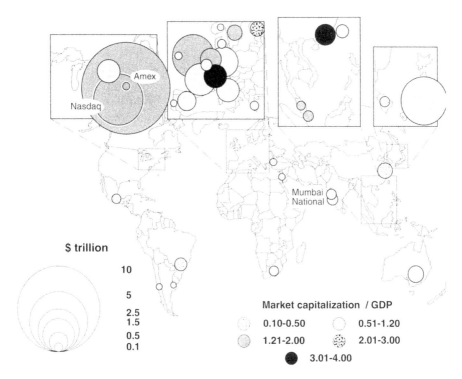

Figure 4.10 Market capitalization of domestic equity, December 2000.

Source: www.fibv.com: Table I.3.B.

Note
Shadings for the US and Indian exchanges are identical.

the world. The outcome is affected, although not decisively, by the long bull market, already broken, which was particularly strong in the USA. The demise of the Japanese stock market is well known and its modest size does not surprise. London's first rank in Europe is also expected, but Paris's relative size to Frankfurt is not. Recalling that, five years earlier, Paris Bourse ranked a clear third in Europe behind London and Frankfurt (or DB), that nothing of substance has been reported in the interval, and that it now exceeds or threatens to exceed them, it appears strange. The most probable explanation is a change in how the statistics were compiled. Hongkong and Helsinki are larger than one might expect. Helsinki is inflated by Nokia. Hongkong is more difficult to explain, but local fronts of Chinese companies contribute (de Prati 1998: 117). The inclusion of the exceptionally numerous warrants in market capitalization is another possibility. But it can also reflect a shortage of other investment opportunities. Switzerland is also large but there the established transnationals offer an explanation. The following year the Swiss blue chips were transferred from SWX to a London-registered joint venture, Virt-x, but that has not changed the statistical compilation.

Related to the GDP, Switzerland, Hongkong and Helsinki rank first for the said reasons. Thereafter come countries with the Anglo-American financial culture. In Continental Europe, state ownership still exists, notwithstanding extensive privatizations, and there is a dearth of institutional investors. Emerging markets tilt towards non-listed companies and limit foreign ownership, which would increase demand and raise prices.

Trading values do not overthrow the world order already established by market capitalizations, but well the rankings within Continental blocks (Figure 4.11). The change of ranks by NYSE and Nasdaq, in particular, is noteworthy. Two reasons can be given. Nasdaq is the primary platform for technology stocks and they were the main force behind the bull market. Nasdaq is also a dealer market and 40–50 per cent of trading can be attributed to that characteristic. When inter-dealer trading is subtracted, Nasdaq descends to the same size class as NYSE. Interesting is the emergence of Bermuda as a stock exchange location, probably the first time

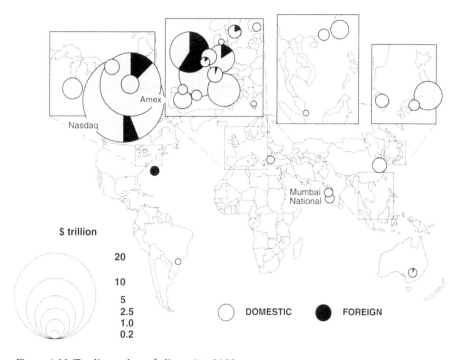

Figure 4.11 Trading value of all equity, 2000.

Source: www.fibv.com: Table I.4.B.

Note
Legibility prevents the display of the foreign share at smaller exchanges.

when a genuine offshore centre has attracted worthwhile trading. The comparatively low values in Germany and Japan can be attributed to the extensive cross-ownership of their companies; 40 per cent and 50–70 per cent are frequently quoted. In Italy, the fiscal privileges formerly enjoyed by large private corporations, and the still extensive state ownership have (had) a similar effect. The very idea that a stock exchange is a place for long-term risk capital rather than speculation has taken time to be accepted. The internal netting of equity orders by banks, some 70 per cent, was unusual in its extent. (Dudley 1997: 82; Hayes and Hubbard 1990: 172; Lucia 2002: 261, 269; Lindsey and Schaede 1992: 49; Sington 1990: 281–282; Szegö and Szegö 1992: 304)

A few words about regional exchanges is appropriate. The US regional exchanges are too small to be displayed, but they have survived thanks to the federally supported Intermarket Trading System which distributes, no matter how imperfectly, order and price information between exchanges (Hasbrouck *et al.* 1993: 27, 31; Metzger 1994: 27; NYSE 1996: 29). The most active users are NYSE members who benefit from lower trading fees and the impossibility of taking a block trade to the non-existent floor, where it might be split by limit orders with execution priority. The Indian twins overshadow a multitude of regional exchanges, in Calcutta and Delhi, for example. Osaka has appeared alongside Tokyo and there are also exchanges in Barcelona and Bilbao. But they are all much smaller than the dominant exchange which testifies to the agglomerating effect of maximum liquidity.

The bulk of trading consists almost everywhere of domestic equities. LSE is the only major organization which claims over one-half of trading value from foreign stock.

> The share is about the same as in the late 1980s (SeaqI). When Continental trading systems were upgraded, the attached tax regimes eased, and trading hours extended on NYSE, foreign trading, and small trades in particular, started returning home where the best prices were available. The migration is not visible in published trading statistics but the widening spread is. When it comes to country-specific figures, LSE in the early 1990s claimed the following shares out of the domestic values: NYSE-listed equities 6 per cent, German 12 per cent, Japanese 18 per cent, French, Swiss, Italian 40 per cent, and Dutch nearly 60 per cent. (Anon. 1993: 34; Blume *et al.* 1993: 228; Cohen 1995b; Dawkins 1996; Jack 1997; Pagano and Roell 1990: 73; Waters 1992b)

NYSE, Nasdaq, DB and Stockholm claim foreign shares of 4–20 per cent. Bermuda is 100 per cent foreign but is quite small. The question is whether these trades are conducted at the recording exchange, i.e. whether it uses the REV system. REV is in use at LSE, Nasdaq and

Stockholm. Nasdaq lists hundreds of foreign shares and ADRs but has also many trading terminals abroad (Figure 4.18). Since it is a locationless exchange/market the alternative reporting system, TSV, is hardly suitable. Its subsidiaries in London and Tokyo are parenthetical in this context. In view of all this, it is difficult to disqualify Nasdaq's 4 per cent share. Stockholm is the natural locus for non-domestic listing of the largest Scandinavian companies. But their numbers are small for a 20 per cent trading share and Stockholm's pioneering role in distance trading should not be forgotten either. LSE has half as many foreign listings as NYSE and Nasdaq together, but a 30 per cent higher trading value. That is too much to originate from London alone. How much is traded elsewhere, then, is anybody's guess but genuine London trades may be less than one-half of the total. Only NYSE, Nasdaq, Bermuda and DB appear, on this account, to keep their foreign shares fully intact.

Trading value related to market capitalization gives *trading velocity* or turnover, a seemingly ideal overall measure of liquidity. The perception is too favourable. Foreign equities cannot be used because their market capitalization cannot be allocated between exchanges. Domestic equities are what is left (Figure 4.12). But their meaningfulness can also be questioned if they are traded widely on foreign exchanges. This is the case with many Latin equities whose trading may be more lively on NYSE than at home.

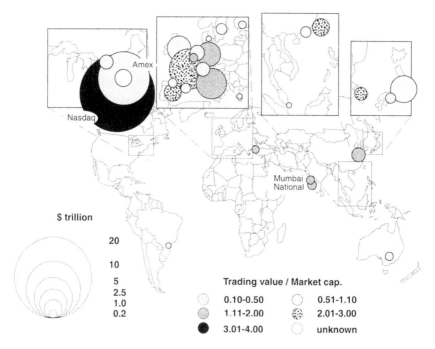

Figure 4.12 Trading velocity of domestic equity, 2000.

Source: www.fibv.com: Table I.6.

Helsinki, dominated by Nokia, is a similar case. Thereafter and overlooking Nasdaq's inflated trading value, the general message is unexpected. Velocity and the implied liquidity is higher on exchanges which seldom figure in financial headlines.

Equities have become the dominant class of securities on most stock exchanges. It has not always been so and, in the beginning, government bonds and bills constituted the bulk of traded script. That can still be the case in emerging markets, Shanghai for example. Debt has since then declined in relative importance but not disappeared completely. There are institutional investors who can, by law or their own bylaws, invest only in listed securities, and prevoyant retail investors may share the same predilection. Listing on a recognized and regulated exchange simply gives the paper a quality stamp. Listings are quite extensive and they accumulate in Europe (Figure 4.13). The reason is eurobonds ('foreign') which are usually listed in Luxembourg and London. Their combined total of foreign bonds, $3.6tr, tallies quite well with the approximate size of the eurobond market. After eurobonds have been subtracted, European activity assumes normal

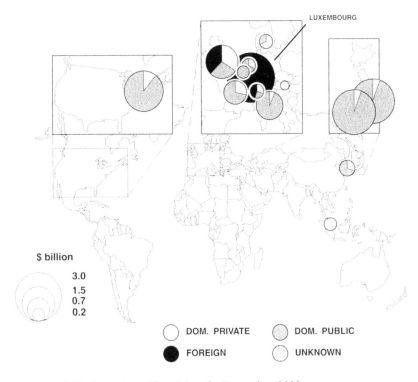

Figure 4.13 Market value of listed bonds, December 2000.

Source: www.fibv.com: Table II.3.B.

Note
Deutsche Börse in 1999.

proportions. There are more private listings than in the USA, where issuers are normally rated. Public listings tend to dominate everywhere, however, because their total stock is so large. Large market value is by no means followed by intensive trading; often it is not. The quality stamp is enough.

Derivatives exchanges

Derivatives exchanges trade futures and options. Futures are for deposits, bills, bonds (interest rate), equity indices, currencies (exchange rate), commodities and commodity indices. Most options are for the exchange's own futures, although options on individual equities may also be available. All of these contracts, except commodity contracts, are here called 'financials'. A derivatives contract normally depends on the real-time price information of a cash exchange. Without the cash exchange's cooperation, the contract cannot survive. A fifteen-second delay in the data stream can be fatal (Lucas 1998). The relative complexity and high price of options compared to futures have made them the mainstay of exchanges irrespective of much smaller numbers and trading values (Figure 3.18). On European exchanges, option contracts can even exceed futures because of the demand by retail investors. Swaps have too many idiosyncrasies to be easily moulded into tradable contracts and, consequently, stay OTC. Commodity contracts reveal the exchange's original business or are booty from merged exchanges which found the going too rough alone. Many, perhaps most, derivatives contracts are traded on derivatives exchanges. But some, and equity-related contracts in particular, are also traded on stock exchanges. What follows will include all contracts, irrespective of the type of exchange they are traded on.

A country seems able to support only one derivatives exchange (Figure 4.14). Where several have survived, the USA and Japan, exchanges have specialized or have the main business elsewhere than with the derivatives.

> The twin Chicago exchanges, Chicago Board of Trade (CBOT) with its partly-owned offshoot Chicago Board Options Exchange (CBOE), the largest in the world, and Chicago Mercantile Exchange (CME) are an anomaly in the derivatives landscape. CBOT is the older of the two, being founded by the Irish ethnic group for agricultural commodities, while CME was put up by the Jewish community to trade livestock products. CME rose to prominence through exchange rate (currency) and index rate futures in the 1970s and the more conservative CBOT was compelled to follow. This historical background has been instrumental for their desire to stay independent and the size of their respective businesses has provided the means to make it happen, much to the chagrin of their largest members, who are the same, and provide 80 per cent of the capital for the separate clearing houses.

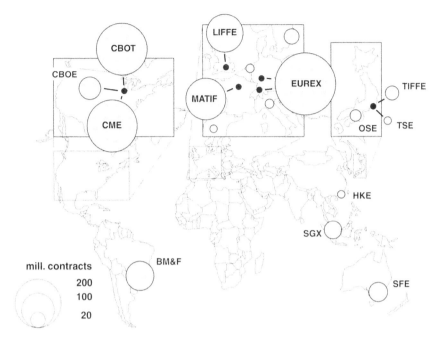

Figure 4.14 Trading volume at major derivatives exchanges, 2000.

Sources: Websites; private communication.

Note
Futures and options of individual equities excluded.

In Spain, the derivatives exchange MEFF was even created with two locations, one in Madrid for index futures and equity options and one in Barcelona for interest rates and currency contracts, a concession to strong regional interests. Scale economies, for members and customers, have normally been large enough to enforce mergers where several exchanges initially existed. Paris Bourse overtook Matif and Monep, the options exchange, and recently Liffe. The German and Swiss exchanges put their derivatives subsidiaries into a joint venture, Eurex. This also applies jointly to stock and derivatives exchanges as elaborated previously (p. 168).

Derivatives are perceived as an American invention, for hedging the annual income of commercial farmers. Europe had a different mentality and commercial, often monoculture, farming was less widespread. Yet, the idea had been implemented much earlier at commodity exchanges, among which the London Metal Exchange may have been the most successful. But it remained there, within the confines of these specialists who, as a group, also faced a declining market after the Second World War when the industry, consolidated into huge transnationals, was able to control raw material markets. The idea had to be imported from the USA in a modern guise, that of currency and interest rate futures. There was no particular hurry either because Europe had a lively interbank market with currency forwards.

It were the British who foresaw the potential and were able to exploit it, as of 1982. It would have been difficult on the Continent because of legislation which equated derivatives with gambling and made contracts unenforceable in courts. It was only in 1995 that the last obstacles were removed, but once the idea was accepted, it was done with vigour. Today, Europe is neck-and-neck with America in numbers of traded contracts. Indeed, it is correct to speak of America as a whole because the Bolsa de Mercadorias et Futuros (BM&F) in Brazil compares with any industrialized world exchange. It used to have a small contract size (as the Korean Stock Exchange today) necessitating a downsized symbol on the map, but this has changed. Asia Pacific has been mostly spared from the frenzy. The start was not too late. Simex came on-stream in 1984, TSE started trading Japanese t-bond futures in 1985, and Tiffe introduced the US t-bond contract in 1989. It was rather a mixture of mentality, administrative practice cum legislation, and the smallish size of many Asian economies which held activity back. Only Japan is able to challenge America and Europe head-on, but there large companies prefer to absorb the market risk rather than hedge it. The cautious attitude to hedging is also demonstrated by Singapore and Hongkong which prefer to excel in banking, forex and asset management, and which actually get much of their business from Japan and the USA.

> The roots of derivatives trading in Singapore are in the former Chinese Gold and Silver Exchange which saw its business wither in the postwar world and had to look for something new. CME came to the rescue, or the other way around. CME was battling with Liffe for eurodollar contracts and wanted to thwart its expansion. To this purpose, CME helped in organizing the renamed Simex into a derivatives exchange, licensed it the three-month eurodollar contract and concluded an agreement for mutual clearing and settling of trades conducted on the partner exchange. Liquidity remained in Chicago, however. Simex's success rests preferably on the Japanese penchant for over-regulation. The outlawing of options on Nikkei 225 and the doubling of initial margin on futures drove one-third of trading from Osaka Stock Exchange to Simex, and there it has remained. (Lapper 1997b; Lee 1998a: 76–77; Shirreff 1994: 34; Terazono 1996)
>
> Reliance on foreign, or copied, contracts has obvious risks, however. Simex felt this bitterly in 1987 when CBOT's night trading session deprived it of over half of t-bond volume. Another reminder came when Taiwanese authorities threatened to cut Simex (and CME) off the real-time stock price data stream, when these tried to launch a futures contract on Taiwan's stock index ahead of the

country's own exchange. Simex has now merged with Singapore Exchange (SGX). (Commins 1987; Davies 1991: 47; Kynge 1997)

Specialization is the key for exchange co-existence in the same country or, increasingly, in the same central time zone. In Spain, it has been implemented by mutual agreement. Elsewhere it has been formed by market forces. The extent of specialization can be made tangible by clustering similar contracts and then displaying the clusters by exchange (Figure 4.15). Three groups are selected, money market (short-term), capital market (long-term) and index products. They are all financial products. The remaining contracts are currencies and commodities. CBOT specializes in capital market products and CME in money market and index products. Eurex has mostly capital market products whereas Liffe has predominantly money market products and Matif indices. After reorganization by the new owner, Euronext, Liffe's and Matif's product offerings will be further rationalized. In Asia, there is very little to rationalize or specialize and the largest exchanges are also in different countries and have separate owners.

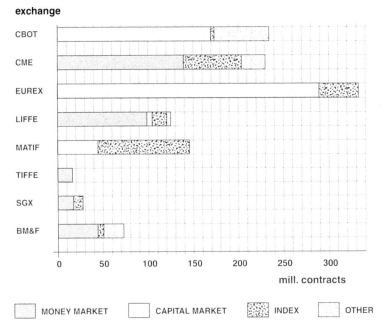

Figure 4.15 Trading by contract class at some derivatives exchanges, 2000.

Sources: Websites; private communication.

Notes
Contracts on individual equities excluded. Money and capital market products not specified at BM&F.

Large derivatives exchanges routinely have twenty or more contracts. Many are experimental, fly-by-night products. Most will never take off properly and the bulk of exchange income comes from a few extremely successful ones. An attempt is made to single out the three top contracts at each major exchange (Figure 4.16). In each case, their aggregate share out of all contracts exceeds one-half, and at three exchanges it is close to 100 per cent. It is easy to understand the care with which these money-spinners are nurtured and the vigour with which attempts to poach them are resisted. Exact copying is not possible because of copyright and the technique is to launch a look-a-like. It avoids the copyright issue but fulfils essentially the same function. Such attempts have almost always misfired, however, and the only truly successful coup has been the homecoming of the *bund* contract from Liffe to Eurex during 1998. The transfer of the Nikkei 225 contract from the Osaka Stock Exchange to Simex was only partially successful, but the destination was also abroad.

Successful countermoves are not made head-on but try to exploit an opening in the competitor's product mix. It can go like this. CME launched the first currency futures in 1972. CBOT imitated the idea with a considerable lag in 1975, and then with an interest rate contract for

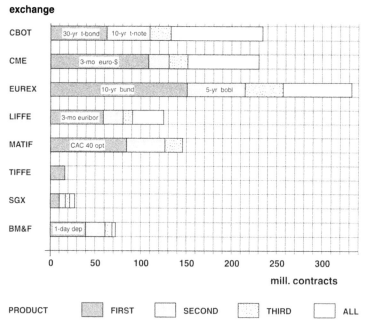

Figure 4.16 Largest contracts at some derivatives exchanges, 2000.

Sources: Websites; private communication.

Notes
Three largest financial products. Contracts on individual equities excluded.

Ginnie Mae bonds. CME countered by introducing the three-month treasury bill contract a year later and the three-month eurodollar future in 1981. CBOT riposted with a thirty-day interest rate contract, but CME offered options on 3-month eurodollar futures in 1985, to be followed next year by the thirteen-week treasury bill contract and crowned by the one-month LIBOR future in 1991. It then turned out that eurodollar futures outcompeted treasury bills, probably because their delivery dates were longer, which facilitated interest rate swaps, and because they were better suited for hedging loans indexed to LIBOR. In a similar vein, when CME launched the S&P 500 index future, CBOT countered by the S&P 500 option through its joint venture CBOE. (Kuprianov 1993a: 188, 199–201; 1993b: 218; Peagam 1993: 96)

Geographical competition

The fundamental relationship between exchanges is competition. The idea is more ingrained at derivatives exchanges than stock exchanges which are much older and possibly more conservative. Their orientation is inherently more domestic, because the main product group is domestic equities and the decision to list or not lies with the companies themselves and not the exchanges. Derivatives exchanges must be more outgoing. There are no ready products and these must be created. One begins with domestic underlyings and if the contract also finds international acceptance it is natural to develop it further. Contracts based on major currencies, interest rates of recognized debt instruments and indices of worldwide following are typical cases. Thereafter follow contracts based on foreign instruments.

The geographical reach can be studied from several angles. The juggling with trade disclosure lags has been commented on earlier (pp. 178–179). Countries from which the exchange receives listings can be mapped. The number of companies or issues are long-term indicators, whereas trading reflects current interest. Internationally oriented exchanges welcome foreign members whose presence will contribute to liquidity. Foreign investors want to follow the activity directly and rent the exchange's terminals. The following presentation is a mixture of these data sets conditioned by their availability. Exchanges are selective in the geographical information they release. For example, trading values by country can be sensitive since they disclose the very topic we are interested in: the exchange's competitive standing. The cases are grouped by the relative location of competitors in the central time zones, American, European and Asia Pacific. This gives two competitive situations – between and within time zones. In both cases stock (cash) and derivatives exchanges are discussed.

Between time zones

In this section, four cases will be taken up. The first one is about the largest, or at least the most high-profile, stock exchanges in each central time zone: NYSE, LSE and TSE. Their influence spheres are mapped by the trading value of foreign equities. The next case is about the distribution of Nasdaq and Swiss Exchange (SWX) trading terminals and gives the investor angle. The third case probes the possibilities of extending trading hours towards a twenty-four-hour market, a strategy for derivatives exchanges. The final case takes up their alliances, which boil down to the swapping of contracts.

NYSE, LSE and TSE are widely seen as the three stock exchanges which *dominate* international equity trading in their respective time zones, and, in combination, dominate the world (Figure 4.17). There is much truth in this perception but, as always, reality is more complicated than that. NYSE apparently dominates Latin America to the extent that local exchanges in Caracas, Quito, Santos and Buenos Aires have atrophied after their best companies listed in New York and took liquidity with them (Caplen 2000; Lapper and Mulligan 2001). NYSE is also important in Northwest Europe where Finland had a banner year, thanks to Nokia; exemplifying the random effect in single-year mappings. NYSE outcompetes LSE in Canada

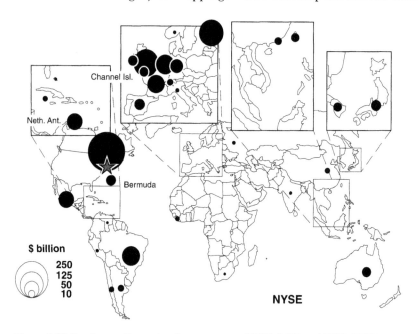

Figure 4.17 Equity trading value by country at NYSE, LSE and TSE, 2000.

Sources: NYSE, private communication; LSE *Fact File* 2001: 18; TSE, private communication.

Note
TSE has a different scale from NYSE and LSE.

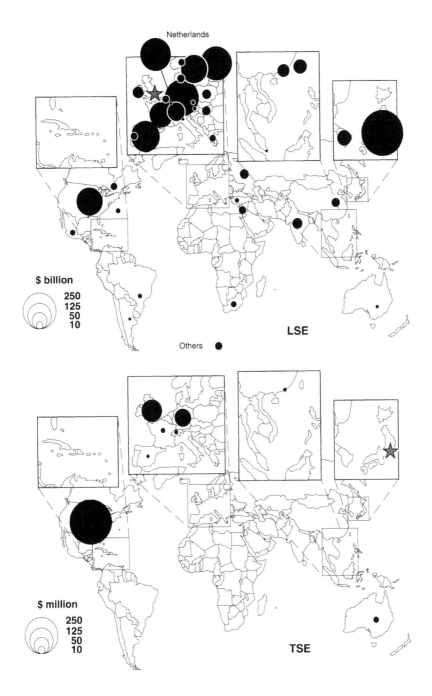

Netherlands

$ billion
250
125
50
10

Others ●

LSE

$ million
250
125
50
10

TSE

and Australia by a wide margin, but elsewhere in the former British Empire, LSE has the upper hand. Most of LSE's business originates from Europe, of course, and it has a reasonable presence in the USA and Japan. By contrast, the trading of foreign equities at TSE is minuscule, concentrating on a few countries and often on banks. It certainly reflects the depressed state of the exchange, which affects domestic and foreign shares alike, but there are other reasons too, like the transaction cost and currency risk. Disillusioned by the lacklustre trading and having baulked at the high cost of maintaining listing, foreigners have departed en masse, giving a blow to TSE's image as a global marketplace (TSE 2001: 42). This leaves NYSE and LSE as the only serious rivals for equities from America, Europe and Asia.

The natural corollary to time zone dominance would be a global exchange, trading in the largest multinational companies. The concept is technically feasible but organizationally problematic. It would make much of the existing capacity redundant and substantially increase the capital needed to trade in, say, the world's 1,000 leading companies. Although some brokers maintain a twenty-four-hour off-hours wholesale market in the world's leading stocks, it is only a supplement to the main market, since investors like to trade while watching the market evolve simultaneously. If the idea ever materializes, NYSE is the exchange with an ambition and capacity to become the global hub for equities from other time zones. Indeed, abroad is the only direction where it still has substantial growth potential. Listing the top one-third of the 2,300 foreign companies which qualify would increase the capitalization substantially. That would make special services possible, such as trading in ordinary shares rather than ADRs and in several currencies rather than just dollars. It would be a big step towards making NYSE a truly global exchange. NYSE specialists are too small for the challenge, but large brokers who hope to win new issue mandates might one day put up the necessary capital. (Grasso 1995; Lambert 1997; Lee 1993)

Listings and trading appear to reflect the exchange angle. The *investor angle* need not be the same. It comes to light in the location of the exchange's proprietary terminals, which allow trading or at least give direct access to the information flow without the intermediation of brokers. Their locations have been made available by Nasdaq and SWX, although the data could not be updated (Figure 4.18).

The locational patterns reveal intermediary and investor preferences for exchange and possibly time zone as well. Nasdaq has a following all over the world, Switzerland included. SWX has a following mainly in Europe, particularly the UK and Germany, and the USA. Latin America and Africa are completely empty. Not a single terminal is recorded in South Africa or Brazil, for example, although both are known as sources of flight capital. Many of the comparatively few faraway terminals ostensibly belong to exchange members (banks), while investor terminals apparently cluster in neighbouring countries. The Swiss Exchange is not a place where offshore

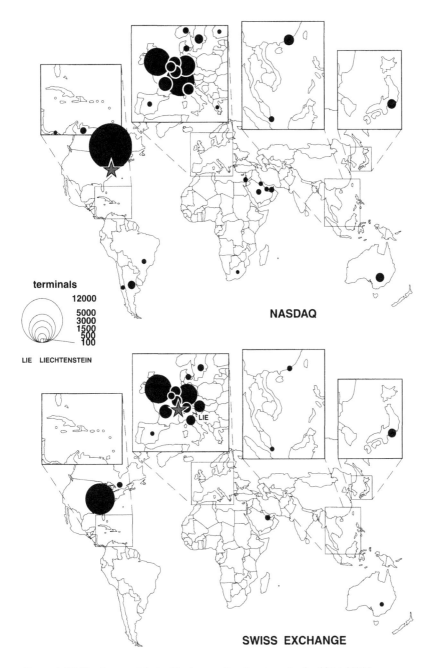

Figure 4.18 Nasdaq and Swiss Exchange foreign terminals, 1994/1995.

Sources: Nasdaq 1996: 34; Swiss Exchange, internal statistics.

Notes
Nasdaq December 1995; Swiss Exchange December 1994.

investors and intermediaries like to operate on a large scale. Their Swiss contacts bypass the exchange. That is what the terminal locations tell. But it is advisable to complement the picture by also looking at the exchange listings. It is certainly possible that foreign investors lease terminals because they wish to trade their domestic equities on Nasdaq and SWX. These are listed abroad for the sake of better liquity, among other things.

The comparison of Nasdaq terminals and listings might suffer from the six-year time difference (Figure 4.22), but not necessarily, because the basic pattern was there already in 1996 and during the past years it has only intensified (Laulajainen 1998: see also Figure 4.13). Such a development cannot invalidate our comparison. For many countries the thesis about trading domestic equities listed abroad appears to hold, at least to a degree. For a definite minority it clearly does not. The ostensible reasons vary. Israel, the Caribbean and Bermuda have the capability and willingness to originate companies but have a modest investor community. Switzerland and the Gulf States are their direct opposites. Although unwilling or unable to originate listings, they have a respectable investor community and it needs terminals.

The Swiss experience is broadly similar. The distribution of terminals compares with the countries from which SWX receives equity and bond listings, the UK and the Caribbean excepted (Figure 4.19). The former has its own LSE and prefers the US exchanges to Continental ones. The latter is a financial turning table and not an investor community. The availability of listable issues also has a bearing. They are not too numerous in Liechtenstein or the Gulf States, so there cannot be many listings either. Domestic listings in Italy are far less than they could be, so their absence on the Swiss Exchange is only logical. India and South Africa had strict exchange controls and consequently little need for foreign terminals.

The above exchanges operate within normal *business hours*. They can afford it because they are not easily dislodged. Small adjustments are always possible. London may add two hours or so at the end and New York at the beginning of the day, for example. The solution works between Europe and North America because the time difference is so small, a mere five hours between London and New York, or six hours between London and Chicago. But it limps with Asia Pacific where the time difference is larger, even from the US west coast, which, in addition, is in a financial shadow.

Smaller or just more aggressive exchange can be really venturesome. Philadelphia SE experimented with twenty-four-hour trading. The CBOT floor night session between 6–9 pm from Sundays to Thursdays attempted to bridge the gap between regular US and Japanese trading hours but was discontinued when the screen chalked four times the volume. The main problem is that trading fades off when normal business hours end. Slow trading does not attract and traders need rest. Derivatives exchanges are also tied to the underlying cash market. In the late 1980s, the trading by

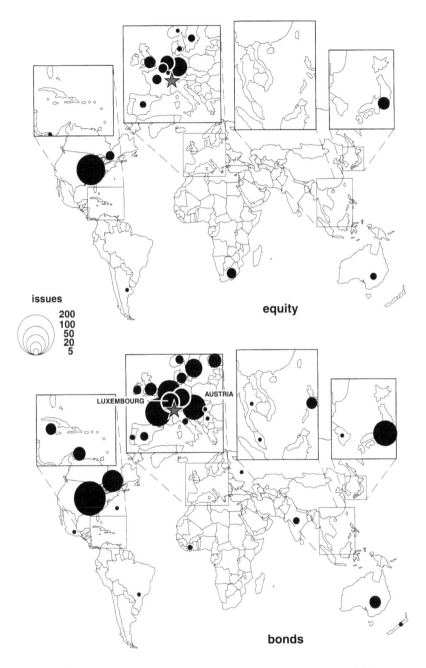

Figure 4.19 Swiss Exchange foreign equity and bonds, December 1994.
Source: Jahresbericht 1994: 54.

CBOT and CME of TSE's Topix and Osaka Stock Exchange's Nikkei 225 index contracts, respectively, never took off, because a simultaneous liquid cash market did not exist. In a time of crisis things are different, but the permanent gain is doubtful, because gains and losses are bound to out-balance each other in the long term. (*BIS QR* Aug. 1997: 36; Durr 1990; Morse 1992a; 1997b)

> When the t-bond contract hit the trading limit at CBOT on 20 October 1987, business shifted to London. Altogether 45,000 con-tracts were traded against less than 10,000 normally. In the evening the business returned to Chicago. S&P futures, by contrast, could not flee, as they were only traded in Chicago (Anon. 1987: 22; Evans 1988: 109).

Derivatives trading hours and their loci are quite variable (Figure 4.20). The typical hours given here are for broad contract groups, not individual contracts, which would make the figure too large. Some groups split between the floor and the screen, others between fixed income and indices. Americans work round the clock but Europeans stick to daylight hours. Americans still value the floor while Europeans have abandoned it for screens. Singapore uses both, although for different products, a

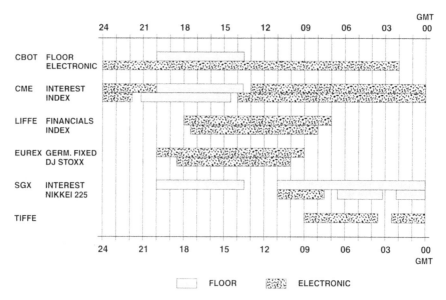

Figure 4.20 Trading hours at major derivatives exchanges, May 2002.

Sources: Websites.

Notes
Time scale runs from east to west following the sun. Trading hours often vary with the con-tract, even radically; the figure offers a broad view only.

transitory phase. There is a considerable overlap between time zones and it often originates from screen trading. The floor night shift at SGX tries to comply with floor trading at CME.

When extended trading hours do not help, it is natural to consider a jointly run trading system. Such ideas raise resistance on the exchange floor and particularly among locals. Loss of volume is suspected, with no compensating balance. The promoters are the large banks and brokers, who see cooperation as a way to cut costs (Lapper 1995b; Raybould 1994: 8).

In the mid-1980s, 95 per cent of world derivatives trading took place in Chicago, which led its exchanges to believe that a global off-hours system anchored in Chicago and uniting the other centres across time zones was just beyond the horizon. CME bit the bullet, cooperated with Reuters in developing a twenty-four-hour electronic trading system, Globex, and organized alliances with other exchanges to run it. Things did not develop as anticipated. Demand outside of the Chicago time zone proved disappointing and regulation could differ dramatically between countries. Globex never properly got off the ground, partly because it was too expensive. About 80 per cent of trading was of Matif's contracts, 6–7 per cent of those involved. Then Globex was outcompeted by cheaper and more modern systems, although it seems to be on the way back in a modernized version. (*BIS QR* May 1997: 23; Campbell 1989b; Khan and Ireland 1993: 5; Massimb and Phelps 1994: 43; Matif 1995, inside folder; Morse 1994; Shirref 1998a: 37)

When twenty-four-hour trading flounders, *alliances*, in practice institutionalized contract swaps, might do the job. The ambition for alliances has a long history. Sydney Futures Exchange (SFE) is believed to be the oldest alliance partner, because it was the first exchange outside the USA to trade financial futures and in a time zone where potential partners were rare. CME and Simex joined up to offer CME's eurodollar contract in 1984. Others imitated. The essence is contract fungibility. A contract opened at an exchange can be closed at the cooperation partner as is the case with CME and SGX (Simex), the mutual offset system. The alternative is clearing link. Trades executed in Tiffe's three-month euroyen contract at Liffe are transferred to Tokyo at the end of the day, and the open interest is held by Tiffe members. These operations make sense at exchanges in different time zones. Within the same time zone, a common settlement price keeps the scales balanced, as agreed by Simex and Tiffe for their euroyen contracts. (*BIS QR* Aug. 1997: 34; Jeanneau 1996: 30–39; Shirreff 1997a: 52; Tiffe 1996: 1–2)

Because cooperation is sought between time zones, and the partners should have approximately equal weight, the available selection is restricted. A set of important alliances from the mid-1990s is instrumental (Figure 4.21). For the sake of legibility, many less relevant exchanges, linkages and products are omitted, such as the identical euroyen futures traded at CME and Simex, CBOT's t-bond contract at TSE, or CME's

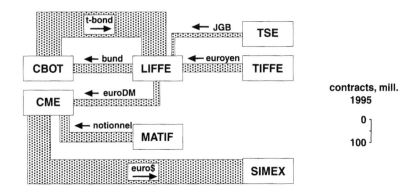

Figure 4.21 Some important alliances between derivatives exchanges, December
　　1996.

Sources: *BIS QR* Feb. 1997: 30.

Note
The contract flow gives trading at the home exchange in 1995.

eurodollar product at Tiffe. An alliance can be considered a success when
trading abroad is about 2 per cent of the volume at home. Because the
partner is in another central time zone, it is natural that trading is during
off-hours. (*BIS QR* Feb. 1997: 29; Corrigan and Morse 1992; Morse 1996)

　Although the figure is both incomplete and outdated, it sheds light on
strategic thinking. Only the short-term eurodollar, euroyen and euromark
futures had a truly global trading interest, the rest were marginal. The
great absentee was DTB, which opted for access points (gateways), mostly
in Europe but also in the USA (Figure 4.3). Liffe and Matif ceded their
best contracts (and some others) to the Chicago exchanges, but got relatively little in return. CME's eurodollar was off-limits for them but not for
Simex, which was more distant and therefore a real partner rather than a
competitor. CBOT's t-bond appeared more promising for Liffe, which
could determine the day's first price, but the fees went to Chicago,
directly to CBOT's members. The problem was CBOT's off-hours trading
system, Project A, in direct competition and cheaper than Liffe's open
outcry. The link was subsequently severed and a new one forged with
Eurex, with the *bund* as the core contract. (Luce and Tait 1997; Morse
1995a; 1995b; 1997a)

Within time zones

A dominant exchange naturally also faces competition from its own time
zone. Does the geographical reach of competitors coincide with the
incumbent's pattern or cover a smaller area? In the former case, challengers need to intensify penetration, in the latter they can also compete

by expanding geographically. The answer is obvious to an extent. Small exchanges list companies from their own country and possibly neighbouring countries. The absolute overlap is modest, but the relative one may be substantial. Large exchanges have extensive, even worldwide, listings and strive for enhanced penetration. What remains is to look at two or more large exchanges in the same time zone. NYSE and Nasdaq are obvious candidates in the American time zone; CBOT and CME would be others. In the European time zone, the major derivatives exchanges, Liffe, Eurex and Matif, fit the bill. The Continent has an oversupply of exchanges and rationalization is in the air. This is easier said than done, and the case of LSE and DB illuminates some of the snags which delay progress. Starting from scratch is no less difficult, as the short history of Virt-x shows.

The comparison between *NYSE and Nasdaq* is conducted through the number of listed issues, disaggregated into ADRs and ordinary shares (Figure 4.22). Both exchanges have global coverage with a presence on every Continent and in most financially important countries. The earlier gaps in Germany and Switzerland are filled in, after companies there have become convinced about the advantages of a US listing and overcome their aversion to comply with the US disclosure and reporting rules. NYSE has a wider presence, though, than Nasdaq, whose listings are heavily concentrated in Canada, Israel and the English-speaking world. NYSE is very strong in Latin America and has made important strides in Italy, Spain and China. One would expect that companies from these countries would prefer Nasdaq because of its easier listing requirements. But companies seeking a NYSE listing are often national champions which value the status which only NYSE can give and possibly obtain a higher p/e ratio as well. For example, Chinese companies in the early 1990s expected a p/e 50 per cent higher than in Hongkong. How expectations then tally with reality varies. The p/e ratio depends on the intensity of trading, and that varies a great deal between individual stocks. Success seems to be connected with the specific industry, market dynamics and how the listing is subsequently managed (Lindeman 1997; Shale 1993b: 40). Some issuers have apparently misjudged the overall situation or neglected the followup, and their script has very little trading. There may also be a time dimension involved. From among the Swedish multinationals with a US listing, only the newcomers Scania and Astra went to the Big Board, while the older generation opted for Nasdaq.

The type of listing, either ADR or ordinary share, is fairly clear-cut. Either one of the modes tends to dominate a particular country, and regional patterns can be visualized. Companies in Canada, Israel, the Caribbean and Bermuda widely follow US accounting and business practices and find little difficulty in listing ordinary shares, while other countries prefer ADRs. From the investor point of view, it is believed that ADRs are demanded by retail customers, smaller institutional investors, US pension funds (only dollar assets) and newcomers to foreign stocks, while

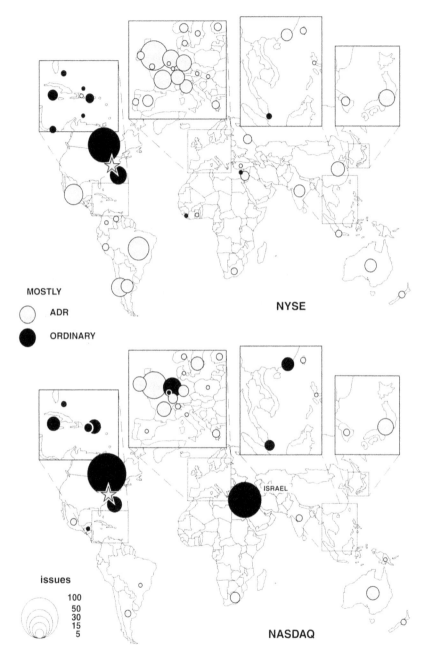

MOSTLY

○ ADR

● ORDINARY

NYSE

issues

100
50
30
15
5

ISRAEL

NASDAQ

Figure 4.22 NYSE and Nasdaq foreign equity listings, March/April 2002.
Sources: www.nyse.com; www.nasdaq.com; private communication.

sophisticated investors prefer ordinary shares at the home exchanges (Adams 1997: 30).

The European case revolves around the leading derivatives exchanges, *Eurex, Liffe and Matif* during 1996–2000. The focus is on interest rate futures because of their large share out of total activity and the fact that options contracts follow them automatically. Eurex is a 50/50 German/Swiss screen-based joint venture, the others are national and made the gradual conversion from floor to screen during this period. Liffe is the oldest, having opened for business in 1982, Matif became operational in 1986 and Eurex in 1990. The age ranking has mattered. Liffe was able to create contracts upon foreign underlyings because nothing was available, the traditional firstcomer advantage. It relied on open outcry, which was the dominant trading technology of the time and apparently suited to the mentality of its free-wheeling trading community. Eurex was a fairly formal institution with roots in the all-electronic Soffex and DB's early electronic trading platform, Ibis. Its labour force consisted of salaried employees rather than entrepreneurs. Matif was located between these two. It had a fair contingent of locals but their influence was not decisive. The French at large excelled in trading technology, as witnessed by the worldwide licensing of their platforms.

The competitive situation in 1996 was such that Liffe dominated both short-term (money market) and long-term (capital market) contracts (Figure 4.23). The dominance rested essentially on its foreign contracts, German and Italian ones in particular. Matif had got going early enough to thwart Liffe's ambitions on its home turf. Italians apparently conceded to the situation. Germans fought back and the struggle was about the *bund* contract which Liffe had launched in 1988. Liffe's market share was about 70 per cent and with it went liquidity, forcing Germans to go to London to trade their 'own' derivative. About 10 per cent of Liffe's volume originated from French institutions and still another 10 per cent from New York and Chicago (Breedon 1996: 8; Corrigan 1993; Fisher 1997a).

Liffe's competitiveness was particularly pronounced in a fast-moving market. German traders cannot take risks, claimed Londoners, theirs is the civil service mentality. So it may have been, but theirs was also the faith in technology. While Liffe stuck to open outcry as the main trading method, DTB/Eurex kept on honing its screen-based system, Xetra, and was finally able to undercut Liffe in trading cost 1-to-4. The difference could be defended in certain difficult-to-trade instruments where the outcome might justify the higher cost, but across the board it was unsustainable in the long run. Liffe's trading community, who owned the exchange, did not relent. Screen trading needs different skills than floor trading and less human labour. It was a question of traders' livelihoods. Eurex's case was greatly facilitated by the support of German banks who were important users of the contract. A six-month fee-holiday was granted to all comers and foreign access points were created. The consent decree

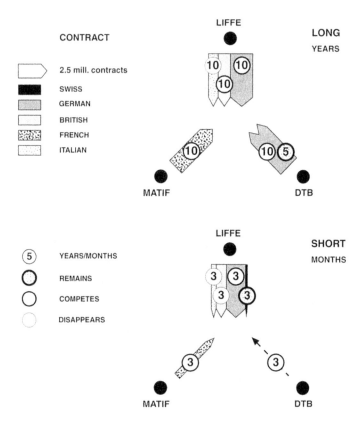

Figure 4.23 Competition in interest rate futures by Liffe, Matif and DTB/Eurex, November 1996 and May 2002.

Source: Iskander 1996; www.liffe.com; www.matif.fr; www.eurexchange.com.

Note
Scales in 1996 and 2000 are different. The contracts are for government bonds and bills. The three-month contract in Frankfurt started trading in 1997. The terms 'remains/competes/disappears' reflect the anticipated effect of the euro.

by CFTC, which allowed trading from the USA as long as the revenue did not exceed 5 per cent of the exchange's total was important. At the same time, the debate between the proponents of floor and screen continued on Liffe. The decisive move came from its own ranks. A former trader who now controlled one hundred trading terminals decided to take his business to Eurex. The end game lasted half a year and by the end of September 1998 the *bund* contract was traded only there. (Clow 1998; Laulajainen 2001; Lee 1998b; Shirreff 1998b)

That was a severe blow to Liffe but not yet the end. What made it menacing, however, was that the coming of the euro on 1 January 1999 would finalize the gradual merging of government debt markets in the EMU

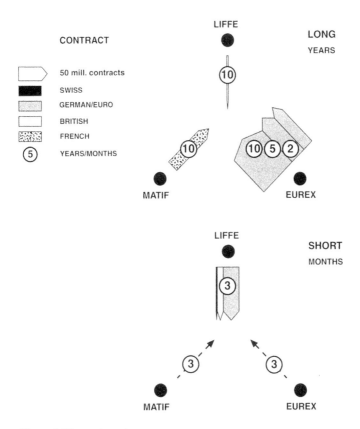

Figure 4.23 continued

area. National contracts would probably be replaced by a EMU-wide one and the most likely candidate was the *bund* contract. Only the British and Swiss contracts would remain and even they might be partially replaced by the *bund*. Another threat was that the German short-term contract would follow the *bund* to Eurex because of scale economies in clearing and settlement. It might have been the end of Liffe. The vision of the *bund* contract as a Pan-European benchmark became a reality but the transfer of the three-month contract did not. The reason was simple enough: the money market was in London and it made sense to stay close to it. Liffe also realized that the old days were over and converted itself into an all-screen exchange in record time. It launched a new trading platform, Connect, which probably outperforms the relatively old Xetra. But it could not repatriate the *bund* contract. Liffe was then transformed into a public company which allowed members to cash their investment but also made the exchange vulnerable to hostile bids.

Matif had remained on the sidelines during the struggle. It kept its national contracts and cooperated in Globex but did not move within Europe. Having been independent it was consolidated with the options exchange Monep and the Paris Bourse. This new entity then formed the core of the international Euronext. It was demutualized and could thereafter use shares for acquisitions. The necessary mass and armoury had been created and it was time for action. The European market as such was saturated and growth could be only by merger or acquisition. Eurex was apparently not for sale and attempts in the mid-1990s to swap contracts and consolidate trading systems and platforms with DTB had floundered. The smaller exchanges were hardly worth the trouble. Liffe was what remained, seriously weakened by the loss of trading and confidence. (Jack 1994; 1996b; Raybould 1994: 28; Shirreff 1997a: 50)

It had several suitors. CME and Nasdaq may have been interested. The Swedish OM offered shares and some cash but was flatly turned down. The bid simply was not credible. But those made by DB, LSE and Euronext were. The final contest took place between LSE and Euronext and, rather unexpectedly, Euronext won. Its bid was slightly lower but it was all cash when LSE made a cash-and-shares offer. Why LSE allowed this to happen is something of an enigma although allegations have been made about earlier cold-shouldering. Liffe was left outside the iX deal (see below) and LSE refused a merger when OM placed its bid. We also recall the reception by LSE when the idea of a derivatives market had been raised two decades earlier. Having completed the coup, Euronext announced its strategy: the derivatives business will be based in London and use the Connect technology; Liffe's management will remain in place. (Boland 2001b; 2001c; Boland and Pretzlik 2001a; 2001b; Pretzlik and Boland 2001; Pretzlik and Nicholas 2000)

What happened with Liffe and the other Euronext constituents is going to happen many times over in Europe. Its thirty-odd stock exchanges do about one-quarter the trading of US exchanges but have a cost base 50 per cent higher. They cannot all survive, not even as venues for small local companies. But consolidation will take time. The USA needed one hundred years to prune the more than 100 exchanges to the current half a dozen. The consolidation of stock (cash) and derivatives exchanges in the same country and city is almost completed in Europe. Cross-border mergers are in order and they are much more difficult. The regulatory and legal environments differ, and so do taxes. Trading systems are different and expensive to develop. Ownership and location affect the respective status of finance centres and raise national emotions. The floundered merger of *LSE and DB* is a case in point. (Baker 2000; Blume *et al.* 1993: 30; Boland 1999; Butler 1999; van Duyn 2000; Evans 1992: 56–58; Luce and Tait 1997; Regas 1997; Shirreff 1997a)

LSE and DB announced in May 2000 their intent to merge under the logo 'iX'. The driving forces in London were a handful of investment banks, responsible for 80 per cent of activity on LSE, and in Germany probably the exchange management because banks, the dominant owners, showed little enthusiasm. The announcement came as a surprise and it took some time before details were released. The incompatibility of the intended partners was soon pointed out. If the exchanges went public, DB's market value would be double LSE's, while the relation was exactly opposite in domestic market capitalization. LSE probably had a larger trading value although published figures were not comparable. Not unreasonably, LSE wanted a 50/50 deal and to achieve it DB agreed to exclude its 50 per cent share in Clearstream from the deal, but decided to keep a similar stake in Eurex. LSE lacked settlement and derivatives units. Blue chip equities were to be listed and traded in London and high-tech, assumedly growth, stocks in Frankfurt, a controversial decision and not least because London collected stamp duty but Frankfurt did not and because block trades had to be reported in London but not in Frankfurt where they were important money-spinners. Neither exchange yet had a central counterparty which is necessary for actor anonymity, but both had linked with different equity indices, the choice influencing investment flow. Interested parties could agree about UK market regulation, which decided the domicile for London. LSE agreed to the Xetra platform which had more local gateways than Sets, although neither was very good for further development. Many obstacles thus seemed to have been cleared away but the most important had been overlooked: the necessity to get at least 75 per cent of votes at LSE. These votes were with the small and medium-sized members and they had not been consulted. What, exactly, the bone of contention was has not been detailed in public. Money was certainly important; a wholesale change is always expensive. It can also have been hurt pride. Anyway, the merger between LSE and DTB collapsed due to resistance by local brokers. Other critical voices were heard from bankers who did not want two separate locations, and fund managers whose Association, representing eighty asset managers with $3.3tr in assets, did not want to lose high-tech stocks to Frankfurt. (Barber 2000; Boland 2000a; 2000b; Boland and van Duyn 2000; Currie 1998; van Duyn 2001; Harnischfeger and Boland 1999; Maguire 1998/1999; McKenzie 1998/1999; Targett 2001)

If cooperation and consolidation do not work, one can launch a completely new exchange, or almost, as the *Tradepoint/Virt-x* example shows. Tradepoint was a British ECN established by large banks, brokers and other ECNs in the apparent purpose of putting pressure on the stodgy LSE. When the exchange tried to raise fees for IDBs, Tradepoint undercut it by 75 per cent and indirectly forced the introduction of a central limit order book. It was classified as an exchange by the UK regulator, and exempted from registration as a national exchange in the USA. But its trading never exceeded 2 per cent of the UK total and many considered it moribund. Then came the Swiss, who gave it a new lease of life.

It is generally agreed that there are 200–300 Pan-European stocks, liquid and deep enough to attract large institutional investors. It has been the ambition of every large exchange to get their listing, trading and settlement. Theoretically, it is a question of low cost and a supportive regulatory environment. The solution, again theoretically, is to have a central limit order book and an electronic trading platform with straight through processing. The large Swiss banks decided to try and got the Swiss blue chips to move from the domestic SWX to a new UK-regulated platform. They came to London because it is the place for cross-border deals and because there they escaped the Swiss stamp tax. The banks' first priority was LSE but when this was refused they turned to Tradepoint. The result was the joint venture, Virt-x. It is cheaper than LSE, DB or Euronext. All major European indices can be traded on a single platform. Users have a choice of whether to clear at Crest, SIS or Euroclear. By the end of August 2002, Virt-x was reaching about 10 per cent of European blue chip trading, but over 95 per cent of it was in Swiss equities. It is too early to give a final judgement but the feeling is that national preferences still matter more than rational business considerations. (Baker 2000; Boland 2001a; Dalla-Costa 2002; Graham 1997a; 1998; Minto 1997)

Conclusion

This chapter has deepened the picture about financial markets because organized exchanges, by their very character, release more data than OTC. They are an important segment of financial markets because the bulk of equity business and a fair share of derivatives are conducted there. The original private clubs with a strong monopolistic position have, in most important countries, been converted to business companies and some have even been listed on an exchange. This has given them the financial muscle to better face challenges from the OTC and ECNs in particular, but has also made them vulnerable to hostile acquisitions. In the process they have outsourced many former functions and discovered that actually only three or four are essential: listing, trading, surveillance and possibly clearing and settlement. Listing by a recognized exchange is still seen as a quality stamp, trading is a revenue source and surveillance is expected by authorities. A clearing house is an important competitive weapon because it shoulders counterparty risk and nets trades.

The core tasks of an exchange are price finding and trade execution. The available techniques group broadly into market marking (dealer market) and auction (order market), and the technical devices are either open outcry or screen. The trend has clearly been from market making to auction and from open outcry to screen. In both cases the reason has been lower cost. Open outcry is labour-intensive and market making requires operating capital from the dealer. Screen trading is technically about the same on exchanges and in OTC. The difference is in the number of participants, amount of information released and surveillance.

ECNs have also taken some market share from conservative or inefficient exchanges although it is thought that their impact will be felt primarily in the OTC. Some commentators speculate that screen trading will smooth out the effect of distance but empirical evidence contradicts this idea.

Exchanges have arisen from the need to collect all possible liquidity on one trading forum. The ideal is that a trade can be executed immediately, it does not move the price no matter how large it is (depth) and if it does the price will come back with a minimum of delay (resilience). The larger the exchange, the better the chances that these qualifications will apply. But measuring the size can be only approximate because reporting systems at stock exchanges differ and contracts at derivatives exchanges are not necessarily comparable. Stock exchanges can be conservative because their hold over domestic equities in financially important countries is at least acceptable. Derivatives exchanges must be more outgoing. They create the contracts themselves and pay a stock exchange for the price data the contracts are based on. Only few contracts are money-spinners, both nationally and within a central time zone, which means that business risk is much larger at derivatives than stock exchanges. Both get the bulk of their business from home. International business seldom exceeds 10 per cent, although it can arrive from all over the world. Listings are the most solid way to attract business, extended trading hours and contract swaps have contributed 5 per cent or less. Established exchanges are very resistant to competition. Where consolidation is overdue national taxation, legislation, different trading and settlement systems delay implementation.

5 Banking

Many types of bank

Definitions

Banks are the intermediaries and participants in most financial transactions. They organize the financial space by developing new products,
markets, trading forums and rule sets. These aspects are largely unknown
to the small investor. S/he knows the bank as an office on a street corner
or in a shopping mall, a place to deposit and retrieve money, make payments and occasionally ask for a loan. This image contains many key
ingredients but is too narrow for professional use. Regulators, in particular, who must monitor and supervise the activity are keen on a comprehensive view from which to carve out their own domain. Our discussion
benefits from a similar vision, and some historical background helps us to
understand the current situation and future trends.

A widely accepted definition is based on borrowing and lending: the
bank is a financial intermediary which accepts deposits and makes loans.
Both activities must be included. But financial intermediaries offer many
other services, and the question is whether any of these others, without
borrowing and lending, would suffice to make an organization a bank.
Germans have taken an extreme stand and also accept bill discounting,
security brokerage, custodial services, fund management, factoring, provision of financial guarantees and fund transfer as bank criteria. The EU
has adopted the German list of banking activities and excluded only insurance broking (Johnston Pozdena and Alexander 1992: 556; Szegö and
Szegö 1992: 330). Definitional variety makes international comparisons
vague. A good example was Salomon Brothers (currently Schroeder
Salomon Smith Barney), the US investment bank (or broker), which was a
bank in Frankfurt but not in London. Much of the apparent variety is
froth, however, hiding comparatively few basic types which appear everywhere although under different names. These types are characterized
either by the products they offer, or by the customers they serve, or
by both.

One possible split is between retail and wholesale banking, the former serving individuals and small businesses and the latter institutions and big corporations. The needs of retail and wholesale customers obviously differ, but the split does not give much indication as to which way. Therefore, a more product-oriented or functional split appears preferable (Figure 5.1). This split is between universal and special banks, to differentiate institutions with a very wide mandate from those focused on a narrow niche. The latter group is obviously more varied than the former, and the types mentioned in this chapter should be understood as examples rather than an exhaustive list. Private banks are in a grey zone. They have similar features to universal banks but their product lines are too narrow to make them fully-fledged members. Islamic banks are more finance companies than banks but noteworthy deposit takers in that part of the world. Each bank type will be given a basic characterization. Added to that are additional features typical for Islamic finance at large, which expands the topic beyond the scope of banking.

Special banks

'Savings bank' is a generic name, about the same as 'savings & loan association' ('thrifty') in the USA, 'building society' in the UK, '*sparkasse*' in Germany, 'cantonal bank' in Switzerland, '*caisse d'epargne*' in France and '*caja*' in Spain. The ubiquitous postbank is essentially a savings bank, although organized under the Postal Service. Savings banks were established to promote thriftiness among less-monied classes, in a period when banking was geared to serving the wealthy and businesses. When the lower layers of society became seriously bankable, their small savings aggregated to retail market shares of 50 per cent and more (Aris 2001; Helk 2001a).

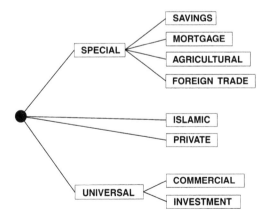

Figure 5.1 Common types of banks.

Source: author.

The social motives of savings banks were reflected in lending, which was largely directed to home loans. The client base implied that most banks were small, and their localized lending made it impossible to spread risk by differentiation. Another weakness was the consolidation of small demand deposits into larger home loans, which led to a serious maturity mismatch. It was logical to create a ceiling organization which smoothed local imbalances and risks, provided clearing, and which has become a fully-fledged commercial bank. The need for depositor security has led to radical solutions. German and Swiss savings banks are owned and guaranteed by states/cantons or municipalities. Their Italian namesakes are often public law institutions, or owned by foundations and associations whose stock is not negotiable. In the USA, the federal government has at times given thrifties extremely generous guarantees.

> The German *sparkassen* have, for many years, inspired strong feelings among the country's private commercial banks and, during the past few years, they have also managed to rock the boat internationally. *Sparkassen* are owned by municipalities who have a legal obligation to keep them operating and to guarantee the deposits. A *sparkasse* cannot issue shares, that is, it cannot be sold, and the latent support will be taxpayer money. A gentle way to support a *sparkasse* is to use its services at mutually favourable terms. It pays below-market interest for municipal deposits and is able to pass the advantage on to its other customers. When needed, it will lend favourably to public projects which might have difficulty in finding other financing.
>
> The next echelon is the mutually-owned *landesbank*, guaranteed by the respective land and this, in turn, by the federal government. Logically, *landesbanken* would enjoy excellent ratings if they care to ask for one.
>
> One *landesbank*, Westdeutsche Landesbank (WestLB), tired of its provincial role and went international, offering investment banking services. That was too much; an internal German issue had become international. WestLB's capital base was sufficient but it fell foul of EU directives of public subsidies. The formal case against them was the subsidized purchase of a housing agency, for which it was fined DM1.6bn ($950m). In the same melée, the German government agreed to abolish state guarantees within a time period, but no more than that. This is only the tip of the iceberg, however, because similar arrangements also exist elsewhere within the EU. (Harnischfeger 1999; Helk 2001b)

Banks that specialize in lending to primary producers in agriculture, fishery and forestry often go under the generic label 'cooperative bank'. '*Rabobanks*' in the Netherlands, '*raiffeisen*' banks in Switzerland, '*crédit agricole*' in France and 'agriculture and forestry' banks in Japan belong to this category. Organic production is plagued by the vagaries of weather and the entrepreneurs, farmers, fishers, and so on, are usually too small to exert significant market power. They sell their products in a basically atomistic market, making them poor credit risks. This fact combined with the producers' political clout has led to the establishment of these specialized credit institutions, which also offer the government a convenient channel for distributing subsidies. Like savings banks, they have normally formed a ceiling organization, essentially a commercial bank.

The maturity mismatch of savings banks is corrected at mortgage banks, which finance their real estate lending with bonds of corresponding maturity. The illiquidity of the collateral has, in some countries, prompted legislation which reserves the sector for these specialized banks. To gain access to the segment, commercial and universal banks have established mortgage subsidiaries.

Banks that specialize in foreign trade, foreign exchange, trust banking, industrial finance, construction, and other large-scale and long-term activity of great national importance are typical of guided economies like China and, previously, the Soviet Union and Japan. It is easier for authorities to guide and control one specialized institution than scores of diversified ones, and scarce resources, financial and human, are thereby utilized better. The Bank of China, Vneshtorgbank, Industrial Bank of Japan, Japanese trust banks and the former Bank of Tokyo (forex, now Bank of Tokyo Mitsubishi) are, or were, among them. But the principle also exists elsewhere. Crédit National in France and Kreditanstalt für Wiederaufbau (KfW) in Germany are other familiar examples. The Bank of New York and the Bank of Boston in the USA have developed into world-class custodians, reaping 70 per cent of their revenue from that business (Authers 1996; Cooper 2002).

Universal banks

Universal banks are, by definition, active in all kinds of banking unless barred by legislation (or by informal understanding, as was the case in the UK). And when they are barred from something, they at least try to participate through subsidiaries and holding companies. In the narrow sense, the label applies only to banks in Continental Europe and its cultural sphere, such as Latin America. In the English-speaking world, and Japan after the Second World War, universal banks were split into two, commercial and investment. Although the split is now a thing of the past, the commercial legacy still lasts.

The justification of a universal bank is in the diversification of risk and economies of scope. The first argument is obvious enough. The second one is less so, as shown in studies on the US banking industry. The very size of large universal banks, essentially based on their extensive branch networks, is the origin of much folklore concerning their power (Figure 5.2). The question is particularly acute in Switzerland and Germany, where the banks are not only large but also internationally active. The United Bank of Switzerland (merged from Union Bank of Switzerland and Swiss Bank Corporation), Crédit Suisse (CS) and Deutsche Bank have an aura which similar banks in neighbouring countries lack. All three dominate issuance and trading at home. The Swiss benefit from their role as asset managers, which gives them considerable placing power. The Germans hold interests in manufacturing and retailing and vote by the proxies of their custody customers, a practice which seems to be on the way out. Many equity stakes are the result of bad loans which were preferably converted to equity rather than written off. This is in sharp contrast to French banks, which invest in industry to cement a relationship and get the partner's banking business. By contrast, the concept of the German house bank which sits on the board of its customers and helps them through thick and thin is nowadays largely a fiction. More truthful is the idea that relationship banking is more entrenched on the Continent than in the USA and UK. In Japan, the renowned keiretsu bank is actually several banks, although less than is usual in the West. The concept has partially crumbled, however, under the onslaught of the banking crisis in the 1990s when keiretsu banks occasionally refused to honour their moral obligations or have been merged into

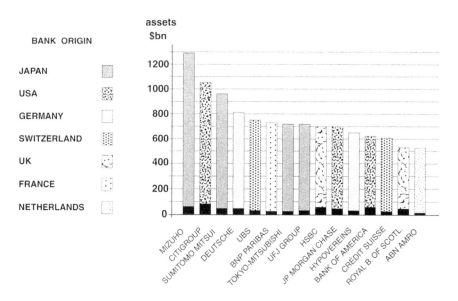

Figure 5.2 Largest bank groups, 2001.

Source: *Euromoney,* June 2002: 114.

Note
Own capital in black.

larger groupings. (Abrahams 1999; Bowley 1998; Edwards and Fischer 1994: 142, 145; Hayes and Hubbard 1990: Table 7.7; Humphreys 1991: 27; Jack 1996; Saunders 1994: 234; Tett 1997a; 1997b)

Where universal banks have been split into commercial and investment halves, the identifiable reason has been the worry that investment banking is inherently more risky than commercial banking, and that depositor money should not be put at excessive risk. The idea gained popular acceptance in the USA during the banking crisis of the early 1930s and gained legal representation with the Glass–Steagall Act in 1933. Existing banks had to choose between the commercial banking and investment banking formats. Most opted for the first alternative and a few split into two, the best-known example being the House of Morgan which was spun into JP Morgan (commercial) and Morgan Stanley (investment).

> The Glass–Steagall Act had its roots in the buoyant 1920s. Companies could finance investments from profits and banks had to find other income sources. One was speculation in stock and money markets and many small investors followed suit, frequently on a 10 per cent initial margin. The frenzy was intense and bankers exploited it by packaging unperforming Latin American loans into bonds and selling them through their securities affiliates. When the stock market plummeted and the country moved into depression, the matter came to light, ruining many small investors. It was a major reason to separate banking from securities business (Chernow 1990: 303–304; Hampton 1996: 82). From a wider perspective, the securities industry hardly deserved its tainted image. Reckless lending to real estate, farming, leveraged acquisitions, developing countries and so on has been equally disastrous as uncontrolled securities underwriting and trading.

In the UK, the separation resulted from a natural selection on which original domicile, whether in London or the provinces, contributed. These were two different worlds, which have met only since the 1980s. Undercover supervision was important, although the traditional 'quiet nod' exercised by the Bank of England does not lend itself readily to quantification. In Japan, the ease of control, combined with acute capital shortage during the Meiji restoration and after World War II were powerful arguments, not just for this specific split but for the extensive segmentation in general. The political and cultural pressure radiating from the USA after the war was also important, specifically in the shape of Article 65 of the Securities and Exchange Law from 1948, which restrained commercial banks and securities houses from entering each other's territories. As in the USA, the ownership limit did not apply abroad and securities subsidiaries in New York, London and elsewhere were a popular way to learn the skills which today are needed at home.

Commercial banks

The term 'commercial bank' only applies, strictly speaking, in the USA and the following lines apply foremost to them. The concept also exists elsewhere, although under a different name: 'clearing bank' in the UK and Australia, 'chartered bank' in Canada, and 'city bank' or 'regional bank' in Japan. The philosophy is that a commercial bank borrows and lends, it offers payment and custody services, but abstains from securities underwriting and trading, which is the realm of the investment bank. At first, commercial banks gave short-term self-liquidating loans. But since trade finance and consumer loans alone do not make a large bank, loan maturities were extended and their assortment expanded, for example, to commercial real estate. When banking started losing ground to securitization, and internationalization gained pace, it became obvious that Glass–Steagall had fenced commercial banking into a stagnant if not an outright declining business.

Fortunately, the wording of the Act allowed interpretation and its watering down started in earnest in the 1960s. For example, the Fed passed a tentative ruling in 1962 that Glass–Steagall did not apply abroad. This made it possible for JP Morgan to start acquiring investment banking skills in its London base, and it became a genuine investment bank within a decade. Government securities, municipal bonds, commercial paper, retail broking and mutual fund management were accepted activities by 1996. Corporate bonds and equity also appeared possible as long as they did not constitute a substantial part of activity, whatever that activity then was – assets, revenue or profits. The Fed, with the backing of the Supreme Court, interpreted that when the bank has a good rating, 25 per cent of total revenue was permissible, a generous percentage for most purposes. The possibility to sell life insurance products over the teller ('bancassurance') was the last barrier to remove, and this happened in the shape of the Gramm–Leach–Bliley Act, in November 1999.

> Whether bancassurance is a boon or a curse can be discussed. Against one-stop shopping and cross-selling of products must be put the lessened transparency of a conglomerate. After the Enron, WorldCom and other similar scandals, investors have become wary. Citigroup and JP Morgan lost one-quarter of their market capitalization in two days late July 2002 while Goldman Sachs, a traditional investment bank, did not (Silverman 2002b).

What still remains is to consolidate the regulators and their accounting rules. For example, commercial banks book loans at their historical value while investment banks mark them to market. (Blanden 1995: 24; Grunfeld 1995; Hayes and Hubbard 1990: 99; Silverman 2002a; Spong 1994: 84–85; Taeho 1993: 243)

Internationally, an earlier law which, for a long time constrained banks from opening branches in other locations or states than their own was more damaging. It prevented banks from reaching a size commensurate with the country's size and inherent potential. Regulatory permission for opening new branches is nothing unusual as such. It is practised in most countries to control competition and pre-empt the banks from competing each other into bankruptcy. But control in the USA went deeper than that, reflecting an ideological cleavage between decentralized and centralized government. The modern era was shaped by the McFadden Act in 1927, which allowed branching by national (federally-licensed) banks according to the law of the state where they were headquartered. Midwestern agricultural states were restrictive, while the Eastern Seaboard and California took a more relaxed stand. Holding companies with subsidiaries offered a loophole until 1956 when the Douglas Amendment prohibited holding companies from other states from acquiring banks unless the state law explicitly allowed it. In practice, states formed regional coalitions to keep outsiders, and particularly large money-centre banks, out. The Civil War South was exceptionally successful and sizeable regional banks were created in the Southeast before nationwide branching was allowed in 1994 and 1997 through the Riegle–Neal Act. This made interstate branching possible, both *de novo* and by merger, but also required that a bank office, after one year of operation, must have the ratio of local loans and deposits at least 50 per cent of the average by banks domiciled in the actual state. (Blanden 1995; Lord 1992; 1996; Mikdashi 1998: 71, 217–218; Spong 1994: 152; Taeho 1993: 229–230)

Investment banks

The roots of investment banks are varied. Some are bankers or merchants who started guaranteeing other merchants' bills, others are outgrown brokerages, but most are products of the Glass–Steagall Act. The term 'investment bank' originates from the USA, while 'merchant bank' is used in the UK and 'securities house' in Japan. With the globalization of US investment banking, the term has become a generic concept, however, while in the USA merchant bank has come to mean a bank which risks its own capital in bridge loans and position taking. Small, limited-function investment banks are called 'boutiques'. They thrive on relationships and the quality of work rather than committing their own capital, and necessarily lose the attached income.

From today's perspective, the Glass–Steagall Act may appear a deplorable market imperfection. For the investment banks, it was a godsend because for decades it protected their independence from the money-centre banks. It also gave them the firstcomer advantage internationally. They were free to underwrite equity and debt issues, trade them, arrange mergers and acquisitions, provide bridge loans for buyouts (LBOs and MBOs), develop products, hone skills and gain strength domestically. When international capital markets opened, they were the best and, backed by a home market which still generates two-thirds of investment bank revenue worldwide, went from victory to victory. Entrenched domestic banks, often much smaller but with all possible connections, could not outsmart the American banks which were selective and expensive, but got deals done (Cave 2002).

Although the letter of the law separated commercial and investment banks, the profound difference was and is cultural. A typical commercial bank thinks nationally, has an extensive branch network supported by largely captive customers, staffed by armies of low-paid clerks in a slow-moving bureaucracy. A world-class investment bank, by contrast, thinks globally, has branches only in major finance centres, seldom employs more than 10,000 people, has a steeply differentiated pay scale and mobile employees, may still be a partnership rather than a corporation, and cherishes its flat and entrepreneurial organization. The bulk of business comes from the Fortune 500 or corresponding, and the activity is advising, organizing, underwriting, trading, broking and possibly fund management rather than borrowing and lending. Its greatest weakness used to be the limited capital base, although this has changed with their acquisition by large commercial and universal banks. (Celarier 1997: 53–54; Parsley 1996: 32)

The entry of commercial and universal banks into the field by opening subsidiaries or acquiring existing investment banks has led to a difficult learning and acculturalization process. JP Morgan mastered it, but needed ten years for the task. Many have failed with the leaving of disgruntled bankers who only too often take the choicest customers with them. Great flexibility and tact are needed in integrating operations. When the merging, or at least co-existence, of the two cultures succeeds, the synergy effects can be considerable. Investment bankers get protection from volatile markets, they can use the placing power of the commercial banking arm, benefit from its asset base and (hopefully) high credit standing, and contribute with a ROE which is easily double that of the commercial part, say, 25–40 per cent against 10–20 per cent in the USA. (Celarier 1996b; Fabre *et al.* 1996; Hayes and Hubbard 1990: 113–114)

Private banks

Private banking is sometimes considered a special form of bank or as a banking service in the way of asset management. Both opinions can be justified. Private banking Swiss style grew up from asset management, while the British style started as banking for wealthy individuals. Either way, asset management is the hub around which other private bank services circulate. But today's commercial banks can also be seen as private banks in a democratic mould. A hundred years ago, comparatively few people had an income which permitted saving, and in this sense private banks are a remnant from bygone days, although a remnant which is full of vigour.

A private bank in the original sense is a partnership where the partners have unlimited and joint liability. This is the only accepted definition in Switzerland, and the idea is that people are most likely to exercise due diligence with other people's money when their own property is at stake. Partnerships are not required to publish accounts and cannot therefore solicit deposits from the public either. The question is whether they need to, as they are well known anyway, and a prospective customer may well need recommendation from an existing one to qualify. The weakness of partnerships is their capital base, which can be augmented only by retained earnings and the acceptance of new partners with fresh capital. Information technology in particular has put heavy demands on the ability to invest and forced the closure, acquisition, merger or listing of private banks. Excluding a handful in Switzerland, private banks today are listed or subsidiaries of large commercial and universal banks. (Dullforce 1990; Gapper 1997; Graham 1996a; Hall and Williams 2002; Riley 1998)

Unlimited and joint responsibility of partners, combined with a narrow capital base, makes private bankers cautious and conservative. Many of their customers share these characteristics. Old money is loyal, looks for wealth preservation and discretion, has unsophisticated objectives, and often prefers offshore. It is necessary to know the customer and his/her family; it is a relationship business. It follows that the most precious asset a private banker can have is a dedicated personnel with an average length of service of ten years and more. For example, does the bank know its employees well enough to be sure of their honesty? This dimension may have escaped Americans in the 1970s when they tried, unsuccessfully, to crack the European private bank market. But being more performance-oriented, they have a following among Asian customers. The Swiss believe that it takes at least seven years to build up the business, and that a presence in Switzerland is then essential. The new client, often an entrepreneur, is less loyal, richer, more active in structuring the portfolio, seeks higher returns and is not afraid of taking short-term treasury positions. Asian and Latin investors are not easily converted to discretionary management, while American customers distinguish themselves with a contentment with standard products but an expectation of borrowing facilities, a legacy of the Glass–Steagall. (Bicker 1996: 28, 31, 37, 44; Ehlern 1997: 46–47, 51–52, 66, 84, 110; Harverson 1995; Kochan 1992: 84; Krayer 1998: 127–130; Rodger 1994; 1995c)

Islamic finance

Islamic finance follows the *sharia*, Islamic law, which is based on the Koran. This forbids interest charged by banks and money lenders (*Surah al-Imran*, verses 130–132). The key word is '*riba*' which covers both interest and usury, a difference which arrived to the English language only in the thirteenth century. The analogy with the Medieval church is not far-fetched, since it considered 'certain' interest to be usury and forbade it, but accepted 'uncertain' interest, the trading profit of our time. The Koran's wording seems rather vague to a Western mind, and even in the Islamic world disagreement about interpretation is rampant. At a national level, Iran, Pakistan and Sudan apply strict rules, Southeast Asia is pragmatic, while the Gulf is in-between. Basically each bank has its own religious board for interpretation, which prevents the emergence of a large homogeneous market. (Khalaf 1995; Premchand 2000)

A simple way to disguise interest is to call it a 'management fee', scale it after risk and let it move with markets. Trading profit is the orthodox way because of the inherent risk, however. A bank accepts a deposit on a partnership basis, uses it for trade finance, and splits the net proceeds with the depositor. The next deal necessitates, in principle, a new agreement. It follows that lending is short-term. That requires good liquidity, which is expensive. Long-term loans and bonds are, in practice, ruled out because few investors are willing to wait for five-to-ten years for the proceeds to mature. If the issuer is a public body, it may have difficulty in defining the particular project and still less in calculating the profit. An equity stake can be considered, but it must avoid companies involved in banking, insurance and alcohol, a corollary of ethical investment Western style. Since conglomerates comprise all kind of activity, any net interest earned on unethical activity, deposits included, is subtracted from dividends and paid to charity. Leasing is marginally acceptable if the bank buys the equipment and sells it in instalments. (Bokhari 2000; Dudley 2001; Khalaf 1994a; Taylor 1996)

Islamic banking or not, there is no real Arab marketplace, but banks stick to their home countries. Bahrain boomed in financing Saudi projects in the early 1980s but has since declined as a cost-effective centre. Financial markets where long-term assets are converted into tradable securities and where daily liquidity can be found are basically off-limits, although a blind eye is turned to them in Bahrain, Saudi Arabia and the UAE (Allen 1995a; 1995b; Evans 1992: 60; Shreeve and Timewell 1990). The lack of regulation and, often, also a lender of last resort is devastating, and serious investors go offshore with Citicorp, UBS and similar. London has preserved its traditional role as the foreign capital of Islamic finance, but there the game is played by Western rules. The Bank of England does not authorize Islamic banks, because they do not offer depositor protection or an agreed rate of return – they are not banks in the Western sense. (Hagger 1993: 108; Khalaf 1994b; Rudnick 1992: 24; Whittington 1995)

Islamic banking is an important force in the religion's heartland and among the educated middle class. Its market share in the Gulf, Jordan and Egypt, where it is an optional way of banking, can reach 30 per cent, and Western banks have opened Islamic tellers at their offices. Malaysia has made great efforts to promote the concept. Bank Negara Malaysia, the central bank, has standardized definitions and products. The first Islamic interbank and cheque clearing system was launched there in 1994, the country has the world's first Islamic stock index and is emerging as a centre for Islamic stockbroking, banking and finance. Yet, the market share, end-2000, was only 2.3 per cent of deposits, although the weight of the Chinese ethnic group should not be forgotten. Muslim communities in Europe and the USA have accepted the concept to a degree and a 15 per cent annual global growth rate is estimated. But the stock of Islamic deposits, at $200bn, is still less than 1.0 per cent of the global total (Table 2.2). For the sake of comparison, in the late 1990s, ethical funds were estimated in the USA at $1tr and in the UK at $2.7bn. (Bank Negara Malaysia, correspondence 2002; Drexhage 1998; Khalaf 1994a; 1994b; Kynge 1996; Premchand 2000; Whittington 1995)

Many types of task

Full range

Banks are needed for financial intermediation. They have two core services: funds transfer and lending. In the former, the bank comes in between the payer and the payee through the benefits of the convenience, speed and security of its service. In the latter, it collects deposits where excess funds are available, repackages them and lends where there is a shortage. Bank lending is paralleled by another system where securities replace loans and markets take over the allocative function (Cargill and Royama 1992: 335).

The relative weights of the banking-based and securities-based systems vary from country to country. There has also been a shift from the former to the latter. Banks are heavily regulated, which makes them expensive. Their credit ratings have, at times, been badly bruised, down to Bs. When financial information has become more widely and easily available, disintermediation has followed. Issuance of corporate bonds, instead of bank borrowing, has rechanelled lending more to individuals, small and midsize businesses and very large syndicated company loans. In the USA, four distinct phases have been identified (Baer and Mote 1992: 530–532):

1 Business companies issue commercial paper and banks respond by offering standby credits off the balance sheet, thereby escaping capital adequacy rules.
2 Consumer credit is largely securitized, following the example of government mortgage agencies.
3 A market for commercial loans takes shape.
4 Commercial loans are being securitized through mutual funds and loan-backed credit instruments.

Banking products that are important for individuals are comparatively few: loans (for whatever purpose), instalment credit (often through credit cards) and payment services. Business needs are more varied. Straight loans and fund transfers are the same as in individual banking. Add to these trade finance and numerous corporate finance products such as loan syndication, project finance, standby credits, underwriting, advising in mergers and acquisitions (M&A), financial guarantees, securities and forex trading, fund management, and settlement and custodian services (Gardener and Molyneux 1993: 137). The multitude of tasks becomes clear in the organization chart of a major bank (Figure 5.3).

In profit terms, many of these somewhat esoteric products can be far more lucrative than plain deposit taking and lending (intermediation, interest business). The $2.1bn profit of Nomura in 1987 was indicative, putting the Japanese securities house at the top of the Japanese corporate league with its renowned car makers and electronics companies (Hayes and Hubbard 1990: 274, 265). The figures available about the two largest Swiss banks and cantonal banks are more detailed and shed light on the underlying structures (Figure 5.4).

The revenues are split into three parts: net interest from intermediation, commissions and trading profits. At the big banks they are approximately equal; at the cantonal banks, net interest dominates. In other words, cantonal banks are much more dependent on retail banking. Yet both groups

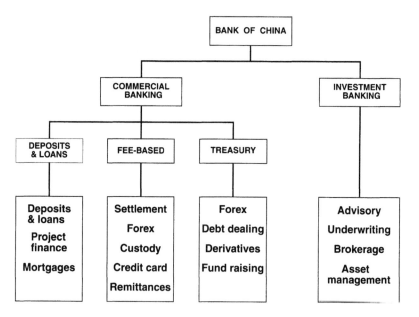

Figure 5.3 Universal bank structure, Bank of China, 2001.

Source: *Euromoney*, September, 2001: 169. Copyright © 2001 of Euromoney Institutional Investor plc, England; used with permission.

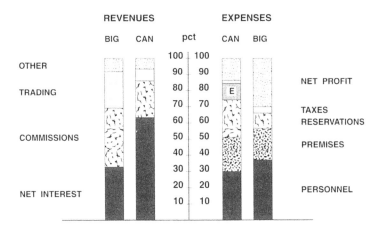

REVENUES   EXPENSES

BIG   CAN   pct   CAN   BIG

E = EXTRAORDINARY

Figure 5.4 Revenues and expenses of the Swiss big banks and cantonal banks, 2000.

Source: Schweizerische Nationalbank 2001: A164–167.

Notes
UBS and Crédit Suisse (CSFB) are classified as big banks.

have extensive domestic branch networks. A retail network is traditionally the foundation of a universal bank, because retail customers, largely individuals but also small businesses, are in many ways captives of banks. They are not too well-informed, avoid risk and may have few alternatives when saving and borrowing. Successful banking strategies can be based on them, as the example of Lloyds TSB in the UK shows. It is one of the four large clearing banks which all aspired to become international banks in the late 1980s, either as retailers or investment banks. After a few years, Lloyds reversed its strategy and kept to domestic retail banking, with excellent results.

For profits, costs are as important as revenues. Personnel and premises weigh heavily but the reasons may vary. In retail banking it is the extensive network manned by hoards of low-salaried clerks; in investment banking it is the high-flyers who take one-half of revenues as salaries and bonuses (Thal Larsen 2002). This dichotomy may also underlie the difference between the big banks and cantonal banks. The shares of premises are about the same, as are the branch networks in absolute terms, but personnel costs take a larger share of revenues at the big banks. The aggregate of personnel and premises cost is 50–55 per cent, also called the 'efficiency ratio', and the rest is, broadly speaking, gross profit. An efficiency ratio of 50 is quite good and only the US banks go below it. In Europe, 70 is considered normal, while Germany's largest universal banks climb up to 80. Their retail operations are also hardly profitable (Lanchner 2000). Gross profits are divided between reservations for bad loans, taxes and net profits. To them come extraordinary items which usually originate from reorganization. Here, taxes are parenthetical. Gross profits are about the same, but their split into reservations and net profit is not. There certainly have been good reasons to make reservations, but their extent is always judgemental. Banking supervision is there to see that the judgement is prudent, but supervisors cannot have the same intimate knowledge of a bank's loan book as the banker.

These rulings are culturally conditioned and intended to smooth matters, which constrains the scope of action. Among them are conventions about the maximum percentage of bad loans considered appropriate and social mores which prevent their sale. The very definition of a bad loan may differ. In the West, a ninety-day delay in interest payment is sufficient. In Japan, the limit is one year and, in China, three years. The sale of collateral may lead to capital gains tax, and a write-off may not be tax deductible. It is the same with reservations. The maximum per year is 1 per cent in China while in Japan it used to be 5 per cent of foreign debt in countries defined by MoF, except for tax relief when it was only 1.5 per cent. Corresponding cultural differences exist between Anglo-American countries, particularly the USA, on the one hand, and the Continent on the other. One bone of contention is hidden reservations. In Anglo-American culture, all assets should be marked to market, to reflect the true situation of the bank. The Continental standpoint is that such practice will lead to unnecessary fluctuation in earnings and in all likelihood strengthen business cycles. When the economy deteriorates, and takes results with it, banks must reduce lending, exactly when it is needed most. Such differences make international comparisons of bank profitability hazardous. They can also be of great practical importance, particularly at mergers and acquisitions. (Baker 1996; Brown Jr. 1994: 175; Cockerill 2000; 2001; Covill 1996a; Evans 1987; Fingleton 1987: 58; Roell 1996: 149)

> The Hongkong and Shanghai Bank Corporation (HSBC) wanted to purchase Marine Midland Bank in Buffalo, NY, in the late 1970s. US banking regulators resisted. One of their arguments was that HSBC did not disclose its true position. It should convert to GAAP, which HSBC found both expensive and unacceptable. Hidden reserves had always been their way of doing business. Regulators agreed; while full disclosure had not been enforced for some small deals, this was a major acquisition. The key regulator was SEC which, by law, has to keep shareholders and investors fully informed. Facing a stonewall, HSBC took its books to a meeting where the discrepancies between its accounting and GAAP were pencilled down and the true position established. It was better than anticipated. At the end of the meeting, the notes were handed in and burned. The acquisition was completed in 1980. Today, the topical notes are printed as a separate section in the annual report. (King 1991: 814, 832)

Returning to the Swiss example, traditional wisdom maintains that Swiss banks are twice as profitable than they report (Koenig 1989: 40). That wisdom, however, is somewhat beside the point. The important fact here is that the revenue from commissions is quite crucial for the banks, and it varies with product and region (Cecchini 1988, cited by Leyshon and Thrift 1992: Table 1). The variance also applies to loan margins, adjusted for maturity and counterparty risk. The following pot-pourri gives a taste of the situation in the mid-1990s. The exact figures may have changed, but the general tenor has not.

- Protected markets, usually domestic, can have excellent profit potential, particularly when compared to international banking. Loan margins in Germany are 0.5–1 per cent over the interbank rate for large firms and 2–3 per cent for smaller ones, against 10 bp for top-quality syndicated loans plus a 5 bp commitment fee elsewhere. (Edwards and Fischer 1994: 141; Iskander 1996; Rose 1994: 16; Spink 1996: 69)
- Project finance, to be paid back from the revenue stream of the project, is riskier and more expensive than a conventional loan, say, 1.0 per cent and over against 0.2 per cent (20 bp) above LIBOR. Regulatory risk in utilities, transportation infrastructure and healthcare in particular can be large (Lapper and Middelman 1996).
- Lending requires own capital and carries a risk. Fund management, by contrast, needs a minimum of own capital and carries practically no management risk. Still, an actively managed fixed-income portfolio commands a fee of 15 bp in the USA (minimum assets, $100m) and 19 bp (minimum assets, £10m) in the UK. The size of portfolios should be observed. With identical sizes the UK might be only 5 bp. Tracker fund fees are perhaps one-fifth of actively managed. (Skorecki 2001; Targett 2001b; Zlotnick 1996: 17)
- Custody is another low-capital activity although competition has depressed fees for US- and UK-based portfolios below 1 bp, whereas the high cost of some emerging markets permits 40–60 bp (Graham 1996b).
- The attached stock lending is more lucrative although risky: 10 bp for US stocks, 25 bp in London, 60–90 bp for German and 75–125 bp for Japanese stocks, and up to 300 bp in some emerging markets (Gapper 1994; Kochan 1993: 113).
- Underwriting of equity is riskier than that of bonds and therefore equity fees are higher, 3–7 per cent in the USA against 1 per cent for investment grade bonds and 3 per cent for junk (Celarier 1996a: 34; Gapper and Cohen 1994; Lewis 1996).
- Underwriting fees for equity are higher in the USA than in Europe where discounts of market price are deeper. The fees are 3–7 per cent and 1–3 per cent, respectively (Gapper and Cohen 1994; Hayes and Hubbard 1990: 214; Lapper 1996; Lewis 1996).

The aim of the game is consequently to establish presence, indeed leadership, in profitable niches, and maintain it. Leadership means that customers contact the bank first and perhaps exclusively. Its view becomes dominant, and knowledge of the product backlog helps in coming to market from windows of opportunity, ahead of competitors. In non-repetitive deals, M&A for example, reputation is important. Niches related to currency and regulation have certain permanence, the rest is transitory. That is particular true in investment banking which is event driven, while commercial banking is more process oriented. Strength in a particular segment comes from a variety of skills and constant alertness is necessary. (Ehlern 1997: 105; Hayes and Hubbard 1990: 81–84)

Some products support each other, offer internal synergies, while others do not. In addition to the products themselves, synergies also arise from common capital, risk management, technology and joint marketing. Brealey and Kaplanis (1994: 51–52, 56) differentiate between twenty-two product categories. To display synergies, they rank banks by category, calculate mean difference in ranking between pairs of categories and arrange the difference in quintiles. The first quintile indicates extensive synergy, and the fifth quintile a limited one. Many product pairs show large synergy. For example, derivative instruments link closely with each other, arranging and dealing have large mutual synergies, and so do underlying instruments and their derivatives. Synergies are so abundant that it is difficult to find clear clusters and, when linked after the first quintile, the proto-clusters gradually form a long-branched chain. There is only one outlier, M&A and portfolio management, which show large synergy only with each other and constitute a very distinct group (Brealey and Kaplanis 1994: 56). The result shows how difficult it is to focus on a consistently profitable segment and indirectly claims that 'Big Is Beautiful', a slogan supported by modern history. When the British equity markets were deregulated in 1986 (the so-called 'Big Bang'), most small firms sold out to large competitors. Few remained independent and none of them has been a success story (Celarier 1996a; Gapper 1997; Riley 1998).

The twenty-two product categories are far too many to be considered here. The solution is to pick up a few proto-clusters which are important, have a strong geographical dimension and offer a fair amount of empirical material that has not been discussed extensively elsewhere in this book. Correspondent banking, lending, underwriting, trading, M&A advising, asset management and custodianship are taken up for discussion.

Correspondent banking

Classic correspondent banking is essentially about fund transfers and trade finance, letters of credit for example. It provides services for banks which lack capacity in a particular geographical region. The basic qualifications of classic corresponding are speed and accuracy in transactions and the willingness to assume associated risks. For both tasks, capital strength is important, because bilateral credit limits and the intra-day credit limits of payment systems can otherwise interfere with timely execution. The balance sheet also affects the ability to raise funds in the markets. Still, the activity is largely fee-based and consequently escapes most of the capital adequacy rules. In addition, a bank having net exports of correspondent services benefits from interest-free compensating balances put at its disposal. This can be a sensitive issue, particularly for US banks, which benefit from the dollar's role as a reserve and trading currency. Correspondent banking is a relatively stable business, because people value relationships and do not like changing clearers. This is the traditional philosophy, while new thinking claims that all products and services must be profitable in their own right. The activity is relatively risk-free which contributes to good profitability, the ROE being at times 30–40 per cent against 15–18 per cent in other services. Trading activities have lately been added to the classic correspondent functions, and the standard investment bank battery is on the way in. It is rather meaningless to try to map correspondent relations. They are available in handbooks and similar, so the problem is not information but the very large numbers and varying intensity of use. A big bank like the former Midland (now HSBC Group), for example, has thousands of correspondents banking with it in London. The total number worldwide used to be 11,000, but most contacts were sporadic and, with the smaller partners, not even reciprocal. (Anon. 1990; Fitzmaurice 1989; Forsyth 1991; Keslar 1987)

Lending – and borrowing

Lending and, previous to it, deposit taking (borrowing) are in many minds the essentials of banking. So it all began, of course, and so it still is in many parts of the world, even in Europe. The lending margin made up 90 per cent of French bank revenues in the mid-1980s and, in Italy, it is still 75–80 per cent. These figures apply to all banks, however, not only the big and internationally well-known ones at which they would probably be lower. Being systemwide, the figures also depend on the definition of 'bank', but that is splitting hairs. The fact remains that figures exceeding 75 per cent are high in our time (Lebeque 1985: 27; Lee 1996a: 140; Moore 1996: 357–358).

Many explanations can be offered, and two appear to have particular validity. The income structure of the country has relevance. Small investors have little alternative to bank intermediation but are their captive customers, while those in higher income brackets have more options (Baer and Mote 1992: 472). Captiveness invites exploitation by offering a low deposit rate in relation to the lending rate. Captiveness does not necessarily arise from poverty alone. It is also the result of regulation. Where mutual funds are banned, private pension plans politically unacceptable, capital markets undeveloped because of high taxation and weak corporate governance and stock exchanges infested with insider trading, savers have little choice. The state may also actively solicit bank deposits by offering tax relief, as happens in France where Crédit Mutuel, Post Office and Caisse d'Epargne offer tax-free, fixed-interest deposits called *Livret Bleu* and *Livret A*, or competitive, but still low, interest rates, as is the case with the Japanese Post Office (Dawkins 1996; Guerrera and Mallet 2002; Jack 1995).

The deposit rate, whether retail, corporate or interbank, is important for international competitiveness. Maximum allowed deposit rates, thought to find their way into low lending rates, were well established in Japan until very recent times and were often quoted as a reason for the international competitiveness of Japanese banks. They undoubtedly were, although, curiously, corresponding rates payable for time deposits in the USA in the period 1935–1980/1986 have not attracted similar comment (Baer and Mote 1992: 504, 515).

How much a deposit rate matters to profitability is more difficult to evaluate, however, because the margin also depends on the lending rate, and the cost of an overstaffed branch network may eat up the better part of the margin. The involvement of the state, foundations or associations does not help either, because the profit motive easily takes a back seat. This was widely the case in the EU in the late 1980s, when ninety-three out of the top 162 banks were not run for commercial profit or to satisfy private shareholders. Not surprisingly, large banks in Europe used to have only half of the American ROE (Celarier 1996a; Gardener and Molyneux 1993: 36; Lee 1997).

Regulation bears on international competitiveness in other ways, too. The minimum capital adequacy ratio of 8 per cent was mentioned in Chapter 2. But it was also mentioned that national authorities can raise and lower it should they feel the need. And they do. When Daiwa Bank was ousted by the US authorities for serious irregularities and thereafter faced punitive rates at the international interbank market, it returned home where the capital adequacy ratio is a paltry 4 per cent.

A more explosive ruling is the minimum reserve deposited interest free at the central bank. Americans even tried to introduce the concept internationally, suggesting that each central bank should impose reserve requirements on their own banks' euromarket activities. The UK and Switzerland opposed, and the idea came to nought (Helleiner 1995: 327; Pilling 2002). The reserve is calculated as a percentage of deposits, and its purpose is to regulate the monetary stock and thereby inflation. It was very common two or three decades ago. For example, the percentage was 12.5 in the UK in 1972, it varied between 12 and 5 per cent in Germany in the late 1980s, depending on the maturity of the deposit, and was 8 per cent for CDs in the USA in 1980. Today, the industrialized West has almost abandoned it. The UK has none. Euroland has 2 per cent for which interest is paid. The USA belongs to a mezzazine layer with 3 per cent, notwithstanding the extensive use of open-market transactions. The transforming world lags by two decades. Russia has 7.5 per cent, and in China banks maintain 13 per cent locally while an additional 5–7 per cent is met on a consolidated basis. (Baer and Mote 1992: 472; Evans 1992: 55–56; Fairlamb 1999; Goldberg and Saunders 1980: 639; Haindl 1991: 154; Roell 1996: 150; Thornhill 1998)

The other regulatory burden, and one of doubtful value, is the deposit insurance premium, to be used for bailing out insolvent banks. The scheme's doubtfulness is due to the fact that available funds are normally insufficient to prevent a severe crisis but still affect competitiveness unfavourably because the premiums, although not excessive, vary with the country. The US rates of 0.21–0.31 per cent and Japanese of 0.12–0.84 per cent, both annually out of deposits, are indicative (Horvat 1998; Spong 1994: 118).

Not unexpectedly, the minimum capital adequacy ratio, reserve requirements and deposit insurance drive banks away from traditional deposit taking and lending. Non-bank competitors benefit correspondingly. General Motors, General Electric and Sears, for example, have better ratings than most banks and make consumer loans faster and cheaper, primarily because they do not need to answer to bank regulators. Car loans was the largest single business of a US bank twenty-to-thirty years ago but has now withered away (Baer and Mote 1992: 479; Chesler-Marsh 1991: 36).

Parallel to the retail market, there is the wholesale market disaggregating into several submarkets such as commercial paper, corporate loans and interbank. The amounts are much larger, customer captivity less and margins thinner. Market transparency is considerably better than at the retail end and actors react more rapidly to emerging opportunities. The top is the interbank market, routinely used for balancing books for the day but also as a source of regular operating capital, albeit of short maturity. For example, Luxembourg-based banks got 75 per cent of their funding in the interbank market in the late 1970s against 40 per cent in the early 1990s, an indication of a change from plain loan booking to deposit taking. The HSBC branch network collected the bulk of Hongkong savings in the 1980s but, rather than lending them to competitors in the local interbank market, transferred surplus funds abroad (Anon. 1993; King 1991: 744).

The London interbank market is structured around the LIBOR (Figure 5.5). At the time we are considering, the British clearing banks and the choicest Swiss, German, French and Dutch banks benefited from the lowest lending rate, 12.5 bp below LIBOR and actually at par with LIBID (London Interbank Bid Rate, for eurocurrency deposits). US banks with ready access to dollar funds seldom came to the market but when it happened it was in large amounts at short notice which drove the rate up. Japanese banks, the large banks in particular, operated aggressively and

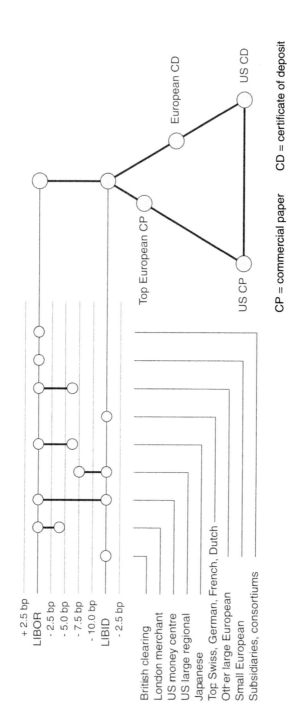

Figure 5.5 **Short-term interest rate structure, 1990.**

Source: Haindl, Andreas, *The Euro Money Market*: Figures 5.1 and 5.2. Haupt, Berne, 1991. Copyright © 1991 of Verlag Paul Haupt, Berne, used with permission.

paid top rates. The structural Japan-premium, 50–100 bp over LIBOR, appeared in mid-August 1995 with Daiwa Bank's debacle in the USA and has persisted once the problems of the banking sector became apparent. 'Other' large Europeans were a heterogeneous group from less recognized banking countries and paid accordingly. Small banks and subsidiaries also paid top rates, the latter because their possible backing by the parent is not founded in law. There were also banks, from Latin America for example, which had no direct access to the market, no matter what they were prepared to pay, and operated through intermediaries. (Baker 1995; Haindl 1991: 150–151; Rafferty 2000)

The interbank market, and LIBID in particular, can be tied to securitized eurocurrency money markets, commercial paper (CP) on the one hand and certificates of deposit (CD) on the other. The lower rates paid for these instruments reflect their better liquidity compared with eurocurrency deposits. The relation is more intimate for CDs than CPs which move comparatively independently from LIBID, at least in the USA (Haindl 1991: 152).

The discussion can also be taken to a more aggregated level and correlate the interbank market by regional and/or economic groupings with corresponding claims of, at most, one year maturity (Figure 5.6). High reliance on short-term funds can be interpreted as a sign of a developed banking system with a constant balancing of accounts, while low percentages provide evidence of borrowing by the real economy, like plants and infrastructure. Other interpretations are also possible.

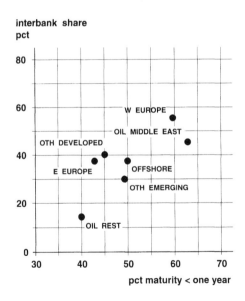

Figure 5.6 Interbank share versus maturities up to one year, December 2000.
Source: *BIS QR* June 2001: Table 9A.

At the country level, the variation becomes larger and explanation more difficult, particularly outside the BIS reporting area. It is partly a question of proper classification and partly a country's economic and political credentials. For example, Lebanon's and Liberia's seats among offshore centres are only conditionally justified and might well suit Liechtenstein and Malta better, although these two are now classified as developed (West) and developing (East) Europe, respectively. The sophistication of Mexico's economy is well ahead of Angola and Libya (other oil-producing countries – 'Oil Rest') and in need of long-term funds. Overambitious governments may enforce development with the help of short-term money. Small and weak economies or political pariahs only have access to short-term interbank money. And so on.

The creditworthiness of the borrower adds additional taste to the soup. This is the classic case of asymmetric information where the borrower is better informed about risks than the lender, a strong case for the house bank system. The ratings of credit agencies are useful, and in the interbank market Fitch IBCA, specializing in banks, comes into its own. In addition, there may be regulatory rulings about the acceptability of borrowers. In the USA, federally-licensed (national) banks can hold only investment grade corporate debt, the appropriate company list being available at the Office of the Comptroller of Currency (Baer and Mote 1992: 504). All diligence notwithstanding, things occasionally go wrong. The loan needs to be renegotiated and possibly the whole company restructured. Such risk is less in the interbank market than in conventional non-bank lending, but the former is also less profitable. It leaves the practitioner more exposed to interest rates and does not give a proper deposit base. There are no free lunches in the intermediation business.

Underwriting

The management and underwriting of securities issues is a major source of banking revenue. Public bodies are, in general, larger issuers than corporations, but handle much of the issuance themselves, through regular auctions, for example, and keep fees low through their negotiating power. Although issuance is lucrative, it is also cyclical and somewhat unpredictable. In the private sector, upcycles arise for similar reasons as physical investment and are often their direct reason. The public sector borrows in downcycles, which counteracts the private sector. But it also has a large 'random' element which is not linked with economic activity as such. The financing needs of the German reunification and 'Reaganomics' in the USA are examples. The privatization of public-owned businesses in Europe was triggered off more by ideology and empty government coffers than substandard profitability.

It is reasonable to assume that domestic issues, whether bonds or equity, are arranged by banks domiciled in the issuing country. This is because they have the best local placing power. Issues directed to international investors are a different story. Now the placing power within the largest investor countries becomes decisive, and their banks are certain to be included. But banks of the issuing country are also part of the syndicate if for no other reason than pressure by authorities and sheer courtesy. To the extent investors prefer their own currencies, the currency of denomination reveals something about the future underwriters (*BIS QR* Aug. 1997: 26–27). The preference is not guaranteed, of course, as interest rate levels, rates of exchange and expectations about their changes play a role. As sales are concentrated in a few countries and currencies, the nationalities of lead managers and coordinators soon become repetitive and the actual banks are selected because of their reputation from previous deals and marketing clout (Figure 5.7).

At the top of the league is a handful of US investment banks, the so-called 'bulge bracket'. They call themselves global coordinators ('bookrunners') and use the book building method. Competitionwise, this means that European banks, Deutsche Bank and Crédit Suisse First Boston (CSFB) excepted, have been pushed to a regional role. The Japanese are there already. It is not simply a question of relative placing power. American investment banks are simply the best because they are unashamedly meritocratic and take great care to recruit only the best talent (Lee 1993: 28–33; Rawal 1997).

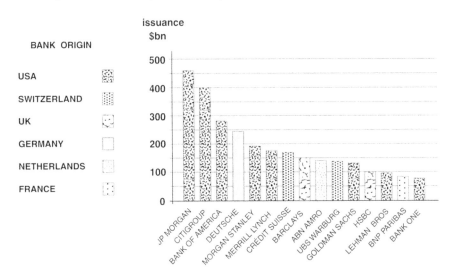

Figure 5.7 Leading debt arrangers, April 2000 to March 2001.

Source: *Euromoney* June 2002: 122.

Note
The rank order of equity underwriting would be different but ten of the fifteen underwriters would be the same (*Investment Dealers' Digest*, 8 January 2001: 54; as quoted in *sigma* 7/2001: 17).

They have won much business by being more prepared than others to organize themselves by industry instead of geography. The reason is obvious. Companies and industries are increasingly global. Buying German equity implies that the investor believes in German competitiveness against other industrial nations. The belief may hold for some industries but not others. Picking the winners in Germany only means concentration on relatively few stocks, instead of diversification as the portfolio theory wants it, and possibly overlooking foreign companies with whom the German manufacturers are in head-on competition all over the world. Specialization by industry, in research, sales and trading, avoids this pitfall. More about investing follows, in the context of asset management.

Another bulge bracket advantage, and one which is far more difficult to neutralize, is the size of the domestic US market. There is only one other market that offers an even modest comparison: the UK. How the Euroland will develop remains to be seen. The home market advantage has allowed the bulge bracket to build up global distribution and trading capability and also to maintain it in adverse local conditions.

Although the rule of issuing and investor and currency country holds in the main, a world-class bank will, nevertheless, be competitive in many surroundings. It may have operated in a host country so long that it has become part of the local banking scene. It is represented all over the world, and countries lacking strong local banks are indifferent to the nationality of the lead manager. It may have strong cultural ties with several countries, the banks domiciled in the former British Empire being the most conspicuous example. Sometimes it is the result of a merger or joint venture.

Crédit Suisse Holdings belongs to the last group. Its base is in Switzerland, but in 1978 it acquired a 40 per cent stake in First Boston, a Massachusetts bank, through a London-based joint venture which it controlled. The subsidiary was renamed CSFB and is equally at home in the USA, the UK and the Continent. In the mid-1980s, pound sterling was an issuing currency to be reckoned with, the Swiss central bank had already taken a relaxed attitude towards Swiss franc issues, Japanese companies were expanding vigorously and issued convertible bonds in the international market, while the reunification of Germany with its monstrous financing needs was still in the future. It was most natural then that the Group was able to win mandates in most of the major issuing countries and currencies plus Australia (Figure 5.8).

Whereas the Crédit Suisse case gives an aggregated picture, Deutsche Telekom's first privatization tranche in November 1996 gives an idea of the geographical complexity of a large issue. Altogether twenty-three banks participated in the underwriting syndicate, many in several capacities. The tranche was estimated to command an approximate price of $10bn, possibly too much to be placed in Germany alone. Being one of the largest telecommunication companies in the world, Telekom was

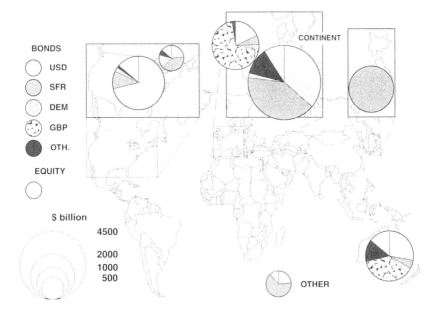

Figure 5.8 New issues by CSFB/Crédit Suisse, 1987.
Source: *Annual Report* 1987.

likely to attract wide interest and a global issue was considered prudent (Figure 5.9). It was decided that the coordinating team should include at least one German bank to handle relations with the issuer and the owner (government). In addition to fees, the bank would gain valuable experience. Since it would have been difficult to exclude either of Germany's two then leading universal banks, Deutsche Bank and Dresdner Bank, both were invited. Although both had investment bank subsidiaries in London, it was still important to also source the skills of a US investment bank. Goldman Sachs, renowned for its team spirit and egalitarian (everything is relative) culture, was given the mandate. The government and Telecom both had their advisers, CSFB and the British N.M. Rothschild, respectively. The placement was organized geographically with Germany, the UK, the Rest of Europe, the Americas and Asia, each having its own team headed by up to three lead managers and two-to-eight underwriting members. Germans were represented in each team. The actual selling was done by dozens of banks. Retail customers were given preferential allocation and a discount of about 1.5 per cent (Covill 1996b: 35).

The issue was oversubscribed by retail customers alone. Thereafter book building to 3,700 institutional investors began, which raised oversubscription sixfold and catalysed a 20 per cent increase of the tranche. Rationing was still necessary, but the final allocation, understandably,

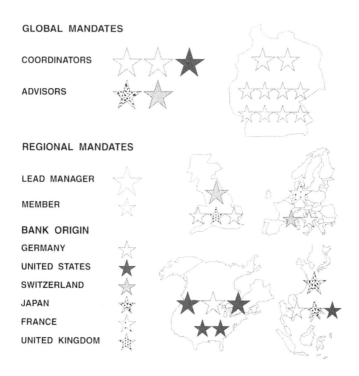

Figure 5.9 Deutsche Telecom IPO underwriting syndicate, 1996.

Source: Fisher *et al.* 1994.

Note
The syndicate was formed in 1994. At that time S.G. Warburg and Kleinwort Benson, lead manager and syndicate member in the UK, respectively, were owned by British interests.

followed broadly preliminary quotas. Germany got 67 per cent (40 per cent retail), Americas 14 per cent, UK 8 per cent, the Rest of Europe 6 per cent and Asia 5 per cent, roughly in proportion to the number of underwriters (Covill 1996b: 36). In view of the oversubscription, it would appear that global placing had been superfluous. The conclusion was premature. The first tranche was planned to be followed by two others, too much for the domestic market alone. Now the path had been opened to the global marketplace.

Trading

Information about the geographical aspects of trading has certain gaps. Trading at exchanges, particularly of equity and derivatives, is well documented. OTC trading of derivatives and forex is surveyed every third year. The weak link is debt. Trade associations which collect the statistics are more interested in the breakdown by currency and instrument than the location of trades. Location can, indeed, also be difficult conceptually, because trading is screen-based and the trading book need not stay put geographically.

The first question is about the location of trading desks. Since the activity is screen-based, one centre per central time zone should be sufficient. It is certainly desirable, because risks can be controlled better when they are centralized. Administrative scale economies are also possible. In practice, however, local regulations may enforce the maintenance of local units. The authorities wish to have the possibility of intervening, and that is much easier when the unit is within their jurisdiction. The centralization of trading differs from the origination of the business, which is best done close to customers. For example, in the mid-1990s, Citicorp had six forex traders in two European centres, London and Frankfurt, against thirty-nine traders in seventeen centres eight years earlier. JP Morgan concentrated all its euro trading in London and closed desks in Paris, Milan and Madrid. It followed that remaining local branches were used as marketing outlets with price discovery in the local currency only (Graham and Timewell 1997: 8).

Suppose that centralization has been taken to its logical end, one trading centre per central time zone, and that trading is global. There are three organizational alternatives: to close books at the end of the day, to transfer them to the next time zone, or to keep the trading desk open twenty-four hours a day. Closing the books in the evening keeps the lines of responsibility clear and simplifies taxation. But if the same position is reopened next morning, transaction fees will be doubled. Possibilities during the night have also been missed. Therefore, the transfer of books to the next time zone tends to be preferred. It has two subcases. Either the receiving zone is allowed, but not required, to close the positions but not open new ones ('defensive trading'), or it has full discretion over the trading book, which is essentially global. Round-the-clock opening avoids these problems but becomes expensive and is justified only where activity is intense. The common weakness of all transfer is the difficulty of allocating profits and losses between locations and dealers.

Full discretion sounds dramatic, but need not be so. It will be recalled that trading in instruments which originate from a specific time zone will, under normal conditions, be most intensive during the business hours of that particular zone. The reason is that relevant news is mostly created there. It follows that dramatic changes in open positions during the business hours of other time zones are the exception rather than the rule. Instrument sensitivity to news from the 'home' zone need not be identical though. It would appear that equities and government bonds are sensitive. Forex is probably less so. It reacts to central bank and government policy measures, but since its price is a ratio of two currencies this blurs the relation. Seriously globalized instruments like the dollar and US treasuries, which are traded round-the-clock by the worldwide financial community, should be most responsive to off-hour news.

The corporate solutions vary. Different internal structures, instrument portfolios, office patterns, executive personalities and temporal fads all play a part. Our empirical data are scanty and mostly from the late 1980s/early 1990s when global trading was properly established. Defensive trading appeared to be in vogue. In the late 1980s, Nomura had separate dealing books in New York, Tokyo and London. At the end of the day a centre passed its book to the next location with strict instructions for defensive trading. Citicorp also passed orders from one time zone to the next. At Bankers Trust, the currency swap book was passed around international offices. An unnamed bank divided its New York forex book between several Asian centres in a temporally staggered fashion in the late 1990s. The pass-on technique may not be suitable for localized currencies, however, because the expertise is only available locally. Some financial institutions kept their forex dealing rooms open twenty-four-hours a day from Sunday night to Friday night. Those not on duty slept with a mini-Reuters by their side in case a call came in the night. HSBC's treasury and capital markets dealing room in Hongkong follows this philosophy today. (Agnes 2000: 360–361; Harverson 1992; Hayes and Hubbard 1990: 281; Humphreys 1987; Kibazo 1990; Langdale 2001: Figure 11.4)

There is a tendency among bankers to specialize in specific currencies, home country currency in particular. As international investors prefer strengthening currencies, bankers' fortunes shift accordingly. Therefore, it is desirable to have skills in several currencies, and this is what differentiates large and small banks. The other differentiating factor is the capability to accept risks. The size of the risk has segmented the market by the size of the dealer. A small bank lacks the name, credit standing and market muscle to run a cost-efficient forex operation alone and relies on large banks, although the coming of electronic trading has radically lessened the dependency. There is also a difference between commercial and investment banks, where a dichotomy exists. Commercial banks offer keen rates for smaller trades, valued by company treasuries which need competitive pricing and the smooth processing of many small deals. Investment banks, by contrast, are ready to explain the intricacies of the market, which becomes expensive but is valued by fund managers. (Adams 1997; Crowe 1995; Fitzmaurice 1990; Gawith 1995b)

Creditworthiness is a key aspect in forex. There are banks routinely settling trades of $1bn and more, per day, with a single partner, and the exposure can last for days, because even spot trades need not settle earlier than the second business day. For such short maturities, the rating of commercial paper is the appropriate benchmark, and what it leaves in the air is covered by plain trust, reflected in the mutual credit lines which market participants grant to each other and which they enjoy from payment systems.

Scale economies find their expression in market concentration. Comparatively few banks are responsible for a large share of the business. In major centres, with hundreds of banks, the top twenty-five or so account for three-quarters of the turnover, and the top five gobble up 44 per cent of the global business. The source does not give their identity but Citicorp, JP Morgan Chase, HSBC, Deutsche Bank and UBS Warburg are good candidates. The HSBC Group alone accounted in one year for over 5 per cent of the global forex market. From a geographical perspective, national biases come well to the fore (Figure 5.10). (*BIS F* 1996: Table F–1; *Euromoney*, May 1996: 60; Fairlamb 1997: 69; Gawith 1995a; Oakley 2002)

M&A advising

If underwriting is cyclical and at times unpredictable, so are mergers and acquisitions. They also respond to economic cycles and are influenced by the political climate, that is, regulation and prevailing mood. Periods of

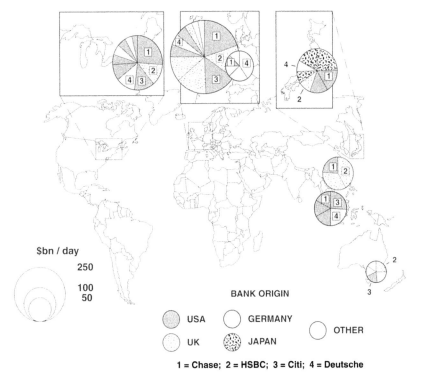

Figure 5.10 The largest forex banks in some major centres, 1996.

Source: Higgins 1996: 29.

Notes
Switzerland and France are not in the survey. Mitsubishi Bank and Bank of Tokyo recorded separately.

intense activity tailgate severe overcapacity, deregulation (legislative or administrative), and easing of financial controls, and are triggered off industrywise by high-profile deals. In friendly deals, the participants may wish to be valued by impartial outsiders. In hostile deals, the aggressor needs a financial war chest and expertise in timing and pricing the bid. The offer must be rejected on objective grounds, and the defendant consequently needs an impartial opinion of its true (higher) value, possible financial means to buy back the aggressor's stake, or as an ultimate measure a friendly acquirer (a 'white knight') committed to running the company with a minimum of disturbance. The participants cannot have all the necessary expertise in-house but rely on external advice, usually provided by banks. Three-quarters of M&As worldwide are also done with advisory help (*The Global M&A Guide to Advisory Services* 1996/1997: 34).

The size of the M&A market has a distinct geographical and cultural dimension. Deals are commonplace in the Anglo-American, securities-oriented culture, while they are more rare in the banking-based Continental atmosphere, and almost non-existent in Japan. Superficially, Japan may look attractive because company market capitalization is often lower than the cash on the balance sheet. What is hiding behind this front is another matter because public disclosure is minimal. But this is also beside the point because there are powerful social mores involved. Equity stakes are taken to strengthen life-long relationships and are not easily broken. Smaller companies are often family-controlled, which restrains deals. The paternalistic relationship between employer and employees does the same: one does not sell people. Payment by shares is subject to two-thirds majority vote on both sides and a hostile bid must, therefore, be made in cash. There is also a stigma attached to hostile bids and few Japanese institutions want to advise them. When deals are made, nevertheless, the advising is done almost free, on a relationship basis. (Lucas 1996; P.A. 2000; Plender 2001)

More legalistic institutional barriers exist on the Continent. In Germany, hostile acquisitions are held in check by the small number of listed companies, bank shareholdings in many of them, and their use of proxy votes, up to 55–60 per cent of the total. The labour legislation also wipes away much of the rationalization motive, because it is forbidden to shed labour in the context of a merger or acquisition. Banks prefer to arrange matters behind the scenes, which has led to accusations of poor corporate governance and the neglect of shareholder value. Similar obstacles, fortified with cross shareholdings, characterize much of Continental Europe. Dutch in particular are extremely well isolated against hostile bids. In France the regulatory body can decide whether the offered price is adequate. There also used to be a social stigma attached to being acquired, an indirect admission of bankruptcy. That, however, has changed since big, very diversified companies have realized that they cannot be champions in every market and started shedding their peripheral parts. This bears some resemblance to the Anglo-American culture, which sees hostile bids as a useful whip for disciplining complacent executives and boards. Logically, the main potential for M&A business is there. (Betts and Hargreaves 2001; Bowley 1997; Edwards and Fischer 1994: 112, 162, 193; Fleming 1999)

The data relate to completed deals and are arranged by target country (Figure 5.11). This slants the fee-generating potential somewhat, because success, whether in aggression or defence, is supposed to generate more fees than failure. There is no information about successful defences, while successful aggressors are mostly Americans and Europeans (Green and Meyer 1997: Table 1). The latter aspect may have significance in cross-border deals unless the aggressor employs a bank in the target country. Since 70 per cent of the deal value is domestic, this is not a serious shortcoming. The figure is highly revealing. The USA constitutes over one-half of the worldwide market with the UK following around the 10 per cent mark. No other country rises above the 5 per cent level, or even approaches the 10 per cent mark in any of the screened years.

The fact that the USA is such a large M&A market means that US banks are dominant in the business, and Goldman Sachs, Merrill Lynch and Morgan Stanley appear to excel themselves year after year. However, bigger is not always better in M&A. The quality of the work is the key issue, and quality is easily equated with a long-standing relationship

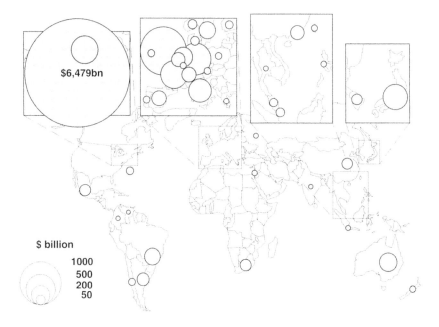

Figure 5.11 Completed M&A by target country, average of 1997–2001.

Source: Courtesy of IFR/Securities Data, London.

between the advised and the adviser. This makes it possible for small boutiques to survive and even prosper, which makes them attractive takeover targets when large but bureaucratic banks try to penetrate the segment. Their weakness of boutiques is that, without a large capital base for the attached underwriting and bridge loans, they must pass this part of the business to larger competitors (Denton 1996).

The discussion can be taken a few steps further in the analytical direction. This is all the more important because the traditional pie chart does not allow too much detail. Therefore, the deal value is related to GDP, to arrive at M&A intensity, and cross-border deals are given as a percentage out of the total (Figure 5.12). The result is displayed as bar diagrams rather than maps because a diagram allows the countries to be arranged into groups. These groups are purely impressionistic, as are their titles, without a shade of numerical stringency (cf. Figure 2.3), and many of the details can be challenged. Still, there is logic and order. M&A intensity is lowest in Asia and highest in the Anglo-American culture, as suggested above. Latin countries are closer to Asia than Anglo, probably because there is not so much to buy. After all, it is the listed companies which are the most exposed and largest targets. Among Continental countries, the variance is large and if anything general can be said it is probably that all the intensive countries are small.

Cross-border shares are a different story. In Asia they are low, as expected, but the same also applies to the USA and Latin Europe. In Asia, the cultural paradigm must hold. The USA is so large that the scant 20 per cent share there is actually quite a lot. Latin Europe must be seen against Germanic Europe, where cross-border deals are twice as important. Can it be that northern Europe is more open to international influence than southern Europe? Or is it that the industrialized, rich north has more interesting companies to buy? Or can it be that the US business establishment, which is responsible for so much deal making, is predominantly of northern stock and feels more comfortable among its own kind? All these explanations, and some others, appear possible and each may contain a grain of truth. The Empires rest on two assumptions: that former colonies still lag in economic development and are not capable to make mergers and acquisitions even domestically, and that former colonial powers still dominate their economies which becomes apparent, among other areas, in mergers and acquisitions. Such speculations can be used as a starting point for a serious study. In this context it is sufficient to record the greatly varying propensity for cross-border deals.

Asset management

Asset management and fund management are widely used as synonyms. Here the stand is taken that fund management is a narrower concept, comprising only financial assets while asset management also includes

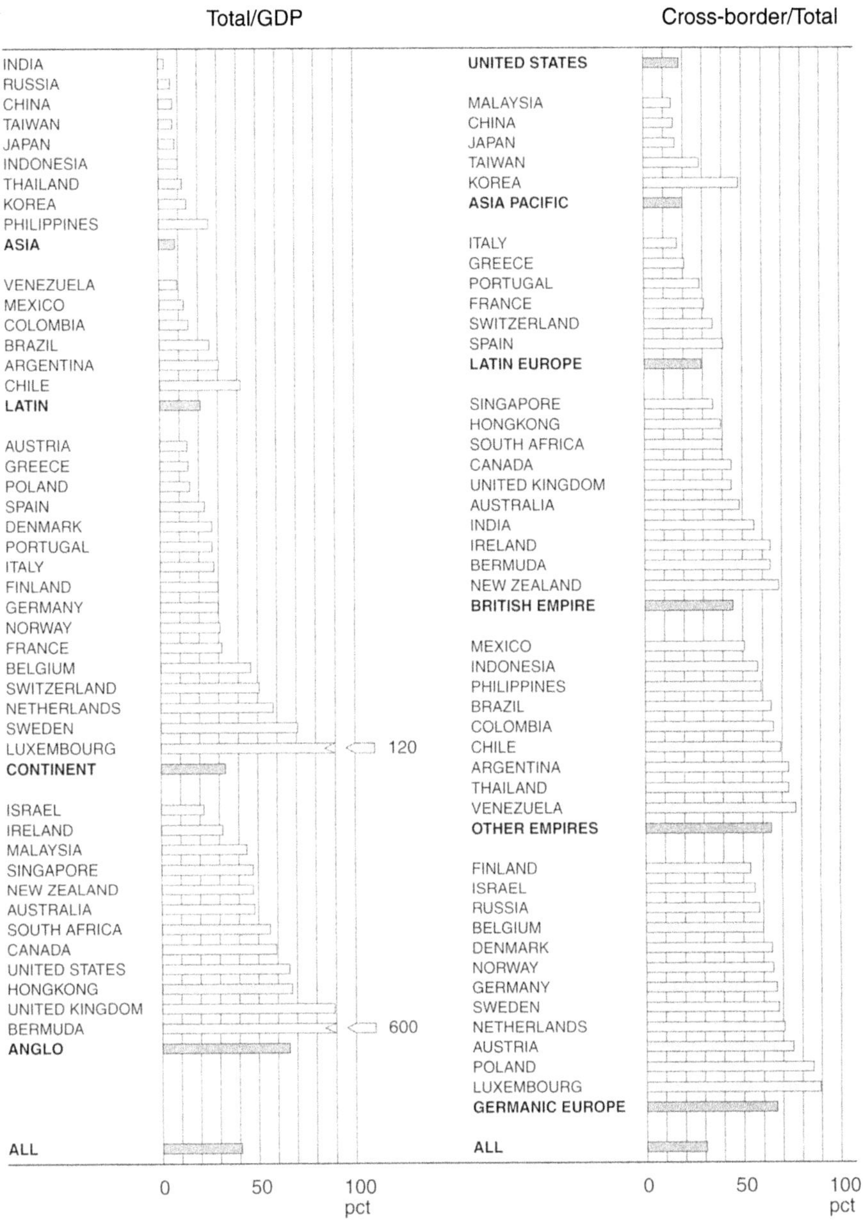

Figure 5.12 M&A intensity and cross-border share by target country, average of 1997–2001.

Source: Courtesy of IFR/Securities Data, London.

Note
Overall entries ('All') calculated as country averages, otherwise the USA would dominate.

non-financial assets, for example real estate which is popular at insurance companies and is often part and parcel of trusts. Commodities would be another possibility, although not for insurers. The attraction of these alternative assets is that they do not correlate closely with securities. In line with the general approach of this book, most of what follows will be about fund management.

Underwriting and M&A are cyclical and subject to political shocks. Fund management is their direct opposite, providing a steady stream of income. Its other attraction is that very little own capital is needed, offering scope for ROE in the 20–30 per cent range. A fund manager's task is to allocate the funds at his/her disposal so that customer criteria for yield and risk are met and perhaps exceeded. This suggests the use of economic criteria in selecting the manager, for example Global Investment Performance Standards (GIPS). The idea originates from the USA and is intended to show the performance of 'composites', portfolio groups with similar investment objects, by disclosing the tenth percentile, the median and the ninetieth percentile. In reality, many management charters are given as much on the basis of relationship as performance. It is less irrational than it appears. It is impossible, in a constantly changing world, to strike an objective balance between yield and risk, and individual funds seldom outperform the market for more than a few years. (Harverson 1995; O'Barr and Conley 1992; Riley 2000)

Customers are organizations and individuals who lack the necessary skills, or time, or realize that scale economies do not make in-house management worthwhile. Pension funds and life insurance companies are important customers in the UK, as are wealthy individuals on the Continent. Small investors can participate in certain financial sectors such as government bonds only through mutual funds and similar because of the high nominal values of instruments. A rule-of-thumb in the industry is that the threshold for economic in-house management is about $1bn, and only $15bn promises good returns. On the other hand, there is also a widespread consensus among hedge fund managers that a fund exceeding $1.5bn becomes unwieldy managerially and loses the ability to exploit emerging opportunities rapidly, which is essential for above average results. (Gapper 1995; Gawith 1995a; Kay *et al.* 1994: 13–14; Zlotnick 1996: 16)

The fundamental approaches of fund management are 'top-down', where macroeconomics dominate, and 'bottom-up', where undervalued stocks irrespective of country come to the fore. The dominant opinion is that allocation between asset classes, and countries and regions, is the most important decision of the year. Over 90 per cent of the performance is achieved there, in the allocation and timing, stock picking is less important. Top-down can be played actively by doing extensive research, or passively by tracking an index. Bottom-up, by contrast, is always an active strategy. Pictet et Cie., the leading Swiss private bank, uses stock picking in

Eastern Europe where sectors and companies are not yet too numerous and finds that intimate knowledge of company histories is a considerable advantage. The choice between active and passive strategies comes down to the time perspective, customer preference and fund manager personality. Active management can be very rewarding in the short term but its value in a longer time perspective is less certain. A seasoned Swiss banker claims that it is practically impossible to exceed 5 per cent interest in real terms in the long run. The fund manager may also face restrictions in his/her choice. Some originate from customers and some from regulators. There are two schools of thought: the prudent person rule, essentially sound judgement, and the rulebook. The UK, the Netherlands and Belgium follow the former and Germany, France and Denmark the latter, for example. The EU as a whole appears to tilt for the rulebook. These different philosophies, along with the availability of instruments, currency risk, and liabilities play a role, and the blend of instruments and regions may differ drastically between countries (Figure 5.13). (AH 2002; Bedford 1998; de Boerr 1989; Ehlern 1997: 205; Kay *et al.* 1994: 26; Krayer 1998: 127–130; Putnam 1996/1997: 55; Vortmüller 2001: 60)

Looking by type of instrument, equities might group into US, European, Japanese and emerging markets, and fixed income would be US treasuries, blue chip corporate bonds, non-US corporate bonds and global high-yield bonds. This classification has an explicit geographical dimension and is preceded by a decision about the regional units and their blend. Countries appear the natural choice if for no other reason than currency risk (Ehlern 1997: 215). Regional groupings such as EU and Euroland have blurred but not invalidated this truth.

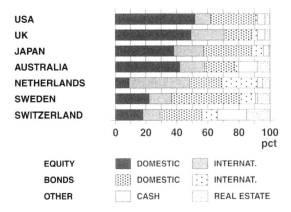

Figure 5.13 Pension asset allocation in major markets, 2000.
Source: Maclaren 2001: 9–16.

Among European equity managers, 75 per cent preferred sectoral and 10 per cent country indices in 2000. Three years earlier, the proportions had been 20 per cent and 50 per cent, respectively. In a regression analysis, sectoral effects gained the upper hand in mid-1998 and had a weight of 5 against country effects of 3 in late 2000 (Tsatsaronis 2001).

The proper blend is influenced by the trade-off between yield and risk, influenced by the correlation between countries. The USA constitutes the baseline because it is generally seen as the motor for other industrialized countries. Most equity markets, particularly those in neighbouring countries, move broadly in step, but not consistently enough to be of practical value. Equity is more capricious than bonds, and a link which functions one day need not hold the next. Market volatility itself may matter. Large markets are correlated better in periods of high than low volatility, and the volatility is normally three times greater during New York trading hours, probably because of the dissemination of relevant news. To attain maximum freedom from such linkages, one must go global. Japan has shown most individuality among the large markets. Emerging if not outright exotic markets are still a safer bet but fragmented and even as a group too small for efficient diversification. One must also be selective. Russia correlates too well with Dow Jones. Brazil is good because of its relative size, liquidity and openness. The Chinese market correlates poorly with the rest of world but the B-sector open for foreigners is quite small and illiquid. (Abken 1991: 17; Barrett 1988; Koshci and Bagramov 1997: 3; Page 1997; Vortmüller 2001: 59)

The alternative strategy is to be an index tracker. This may not be the first choice for a bank but in practice they are important trackers. For example, Barclay's Global Investors with $801bn of assets under management is the largest tracker fund in the world. Globally, trackers manage $2.3tr or some 6 per cent of institutional funds, although the percentage varies tremendously between countries (Table 2.3). Another source puts it at 35 per cent in the USA, 25 per cent in the UK but only 5 per cent or so on the Continent. Tracker funds are a phenomenon of the past ten years and their popularity is at least partly due to managerial problems at bulging public funds, where modestly paid staff are about to be swamped by the daily influx of millions of dollars. The performance is, by definition, average or maybe less. There is, namely, an inbuilt weakness in a tracker's target, to follow the index. When a share goes up in price its weight in the index increases and necessitates purchase. When it goes down the opposite reasoning applies. With bonds the mechanism is slightly different. When more bonds are issued the issuer's ability to service the debt weakens. But larger outstandings mean an increased weight in the index and enforce purchase. The fund is condemned to buy high and sell low. Otherwise, it is quite undramatic. When errors are made they mostly originate from changes in index components. A hybrid fund has a passively managed core and actively managed satellites. (Capon 1997; O'Barr and Conley 1992; Skorecki 2001; Targett 2001a; 2001b)

Geographical information about fund management is very approximate, being based on the domiciles of managers or their holding companies (Blattner *et al.* 1996: 35, 90). Banks and brokers are an important group with a blend of organic and purchased units on their roster. For example, the largest UK fund managers are foreign-owned: Mercury Asset Management by Merrill Lynch and Phillips & Drew Fund Management by UBS (Cooper 1998). Then there are independent specialized managers such as the US group Fidelity with units all over the industrialized world, or Calpers (California Public Employees' Retirement System). Added to that comes in-house management. The largest managers are huge, internationally active organizations with operational units in several locations, some carefully chosen, others a historical legacy.

> Deutsche Bank has three management units, one in London, one in New York and one in Frankfurt. UBS covers the globe with eight units in Zurich, London, New York, Chicago, Bahrain, Singapore, Hongkong and Tokyo. Barclay's Global Investors is headquartered in San Francisco, the traditional centre of US west coast, although it gets 40 per cent of funds from outside the USA. Goldman Sachs Asset Management has a logical geographical setup: US debt and equities in New York and Florida, European equities, global debt and forex in London, Japanese equities in Tokyo, Asian ex-Japanese equities in Singapore, emerging markets in London, Singapore and New York. Shenyin & Wanguo Securities Co., the largest securities company in China, has its fund management unit in Singapore. (Capon 1998/1999; de Prati 1998: 44, n. 64; Targett 2001b; www.ubs.com)

These examples suggest that large, well-known finance centres are the choicest locations. One reason is research, which benefits from local expertise, gauging the sentiment of the market and the credibility of information; and timeliness, tantamount to same time zone. Taxes and estates are also best handled locally, while trust needs another type of expertise and is centralized. It can also be rephrased: proximity to the market applies in wholesale management and proximity to customers at the retail end. Shifting to the numerical paradigm, statistical analysis suggests that the attraction of a country as an asset management location is positively affected by high interest rates, share of managers' own capital and banking secrecy. Taxes, commission fees and political stability escape estimation, as does reputation. (Blattner *et al.* 1996: 47; Ehlern 1997: 215, 251–252)

Considering the vagueness of locational information, Figure 5.14 can be reproduced unchanged from this book's first edition. The total assets are allocated to the parent's home country and the share reportedly managed abroad is indicated as a segment. The concentration of fund management in a handful of countries is as peaked as that of institutional investors (Figure 2.8). The USA and Japan are the largest individual bases, as can be expected. The UK is neck-to-neck with Switzerland but cannot match Euroland. Here the difference between assets originated and those managed becomes apparent. Switzerland cannot compete with the UK, which is over ten times larger, as an originator but it can meet the challenge as a manager. The Netherlands is much larger than Belgium, thanks to its pension funds, while Italy is marginal, quite in line with its meagre institutional assets. Offshore centres and Luxembourg play no visible role, ostensibly because their funds are parts of organizations domiciled elsewhere. The tiny principality of Liechtenstein is comparable to Spain.

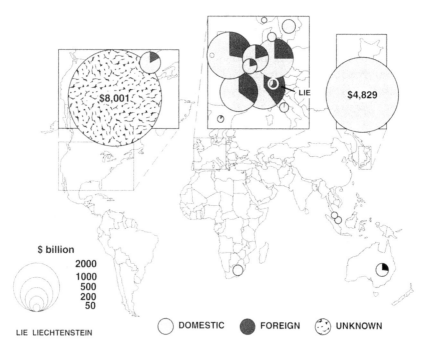

Figure 5.14 Assets under discretionary management, 1995/1996.

Sources: *Nelson's Dictionary of Investment Managers* 1996: II 4931–4932; Sirius 1996.

Note
US fund managers in *Nelson's Directory* (1995) are made comparable with the 250 non-US managers listed by InterSec Research Corp. (Sirius 1996) by applying InterSec's cut-off point ($7,765m) and thereafter excluding all funds which explicitly or obviously have a non-US parent. About 200 US managers remain.

Switzerland has appeared on these pages several times as an important banking and asset management centre. Considering its population base, five million, and the fact that it is not a plain booking centre, the role is simply exceptional. The standard explanation is the country's political and economic stability, banking secrecy and operational efficiency. It has been an appreciated refuge in a volatile and insecure world. The return on assets left for management may have been mediocre, but for clients who prefer safety to earnings it has been sufficient. That status has not come overnight. Its roots are in the First World War when Switzerland and the Netherlands were the only countries in Europe which maintained gold parity intact. The country developed its first banking law in 1934 which, among other things, codified the customary banking secrecy to better protect foreign depositors who were persecuted for race or political opinion. During the Second World War, the Swiss franc kept its value and was freely convertible. Switzerland was also almost the only free market for gold, a service which later on has been equated with money laundering. Trust in the country's currency and its banking system originates from those days. After the war, foreign money flowed in and, although it was invested mostly abroad, the flow was so large that it threatened to ruin the country's export industries. There was a period in the 1970s when the central bank imposed a 2 per cent charge on recent increases in foreign balances and it was only in 1980 that interest was again paid on franc deposits of non-resident foreigners. (Cassis 1995; Marguerat 1995; Rogge 1997: 109; Schwander-Auckenthaler 1995: 151)

These facts usually go unmentioned while attention is focused on banking secrecy. Its importance is undeniable irrespective of the growing weight of institutional investors. But it is not impenetrable and has been loosened in recent years.

Two cases have assumed high profiles: the disclosure of 3,687 dormant Holocaust accounts in 1997, and the consent in 2001 to pay the 35 per cent withholding tax of US citizens as a lump sum without, however, revealing the identity of the account holders. In the first case the banks complied after having lost 22 per cent of their normal US business during a two-month boycott, but emphasized that it will be a one-off event. In the second case the penalty was to discontinue doing business in the USA altogether. The 90 per cent share of the US traffic in the Swiss wholesale payment system gives an idea of the seriousness of the threat. (Authers 1997; Cramb 1999; Willman 2001)

The principle, nevertheless, is clear: breach of banking secrecy is a criminal offence, that is, in the domain of the public prosecutor. So is tax fraud, but not tax evasion (non-disclosure). The same rules apply to citizens and foreigners. Banks are obliged to give assistance in criminal cases. If the investigator is a foreign authority, criminality must exist in both countries, which protects against tax evasion, foreign contraband and foreign corruption. On the other hand, the prosecution can also be a fake, staged as a refined form of robbery. The cooperation of the Swiss public prosecutor is always necessary. All this sounds very reassuring but then comes the sting in the tail; no assistance is given if the release of information would cause considerable damage to the Swiss economy. Nor do authorities have an obligation to release internal information. Numbered accounts exist but the beneficiaries are known to the bank. B-accounts, to be opened by a lawyer on behalf of unnamed depositors, were abolished in 1990. The Swiss also point out that the forty recommendations of the Financial Action Task Force on Money Laundering (FATF) rest essentially on Swiss laws and practice. The main thing is that banks shall know their customers and notify authorities about suspects. The first year that money laundering legislation was in force brought 160 such cases of which 107, involving SFR236m, went to the prosecutor. The problem may be less in the principles than the resources available for their implementation, because most law enforcement is on the cantonal level. These are the facts. Then come the perceptions. Foreign police authorities lament the impossibility of getting information from Swiss banks while many customers compare the banking secrecy with Swiss cheese. (Authers 1997; Birchler and Rich 1992: 418–419; Blattner *et al.* 1996; Fleck 2001; Hall 1999; Mellow 1999; Schwander-Auckenthaler 1995; Rodger 1995a; 1995b; 1995c)

Be that as it may, assets coming to Switzerland for management show no signs of drying up although the market share is slowly declining. They are by no means all flight capital, and all flight capital is not criminal money. Insufficient protection of property, high inflation, high taxes, forthcoming currency control, poor bank systems and extortion are other reasons that feed capital flight. That kind of capital comes from the super-rich and is intended for long-term investment. Short-term flight capital originates from merchants and entrepreneurs, and leaves Switzerland as easily as it arrives. During the Kuwait crisis, $15bn was flown from the Middle East during the first two weeks of August 1990 alone. When the war was over, large sums were repatriated. Roughly one-third of managed assets belongs to institutions and the rest to individuals, foreigners being in the minority in both groups (Figure 5.15). (Bischofberger 1996: 124; Graham 1997; Kochan 1992: 86; Lewis 1990; Schwander-Auckenthaler 1995: 32, n. 76, 129, 153, n. 45)

Most deposits are of the conventional type, and only some $200bn, about 12 per cent, are of the fiduciary variant (*Treuhand*). There is good reason to assume that *Treuhand* is used for tax evasion. For that to be possible there must be a written contract, the bank manages everything in its own name, the customer assumes the credit, transfer and currency risk, pays a maximum of 1 per cent in commission and receives all revenues. In that case the customer pays no Swiss withholding tax. The interest in *Treu-*

hand here is not the possibility for tax evasion, however, but that its origins and destinations offer an unusual insight in the turning table role of a finance centre (Figure 5.16). (Blattner *et al.* 1996: 100; Schwander-Auckenthaler 1995: 115, 119)

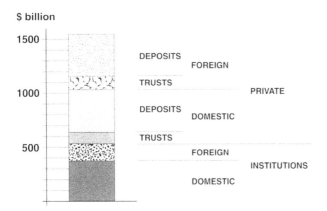

Figure 5.15 Assets managed by Swiss banks, December 1991.

Sources: Gehrig 1992: Table 2; Scheuenstuhl and Spremann 1992.

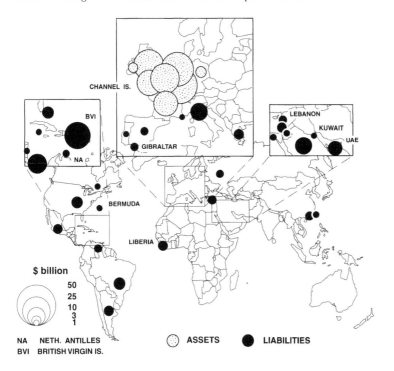

Figure 5.16 Swiss *treuhand* net assets by country, December 2000.

Source: Schweizerische Nationalbank 2001: Table 38.

For expositional clarity, the country figures are given net, that is, claims and liabilities are netted against each other. This matters mostly in Europe, where Germany and France have large balancing entries, and some Caribbean territories, but elsewhere countries fall neatly into net importers (assets) and exporters (liabilities). Stated simply, Swiss banks attract monies from all over the world, particularly the Caribbean and the Middle East, and channel them to a few countries and territories in Northwest Europe. Prominent among them are the Benelux countries but also Jersey, partially because of their low, even zero, taxes. Since Figure 5.16 covers only *Treuhand* assets, its message cannot be extrapolated too far. For example, there are certainly African countries other than Liberia which are net exporters of finance capital.

A quite special segment of fund management are *high net worth individuals* (HNWI); persons with a minimum of $1.0m of liquid financial assets. They number about 7.2 million and are worth $27tr or one-quarter of worldwide financial assets, estimated to grow at 15 per cent a year (Table 2.2). When the average management fee is about 1.0 per cent and shows little cyclicity, the interest of asset managers is easy to understand. An estimated 4,000 organizations try to exploit the pool. One-third of the HNWI assets are offshore, that is, outside the country of origin, although the share is decreasing rather than increasing (Figure 5.17). Falling tax rates are the simplest explanation, but the authorities have also been busy

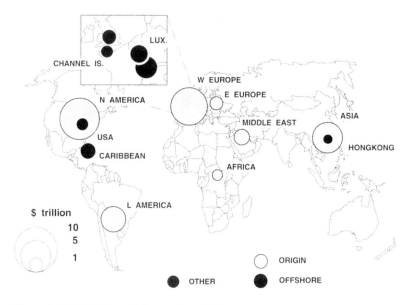

Figure 5.17 HNWI wealth by region, 2000.

Source: Schierenbeck 1998: 18; *World Wealth Report* 2001.

Note
Distribution among offshore centres as in 1996.

plugging loopholes for people who wish to enjoy the security and amenities onshore but prefer keeping their money in a low-tax offshore location (Ehlern 1997: 48; Graham 1997; *World Wealth Report* 2001). More about that in Chapter 7.

The relative weight of originating regions approximately reflects the tripod structure of the financial world: North America, Western Europe and Asia-Pacific. Latin America and the Middle East can be added. Their apparently modest financial resources are compensated by the extremely peaked wealth distribution. Political instability and the poor state of many economies also contribute. Asia is plagued by suffocating bureaucracy and occasionally confiscatory tax regimes; for example, the Japanese inheritance tax for estates exceeding ¥2bn is 70 per cent, on a level with British taxes just after the Second World War, the time when the modern offshore industry was born (Tett 1997c). Offshore wealth has a tendency to remain within its own central time zone, although not entirely (Figure 5.18). Asia lacks strong offshore locations which pushes money to Europe and America. Americans, and Latin Americans in particular, also come to Europe where Switzerland is the main destination.

Figure 5.18 Offshore customer origin in private banking, mid-1990s.

Source: Ehlern, Svend, *International Private Banking*: Exhibit 35. Haupt, Berne, 1997.
Copyright © 1997 of Verlag Paul Haupt, Berne; used with permission.

The attraction of Switzerland is not only in its banking secrecy. Swiss banks are part of the package, and when it comes to asset management private bankers take the front seat. Their strength lies in efficient, fast and error-free service, in which they are absolute market leaders, and in safety and secrecy, where the culture of confidentiality helps as much as legislation. Swiss bankers are also cosmopolitan, more so than their colleagues in other countries. Parenthetical staff turnout is an additional tout. The shortcomings are in know-how and inflexible management hierarchy. There are also complaints about high charges and erratic performance. (Hall 1998; Paneldiskussion 1998: 140–147; Stewart 1998)

Once in Switzerland, a private bank should probably locate in Geneva, which is the main centre, much more so than Zurich. It is the natural tourist spot and gateway for customers from the Middle East, Latin America and France because of the language, scenery and closeness to the Alps. Even the big banks, domiciled in Zurich, do as much business in Geneva than 'at home'. Julius Baer, a Zurich-based private bank, specifically purchased a Geneva bank to be close to the French- and Italian-speaking market. Italians, however, are best accessed from Lugano, which is Switzerland's third largest banking centre and whose sixty-odd banks, half foreign-owned, specialize in fund management. This may create the impression that private bankers seek each other's company to create economies of scope. Exactly the opposite is true: they avoid each other and thereby minimize unwanted attention. (Rodger 1995c; Wallace 1987: 62; Williams 1995)

Swiss banks are best at home and offshore; this arrangement has proved to be sufficient, and an onshore presence has not necessarily been appreciated. For example, Germans have preferred offices on Swiss rather than German soil. Smaller private banks as a group rely heavily on offshore. It is only in recent years that UBS and Crédit Suisse have increased their onshore private banking network on a large scale. It has not been an outrageously profitable investment. Onshore banking is much more capital intensive than offshore and there are many established competitors. But they must follow the customers, and these are gravitating back home. A case in point is the recent Italian tax amnesty which made Italians repatriate hidden monies. Much of the outflow was captured by UBS and Crédit Suisse in their Italian offices. (Hall 2002a; 2002b; Rogge 1997: 215)

Custodianship

Fund management is a proactive business in which the manager is largely free to make his/her own decisions within the limits of the charter, and is held responsible for them. In the meantime, somebody has to do the attached paperwork and take care of the securities. This is the job of the custodian. For that s/he needs an expensive infrastructure of vaults and information networks, particularly when operating on a global scale. This is compensated by a stable income stream and custody relations lasting, on average, ten years. Changing a custodian is simply too expensive to be practised frequently (Cohen 1995; Lewis 1991: 58).

The most basic custody includes the settlement of trades (payment and collection of money and securities) and the keeping of script in a safe place. Safekeeping has somewhat faded into the background with the coming of dematerialization but where ownership and settlement are still paper-based, it means literally keeping the script in a bank vault. Safety also has a legal aspect. In most jurisdictions, even without specific trust legislation, securities under custody are retrievable in full should the custodian go into receivership. By contrast, the cash portion of assets would probably have to join the line with general creditors.

Once the securities are under custody, it is logical that the custodian performs other related tasks like collecting interest and dividends, handling tax reclamations, managing cash, informing about corporate matters such as stock splits, rights issues and general meetings. Upon request performance measurement, asset valuation and daily reporting, and stock lending can be added to these. In cross-border business, forex operations are an integral part of payment services and cash management. In revenue and profit terms, real-time reporting has become crucial, anticipating competition from information vendors like Reuters and Bloomberg. Currently, settlement vendors such as Euroclear and Clearstream also offer most of the standard custodian services. The main competition, however, comes from fund managers, who often prefer doing their own custody (Buckley 1995).

Competition has pushed custodians to offer risky services. The securities lying otherwise idle offer an opportunity to make an extra buck through stock lending. The activity has been explained on page 121 and need not be repeated here. Usually there is a guarantee that dividends and tax rebates are paid on set dates. This is welcome to the client who knows when the monies will be available for further investment. But the custodian accepts a credit risk and a country risk, because the authorities may intentionally stall timely payment. Big, powerful custodians can make quite a difference here. More risky is settlement guarantee, because nobody can enforce a settlement, and at failure or delay the custodian must step in and purchase the security, accepting market risk. Some customers require costly measures from the custodian like exercising proxy voting at company general meetings. This is part of the corporate governance drive which started in 1987 when Calpers realized that it could not sell a poorly managed company which was in the index it followed. The shares must be registered well in advance and personal attendance with an attached entry fee may then be necessary. In Japan, 85 per cent of all annual general meetings are held on the same day, attendance must be announced two weeks and instructions on voting made ten days in advance. (Cohen 1994; Dickson 2000; Kochan 1993; Targett 2001c)

Most custody was domestic until the late 1970s and cross-border activity is simply a reaction to the changing needs of institutional investors. The real breakthrough occurred during the 1987 stock market crash, when investors and traders faced huge losses because settlement systems were unable to cope with the stress. By then the international market consisted of about twenty countries, which ten years later had grown to up to sixty, justifying the label 'global' for those custodians who offer the service all over the world. The assets under custody, Japan excluded, can be estimated at $45tr worldwide, of which $11tr are cross-border. Japan is exceptional. Custody there has been the realm of trust banks and practically all-domestic. (Freeman 1990; www.globalcustody.net; Lewis 1997; Warner 1994: 54)

Custodians welcome globalization because the most profitable activities are across markets and products, while operation with a single product in a mature market hardly breaks even. Global activity needs an extensive network of service points, at least one per country, and only the largest banks can offer them. Some opt for their own network in major markets, which gives consistency and control, in pricing for example. In smaller markets, the task is given anonymously to another bank but labelled under one's own logo ('white labelling'). The alternative philosophy is to employ local banks as subcustodians throughout because they are familiar with local conditions. Selection criteria are credit rating, quality of staff and willingness to admit errors, for example when failed trades are cleared. Some banks also have market shares, which make them very difficult to dislodge. HSBC and Standard Chartered Equitor have shares of 40 per cent and 30 per cent in Asia, respectively. Citicorp, Banco Santander and Bank of Boston are strong in Latin America, Chase (formerly Morgan Stanley and Barclays before that) in Africa, ING Bank and Creditanstalt (now Bank Austria) in Eastern Europe, and Paribas in France. Which alternative becomes cheaper is a contested issue. Customer preferences naturally play a role and in large countries it may be advisable to distribute volume and risk by using several subcustodians in parallel (Figure 5.19). (van Duyn 1994; Gapper 1994; 1996b; Hyam 1997; Middelman 1996; Morris 1996)

The other dispute concerns the organizing principle, functional or geographical. While geography seems to be on the retreat and product-based organization ascending in general, in custody, geography defends its position. HSBC with $1,060bn assets in custody worldwide has organized itself along geographical rather than functional lines, achieving lower fail rates and upgraded productivity. The customer interface is obviously where the fund managers are, while the back office can be located almost anywhere, or outsourced. US custody banks have a substantial presence in London, but Chase does the processing in Bournemouth, Bank of New York in Brussels, and State Street Bank in Quincy, MA (Gibson 1997; Kochan 1996).

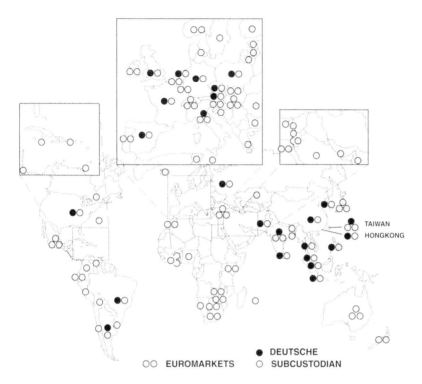

Figure 5.19 Deutsche Bank custody units, 1998.

Source: *The Global Custody Yearbook* 1999: 21.

The necessary information network requires investment in short-lived technology to the tune of $300m per year. Scale economies are considerable, and many insurers and banks with $200bn and less of assets in custody have found it prudent to withdraw. State Street, which specializes in the US market, claims that $1,000bn is the current threshold. This is a very high figure and makes one wonder whether custodians are properly capitalized for it. The answer is tentatively negative. The largest assets in custody are already so large that no conceivable capital will cover them (Figure 5.20; compare with Figure 5.2). The issue cannot be avoided by referring to custodians as mere agents. When they issue payment instructions, they are principals and fully responsible. When scale economies are combined with the need of a worldwide network, the logical result is heavy market concentration. The five biggest banks control about 60 per cent of global custody, Japan excluded. The key word then is 'global' because many large custodians operate predominantly in the domestic market. On the other hand, custodians can be far more specialized. Bank of New York and State Street are technology-intensive and serve mutual funds. Bank of Tokyo–Mitsubishi and formerly Barclays have tailored their output for

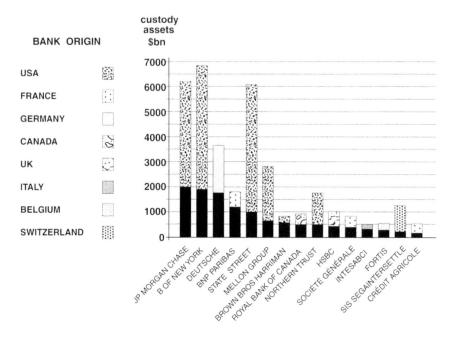

BANK ORIGIN

USA

FRANCE

GERMANY

CANADA

UK

ITALY

BELGIUM

SWITZERLAND

Figure 5.20 Largest global custodians, March 2000.

Source: www.globalcustodynet.com. Copyright © 2002 of BDG Communications, used with permission.

Notes
Cross-border assets in black. Japanese trust banks excluded because the market has, in practice, been closed to foreigners. Citibank does not disclose global assets which were believed to be $1,600bn in September 2000.

wholesale clients. Northern Trust Co. caters for pension funds. Brown Brothers Harriman accepts only customers with a minimum of $1bn, eight times the typical custody. (Anon. 1995; Featherstone 1997; Gapper 1996b; 1996c; www.globalcustody.net; Goenfeldt 2001; Ioannou 1990; Middelman 1996; Targett 2000; Timewell 1995; Warner 1994)

Follow the trade – and money

Why expand abroad?

The approach in this book is international. Therefore it is natural to query why banks expand abroad. The underlying reason, of course, is the desire to make money, but we are interested in more detailed and refined explanations. A difference must then be made between things that make international expansion possible and others which make it worthwhile. Among the first, the deregulation of exchange rates, capital movements and banking in general stands foremost. Among the second, a difference must be made between retail and wholesale banking.

Global banking is a recent phenomenon. In the early 1970s, most of the world's largest banks were still only important actors at home. Abroad, they used correspondents and branches to give core services such as trade finance to their national customers. The change came with deregulation which made true internationalization possible and was boosted by a number of push factors. Banking lost much of its traditional relationship character and became deal-oriented. That gave foreigners a chance as never before. Non-banks increased competition which blurred the distinction between credit and capital markets. Technical networking tied geographically separate markets together and enhanced the negotiability of debt instruments. Increased volatility of exchange rates extolled the virtues of local deposits, while the 1987 market crash showed the importance of diversified portfolios. (Ehlern 1997: 27; ter Hart and Piersma 1990; Rogge 1997: 204–205)

Having serviced domestic exporters, internationally active banks saw new opportunities. They had superior in-house know-how and surplus deposits to place. Interest rates were higher and regulation, such as reserve requirements, interest rate ceilings, issuance queues, stamp taxes and many others, was less onerous abroad. But there were numerous constraints. Entries usually require reciprocity. The EU is an exception to this but only within its own borders. There are cultural differences. Markets are often saturated and serious entry may be possible only by purchasing an existing bank. But many banks are not for sale, no matter what price, and when they are, the central bank must give its acceptance. All these circumstances are subject to change and the timing of entry depends on windows of opportunity. (Ehlern 1997: 146; Goldberg and Johnson 1990; Goldberg and Saunders 1981)

The varying conditions and adaptation to them can be illuminated by the post-war internationalization of Japanese banks, irrespective that it has been a guided process with the MoF at the helm. Haga (1999) identifies four phases, each with a different geographical imprint. From the Peace Treaty in 1952 to the end of the Bretton Woods system in 1970, the Bank of Tokyo (forex bank) led the pack by opening offices worldwide in forty-five cities to support the export drive, while other city banks stayed in New York, London and Los Angeles. Bretton Woods ending and euromarkets on the front page was the hallmark of the 1971–1980 period, with New York–London–Hongkong as the standard locational triad. When the appreciating yen allowed more playground during 1981–1990, emphasis was shifted to the USA and the Continent at large, in anticipation of NAFTA and the EU. War-torn Beirut was replaced by Bahrain. China was not yet a major force to be reckoned with. Deregulation in Asia started in earnest as from 1991 and it was time to open representative offices there. In every phase, the needs of Japanese manufacturers were paramount and the host-country banking opportunity took a back seat. Locally, as in California, it may have been noteworthy, however (Yamori 1998).

Technically, there are many ways to enter a market. The simplest way is to open a representative office to show the flag, collect information and negotiate deals. If the host country recognizes the concept of agency it can be used in money markets and payment systems. It not, branch is the next step, to book loans for domestic and possibly also non-domestic customers. It may be allowed to take deposits although not necessarily at the retail level. For this a subsidiary is necessary. Thereafter the newcomer is in full-scale competition with local banks. (Heinkel and Levi 1992; Tickell 1994)

In strict numerical terms, the concept of global banking may be oversold. Few banks make more money abroad than at home. Among the fifty largest international banks, only Standard Chartered, Crédit Suisse Holdings, Banque Indosuez and HSBC get more than one-half of their revenue from abroad. And in the USA, only JP Morgan Chase and Citicorp have a global vision. The rest put America first (Mikdashi 1998: 72; Shapiro 1998).

There is also terminological confusion in so far that the words 'global' and 'international' are used as synonyms, or almost, global being simply a more extensive concept than international. But the matter can be seen from a functional angle: a global bank funds its operations locally while an international bank takes deposits in one country and makes loans in another (McCauley *et al.* 2002). It means that transfer risk is substituted by country risk. The difference is measured by the ratio:

> locally funded foreign claims/(cross border claims + local claims abroad),
> in which locally funded claims are measured by min (local claims, local liabilities) booked by the bank's foreign affiliates.

The ratio equals one for a pure global bank and zero for a pure international bank. It can be calculated either by bank nationality or by country. In countries with a currency board, the BIS consolidated data underestimates global banking because there is no information about local positions in foreign currency. On average, banks are halfway between global and international (Figure 5.21). The global variant is widely accepted by banks domiciled in high-profile banking countries while the international variant appears to be the choice on the Continent and in Asia Pacific. A tentative explanation on the Continent is the existence of many competing finance centres, the integrated interbank money market, and the reluctance to enter neighbouring retail markets. Countries in Asia Pacific have few international liabilities and can therefore keep foreigners away from their credit markets.

Retail banks expand because the home region is saturated, because the

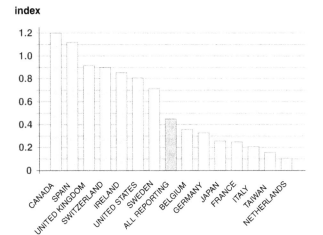

Figure 5.21 Globalization of international banking by bank nationality, September 2001.

Source: McCauley, Robert N. *et al.* 2002: 41–51. Copyright © 2002 of the Bank for International Settlements, Basle; used with permission.

Notes
Local claims in local currencies/(cross-border claims in all currencies + local claims in foreign currencies). Due to data shortcomings the theoretically preferable ratio (in text) has not been feasible. One consequence is ratios exceeding 1.0.

interest gap between deposit taking and lending is more attractive abroad and because there is a large bankable expatriate community. However, in most countries, retail banking has been reserved for nationals, if not by law then by administrative practice. The USA has been comparatively open for foreigners. The EU has followed suit but only internally. Much of Asia has been restrictive but is now opening. But apparent openness may be just that, apparent.

When HSBC acquired Marine Midland Bank it met stiff resistance from the New York State Bank Superintendent who was against foreign banks making acquisitions in the USA. To escape her authority, Marine Midland withdrew from the state banking system and became a national bank with the Comptroller of Currency as the highest regulatory authority (King 1991: 818, 891).

Foreign asset managers have had difficulty in keeping the Japanese assets they have acquired. Goldman Sachs garnered in 1998 ¥1,600bn but lost 60 per cent of them in two years. Fidelity, having purchased parts of the bankrupted Yamaichi Securities, imposed a six-month lockup period on one fund. At the end of the period, 40 per cent of monies were withdrawn (Tett 2000).

Since China became a member of the WTO, foreign banks are allowed to open branches. The number, however, is limited to one branch per year and its capital must be at least RMB60m or $72.3m. Compare this with the $1.5m cost of a typical US branch with a deposit base of $50m (Kynge 2002; Orlow *et al.* 1996).

The retail banking market is like retail trade, apparently well saturated by domestic companies but in reality covered by a fair number of organizations with very diversified offerings and skills, and sometimes dominated by a sleepy cartel. If the foreigner can offer innovative services at competitive prices, a greenfield entry is possible. The most promising segment is high income brackets, most responsive to novelties and possibly dissatisfied with outdated services in a conservative environment. Citicorp focused on this and succeeded in creating a worldwide network of retail desks in its offices. The usual way of making entry is mergers and acquisitions, however. Unfortunately enough, analytical effort has been directed on M&A in general without making a difference between retail and wholesale (perhaps even private) banking, as would appear relevant.

Once a merger is consummated, the parts must be integrated. In retail banking, that can be a real challenge because of the looming redundancies. When the purchase is made outside current operational territory, the situation is less acute, but otherwise 40 per cent is quite possible. That, indeed, is a typical rate in domestic US mergers, achieved within two-to-three years. Half of that sounds ambitious in Europe, where staff levels are normally reduced through natural attrition. The slower rate as such would be acceptable were it not that the younger, more energetic but less well-paid staff are affected disproportionally (Lee 1996b: 31).

Few of these deals have really prospered. One of them is Banca d'America e d'Italia, purchased by Deutsche Bank and routinely mentioned in this context, although the deal was actually made to enter wholesale banking. Culture, corporate and national, is the main problem and it is not easy to generalize in which way it works. The difference between British and French styles is substantial and well-known. HSBC with all its international experience and having established a solid foothold in the UK, needed almost a decade to cross the Channel, the first British clearer ever (see page 292). It is not only retailers who must observe the cultural dimension; British merchant banks, reportedly, preferred a Continental purchaser to an American one. The happy partners seem to be overwhelmingly from neighbouring countries. The Pan-Nordic Nordea appears to work, as does the Belgian–Dutch Fortis and the Belgian–French Dexia. (Anon. 1996; Delamaide 1990: 34–36; Fisher 1996; Grunfeld 1995; Hultman and McGee 1990: 72; Lee 1996b: 34; Pretzlik 2000)

Wholesale banking is fundamentally different. Presence rests initially on servicing home-country clients in their export and direct investment (FDI) with forex, trade finance and lending. Entry into a major finance centre can also have the sole purpose of escaping the small size of the domestic market, its regulation and taxes. Since foreign trade is largely a bilateral phenomenon between neighbours, most foreign entries are made in neighbouring countries. The result is regional banking clusters.

The validity of foreign trade and FDI as an explanation has been formally tested by, among others, Brealey and Kaplanis (1994). As large economies generate large trade and FDI, the size effect must be neutralized either by introducing GDP as a separate variable or using it as a scaler. Regression technique with countries as observations shows that parent-country GDP has more explanatory power than host-country GDP, and that trade overshadows whatever effect FDI might have. R-squares of 0.34–0.49 are reported. The results are similar to those obtained by Goldberg and Johnson (1990) about the USA. When trade is accounted for, regional patterns largely disappear. Large positive deviations indicate finance centres and negative ones indicate discrimination against foreigners. Singapore, Switzerland, the UK and the USA belong to the first group, India and Turkey to the second. Indonesia is an anomaly in the first group because of its many private banks, and Holland in the second group because of its very large banks.

Some countries host hundreds of foreign banks, most of which are in the wholesale business. The comparatively short time span (one decade) when the inflow may have taken place suggests that entry and exit are generally easy. This is true in so far that opening a representative office or branch can be achieved in a matter of weeks or months. Expatriate staff can fill the executive positions and clerical labour is hired locally. Their numbers are sufficiently small to make a closedown relatively painless, and the premises can be subleased without difficulty. In a world-class finance centre like London, the annual turnover is easily 5 per cent of the stock. In other words, although entry and exit may be easy, staying and prospering in a foreign location can be difficult enough, particularly for smaller and weaker banks. Among market leaders, positions are more stable, as temporal matrices about their ranking by financial product indicate (Brealey and Kaplanis 1994: 47–49).

At the top of wholesale banking are *investment banks*. Their comparative advantage is in underwriting, M&A advising, fund management and custody, all activities which need large market potential. Competition within the top league has been fuelled by the widespread belief in the mid-1990s that in a decade or so only four or five would be left on the global scene, while the rest were reduced to niche and regional roles, or simply disappeared, a vision which has by and large been substantiated. Americans lean on their domestic market, the largest and most innovative in the world, and the skills honed there. Europeans and Japanese used to benefit from their large balance sheets, but particularly the Japanese have not shown the skill commensurate with their money, and their banking industry at large still suffers from the aftermath of the real-estate bubble of the late 1980s.

To gain global status, both Europeans and Japanese alike need a solid foothold in the USA. Glass–Steagall used to constrain this but is now a thing of the past.

> Deutsche Bank had licences in the USA from the SEC both for invest-ment and commercial banking. When it took an equity stake in Morgan Grenfell, a London merchant bank, in 1984 it kept the stake below 5 per cent for two years in order not to risk the displeasure of the SEC. And when it completed the acquisition in 1990, it sought the SEC's approval in advance. When Crédit Suisse took a 40 per cent stake in First Boston in 1978, it was possible only because the deal went through the London-based joint venture CSFB. (Delamaide 1990: 34–36; Fairlamb 1998; Fidler and Bush 1988; Gall *et al.* 1995: 849–850)

That is the regulatory part. The real test is operational. The current wisdom is that it is comparatively easy to gain market share in bond trading on the strength of a strong balance sheet and international repu-tation, but it alone does not make for success. Equity is already harder to crack because it is more based on research. Therefore, the placing of Daimler-Benz's rights issue by Deutsche Bank in January 1994 was regarded as a landmark. At least Deutsche had placing power for German equities. At the top of the scale comes M&A, which rests on long-term rela-tions and trust. A sensible way to enter this elite group is, therefore, to buy an established house if any are available.

> That, exactly, was what Deutsche finally did. Its attempt to build a US business from scratch had been a long-drawn affair and cost it $3bn. A large part of that money had been spent in hiring local talent at prices which were considered exorbitant even by Wall Street standards. Results did not correspond with expectations, however. To make progress, Deutsche then purchased Bankers Trust, a medium-sized investment bank, for $10bn in 1998. Rumours about an attempted merger with JP Morgan circulated and analysts pointed out that Merrill Lynch would have been a worthy partner, at an estimated price of $30bn. Deutsche's weakness in this game was its large indus-trial holdings, estimated at 45 per cent of market capitalization and an eyesore to Americans who see manufacturing as an obstacle to prof-itable banking business. Deutsche was unable to sell the holdings because of the then confiscatory capital gains tax at home. (Barber 1998; Bowley 1998)

So, entry into the USA is possible. What about success? Historical evidence is not encouraging. Crédit Suisse and now Deutsche are the only European groups with a significant investment banking presence there, and appear to also have staying power. Americans have had similar experiences in Europe. When they invested in the UK by acquiring merchant banks, brokerages and other intermediaries before the latest major deregulation in 1986, no-one made a killing. Their strong position is the result of superior skills in M&A, worldwide placing power and hard work since the 1960s and 1970s. (Celarier 1996b: 38–40; Corrigan 1997; Denton 1996; Gapper 1996a; Hall 1996; Neish 1996: 60; Plender and Fisher 1995; Shirreff 1995: 26)

Aggregate patterns

Understanding the overall patterns necessitates the selection of a suitable indicator. The core information appears to be assets or loan portfolio, by country if the angle is aggregate and by office if the interest is in networks. Since assets and loan portfolios understate investment banking, they might be supplemented, or replaced as the case may be, by revenue. The number of employees would be a compromise between the two. Such information may be available by country but certainly not by office. Even the number of offices, by country or metropolitan area, may be available only through a tedious survey at banking regulators and similar. In practice, the global analyst is likely to accept the number of banks (companies) as an approximation. The practice is fraught with pitfalls because of the range of sizes and functions.

In London in the mid-1990s, when a thorough count was made, 20 per cent of foreign banks had at most three employees, while Citicorp, which was also in retail banking, and Deutsche Bank had almost 6,000 each. In the USA, there are half a dozen functionally different 'banks'. Commercial and investment banks are the most important segments. Edge corporations accept deposits through their subsidiaries abroad and are, in that sense, banks. Agencies, export trading companies and representative offices also link with cross-border trade and banking but are not legally banks. The US system may well be more complicated than in most other countries, but it serves as a reminder about the potential variability of the global banking scene. (Brealey and Kaplanis 1994: 2–3; Graham and Timewell 1997: 10; Rose 1994: 52; Spong 1994: 161–166; Taeho 1993: 233, 293)

The scene is neatly abstracted by the presence of the 1,000 largest banks (Figure 5.22). They are recorded here by both parent and host country, while domestic operations are omitted. The most important banking countries and territories are displayed separately, the rest are aggregated by region. The markers of parent and host regions are superimposed to create an immediate impression of net surplus or deficit.

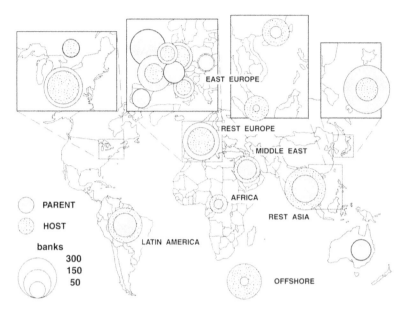

Figure 5.22 Presence of the largest 1,000 banks, 1993.

Source: *Telerate Bank Register* 1992 as cited by Brealey and Kaplanis 1994: Table 3.

Notes
Japan is parent to more banks than it hosts, Singapore hosts more than it originates, in Australia and Canada the numbers are almost equal. The source uses the term 'offices' when 'presence' would be preferable. On average there are 2.5 'presences' per bank.

The main features are clear and logical. Old industrial countries generally originate more banks than they host. Exceptions are recognized banking centres such as the UK and Switzerland, where the numbers are about equal. Switzerland's balance is partly based on strict reciprocity when granting licences to foreigners. The same may apply in Australia, Canada, Spain and Eastern Europe, although it is equally plausible that banking in some of them is in a transitory phase. The fact is that everywhere in the industrializing and developing world, hosted banks outnumber originated ones. Their own banks are still too weakly capitalized, or small, or regulated, to make foreign entries attractive or even possible. An extreme case is the entrepôt cities Singapore and Hongkong, and offshore centres, attractive as locations but far too small to originate an equal number of banks.

Obviously there are *national biases* at work, based on trade connections, capital availability, regulatory burdens, geographical proximity, kinship and whatever. They can be illuminated with the help of deposits, or claims when seen from the lending angle (Figure 5.23). Central bankers, regulators and tax authorities do not like cross-border deposits. They complicate

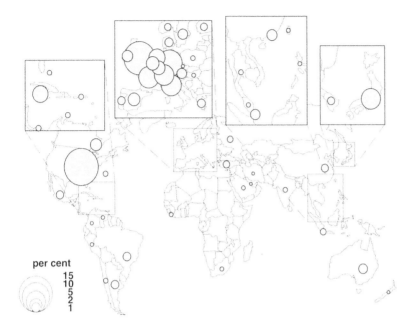

Figure 5.23 Consolidated international claims, country pattern, December 2000.
Source: *BIS QR* June 2001: Table 9B.

monetary policy, circumvent regulation and evade taxes. But one cannot do without because deposits also finance trade, diversify default risk and exist as compensating balances with correspondents. So, where do the deposits go? They very much prefer locations without exchange controls and capital flow constraints, low taxes (also withholding) and duties, and a fair legal system. Tax evaders also look for banking secrecy, institutions for deep and active financial markets, and small investors proximity and deposit insurance. There is a mutual dependence, banks locate where deposits accrue and the other way around. The non-bank share out of all cross-border claims (or deposits) varies markedly (Figure 3.5). (Alworth and Andresen 1992; ter Hart and Piersma 1990)

There have been many attempts to explain the mechanism statistically and here is one of them (Alworth and Andresen 1992). The dependent variable is the log of non-bank dollar deposits of country i in country j. Three sets of explanatory variables are used: outward deposit decision, bilateral variables and location attractiveness. In a two-stage least square regression, the number of banks is first regressed against exogenous variables, whereafter the estimated value so purged of endogenous effects is used with other variables to explain the deposits. As can be expected, centres with high interbank lending attract non-bank deposits, as do bilateral trade and number of banks. Stock market and bank secrecy are important, and a dummy differentiates Japan from other countries. Taxes, unexpectedly, lack significance. When different runs are made for onshore and offshore, R-squares reach the respectable heights of 0.59 and 0.73, respectively.

To make the picture more tangible, the worldwide presence of the six largest lending countries is examined. Specifically, the lending is done by the bank holding companies domiciled in these countries, irrespective of the location of the operational units actually making the loans. In the BIS terminology, we make use of consolidated data by bank nationality. The aggregate lending of these six countries is 55 per cent out of the global and their relative standing is evaluated in fifty-five countries (Figure 5.24). It is interesting to observe the large market shares of German and Japanese banks, and contrast them with the recognized banking nations, the USA, Switzerland and the UK. Because the data is consolidated, intragroup lending is outruled but interbank lending is not. Among many possible explanations, the extensive dollar-based trading connections of German and Japanese exporters come first to mind. They need trade finance and the natural suppliers are domestic banks. Americans invoice mostly in dollars and do not need correspondent accounts in the same extent as other nations. Their presence is also often in the shape of investment banks and these are not large lenders.

In the first edition of this book, the geographical evaluation was made with the help of six parallel figures, each displaying the claim pattern of a particular country. The figures were easy to interpret separately but their visual comparison was difficult. Now a technique which neutralizes the size differences of the lenders is used. Otherwise Germany, with its 17.8 per cent market share, would dominate in most countries and would, for example, push Americans away from Latin America which, however, is

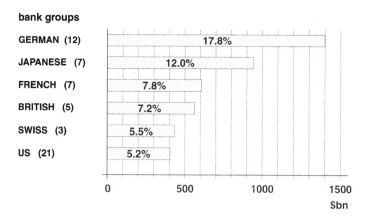

Figure 5.24 Consolidated international claims, largest creditor countries, December 2000.

Source: *BIS QR* June 2001: Table 9B.

generally recognized as US banking territory. The claims against debtor countries are expressed in percentages, for each lending country separately (totalling to 100.0) and then for worldwide lending, i.e. also by other than the sampled countries. A lender's score in a debtor country is derived by subtracting the aggregate percentage from its individual percentage. The score tells whether the lender's relative presence is above or below the average. Finally, each debtor country is allocated to the lending country with the highest positive score. That lender dominates the debtor country in a relative sense. By definition, a lender cannot dominate itself (Figure 5.25).

The picture created from the scoring technique contains many familiar and some unfamiliar features. US lenders dominate the Americas, the Caribbean excepted, and the northern part of Asia Pacific. This is as one would expect. But they are also in the North Sea area and around the Indian Ocean which runs against conventional wisdom. Although their market share is smallest among the six largest lenders they dominate, in a relative sense, almost half of the countries scored. The Germans have a smaller but compact territory: Luxembourg, Eastern Europe, the Baltic area, Russia, Turkey and a few small Atlantic countries. It is almost as if one

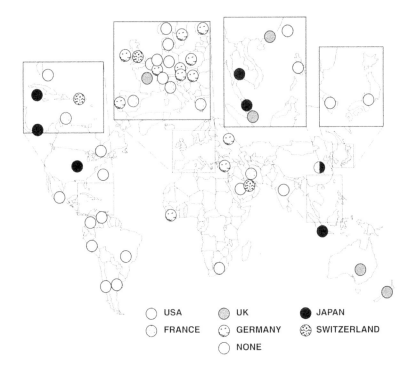

Figure 5.25 Consolidated international claims, relative presence, December 2000.
Source: *BIS QR* June 2001: Table 9B.

had turned the clock back one hundred years. The Japanese are strong in the southern part of Asia Pacific, the USA and the Caribbean, the familiar places. The French are in the Mediterranean, Iran and the Netherlands Antilles; the British in their former colonies in Asia Pacific plus France. China is contested by the Japanese and French. Swiss dominance is unexpected but logical: the UK, Bahrain and the British West Indies (Virgin Islands). For a small country without empire building instincts, past or present, but having a strong banking industry, these are natural places to be. London is the finance centre of its central time zone (see Virt-x on pages 223–224), Bahrain is the banking centre of the Middle East and the British Virgin Islands is the place for trusts and International Business Companies. Then there is an anomaly. No country dominates Switzerland in the sense that all its scores are negative. This can be traced back to some technical operations of the Swiss banks in the London market and is of no consequence here. (BIS, private communication)

The philosophy of a dominant lender makes it possible to outline banking territories. But it also abstracts complicated matters to the utmost. A lender's presence in the countries which it does not dominate is ignored. The competitive relations of the six lenders is likewise overlooked. A compact way to account for these shortcomings is to calculate Pearson correlation coefficients with the country scores as input. To achieve maximum transparency the output is given as a figure rather than a table and only significant coefficients are indicated (Figure 5.26). The split between significant and insignificant relations is comparatively sharp,

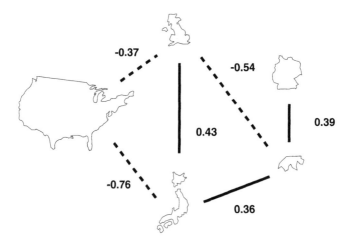

Figure 5.26 Consolidated international claims, correlations of relative presence, December 2000.

Source: *BIS QR* June 2001: Table 9B.

Note
Only significant correlations at the 0.01 level, two-tailed test.

the 'largest' insignificant coefficient being −0.21. It also follows that the difference between significant positive and negative correlations is pronounced. A positive coefficient obviously means that the countries have similar patterns and the other way round. How this should be interpreted in competitive terms is less clear. Can it be that dissimilar patterns mean avoidance? If so, one can claim that avoidance is the result of sound judgement; potential competitors see no point to clash head-on. The relative strengths are well understood and unlikely to be overturned. Similar patterns (positive correlation) then appear to indicate coexistence. They do but they stand equally well for simultaneous absence. Both possibilities are equally important and they both exist, for example, in the correlation between Japanese and Swiss banks. Neither is strong on the Continent nor Latin America, but well in the UK, the USA and parts of Asia Pacific. The same holds for the Japanese–British relationship. The German–Swiss relationship is the most difficult to pinpoint regionally. Considering their geographical and cultural closeness it appears natural that they follow similar lending patterns but that is as far as one can go without a special study. For the sake of perspective, it is also good to remember that until the second half of the 1970s, that is, before globalization had gained momentum, Swiss and German banks did not enter each other's turf physically (Rogge 1997: 205, footnote).

Corporate patterns

Most of the preceding narrative has been aggregated. Aggregation, by its very nature, conceals things to some extent. The details must be classified by some principle and a principle which suits one purpose may not suit another. Various countries and data vendors aggregate data according to their own needs, and the analyst gets frustrated when trying to compare and conciliate information from various sources. This last subchapter goes into some detail on the basis of published information and describes two of the most internationalized banks in the world. What they have done can be extrapolated to other aspiring banks. And what they have not done may well be beyond the possible.

Citigroup is a US financial conglomerate with $1,051bn assets (2001), created in 1998 by the merger of Citicorp, a holding company of commercial and trust banks, and Travelers Group, a collection of investment banks, brokerages, credit card and insurance companies. Citicorp was incorporated in 1812, obtained a national charter in 1865, opened its first foreign branch in Buenos Aires in 1913, and was up to over 100 by 1930. Today it operates some 1,500 branches in 102 countries. It is the only US bank with a noteworthy retail presence abroad. It has about 62 per cent of the conglomerate's assets, 59 per cent of the $80bn revenue net of interest expense and 75 per cent of the 200,000 or so employees. It is our actual topic of interest, but because its geographically interesting data is consolidated with the rest of the group, the actual treatment is about the whole group. (Blanden 1995; Brown Jr. 1994: 144–145; Eade 1996: 47; www.citigroup.com)

Citigroup revenue splits approximately 60/40 between retail and wholesale operations. Retailing includes a 10 per cent private banking segment, the rest divides evenly between conventional retail banking and bank and charge card issuance, in which Citicorp tops the world league. Wholesale banking comprises, in roughly equal shares, transaction services, securities and derivatives trading, bank lending, and other capital market activities including issuance. The core customers are 2,200 multinational corporations in developed countries, although growth is mostly in the emerging markets. Geographical breakdown can be made for 80 per cent of revenue and even then approximations are necessary. The company simply does not see its business in strict geographical terms and there are activities which are hardly possible to allocate meaningfully between regions. The main features are obvious nevertheless (Figure 5.27). About one-half of the revenue comes from Anglo-America, primarily the USA. Elsewhere, all the regions are about equal. Noteworthy is that Japan and Mexico are large enough to constitute independent regions. It is believed that the retail share is nowhere less than 50 per cent. This is in sharp contrast to most internationally active banks, whose retail presence abroad is limited to a few countries, perhaps a single country. Colour can be added by replacing regions by countries. That necessitates substituting labour force for revenues.

Practically all countries where foreign banks are allowed to operate are on Citicorp's roster and all of them are suited for wholesale banking (Citicorp AR 1995: inside front cover). The 2,200 core customers need banking services all over the world, are big accounts and do not need expensive branch networks. The branches are in the largest cities, a hierarchical rather than contagious strategy in retailing terms, and a natural choice for a foreigner who prefers organic growth to acquisitions and whose expansion in a host country may be constrained by authorities. At the other end of the scale are standard retail operations which need extensive branch networks and thrive best where a solid middle-class customer base exists. The card business needs the same customer base but can survive without many branches. Private banking, by contrast, resembles more wholesale banking and emerges in quite unexpected countries like Ivory Coast, Kenya, Peru and Senegal. It is a sobering experience to realize that Citicorp classified Scandinavia in 1995 as an emerging market, together with Eastern Europe and Africa. Obviously, the rigid idea of rich industrialized and poor developing countries does not hold in Citigroup's world.

There are countries and territories where presence is larger than their per capita income would suggest. The explanation is twofold. First, every country has its elite and most have their middle class, and these generate

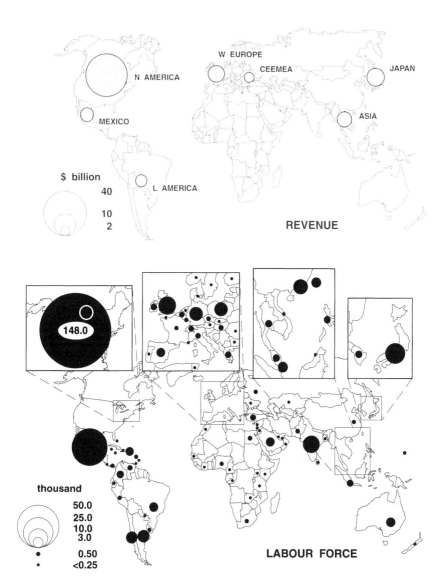

Figure 5.27 Citigroup revenue and labour force, 2001–2002.

Source: www.citigroup.com; private communication.

Notes
About 20 per cent of revenue (2001) remains unallocated. Offices (May 2002) with retail and wholesale functions.

Citigroup's private banking and retail customers. Second, Citicorp has been in some of these countries for a century and has had time to develop its business. Tracking the entry sequence of a hundred-year-old corporation with numerous merged and acquired parts is an undertaking full of risks, but available evidence tells us that Asia Pacific and India were entered in 1902, as was the UK. Argentina, Brazil and Chile were entered during 1914–1916, Spain followed in 1917 and Germany in 1926. All of these countries have respectable labour forces and, by extension, business too. Of course, a long presence in a country is not always tantamount to a large presence. France was entered in 1906 but the labour force is only 20 per cent of Spain's. Poland was entered in 1991 but its labour force already compares with Germany's. The explanation is simple. Citigroup purchased Poland's largest commercial bank. It did the same in Mexico in 2000, and got its largest foreign subsidiary with 37,000 employees.

The other example is the *HSBC Holdings*, a British financial holding company with $696bn assets (2001) with origins in Hongkong and Shanghai, where offices were opened in 1865 under a special charter which allowed Hongkong rather than London as a headquarter location. The bank remained an eastern force until the 1950s, when overexposure to the crown colony and its textile industry pointed to a need for geographical diversification. A worldwide scan was made with rather disappointing results. Australia and Canada were protectionistic and so was the Continent, in addition to being over-regulated and well served by its own talent. Central West Africa was saturated by British banks and, after independence, the new countries gave priority to domestic banks. Only the USA was attractive because it offered dollar assets in a dollar-hungry world. (*HSBC History* 2000: 5; *HSBC Holdings* 2001: 9–11; King 1991: 498–528, 693)

But before anything could be done about it, events elsewhere called attention. HSBC was in intense competition all over Asia with Chase Manhattan which showed interest in a small bank in India and Malaysia. HSBC pre-empted by purchasing the bank in 1959. In the same year another defensive acquisition became necessary, when an investor group tried to buy the British Bank of the Middle East, strip its assets and sell the branches to HSBC, which did the bulk of its Middle East business through the bank. For example, Kuwaiti authorities kept half of their money there. With the purchase came a chain of retail branches in Cyprus. A few years later a banking crisis erupted in Hongkong. HSBC was not seriously affected but Hang Seng Bank, the colony's second largest, was about to flounder in a run. Chase offered help but Hang Seng preferred HSBC, because of its local roots, and sold it a majority stake in 1965. These three deals illuminate the difference between corporate strategy and the realities of the marketplace. Diversification had taken a beating although it was only in 2000 when acquisitions in Asia became topical again, in a small way. Two of them were part of the private banking drive, PCIB Savings Bank in the Manila area and Taiwan's leading asset manager China Securities Investment Trust Corp. in 2001, to be followed by an 8 per cent stake in the Bank of Shanghai. HSBC had returned to its roots. (*HSBC History* 2000: 10–12, 20–22; *HSBC Holdings* 2001: 9–11; King 1991: 529–539, 701–706)

In the meantime, the USA had lost some of its allure because of the squeeze of foreign lending which gave birth to euromarkets, and was only seriously reconsidered in the late 1970s. The only realistic and reasonably attractive target was Marine Midland Bank in upstate New York, 60 per cent of HSBC's own size. The deal came to fruition in 1980 after two years' intense wrangling. It would almost certainly have failed had American competitors not been thwarted from bidding by the Glass–Steagall. The US presence was then strengthened in 1999 by the acquisition of Republic New York Corp, number three deposit taker in the New York metro area and strong in the high income brackets. (*HSBC History* 2000: 26; *HSBC Holdings* 2001: 9–11; King 1991: 851–859)

It was something of an anomaly that a British bank, although head-quartered in a colony, had only a parenthetical presence in the mother country. HSBC tried to correct that, but its attempt to acquire the Royal Bank of Scotland in 1981 was thwarted by both the Scottish national sentiment and the Bank of England, the latter formally on regulatory grounds. As in the USA, British authorities had doubts about the stringency of banking regulation in Hongkong and pointed out that the territory lacked a lender of last resort. HSBC persisted, took a 14.9 per cent interest in Midland Bank in 1987, one of the four British clearers but weakened by a failed entry in California, and swapped with it operations in the Far East and on the Continent. A merger was in the air but large losses by the prospective partners put it on the back-burner. A fresh attempt was made in 1992 and then in competition with Lloyds Bank, another clearer. Lloyds' offer was in cash and HSBC's mostly in shares which tilted scales in Lloyds' favour. But Lloyds would have doubled market share in the small and medium size customer segment and that prospect suggested lengthy monopolistic investigations. HSBC got its deal. It now had a solid base in the UK, the handover of Hongkong to China was pending and headquarters were duly transferred to London. All its global drive notwithstanding, HSBC had remained Hongkong's largest retail bank and the deposits it could not invest locally found ready use elsewhere. That had not gone unnoticed by Chinese authorities and their reaction was carefully followed during the Midland talks. (Barchard *et al.* 1992; *HSBC History* 2000: 17; *HSBC Holdings* 2001: 9–11; King 1991: 891–896; Peston 1992a; 1992b; Peston and Holberton 1992; Waters *et al.* 1992)

The deal had a high profile because of its location and size, the characteristic of a meaningful retail operation. But it also included less-noticed elements: Samuel Montagu in London, Trinkaus & Burkhardt in Düsseldorf and Guyerzeller Bank in Zurich, all with solid private banking business. The opportunity was developed further. Measures in the Philippines, Taiwan and New York were mentioned above. The Continental business was expanded by acquiring Safra Republic in Geneva and Luxembourg (1999), Crédit Commerciale de France (2000) and Baque Hérvet in the Paris area (2001). They were not necessarily banks for HNWIs only but also investment and commercial banks, accepting deposits from the upper middle market. As a group they made up a formidable force and involved a serious entry onto francophone soil, the renowned cultural gap notwithstanding. (*HSBC History* 2000: 17; *HSBC Holdings* 2001: 9–11)

HSBC could also record progress in the former dominions. Canada, Australia and New Zealand had been carried along with the globalization wave and opened their markets for foreign banks in the 1980s. HSBC consolidated existing operations and made greenfield entries elsewhere. The subsequent growth has been both organic and by acquisition. (*HSBC History* 2000: 11, 26; *HSBC Holdings* 2001: 9–11; King 1991: 891)

HSBC in the mid-1990s had substantial presence in most of the major regions. Latin America, Africa and the former Soviet Union remained: all of them volatile and unpredictable, and also comparatively small markets, their physical size notwithstanding. Probably the most promising of them, economically and culturally, is Latin America, and the Marine Midland and Midland Bank deals had given some exposure to the continent. The main thrust was directed there. It took the shape of two purchases in 1997, Grupo Roberts of financial services based in Buenos Aires, and the 1,300 branches of Banco Bamerindus do Brasil. (*HSBC History* 2000: 26; *HSBC Holdings* 2001: 9–11; Pretzlik 2000)

By late 2001, the company had grown to 180,000 employees and some 6,000 offices in eighty-one countries, a narrower but deeper geographical presence than Citicorp's. That is natural for a financial intermediary emphasizing the retail rather than wholesale market. The difference in emphasis also reflects a deeper cleavage, British banks started in Southeast Asia as retailers but US banks as wholesalers. (*HSBC Holdings* 2001: 7, 26, 48; Cooke 1995: 47)

The geographical diversification has been extremely successful (Figure 5.28). Hongkong is important as it always has been with one-half of profits, thanks to a retail banking cartel. But assetwise it does not dominate any more. Western Europe is two-thirds larger and North America 'only' one-quarter smaller. The office networks tell a different story: in Brazil they are greatly overblown in relation to the asset base. There are fewer assets per office in Europe than North America, while Hongkong has the most. The ranking may reflect the relative ease of shedding superfluous labour, difficult in Brazil and easy in Hongkong. But it correlates with population density, too. Hongkong is a densely built city, New York

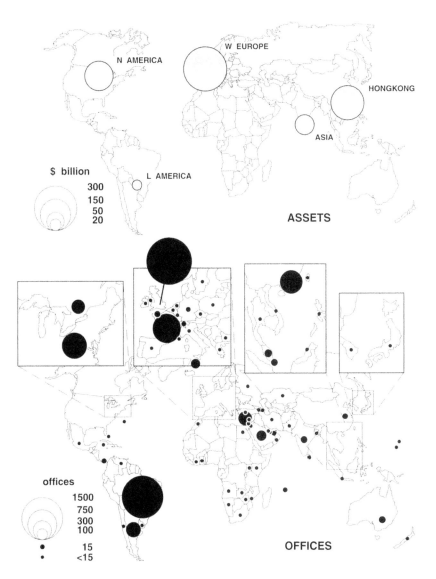

Figure 5.28 HSBC Group assets and offices, December 2000 and 2001.

Sources: *HSBC Group: a Profile* 2000: 8; *HSBC Holdings Annual Report and Accounts* 2001: 48, 84.

Note
In Saudi Arabia, a 40 per cent stake.

and Buffalo dominate the US presence, while European operations cover large swatches of semi-rural areas. The breakdown also disguises differences between countries and regional business mixes. For example, the Swiss ratio assets/offices exceeds Hongkong's forty-five-fold. As two-thirds of assets are loans covered by deposits, the ratio functions as a rough measure of profitability. Big is not always beautiful.

Conclusion

This chapter about banking is the one where the actor perspective becomes particularly apparent. The label is 'banking' rather than 'financial intermediation' because banks are a tangible concept uniting all relevant activities. How the field is then organized into operative units varies between countries and in time. Operational efficiency and regulatory needs can be difficult to conciliate and the outcome ultimately depends on political judgement. When all activities are collected under one roof, the universal bank alternative, operational efficiency is believed to be at its maximum. The size gives resistance to shocks and allows large undertakings without undue risk. The bank avoids the imperfections of external markets because both sellers and buyers come to it and because it has full selection of financial products. But it must be on its guard that the internalized markets do not lag behind the external ones in terms of efficiency. And it must tread the thin line of supporting loss-making activities or shedding them. These caveats also interest the regulator who is in charge of the fairness and soundness of activity. A large universal bank is more difficult to supervise than a specialized one, which leads to the creation of specialized banks. It is not only technical regulation that leads to such solutions but also wider economical goals such as the focusing of scarce resources and the mobilization of small savings.

Some twenty services can easily be differentiated. From among them, seven have been selected, partially by aggregation. Corresponding, lending, underwriting, trading, M&A advising, asset management and custodianship cover most banking activities. Their very different potential to create revenue and profits has been underlined. The geographical ambition has been twofold: to give an overall global picture and to emphasize features of great practical importance. The London interbank market, the role of US bulge bracket in M&A advising, and Swiss private bankers as asset managers are examples. Since the overall picture is tantamount to markets at large, and since markets have already been described in Chapter 3, the discussion here has been given some analytical colour. That has happened by grouping countries by M&A intensity, pointing out the difference between global and international banking, calculating the relative presence of the largest lending nations in debtor countries, and outlining statistical models of bank foreign entries and cross-border deposits. These aggregate treatises have, finally, been rounded out by short cases about the spatial expansion of two global banks. It is doubtful whether such behaviour has been adequately described by current models.

6 Insurance

Purpose and products

Insurance is included in this book for several reasons. It is an essential, and at times a major, part of finance centres. It creates substantial reserves which are invested in financial markets. It handles risk, an integrated element of the financial system at large. There is currency risk in foreign trade, credit risk in lending, market or price risk at exchanges and so on. Internal risk, in payments and lending for example, is handled by introducing controls and exercising due diligence. External unsystematic risk is handled by diversifying into assets and liabilities which do not correlate with each other. Systematic market risk cannot be diversified away but is hedged, that is, unloaded onto somebody else who is willing to assume it. Hedging is a kind of insurance, although the word is conventionally reserved for the handling of physical risk.

The risks for which insurance is bought may concern life, health, employer liability, product liability, environment, business interruption, property and so on. Their origin may be, for example, old age, sickness, accident, energy production and transportation, machinery breakdown, fire, flood, windstorm, earthquake, burglary or theft.

Insurance claims are triggered by occurrences. Some, like theft, include only one risk, while others, like earthquake, normally include several. The shock waves of an earthquake destroy buildings and these bury people, damaged gas lines set fires ablaze, business gets interrupted. The separation of sub-risks under the general heading of 'quake' may be difficult. The same applies when the occurrence covers an extended period, like creeping pollution.

Many types of occurrence, like car accidents, are fairly frequent, and the ensuing claims are small, easy to quantify, and can be settled within twelve-to-eighteen months. Frequency makes the use of statistical techniques possible. When the size of claims increases, they become less frequent and their final settlement takes a longer time, up to decades ('long-tail business'), as may be the case with employer liability and professional malpractice. Statistical fact-finding becomes difficult and intuition gains ground.

Claims for cars, homes and deaths are familiar from everyday life and need no elaboration. Although the claim total may be substantial, it is in proportion to the size of the economy and its ability to pay. Therefore, this type of risk is normally insured domestically. The opposite end, large industrial risks such as aeroplanes, power plants and fishing fleets, may be too large to be absorbed as a whole by the domestic insurance industry and are offered to the international market either as direct risks or through reinsurance. Because the angle here is international, such risks loom larger than their actual impact would warrant.

When potential claims escalate, it is appropriate to speak of catastrophe risks. Earthquakes, windstorms, floods and certain energy risks like oil platforms are well-known examples. Consolidated claims from a single occurrence can exceed $1bn, the $15.5bn from hurricane Andrew in southern Miami and along the Louisiana coast in 1992 being a landmark for many years (Smith 1996: 20). It is still far from a nightmare scenario. A Californian earthquake or a class five hurricane in Miami could easily cost $50bn and make a big hole in the $200bn equity and reserves of US non-life insurers (Denney 1995; *sigma* 5/1996: 4). Still worse, the trend is rising because people increasingly settle in attractive but catastrophe-prone areas, and because the climate has lately become warmer and more capricious (Figure 6.1).

To that has recently been added large-scale terrorism, whether outright malicious or one tilting towards mockery. The attack on the World Trade Center (WTC) is the current high mark of the former, the computer virus 'I love you' of the latter. The losses are estimated at $35bn–$50bn and more than $1bn, respectively, the former insured and the latter not (Coburn 2001/2002; *sigma* 2/2001). The WTC incident, in particular, raises the sceptre of urban risks, a nightmare because of their size and multitude; twenty-two insurance categories being anticipated in that particular case.

A closer look at catastrophe risk shows that the economics are also a question of the yardstick one uses. Conventional risks are manageable when put against the paper losses routinely created at exchanges, the daily fluctuation of US capital markets in the mid-1990s being, for example, $130bn. It appears natural, then, that insurance monies will, in the long term, be supplemented by the resources available in the financial markets proper. The beginnings of a futures market in catastrophe insurance already exist at the Chicago Board of Options Exchange. Its regional Catastrophe Risk Contracts (CATs) hedge exposures in Eastern US, Northeast, Southeast, Midwest, West, California, Florida, Texas and nationwide, and augment Eastern September hurricane and Western annual earthquake contracts. The cover is for the yet emerging claims from a catastrophe which has already occurred. Catastrophe bonds offer similar cover. The idea rests on the fact that the size of the losses accumulates gradually

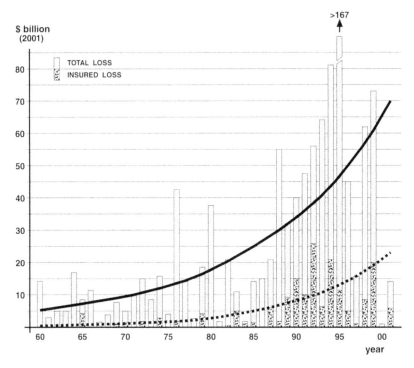

Figure 6.1 Losses in great natural catastrophes, 1960–2001.

Source: Munich Reinsurance Company, *Topics, Annual Review of Natural Catastrophes* 1996: 7; 2001: 14. Copyright © 1996, 2001 of Munich Reinsurance Company, Munich; used with permission.

(Figure 6.2). The trick is to guess how much and how soon. So far the reception of financial instruments has been muted because conventional insurance has been less expensive (Anon. 1995; *sigma* 5/1996: 4, 21).

Risk cover is obtained by paying an advance premium. Premium income is the insurer's sales revenue. It is still gross because sales costs, like brokerage and the premium paid to reinsurers, must be subtracted to arrive at the net premium income. Net premium is available for claims, administration expenses, build-up of reserves and investment. The funds to be invested depend essentially on the time lag between payment of premiums and settlement of claims. Investment, naturally, gives investment income. It is quite normal for the net premium to be so low that it does not cover claims and administration costs, and that profit depends on investment income (Figure 6.3). Insurance is then 'written for investment'. The degree of the dependency is routinely given by: combined ratio = (claims + administration)/net premium.

The description applies to direct insurers. Since a risk may be too large to be carried safely alone, the burden is shared. Either several insurers

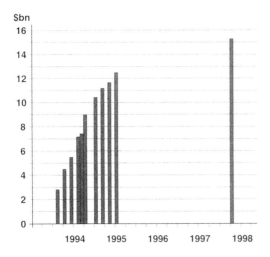

Figure 6.2 Development of loss estimate at Northridge earthquake.

Source: Munich Reinsurance Company, *Topics, Annual Review of Natural Catastrophes* 2001: 35. Copyright © 2001 of Munich Reinsurance Company, Munich; used with permission.

Note
Northridge earthquake took place on 17 January 1994.

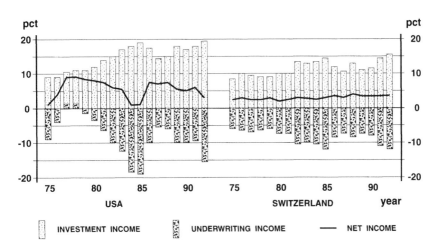

Figure 6.3 Return on net premium in non-life insurance, 1975–1992.

Source: Swiss Re, *sigma* No. 1/1995: Figures 2 and 7. Copyright © 1995 of Swiss Reinsurance Company, Zurich; used with permission.

Notes
The small variation in Switzerland results from regulation, abolished by 1997.

participate or part of the risk is ceded to reinsurers. Thereby the pool of those affected is increased so that the law of large numbers operates better. The cession can be based on a treaty which covers specific risks of an insured party or it is facultative, which allows the reinsurer to select the risks s/he wants to cover case-by-case. The cover is either proportional, i.e. a certain percentage, or it covers an agreed layer of the risk. Excess-of-loss (XL) is one possibility, another is stop-loss. The former refers to a monetary amount exceeding an agreed limit and ends at a ceiling. The latter meets the claims above a certain loss ratio but leaves the amount open. The share ceded tends to increase (and retention decrease) with the size and unpredictability of risk. Small and new insurers with limited reserves also cede a larger share than large and established ones. When reinsurers themselves cede part of their risk, the term is 'retrocession'.

Insurance business is subjected to economic cycles. Cyclicity partly reflects the investment income, be it from bonds, shares, real estate or mortgage, but primarily the interplay of insurance demand and supply. Exceptional losses alert minds to the desirability of insurance cover and increase demand. Demand also reacts to the relative merits of alternative insurance and investment vehicles at the insured's disposal. Life policies often contain a sizeable savings element because of their favourable tax treatment. Supply reflects the anticipated return on insurance capital compared with other investment opportunities. Cyclicity is smaller in the mass market, where policies are numerous, individual risks modest and regulation tighter than in large risks, where premiums can be halved or doubled from one contract year to another.

Cyclicity combined with weak profitability and an excessive or unpredictable claims history may lead to unavailability of insurance cover. Among risks which are difficult or impossible to place are terrorism, environmental, professional malpractice and certain employer liability. Terrorism is an old curse in Europe. Governments there have been compelled to intervene, and the city areas of several European capitals are essentially insured by them. The other categories are more a US problem because of the excessive and increasing damages decreed by courts, and where retroactive 'deep-pocket' legislation about polluted plant sites is in force. The solution, widespread in property and casualty risks, is to seek alternative insurance. Its share in the commercial (as opposed to personal) sector is approaching one-half of premiums (*sigma* 2/1999). The same also applies when the insured considers premiums excessive, possibly because of an unusually good claims record. It can leave the risks uninsured and absorb damages, rational in very large organizations although at the cost of downgraded risk consciousness. It can form its own insurance company, so-called 'captive', and it can join a mutual insurance club. Mutual clubs, so-called P&I (protection and indemnity) Clubs are crucial in shipping, where they participate in about 90 per cent of ship hulls insured. Europe lags behind the US in alternative risk transfer because of technological lag, availability of capacity and more regulation.

Insurance is a regulated industry. The three pillars are authorization, capital reserves and surveillance. The main purpose of regulation is to protect the insured, to guarantee that the insurer can meet all valid claims. To achieve this, the insurer's capital reserves must be in sound relation to the risks written. The reserves consist of equity and technical reserves. At established companies, the latter are easily three-to-five times the former. The technical yardstick is the solvency ratio = capital funds/net premiums. The way it is calculated and the minimum required by regulators varies between countries and also depends on the kind of insurance written. The other purpose is to protect domestic economic interests from foreign competition. Both purposes are to some extent conciliatory, as it is easier to monitor domestic than foreign companies. Insurance for international transports (marine, aviation and transport, or MAT) is the least protected segment, followed by reinsurance. They have truly international, even global, markets. Although it may happen that the first placement must be made at a national insurer, this has seldom sufficient capacity and surplus lines will be ceded abroad. Mass markets like motor, accident and life are the most protected ones, having compulsory guarantee funds and state guarantees, both signs of consumer protection.

Licence applications can be a hurdle. In the USA, although basically an open market, separate authorization is needed in each of the fifty states, which all have their own rule sets. It takes years to complete the full ritual, and an entrant might seriously consider buying an established company. In the UK, which is lightly regulated by European standards, the authorization process takes six months, while offshore centres such as Bermuda, Dublin and Luxembourg manage with four-to-nine weeks. In the EU, authorization in one country automatically gives access to all the others, but it does not give exemption from their national surveillance and tax legislation. Latin America at large welcomes foreign insurers while Asia is protectionistic. As can be anticipated, the most regulated and protected markets are also the most profitable ones (Figure 6.4). Whether they also are the safest ones for insureds is less certain. There has not been a single insurer insolvency in Germany for thirty years, while in Japan a life insurer was suspended from business in 1997 when its solvency margin slid below the regulatory minimum. It had sold life policies with a guaranteed savings element and not foreseen the decline in government bond rates (*sigma* 6/2000). Swiss life insurers currently face a similar dilemma.

Much of the basic classification routinely used in insurance has indirectly come out already in our discussion. The first split is into private insurance and social security provided by the authorities. This report discusses only the private sector. It is divided into direct and reinsurance. Both are further split into non-life and life segments. Accident and health insurance are in the grey zone. In Europe they are included in non-life,

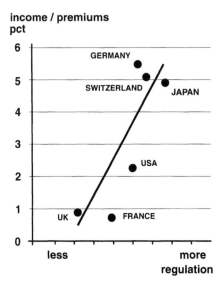

Figure 6.4 Return on net premium relates to regulation, 1975–1992.

Source: Swiss Re, *sigma* No. 1/1995: Figure 13. Copyright © 1995 of Swiss Reinsurance Company, Zurich; used with permission.

while in North America and Japan they are in the life segment. Here, the European practice is followed in global statistics and national practice in short overviews. In non-life, the major subsegments are motor, fire/ property, liability and MAT. Motor, in particular, dominates premiums in many countries. A parallel grouping is into the conventional (or tradi- tional) and alternative market.

'A rich man's industry'

Demand for insurance grows with increasing wealth. Since a varying share is met by the public sector and since this report handles only the private industry, the relative sizes of country markets sometimes deviate strongly from what might be expected from their national economies. The vari- ation is greatest in life insurance and is reinforced in many countries by the imbedded savings element.

The relation with wealth also makes the richest Continents and coun- tries the world's main insurance markets (Figure 6.5). As to their relative sizes, caution is warranted. In the first edition of this book, they were about equal. In 2000, North America had overtaken the other two and Asia is trailing Western Europe. The explanation is simple: a stronger dollar and weaker yen. In local currencies, the changes have not been so great, although the relative growth of life premiums in Western Europe,

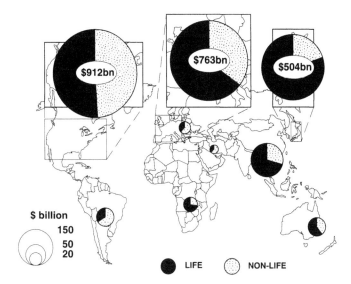

Figure 6.5 Gross direct premium income, 2000.

Source: Swiss Re, *sigma* No. 6/2001: Table I.

Notes
Japanese life insurers Kampo and Zenkyoren included.

and also North America, should be mentioned. Again, the explanation is simple: enhanced importance of the savings element prompted by the gradual demise of the pay-as-you-go pension system. Structurally, the Western economies are approaching the Asian ones. As the market was in 2000, the life premiums were almost the same, whereas non-life premiums in North America were more than half of the global total.

When attention is turned from Continents to countries, it is rational to bring them to a common basis by calculating two ratios:

- density = gross premium/person,
- penetration = 100 × gross premium/GDP.

Insurance *density* is interesting as a marketing signal because it gives a monetary indicator (Figure 6.6). There is a declining gradient from the rich northwest Europe, actually part of a larger Atlantic gradient with the USA as the western apex, tapering outwards in all directions. A more vague, low-intensity gradient can be visualized in Asia, with a patchy ridge in the Pacific Rim and declining westwards. The very low values in the valley between the two peaks centred in northwest Europe and the Rim, respectively, can partially be related to cultural factors. It is largely the Islamic world governed by *sharia* which forbids interest-earning business

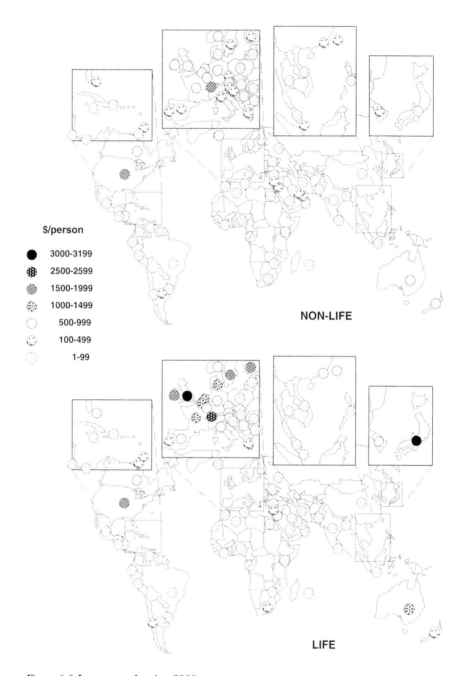

$/person

●	3000-3199
⊛	2500-2599
▨	1500-1999
◍	1000-1499
○	500-999
◔	100-499
○	1-99

NON-LIFE

LIFE

Figure 6.6 Insurance density, 2000.
Source: Swiss Re, *sigma* No. 6/2001: Table VIII.

and treaties whose fulfilment depends on uncertain future events, which are the very core of insurance (Rakiya 1999: 6–10; *sigma* 4/1996: 11). That is a fateful ruling because it hampers the accumulation of long-term investment capital, the foundation of economic development.

Scrutinized by country, the non-life half of Figure 6.6 is more regular than the life half. The per capita value of the vehicle park, building stock and factories cannot differ so dramatically between industrialized countries. Third-party traffic insurance is compulsory, home insurance covers fire, burglary and often some form of natural catastrophe. The economic rationale is easily visible and the decision fairly uncomplicated. What complicates this neat picture somewhat is that health premiums are included and that the social safety net offered by public bodies varies so much. The band of error can be made tangible by reference to the USA, where 15 per cent of GDP are spent on healthcare. One-third of this is financed by private insurers (*sigma* 2/1998). The country also tops, together with Switzerland, the non-life country ranking.

The variation is considerably larger in the life segment. In industrialized societies the benefits of public social security weigh heavily. Italy, France and Germany, for example, are known for their generous pension schemes. The UK and Japan are their opposites. To that come alternative saving possibilities, tax-exempted bank accounts and high-yield government bonds, for example. Where these do not exist, a life policy with a substantial savings element may be a good solution; except where it happens to be heavily taxed, as in Italy. Definitional matters add to the confusion: in Germany, pension funds do not fall under the concept of life insurance. And in the USA mutual funds are difficult competitors to pension funds.

Penetration outlines the relative burden placed on the national economy for the chosen level of insurance cover. There, too, material wealth comes to the fore (Figure 6.7). Average figures can be read from S-shaped regression curves. They begin at the 0.5–1.0 per cent level, the life curve below the non-life curve, typical for nascent markets. The non-life curve levels off at the 3 per cent mark while the life curve continues its rise. The widespread use of a life policy as a savings instrument is the main reason. Figures from countries where the savings element plays a secondary role suggest that pure life risk is valued at roughly 3.0 per cent, the same as the non-life risk. The cut-off at the 4 per cent mark is a mere convention, as is apparent by looking at the country figures (Figure 6.8). Against the downsizing of social security in Western Europe and the shrinking family size in industrializing Asian economies, the difference between Japanese or British levels and this 3 per cent mark can be taken as a rough indicator of long-term market potential.

The geographical order seen in insurance density is partially wiped away in insurance penetration. The Atlantic and Asian gradients can be visualized with some goodwill but they are less regular and there are

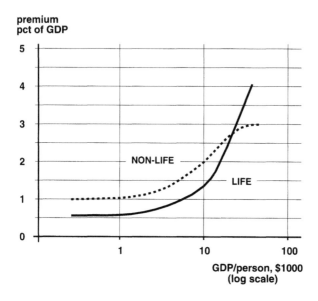

Figure 6.7 Insurance penetration relates to living standard, 1999.

Source: Swiss Re, *sigma* No. 4/2001: Figures 7 and 8. Copyright © 2001 of Swiss Reinsurance Company, Zürich; used with permission.

anomalies in the margins. The bright side is that well-known national features became apparent. The high marks scored by South Africa, Japan and Korea in the life sector are typical, the result of a substantial savings element. Such policies produced some 30 per cent of Japanese and Korean non-life premiums in 1994. Not only gaps in the social security system but also the dismal level of investment return from bonds and equity have led to their popularity (*sigma* 4/1996: 21; 6/1996: 15–16). In the non-life sector corresponding practices are common. Maturity-fund policies return 80–100 per cent of premiums to the policy holder at the end of the term if claims do not exceed an agreed level (*sigma* 8/2000).

In non-life insurance, one would expect a much closer link to the role of capital-intensive industries in a country's economy and its exposure to natural hazards than appears to be the case. Territories with a modest industrial base like the Bahamas and Barbados outdistance Scandinavia, for example. Of course, capital-intensive industries need not contribute to the GDP in proportion to their insurance value, nor are natural catastrophes fully insurable. Although natural catastrophes are widespread, the insurance market they create is too concentrated to allow meaningful diversification (Figure 6.9). And although more than 40 per cent of worldwide non-proportional catastrophe reinsurance premium originates from the USA, only 20 per cent of possible Californian property losses, for example, are actually insured (*sigma* 5/1996: 7–8). California is not a

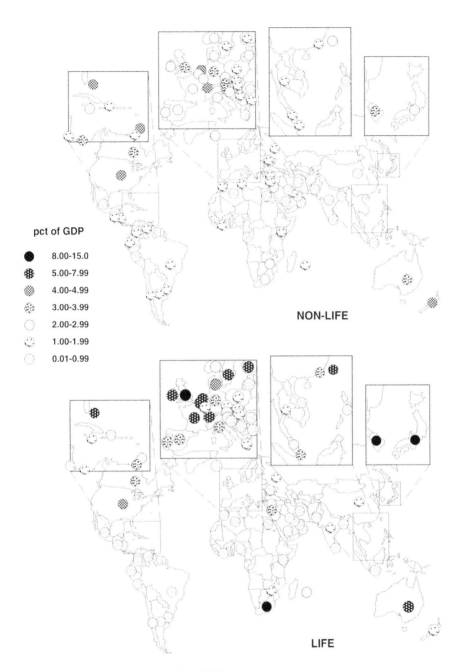

pct of GDP

●   8.00-15.0
⬤   5.00-7.99
⬤   4.00-4.99
⬤   3.00-3.99
○   2.00-2.99
◌   1.00-1.99
○   0.01-0.99

NON-LIFE

LIFE

Figure 6.8 Insurance penetration, 2000.
Source: Swiss Re, *sigma* No. 6/2001: Table IX.

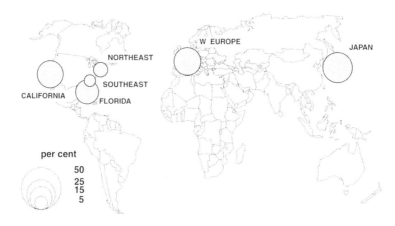

Figure 6.9 Geographical exposure of catastrophe risk, 2000.
Source: Jenkins 2002: 39.

singular case. Notwithstanding earthquakes, tsunamis and windstorms, much of Japan's building stock is uninsured, retentions by the insured are large, and the ultimate earthquake reinsurance is provided by the government, i.e. it is external to the private insurance industry. In the Kobe earthquake, 1995, damages were $82bn but insurance claims only $2.5bn, a low percentage compared with the 30–60 per cent range, normal for catastrophes in industrialized countries (Terazono 1995; *sigma* 2/1996: 6). More than that, the maximum indemnity payable by all insurers to all policyholders per event is decided annually by the Diet. At the time of the quake, it happened to be about $18bn (*Non-life Insurance in Japan, Fact Book* 1994: 37). In France the problem has been solved in an elegant way. Everyone with property insurance is automatically covered against all natural catastrophes except windstorms. It is sufficient that an incident is declared as a catastrophe in the French Official Journal. Reinsurance is ultimately offered by the government (Jack 1996).

Towards international horizons

The preceding tables and figures have not differentiated between domestic and foreign writing. The distinction is important for the international and global approach of this book, while the various aspects of foreignness contribute to conceptual confusion. 'Foreign' can mean insurance written abroad, in the country where the risks and the insured parties are located, foreign-owned local writing; or it can mean insurance written from outside the country of location, pure cross-border writing. Cross-border writing can be practised by domestic as well as foreign-owned insurers. It primarily targets larger non-life risks, or is reinsurance. Direct insurance written locally should not differ from the activity of domestic insurers. Historically, it has been a larger business than cross-border writing but the EU's Pan-European passport may have changed that.

The advantages which a foreign-owned insurer is believed to bring to the host country are its capital resources, possibly exceeding those locally available, and its better know-how of particular risks. This applies in an emerging market. In a mature market, its presence will facilitate the diversification of risk, although the same effect can also be achieved through reinsurance. Most countries do not seem to appreciate these advantages too much but try to constrain the entry of foreigners. They suspect foreigners' ability and willingness to honour claims and fear that precious capital will leak out of the country. Entry is likely to be a time-consuming process rather than an on-off event. It will begin by the removal of obligatory cessions to government reinsurers or domestic pools, continue by a cross-border reinsurance licence, proceed to minority and then majority holdings in local companies, to be followed by the opening of local subsidiaries (independent legal entities) and thereafter branches (dependent on cross-border parent), and end with a licence to sell products directly from abroad (*sigma* 4/2000: Figure 4). Each phase in the chain is equally valid as a reference point. The choice here is majority holding and the purpose is to exemplify differences in foreign influence by country (Figure 6.10). The data are from larger emerging markets, with less than $13,000 per capita GDP and at least $500m gross premium income from direct insurance, plus South Africa. Their growth is twice that of mature markets which makes participation most desirable. The former criterion excludes territories like Hongkong and Singapore from the population.

The topical countries are grouped as Latin America, East Europe and Asia with foreign shares of 47 per cent, 41 per cent and 12 per cent, respectively (*sigma* 4/2000: 3). These shares also include companies with foreign minority of at least 20 per cent but the exact ownership criterion is immaterial to the overall picture. Latin America has taken a liberal attitude towards foreign insurers because its ability to generate capital is insufficient for its needs. The population may also have more faith in foreign than local life insurers. East Europe has lived for many years under the legacy of state-owned monopolies which may still collect half of the premiums. The countries displayed here are those where the deregulation has proceeded furthest with entry into the EU in mind. Asia continues to be comparatively closed and this applies particularly to the large markets. The prevalence of corporate conglomerates allows in-house insurance. High savings rates have moderated the need for foreign capital. Protectionistic and dirigiste attitudes may sit deeper than elsewhere. In India, a foreigner cannot exceed 26 per cent out of total equity, and in China operations must have at least $24m (Rmb200m) capital in each city.

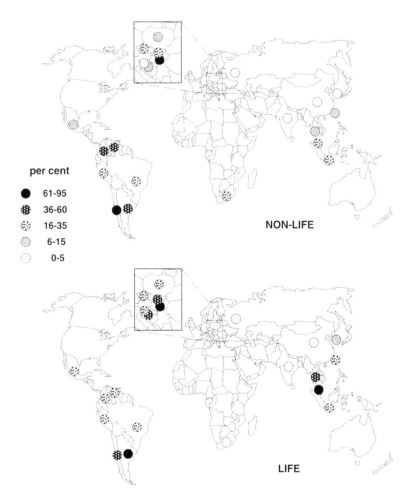

Figure 6.10 Foreign share of direct premiums in large emerging markets, about 1999.

Sources: Swiss Re, *sigma* No. 4/2000: Figures 6, 8, 10 and Table 13; Feller 2001/2002.

Note
Only companies with foreign majority.

That is a lot, recalling that the minimum capital of a catastrophe insurer in Bermuda, known for its strict supervision, is $100m (Feller 2002).

Cross-border operations are a much simpler story. Total premiums out of the global grand total in 2000 were 2.2 per cent in non-life and 0.7 per cent in life insurance. The non-life sector is dominated by the UK and the life sector by Ireland and Luxembourg (*sigma* 6/2001: 5). Luxembourg gets its business from Belgium and Ireland makes use of the Pan-European passport. The British activity, called 'home–foreign' in the vernacular, also extends overseas. It is mostly Lloyd's of London, the insurance market, which has a licence for direct insurance in about sixty countries and all of the US states, a testimony of its long history and readiness to accept unconventional risks.

In reinsurance, foreigners normally play a larger role than in direct writing. It may be difficult to find the necessary cover at home, and it is desirable to spread large risks far and wide. Smaller companies in particular must seek cover from reinsurance. Therefore, in markets dominated by them, the share of premium ceded to reinsurers tends to be larger than otherwise. Market concentration, measured by the herfindahl index, is unable to grasp this need because it leaves the market size undefined. Several large companies can operate in a large country, and yet the concentration remains modest. Countries with large, even catastrophic, risks, whether natural or man-made, such as oil platforms, are potentially large international markets. For this to be realized, insurance cover needs to be sought for in the first place, and the market must be open for foreigners to operate.

The emphasis of activity is in the non-life sector with four times more premiums than life. Since the life sector is larger in direct insurance this means that the cession rate is much higher in non-life than life. The statistical properties of life risks are 'better' than those of non-life risks and make cessions less important. Approximate figures are 14 and 1.5 per cent, respectively for non-life and life, fairly stable when aggregated over continental regions but variable by country (*sigma* 9/1998: 5). The London non-life market has many small foreign-owned companies and cedes about 30 per cent, often to parents abroad. The Japanese figure is only 4 per cent because the companies are large. German insurers, out of sheer conservatism, write predominantly proportional rather than selective treaty reinsurance, which leads to large cessions. The providers are increasingly large, multinational groupings which have expanded to all major markets to diversify risk and exploit market openings (Figure 6.11). The main vehicle has been acquisition: Americans purchasing insurers in Germany, Germans and French in the USA, Swiss in the UK and Italy and so on (*sigma* 9/1998: 11). The targets have been large companies giving substantial market share. It follows that a company's domicile becomes less relevant for the location of its business. Swiss Re gets 85 per cent of its premium abroad, it and Munich Re write one-half of the French premium, whereas Axa has only one-quarter of its business at home, actually less than in the USA (Bolger 1999; Challis 1996). Rather than plunging into this jungle of criss-crossing market shares, it is more fruitful to consider a few key markets in detail.

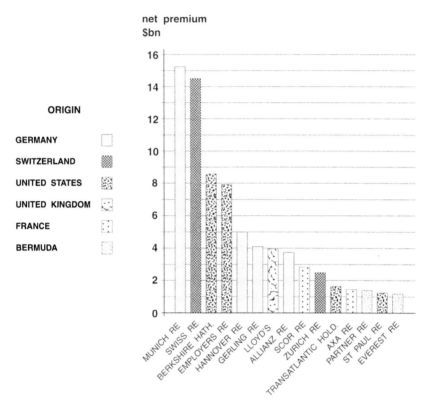

net premium
$bn

ORIGIN

GERMANY ▢

SWITZERLAND ▨

UNITED STATES ▩

UNITED KINGDOM ▨

FRANCE ▨

BERMUDA ▢

Figure 6.11 Largest reinsurance groups, 2000.
Source: Reactions, March, 2002: 32.

The London Market – old but resilient

It is noteworthy that the UK does not figure more strongly among the top fifteen reinsurers, its market size and deep international involvement notwithstanding. The market's unusual structure may help to explain this. There is a clear division between domestic and foreign business, the non-life split between them being about 60/40. The potential reinsurance market is thereby almost halved, and internationally active reinsurers also compete keenly for the domestic half. Many are subsidiaries of foreign groups.

The foreign business is essentially done in and from London, where the activity is concentrated almost exclusively in the financial district (the City or Square Mile). The physical core can be cited as the buildings of Lloyd's and the International Underwriting Association of London (IUA) a stone's throw away. In total, about 120 companies and seventy-five Lloyd's syndicates with almost $40bn capacity/capital are within a five minute's walk. The physical closeness, unrivalled elsewhere except perhaps for some offshore centres, is a substantial competitive advantage when it comes to placing unusual risks through brokers, in need of face-to-face negotiation. Not unexpectedly, such risks are a London speciality.

Insurers organized around IUA are called the 'company market' because the members are conventional limited companies (Figure 6.12). Lloyd's of London, by contrast, is originally a market where individuals, arranged in syndicates, write insurance. Lloyd's and the company market

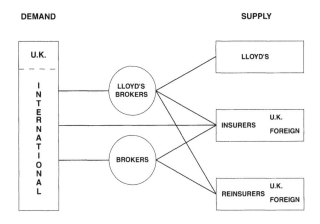

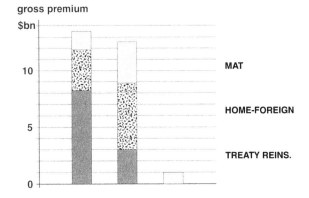

Figure 6.12 Structure of the London Market.

Sources: Swiss Re, *sigma* No. 2/1995: Figure 1; *sigma* No. 3/2002: Table 2. Copyright © 1995; 2002 of Swiss Reinsurance Company, Zurich; used with permission.

Notes
Home–foreign = Non-marine direct cross-border and faculty. London market risks written from outside and UK risks written from London are not included. The net effect might add $4.5bn to the premium total.

are of roughly equal size. There is a fair degree of specialization between the two. Lloyd's is particularly active in MAT and direct catastrophe insurance, and IUA in non-marine treaty reinsurance. A looser grouping are the P&I Clubs, which insure ship hulls and cargoes on a mutual basis against risks not covered by Lloyd's and companies' policies.

The London Market is exceptional in having underwritten risks globally for several centuries. It is a non-life market which relies on brokers and where risks are jointly written, perhaps a necessity in business which often revolves around risks which are difficult to place, such as catastrophe reinsurance, energy, political, ransom and professional malpractice. The global market shares of 3 per cent in direct insurance and 15 per cent in reinsurance are not overly impressive but when calculated from typical London business, the picture changes: in aviation, 40 per cent; in offshore oil and gas rigs, 60 per cent; in P&I clubs, 70 per cent; and dominance in other marine insurance. It has 20 per cent market shares in Japanese reinsurance and US excess and surplus lines. Although located in the UK, it is not a particularly British market; actually the opposite. The company market has always been a place for foreigners but now they are also about to gain majority position at Lloyd's. In a way that is a welcome sign because it demonstrates the market's international attractiveness. A particular strength is the expertise of its legal profession, sourcing from the vast resources of case law.

Less welcome is that London has lost one-half of its market share to offshore, and Bermuda in particular. Much activity is in segments where growth is slow, such as marine and aviation. Its cost base has been too high, 45 per cent of premiums going into administration and only 55 per cent for covering the risks. Measures have been taken by consolidating claims handling into a joint venture, Insure, and accepting business without the intermediation of brokers. The results take time to materialize. Many London insurers are smallish and therefore considered risky in troubled times. Consolidation has been the natural response but it has only kept pace with the outside world. There has been much imprudent underwriting with heavy loss of capital as a consequence. Complaints of unfinished work appear frequently. The size of retrocession to foreign parents is also a weakness. (Ballantine 2001; Dawkins 1997; Goddard *et al.* 2001/2002; Murray and Kritz 1996: 28; *sigma* 3/2002: 4–5, 8)

Although brokers are expensive they also provide an indispensable service in placing complicated risks which need face-to-face negotiation and which are so large that nobody wants to write them alone. It helps when there is a broker who is familiar with the insurers' specialities and rates, and who has the patience to accumulate full cover from smaller lines, say down to 5 per cent. For his trouble the broker collects a fee, 15–30 per cent of the premium in direct business and 5–10 per cent in reinsurance, which s/he may share with other intermediaries. The 140 brokers increasingly represent large houses, the three largest having

60 per cent of the London Market. They are in no way constrained to the London Market but can place the major part of their business elsewhere. (Carter and Falush 1994: Table 1.5; *sigma* 3/2002: 18)

Lloyd's of London, like so many City institutions, has its origin in a seventeenth-century coffee house which offered a meeting place for shipowners and financiers for chartering shipping space, selling and insuring cargoes. Originally, insurance cover was provided by individuals, but with increasing risks they formed syndicates, today's underwriting units. The members, called 'Names', remained responsible for all liabilities with their whole property, nevertheless. But they could write off possible losses against tax, a benefit which became important after the Second World War, when the income tax rate was at times 90 per cent. The concept has remained reasonably intact to this day, and one may wonder how it has been able to survive competition by limited companies with their seemingly unlimited capital base. A plausible answer is that limited companies, following some early scandals, were outlawed in the UK for most of the eighteenth century and that Lloyd's was, in the meantime, able to establish a reputation and professionalism which were not easily dislodged.

A difficult risk in which a Lloyd's syndicate has taken the first share ('line') and set the first premium for others to follow ('lead underwriter') is easily placed elsewhere, in Zurich, Paris or Bermuda, for example. The other explanation is the aura of, until recently, impeccable financial security. Without the unlimited liability of its Names, Lloyd's would have needed about three times its book assets to offer the same implied rating. That, however, is history. Following the profitability crisis of the late 1980s and early 1990s, and the consequent introduction of corporate capital, Lloyd's got its first explicit credit rating ever, A+ by S&P. This cleared the air but, recalling that 40 per cent of its premium income comes from reinsurance and that its largest competitors score higher ratings, it also underlines the competitive disadvantage (Adams 1997c; Feldstead 2001; *sigma* 2/1995: n. 9).

Names are organized into syndicates which are the operational units. The membership lasts one year at a time, whereafter the Name can switch over to another syndicate, for the obvious benefit of skilled underwriters and managing agents. Because there is a time lag between occurrences and the settlement of claims, books are kept open for three years before reserves are set aside for open and unrecorded claims, profits distributed and Names freed from liability (Adams 1997b; Atkins 1996a). Three years were sufficient as long as risks were uncomplicated but has proved impracticable with the coming of long-tail, high-risk business. Accelerating catastrophe claims, the hardening stand by US courts towards liability risks and reckless writing of excess-of-loss reinsurance led in the early 1990s to a situation where numerous syndicates were unable to close their books. Indeed, having lost more than £8bn since the late 1980s, Lloyd's came to the brink of bankruptcy. The crisis led to decline in underwriting capacity and prompted the acceptance of limited companies as members, from 1994 (Figure 6.13). That created a two-tiered structure followed by conflicts of interest. The almost 900 corporate members find the administrative effort in handling the accounts of some 2,800 Names excessively expensive, with a regulatory apparatus larger than at the Department of Trade and Industry. They detest the mutualization of losses which supports the entrepreneurship of small syndicates. They want to replace the archaic three-year accounting period with the GAAP standard. But, although having almost 90 per cent of underwriting capacity, they are soundly outvoted by Names when it comes to decision making. In the long term, the Names can hardly prevail, however, and the gradual merging of Lloyd's and the company market is well on the cards. (Adams 1997a; Dyson 2002; Mayer 1997; *sigma* 3/2002)

The progress notwithstanding, Lloyd's is not out of the woods yet. The future is intimately connected with the US marketplace. The capricious nature of its courts when decreeing liability damages is the main stumbling block, and the tendency has become worse rather than better. The retroactive (pre-1986) legislation about polluted industrial sites has a guesstimated price tag of $260bn and asbestos claims are guesstimated at $60bn–$70bn. Although only a fraction of the total bill will fall on Lloyd's doorstep, its size is sufficient to put the existence of the organization into jeopardy again. To escape the menace and make up for old misdoings Lloyd's transferred, at the regulator's consent, an estimated £11bn ($18bn) of old liabilities to a new company, Equitas, and negotiated a

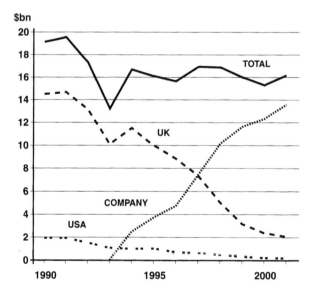

Figure 6.13 Lloyd's capacity by major origin, 1990–2001.

Source: Courtesy of Lloyd's of London.

compensation agreement with the Names affected at a price of £6.2bn. It is uncertain, however, whether Equitas is able to shoulder the burden placed upon it, which keeps the effort in a grey zone. (Adams 1997b; Leonard 2001/2002; Mayer 1997; *sigma* 2/1995: 25)

Lloyd's capital ('capacity') used to originate mainly from the UK but also from the English-speaking world at large. The Commonwealth countries were on the same level as the USA, closely followed by South Africa and Ireland. That changed with the coming of corporate capital. Most of it originates from the USA, either directly or through Bermudan companies, with a sprinkling from Australia and Germany. Premium income, instead, is split pro rata between the UK, North America and rest of the world (Figure 6.14). The large dependence upon the US market is witness to its size and relative openness. It also introduces a considerable market risk, because foreigners have no influence on American legislation and administrative practice.

The US market – the international honeypot?

The USA, being the world's largest insurance market and one where discrimination against foreigners is minimal, appears a real international honeypot – or almost. Surprisingly, the market's curse is stifling and intensifying regulation, thought to protect consumers and stimulate competition. The regulation has an important structural element in the fact that

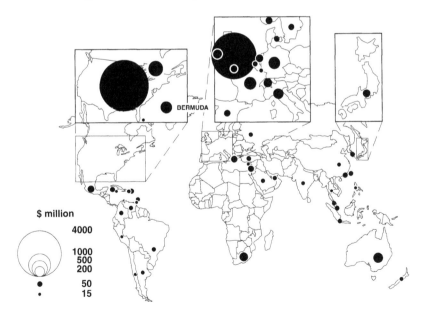

Figure 6.14 Lloyd's gross premium income by country, 2000.

Source: Courtesy of Lloyd's of London.

the insurance industry falls under the jurisdiction of individual states rather than federal authorities. As state regulations vary, an entrant, whether out-of-state or foreign, must file a separate licence application in each of them. Admission into all fifty states with attached seasoning periods and temporary bans on new admissions may take up to ten years (Pomerantz and Nilsen 1995: 98). Thereafter come applications of rates and policies. The approval system has two extremes: (1) obligatory prior approval and (2) subsequent approval with the supervisor intervening only when regulations are violated.

The property and casualty market is the main target of foreign insurers and this review is limited accordingly (*sigma* 1/1997). Its premium income exceeds Europe's by 25 per cent, and almost 40 per cent of it originates from California, New York, Texas, Florida and Pennsylvania. Peculiar to the casualty market, although unusual by world standards, is the 55 per cent share of long-tail business. The market splits into a traditional segment and an alternative one. The alternative share, particularly in commercial lines, is larger than in any other country at 45 per cent (*sigma* 2/1999). The segment started growing in 1987, when a sharp increase in premiums, following catastrophe losses, triggered an exodus of insureds with good loss histories from the traditional segment. The traditional segment is divided into an admitted market and excess and surplus lines. Excess and surplus are risks which are impossible to place at the admitted insurers and are consequently also open to non-admitted companies whose regulation is comparatively lenient. Although important internationally, excess and surplus are only 3.5 per cent of the admitted market (Ballantine 2001). The restricted availability of reinsurance cover for catastrophe risks has led to direct state involvement in states such as Florida, California and Hawaii.

The existence of excess and surplus lines has much to do with price controls. The ideology is that insurance cover should be available for all risks, for everybody, and at a reasonable price. That can only be achieved, if at all, by regulating prices and enforcing the writing of unprofitable business. When the prices accepted by authorities are too low, the admitted market gets divided into free and residual, that is, unprofitable, market. Prolonged unprofitability leads to unavailability of cover and inability to pay claims. The authorities, often directly elected, are tempted to make the insurance licence conditional on also writing unattractive insurance. This applies particularly to the mass market, where residual shares can be substantial. For example, in personal auto, the residual market varies between 0.5 and 50 per cent by state, and in workers' compensation, it grew from 5 to 25 per cent during 1985–1994. Profitable lines cross-subsidize this business. It happens that insurers retreat, at least temporarily, from states where cross-subsidies are excessive. Some flee offshore, Bermuda and the Caribbean in particular. If a foreigner, nevertheless, decides to go after private customers, s/he needs deep pockets.

Owned distribution network is highly desirable, and the larger it can be made the better. Brokers and multiple agents are for corporate customers. (Authers 1996; *sigma* 4/1994: 32, 36; 1/1997: 15–16, 19)

The state-by-state variation in regulation and surveillance easily leads to an uneven playing field between companies and duplication in bureaucracy. As federal intervention is not possible, state commissioners have formed a private association, the National Association of Insurance Commissioners (NAIC), which gives guidelines about regulation and minimal standards, and exercises control over state surveillance resources. The weights which are used to scale investment risk and reinsurance cover provide an example. Treasury bonds carry zero risk; other bonds vary between 1 and 30 per cent depending on the credit rating of the issuer; shares are 15 per cent; real estate and reinsurance 10 per cent; and international insurance subsidiaries, a wholesome 50 per cent (*sigma* 4/1994: 13). The last figure hampers the internationalization of US insurers.

States are under no obligation to follow the guidelines, but non-compliance leads to a renewed solvency investigation each time an insurer domiciled in a non-complying state applies for a licence in a complying one. The great majority of states comply, although there have been important outsiders. For example, New York, Pennsylvania and Vermont either had not complied or had been excluded from among the accredited states as of year-end 1993. The inclusion of Vermont among important states depends on its role as a domicile of onshore captive insurers.

Captive insurance companies are a core segment of US foreign involvement. Another segment is foreign insurers writing excess and surplus lines and reinsurance. Where, exactly, the cover comes from is not always clear, although the London Market, and Lloyd's in particular, plays a role in excess and surplus, as do some offshore finance centres. Among them, the Cayman Islands is known as a location for professional malpractice cover and Bermuda for captives and catastrophe risks. As a captive insurance company is a common vehicle for writing professional malpractice insurance, it is impossible to draw an unambiguous line between the two.

Reinsurance statistics are more readily available and they support earlier statements (Figure 6.15). One-third of the market, affiliated companies, is internal to large insurance groups, the rest are independents. Bermuda and the Caribbean represent offshore centres. The UK can be equated with the London Market. Germany and Switzerland are the homes of world-class reinsurance companies and the rest belong to the medium league. When a disaster occurs, the losses are distributed accordingly (Figure 6.16). The country shares are by no means stable, and trouble at one location is rapidly reflected at the competitive international marketplace. A classical example is Bermuda's overtaking of the UK in the 1980s, a result of capacity shortage at Lloyd's (Figure 6.17).

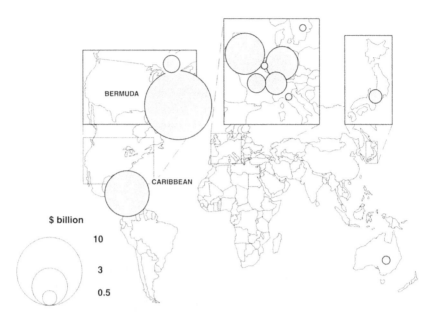

Figure 6.15 US premium income ceded abroad by destination, 2000.

Source: *Survey of Current Business*, November, 2001: Table 6.4.

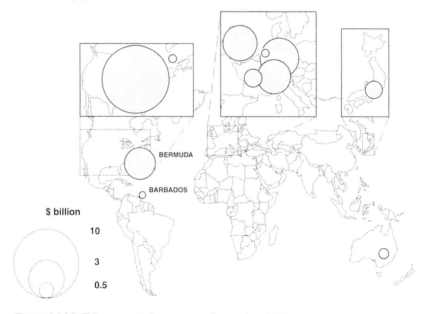

Figure 6.16 WTC exposure by country, December 2001.

Source: *Global Reinsurance*, December/January, 2001/2002: 34–39.

Notes
High estimates. Minimum $50m. Two-thirds by reinsurers, the rest by direct insurers.

**premium ceded
abroad, pct**

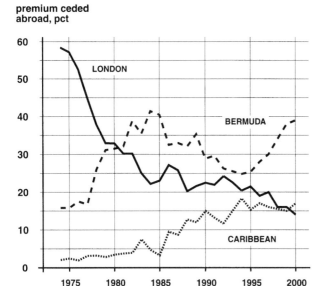

Figure 6.17 US reinsurance premium ceded abroad by major destination,
1974–2000.

Sources: Carter and Falush 1994: Figure 6.3; *Survey of Current Business* 1995–2000, Tables
6.1 to 6.4.

Captives – the exotic alternative

Captive insurance companies are established by large multinationals and
professional bodies to handle in-house insurance in segments where commercial insurance is excessively expensive and unpredictable, insufficient
or outright unavailable. Lower taxes contribute, since in most countries
insurance premiums are tax deductible, whereas reserves to pay future
damages are not. To that has lately come better control, of investment
policy for example, and more convenient collection of premiums worldwide. Because claims are own, their handling is simple and inexpensive.
Costs are about 5 per cent of premiums against 35 per cent or more
without captives. A captive company can offload part of the risk onto the
reinsurance market, which the parent cannot access. The standard practice is that insurance is taken in an unaffiliated local company (fronting),
which reinsures in the insured's captive for a 5–10 per cent share of premiums. Fronting helps to keep the taxman at bay, since premium paid to
the local insurer is arguably external to the corporation. Captives have
existed for at least 150 years, and many a conventional insurer traces its
origin back to them. The first single-parent captive may have been established in Copenhagen in 1919 and the first offshore firm in Guernsey in

1922. Their popularity, on the other hand, is a recent phenomenon, the number having grown threefold during the past ten years. (Corroon 1994; Leonard 1998; Moore 2002; Woodman 1996)

There is normally an overall business plan. For example, smaller operational risks with high transaction costs are absorbed by the parent, the captive assumes catastrophe risks and seeks reinsurance for the layers it does not want to retain. The minimum annual premium for making a single-parent captive worthwhile is variously estimated as between $1m and $8m. The estimate depends on location and time, offshore is lower than onshore, and the trend is towards smaller minimums. A captive may have several owners, and it can write third-party insurance, preferably for the parent's customers with familiar risks. When third-party business becomes important, the captive is likely to end up in the domain of commercial insurers and face more stringent regulation. On the other hand, tax authorities may require a minimum share of third-party writing in order to consider premiums paid by the parent as tax deductible. In the USA, the formal limit is 30 per cent. Larger open market risks are then juxtaposed with a lower tax rate. When a captive has several owners it is desirable that one's financial difficulties do not contaminate others. This can be achieved by establishing a Protected Cell Company (PCC) in which the funds of each co-owner are separated from each other. So far PCC is an offshore construction and has not been tested in onshore courts (Freeman 2002).

Globally, captive premiums are $18bn–$20bn or some 8 per cent of the property and casualty market (Leonard 1998). Practically all captives originate from the industrialized world (Figure 6.18). They have been more popular in the USA and Europe than Asia because of the close ties between industrial and financial companies there. With the dismantling of the *keiretsu* banking philosophy, this is bound to change, however. Captive destinations have overwhelmingly been small zero- or low-tax offshore territories, often British dependencies (Figure 6.19). Onshore destinations, that is, located within the country of origin, have a share of about 10 per cent or less. An onshore captive is more expensive and complex to set up and operate than its offshore cousin, but it avoids fronting fees and ceding commissions, is more likely to benefit from tax treaties, and is easier to control by the parent (Caine 1994). Offshore tax advantages have also come under the intensifying scrutiny of onshore tax authorities.

Why some offshore locations prosper but not others is actually a question to be discussed in the context of finance centres. Political and social stability, absence of capital and exchange controls, flexible tax regimes, credible but not stifling regulation, rapid licensing, acceptable cost, familiar language, solid legal, accounting and communication infrastructure, all can be included as general requirements (Caine 1994; Day 1996: 47).

The fundamental issues relevant for captives are the 'realness' of location, the legal validity of ceding risk essentially to oneself, and the possibil-

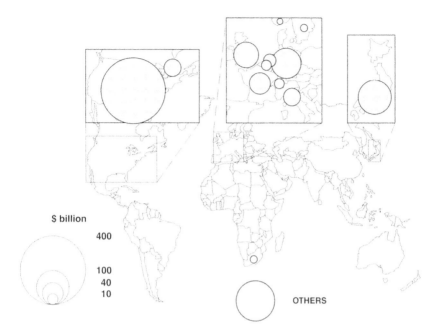

Figure 6.18 Major captive origins, 1997.

Source: Leonard 1999: IV.

Note
By non-life premium.

ity of trading insurance with third parties. Direct captives are often not allowed, and where they are, may encounter difficulties in finding reinsurance, but cannot do without because of their generally small size. This makes fronting by a local insurer necessary. When abroad, local carriers also have the vernacular, connections and familiarity with the culture. Solutions to the ability to trade insurance can normally be found in industrialized countries, but in the developing world protectionistic and currency issues may bar the use of offshore captives.

The 'realness' of location is more than a question of minimizing taxes. It is also a question of writing insurance legally in the first place. Dublin's and Luxembourg's advantage over Guernsey and the Isle of Man, for example, is that Pan-European risks can be written there while the latter are outside the EU (except for goods trade) and can write only UK risks. Closeness of control plays a role, and 'wrong' management level in a 'correct' location can spoil all the ingenuity of the arrangement. France, Italy and Spain use the day-to-day management as the criterion for domicile while the UK, Ireland, Belgium and Germany look for the captive's highest management, its board meetings. The solution may then be a management company in the offshore location, preferably a nearby one

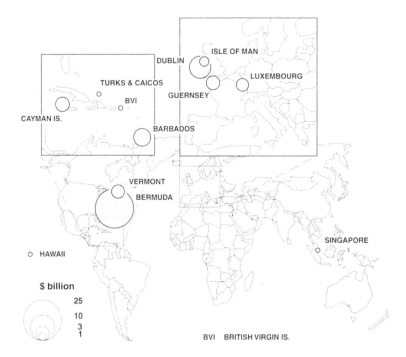

Figure 6.19 Major captive locations, 2000.

Source: Pierce 2001/2002: Figure 2.

Notes
By net premium. Bermuda only Class 1–3 companies.

for ease of communication. But there are limits, because territories of 10,000 inhabitants simply lack the human resources to develop into true management centres. It takes Bermuda, with its 65,000 population to find the 2,000 persons who worked in insurance there in the mid-1990s. Of these, 630 were employed by the twenty-four management companies handling about 1,050 captives (*Captive Insurance* 1995: 249–256).

Taxes are naturally a *conditio sine qua non* for offshore locations. Superficially, they are simplicity itself: the fewer the better. Indeed, the traditional offshore domiciles are zero-tax locations for external business. The flip side is that such business is subject to full tax outside the offshore location itself. Therefore, it may be more advantageous to pay some tax, say 10–20 per cent, and become party to double taxation treaties which allow the parent to deduct premiums paid from its taxable income. Solvency rules place a ceiling on the premium which can be written on a given capital, that is, the interest which the capital can earn. Reserves of at least 20 per cent of net premium are a common benchmark, although the variance is substantial depending on the size and type of risks written.

Insurance accounting principles, particularly the building of reserves, also vary greatly from country to country, and a captive obviously prefers to follow the practice of its parent. The offshore location, however, may have its own ideas about the preferable accounting system. In Bermuda, the US GAAP system or Canadian principles are used, while captives in Luxembourg and Dublin follow EU accounting directives.

Specifics are decisive in each competitive relation. For example, Germans are attracted to Dublin because of its low cost, tax included, flexible Anglo-Saxon accounting rules and speediness of licensing. Luxembourg cannot compete on these dimensions but gets Belgian and French business because of language advantages and the opportunity to build catastrophe reserves in reinsurance. Indeed, reinsurance has become Luxembourg's forte, since reserves can be created there up to twenty times the net premium income, almost tantamount to infinite tax deferral (Osborn 1988: 56).

The Bermudan market – the salty challenge

Bermuda is Britain's oldest colony but has enjoyed self-government since 1620. It became a parliamentary democracy in 1968, and overwhelmingly rejected independence in a referendum in 1995. Although both major political parties agree that non-Bermudan insurance companies should operate tax-free, at least until 2016, the referendum, nevertheless, shook confidence in the territory's stability. Zero tax is certainly an attraction, but plain tax evasion is discouraged by the exchange of tax information with the USA. The legal system is based on British common law and supported by 160 lawyers and 450 chartered accountants, about one-third and 90 per cent, respectively, of the London Market figures (Carter and Falush 1994: 20). The final court of appeal is the Privy Council in London. Three local banks offer international banking services, including global custody. There are daily air connections to the US east coast and scheduled flights to the UK and Canada. However, a round trip from Europe takes several days, dampening interest from that quarter. Incorporation is by registration, normally within two weeks, or two days in urgent cases. When billions of risk capital enter the market within a few months of 'mega-catastrophes' like the WTC incident, speediness is a considerable competitive advantage. Innovation is encouraged and new standards are created. Various forms of alternative risk transfer (ART) were accepted early, PPCs are possible without separate legislation in every separate case, electronic signatures using the Quo Vadis system are legally binding. The attitude is 'can do'. (Evans 2002; Goddard 2002)

The weaknesses are those of small size: 65,000 people on 55 square kilometres. A metropolis would support more air connections than Bermuda ever will. Real estate is in short supply and extremely expensive. Social life is confined to small groups of people. Entry of expatriates is controlled, a maximum of two children per family, for example. The labour pool is restricted, which excludes mass markets, direct motor and life insurance, for example. The shortage also makes itself felt at higher intellectual levels. The legal profession cannot possibly compare with the resources available in New York and London and planeloads of documents and legal teams are shipped every week to the island (Goddard 2002; Jenkins 2002; Kilgour and Coull 2002).

Insurance business has grown by adapting to developments onshore. The beginning was slow, the first international insurer opening for business in 1948, and their number reaching ten only in 1960. The first wave were US captives, which came in the 1960s to accumulate tax-free reserves and escape the fragmented home market (Atkins 1996b). Many also arrived from the Bahamas, where the government in 1969 wanted to regulate and tax local insurers without clearly exempting offshore business. Captives were followed by US liability insurers in the 1970s, but when Bermuda introduced new insurance legislation, the tide turned to the Cayman Islands (Luce 1997; Peagam 1989: 59, 65, 70). The liability market then practically dried up in the mid-1980s following escalating damages and retroactive pollution legislation in the USA. A string of severe natural catastrophes in the late 1980s and early 1990s, with claims in the billion class, hit that segment. About $10bn, or 30 per cent of worldwide catastrophe capacity, was withdrawn during 1987–1992, over 20 per cent of it due to hurricane Andrew alone. The shortfall was partially replaced by raising over $5bn capital in New York in 1993–1994 and placing it in Bermudan companies. Another $7bn followed the WTC incident (Atkins 1996b; Chichilnisky 1996: 68; Moore 2002; Smith 1996: 20). London, the traditional reinsurance centre, simply could not compete.

The capital inflow has made Bermuda the location to buy cover against large risks, excess and catastrophe. Its estimated 25 per cent global market share in property catastrophe reflects this and its role exceeds that of London and New York. It is even claimed that practically all publicly-quoted US reinsurers have relocated to Bermuda. The maximum cover granted is within a range of $65bn–$85bn, in one exceptional case $500bn, which makes it difficult to find reinsurers at a reasonable cost. After all, catastrophe reinsurers nowadays habitually expose 'only' 5–6 per cent of their capital to a single risk. They might also go into receivership and, as premium is paid in advance, risk retention becomes attractive. It follows that the ratio premium/capital is unusually low, varying between 0.5 and 1 against the more conventional 2. Risks of the indicated magnitude can only be written by well-capitalized companies. The minimum statutory capital for catastrophe writing is $100m, twice that of the largest Japanese commercial reinsurer. In practice, the minimum is more likely to be $400m, however. This suits Bermuda well, because a lot of activity is generated by a small number of companies. (Chichilnisky 1996: 68; Leonard 1998; Smith 1996: 20–21)

As implied, specialization in catastrophe risks rests much on the catastrophe proneness and wealth of the USA. It is simply the largest open catastrophe market in the world, with 40 per cent of premiums. Insurers would be only too happy to diversify to other Continents, but this is possible only to a limited extent (Figure 6.9). Japan, the obvious target, is for all practical purposes a closed market, very likely to its own disadvantage. Instead, diversification in Bermuda has followed other avenues, MAT, satellite and membership at Lloyd's, where leading Bermudians have about 15 per cent of capacity. The era of Bermudan uniqueness is fading away. (Jenkins 1997; *sigma* 6/1995: Figure 10; 3/2002: Appendix)

Overall, the equity domiciled in Bermuda was $59bn in 2000 and total capital base $146bn against which $38bn of premium was written (Lines 2002: 22). These figures are two-to-three times those of Lloyd's and probably exceed all of the London Market as well. There is no firm information about domiciled funds, and the suggested $200bn–$250bn is only a guesstimate. Their actual management is mostly done in New York, London and other conventional finance centres. Efforts to attract mutual funds and similar to the Bermudan Stock Exchange have largely been unsuccessful. The island is too distant for such business and, considering the increasing links with London, possibly approaching the limit of its potential.

Conclusion

Insurance is, to a degree, an outlier in a financial context. It undoubtedly belongs to financial services but its approach is fundamentally different from banking, the major sector. Where banking does its best to avoid risk, insurance makes its money by chasing and valuing it. Insurance's role in this book has been threefold. It has probed the origins of a major source of investment capital. It has touched the surface on a particular segment of retail finance. And it has shed light on the competitive forces between onshore and offshore. This final aspect is the central theme in the following chapter.

7   Finance centres

Evolution

Many finance centres have repeatedly turned up on the preceding pages. The easy way of identifying the top twenty of them would consequently be to pick up the most frequently cited names and be done with it. We will try a more analytical approach, however, and will take a closer look at the underlying factors, practical indicators, centre hierarchy and specialization. We will also observe that many locational factors are essentially political and 'easy' to change, which gives odd territories a chance to become offshore centres.

The basic question about international finance centres undoubtedly relates to their birth: how did they come about? The absence of a widely accepted definition complicates the answer (Reed 1981: 3). And a logical definition may be impossible because the question is implicitly about a large international centre. But where international business is large in volume terms, it can still be modest in relation to the domestic one, and the other way round. There is certainly no simple answer (Bindemann 1999: 4–19). What aspects are fundamental and what are complementary? There seems to be a consensus about the information functions. When fully developed, centres are first and foremost communication and management hubs, they lend abroad and function as cross-border clearing houses (Kindleberger 1974: 57). And when still embryonic, they enjoy an information advantage about local opportunities, business cultures and personalities. This advantage is unlikely to be directly converted into financial pre-eminence, however. Once the centre is up and running, the wealth of available information certainly attracts, but this was not necessarily so at the start.

New York was a wholesaling city before it became a financial city; financial intermediation attracted the headquarters of national corporations, and that led to financial pre-eminence. But the wholesaling functions were decisively dependent on New York's logistical and information advantage. It offered a convenient gateway to the vast American interior, and it was the first place on the way in from Europe offering that possibility. New York is by no means the only example. London, among the world's finance hubs, can also thank its origin for its logistical advantage within England. Singapore, inheriting the role of many previous entre-pôts, was intentionally established at a focal point of international ship-ping routes. Shanghai also has an excellent logistical location, but its ability to outcompete older trading cities was decisively helped by it being a stronghold of foreign interests, a safe harbour in a country infested with civil strife. Hongkong's logistical weakness was more than compensated for by its gateway role during China's trade embargo after 1949. Tokyo was originally a military outpost and a strictly administrative city, which rose to prominence by being the focal point of the largest cultivated plain in Japan. The centralizing power of a modern state got its confirmation in finance centres like Berlin and St Petersburg. Although the latter had a logistical advantage of a kind, its financial dealings originated from its political role. When the role was lost to Moscow, finances followed suit and have not returned. Corresponding contests for national supremacy abound: Osaka no more challenges Tokyo, Toronto has surpassed Mon-treal, Sydney has outdistanced Melbourne, Zurich is doing the same to Geneva, and Frankfurt is competing Munich into insignificance.

The development chain has sufficient regularity to inspire a five-stage evolutionary hierarchy (Reed 1981: 57) in which a centre serves

1   its immediate surroundings,
2   an area wider than the local one,
3   the national space,
4   contiguous countries and political dependencies,
5   finance centres worldwide.

While there is evidence of such evolution (Labasse 1955; Lord 1987; 1992), the view that national dominance is a precondition for international promi-nence may be too rigid. The best evidence to the contrary comes from large industrializing countries where the communication and transportation network is yet to be completed and where regional loyalties remain strong. Mumbai, Sao Paulo and Shanghai have recognized international status but face keen national competition from Calcutta, Rio de Janeiro and Beijing, respectively. The increasingly important offshore centres are still more diffi-cult to fit into Reed's evolutionary scheme. They simply obey other laws.

The basic function of an emerging finance centre is banking, first retail and thereafter wholesale banking. Recalling this, it is easy to accept Reed's (1981: 55) claim that being a banking centre is a preliminary and neces-sary phase on the way to becoming a true finance centre. Portfolio man-agement is another key function, because it rests on large amounts of liabilities and, indirectly, trust in the centre's ability to take care of them professionally. The practical caretaking means that there are monies to be placed which attracts borrowers and catalyses organizational arrangements such as bond auctions and stock exchanges. The third pillar would be insurance. Its immediate linkage is with physical trade and manufacturing but premiums which are not immediately needed for paying damages lead unavoidably to portfolio management.

An established banking centre is thought to be permanent and hard to dislodge (Reed 1981: 54). Ostensibly, this role is identified with the head-quarter location of major banks. By analogy, the chances for new banking centres to emerge are small (Grubel 1989: 74). Locations with ample hinterlands have already been occupied and incumbents are likely to pre-empt challengers. These opinions appeared plausible at the time and in the environment (the USA) where they were conceived, but their validity may be reduced today. Financial deregulation has made bank mergers easier and more frequent. If a merged bank must select between existing headquarter locations, the relative standing of the centres may change. And when banks are large, the shifts will also be large. Of course, many 'mega-mergers' such as between Manufacturers Hannover Trust, Chase Manhattan and Chemical Bank in New York, Mitsubishi Bank and Bank of Tokyo in Tokyo, and Hongkong and Shanghai Bank and Midland Bank in London involved no headquarter changes. But the intensive merger activity of Nations Bank and First Union has raised the banking profile of Charlotte, NC radically. And the acquisition of First Interstate in 1996 by Wells Fargo considerably strengthened San Francisco as a banking centre at Los Angeles' expense, whereas the purchase of Bank of America by Nations Bank in 1998 weakened it. The transfer of HSBC's headquarter from Hongkong to London in 1993 also belongs to the shifts which have the capacity to affect a banking centre's status. The opinion is thus open to debate. (Authers 1997: 13; 1998; Choi *et al.* 2002; Lord 1996: 210)

By analogy, a centre's fund management role is considered less firm than its banking status (Reed 1981: 54). But, theoretically, it is a matter of sunk costs. They and indivisibilities make the relocation of any activity far from marginal, and the new location must offer advantages which are likely to remain (Davis 1990: 3). That applies to fund management and banking alike. Transfers of fund business to alternative centres have, of course, occurred. Substantial funds escaped the Swiss withholding tax and relocated in Luxembourg in the 1970s. The same was repeated when Germany introduced a 10 per cent withholding tax in 1989 and then raised it to 30 per cent in 1993. When the Bahamas and Bermuda were left outside the sterling area in 1972, many trust funds were transferred from there to Jersey. Changes in the UK tax legislation then triggered a reverse flight from Jersey to the Cayman Islands in the 1980s. These movements were between offshore locations, or almost, and may consequently be a partial proof only. But there are other examples. Dresdner Kleinwort Benson in the late 1990s merged its three asset management units in San Francisco rather than in London. Since the relative sizes and corporate histories of the merged parts played a role, the consolidation may not properly reflect the cities' competitive power, however. More thought-provoking is the transfer of BZW's fund management arm from London to San Francisco, notwithstanding the fact that the transferred unit was an index tracker rather than an active manager. Both transfers were made by important banks. (Dugan 1989; Fisher and Luce 1997; Hampton 1996a: 11; Schwander-Auckenthaler 1995: 33, n. 76)

Indeed, much fund money is actually managed by banks themselves, which creates an interdependency. The loss of the former leads to the hollowing out of the latter, the role of a centre's banking status. Banks may also transfer part of their banking business abroad. The emergence of the eurodollar market in London in the 1960s is a case in point. Headquarters did not move, but their role diminished.

From a wider angle, it is a misconception to think that fund management is exceptionally concentrated and somehow the exclusive realm of major international centres. There is overwhelming evidence from the USA that comparatively small centres can also have substantial funds under management. Hartford, CT, the US insurance company 'capital' is one of them (Graves 1998; Green 1993; Green and Meyer 1992). Institutional equity holdings by major city in 1993/1994 provide additional evidence, now on a global scale (Figure 7.1). The identified holdings aggregated to $7.4tr or one-half of the then-global equity market.

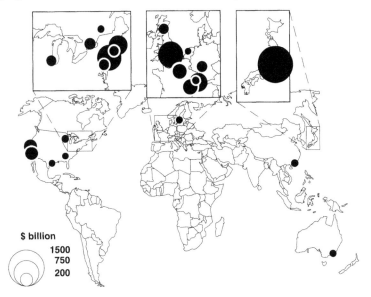

Figure 7.1 Institutional equity holdings by major city, 1994.

Source: Vogt 1995. Courtesy of Technimetrics, New York.

Notes
The source lists only the twenty-five (world), fifty (North America) and twenty-five (Europe) largest management centres. Newark consolidated with New York. Allocation is by fund domicile rather than actual management. More recent figures about the largest cities are available in Bank of England 2002: Chart 22. Tokyo has lost in relation to London and New York.

Centres in the USA, Japan, the UK and Switzerland figure prominently, as indeed they should. Unexpectedly, no offshore centre is displayed. Dublin, Luxembourg and Liechtenstein are among the twenty-five European centres, but their role is modest. Funds domiciled there may prefer another type of investment than equities. Not all of them need be classified as institutional either. In true offshore, the willingness to make any disclosure should be minimal. At the city level, the concentration of management in Tokyo, London, New York and some other international finance centres is expected. But even secondary cities such as Houston, Montreal, Edinburgh and Basle house respectable fund assets. One can sense strong regional identities, the necessity to be close to the customer base. Such centres can have considerable staying power but are hardly serious competitors of world-class management centres. They can ultimately cede management function but seldom receive one.

All over the world

What makes a finance centre?

The ability to collect, exchange, rearrange and interpret information is the most persistent characteristic of an international finance centre. Collection depends largely on factors external to the centre: convenient river crossings and economic shipping routes in the early days; railroad hubs, ground cables and motorways later on; and flight connections and satellite communication today. The exchange, rearranging and interpretation, in contrast, is up to the centre itself.

These tasks are tremendously facilitated by the possibility for personal, face-to-face contact. The more complicated a deal, the more important face-to-face contact becomes. Large issues, syndicated loans and M&As, involving numerous lead managers and many layers of debt, are impossible to arrange electronically from a distance. The risk of a leakage would also increase dramatically. Teams of twenty or more persons meet several times in negotiations lasting late into the night. With time at a premium, it would be far too cumbersome to prepare detailed contracts in writing, so even large transactions are consummated by word of mouth and a handshake. The paperwork comes later on. A word once broken is long remembered and leads to ostracism by peers. Also, much worse things can happen. A renowned case is the competitive acquisition of Getty Oil by Texaco and Pennzoil, during which an allegedly binding handshake was broken and subsequently led to a court verdict for damages exceeding the culprit's net assets (Petzinger Jr 1987: 435–436). Trust is extremely important and is built up best face-to-face; as one banker expressed it, there is a need 'to be able to look the other participants in the eye, observe their behavior, assess their character, and evaluate their competence' (Reed 1981: 68). It is not out of place to consider relationships and the subsequent trust as a sunk cost, more important in complicated products than commodities, primary issuance than secondary trading (Davis 1990: 6).

Where, then, does electronic communication come into the picture? Within centres, electronics first and foremost supplement face-to-face, substitute it to some extent, but are not able to dethrone it. The aggregate volume of face-to-face has, in fact, increased (Thrift 1994: 351). Between centres, the effect has depended on the financial product. In commodities like forex and government bonds, it may have helped spatial concentration, whereas in specialized products like equities the outcome has depended on their following by the financial community, whether local or continental. In general, strong centres have been able to extend their spheres and outcompete weaker ones, so far protected by distance. While the number of international centres will decline, it is unlikely that the minimum will ever be less than three or the number of central time zones.

The apparent reason for larger concentration is enhanced liquidity. A broker may need to be close to customers but a trader is where information flows freely, and that means centralization. This makes trading centralized while origination remains dispersed, and the growth of securitization encourages this divergence. Buyers and sellers simply wish to operate in the most liquid market, and both liquidity and efficiency grow with the number of participants. This leads to increased competition, which promotes the build-up of expertise and stimulates innovation. Physical closeness is not an absolute necessity but it helps when keeping an eye on competition, learning from it, and poaching its employees should the need arise (Agnes 2000, 356–359; Brealey and Ireland 1993: 24; Davis 1990: 7; Grote *et al.* 2002; Thrift 1994: 336).

Information advantages are shared by many locations, and chance, or political fortune, decides which one will rise to national dominance. But that is something quite different from international pre-eminence, and only a handful can boast that position. Among the pre-First World War centres, London and Paris, and in the eighteenth century, Amsterdam, are the standard examples. New York joined the club after the First World War when Amsterdam had already declined to the second league. What characterized these centres was their ability to export financial capital. Some was sourced from abroad but the bulk was generated domestically. Nothing was more natural than seeing this ability as the necessary condition for an international finance centre. Our time is less certain about that, although the link between foreign direct investment and certain financial services, such as the management of cash positions, opening of foreign offices and dissemination of information is readily acknowledged (Reed 1981: 52).

Our uncertainty originates from the post-Second World War experience. No country has been a consistent capital exporter since 1945. The USA made a good start but did not press on with it. When its leadership began waning visibly, it resorted to regulation rather than competition. When Japan rose to a similar position, its reaction was very much the same, regulation rather than open competition. The UK was impoverished and in no position to maintain its former role as a capital exporter. But it was able to bounce back as a host for the worldwide financial community. An important reason was that the former links between invoicing or issuing currency and the lending country or country of issuance, ownership and trading, were gradually severed (Davis 1990: 10; Gardener and Molyneux 1993: 144). Another reason was the need for a finance hub in the European time zone. There was no compelling reason for a single hub, as is shown by the current Asian time zone, but the UK saw to it that it came about anyway.

The negation of capital exports cannot be taken too far, of course. It is a powerful argument for the existence of a finance centre, but it is not a necessary condition, a *sine qua non*. Since banking is an important part of a finance centre, the reasons which lead to the proliferation of banks are relevant. Foreign trade and foreign direct investment have explanatory power. FDI, of course, is a special aspect of capital export but trade finance is not. Since bankers wish to participate in debt issuance, they need presence in the issuing location. In other words, not only capital exporters but also consistent importers attract financial intermediation. The large-scale entry of Japanese banks and securities houses into New York, originally to intermediate the US government debt to their clients at home, is a case in point.

Add to the deep undercurrents and macroeconomic factors the policing of the actual markets and their regulation. A country or a city cannot normally enforce a decision on a suitable location upon foreigners but can facilitate it by removing unnecessary barriers. That is what the UK did in the 1950s and onward. It opted for a light regulation of those financial dealings which did not directly affect its domestic economy. The choice is usually seen in the light of a shrewd, long-term strategy. It is equally possible to see it as a valiant effort to make the most of a difficult situation: how to employ a youth who was emotionally inclined to have an administrative job in an empire rather than a career in manufacture. Or, it can be seen as a logical continuation of deep-rooted traditions in liberal thinking, political as well as economic. Be that as it may, in a heavily regulated world, London appeared as a free town. Its serious financial decline was also of comparatively recent date, which meant that the skill base was still there to respond to an opportunity when it turned up.

The concept of regulation and supervision is many-faceted. It includes exchange and interest rate controls, interest-free minimum reserves at the central bank, minimum capital/asset ratios, compulsory insurance schemes, direct taxes on capital gains, income and profits, withholding taxes hopefully repatriated without undue delay, turnover taxes, stamp duties, compliance officers, ex-post reporting, advance reporting with time delays, and an inexhaustible inventory of banned and non-ethical practices. To this may be added the impartiality and consistency of the administration, no less important than its sheer volume. Indeed, they are a special aspect of security, which is the keystone of all financial dealing. (Davis 1990: 5; Reed 1981: 85–86)

This flak indirectly suggests that the less regulation, the better. Within reasonable limits this is true. International finance centres are for the wholesale, or 'high', finance, which should be prepared to take care of itself, the *caveat emptor* principle of English law. It has little need for the regulatory apparatus, much of which has been created for the protection of the small investor and which is internationally more a nuisance than a blessing. The US reporting and disclosure requirements are often seen in this light by foreigners. A possible solution is to apply different sets of rules internationally and domestically. This, indeed, has been the case in many small offshore centres. There the two poles of the financial spectrum are so distinct that regulatory separation is quite painless. In larger territories with diversified economies and vibrant entrepreneurial communities, care must be taken to avoid competitive distortions between the liberalized and regulated sectors.

Although regulators get easily criticized by impatient intermediaries, the financial system would be unable to cope without them. One needs only recall a spate of recent scandals to see the truth of this: the emptying of the Maxwell pension funds through Liechtenstein foundations; the ostensible fraud and certain mismanagement of the BCCI domiciled in Luxembourg but operating primarily from London; the reckless derivatives trading of Barings Securities in Singapore in spite of the city's renowned regulatory structure; the fraud and forgeries at Daiwa Bank in New York and the blindfolded lending by first-rate money centre banks to LTCM, an unregulated hedge fund which allegedly threatened the stability of the US banking system. In each case, the regulators were unable to detect and cleanse the misbehaviour in time. But without any regulation, such incidents would be much more numerous. Thus, regulation is about people (Baker and Urry 1995; Gapper and Denton 1996; Lascelles *et al.* 1991; Marshall 2002; Rodger 1994; Shirreff 1997; 2000). But so is the functioning of a finance centre at large. First comes the workforce of intermediaries. The wholesale business needs only small numbers but places high demands on skills and commitment. At the retailing end, the numbers are large but skills modest. Details vary enormously from country to country. Some offer a formal banking education, others rely on college graduates, and a few favour on-the-job training. But all require a fair command of the English language in international operations. English is the *lingua franca* of contemporary financial intermediation, and centres without an adequate supply of speakers cannot achieve international pre-eminence.

The difference in skill levels should not disguise the fact that the vast retailing masses offer both a recruiting ground for the high finance and a safety net for those who cannot make it in the cut-throat international competition. The importance of human resources comes strikingly into focus in small offshore centres, which must import qualified labour and subsequently constrain business when their capability to absorb more people gets exhausted. Even in world-class metropolises, the very best of people may be in short supply and must be imported. It is then up to the authorities to supply them with work permits.

At that level, pay scales, often cited as a location factor, mean little. The key thing is to get things done, and the pay is related to achievement rather than seniority or formal position. At lower levels, the labour cost matters but so does its productivity and flexibility, the ease of hiring and firing. It is no good having modest labour costs if the workforce is permeated by a civil service mentality and unavailable because of implied life-time employment (Riley 1991).

The next echelon of people are found at accounting, law and technology firms. They are indispensable for the proper functioning of a centre but less visible than the financial staff. They are simply assumed to be available in sufficient numbers and skills, which may or may not be the case. London and New York clearly benefit from the fact that much international dealing is based on their respective national and state laws. The Big Three accounting federations are widely represented all over the world, but their roots are in the UK, USA and the Netherlands, which gives these countries a competitive edge. By contrast, countries in the process of transforming into market economies are still building up their legal and accounting infrastructure.

A centre's physical structure and its office and living cost are comparatively easy to quantify and, therefore, a target of frequent comment. They are not unimportant, and there is much anecdotal evidence on how financial intermediation reacts to high cost by moving to less expensive locations. But again, it is a balancing act between revenue and cost. If business is buoyant and profitable, it is also capable of paying rents and other expenses. And in most cases there are counterforces at work. High rents stimulate new buildings, residential and back office activities relocate further from the business hub, transportation systems are upgraded and so on (Davis 1990: 11). It is only the absolute shortage of space, effective in a handful of offshore locations, which can permanently clog the development of an otherwise vibrant international centre. Lifestyle? Executives surveyed in London did not value life quality too much: 'I go everywhere when money is there' (Häuser *et al.* 1990: A41).

That is one possible angle, but it is not the only one. Others include: 'I have never heard of anyone refusing to come to London' (Yassukovich, cited in Warner 1997: 26); or 'Ultimately finance centers are where people want to work' (Fisher and Luce 1997).

It is up to everybody to make the choice.

Identifying them

Once the locational pros and cons have been derived at the conceptual level, it is natural to look for tangible proxies and try to quantify the relative central power by centre. The effort has a strong academic flavour, because many important factors are hardly measurable, or at least commensurate, and because the approximate relative status of major onshore centres is intuitively obvious. Their offshore cousins, on the other hand, may be more difficult to craft into an overall framework.

The main activities found in international finance centres are lending, securities issuance and trading, fund management and possibly insurance. Securities comprise bonds and equity and constitute the underlying instruments for derivatives. Most script is domestic, but the share of issues intended for international investors is growing. Trading takes place at formal exchanges and OTC. Customers can be foreigners as well as nationals. Trading need not be tied to a particular location, although this is still the standard in exchange-based trading. OTC trading and issuance (or derivatives writing), in contrast, can be dispersed as well as centralized at the city level, although the specific location may be ambiguous. For example, the Deutsche Telekom IPO can be allocated to its headquarter location (Bonn), the location where the bookbuilding was done (Frankfurt), or split between the headquarter locations of the global coordinators (Frankfurt and New York). Securities houses and most wholesale banks underwrite issues, write derivatives and are involved in trading and the ensuing settlement. All banks engage in lending, long and short term, domestic and international. They also buy and sell forex and offer payment services. Many give investment advice, offer fund management and provide custody. The scope is wide and many an activity has only been superficially registered on a global scale.

The practical solution, then, is to use what is available and turn a blind eye to the white spots. Typical indicators are the number of banks, their assets, international bank loans, exchange capitalization, number of contracts traded, number of listed companies, number of members, issuance of new script, share of foreign equity trading, forex trading, share of derivatives out of all trading, funds under management and so on (Scholtens 1992). The list can be made very long, and the analytical problem is the mutual weighing and joining of indicators into an overall ranking score.

These practical difficulties suggest using the plain number of banks as a rapid check, notwithstanding the differences in definitions, bank sizes and the time of recording which make figures approximate. In fact, it may be difficult to find two sources, at face value perfectly reliable sources, which would agree even approximately in their estimates. Only foreign banks are included, which may or may not be advisable depending on the banking structure of the particular country. A sample of well-known centres is selected during two time periods (Table 7.1). Onshore and offshore are

Table 7.1 Number of foreign banks in some banking centres, since early 1990s

Onshore	1990–1995	2000–2002	Offshore	1990–1995	2000–2002
London	520	480	Cayman	>600	580
New York	340	260	Bahamas	350	250
Paris	170	180	Luxembourg	220	190
Frankfurt	150	130	Singapore	220	120
Tokyo	90	140	Hongkong	130	170
Shanghai	n.a.	50	Bahrain	40	50
Moscow	n.a.	40	Labuan	40	60

Sources: Onshore: Bank of England 2002, Chart 9; Batchelor *et al.* 2002; Brown 1997; Choi *et al.* 2002; Graham and Timewell 1997; Montagnon and Walker 1995; Rose 1994a: 42; Russia 2002: 46. Offshore: Anon. 1992; Bounds 2001; Coggan 1996; Crisell and Alberga 1995: 130; Crisell 2002: 76; Dudley 1996: 125; Gray 1997; Shirreff 1995b: 82; www.bma.gov.bh 2000: 24; www.cssf.lu. 2001; www.earnshaw.com, Shanghai Phone Book 1996; www.info.govhk/ hkma/ar 2001; www.mas.gov.sg 2002; www.transnationale.org 2002.

Notes
Different sources can give widely varying estimates. Figures are rounded. Cayman also includes managed banks, London and New York rep. offices. Hongkong and Singapore (2002) exclude rep. offices. Bahrain had eighty banks in the mid-1980s.

kept apart because they follow partially different rules. Change in numbers is subject to a wide margin of error depending on definitional matters. The decline in London and New York reflects bank mergers and the withdrawal of Japanese and Russian banks because of domestic problems; decline in Luxembourg can be traced to the loss of competitive advantage because of streamlining within the EU. The location of the European Central Bank has not helped Frankfurt because it is the intervention market only for Germany. The French figure can be doubled by using a French source (Simon 2000: 23). The Cayman Islands and Bahamas have tightened regulation.

There is little difference between the number of foreign banks onshore and offshore. Two interpretations are possible. Either bank numbers alone do not differentiate between heavy-weight finance centres and 'short-term parking lots' or outright booking centres. Alternatively, many offshore centres have reached levels commensurate with traditional heavyweights. Our view tilts more towards the first interpretation. The reasons become obvious later on.

Reed (1981) has attacked the problem in a seminal study which covers the period 1900–1980. The study is in three steps. First, centre clusters are derived by hierarchical classification. Second, the result is verified by discriminant analysis which indicates the important variables and ranks the centres (Reed 1981: 14). The third step involves the testing of national variables for possible relevance to a centre's rank (Reed 1981: 43). Only the first two steps are considered here in any detail. International relevance, consistency and temporal access were instrumental in the choice of classification variables. Aggregate assets, for example, were rejected, as they do not necessarily tell much about a centre's international status. Data availability necessitated splitting the period into two overlapping sub-periods: 1900–1980 and 1955–1980. The first sub-period was covered by five variables, about bank headquarters and offices, indicating a banking centre. The second sub-period had four additional variables, concerning foreign assets, liabilities and linkages, and was seen in terms of a finance centre (Reed 1981: 10–12). The variables overlooked, among others, securities issuance and trading, and the institutional infrastructure (Reed 1981: 37).

As our emphasis is on modern times, only the results in 1980 are commented on. The cluster analysis grouped the eighty centres into five classes, and the subsequent discriminant analysis supported the result with 92 per cent correct classifications. The most powerful discriminating variables were foreign assets and liabilities, followed by local bank headquarters and the ratio of local bank branches/direct links abroad (Reed 1981: 26, 129–130). This is as could be expected. A surprising feature was the relative scores of the top centres, where London vastly exceeded its nearest competitors, New York and Paris (Figure 7.2).

When subjected to the third phase of the analysis, the eleven top centres were found to be:

1   headquarter locations of large international banks;
2   managers of large foreign assets and liabilities;

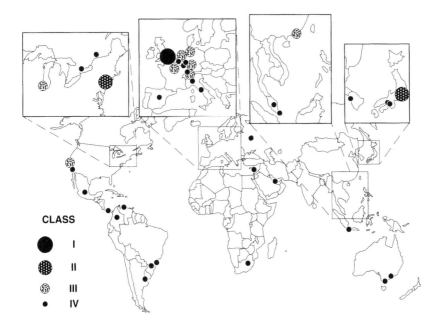

CLASS

●   I

◉   II

◉   III

•   IV

Figure 7.2 Finance centres, 1980.

Source: Reed 1981: Table A.7.

3   net suppliers of FDI capital;
4   close to large manufacturers;
5   intensive users of international telegraphic facilities. (Reed 1981: 60)

In other words, some of the conceptually relevant factors above are substantiated in this way. Reed has, in a subsequent study (cited in Thrift 1987: 209), developed the classification further and modified the ranking somewhat. For example, New York has been raised to the highest class, which it occupies together with London.

Obviously, quantitative studies like Reed's depend heavily on their input. Some variables may be subject to large variation within a period of a few years. The assets of Japanese banks, inflated by the unprecedented boom in real estate prices in the late 1980s, are a case in point. They were paralleled by a corresponding boom in the market capitalization and trading value of Japanese stock exchanges. Both are now a thing of the past and were superseded in the 1990s by an equity market boom in the USA and Europe. None of them affected Reed's study but they serve as a reminder. Another aspect which easily escapes aggregate ranking is the specialization of centres. It is not sufficient to input a wide range of data – which may not be available anyway. It also needs to be weighed by importance. If the volume of foreign banking assets and the trading value of foreign shares are important, is their relative importance equal or should they be weighed, and how? But ability to answer that question actually obviates much of the effort in the first place. If the weights are known or can be derived independently, all that remains is to apply them and total the products. The reasoning becomes circular and is of doubtful analytical value.

What can be still more fatal is the inclusion and exclusion of centres. An urban geographer would hardly consider Kobe separate from Osaka in a global study. And a financial analyst would probably include Geneva in a study which also displays Basle and Panama City as international finance centres (Thrift 1987: 209). The problem is that many banks in Geneva with worldwide fund management were private in 1980 and consequently coy about their dealings, while those in Panama City were captured by the national statistics.

Since it is so difficult to derive a comprehensive and consistent ranking of finance centres on the global scale, it is as well to proceed in the opposite order: pick up the recognized leaders, describe their strong and weak sides, and look around for challengers.

A tale of three cities

Tied to the time zones

A basic feature of contemporary global finance is that there are three interlinked time zones centring on North America, Europe and Asia Pacific. People in these zones prefer to work during daylight hours, which means that there is only limited or no time overlap between them. Various scale economies promote the existence of a dominant hub within each central time zone. The overwhelming size of the US economy within the American zone has made the national centre, New York, the zonal hub. Within the European zone the pre-eminence of London has been more open to challenge because of the smaller size of the UK economy. This weakness has been compensated by an inherited skill base and a conscious policy to preserve as much of the traditional position as possible. In Asia Pacific, Japan repeats the American pattern by generating some 60 per cent of the time zone's aggregate GDP. It is natural then that the national hub Tokyo is seen as the third pole of the global order.

The time differences in this chain, New York–London–Tokyo–New York, are five–nine–ten hours. It means that only New York and London can communicate directly during a normal working day, and even then the overlap is only three hours. As the international financial community is renowned for its solid work ethic and long hours, the actual limits are less rigid. But even so, the window of opportunity for direct communication is not very wide. It means that many relatively routine matters which are normally decided in one day now need two, a good reason for opening an outpost in the other time zone. Another aspect giving flexibility to the global system is that London and Tokyo have realistic alternatives on the mainland. Paris or Frankfurt and Hongkong or Singapore, respectively, can fill some, or the same, or more, of the functions that the accepted time zone hubs perform, and when this happens simultaneously the time differences become six–seven–eleven hours. This alternative situation further upgrades Europe's relative position and makes it the world-wide central time zone. With this background, it is reasonable to accept New York, London and Tokyo as the time zone hubs.

In aggregate, these three account for some 40 per cent of international bank lending, and London and New York combined roughly 70 per cent of equity trading outside the home country. Then come fields like eurobond issuance and trading, international fund management, OTC derivatives trading, forex trading, international insurance, and bullion trading, in which the combined market shares are similar but the activity usually more concentrated in London. The impression then is that London is largely an international centre, while the other two are predominantly domestic, although New York is far more international than the insular Tokyo.

At face value, there is very little to add. London occupies the top slot and that is it. But from a wider perspective some of its position also reflects Europe's political fragmentation. All intercontinental connections notwithstanding, much of its foreign business is still European. In a truly united Europe, that business would be statistically domestic, or return to its origins, or simply disappear. Assume similar development in North America (NAFTA) and Asia Pacific, and the effects on New York and Japan would be far less dramatic because of less fragmentation, Caribbean mini-states excluded.

Even with this reservation, the standard question is, why do New York and Tokyo not do better than they actually do? And the equally standard answer is because US and Japanese authorities and politicians at large give clear priority to domestic issues and may, at times, be openly critical of the views and wishes of the international financial community whose interests need by no means coincide with the national ones. The American and Japanese attitudes are also very human. Their economies are enormous and, particularly in the USA, international trade and finance continues to play a comparatively modest role, some 10–15 per cent. In Japan, the belief that good administration is vastly superior to capricious market forces is very strong, an attitude deeply resented by the financial community. Administrative action easily distorts competition, complicates matters, takes time to comply with and may become costly. In addition to these general viewpoints there are a number of specific troubles, which will be our next topic.

New York – unused potential

The economic muscle of the USA since the Second World War should have guaranteed New York the unquestionable top slot among world-class finance centres. This has not happened. The American political establishment is essentially regional with limited nationwide interest in promoting cities which belong to the jurisdiction of other states (Helleiner 1993). There is also a certain wariness towards the financial world, a legacy from the Depression years, the heyday of large trusts, and, still more fundamentally, of a simple agrarian society. Big cities are the financial meeting points, and curbing the power emanating from them has at times been an important political goal. We have met it in the context of the Glass–Steagall and McFadden Acts (Chapter 5, pp. 231 and 233). The New York banking community was the obvious adversary, and this confrontational relationship was easily transferred to international matters. The International Monetary Fund and World Bank were located in Washington, DC, close to the political power but away from the commercial hub. With similar logic, the main intervention market of the Fed could also have been located there rather than in New York. Such thinking is window dressing in a sense, of course, because the IMF and World Bank do not participate in the wide array of banking activities; they only issue bonds and lend. But local politicians could be equally non-supportive. The state of New York allowed foreign banks to open full service branches only in 1961 (Reed 1981: 32). Protectionism or political in-fighting?

New York's international competitiveness in general suffered from domestic rigidities which banks could avoid in London, the only serious challenger. Foreigners in London did not have interest-free reserves at the central bank, they could choose any capital/assets ratio they wished, and they did not pay deposit insurance. These items made up a competitive advantage until the early 1970s when London tightened its regulation. They did not matter so much as long as New York was able to supply capital, but this capability was visibly weakening as from 1962. Authorities reacted by putting an interest rate equalization tax on foreign issuance in July 1963, which virtually closed New York's capital market for foreigners. It was followed by 'voluntary' guidelines and then a tax for cross-border lending in 1965. They could not restore the balance, interest rates rose, and a new factor came into play. US banks had, since 1937, faced an interest rate ceiling for deposits, to constrain cut-throat competition. It worked as long as international interest rates did not exceed the ceiling, but when they did in 1966, banks went abroad and borrowed there. The lenders were oil producing and socialist countries who did not want to risk their money being frozen by US authorities for political reasons, and US companies who received better interest abroad than at home. The main loser was the State of New York, but it was only in the late 1970s that it succeeded in reversing the federal policy. By then, London had consolidated its position as the hub of euromarkets. (Blume *et al.* 1993: 70; Corrigan 1997; Hampton 1996a: 5–58, 79; Morris and Walter 1993: 39; Reed 1981: 27; Sele 1995: 59–60)

That New York, nevertheless, has been able to do so well internationally depends on its role as a dollar source (correspondent accounts) and its ability to supply capital once restrictions had been lifted. No other country can match the amounts nor has the same appetite for unorthodox and risky debt than the USA. That debt is overwhelmingly intermediated by banks in New York. The international leadership of NYSE is just another expression of this ability.

Another competitive vehicle is International Banking Facilities (IBFs), mostly in New York and Miami, created in December 1981 at the behest of New York banks and the New York Clearing House Association. The purpose was to attract expatriate monies back home and avoid the many onshore restrictions and, in addition, to save state and local taxes, some 18 per cent. The creation of IBFs can also be seen as a result of the refusal by the UK and Switzerland to introduce reserve requirements on euromarkets as suggested by the Fed, and the realization that competition with offshore was possible only on its own terms. The measure became a success, $64bn being repatriated within one month, and in three years the amount had risen to $200bn. In recent years, IBFs' share out of total US cross-border lending has varied between one-third and one-half. American banks transferred monies from the Bahamas, Cayman Islands and London, and foreigners from other US businesses, becoming IBFs' largest users. The flip side is that IBF and its clones impede the central bank's monetary management and reduce domestic competition. (Häusler 1994: 13; Helleiner 1995; Rose 1994a: 26; Sele 1995: 206–209; Ungefehr 1990a)

Conceptually, an IBF is an offshore centre operating onshore. Physically, it is a separate set of books at a bank's normal premises allowing the bank to operate on its entire capital and not just that of a subsidiary. Funds in these books can be in any currency, they are exempted from reserve requirements, interest rate ceilings, withholding tax, state and local taxes, the forty-eight-hour withdrawal notice and interstate branching restrictions (now abolished). But IBFs cannot escape all red tape, since the international side must be kept apart from the more regulated domestic side. At-sight instruments are not allowed, time deposits and withdrawals must be at least $100,000 and they can be taken only in the interbank market from non-bank foreigners, loans must be external to the USA, instruments are not negotiable, and deposit insurance applies. And then there is the risk, much resented by foreigners, that the monies are exposed to the investigation and possible freezing by the US authorities. They are not truly offshore. (Johns and Le Marchant 1993: 75; Rose 1994a: 24; Taeho 1993: 192; Willman 2001b)

London – flexible and liberal

When American multinationals decided to keep their dollar funds abroad in the 1960s, these went mostly to London. Thereby the world's premium reserve currency was partially placed beyond the reach of its domestic authorities. These authorities wanted to interfere but realized that a ban on US banks keeping eurodollar accounts abroad would force them out of foreign markets altogether. Americans were not the firstcomers to euromarkets, however, as socialist countries had been there a decade earlier, although their impact had been comparatively modest. The normal practice is that dollar funds are deposited in the USA, mark funds in Germany, yen funds in Japan and so on. Unfortunately enough, they also come under the jurisdiction of national authorities who can constrain their use in various ways, and at worst expropriate them. This was a very real concern for the socialists during the Cold War era, and it became a similar concern for the oil-exporting Arab countries after December 1973, when the first large increase in oil price was implemented, to punish the USA for helping Israel in an ongoing war. The worry was not unfounded, as the freezing of Iranian government assets in November 1979 showed, a countermeasure against the hostage crises. The socialists kept their dollar funds outside the USA and so did the

Arabs. To be on the safe side, the latter preferred short-term and even day-money deposits. After all, international banking in London was dominated by US and British banks. (Chernow 1990: 545; Haindl 1991: 50; Reed 1981: 54, 79)

Once the idea took root that financial dealings can be located outside the jurisdiction in whose currency they are denominated, other currencies joined the bandwagon. Eurodollars became eurocurrencies, and the prefix 'euro' gradually became a generic term because other Continents, Hongkong, Singapore (asiadollars), the Bahamas and Cayman Islands, for example, increasingly participated. The bulk of the business, however, stayed in London. Forex, of course, benefited greatly from these markets. It was not only deposits. Securities such as bonds, medium-term notes and commercial paper were also issued as euro instruments. All these good things happened before New York could hit back by freeing capital exports and opening IBFs. By that time London could no longer be dislodged. (Gardener and Molyneux 1993: 146; Haindl 1991; Hayes and Hubbard 1990: 224; Lee 1996; Martin 1994: 257–259)

But why London and not some other European location? A multitude of factors have been suggested but only a few rigorous comparative studies about London and its competitors seem to have been published (City Research Project 1995; Häuser *et al.* 1990; Rose 1994b). The choice was not so obvious in the early 1960s. Paris, Geneva, Zurich and Luxembourg were all considered, and Euroclear and Cedel, the settlement organizations, were actually located on the Continent.

> The problem with London was its parochialism and disorganization. Foreigners could not sell bonds on the UK market, which was part of the sterling area, and the country's credit rating was so poor that its debt could not be placed abroad. The stock exchange did not accept foreign members. It gave 15 per cent of a new issue to jobbers who had no placing power. There were strikes and power cuts and some people remember having to work by the light of a kerosene lamp. The taking of office by the Labour government in March 1974 catalysed a Swiss bank to open an office in Luxembourg in case the bank's operations were hampered in London. Fortunately for London, it had the syndicated credit market which had left Switzerland where authorities refused to exempt eurobond trading from stamp duty, which UK authorities did. (Chernow 1990: 636; Rogge 1997: 213–214; Shirreff 1999: 31, 34)

The strengths, however, gradually prevailed. At the most trivial level, Americans could operate in their own language when coming to London and Arabs did not need to learn a new one. Many historical factors weighed heavily. The Empire, once a quarter of all mankind, had been financed from London. Many of its current elites had obtained their higher education in England and now formed an invaluable network of contacts. The Empire had also been groomed in the tradition of English case law, which could be put to good use in the new financial world. Thanks to the capital amassed during England's early Industrial Revolution, the City had financed much of the infrastructure in the Americas. This had provided valuable experience. The liberalistic and free trade traditions facilitated regulatory moderation even in the darkest days after the Second World War, and when economic horizons brightened, the lifting of restrictions was soon started. Exchange controls for financial transactions not linked with the UK economy were officially abolished in 1958, and the last remains went in 1979. People realized that the government is not going to close the eurodollar market and moved large parts of it from the offshore to London. As a final measure, London in October 1986 cut tax rates, stabilized the pound, scrapped fixed commissions at the exchange, allowed unrestricted entry to it, and established the SeaqI trading system free of stamp duty, in a major deregulation move coined as the 'Big Bang'. That ensured London's survival as an international finance centre although it destroyed many a weak British house. (Chernow 1990: 673; Hampton 1996a: 56; Peet 1992)

Foreigners have come to the City to do things which they cannot do at home. And they have come from all over the world (Figure 7.3).

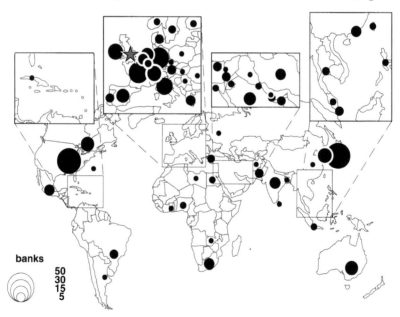

Figure 7.3 Foreign banks in London, February 1996.

Source: Bank of England 1995/1996: 46–47.

Notes
Representative offices excluded. The last published listing by country in 1997/1998 is practically identical.

Continentals arrived in the 1970s. Swiss banks issued script denominated in foreign currency and thereby avoided the domestic stamp duty. Germans came to trade in derivatives which were subjected to gambling laws at home. Japanese arrived in droves in the 1980s to escape stifling, expensive and anti-competitive regulation of bond issuance. London was, for them, a huge offshore centre. It had few legal barriers to banking and regulators could follow sound judgement as much as a rule book. To cite an example, non-British banks accounted for almost one-third of all lending to UK residents in 1991, a share difficult to imagine in most medium-sized industrialized countries (Gapper 1996; Tickell 1994).

The City is well aware of the competitive aspects of regulation and supervision, and sees with some concern the ongoing deregulation elsewhere: the end of the Glass–Steagall legislation in the USA, the widespread disappearance of withholding taxes, the simplification of government bond issuance, the lowering of minimum reserve ratios and so on. Having deregulated most of what can be deregulated, the City seems to have little left to offer (Rose 1994a: 50). The concern may be premature. Old structures are dismantled abroad but new ones are simultaneously put in place. In the words of a seasoned practitioner:

> The many threatened practices ... such as rules that issues in euros be underwritten in Frankfurt, are the very stuff of which London's market pre-eminence is made. The more restrictions the better. London has always been the beneficiary of the attempts of other markets to attract business by decree.... London has never been part of domestic clearing arrangements in either the US or Germany. London is the largest centre for dollar-denominated transactions outside the US, and the *bund* contract on Liffe is the dominant deutschmark derivative product.
>
> (Yassukovich 1996)

With six years' hindsight and the exclusion of the last statement, it still holds.

London's role as a fund manager is an essential part of its international status. The foundations are in the domestic pension system, by now fully funded. The Scots developed the basic skills (as in accounting) over a century ago; these have been honed further, and made London the largest centre for international fund management with well over $3tr in portfolio assets. At least one-quarter of these monies are managed for foreigners and then predominantly for wholesale customers because retail funds started gravitating towards the low-tax Luxembourg, from 1988, when the Luxembourgers had got their Ucits legislation in place. International funds act as a magnet for international equity offerings and these bring additional liquidity to an already liquid market, not only at the stock and derivatives exchanges but also OTC dealing in eurobonds, swaps and currency forwards. (Anon. 1993a; Corrigan 1995; Lapper 1996; Riley 1997)

Tokyo – insular and regulated

Tokyo, the third pole of the global triad, is London's opposite. Where London is liberal, flexible and cosmopolitan, Tokyo is conservative, rigid and insular. As so often, the roots lie deep in history. The country opened to the outside world a good hundred years ago, spent the next 70 years building a modern industrial base, rebuilt its industry and most of its cities after a lost war and became a fairly consistent net exporter of capital only after the mid-1970s. Such a history is not very conducive to the emergence of an international finance centre. Add to that a culture which adores seniority and authority, avoids direct confrontation at all costs, has consequently a parenthetical legal profession and follows an ideal of benevolent, paternalistic authorities. Spice it with a language which, in syntax and vocabulary, is so fundamentally different from English that its real thinking may be impossible to translate into fluent everyday English and will certainly lose subtle nuances conveyed by the *kanji*-script. Then it becomes understandable why Tokyo languishes as an international finance centre.

Tokyo's achievements result from Japan's giant economy and its technical sophistication. Its share of international banking used to be about the same as London's, 15–16 per cent. Its stock exchange widely surpassed NYSE in market capitalization and trading value in the late 1980s, although it has now returned to the third slot (after Nasdaq). Its technological sophistication, for example in settlement, is second to none. But the shallow internationalization comes to light in the parenthetical presence of foreign listings at TSE, the weak performance of its fund managers, the flight of corporate bond issuance to London and New York, and derivatives trading to Singapore. Much of the international business in Tokyo comes from foreigners who wish to exploit its weaknesses rather than use it as a springboard for operations in Asia. Obvious as the weaknesses have been, their exploitation has taken time to materialize. Foreign brokers seem, by now, to have made a breakthrough with one-quarter of all trading on TSE. Fund managers have been given a toehold although only in a limited segment. Underwriting, as usual, has been practically off-limits. (Corrigan 1994; Lascelles 1989; Peston 1992; Tett 1997a)

The loss of business to foreign centres was sufficiently disturbing to catalyse Japan into following the US example and creating its own Offshore Market in 1986. Like its US counterpart, IBF, the JOM is also free from reserve requirements, interest rate controls, deposit insurance and withholding tax. But only authorized banks can use it, it is exposed to full local and national taxes, the stamp duty applies and reporting is heavy. On the face of it, JOM was a significant success; recording $400bn assets within two years, and one-third to one-half of Japan's cross-border lending since then. But it has also been claimed that much of the activity is inter-office and plain window dressing towards authorities, and that big banks get the same benefits at less cost in Hongkong. Fortunately enough, JOM competes less with nimble offshore than regulated foreign onshore, and its main effect has been the repatriation of funds from New York. (Hampton 1996a: 63; Rose 1994a: 27–28; Ungefehr 1990b)

Although the lack of a broad skill base contributes to Tokyo's languish-ing, the real roots are in the Ministry of Finance, which has been respons-ible for the financial markets. Sceptical about the self-correcting ability of market forces, it kept tabs on the development and guided it as seemed fit. Change was by consensus and consequently gradual, so as to not upset the overall balance and deprive people of their livelihoods. Competitors could not be taken by surprise in Japan, because applications for new financial products were circulated among all interested parties and became common property before launching. That fared badly with inter-national finance, which is more about cut-throat competition than any-thing else. Frustrated foreigners used to claim that everything is forbidden unless it is explicitly admitted (Brown 1994; Hutton 1995b).

An important factor in Tokyo's competitiveness has been its cost level. It used to top the global league in the late 1980s but has come down since then, at least in relative terms. But each expatriate with a family in Tokyo still costs $1m a year, and the question is whether enough business can be generated to cover that. Authorities expect to be addressed in the vernac-ular but the necessary skills are in short supply among foreigners. The most talented Japanese avoid foreign employers for various cultural reasons and the foreign company knows that dismissing an employee can take a year and attracts devastating publicity. When the financial Japan then went into a tailspin in the early 1990s, business started moving abroad. Listings were made in New York and Hongkong. Trading in equi-ties shifted to London. Singapore got a large chunk of Osaka's (but not Tokyo's) derivatives business. Many borrowers went to the euroyen market to escape the turnover tax in Tokyo. Some speculated that Tokyo's foreign financial community would be transferred wholesale to Hongkong and Singapore. That did not happen, however. The competitors were approaching Tokyo's cost level and Japan continued to have 60 per cent of the Asia Pacific economy (Baker 1995; Hutton 1995a; Rafferty 2000).

But Tokyo's weaknesses came to haunt the politicians and authorities. With the country's financial system under strain from a slower economy and past financial excesses, minds were open for a thorough reform. When it actually happened is conjectural. Fixed commission for largest transactions were officially abolished in 1994, and the last remains went in 1999. The walls between banking, insurance and securities companies were demolished and the repo market created in 1996. From then on, stocks could be traded outside stock exchanges and foreign financial institutions could acquire domestic ones. Securities transaction tax was abolished, netting became legal, remaining forex controls were removed and commissions at TSE freed in 1998. Innovation meeting prudential principles and not being explicitly prohibited became positively permitted. As a Japanese reform, the change has been shockingly profound and it was aptly coined the 'Big Bang', after its UK namesake in 1986. (Hamlin 2000; Lapper 1997; Robinson 1997a; *sigma* 7/2001: 35; Tett and Nusbaum 1999)

Of course, sceptical voices have also been raised: announced reforms had previously been watered down and, indeed, some substance for such thinking has emerged. Forex reforms abolished reporting on cross-border transactions above ¥5m, but the MoF decrees that everything above ¥2m must be reported to the tax office for monitoring. Withholding tax for foreign investors remains in place. From April 2001, all property and financial assets should be marked to market, corporate accounts be on a consolidated basis, and deficits in corporate pension schemes be disclosed. But when large-scale bankruptcies threatened domestic banks, the rules were temporarily suspended. When the Nikkei 225 index threatened to pass a critical limit just before the close of the accounting year, a quiet voice at the phone suggested a short holiday for shorting tactics to avoid putting unnecessary pressure on bank balance sheets. After all, banks are there to support the national economy and not to maximize shareholder value. FSA, the regulator, decrees that if a bank has five different licences each segment must be kept separate with its own street address, and have its own compliance department. There is a dearth of competent financial lawyers, primarily because the government has deliberately kept the number of bar examinations down. Foreigners can set up joint law ventures but cannot hire Japanese partners directly. The economy is one-half of the US but the auditors count only 3–4 per cent of their US numbers and most work with compliance rather than auditing. Rome was not built in a day and such bottlenecks and distortions are not that unusual; most countries have them in one form or another but they are not conducive to a world-class finance centre. (*BIS QR* Aug. 1997: 24; Ibison 2001; Irvine 1999; Robinson 1997b: 15; Tett 1997a; 1997b; 1998; 1999; Tett and Ibison 2001)

The world order challenged?

The Calm Atlantic

The New York–London–Tokyo triad has been so dominant for so long that it may appear secure for the foreseeable future. Financially that may be so. The challenge is more likely to come from politics. The forces of change are currently most visible in Europe, but the undercurrent may be strongest in Asia.

New York is the best established of the three. It does not lack domestic competitors, among which banks in Chicago, San Francisco and Los Angeles, the great derivatives exchanges in Chicago, fund managers in New England, and the international banking community in Miami are prominent. But these competitors are much smaller and narrowly focused, largely lacking the synergy effects and solid infrastructure which are so indispensable for a global centre. The British are very definite when they claim that the only centre which measures up to London's range of commercial, legal and accounting facilities is New York, and that there is no other comparable international competitor (Rose 1994a: 56). That, of course, also settles the matter for the other centres within the time zone such as Toronto and Sao Paulo.

London certainly is the most exposed among the three. It lacks New York's and Tokyo's domestic base, and addressing EU in such terms is wishful thinking for a long time to come, quite irrespective of the British membership in EMU or not. Its serious competition on the Continent are Frankfurt and Paris, and the three will be the topic of the following evaluation. Frankfurt and Paris are first compared with each other, whereafter the 'winner' will be considered against London. The approach by Bindemann (1999) is essentially similar although in reverse order.

From a historical perspective, Paris is vastly superior to Frankfurt. It has been an important banking centre since the nineteenth century and, in 1939, was an international linchpin, together with New York and London. In Germany, all important dealings were concentrated in Berlin, which was the location of the central bank and where the large banks had their headquarters. Frankfurt's chance came after the Second World War, initially because the US military administration happened to be there and supported it against Hamburg, and subsequently when the future Bundesbank was located there. Both these facts had long-term implications. Military presence meant intensive air traffic and made Frankfurt the unquestionable air hub in Germany. The central bank pulled bank headquarters to the city, and with them came securities trading and later on the derivatives exchange. Bundesbank's reputation as a stalwart of monetary policy, uncontaminated by political winds, and combined with deutschmark's role as the second reserve currency could be used as levers when negotiating the location of the future European Central Bank (ECB). At this stage also federal authorities awakened and started promoting 'Finanzplatz Deutschland' in Frankfurt by implementing long due legislation. (Holtfrerich 1999: 220–238; Kindleberger 1993: 409; Rose 1994a: 8)

Paris's trump card is the staunch support which it has long received from the government. Legislation which transformed the stock exchange into a modern institution was enacted earlier than in Germany. The same holds for derivatives exchanges. The issuance of government bonds has been more consistent and innovative. The rule set for the full conversion of domestic-currency securities into euro was in place much earlier than in Germany. The acquisition of Liffe by Euronext was a real coup, although its significance for Paris as a finance centre is uncertain. Can Euronext transfer Liffe's business to Paris or will the opposite happen? The European Central Bank was lost to Frankfurt, but everything possible was done to constrain its powers and channel the monetary policy through national central banks. With the coming of euro, Germany also lost its currency advantage. The elitist *grand écoles* are more suited for grooming future *cadres* in high finance than the egalitarian German education. Quality of life is undoubtedly better in the metropolitan Paris than the half-a-million Frankfurt, although this comes at the expense of higher living costs. (Häuser *et al.* 1990: 23, 40, A37; Rousset-Deschamps 2002)

What Frankfurt has that Paris does not is the specific weight of an economy 40–50 per cent larger. The tardiness of modernizing the German financial sector may have originated from an indifference towards an industry with a shadowy image, the difficulty of coordinating interests in a federal structure, or shrewdness in not ruffling feathers in France. Now, when the task has been mostly completed, it is difficult to see how the larger economy can fail to make its weight felt. All its flair notwithstanding, Paris lacks the implicit backing of the global financial community and cannot, therefore, offer a proper counterweight to London. Frankfurt, for a short while, appeared to have a chance.

The competitive core between Frankfurt and London is in liquidity and synergies. On both counts London wins hands down, German instruments excepted. In such crucial activities as cross-border lending, asset management and OTC trading, London can show two-to-three times more activity than Frankfurt. In forex, it is almost six times bigger. Thereafter the contest revolves mostly around labour issues and the long-term role of the ECB. The simple fact that London has as many people in financial services as is the entire population of Frankfurt actually tells most of the story. The picture can be sharpened by Frankfurt's lower executive salaries and higher taxes, which certainly do not attract talent. Clerical staff, in contrast, are twice as expensive in Frankfurt as London and the rigid labour practices with ensuing civil servant mentality can be a real nuisance. Employees are generally tied to three-year contracts, and for overtime written permission from the work's council is necessary. (Batchelor *et al.* 2002; Covill 1996; Evans 1992: 56–58; Grote *et al.* 2002; Häuser *et al.* 1990: 19)

London's gravest weakness is probably the three-to-four times higher housing cost, which in practice means much longer commuting distances in a dilapidating transportation network. The stamp duty in securities trading is another handicap but in a keen competitive situation it would disappear. Pure trading costs are not so bad and operating costs are not seen as particularly important when juxtaposed with excellent liquidity. Although the UK did not join EMU, it was not excluded from the Target settlement system, only its overnight lending facilities. None of these handicaps, alone or in combination, is sufficiently potent to turn the tables in Frankfurt's favour. (Brealey and Ireland 1993: 25; Häuser *et al.* 1990: 31, A16; Lascelles 1999; Simon 2000: 23; Tett and Gowers 1996)

The key issue about the ECB is its primary intervention market which need not be in the same location as the bank. And it is not, because the function has been delegated to the national central banks which are supposed to act in a coordinated way. That may well have been the only politically feasible solution in the short term, and on that count Frankfurt undoubtedly lost. But in the long term, the decision can be changed if the EMU has staying power, which is still an open question. However, the creation of a single intervention location does not automatically mean that it will overtake London as the foremost European finance centre. Enhanced communications mean a good deal and lobbying can be outsourced to specialists, as has happened in Washington, DC and Brussels. (Häuser *et al.* 1990: 22–23; Rose 1994a: 54)

Then there are such soft issues as London's marginal location in Europe, its non-European ambiance and its modest weight in Latin countries (Häuser *et al.* 1990: 8). These cannot be taken seriously. With modern communications, a difference of 300 km can hardly matter much. What London lacks in European ambiance, it certainly wins in the global variant. And its Latin community is no less numerous and representative than Frankfurt's.

So, what has London to fear? Perhaps nothing, at least not in the eyes of Mr Yassukovich (p. 347). From a historical perspective, the shift of a Pan-European financial centre, from Firenze (Florence), Antwerp, Amsterdam or Paris has been the result of major political disasters rather than conventional competitive factors which are our realm.

Stormy Pacific?

Tokyo could rule over Asia Pacific financially if it wanted to, which it does not – at least not so far. This has left the field outside Japan open for contenders and makes it difficult for Westerners to decide how they should place their bets. The choice between Tokyo and Hongkong, in particular, can be difficult, and some intermediaries have been leapfrogging between the two (Cooke 1995b). As long as China was isolated politically, Hongkong was the natural gateway into the country, in the same way as New York in the nineteenth century was the gateway to the USA. When China's economic opening began in 1979, one could count on Shanghai making a claim for regional supremacy sooner or later. At the southern end of Asia Pacific is Singapore, in the same time zone as Hongkong. It is too small to aspire to a regional hegemony but offers an alternative to the large Japanese and Chinese centres whenever regulation and costs there become unbearable. The remaining centres expressing wider ambitions,

Seoul, Taipei, Bangkok, Kuala Lumpur and Sydney, have so far given only scant proof that they really want, or are able, to proceed on the road which leads to international financial pre-eminence. Our discussion will consequently dwell on Hongkong, Shanghai and Singapore.

Hongkong is the economic giant of southern China, with a money supply 28 per cent and currency reserves 65 per cent of the mother country's at the end of 2000. It is China's largest container port, far exceeding Shanghai, and its FDI reaches 42 per cent of its mighty competitor (*BIS QR* Sept. 2001: Table 1; *IFS* 2002; Rahul 2001). The city was established as a trading post and prospered as such. It assumed its current role after the regime shift in China in 1949, when Shanghai industrialists took their money and machinery and flocked to the British colony for safety. They were followed by millions of refugees offering a seemingly inexhaustible supply of cheap labour. That built the early economic foundation for which the British provided the infrastructure. China was subjected to an onerous trading embargo by Western powers but that could be circumvented by forwarding shipments through Hongkong. The colony duly became the main gateway to China, and a location for trading companies and observation outposts. It had no financial regulator, central bank, nor double taxation treaties, and was essentially an offshore centre.

This was fertile ground for financial intermediation, readily exploited by Japanese who came to dominate wholesale finance. Many transactions were arranged in Hongkong although booked in Singapore which had abolished withholding tax on foreign currency income in 1968. It was also fertile ground for doubtful financial practices, and it took several banking and exchange crises before regulation was brought up to onshore level in the early 1990s. Intermediation was helped tremendously by a stock of lawyers, accountants and executives who were mainly locals but trained in Western ways and fluent in English. These were rare qualities in Asia Pacific and allowed Hongkong to play a regional role. It became the major location for Asian regional headquarters, and one-half of major companies have opted for it. This is tantamount to corporate finance and one reason why the territory occupies one of the top slots in forex trading. Drawing on Singapore's deposits it also became a leader in fund management and loan syndication. It was the only place in Asia in the 1980s where large non-Japanese Asian companies could raise funds locally. China's economic opening allowed Hongkong to expand its influence to the neighbouring province Guangdong and beyond. Over half the local Hongkong banks have some presence in China, and 25 per cent of its notes are circulating in southern China. As the territory will preserve its note issuing right for some time to come, its economic grip is likely to be maintained. (Cottrell 1988: 143; Goodstadt 1988; Hayes and Hubbard 1990: 251; King 1991: 702–703, 740–741; Peet 1992; Reid 1988: 217; Sele 1995: 64, 91, 122, 138–139; Shirreff 1997: 63; Ungefehr 1989c; Warner 1994: 56–57)

At home, banks benefited from bulging trade finance, booming savings, an interest rate cartel for deposits below HK$500,000 and very few bad loans. There is little disintermediation and interest income can reach 80 per cent out of the total. As a result, a 30 per cent ROE has been quite standard (Gapper 1994). The exchange, consolidating stocks, futures, and clearing and settlement depends heavily on retail customers because of a lack of institutional investors. The bulk of market capitalization used to be of local origin but the 1997 reunification triggered capital flight and one-half of the capitalization moved to Bermuda. The remaining companies depend heavily on China proper for their business ('China plays'), or have Chinese backing, although incorporated in Hongkong ('red chips'). One possibility is to buy a publicly quoted Hongkong company, change its logo and issue shares in its name. If it is a joint venture, the effective Chinese tax rate is halved. Then there are pure Chinese companies which have their H shares listed in Hongkong where they get a better p/e ratio than at home. They have been screened by Beijing before listing and get another, very thorough scrutiny by the exchange authorities. It follows that they are reasonably safe risks. They have no definite lifetime as joint ventures do in China, they follow International Accounting Standards, and they must inform about market risks in China: forex controls, tax legislation, share market and its liquidity, company law, accounting rules, legal system. The H-market is also liquid. But to become a really significant stock market, Hongkong needs a large-scale flotation of Chinese assets. That will put it in direct confrontation with Shanghai. (Boland 2000; Crisell/Evans 1995: 110; Hyam 1997: 10; Lucas 1998; de Prati 1998: 117, 119, 136, 168–169; Spencer 1995: 29; Vortmüller 2001: 82, 185–188, 195, 202–203, 230)

Shanghai can recall a financial past far superior to Hongkong's. Its decline came with the People's Republic in 1949. Domestic banks were nationalized or closed and the foreign banking community expelled, save for four banks. The stock exchange lost its function and was closed. When the economic reorientation began in 1979, Shanghai, the hotbed of political radicalism, was initially sidestepped. This policy was subsequently reversed and today the city has one-half of all foreign banking assets in China, plus a vibrant stock exchange (Anon. 1995a).

What these facts hide is that financial operations are heavily regulated, the regulation relies much on administrative judgement, a reliable legal infrastructure is still in the making, and standard financial and linguistic skills are largely lacking. According to a local university spokesman, the city needs almost a generation to give enough people the necessary skills in English and overseas experience (Harding 1997b). There is also uncertainty about the future location of the intervention market. Today it is in Beijing which is the domicile of the People's Bank of China. But when market forces are allowed a free play, the bipartition between the domicile and the financial hub, that is, between Beijing and Shanghai, needs to be solved. In the USA, the solution has been to move the intervention market to the financial hub while keeping the formal domicile in the capital. That need not be the Chinese solution, however, because information technology may have rendered the locational question irrelevant when it arises. Today, it would still matter as the location of foreign banks suggests, representative offices gravitate to Beijing and branches to Shanghai (Kennedy 1995).

Foreign bankers used to complain that their activity was restricted to trade finance and that they, with four exceptions, could not deal in local currency. The latter fact exposed them to currency risk and deprived them of the presumably inexpensive retail deposits. These constraints have been or will be removed with China's entry to the WTO but at so onerous terms that foreign banking will remain a marginal force in Shanghai for a long time to come.

The situation at the stock exchange is rather similar. Trading is mostly in bonds, the listed companies have been selected evenly from all provinces according to a government quota and are smaller and of lower quality than in Hongkong, if only for less stringent accounting standards. Foreigners and Compatriot Chinese (inhabitants of Hongkong, Macao and Taiwan) can deal only in B shares, a marginal and largely illiquid market, of little interest to institutional investors. The Chinese market proper in A shares is very liquid, trading at a 70–80 per cent price premium over the B market. The sectors will certainly merge but hardly before the currency becomes freely convertible. These hassles notwithstanding, the exchange has attracted some fifty foreign brokers out of the total of over 700. The derivatives exchange was closed for an undefined period following a rampant and grossly illegal speculation bout, testifying both to the exchange's inability to regulate itself and the government's determination to keep a tight rein on the activity. The exchange faces no serious challenge by its namesake in Shenzhen which deals in smaller, local companies and has discontinued new listings, in anticipation of being converted into a Nasdaq-type high-tech and growth company exchange. Competition comes preferably from two trading networks used by institutional investors, while the physical exchange is a place for retail customers. (Harding 1997a; Irvine 1997: 24; McGregor 2000; Montagnon and Walker 1995; de Prati 1998: 47–52; Spencer 1995: 29; Timewell 1994: 36; Vortmüller 2001: 12, 62, 67–68, 96)

Singapore has a 200-year long history as an entrepôt, but its development as a finance centre began only in 1968, in response to a government survey among foreign bankers. The asiadollar market became Singapore's forte and attracted numerous foreign banks, active in syndicated credit and trade finance, and controlling one half of loans and deposits in S$. The asiadollar market has, in the meantime, grown to over $300bn. They are external, short-term, interbank monies, the city's modest size setting limits to the accumulation of domestic funds. The use of S$ as an international reserve currency has been actively discouraged, because currency speculation could seriously disrupt the country's monetary order, although that is slowly changing. (Coggan 1996; Grubel 1989: 70–72; Kynge 1997b; Roberts 1994: 102; Sele 1995: 138–139; Shirreff 1995a: 85; 1995b: 80; Ungefehr 1989b)

Such restrictions mean little for many financial activities. Low taxes, competent regulation and low criminality are attractive. Non-residents pay no withholding tax and Asian Currency Units pay only 10 per cent tax for offshore income. The competence of the Monetary Authority of Singapore is legendary and has helped the city state to gain forex business at Hongkong's expense; in forex it is important to know who the counterparty is. A further lift has come from the numerous treasury operations which have fled Hongkong's cost level. The maturing of exotic currencies has also been helpful. Standard Chartered, for example, relocated options and forex derivatives teams from London to Singapore. In fund management, the city has been slowly creeping into Hongkong's role as a regional centre, but is handicapped by the small size of domestic funds, one-third of Hongkong's. The workforce compares well with Hongkong's in skills and is also bound to remain that way. Expatriate executives stay longer at their jobs and may even be cheaper than locals. The problems are in recruiting and retaining staff at the clerical level and the withering of entrepreneurial instincts, a result of strict controls and secretive regulation. (Caplan 1987: 81; Coggan 1996; Franck 1997: 4; Handley 1998: 158–159; Kynge 1997a; Lowenstein 1990: 66, 73; Shale 1993: 42; Shirreff 1997: 60)

Domestic banks are small and, until 1999, well protected from foreign competition. Chinese banks are expected to leave for Hongkong when the yuan becomes more liquid. The small size of the domestic economy draws narrow limits around capital markets. A balanced government budget and the dominance of large multinationals in manufacturing limits bond issuance. The compulsory pension fund has invested mostly abroad or in government projects which do not trade. Listings on the stock exchange depend as much on the character of the directors as the financial statements of their companies. It may be fine in local circumstances but works less well internationally. Smaller domestic companies are family-owned. Foreign companies can list in their own currency but few do. Competitive listings with the Kuala Lumpur SE have sapped energies but given no lasting results. The derivatives exchange, now merged with the stock exchange, made its name by trading US and Japanese products in the right time zone and regulatory environment. But none of its contracts are based on domestic products. (Cockerill 2002; Lowenstein 1990: 73; Shale 1993: 43; Shirreff 1995b: 81)

This description can be rounded out by a comparatively recent analysis of the region's banking system (Figure 7.4). The analysis is based on the idea of dominance. If banks headquartered in centre A have more offices

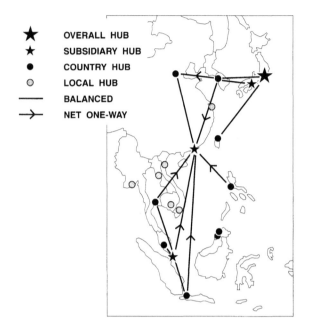

★   OVERALL HUB
★   SUBSIDIARY HUB
●   COUNTRY HUB
○   LOCAL HUB
──   BALANCED
→―   NET ONE-WAY

Figure 7.4 Banking system in Asia Pacific, 1995.

Source: Haga, Hirobumi, 'Banking centres and the network of international banks in Pacific Asia', Figure 7. *Asian Geographer* 1997: 16 (1–2), 1–20. Copyright © 1997 of Dr Hirobumi Haga, Kyushu Sangyuo University, Fukuoka; used with permission.

Notes
Relation between centres is balanced when both send about equal number of offices to each other. Tokyo dominates (not shown) all subsidiary and country hubs except Seoul and Taipei.

in centre B than the other way round, A dominates B. When the numbers are about equal, the relationship is balanced. The measurement implies that all the banks are of the same character and about the same size. Otherwise, the possibility of a bias exists: a wholesale bank will open few offices and a retail bank will open many, other things being equal; where ten small wholesale banks will open ten offices in a centre, a wholesale bank ten times larger will open only few, maybe just one. Such biases are not serious in the comparatively simply structured Asia Pacific, but in North America and particularly Europe they should be accounted for explicitly.

The figure displayed here is heavily simplified from the original. Only the capital cities plus some other key hubs, i.e. Osaka, Shanghai, Hongkong, Labuan and Ho Chi Minh City, are identified. Tokyo dominates the whole system, Seoul and Taipei excepted, which makes corresponding markers superfluous. When it has no offices in a particular city, it exercises dominance through another hub. Osaka replicates Tokyo to an extent, which partially results from the Japanese custom of having double headquarters. Hongkong attracts offices from all over the region, it is the dominated city. In view of the previous description, this appears strange but the explanation is logical. There are some large banks, which reduces the need to open numerous offices in other centres, and Hongkong's role as an offshore centre means that the number of originated banks is much smaller than of hosted banks (see Figure 5.22). Shanghai assumes a modest role in this seven-year-old system. A new analysis is needed to define its contemporary position and then particularly in relation to Beijing and Hongkong. Singapore is the unquestionable hub of the south. But there is also a subsidiary hub, Bangkok, which dominates the surrounding local hubs.

Nothing in this account, neither the formal system nor the description preceding it, suggests that Tokyo's leading position would be threatened in the medium term. The same applies to Hongkong. Speculation that its traditional business would be muddled by administrative interference from Beijing has come to nought. Such prophesies might better fit Shanghai once its own financial skills, the full convertibility of the yuan, and the unconstrained admission of foreigners allow it to spread its wings. That still lies in a distant future. Singapore is basically an offshore centre living on the shortcomings of its larger neighbours. It continues to look after Southeast Asia, while Hongkong looks to China, Taiwan, Japan and possibly Korea. Hongkong's true international peer group, however, is London and New York rather than any of the Asian centres, even Tokyo.

Offshore – slim and trim

A love–hate affair

Offshore centres are given more than their fair share of space here. The lack of systematic treatment of their specific features elsewhere in the text warrants it.

The image of offshore centres in the mind of laypeople is not the best: zero-tax locations for tax avoiders, speculators and twilight figures; less finance hubs than booking centres and legal domiciles where one single management company handles scores of trusts and funds. Central bankers also have negative feelings: that offshore centres are free riders at the expense of the domestic markets of international reserve currencies (Häusler 1994: 11). The physical setting is no less irritating to stressed city dwellers, faraway tropical paradises or close by anachronisms from bygone days, putting up barriers for retired people to live in quietly and attractively. These shibboleths are true to some extent, but they are only part of the picture.

Geographically, everything which is separated by a body of water is 'offshore', while economists reserve the term for financial structures which follow different rules from the main body of the economy and are separated from it. Accepting the latter definition, IBF and JOM are clearly 'offshore'. So are euromarkets. The same label is attached to countries and territories which are part of the mainland, but whose economy is largely geared to the needs of the international financial community. Liechtenstein and Luxembourg are typical examples. Switzerland is sometimes seen in these terms irrespective of its size.

Whatever the exact definition, offshore centres play an important role in global finances. In 1980 it was estimated that one-third of eurocurrency markets were 'offshore'. Ten years later a more dramatic estimate was made: one-half of the world's money stock either resides or passes through tax havens (Johns and Le Marchant 1993: 78; Kochan 1991: 73). Such estimates, however, omit the average time of residence, which is shorter than onshore. What, exactly, is included geographically and asset-wise is not revealed either. Both estimates are also ten-to-twenty years old. More recent figures were given in the context of HNWIs, a total of \$9.0tr in 2000. They included Switzerland, the UK and USA, a total of \$4.2tr, which leaves \$4.8tr for genuine offshore. Another recent source puts the figure at \$6tr (*Libération*, 8 March 2000). Both figures match reasonably well with our estimate which is mostly collected from occasional comments in trade press (Table 7.2). Several reservations are necessary, however. It is often unclear which items are included in the disclosed data, only fund monies, bank deposits, all trust assets which also include other than financial assets and so on. Assets in Hongkong have been taken directly from HNWI calculations. The HNWI estimate for Luxembourg

Table 7.2 Assets managed offshore, about 2000

Territory	$bn	Source
Cayman Islands	750	Martinson 1998
Bahamas	1,094	James 2001
Bermuda	146	Lines 2002
Caribbean	1,990	
Dublin	80	Murray-Brown 1999
Jersey	480	Peel 2000b
Guernsey	150	Cobb 2001
Isle of Man	150	Peel 2000c
Luxembourg	875	www.cssf.lu 2002
Liechtenstein	70	www.bankenverband.li 2002
Monaco	65	Mallet 2001
Europe	1,870	
Mauritius	4	Anon. 1999
Singapore	216	Cockerill 2002
Hongkong	450	Figure 5.7
Asia	670	
Total	4,530	

was $1.62tr while the figure here is $875bn and includes only investment funds. Bank deposits would add another $480bn but part of them are interbank. It is interesting to recall that the estimate by Pouzin (1995) from the early 1990s, given in Table 7.2 of the first edition, was $5tr but also included ship registers, about $1.0tr. This gives an idea of the accuracy of estimates like ours. The conclusion is that offshore assets in a narrow sense are about 5 per cent of total financial assets.

Although offshore flight capital is nearly as old as money itself, the contemporary centres are essentially a phenomenon of the past forty-to-fifty years. Three forces were instrumental in their proliferation. US banks could get a better interest rate spread abroad and avoid restrictions at home. Once abroad they created euromarkets. The other factor was excessive income taxation, with marginal tax rates of 90 per cent and over. Capital gains were often taxed separately, and the rates were much lower. This created the incentive to convert income to capital gain and book as much income as possible in low-tax jurisdictions. Tax was payable when the monies were repatriated onshore, but cash flow advantages were still recorded. In addition to traditional tax planning came the market created by expatriate labour, in plain ascendancy with the globalization of businesses. Much of this labour works in short-term tax-free contracts in countries with no retirement benefits or double-taxation agreements. Or, if taxes and agreements do exist, the tax bases and fiscal boundaries (national, worldwide) are likely to vary. It is important then to create a nest egg for unemployment periods between contracts and old age. This can be done best in a low-tax offshore location. The name of the game is low tax or none at all.

In the long run this was too easy. Tax authorities started plugging the loopholes, new offshore centres intensified mutual competition and customers began looking for higher returns in addition to lower taxes. Simple tax havens consequently specialized, in banking, investment funds, fiduciary activity, company formation, treasury operations, trading, insurance and so on. Some became locations for conducting third-country operations, others for accessing capital and money markets, and some for sheltering earnings and savings. For example, Jersey and the Bahamas concentrated on offshore banking, Bermuda and Guernsey on insurance, while company formation was left to the British Virgin Islands and the Isle of Man. Specialization led to a skill-based hierarchy. Offshore company registry with a low value added was at the lowest level, while banking and insurance were high-order industries. When a centre developed its skill base and infrastructure, it also shed lower-order activities to newcomers and adopted higher-order tasks instead. For example, credit life insurance (lending against insurance policy) was originally handled in the Bahamas, then it moved to the Cayman Islands and then to Turks and Caicos, fleeing restrictive regulation. (Johns and Le Marchant 1993: 18–19; Peagam 1989: 104; Roberts 1995: 251)

Much of what happened was due to pure chance or, rather, inherited circumstances for which nobody had, until then, given much thought. Jersey and Guernsey (the Channel Islands), and the Isle of Man offer a superb example thanks to a thorough analysis by Johns and Le Marchant (1993). Each of them is a self-governing body under British sovereignty. The political constellation allowed them to escape many burdensome obligations and charge the modest income tax rate of 20 per cent. Their beginnings were as sterling and subsequently eurodollar offshore centres with a ready access to the city of London. Jersey then specialized in banking and Guernsey in insurance and trust business. It was rather accidental.

Banks went offshore first and the Jersey authorities, who were looking for diversification from agriculture and tourism, got hooked on them. Guernsey, in contrast, made no conscious effort to become an offshore centre but became involved more by accident and through its closeness to Jersey. Banking in Jersey boomed and gradually exhausted the island's labour force, real estate and absorption capacity in general. A one-year ban on new bank entries was introduced in 1973. The overspill went to Guernsey. Jersey hardly participated in the rising groundswell of offshore captives in the 1970s. It suffered from outdated legislation and insurance companies could be incorporated there only from 1982. It followed the French tradition and had no developed trust law either before 1984. Guernsey, consequently, had a field day with captives and also started receiving trust funds, for example, from European civil law countries. Today, it collects insurance premiums corresponding to 10 per cent of Bermuda's, which has both captive and catastrophe insurance (Leonard 1997).

The Channel Islands were in the ascendant and could afford to become choosy. Entries from geographical areas and business fields still weakly represented were given priority. So were quality institutions from well-regulated countries and companies promising a good profit/labour ratio. Over 90 per cent of banks in Jersey were among the world's top 500 in 1992, and a new licence was given only to those making at least £50,000 pretax income per employee. One way to achieve the income target was to introduce managed banks, essentially large individual accounts managed by a resident bank. Guernsey followed suit and welcomed only banks which were household names in their own countries. Most of its banks focus on private banking. There was only one adversity. Attempts to attract Japanese banks practically failed, since the Japanese prefer the Cayman Islands and British Virgin Islands. (Johns and Le Marchant 1993: 136; Marriott 1995: 16; Riley 1995)

The Isle of Man was left behind in this race. Its starting position was much weaker. Its legislative and budgetary autonomy was less. Its 40 per cent income tax was brought down to 20 per cent only in 1980. Its usury legislation was outdated, making it difficult to charge market rates for lending and services. Its authorities moved slowly and seemed to lack the skills of promoters and regulators. Some financial scandals generated bad publicity, which took a decade to fade away. The island was mainly used by UK residents, and then from the less affluent central and northern parts. Non-resident and exempt companies and a shipping register, comparatively simple activities with a low value added, became its forte. The comparatively large population of 75,000 has allowed back-office operations, another low-value activity. (Cobb 2001; Graham 1998; Ungefehr 1989b)

These lines give an inkling of what customers expect from an offshore centre. But there is more to it than just low taxes and a certain skill base. An offshore centre must also be politically stable, without exchange controls and other fiscal barriers for non-residents, without minimum reserves for banks, convenient to visit repeatedly, maintain strict secrecy – whether by law or custom – with a minimum of reporting, have legal, accounting and banking services, respectable regulation, rapid company formation and a reasonable cost level. (Crisell and Ellis 1995: 4–6; Crisell and Fitzgerald 1995: 30; Grubel 1989; Johns and Le Marchant 1993: 30–32)

Safety first

Mini-states with a non-party political system geared to continuity and stability are ideal. When they, in addition, can look to a large, benevolent neighbour as a guarantor of regional peace, an extra layer of safety is provided. The Cayman Islands is probably as close to that as is conceivable. It is a 35,000-inhabitant British Crown colony which shuns independence but minds its own affairs, does not want change and makes politics about personalities rather than principles. The Bahamas, in contrast, provides a cautionary example. The country gained independence from the UK under a populistic leadership in 1973, experienced an acrimonious struggle between the white minority and black majority, got involved in a drug trafficking brawl with the USA, was branded as a major money laundering centre, and radically raised its banking licence fees. New offshore business dried up and the old one shifted wholesale to the Cayman Islands and Jersey, among others. The industry was saved because of the country's closeness to the USA. It was too convenient a base to be abandoned and strict law enforcement has brought business back. (Fidler 1996; James 1997; Ungefehr 1987)

Should stability fail, it is valuable that the location can be left at very short notice, that the transfer of business can be affected without unwinding the company or trust and that the law both in the old and the new jurisdiction permits this. An extreme vehicle is a so-called 'escape (or flee) clause'. It automatically triggers relocation when a particular event occurs. Its strength is speed of movement. But automation may create vagueness. Has the particular event really happened and did it go unnoticed? The alternative is that a denominated person makes the decision ('forms an opinion') but s/he also escapes all control. Such ideas seem distant in the academic world, but when Iraq invaded Kuwait in 1990, the National Bank of Kuwait was immediately relocated to London, although neither is considered an offshore centre. (Crisell/Olesnicky and McKenzie 1995: 47; Johns and Le Marchant 1993: 236)

There is one particular category of money, however, which is not safe offshore: criminal money, money earned in drug business or earmarked for terrorism then takes a special position. The worldwide coordination to combat money laundering currently rests with the Financial Action Task Force (FATF), an independent organization aligned with the OECD. It has released twenty-eight recommendations, follows their implementation, and lists offenders. That new offshore centres such as Nauru, the Cook Islands and Niue (pop. 2,000) are alleged to tolerate criminal activity is hardly astonishing. But established onshore countries have also been lambasted, including Russia, Israel, Hungary and the USA. The most serious sanction so far has been intensive surveillance and transaction reporting. Noteworthy is the vacillating US attitude. In 1999 Congress rejected legislation intended to tighten know-your-customer rules, which made European banks regard payments from the USA with suspicion. But after the World Trade Center attack, it froze alleged terrorist accounts at home and urged other countries to follow suit under threat that their own funds in the USA might be frozen. (Crisell/Cox 2002; Peel 2000a; 2001; 2002; Willman 2001a; 2001b)

The practical work remains with national authorities and the financial community. Bankers are required to inform authorities of suspects and they normally agree, sometimes with very tangible results. Since the Cayman Islands started fighting money launderers in 1992, 500 suspicious drug-related transactions were scrutinized within a few years, of which 80 per cent were positively identified. Two local banks were closed down and practically only subsidiaries of major banking groups were left. In Jersey, about 300 reports are made annually, but only 5 per cent led to police investigation. On the global scale the problem is far from being solved, however. The launderers only relocate themselves. They migrated from the Channel Islands to the Caribbean, from there to the Indian Ocean and have now arrived at the South Pacific. The Seychelles at one time promised immunity for all criminal charges once at least $10m has been invested locally. (Fabre and Jacquin 1996: 61; Graham 1997; Hampton 1996b; James and Fidler 1997; Jeune 1997; Johns and Le Marchant 1993, 178)

Zero tax – or almost

Many offshore territories do not have tax for external, or any, income, and, logically, they have minimal or no tax laws. The rest usually criminal-ize tax fraud, possibly evasion, but not avoidance. The difference between the three is vague but avoidance can probably be equated with tax planning, evasion with non-disclosure, and fraud with the forgery of accounts, for example. Onshore, interpretation can be more strict, however. In Germany, France and Italy, an offshore company put up for the sole purpose of minimizing tax is considered fraud. Now the offshore is asked to cooperate with foreign countries in tax-related investigations, many of which have no basis in their own law. The usual form of cooperation is the disclosure of bank accounts or at least the income accrued on them. Offshore territories object unless the case is about drug trafficking, terrorism and similar serious crimes. But in practice they are usually compelled to cooperate because important onshore countries have the capacity to retaliate in many ways. It is also a cat-and-mouse game because a stated criminal case can be a simple 'fishing expedition' by the taxman who hopes to find evidence for further investigation. In a historical court case, the Danish tax authorities won the right to seize confidential documents in the Isle of Man, while similar requests they made in Switzerland and the UK were rejected. The court order was allegedly won by claiming a fraud investigation. (Crisell/Palmer 1995: 14; Hampton 1996a: 34; Johns and Le Marchant 1993: 106; Rice 1996)

It has become fashionable to belittle the importance of low taxes to offshore centres. This is window dressing, although tax weighs much less in wholesale than retail business. But still, no offshore centre can exist without tax benefits. Two examples will bring the message home.

When it became known in October 1982 that, investigation notwithstanding, no new action was to be taken in the UK tax treatment (income versus capital gains tax) of monies which were shifted between funds in the Channel Islands, deposits there increased 40 per cent during the next three weeks. When action was finally taken as from January 1984, one Rothschild fund plummeted from $1,000m to $290m. Many mutual funds simply went to the Cayman Islands (Johns and Le Marchant 1993: 99–100; Peagam 1989: 65).

The real issue nowadays is not plain zero tax but what the optimal tax percentage is. The correct figure depends on circumstances, and places like Jersey and Mauritius allow their customers to decide which percentage suits them best. If the customer is an individual with permanent residence in another offshore jurisdiction, zero tax may make sense. The problem is that offshore centres generally offer limited investment opportunities, and that the exemption is only for external business. Normal tax is payable onshore, and a company incorporated in a zero-tax territory cannot benefit from double taxation treaties. For example, London has some difficulty in competing for Middle East money, because people there pay no income or capital gains tax. Many countries go still further. They simply refuse to conclude double taxation treaties with zero-tax territories. But it also goes in the opposite direction. Jersey, for example, has never sought double taxation treaties except with the UK, since they complicate fund management. (Crisell/Bikoo 1995: 204; Crisell/Palmer 1995: 14; Johns and Le Marchant 1993: 153; Slaughter 1995; Stuart 1996; Ungefehr 1989a)

A multinational company sees the matter from a different perspective. It creates an International Finance Company (IFC) to collect and redistribute cash flows. The International Financial Services Centre in Dublin is a typical location and works as follows.

A Canadian firm sets up an Irish subsidiary and finances it with a loan for which the subsidiary pays interest. Since there is a tax treaty between Ireland and Canada, no withholding tax is taken in Ireland. The tax is payable from the parent's net income in Canada and subject to the usual deductions there. The Irish subsidiary lends further to a US subsidiary. Because the USA and Ireland also have a tax treaty, there is no withholding tax in the USA for this interest either. The tax is payable from the Irish subsidiary's net income at a rate of 12.5 per cent. (Crisell/Jennings and Cundy 1995: 27–28)

An ideal location for an IFC is a normal tax territory with numerous tax treaties and a special provision for holding companies and free zone areas. The UK, Austria, Belgium, Denmark, Luxembourg, Spain, the Netherlands and Switzerland lead the pack (Figure 7.5). Exemption from withholding tax is particularly important.

Unexpected possibilities emerge. Belgium and the Netherlands both have 25 per cent withholding tax but it can be cut to 5 per cent and 8.3 per cent, respectively, through tax treaties with Mauritius and the Netherlands Antilles (Crisell/O'Reilly 2002).

Because all operations are internal to the corporation, normal equity/asset ratios (solidity) play no role. The lower the ratio, the more profitable the IFC. Switzerland and Luxembourg are very liberal in this respect and therefore popular locations, although the former is handicapped by its high withholding tax (Kochan 1991). The benefits can be in several layers.

US banks and corporations used to borrow in the eurobond market through a shell company in the Netherlands Antilles which was guaranteed by the US parent. The shell re-lent to the parent and received the interest, free of the 30 per cent US withholding tax. It paid a low tax in Curaçao, for which the US parent claimed tax credit at home. Since bond purchasers in Europe and Japan received their interest

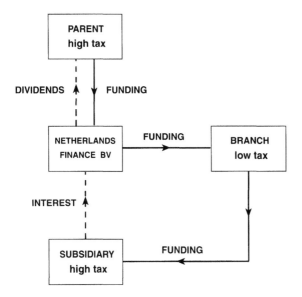

Figure 7.5 The Netherlands holding company in a corporate structure.

Source: Jennings, Simon and Cundy, Mark, Rawlinson & Hunter, London, 'International financial centres and free zones', Figure 1. In: Crisell, Michaela (ed.), *Offshore Finance Yearbook 1994–95*: 26–28. Euromoney Institutional Investor, Colchester. Copyright © 1995 of Euromoney Institutional Investor plc, England; used with permission.

free of the Antilles withholding tax, they accepted a lower interest rate, which was to the benefit of the US borrower. In 1981 the territory reaped more US-source income than Switzerland. The feast ended when the USA abolished withholding tax for foreigners in mid-1984. (Peagam 1989: 75; Ungefehr 1988b)

Tax treaties also have their weak sides. The most formidable is that they are a trading object and must be paid for by concessions. The fewer the treaties, the fewer the concessions. And concessions always have a flip side.

In the mid-1980s, Barbados signed a tax information agreement and double taxation treaty with the USA, which over-rode domestic bank secrecy law. The benefits Barbados reaped in exchange during a ten-year period did the island little visible good, and it is languishing far behind its more cautious Caribbean peers. (Peagam 1989: 31; Ungefehr 1988c)

Therefore, Liechtenstein, for example, has double taxation treaties only with Austria and Switzerland. Treaties can also be revoked, even unilaterally. That happened to the British Virgin Islands, Netherlands Antilles and

Barbados whose treaties were wholly or partially withdrawn by US authorities in the 1980s, an action which almost killed the Netherlands Antilles
as an offshore location (Crisell/Wanger 1995: 15; Fidler 1995; Johns and
Le Marchant 1993: 86; Peagam 1989: 75).

> The cat-and-mouse game never ends. The most recent ploy by US
> multinational corporations is to move headquarters to Bermuda and
> convert the onshore business into a subsidiary. A subsidiary is first
> established in Bermuda, whereafter it and the US parent exchange
> shares. The corporation is from now on domiciled in Bermuda and
> owns all assets, foreign subsidiaries included. Since the new parent is
> not a US corporation, only its US subsidiary pays taxes there. The rest
> gets the tax rate cut from 35 per cent to less than 11 per cent. The
> avoidance is too obvious and legislation to discontinue the practice is
> in the making. (Gift Mullins 2002; Crisell/Williams 2002)

It appears, however, that offshore centres have gone too far and the
long-pending counter offensive by the OECD is ongoing (OECD 1998;
2001). Low-tax territories have been placed into three groups, based on
the tax benefits they grant and their reluctance to provide information to
foreign authorities. The original list included the major European offshore centres, Hongkong and Singapore, in Group I. It is not without
irony that Dublin and Singapore found themselves in this group. Dublin
enjoyed the EU's temporary tax benefits instead of subsidies and Singapore, with Jersey, was the only jurisdiction which refused BCCI a banking
licence, regulatory prudence but not a tax credit. The Group II included,
among others, Monaco, Gibraltar, Bahrain, Barbados and Bermuda.
Stereotype 'tax offenders' such as the Bahamas, British Virgin Islands,
Cayman Islands, Cyprus, Lebanon, Liechtenstein, Mauritius, Netherlands
Antilles, Panama, Seychelles and Vanuatu comprised Group III. With a
slight generalization, the further a territory was from Europe and Japan
the more suspect were its activities. The core issue was secrecy. The offshore centres were asked to disclose internal information under threat of
transaction and tax penalties. Many important centres with little political
muscle have complied and resistance comes primarily from Switzerland
and Luxembourg, OECD members themselves. The US Internal Revenue
Service, in the meantime, has carried out its own crusade but against
financial intermediaries rather than jurisdictions. It insists that only
organizations who repatriate withholding tax on income earned by US
taxpayers abroad can do business in the country. About 5,500 organizations have complied. (Handley 1998: 159; Hunt 2002; Wells 2002;
Willman 2001a; Wright 1998)

Secret and trustworthy

For offshore centres to fulfil their purpose of being safe havens for financial assets, they must resort to considerable secrecy. But the question of
what to hide and what to disclose is actually a very thorny issue. Criminal
money has been outlawed almost everywhere, at least in theory if not in
practice. Tax dodging is already a much more controversial issue,
although the trend appears to be towards tax treaties and exchange of
information. But should financial intermediaries also conduct data search
even when a tax collector or an executor cannot specify the assets to look
for? The law varies and offshore law generally gives far better secrecy
against unwanted investigators than onshore law.

The breach of banking secrecy is, in most places, a criminal and not
only a civil offence. It may be possible that only the registered trustee
knows the beneficiaries of a trust and that s/he need not disclose them.
Matters become more controversial if the identity of company directors
and shareholders can also be kept secret. It is often sufficient with one
shareholder. Thereafter rulings that no director need be resident in the
domicile, that there need be no annual general meeting (AGM), audit or
filing of documents appear quite logical. If, however, an AGM is held, it
can take place abroad and electronically or by phone. These are a sample
of the many possibilities which can be selected by an offshore centre, and
which can also be changed when circumstances warrant it. The structures
can be and are used by criminals, but the original purpose was not that;
they were intended for people who were secretive by nature, avoided creditors, current and future, or who wanted to flout inheritance rules which
they found unfair. Therefore, it is understandable that institutional business like eurobonds and mutual funds considers banking secrecy in its
strict form rather irrelevant. (Crisell 1995; 2002; Luce and James 1997;
Rodger 1994)

The traditional vehicle for estate protection and planning is a trust, a
legal structure in which a settlor provides funds to be managed by a
trustee according to the settlor's instructions for the well-being of a beneficiary (Crisell/Garnham 1995: 7). Obviously, protection can be gained
only when the trust has been established before the topical event takes
place. A fairly typical structure for a private investment company consists
of a trust governed by Jersey law with a trustee in the Isle of Man. The
trust owns companies in the British Virgin Islands. One company has
accounts in Zurich and New York, another owns a flat in San Francisco
and a third has a home in Marbella. That makes five legal entities together
and goes some way towards explaining why small offshore centres have
those monumental company registrations. The current figure in the
British Virgin Islands is 300,000 and in Liechtenstein 75,000 (Courtenay
1996a; Crisell/Bennett 1995: 2; www.transnationale.org 2002).

Trusts can normally be created only in territories which follow common law (as opposed to civil law). French islands, for example, suffer from the mainland's civil code. In Islamic countries trusts are beyond the pale, of course. The Continent is ambivalent because of its civil law tradition. German, French and Italian courts recognize trusts already in existence. The problems arise with tax authorities, although their resistance is gradually crumbling. Countries with a sizeable offshore business are positive, to state it simply. Gibraltar follows the English law and has trusts. Liechtenstein also has trusts (*anstalt, stiftung*) in the positive law and allows their creation according to the English or US law. Swiss law does not know the concept but permits trust creation when it happens under some other law. Monaco enables persons whose national law includes trust law to create trusts recognized and enforced by Monaco law. The variety implies that, although the fundamental idea is the same, the settlor should give some thought to the variant s/he prefers. (Anon. 1997; Courtenay 1996a; Crisell/Ellis 1995: 5; Crisell/Montegriffo 1995: 15; Crisell/Wanger 1995: 174; Crisell/Woolf 1995: 210; Hampton, 1994: 247; Kochan 1992: 85)

Whatever the legal niceties and current administrative practice, residence in a civil-law or Islamic country can easily make trusts a sham. It is also wise to keep trust assets in a common law country and preferably one which is powerful enough to resist political pressure for disclosure. In actual practice, the immediate tax and regulatory benefits of mini-states make trustees optimistic. Merrill Lynch, for example, has located its trust business in the Cayman Islands and Chase has its in the Channel Islands. When the trustee has offices in several jurisdictions, the risk of cross-border pressure is clearly increased. Activity somehow linked with the USA is in a high-risk zone because of the country's litigious culture. (Courtenay 1996b; Crisell/Garnham 1995: 9; Crisell/Ingham 1995: 13; Crisell/Harris 1995: 33; Crisell/Mirecki 1995: 42)

Escaping regulation

Once taxes and secrecy have been accounted for, the best card offshore centres have in competition with the onshore is regulation. When listed, the gamut of onshore regulation becomes amazingly long and it all plays into the hands of offshore centres: ideological antimarket bias, currency controls, rules of minimum reserves, capital adequacy, liquidity, banking laws, company laws, loan and country concentration, permissible business and complicated inspection procedures (Johns and Le Marchant 1993: 4–8, 81–82).

Offshore capitalizes on them by offering flexibility. It is not only investors who value it. Expatriates changing jobs between different tax jurisdictions, i.e. varying tax bases, rates and fiscal boundaries, appreciate the flexible pension plans and life assurance of offshore. They are possible because the regulation is so light. First and foremost there are no exchange controls. There are no reserve requirements or capital adequacy rules. Possibly the onshore parent provides a letter of comfort, guaranteeing the subsidiary's dealings, but it is not legally binding. Investment fund gearing is allowed, as are risky investment objects like commodities and derivatives. Companies with a minimal management structure, absentee directors, electronic board meetings and no audit or filing requirements can be formed. There is less labour legislation, lower social security, less and more rapid bureaucracy, all of which saves costs. An International Business Company is incorporated in the British Virgin Islands on the same day. In Western Samoa it can be done within an hour, and an international company name can be approved within five minutes. Obviously, no fit and proper scrutiny of the directors is possible but the flexibility cannot be denied. (Crisell/Adams 1995: 117; Crisell/Lead 1995: 255; Johns and Le Marchant 1993: 26, 35, 58; Roberts 1994: 99)

The Cayman Islands are a typical example of an offshore centre which has prospered because of its regulatory moderation rather than just low taxes. Its banking business rests on eurodollars and, since the currency is pegged to the US dollar, there is no point in having minimum reserve requirements, particularly when one half of its banks have fled the US requirements. When Japanese loans in Mexico went sour in 1987 and could not be written down properly at home they were transferred to the Cayman Islands. It is one of the major domiciles of hedge and mutual funds in the world. Most are attracted by the Caymans' regulation, light by the standards of Luxembourg and Dublin. When Bermuda revamped insurance regulation, new captives went to the Caymans and started an insurance boom there. At home, US insurance companies have maximum premium limits by state. When a limit is reached, additional premiums are diverted to a captive offshore. The Cayman Islands are a frequent choice. It does not limit the volume of business a captive can write, nor its risk exposure, and has no solvency requirements. Yet, it was the first Caribbean territory to have offshore insurance legislation, in 1979. (Luce 1997; Peagam 1989: 59, 65, 68; Ungefehr 1988a)

The emphasis on flexibility and the minimum of rules easily gives the impression that less is better. Again, it depends on the customer and the need. Dirty money certainly agrees. Clean money probably values a suitable dose of professional regulation because it is nice to find one's funds there after six months' absence. Enhanced regulation can do real wonders in cleaning the stable.

> When the Bahamas introduced the licensing and supervision of banks in 1965, their numbers declined in two years from over 600 to just ninety. Montserrat used to sell banking licences to all-comers and attracted large-scale fraudsters intent on operating in the USA. In the ensuing clean-up, 317 of the 350 banks were closed down in March 1990. (Anon. 1987: 7; Kochan 1991: 74)

Not only are funds safer, transactions with onshore also become easier. Both can be used as a sales argument when attracting new customers, since track records of offshore centres vary considerably. Jersey proudly points out that it refused BCCI a banking licence, while London was fooled and damaged its reputation. Many 'old' centres have found it rational to tighten regulation and supervision to gain quality business. The Cayman Islands, for example, do not issue banking licences easily if the applicant is not regulated and supervised in a recognized country. OECD membership, in particular, gives a kind of legitimacy to a finance centre (Johns and Le Marchant 1993: 251, 263). Still, it is important to know the actual business partner. It is not very likely that the century-old Bank of Bermuda has anything to hide or that a subsidiary of Barclay's Bank would be more risky than its parent in London.

Light regulation may not have a particular purpose. It is also a question of resources, money and skills. The assets of Liechtenstein trusts and foundations were largely held outside the country and managed from there, because there are too few local banks and professional fund managers. With good reason. The Liechtenstein company which managed the Maxwell pension funds and allowed them to be emptied of most monies openly admitted that the task exceeded its capabilities. It was impossible for it to follow all the 400 subsidiaries involved. The Isle of Man has similar experience. Its banking supervisors were inexperienced, careless and understaffed, which resulted in two unrelated bank failures in 1982 and the discovery that a third intermediary had succeeded in taking £1.5m of deposits, although its own capital was only £2 (two pounds sterling). Once bitten, twice wise. When things had been straightened out ten years later, new principles ruled out private banks. Changes in their ownership were considered too difficult to control. Similar insight on the part of the Luxembourg central bank might have saved the world from the BCCI debacle. Having delivered all this flak on failed regulators, it must be admitted in all fairness that regulation is more difficult offshore because innovation traditionally originates there. (Johns and Le Marchant 1993: 200–201, 206, 266; Rodger 1993; 1994)

Clustering and competition

There are at least sixty mini-states and territories functioning as offshore centres. Many of them are parenthetical or emerging, with predominantly low-order functions, and only a handful are important on a world scale. The Bahamas, Bermuda, British Virgin Islands, Cayman Islands, Jersey and Guernsey (Channel Islands) undoubtedly belong to the top league. Luxembourg and Switzerland are also very important but either too regional or large to have quite the right image. Theoretically, offshore activity should reflect the time zones and main sources of financial wealth. This would divide the world into four main regions: the Caribbean,

Europe, Middle East Gulf and Asia Pacific. According to this theory, each has its 'money box' centre: Panama, Switzerland, Bahrain and Hongkong, surrounded by a group of secondary, turntable centres (Johns and Le Marchant 1993: 16–17).

The idea is attractive, but it is difficult to agree with many important details (Figure 7.6). The Gulf is a respectable source area, but there are not too many satellites of any significance around Bahrain, which is rather a satellite to Europe and a base for collecting petrodollar deposits. Asia Pacific has a stronger showing, but even it is a source more than a cross-road. Whether Hongkong and Singapore are really offshore is a moot question considering their vast real economies and the latter's strict regulation. Low taxes alone do not yet make an offshore centre. Wealthy Asians may also find better use for their money in entrepreneurial activity, or seem to prefer the professionalism and relative safety of North America and Europe. The Cayman Islands, Bahamas and British Virgin Islands are too specialized to constitute a hub. Panama after Noriega hardly qualifies. Switzerland is very viable in many sectors, but its taxes and regulation do not quite suit the concept. It, Luxembourg and the Channel Islands complement and compete but do not dominate each other. It is simply difficult to see that any zone has a dominant offshore hub with a set of

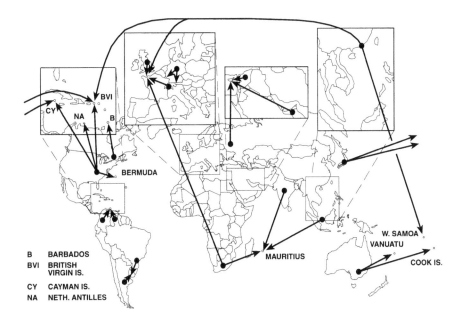

Figure 7.6 Onshore/offshore connections, late 1990s.

Sources: Anon. 1995c; 1999; Crisell/Hooper 1995: 244; Cooke 1995a; Courtenay 1996a; 1996b; Hope 1995; Johns and Le Marchant 1993: 136; Marriott 1995: 16; Peagam 1989: 76; Riley 1995; 1996; Roberts 1994: 102; Stewart 1996: 129–130, 152; Stuart 1996.

subordinate satellite centres. There certainly are clusters but hardly a clear hierarchy.

Some of the clustering can be explained by the need for physical communication. Suppose that daily management is onshore, while the fund is domiciled offshore. Legislation there may require a certain number of board meetings per year and at least one shareholder meeting. It is possible that neither proxies nor phone meetings are permitted. Then the frequency and time of flight connections become an issue and close-by locations gain in attractivity. This is the managerial aspect. Private investors may be wise to meet the people who manage their assets at least once a year in person and, again, it is helpful if the meeting is nearby. Many offshore centres have tried to facilitate things as much as possible by permitting non-resident directors, a minimum of board and shareholder meetings, meetings onshore, electronically or by phone. So it is not only the desire for maximum secrecy which is behind such practices – and established centres, such as the Cayman Islands and British Virgin Islands, have selected this strategy, which may explain some of their popularity among Asian customers, the long distance notwithstanding. But all actors are not attracted. These locations are too distant for retail funds, even for Americans, and managing the funds from a remote offshore is too troublesome. (Crisell/Adams 1995: 118; Crisell/Alberga 1995: 133; Luce 1997: 13)

Within a cluster there is often some specialization backed by historical chance, suitable legislation, innovative thinking or plain imitation. The last alternative is clearly the worst, because it rules out the firstcomer's advantage and the exploitation of market niches. It is no wonder that Turk and Caicos did not make great strides as a trust and insurance centre with laws borrowed from Jersey and the Cayman Islands, respectively (Peagam 1989: 110). Specialization means that competition between offshore centres is at two levels: global, between high-order functions, and regional, between low-order ones. For example, the Caymans' banking competitor is the close-by Bahamas, but in captive insurance the competitors are the distant Bermuda, Guernsey and Dublin. The current market leaders in trust business are Jersey, the British Virgin Islands and Cayman Islands, and possibly Liechtenstein (Crisell/Palmer 1995: 17; Hampton 1996a: 23; Kochan 1992: 85; Roberts 1994: 99).

In Europe, the competition for retail fund management rages between Luxembourg, Dublin, the Channel Islands and the Isle of Man. EU legislation and regional policy underpins it. The marketing of open-ended investment funds (Ucits) by EU-domiciled bodies under a home country licence was made possible by the Second Directive in 1989. Luxembourg was a major beneficiary. In contrast to the Channel Islands, which largely follow the UK legislation, monies in Luxembourg can be switched between investment funds without any tax liability. That was the main selling point. Another was that Luxembourg is inside the EU, while the

Channel Islands and Isle of Man are not and must negotiate with each member country about access to its market. Of course, the EU is not all plain sailing. A member can deny market access to products which are against the 'public interest', taxation may discriminate against foreigners and contractual law is still non-standardized (Johns and Le Marchant 1993: 56; *sigma* 7/1996: 10).

A further blow to the islands was the creation of the International Financial Services Centre in Dublin in 1988, after ten years of hard lobbying. It is within the EU and was sanctioned to charge only a 10 per cent corporate tax for non-Irish business for a limited period. Ireland is in the EU's poor margin with high unemployment and qualified for economic support. It preferred a low tax rate rather than outright subsidy. This, combined with skilled and inexpensive labour, attracted a wide range of businesses. In finance, the gain has been retail funds from the Channel Islands and Isle of Man, and captives from Luxembourg. Its progress was grudgingly tolerated in view of the time-constrained tax. But not to be browbeaten, the country replaced the tax in January 2003 with another one, which applies to all companies but is no more than 12.5 per cent. What it cannot avoid, however, is the EU's legislative net in which it is trapped together with Luxembourg. The Channel Islands' own future, in contrast, will be less of selling financial services within the EU than offering them to its expatriates. Since the islands thrived within the isolated sterling area, they should be able to do the same outside the EU. (Ballantine 1999; Burns 1997; Burt 1995; Goddard 2002; Johns and Le Marchant 1993: 148, 267–269; Murray-Brown 1997; Riley 1996)

Luxembourg – the minnow superpower

The specialization of offshore centres applies foremost to traditional offshore, although even among them diversification is attempted whenever possible. Larger territories have more scope but also other interests to look after and must find a balance between them and the offshore. Their larger size is more likely to arouse the jealousy of neighbours and they must, consequently, tread more carefully than an island paradise. In order to get an idea of how a larger onshore/offshore centre comes about and how it functions, a case is selected from the Continent.

Some doubt was expressed above whether Switzerland is a true offshore centre. Its intermediary role is considerable, but its economy is also too large to qualify as traditional offshore. If Switzerland is disqualified then Luxembourg with its 90 per cent estimated share of the remaining Continental offshore assets rises to absolute dominance there. The underlying advantages are similar to those of the Channel Islands: location in the wealthy heart of Europe, easy access to the financial markets of its neighbours, and political freedom to make its own decisions. The tolerance shown by affected neighbours has partially rested on Luxembourg's previous dependence on the steel industry. Financial services were, as in Dublin, a welcome alternative to EU subsidies. By now, they have become the territory's largest industry with 30 per cent of GDP. (Garner 1997; Garton 1996; Pieretti 2002)

Luxembourg, for its part, has been willing to exploit the unfolding opportunities. The main policy parameters have been strict banking secrecy and a tax system targeting specific financial sectors. Its Continental competitors, Andorra, Gibraltar, Liechtenstein and Monaco, are too small to put up the necessary infrastructure, too weak to hold their own against hostile treasuries, or too late to get their hands on the big money. Luxembourg, with its 450,000 population, has the workforce size to be more than a mere booking centre. Although there are limits. The country can muster a reasonably skilled labour force for private banking, but its funds are managed from London with a Luxembourg bank as a custodian. (Anon. 1995b; Humphreys 1987; Pieretti 2002)

The feast began in the mid-1960s, when German banks started establishing subsidiaries in Luxembourg. Minimum reserve ratios were high in Germany, Luxembourg had none, and Germany had abolished controls for capital exports in the 1950s. Reinsurance companies were attracted by the generous non-taxable provisions and largely avoided the 40 per cent corporate tax. The ensuing capital inflow was instrumental in the emergence of Luxembourg as a major euromarket location, and its stock exchange became a platform for listing bond issues. The debt crisis of the mid-1980s then shifted much of the activity to London. Much but not all, because Deutsche Bank and Dresdner Bank still arranged almost all their syndicated loans from Luxembourg in the mid-1990s, i.e. before they had acquired investment banks in London. Since then, the primary market appears to have withered away because the domestic banks are too small to be anything other than co-managers. Bankers also see their future role in the private banking segment. (Crisell/Geggan 1995: 181; Fisher 1996; Laurie 1988: 46; Mann 2002a; Roberts 1994: 103; Rogge 1997: 214; Rutter 1998; Saunderson, 1994)

For private banking and ensuing fund management the tax laws, withholding tax in particular, of the neighbouring countries have been important. It started with the Swiss 35 per cent withholding tax in the 1970s. A substantial transfer of capital to Luxembourg took place, because a Luxembourg holding company is tax-exempt on dividend, interest income, capital gain and surplus from possible liquidation. Germany also introduced a withholding tax on capital income in 1989. It was only 10 per cent initially but was raised to 30 per cent in 1993. The ensuing capital flight is estimated at $100bn on the first occasion and $150bn–$200bn on the second. Luxembourg's share of the flows can only be guessed, but $20bn and $70bn have been mentioned for 1992–1993 and 1993–1995, respectively. One thing is certain, that banks in Germany openly advertised their tax-free Luxembourg funds. It was quite legal to invest in them as long as one declared the investment in taxation. The changed funding of Luxembourg banks reflected the inflow, some 75 per cent at the inter-bank market in the late 1970s but only 40 per cent in 1993. (Anon. 1993b: 34; Blanden 1987: 35; Dugan 1989: 83; Fisher 1996; Irvine 1995; Pouzin 1995: 68; Stewart 1996: 129)

Most German clients are comparatively small fry, their assets averaging $350,000, but they are numerous. They prefer Luxembourg to Switzerland because of taxation, and because the small investor worth less than $2m reportedly gets better service there. They value banking secrecy, which keeps the tax collector at bay and which can be lifted only by court order for a crime which has been prosecuted at home and which is also a crime in Luxembourg. As in Switzerland, tax fraud is a criminal offence, but tax evasion is not. That is what stands in the books. But then there is the psy-chological side. The SEC tracked down Marcos's money in Switzerland and repatriated it, while the British authorities drew a complete blank in Luxembourg when investigating the funding sources of British miners. Of course, Marcos was prosecuted for fraud, while the British investigation was for tax avoidance. But such finesse easily escapes casual observation and what remains is the image. In one respect the Luxembourgers have been compelled to capitulate, however. They, as the Swiss, pay the with-holding tax of their US customers as a lump sum to the Internal Revenue Service. (Barrett 1988; Crisell/Geggan 1995: 180; Fisher 1996; Humphreys 1987)

As can be deduced from the above, Luxembourg banks collect deposits mostly from Western Europe. The figure for liabilities, roughly the same as deposits, was 78 per cent, end-December 2001 (www.bcl.lu, Banking Statistics, Table 4.1.1). Offshore centres and 'other' both had 7–8 per cent. The resting 7–8 per cent was scattered all over the world. The pattern is very simple and supports the general idea that Luxembourg plays a strictly regional role (see Figure 5.18).

All monies which came to Luxembourg did not go to bank accounts. Bonds had their own supporters, and among them the proverbial Belgian dentist figured prominently. Her/his role depended on the parity of the Luxembourg franc with the Belgian franc and the 25 per cent withholding tax on Belgian government bonds. The dentist paid no tax for bonds issued in Luxembourg and the issuer was able to negotiate a discount because of the tax difference. It probably did not need francs and these were swapped into dollars. Three-quarters and more of Luxembourg bonds were placed with middle-aged Belgians who purchased by name recognition and hardly discriminated between subordinated and non-subordinated debt, making Luxembourg a favoured market for banks to raise subordinated debt for the Tier 2 capital. The market absorbed only small issues but did it at regular intervals and was, therefore, a half-way post between expensive bank loans and inaccessible large international issues. (Brady 1991; Eade 1996; Garner 1997; Humphreys 1990; Irvine 1995)

The bond business has lost much of its former allure, however, and the dentist has redirected investment to mutual funds and life policies. S/he may find them in Luxembourg, but the logic is less straightforward than it used to be. Anyway, Luxembourg retail funds got a powerful boost from EU legislation which allowed EU-wide marketing of Ucits and which became law in Luxembourg in 1988. Since then, Luxembourg has become the second largest fund domicile in Europe with total assets of €950bn, half of them in Ucits, and a market share of 20 per cent. But thereby the grand duchy has reached a limit which appears prudent from a political angle. It has also got Dublin as a competitor. But it has other cards in the sleeve. Hedge funds are moving in. So far they have been compelled to negotiate with regulators case-by-case but a new regime is forthcoming. Venture capital will receive its tailor-made rules, and Qualified Institutional Buyers have joined the legislative queue. (Barrett 1988; Mann 2002b; Stewart 1996: 129)

As the narration suggests, most fund assets originate from the neighbouring countries (Figure 7.7). This statement rests on the assumption that the promotor domicile and the asset origin coincide. Where the promotor has got the monies from is, of course, unknown. It is not unreasonable, however, to assume that funds originating from Switzerland and the USA are primarily institutional assets, perhaps hedge funds. It is equally

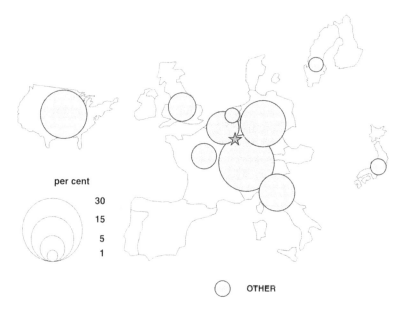

Figure 7.7 Origin of Luxembourg investment fund assets, March 2002.

Source: www.cssf.lu, OPC statistics.

Note
Total assets €967.7bn.

probable that German and Belgian assets are retail funds. French presence is much smaller than the image offered by English-language media, actually smaller than assets originating from Italy and the UK.

Luxembourg has benefited from EU membership in the form of Ucits legislation. But in some other respects the membership has been detrimental. The country has been compelled to implement minimum reserves and cannot pay better interest on deposits any more. The pressure to abolish banking secrecy is intense and, to have a negotiating lever, it has teamed with the UK in putting forward a 'coexistence model', which would decree countries with banking secrecy to introduce withholding tax and let the rest exchange information. It may be possible to negotiate such questions into insignificance, but the country's rising labour cost is more like a tidal wave, mounting and seemingly unstoppable. Its core is the smallness of the local labour force propped up by heavy commuter traffic, and spiced with salaries which are both indexed and based on seniority rather than performance. (Buckley 1996; 1998; Covill 1999; Eade 1996; Evans 1996; Garner 1997; Mann 2002b; 2002c)

Conclusion

This chapter has done several things: defined criteria for onshore finance centres, identified the most important of them, made a simple comparison for central time zone supremacy, and reviewed the birth, activity and spatial order of offshore centres.

Conceptualizing about finance centres is easy but finding empirical proxies is difficult. Some highly relevant data, such as managed funds, are available by company rather than centre. Banking and OTC statistics are released by country and, in countries with several important centres, their allocation is arbitrary. The volatility of equity figures is well known. Size differences between banks make their numbers, the traditional indicator, a doubtful measure. Holding companies have the capability to disguise information. In addition, these data are not commensurate. For example, is $1bn of bank deposits worth as much as $1bn of equity capitalization, and will the adding of bank deposits and managed funds lead to double counting? There are no easy answers and certainly not at the world scale. Monetary flows between centres would be a direct measure, if only they were available. Thereafter it would be a simple thing to derive dominance relationships between the network nodes, finance centres, with the help of standard graph theoretic techniques.

Lacking these data and cognizant of the approximate pecking order in each central time zone, the discussion has compared the hubs and evaluated likely challengers. New York and Tokyo rest safe because of the strength of their domestic economies. London lacks this foundation and is, consequently, the most international of the three. New York does not have a realistic challenger. Nor has London in the short term. Frankfurt and Paris formally fill that role but their chances to unseat London are downgraded by their keen mutual competition. Tokyo's challenge comes from Hongkong and Singapore and, in future, from Shanghai. Since Shanghai must conciliate domestic and foreign roles, it will be in the same position as New York and Tokyo are today. Therefore, its ability to challenge Tokyo will depend on the relative sizes of the national economies.

Offshore centres depend on safety, secrecy, minimum tax and minimum regulation. These ingredients are mixed in suitable proportions and put to the marketplace. Firstcomers pick the best customers, advance in the value chain, and leave commoditized products to newcomers. The concept functions best in a small autonomous territory, because of the difficulty of accommodating offshore with standard economy. When it exists onshore, as euromarkets, IBFs and JOM show, it is in a diluted form. Offshore thrives close to a major capital source, and only when its capacity to provide the service has been exhausted, will more distant territories have a chance. It survives at the quiet consent of the onshore, and the apparent unwillingness to put an end to it illustrates both the need for this type of financial service and the strength of vested interests protecting it.

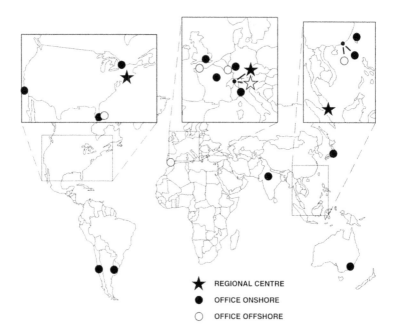

★   REGIONAL CENTRE
●   OFFICE ONSHORE
○   OFFICE OFFSHORE

Figure 7.8 Private banker's world, mid-1990s.

Source: Ehlern, Svend, *International Private Banking*: Exhibit 74. Haupt, Berne, 1997. Copyright © 1997 of Verlag Paul Haupt, Berne; redrawn with permission.

Note
The duality of Swiss private banking is reflected by regional centres in Zurich (headquarters) and Geneva.

In practical life, onshore and offshore, dominant and subsidiary, inter-mingle. The geographical structure of a hypothetical Swiss private bank reflects this (Figure 7.8). There are three regional centres, one for each central time zone, usually one onshore centre per major country, and some offshore centres dispersed between the central time zones. The USA has two country centres in addition to New York, but that in Miami is actu-ally for Latin America. The hierarchy is not rigid because the centres fill different functions. Asset allocation, trading and lending, that is, produc-tion functions, are centralized while service functions are delegated to local offices. These have a box seat to follow local media and policies, can react to them rapidly, understand the mentality and have a marketing role. They may be mere representative offices advising about products available offshore but not in the topical country.

8   Outlook

The narration has come to the end and it is time to pull the strings together. Finances are at the ideological crossroads. In plan economies, they used to be an accounting system, nothing else. In market, if not outright capitalistic, economies, financial markets are the primary allocation mechanism. They not only allocate production resources but also much of the production surplus. The advocates are happy to believe that the system is meandering towards general prosperity. The protagonists believe that the theoretical end point is that all the resources and all the surplus will end up in the hands of one single capitalist. We do not take sides in this discussion. Ours is the banker's view, the technocratic angle. A banker is a professional, not a crusader. Asking him/her where the system is heading is the same as asking where democracy is heading: hopefully to increased democracy, although not necessarily anywhere in particular. Democracy is simply a way of handling matters and so are banking and financial markets. They are more 'efficient' when allowed free play, but they do not necessarily maximize the welfare function.

Another topic which raises strong feelings, although within the financial community itself, is the superior financial system, based either on bank lending or securities markets. The English-language literature and media firmly support the latter alternative, because of its efficient allocative function. All relevant information is supposedly reflected in prices, and actors can base decisions upon them. There is no denial that the securities-based system has gained terrain on the Continent and in Asia Pacific although from a comparatively low start level. But banks continue to prosper in the retail business, and they are also competitive in wholesale finance by forming syndicates, which in certain respects are a more efficient vehicle than bond issues. Lending syndicates actually constitute a miniature quasi-market because the members bring with them a range of views which the lead manager cannot ignore. Bank lending is also less exposed to market fluctuation than securities markets which should contribute to social welfare. There are thus pros and cons, and it is doubtful if a clear ranking can ever be made. It may be more a question of people's mentalities and historical experience than an unambiguous choice between superior and inferior.

Prosperity in the world is growing. There has not been a major war between the rich industrialized countries for half a century. Large parts of the industrializing world have also lived in relative peace. This is conducive to economic growth. Some of the growth is due to the population increase. More hands and brains mean a larger output. The exhaustion of global resources which might put an end to this has not yet materialized. If it ever does depends a good deal on the human race itself.

Although the trend lines are delightful it is important to maintain perspective. The financial world; is not the real world; it only reflects the real world. Some might call it a mirage world. The market values of financial instruments are not the demand and supply of goods and services. They are only a reflection, presumably aggregated over time and discounted to the present moment. Marking a bond, or share, or derivative to market is a snapshot of the constantly changing perception of the aggregate demand and supply, and the attached value of time, the discounting multiplier. The recorded profits and losses are only on paper until the actual sale or purchase has been effected. The revenue is recorded in money, which also seems to be changing in value, sometimes more and sometimes less, depending on the benchmark we wish to compare it with, the US dollar or a hamburger meal.

A number of questions were raised in Chapter 1 about the place of finances in geographical writing, all of which addressed the broad issue whether the geographical angle has any relevance in the financial world of our time with its electronic communications. In particular, which role the friction of distance and the homogeneity of the geographical surface play.

The simple answer to the question of friction is that it still applies. Powerful evidence for it is offered by the geographical pattern of share ownership, company listings and onshore–offshore relations. It is true that world-class exchanges and well-positioned offshore centres attract business from every corner of the world. But the amount of business they solicit tapers off with increasing distance, other things being equal. The explanation, at the most trivial level, is that the extension of action radius requires an effort raised to second power if intensity per area unit is to remain unchanged. Usually the necessary effort cannot be produced, with lower intensity as a result. Two evolutionary observations, the first based on opportunities and the second on initiative, add some sophistication.

All exchanges and offshore centres have started by exploiting nearby opportunities. When these became exhausted, the net was thrown wider, the systems got more polished, the reputation grew and business came from further afield. But a wide trade area is not the first option because of the increased cost. Longer distance brings with it larger phone bills, increased travel, shorter business hours in the east–west direction, often cultural barriers and all kinds of initial learning costs. Then comes the second explanation and it links with the first one. Each new exchange and centre relies initially on local initiative. Brokers in a city see enhanced possibilities for profit by coordinating their activity and raising their profile under the guise of an exchange. Fund managers look across the water and see in the horizon a lone island which by some twist of fate enjoys autonomy or even independence but lacks the means to support itself. It is overjoyed to receive the labour opportunities and registration fees which the funds will bring with them. The managers will not go further than that. There is no reason, since the island is only too happy to meet their modest wishes: a minimum of taxes and controls. If the exchange and the island play their cards properly, it will not be easy to take business away from them. A distant competitor finds itself a priori disadvantaged.

The vision of electronic messages criss-crossing the globe not only creates the illusion of zero friction; it also creates the illusion of a homogeneous communication and transaction surface. In reality, the surface is anything but homogeneous. Some non-homogeneity can be directly related to geography. Centers of financial activity are found in large population agglomerations, separated by rural areas, deserts, mountain chains and oceans. This creates breaks in the financial space, intensified by the three stylized eight-hour time zones. In their shear zones, the flow of money and information gets easily interrupted for a while. Exchange floors get vacated. Meetings are postponed to the next day. Brokers stop answering phones and leave the office. Traders close their positions or transfer them to the next time zone, which may have different priorities and valuations. Payment systems stop receiving orders and start processing them. It is the basic time–space set-up, although the movements concern money more than people.

That is the physical or physically conditioned geographical surface. But then there is a strictly man-made surface comprising the whole gamut of taxes, laws, rules, standards and conventions which legislators, authorities and the financial community itself have found appropriate to decree and agree on. That surface is crammed with discontinuities and anomalies which both retard and speed, discourage and encourage, monetary and information flows. They retard when it takes time to apply a complex rule set, and they speed because some conventions are created for that very purpose. They discourage when high taxes and costly compliance make activity uneconomic, and they encourage and attract when the rule set is designed to meet a particular need like secrecy, accumulation of reserves and risk-taking.

These anomalies probably increase the aggregate volume of money flows. The basic case would be something like the classical transportation problem. There are a number of sources and sinks, each with a net surplus or demand for funds, and the corresponding interest rates for lending and borrowing. The pairwise interest rate differences reflect the propensity that a particular flow will materialize, and the inverse is taken from each difference to suit the solution technique. The solution gives a set of money flows during a time period. Since the timescale of financial transactions is an order of magnitude shorter than that of physical shipments, the time period cannot be too long, certainly not longer than a month. Impose upon this simple scheme a regulatory structure which can be converted into interest rate equivalents, issuing costs and withholding taxes for example, and the solution will change. Impose upon it another structure which cannot be converted into these equivalents, bans for example, and the surplus and demand volumes will change and new nodes get activated.

Most of this is only theory and close to practical impossibility because of very considerable data problems. It might work temporarily, since monthly statistics are commonplace. Regional disaggregation is already more problematic, as is shown by the 'errors and omissions' line of national accounts. But the real hurdle is the varying interest rates reflecting the specific features of each loan and issue. Why, one might ask, take the matter up in the first place? Primarily to indicate the imbedded connection between familiar transportation flows and the more esoteric money flows. The geographical dimension is there, it only needs to be exposed.

The preceding lines have touched each of the three main themes of geography, spatial differences, processes in space and spatial interaction. There are spatial differences in capital availability and need, interest rates, and rule sets. Ample evidence has been produced about them. Then there is the process by which banks, exchanges and finance centres expand and intensify their trade areas. A few figures and some pages of text, about banks and finance centres, have been produced. More can be found in the literature and particularly about banking, for which databases are available. In contrast, spatial interaction has been substantiated by figures and comments more fully than the fragmentary database would actually warrant. As has already been suggested, it can be difficult to push the frontier further and it may be wise to leave the field to econometricians. Should that happen, there are still a great number of interesting research topics which have so far received no or only fleeting attention.

Foreign bank deposits might be a soft start. How do they relate to domestic deposits in size and maturity? How did they develop over time? There should be a sharp difference between onshore and offshore. The amount of deposits should reflect the central bank interest rate. There might also be a relation between onshore withholding taxes and offshore deposits.

The internationalization of fund portfolios belongs to the same class of conceptually simple but empirically very fundamental questions. The process has been going on for at least two decades, and there is little doubt that it will continue. More enigmatic is how the international monies will be allocated regionally and by country. For example, the contrast between Asia Pacific and Latin America, where flows have shifted according to the respective growth rates and default histories, would be worth a closer look. Since funds do not lend but rather invest in securities, real estate and commodities, the financing structures of borrower countries come to light here.

Possibly more marginal in geography are changes in the denomination currencies of international bond issues. The dollar is the largest currency, but its dominance has been gradually eroded by the mark/euro and the yen. The remaining currencies have behaved more erratically, although an exploratory study might discover aspects of geographical interest. Disaggregation by the country of issuer obviously gives additional colour.

Interest on spatial processes might trigger analyses about the formation of captive insurance companies, the development of trading in foreign shares at major stock exchanges and of electronic bond trading platforms. Captives would combine a number of geographical aspects: the spreading of the concept itself, its search for suitable domiciles among offshore centres, and the widening of their trade areas. Listings and trading values at stock exchanges would basically display the same features. NYSE would offer an outstanding case, since it openly courts big companies all over the world. What has it actually got, how much is left and what are the chances of reaching a 99 per cent coverage, for example? If NYSE can do it, then the decades-old dream of a single global marketplace has come a good bit closer to reality. Electronic bond trading would be a valuable contribution because the expansion is still half-way and the study consequently has more than mere historical interest.

Stock exchanges, being the major forum for issuing shares and trading in them, constitute an essential piece in the armoury of an international finance centre. They are supplemented and paralleled by derivatives exchanges, although derivatives are mostly traded OTC. OTC dealing and spot forex largely belong to the realm of banks and fund managers, which constitute the other two pillars of a finance centre. The American time zone has its established hub in New York. The situation is more fluid in Europe, and in Asia Pacific it is quite fuzzy in the long term. This is onshore. Offshore is no less fluid, partly because the rate of wealth generation is more rapid in Asia Pacific than in America and Europe, partly because offshore has come under intense pressure by authorities for its secrecy. It will not disappear because differences in tax systems, its fundamental *raison d'être*, will not disappear but it may well develop into a parallel financial system, with products designed to disguise income and wealth and locations away from the doorstep of the tax-hungry onshore.

The traditional concept of a finance centre is a cluster of facilities in a fixed location but it need not last forever. The technology which permits dealing from a distance has been available for some time and has been used primarily OTC. Its application at exchanges is of more recent date but is now also well established there, making the difference between OTC and exchange mostly organizational. What still speaks for a clustered location is informal market intelligence and the need for face-to-face negotiation in large, complicated transactions. Such deals are not so frequent, however, that they alone would enforce clustering. Market intelligence remains, but it has a counterforce; the concentration of risk and subsequent exposure to terrorist action and natural catastrophes. Terrorist action has always existed, although the World Trade Center attack gave it a new, apocalyptic face. Earthquakes with attached tsunami waves are another tangible threat. The Japanese have responded by building a stand-in capital close to Kyoto. It may be a sufficient safeguard against quakes, but against terrorism only spatial dispersion will really help. If matters ever go that far then the familiar finance centre will be a thing of the past.

The declared goal of this book was to establish a benchmark against which special geographical studies can be projected. The feeling is that this goal has been achieved. The feeling was strongest when Chapter 2, about the playground, had been completed. Its preparation gave an idea of the relative magnitudes of various financial stock and flow variables which could then be used in later contexts as a basis of comparison. The actual operation of financial markets was the topic of Chapters 3 and 4. Chapter 5, on banking, gave the actor's perspective. These chapters are probably the core of the book and should go a long way in giving a detailed explanation as to why it is so difficult to generalize about financial transactions and why the actors have such a propensity to agglomerate. Chapter 6, on insurance, offered an introduction to a sector bound to be integrated more closely with the financial mainstream. The propensity for geographical agglomeration was subjected to an extended discussion in Chapter 7, about finance centres, onshore and offshore.

Important developments, which were established wisdom when the foundations of the study were laid in the late 1980s, became outdated during its course. The streamlining of the German financial system and the budding deregulation of the Japanese one, the outdistancing of derivatives exchanges by OTC trading and their subsequent bouncing back, the births of Eurex and Euronext through mergers, the large-scale transfer of trading from exchange floor to screen, the numerous mergers of major financial intermediaries, the rise of Bermuda to the front line of insurance centres, and the entry of corporations as members into the Lloyd's insurance market are some of them. It follows that when a decade has passed from the printing of this book, it will still be useful for general orientation but unfit for encyclopedic use. That is simply the nature of things.

The work widened the author's view and made him better understand the physical expansion, and also contraction, of industries and companies.

The financial background, and markets in particular, showed where the real economic power rests and how much corporations are subjected to the vagaries of their financial environment. It is difficult to think that proper economic geography can be practised without a basic understanding of the financial mirage world which embraces the countless plants, stores and offices, large and small, in every human settlement in its web.

Bibliography

The references are divided into two parts. In the first part are publications by the Bank for International Settlements which are extensively used throughout the book. In the second part are references which can normally be linked with a specific part of the book. These are listed by chapter to avoid having an excessive number of articles by some very productive financial journalists collected in one mammoth string, creating obvious problems for referencing. Sources fully referenced in figure and table captions are not referenced here again.

AR = Annual Report
ä, ü and ö listed as a, u and o.
Financial Times (European edition) and *Institutional Investor* (international edition).

Bank for International Settlements

Bank for International Settlements (*BIS AR*) (1993/4–2002/3) *Annual Report*. Basle.
—— (*BIS QR*) (1994–2002) *Quarterly Review, International Banking and Financial Market Developments* March, June, September, December. Basle.
—— (*BIS F*) (1996, 2002) *Central Bank Survey, Foreign Exchange and Derivatives Market Activity 1995, 2001* May, March. Basle.
—— (*BIS S*) (1996) *Settlement Risk in Foreign Exchange Transactions* (Alsopp Report) (1996), March. Basle.
—— (*BIS P*) (1996, 2001) *Statistics on Payment Systems in the Group of Ten Countries* December, March. Basle.

1 Introduction

Abraham, J.P., Bervaes, N., Guinotte, A. and Lacroix, Y. (1993) *The Competitiveness of European International Financial Centres*. Research Monograph in Banking and Finance M93/1. Institute of European Finance, Bangor.
Ackrill, Margaret and Hannah, Leslie (2001) *Barclay's, the Business of Banking 1690–1996*. Cambridge University Press, Cambridge, UK.
Agnes, Pierre (2000) 'The "end of geography" in financial services? Local embeddedness and territorialization in the interest rate swap industry'. *Economic Geography* 76 (4), 347–366.

Ahearne, Alan G., Griever, William L. and Warnock, Francis E. (2002) 'Informa-
tion costs and home bias: an analysis of US holdings of foreign equities'. The
Federal Reserve System, International Finance Discussion Paper 691, updated.
Journal of International Economics, forthcoming.

Ahnström, Leif (1973) *Styrande och ledande verksamhet i Västeuropa: en ekonomisk-
geografisk studie*. Almqvist & Wiksell, Stockholm.

Ali, Muazzam (ed.) (1996) *European Perceptions of Islamic Banking*. Institute of
Islamic Banking and Insurance, London.

Alworth, Julian S. and Andresen, S. (1992) 'The determinants of cross-border non-
bank deposits and the competitiveness of financial market centres'. *Money Affairs*
5 (2), 105–133.

Bachmann, Thomas (1976) *Zur Standortwahl von Investmenttrusts*. Haupt, Bern.

Bank of England (1999) 'The City since the launch of the euro'. *Practical Issues
Arising from the Euro* December, 10–16.

Banque de France (2000) *Annual Report*.

Barber, Tony (2002) 'A tale of two complementary cities'. *Financial Times* 12 June,
III.

Beaverstock, J.V. (1996) 'Subcontracting the accountant! Professional labour
markets, migration, and organisational networks in the global accounting industry'. *Environment and Planning* A28, 303–326.

Bennett, R.J. (1980) *The Geography of Public Finance*. Methuen, London.

Bernet, Beat (1995) 'Aspekte produktionstopologischer Entscheidungen in
Banken'. In: Geiger, Hans und Spremann, Klaus (Hrsg) *Banktopologie* 27–55.
Haupt, Bern.

Berton, Lee (1999) 'Countdown to harmonization'. *Institutional Investor* June,
101–103.

Bicker, Lyn (1996) *Private Banking in Europe*. Routledge, London.

Bindemann, Kirsten (1999) *The Future of European Financial Centers*. Routledge,
London.

Blattner, Niklaus, Gratzl, Benedikt and Kaufmann, Tilo (1996) *Das Vermögensverwaltungsgeschäft der Banken in der Schweiz*. Haupt, Bern.

Blumer, Andreas (1996) *Bankenaufsicht und Bankenprüfung*. Haupt, Bern.

Brealey, R.A. and Kaplanis, E. (1994) *The Growth and Structure of International
Banking*. City Research Project Report XI, London Business School.

de Brouwer, Gordon (2001) *Hedge Funds in Emerging Markets*. Cambridge University Press, Cambridge, UK.

Buch, Claudia M. and DeLong, Gayle (2002) 'Cross-border bank mergers: what
lures the rare animal?' Presentation at the SUERF Conference, *Geography and
Banking and Financial Markets*. Bank of Finland, Helsinki, September.

Budd, Leslie (1999) 'Globalisation and the crisis of territorial embeddedness of
international financial markets'. In: Martin, Ron (ed.) *Money and the Space
Economy* 115–137. Wiley, Chichester.

Calomiris, Charles W. and Schweikart, Larry (1991) 'The panic of 1857:
origins, transmission and containment'. *The Journal of Economic History* 51 (4),
807–834.

Chambers, William J. (1997) 'Understanding sovereign risk'. *Standard & Poor's
Credit Week* 1 (January), 9–18.

Chernow, Ron (1990) *The House of Morgan*. Simon & Schuster, New York.

Choi, Sang-Rim, Tschoegl, Adrian E. and Yu, Chwo-Ming (1986) 'Banks and the world's major financial centers, 1970–1980'. *Weltwirtschaftliches Archiv* 122 (1), 48–64.

Choi, Sang-Rim, Park, Daekeun and Tschoegl, Adrian E. (2002) 'Banks and the world's major banking centers, 2000'. Wharton Financial Institutions Center, Working Paper 02-36, mimeo, July. University of Pennsylvania, Philadelphia, PA.

Clark, Gordon L. (1998) 'Pension fund capitalism: a causal analysis'. *Geografiska Annaler* 80B (3), 139–157.

—— (2000) *Pension Fund Capitalism.* Oxford University Press, Oxford, UK.

—— (2003) *European Pensions and Global Finance.* Oxford University Press, Oxford, UK.

Clark, Gordon L. and Wójcik, Dariusz (2002) 'How and where should we invest in Europe? An economic geography of global finance'. Mimeo, University of Oxford.

Cobb, Sharon C. (2001) 'Globalization in a small island context: creating and marketing competitive advantage for offshore financial servives'. *Geografiska Annaler* 83B (4), 161–174.

Cobham, David (1992) *Markets and Dealers: The Economics of the London Financial Markets.* Longman, London.

Code, William R. (1991) 'Information flows and the process of attachment and projection: the case of financial intermediaries'. In: Brunn, Stanley D. and Leinbach, Thomas R. (eds) *Collapsing Space & Time* 111–131. HarperCollins, London.

Cohen, Benjamin J. (1998) *The Geography of Money.* Cornell University Press, Ithaca, NY.

Committee on the Global Financial System (2001) *The Implications of Electronic Trading in Financial Markets* (January). BIS, Basle.

Corbridge, Stuart and Thrift, Nigel (1994) 'Money, power and space: introduction and overview'. In: Corbridge, Stuart, Martin, Ron and Thrift, Nigel (eds) *Money, Power and Space* 1–25. Blackwell, Oxford.

Covill, Laura (1999) 'Making the move to centre stage'. *Euromoney* March, 75–77.

Crisell, Michaela (ed.) (1995) *Offshore Finance Yearbook 1994–95.* Euromoney Publications, Colchester, Essex.

—— (2002) *Offshore Finance Yearbook 2002/2003.* Euromoney Publications, Colchester, Essex.

Currie, Anthony (2000) 'Miami spice'. *Euromoney* March, 122, 124.

Czinkota Michael P., Ronkainen, Ilkka, and Moffat, Michael H. (1994) *International Business* 3rd edn. Dryden, Fort Worth, TX.

Dahm, David M. and Green, Milford B. (1995) 'Transnational branch banking 1976–1986: an empiricist's approach'. In: Green, Milford B. and McNaughton, Rod B. (eds) *The Location of Foreign Direct Investment* 191–221. Avebury, Aldershot.

Daniels, John D. and Radebaugh, Lee H. (1995) *International Business.* Addison-Wesley, Reading, MA.

Daniels, P.W. (1993) *Service Industries in the World Economy.* Blackwell, Oxford, UK.

Daniels, Peter W., Thrift, Nigel J. and Leyshon, A. (1989) 'Internationalisation of professional producer services: accountancy conglomerates'. In: Enderwick, Peter (ed.) *Multinational Service Firms* 79–106. Routledge, London.

Davis, E.P. (1990) *International Financial Centres – An Industry Analysis.* Discussion Paper 51 (September), Bank of England.

Davis, E.P. and Latter, A.R. (1989) 'London as an international financial centre'. *Bank of England Quartery Bulletin* 29 (November), 516–528.

Davis, Samuel G., Kleindorfer, George B., Kochenberger, Gary A., Reutzel, Edward T. and Brown, Emmit W. (1986) 'Strategic planning for bank operations with multiple check-processing locations'. *Interfaces* 16 (6), 1–12.

Diamond, Barbara B. and Kollar, Mark P. (1989) *24-hour Trading*. Wiley, New York, NY.

Dicken, Peter (1998) *The Global Shift*. Chapman, London.

Economides, Kim, Blacksell, Mark and Watkins, Charles (1986) 'The spatial analysis of legal systems: towards a geography of law'. *Journal of Law and Society* 13 (2), 161–181.

Edwards, Jeremy and Fischer, Klaus (1994) *Banks, Finance and Investment in Germany*. Cambridge University Press, Cambridge, UK.

Ehlern, Svend (1997) *International Private Banking*. Haupt, Bern.

Fairlamb, David (1999) 'Dueling markets'. *Institutional Investor* May, 32–40.

Frankel, Richard and Lee, Charles M.C. (1996) 'Accounting diversity and international valuation'. NYSE Working Paper 96-01, 18 March, 17.

Fry, Maxwell J., Kilato, Isaack, Roger, Sandra, Senderowicz, Krzysztof, Sheppard, David, Solis, Francisco and Trundle, John (1999) *Payment Systems in Global Perspective*. Routledge, London.

Gall, Lothar, Feldman, Gerald D., James, Harold, Holtfrerich, Carl-Ludwig and Büschgen, Hans E. (1995) *Die Deutsche Bank 1870–1995*. Beck, München.

Gardener, Edward P.M. and Molyneux, Philip (1993) *Changes in Western European Banking*. Routledge, London.

Geiger, Hans (1995) 'Die Zeit als Gestaltungselement der Bankproduktion'. In: Geiger, Hans and Spremann, Klaus (Hrsg), *Banktopologie* 57–75. Haupt, Bern.

Giddy, Ian H. (1994) *Global Financial Markets*. Heath, Lexington, MA.

Giddy, Ian, Saunders, Anthony, Walter, Ingo with others (1993) *Cross-Border Clearance, Settlement, and Custody: Beyond the G30 Recommendations* 5–8 June. Morgan Guaranty Trust Co. of New York, Brussels Office.

Goldberg, Lawrence G. and Saunders, Anthony (1980) 'The causes of U.S. bank expansion overseas'. *Journal of Money, Credit and Banking* 12 (4), 630–643.

—— (1981) 'The determinants of foreign banking activity in the United States'. *Journal of Banking and Finance* 5, 17–32.

Goldberg, Lawrence G. and Johnson, Denise (1990) 'The determinants of US banking activity abroad'. *Journal of International Money and Finance* 9, 123–137.

Goldberg, Michael A., Helsley, Robert W. and Levi, Maurice D. (1988) 'The location of international financial activity: an interregional analysis'. *Regional Studies* 23 (1), 1–7.

Goodwin, William (1965) 'The management center in the United States'. *The Geographical Review* 55 (1), 1–16.

Graves, William (1998) 'The geography of mutual fund assets'. *Professional Geographer* 50 (2), 243–255.

Green, Milford B. (1993) 'A geography of institutional stock ownership in the United States'. *Annals of the Association of American Geographers* 83 (1), 66–89.

Green, Milford B. and Meyer, Stephen P. (1992) 'A temporal, spatial and functional view of investment companies in the United States'. *The East Lakes Geographer* 27, 48–64.

—— (1997) 'International acquisitions: host and home country explanatory characteristics'. *Geografiska Annaler* 79B, 97–111.

Grinblatt, Mark and Keloharju, Matti (2001) 'How distance, language, and culture influence stockholdings and trades'. *The Journal of Finance* 56 (3), 1053–1073.

Grote, Michael H., Lo, Vivien and Harrschar-Ehrenborg, Sofia (2002) 'A value chain approach to financial centres – the case of Frankfurt'. *Tijdschrift voor Economische en Sociale Geografie* 93 (4), 412–423.

Grubel, Herbert G. (1989) 'Multinational banking'. In: Enderwick, Peter (ed.) *Multinational Service Firms* 61–77. Routledge, London.

Haga, Hirobumi (1997) 'Banking centres and the network of international banks in Pacific Asia'. *Asian Geographer* 16 (1–2), 1–20.

—— (1999) 'Changing networks of Japanese banks among mega-cities in the world'. In: Aguilar, Adrián G. and Escamilla, Irma (eds) *Problems of Megacities: Social Inequalities, Environmental Risk and Urban Governance* 117–129. Universidad Nacional Autónoma de México, Mexico City.

—— (2002) World System of Cities in Terms of Overseas Office Locations of Transnational Banks. Unpublished PhD thesis, Geoscience Doctoral Program. University of Tsukuba.

Haindl, Andreas (1991) *The Euro Money Market*. Haupt, Bern.

Hampton, Mark P. (1994) 'Treasure islands or fool's gold: can and should small island economies copy Jersey?' *World Development* 22 (2), 237–250.

—— (1996) *The Offshore Interface, Tax Havens in the Global Economy*. Macmillan, London.

Handley, Paul (1998) 'Singapore's Big Bang'. *Institutional Investor* September, 157–164.

Hanink, Dean M. (1994) *The International Economy*. Wiley, New York.

ter Hart, H.W. and Piersma, J. (1990) 'Direct representation in international financial markets: the case of foreign banks in Amsterdam'. *Tijdschrift voor Economische en Sociaale Geografie* 81 (2), 82–92.

Hau, Harald (2001a) 'Location matters: an examination of trading profits'. *The Journal of Finance* 56 (5), 1959–1983.

—— (2001b) 'Geographic patterns of trading profitability in Xetra'. *European Economic Review* 45, 757–769.

Häuser, Karl, Götz, Ralf-Joachim, Müller, Johannes and Grandjean, Birgitt (1990) *Frankfurts Wettbewerbslage als europäisches Finanzzentrum*. Institut für Kapitalmarktforschung, Johann Wolfgang Goethe-Universität, Frankfurt am Main.

Häusler, Gerd (2002) 'The globalization of finance'. *Finance & Development* March, 10–12.

Hayes, Samuel L. III and Hubbard, Philip M. (1990) *Investment Banking, A Tale of Three Cities*. Harvard Business School, Boston, MA.

Heinkel, Robert L. and Levi, Maurice, D. (1992) 'The structure of international banking'. *Journal of International Money and Finance* 11, 251–272.

Helleiner, Eric (1993) 'The challenge from the east: Japan's financial rise and the changing global order'. In: Cerny, Philip G. (ed.) *Finance and World Politics* 207–227. Edward Elgar, Aldershot, Hants.

—— (1995) 'Explaining the globalization of financial markets: bringing states back in'. *Review of International Political Economy* 2 (Spring), 315–341.

Heller, Daniel (1995) 'Lieferung gegen Zahlung in der Schweiz: die Verbindung zwischen SWX, SECOM ind SIC'. In: Geiger, Hans und Spremann, Klaus (Hrsg) *Banktopologie* 103–110. Haupt, Bern.

Hepworth, Mark (1991) 'Information technology and the global restructuring of capital markets'. In: Brunn, Stanley D. and Leinbach, Thomas R. (eds) *Collapsing Space & Time* 132–148. HarperCollins, London.

Holtfrerich, Carl-Ludwig (1999) *Frankfurt as a Financial Centre*. Beck, München.

Huang, Chi-fu and Litzenberger, Robert H. (1998) *Foundations for Financial Economics*. Prentice-Hall, Englewood Cliffs, NJ.

Hudson, Alan C. (1999) 'Off-shores on-shore: new regulatory spaces and real historical places in the landscape of global money'. In: Martin, Ron (ed.) *Money and the Space Economy* 139–154. Wiley, Chichester.

Huhne, Christopher (1996) 'Rating sovereign risk'. *Bank of England Stability Review* 1 (Autumn), 31–37.

Hultman, Charles W. and McGee, L. Randolph (1990) 'The Japanese banking presence in the United States and its regional distribution'. *Growth and Change* 21, 69–79.

Johns, R.A. and Le Marchant, C.M. (1993) *Finance Centres, British Isle Offshore Development Since 1979*. Pinter, London.

Johnson, Omotunde E.G., Abrams, Richard K., Destresse, Jean-Marc, Lybeck, Tonny, Roberts, Nicholas M. and Swinburne, Mark (1998) *Payment Systems, Monetary Policy, and the Role of the Central Bank*. International Monetary Fund, Washington, DC.

Jöns, Heike and Klagge, Britta (1997) *Bankwesen und Regionalstruktur in Ungarn*. Institut für Stadt-und Regionalforschung, Heft 16. Österreichische Akademie der Wissenschaften, Wien.

Karyotis, C. (1999) *La place financière de Paris*. Banque éditeur, Paris.

Kaufman, George G. (ed.) (1992) *Banking Structures in Major Countries*. Kluwer, Dordrecht.

Kay, John, Laslett, Robert and Duffy, Niall (1994) *The Competitive Advantage of the Fund Management Industry in the City of London*. The City Research Project Report IX (February). London Business School, London.

Kellerman, Aharon (2002) *The Internet on Earth*. Wiley, Chichester.

Kerr, Donald (1965) 'Some aspects of the geography of finance in Canada'. *The Canadian Geographer* 9 (4), 175–192.

Kerr Christoffersen, Susan and Sarkissian, Sergei (2001) 'Location overconfidence'. Paper read at the EFA Barcelona meeting. SSRN Electronic Paper Collection.

Kilgus, Ernst and Hirszowicz, Christine (Hrsg) (1992) *Der Finanzplatz Schweiz im Spannungsfeld der internationalen Entwicklungen*. Haupt, Bern.

King, Frank, H.H. (1991) *The Hongkong Bank in the Period of Development and Nationalism, 1941–1984* Vol. IV. Cambridge University Press, Cambridge, UK.

Klebaner, Benjamin J. (1990) *American Commercial Banking*. Twayne, Boston, MA.

Klimanov, V.V. and Lavrov, A.M. (1995) 'Problemy ekonomiko-geografitsheskaya izuchcniya bankovskoi sistemy Rossi'i'. *Vestnik Moskovskogo Universiteta*, Seriya 5, *Geografiya* (2), 31–39.

Kynaston, David (2001) *The City of London: A Club No More: 1945–2000*. Chatto and Windus, London.

Labasse, Jean (1955) *Les capitaux et la région*. Colin, Paris.

—— (1974) *L'espace financier*. Colin, Paris.

Langdale, John (1985) 'Electronic funds transfer and the internationalisation of the banking and finance industry'. *Geoforum* 16, (1), 1–13.

—— (2001) 'Global electronic spaces: Singapore's role in the foreign exchange market in the Asia-Pacific region'. In: Leinbach, Thomas R. and Brunn, Stanley D. (eds) *Worlds of E-Commerce: Economic, Geographical and Social Dimensions* 203–219. Wiley, Chichester.

Laulajainen, Risto (1999) 'Subnational credit ratings – penetrating the cultural haze'. *GeoJournal* 47 (4), 501–510.

—— (2000) 'International finance and its regulation'. In: Clark, Gordon L. *et al.* (eds) *The Oxford Handbook of Economic Geography* 215–229. Oxford University Press.

—— (2001) 'End of geography at exchanges?'. *Zeitschrift für Wirtschaftsgeographie* 45 (1), 1–14.

Laulajainen, Risto and Johansson, Kristina (2000) 'Payment systems – the geographical dimension'. *Tijdschrift voor Economische en Sociale Geografie* 91 (1), 31–43.

Lee, Roger and Schmidt-Marwede, Ulrich (1993) 'Interurban competition? Financial centres and the geography of financial production'. *International Journal of Urban and Regional Research* 17, 492–515.

Lee, Ruben (1998) *What is an Exchange?* Oxford University Press, Oxford, UK.

Lévy-Leboyer, Maurice (ed.) (1995) *Les banques en Europe de l'Ouest de 1920 à nos jours*. Comité pour l'histoire économique et financière de la France, Paris.

Leyshon, Andrew (1995) 'Geographies of money and finance I'. *Progress in Human Geography* 19 (4), 531–543.

—— (1997) 'Geographies of money and finance II'. *Progress in Human Geography* 21 (3), 381–392.

Leyshon, Andrew and Thrift, Nigel (1992) 'Liberalisation and consolidation: the Single European Market and the remaking of European financial capital'. *Environment and Planning A* 24, 49–81.

—— (1995a) 'European financial integration'. In: Hardy, Sally, Hart, Mark, Albrechts, Louis and Katos, Anastasios (eds) *An Enlarged Europe* 109–144. Jessica Kingsley, London.

—— (1995b) 'Geographies of financial exclusion: financial abandonment in Britain and the United States'. *Transactions of British Geographers* NS 20, 312–341.

Linge, G.J.R. and Schamp, E.W. (1993) 'Finance, institutions, and industrial change: spatial perspectives'. In: Schamp, E.W., Linge, G.J.R. and Rogerson, C.M. (eds) *Finance, Institutions and Industrial Change: Spatial Perspectives* 1–38. de Gruyter, Berlin.

Lord, J. Dennis (1987) 'Interstate banking and the relocation of economic control points'. *Urban Geography* 8 (6), 501–519.

—— (1992) 'Geographic deregulation of the U.S. banking industry and spatial transfers of corporate control'. *Urban Geography* 13 (1), 25–48.

Lord, J. Dennis and Lynds, Charles D. (1984) 'Market area planning strategy: an example of interstate banking markets in the USA'. *GeoJournal* 9 (2), 145–154.

Lucia, Maria Giuseppina (1999) *La geografia finanziaria, mercati e territorio*. Pátron Editore, Bologna.

Lührig, Alexander und Spremann, Klaus (1995) 'Target'. In: Geiger, Hans und Spremann, Klaus (Hrsg) *Banktopologie* 119–165. Haupt, Bern.

Martin, Ron (1994) 'Stateless monies, global financial integration and national economic autonomy: the end of geography?'. In: Corbridge, Stuart, Martin, Ron and Thrift, Nigel (eds) *Money, Power and Space* 253–278. Blackwell, Oxford.

—— (1999) 'The new economic geography of money'. In: Martin, Ron (ed.) *Money and the Space Economy* 3–27. Wiley, Chichester.

McCauley, Robert N., Ruud, Judith, S. and Wooldridge, Philip D. (2002) 'Globalising international banking'. *BIS Quarterly Review* March, 41–51.

Mikdashi, Zuhayr (1998) *Les banques à l'ère de la mondialisation*. Economica, Paris.

Mishkin, Frederic S. and Eakins, Stanley G. (1999) *Financial Markets and Institutions* 3rd edn. Addison Wesley, Reading, MA.

O'Brien, Richard (1992) *Global Financial Integration: The End of Geography*. Council of Foreign Relations Press, New York, NY.

O'hUallacháin, Breandán (1994) 'Foreign banking in the American urban system of financial organization'. *Economic Geography* 70 (3), 206–228.

Palm, Risa (1971) 'Catastrophic earthquake insurance: patterns of adoption'. *Economic Geography* 47 (2), 119–131.

Park, Y.S. and Zwick, J. (1985) *International Banking in Theory and Practice*. Addison-Wesley, Reading, MA.

Peagam, Norman (1989) 'Treasure Islands'. *Euromoney* Supplement, May.

Peet, John (1992) 'Financial centres: Rise and fall'. *The Economist* 27 June.

Porteous, David J. (1995) *The Geography of Finance*. Avebury, Aldershot.

—— (1999) 'The development of financial centers: location, information, externalities and path dependence'. In: Martin, Ron (ed.) *Money and the Space Economy* 95–114. Wiley, Chichester.

Portes, Richard and Rey, Hélène (2001) 'The determinants of cross-border equity flows'. National Bureau of Economic Research Working Paper 7336. Cambridge, MA.

Power, Dominic (2001) 'Information and communication technologies and the integration of European derivatives markets'. In: Leinbach, Thomas R. and Brunn, Stanley D. (eds) *Worlds of E-Commerce: Economic, Geographical and Social Dimensions* 241–255. Wiley, Chichester.

de Prati, Christian F. (1998) *Chinese Issuers in International Capital Markets*. Haupt, Bern.

Rahul, Jacob (2001) 'Territory falls prey to a bout of insecurity'. *Financial Times* 16 October, IX.

Rakiya, Ibrahim (ed.) (1999) *Directory of Islamic Insurance*. Institute of Islamic Banking and Insurance, London.

Reed, Howard (1981) *The Preeminence of International Financial Centers*. Praeger, New York.

Reid, Margaret (1988) *All-Change in the City*. Macmillan, London.

van Rietbergen, Ton (1994) 'The insurance sector in geographical perspective'. *Tijdschrift voor Economische en Sociale Geografie* 85 (3), 263–268.

—— (1999) *The Internationalization of European Insurance Groups*. Nederlandse Geografische Studies 250, Utrecht University.

Roberts, Susan M. (1994) 'Fictitious capital, fictitious spaces: the geography of offshore financial flows'. In: Corbridge, Stuart, Martin, Ron and Thrift, Nigel (eds) *Money, Power and Space* 91–115. Blackwell, Oxford.

—— (1995) 'Small place, big money: the Cayman Islands and the international financial system'. *Economic Geography* 71 (3), 237–256.

Robins, Brian (1987) *Tokyo, a World Financial Centre.* Euromoney Publication, London.

Rogge, Peter G. (1997) *The Dynamics of Change, Swiss Bank Corporation 1872–1997.* Friedrich Reinhardt Verlag, Basle.

Ross, Stephen A., Westerfield, Randolph W. and Jaffe, Jeffrey (2000) *Corporate Finance* 6th edn. McGraw-Hill, New York, NY.

Sarkissian, Sergei and Schill, Michael J. (2001) 'The overseas listing decision: new evidence of proximity preference'. Unpublished paper, McGill University and University of Virginia, June.

Sassen, Saskia (1991) *The Global City.* Princeton University Press, Princeton, NJ.

Schierenbeck, Henner (1998) 'Private Banking in der Schweiz – Märkte, Kunden, Geschäftskonzeptionen'. In: Basler Bankenvereinigung (Hrsg) *Private Banking – Die Herausforderung für den Finanzplatz Schweiz* 3–51. Haupt, Bern.

Scholtens, L.J.R. (1992) 'Centralization in international financial intermediation: theory, practice, and evidence for the European Community'. *Banca Nazionale del Lavoro Quarterly Review* 182 (September).

Sele, Cyrill (1995) *Standortkonkurrenz zwischen Finanzplätzen unter besonderer Berücksichtigung des Offshore-Geschäfts – der Fall Liechtenstein.* Haupt, Bern.

Semple, Keith R. (1973) 'Recent trends in the spatial concentration of corporate headquarters'. *Economic Geography* 49 (4), 309–318.

Shirreff, David (1999) 'Heroes and villains'. *Euromoney* June, 31–48.

sigma (1987–2002) *Economic Studies.* Swiss Reinsurance Company, Zurich.

Simon, Pierre (2000) 'Forces et faiblesses de la place de Paris'. *Problèmes économiques* 2.674, 19 juillet, 19–25. La Documentation française.

de Soto, Hernando (2001) 'The mystery of capital'. *Finance & Development* March, 29–33.

Spremann, Klaus (1995) 'Banktopologie'. In: Geiger, Hans and Spremann, Klaus (Hrsg) *Banktopologie* 17–26. Haupt, Bern.

Stoakes, Christopher (1995) 'All mapped out'. *Euromoney* December, 25.

—— (1999a) 'Default rules in black and white'. *Euromoney* May, 28.

—— (1999b) 'Questions of seniority and majority'. *Euromoney* September, 33.

Thrift, Nigel (1987) 'The fixers: the urban geography of international commercial capital'. In: Henderson, Jeffrey and Castells, Manuel (eds) *Global Restructuring and Territorial Development* 203–233. Sage, London.

Thrift, Nigel and Leyshon, Andrew (1994) 'A phantom state? The de-traditionalization of money, the international financial system and international financial centers'. *Political Geography* 13 (4), 299–327.

Tickell, Adam (1994) 'Banking on Britain? The changing role and geography of Japanese banks in Britain'. *Regional Studies* 28 (3), 291–304.

Tsatsaronis, Kostas (2000) 'Hedge funds'. *BIS Quarterly Review* November, 61–71.

Turner, Philip (1991) *Capital Flows in the 1980s: A Survey of Major Trends.* BIS Economic Papers 30, Basle.

Ungefehr, Friederike (1987) 'Offshore-Zentren (I): Bahamas'. *Die Bank* (10), 562–565.

—— (1988) 'Offshore-Zentren (II): Cayman Islands'. *Die Bank* (1), 33–34.

—— (1988) 'Offshore-Zentren (III): Die Bermudas'. *Die Bank* (2), 81–83.

—— (1988) 'Offshore-Zentren (IV): Panama. *Die Bank* (5), 282–285.

—— (1988) 'Offshore-Zentren (V): Niederländische Antillen'. *Die Bank* (8), 446–449.

—— (1988) 'Offshore-Zentren (VI): Barbados'. *Die Bank* (11), 629–632.

—— (1989) 'Offshore-Zentren (VII): Die Kanalinseln'. *Die Bank* (2), 105–109.

—— (1989) 'Offshore-Zentren (VIII): Isle of Man'. *Die Bank* (4), 210–213.

—— (1989) 'Offshore-Zentren (IX): Zypern'. *Die Bank* (6), 340–342.

—— (1989) 'Offshore-Zentren (X): Singapur'. *Die Bank* (7), 392–395.

—— (1989) 'Offshore-Zentren (XI): Hongkong'. *Die Bank* (10), 572–575.

—— (1990) 'Offshore-Zentren (XII): Vanuatu'. *Die Bank* (4), 225–227.

—— (1990) 'Offshore-Zentren (XIII): International banking Facilities in den USA'. *Die Bank* (8), 464–468.

—— (1990) 'Offshore-Zentren (XIV): Japan Offshore Market'. *Die Bank* (11), 635–637.

Vital, Christian (1995) Swiss Interbank Clearing (SIC): 'Erfahrungen und Einschätzungen'. In: Geiger, Hans and Spremann, Klaus (Hrsg) *Banktopologie* 79–94. Haupt, Bern.

Vortmüller, Claudia (2001) *Going Public in China* [in German]. Haupt, Bern.

Warf, Barney (2002) 'Tailored for Panama: offshore banking at the crossroads of the Americas'. *Geografiska Annaler* 84B (1), 33–47.

Warf, Barney and Cox, Joseph C. (1996) 'Spatial dimensions of the savings and loan crisis'. *Growth and Change* 27 (Spring), 135–155.

Warf, Barney and Wije, Chand (1991) 'The spatial structure of large U.S. law firms'. *Growth and Change* 22, 157–174.

Waters, Richard (1996) 'The world according to US GAAP'. *Financial Times* 1 February, 22.

Wong, Douglas and Leahy, Joe (2001) 'Big changes are on the horizon for Singapore's financial landscape'. *Financial Times* 21 June, 16.

Wood, Philip R. (1995a) *Comparative Financial Law*. Sweet & Maxwell, London.

—— (1995b) *Principles of International Insolvency*. Sweet & Maxwell, London.

Wooldridge, Philip D. (2002) 'Uses of the BIS statistics: an introduction'. *BIS Quarterly Review* March, 75–92.

Wright, April and Liesch, Peter (1995) 'The location of foreign banks in Australia'. In: Green, Milford B. and McNaughton, Rod B. (eds) *The Location of Foreign Direct Investment* 175–190. Avebury, Aldershot.

Yamori, Nobuyoshi (1998) 'A note on the location choice of multinational banks: the case of Japanese financial institutions'. *Journal of Banking & Finance* 22, 109–120.

Yasenovsky, Vladimir (2000a) 'Tipy bankovskoi kul'tury'. *Kredit Russia* 10, May, 6–13.

—— (2000b) 'Bankovskie sistemy zarubezhnoi stran'. *Kredit Russia* 11, June, 15–20.

—— (2000c) 'Rynki dolgovyh tsennyh bumag v razlitshnyh stran'. *Kredit Russia* 12, June, 9–13.

Zimmermann, Theo (1998) 'Vom Schweizerischen Bankverein zur UBS, die Reorganisation einer Grossbank von 1990–1998'. In: Popp, Werner and Zimmermann, Theo (Hrsg) *Strategie und Innovation in Universalbanken* 69–82. Haupt, Bern.

2 Playground

Abrahams, Paul and Tett, Gillian (1997) 'Japan reaps what it sowed'. *Financial Times* 1 December, 17.

Allen, Robin (1996) 'Pressures mount as oil states dither'. *Financial Times* 8 November, II.

Althaus, Sarah (1999) '"Minnows" needs met by locals'. *Financial Times* 25 October, VIII.

Anonymous (1995) 'Where are the players?'. *The Banker* December, 35–39.

—— (1998) 'Euro Libor vs Euribor'. *ISMA Euro Zone Extra* 1, April, 11.

—— (2002) 'A fresh look at rules for energy and finance'. *Financial Times* 19 February, 15.

Authers, John (1997) 'Victim of its own success'. *Financial Times* 22 January, 13.

Bank of England (1998) *Practical Issues Arising from the Introduction of the Euro* 8.

—— (2001) *Practical Issues Arising from the Euro* June, 30–31.

Banque de France (2000) *Annual Report*.

Beard, Alison (2002) 'Patriot Act put on compliance pressure'. *Financial Times* 26 June, III.

Beers, David T. and Cavanaugh, Marie (1997) 'Sovereign credit ratings: a primer'. *Standard & Poor's Credit Week* 16 April.

Berton, Lee (1999) 'Countdown to harmonization'. *Institutional Investor* June, 101–103.

Biltoft, Karsten (1996) 'A revolution in securities markets' structures?'. *Financial Market Trends* 65, OECD.

Blanden, Michael (1990) 'English speakers required'. *The Banker* August, 20, 23.

Blumer, Andreas (1996) *Bankenaufsicht und Bankenprüfung.* Haupt, Bern.

Brady, Brooks and Bos, Roger J. (2002) *Record Defaults in 2001, the Result of Poor Credit Quality and a Weak Economy.* Special Report (February). Standard & Poor's, New York.

Brady, Simon (1990) 'Basle turns the screw'. *Euromoney* September, 149–153.

Brice, Martin (1995) 'Mexican crisis makes its mark'. *Financial Times* 14 September, 6.

de Brouwer, Gordon (2001) *Hedge Funds in Emerging Markets.* Cambridge University Press, Cambridge, UK.

Brown, David (1996) 'Strategy for a single entity'. *Financial Times* 29 October, III.

Burt, Tim and Rice, Robert (1997) 'Weighted against outsiders'. *Financial Times* 14 February, 11.

Bush, Janet (1990) 'This line against co-men'. *Financial Times* 19 June, 19.

Cantor, Richard and Packer, Frank (1995) 'Sovereign credit ratings'. *Current Issues in Economics and Finance* 1 (3), June, 1–26. Federal Reserve Bank of New York.

Catán, Thomas (1999) 'US banking faces clean sweep over money laundering'. *Financial Times* 22 December, 6.

—— (2002) 'Argentina's vision of private pension system in tatters'. *Financial Times Fund Management* 29 April, 7.

Catán, Thomas and Burns, Jimmy (1999) 'NY laws may apply in probe of laundering'. *Financial Times* 15 September, 2.

Celarier, Michelle (1995) 'Clipped'. *Euromoney* December, 42–46.

—— (1998) 'Collateral damage'. *Euromoney* November, 38–41.

China Statistical Yearbook 2001. Beijing.

Clow, Robert (1998) 'Risk rediscovered'. *Institutional Investor* October, 29–32.

Coggan, Philip (1995) 'Mighty humbled but they're here to stay'. *Financial Times* 4 December, 29.

—— (1996) 'Obstacles to integration'. *Financial Times* 16 February, IV.

Corrigan, Tracy and Harris, Clay (1997) 'Thundering herd comes storming in out of the blue'. *Financial Times* 20 November, 18.

Covill, Laura (1996) 'Playing second fiddle'. *Euromoney* March, 100–104.

Currie, Antony (1997) 'As safe as the Bank of Europe'. *Euromoney* June, 10.

Dawkins, William (1996a) 'A currency for business'. *Financial Times* 28 March, III.

—— (1996b) 'A big bang in slow motion'. *Financial Times* 10 December, 15.

Denton, Nicholas (1995) 'Stepping on to private territory'. *Financial Times* 21 June, III.

Dickson, Martin (2000) 'Tremors in the City'. *Financial Times* 7 April, 14.

Dudley, Nigel (1997) 'Time to bring the money home'. *Euromoney* May, 97–100.

Dugan, Ann (1990) 'The old guard faces retirement'. *Euromoney* July, 119–122.

Durr, Barbara (1990) 'Chicago shakes hands with the SEC'. *Financial Times* 18 April, 28.

Eaglesham, Jean (1999) 'Cruising in home waters'. *Financial Times* 17 August, 11.

Economides, Kim, Blacksell, Mark and Watkins, Charles (1986) 'The spatial analysis of legal systems: towards a geography of law?'. *Journal of Law and Society* 13 (2), 161–181.

Edwards, Jeremy and Fischer, Klaus (1994) *Banks, Finance and Investment in Germany*. Cambridge University Press, Cambridge, UK.

Ensor, Benjamin (1996) 'Resisting the seduction of scale'. *Global Investor* July–August, 24–27.

—— (1998) 'High-yield's virtuous circle'. *International Bond Investor* Spring, 2–6.

European Insurance in Figures, 2001. Comité Européen des Assurances, Paris.

Evans, Garry (1991) 'Big choices for the little European'. *Euromoney* October, 20–24.

—— (1992) 'Bundesbank clings to power'. *Euromoney* April, 55–58.

—— (1997) 'Can Ujiie clean up Nomura?'. *Euromoney* June, 52–57.

Evans, Jules (2002) 'Double Grammy blocks effort to regulate energy derivatives'. *Euromoney* May, 13–14.

Fidler, Stephen (1996) 'Back to a straight and narrow path'. *Financial Times* 7 June, I.

Fidler, Stephen and Burns, Jimmy (1997) 'Illicit drugs trade is put at $400bn'. *Financial Times* 26 June, 4.

Fisher, Andrew (1996) 'Germany's stock answer'. *Financial Times* 22 October, 13.

Gadanecz, Blaise and von Kleist, Karsten (2000) 'The international banking market'. *BIS Quarterly Review* August, 13–19.

Gallatin (1992) 'Nothing to lose but their chains'. *Euromoney* September, 58–60.

Gapper, John (1995) 'Basle model for banking safeguards'. *Financial Times* 13 April, 22.

Gapper, John and Denton, Nicholas (1996) *All that Glitters, the Fall of Barings*. Hamish Hamilton, London.

Graham, George (1997a) 'Regulator pledges vigilance over City'. *Financial Times* 29 October, 10.

—— (1997b) 'Taking a painful road to European dominance'. *Financial Times* 9 December, 18.

Graham, George and Martinson, Jane (1997) 'Handful of firms set for a dominant role'. *Financial Times* 20 November, 18.

Hall, William (1999) 'How to launder $1m'. *Financial Times* 27 October, V.

—— (2002) 'Top Swiss hedge funds head to the provinces'. *Financial Times Fund Management* 17 June, 8.

Hamilton Fazey, Ian (1998) 'World banking system is a "money launderers' dream"'. *Financial Times* 26 May, 7.

Hargreaves, Deborah (1989) 'Regulator under pressure'. *Financial Times* 8 March, IV.

—— (2001) 'Pan-Europe pipe dreams start to fade'. *Financial Times* 17 May, VII.

Harverson, Patrick (1994) 'Bankers breathe a little easier'. *Financial Times* 16 November, II.

Herzel, Leo and Shepro, Richard W. (1988) 'Lessons from Delaware'. *Financial Times* 7 April, 27.

—— (1990) 'SEC bids for index futures'. *Financial Times* 14 June, 27.

House, Richard (1997) Make way for the megaregulator'. *Institutional Investor* September, 55–61.

Humphreys, Gary (1992) 'Old guard under siege'. *Euromoney* April, 45–50.

Industry of Free China (2001). Council for Economic Planning and Development, Executive Yuan, Taipei.

Institutional Investors Statistical Yearbook 2001 (2002). OECD, Paris.

International Financial Statistics (IFS) (2001). International Monetary Fund, Washington, DC.

Investment Company Institute Fact Book, 2001. New York.

Irvine, Steven (1998) 'Caught with their pants down?'. *Euromoney* January, 51–53.

Iskander, Samer (1996) 'Quest for a benchmark may be over'. *Financial Times* 22 November, VII.

Jack, Andrew (1996) 'Stage set for financial reforms'. *Financial Times* 10 December, III.

Jacquin, Jean-Baptiste et Pouzin, Gilles (1995) 'Rating: des notes à la tête du client?'. *L'Expansion* 6/19 mars, 70–73.

Japan Statistical Yearbook (2001). Tokyo.

Kelly, Jim (1997) 'World accounting wins more converts'. *Financial Times* 9 June, 4.

Klapwijk, Philip *et al.* (2002) *Gold Survey 2002.* Gold Fields Mineral Services Ltd, London.

Lambert, Richard (1988) 'Two days in October'. *Financial Times* 13 February, I.

Lee, Peter (1992) 'How to exorcise your derivatives demons'. *Euromoney* September, 36–48.

—— (1993) 'The start of a global bulge bracket'. *Euromoney* April, 28–33.

—— (1994) 'All change: Equity'. *Euromoney* June, 89–101.

—— (1996) 'Developing a taste for equity'. *Euromoney* July, 139–144.

Leyshon, Andrew and Thrift, Nigel (1997) 'The regulation of global money'. In: Leyshon, Andrew and Thrift, Nigel (eds) *Money/Space, Geographies of Monetary Transformation* 59–81. Routledge, London.

Mackintosh, James (2001) 'Financial watchdog unleashed and ready to bite'. *Financial Times* 23 November, 9.

Marshall, Julian (2002) 'LTCM: a cautionary tale'. *Euromoney* January, 107.

Massey, Katy (1997) ' "Rocket scientists" fly high'. *Financial Times* 31 January, IV.

McDonough, William J. (1993) 'The global derivatives market'. *FRBNY Quarterly Review* Autumn, 1–5.

McGregor, Richard (2001) 'Spotlight falls on China's private funds "grey market"'. *Financial Times* 9 July, 4.

Mercer, William M. (2000) *European Pension Fund Managers' Guide, 2000*. April. Mercer Investment Consulting.

Mikdashi, Zuhayr (1998) *Les banques à l'ère de la mondialisation*. Economica, Paris.

Miller, Suzanne (1997) 'Big Argentine companies with bad addresses...'. *Euromoney* June, 111–114.

Moir, Christine (1996) 'Once more unto a breach'. *Financial Times* 16 February, III.

Moody's Investor Service (2001) *Ratings List*. Country Ceilings for Foreign Currency. 29 November.

Moore, Philip (1991) 'Cleaning up the town hall mess'. *Euromoney* April, 31–33.

Morse, Laurie (1992) 'New law lifts uncertainty'. *Financial Times* 8 December, IV.

Mulligan, Mark (2001) 'Mixed results for pioneer private pension systems'. *Financial Times* 19 March, IV.

National Accounts of OECD Countries, Vol. 1, 1989–2000. OECD, Paris.

Nossel, Sean (2001) *SA Life Assurance*. Fleming Martin Securities Ltd, Johannesburg.

O'Barr, William M. and Conley, John M. (1992) 'Managing relationships: the culture of institutional investing'. *Financial Analysts Journal* September–October, 21–27.

Osborn, Neil and Evans, Garry (1988) 'Cooke's medicine: Kill or cure?'. *Euromoney* July, 34–54.

Plender, John (1998) 'Western crony capitalism'. *Financial Times* 3 October, 6.

Putnam, Bluford (1998) 'The long-term lessons of long-term capital'. *Global Investor* November, 48–50.

Rafferty, Kevin (2000) 'Playing a whole new ball game.' *Euromoney* August, 32–35.

Reading, Brian (1998) 'Japan's system of favours for bureaucrats is to blame'. *Financial Times* 8 August, XXI.

Rice, Robert (1995) 'Urge to merge over the Atlantic'. *Financial Times* 16 October, 16.

Schwander-Auckenthaler, Katharina (1995) *Missbrauch von Bankgeschäften zu Zwecken der Geldwäscherei*. Haupt, Bern.

Scott, Hal S. (1992) 'Supervision of international banking post-BCCI'. *Georgia State University Law Review* 8 (3), 487–510.

Shakir, Imran (1999) 'Revisiting Islamic financial products'. In: Rakiya, Ibrahim (ed.) *Directory of Islamic Insurance* 98–100. Institute of Islamic Banking and Insurance, London.

Shirreff, David (1994) 'MoF clings to the same old levers'. *Euromoney* February, 32–38.

—— (1996a) 'The human factor'. *Euromoney* January, 30–35.

—— (1996b) 'The agony of the global supervisor'. *Euromoney* July, 48–52.

—— (1998) 'The eve of destruction'. *Euromoney* November, 34–36.

sigma 7/1995, *Development of Insolvencies and the Importance of Security in the Insurance Industry*. Swiss Reinsurance Company (Swiss Re), Zurich.

—— 6/1997, *Low Claims Ratios and Overcapacity Force Prices Downwards*. Swiss Re, Zurich.

—— 8/1998, *Financial Difficulties of Public Pension Schemes.* Swiss Re, Zurich.

—— 6/2001, *World Insurance in 2000.* Swiss Re, Zurich.

Simonian, Haig (2001) 'Germany aims for unified finance market supervision'. *Financial Times* 12 April, 2.

Standard & Poor's Risk Solutions. S&P Credit Indices by Rating Category. Week ending 3 May 2002.

Stewart, Jules (1997) 'A veil of tiers'. *Euromoney* May, 119–123.

Stoakes, Christopher (1995) 'All mapped out'. *Euromoney* December, 25.

—— (1996) 'Divided by a common language'. *Euromoney* December, 28.

—— (1999a) 'Default rules in black and white'. *Euromoney* May, 28.

—— (1999b) 'Questions of seniority and majority'. *Euromoney* September, 33.

Targett, Simon and Gimbel, Florian (2002) 'Investors to fight tax barriers'. *Financial Times Fund Management* 22 April, 1.

Tassel, Tony and Guerrera, Francesco (2002) 'A pensions passport faces local customs test'. *Financial Times Fund Management* June, 3.

Tett, Gillian (1997) 'Nomura hit by suspension'. *Financial Times* 31 July, 12.

—— (1998) 'Crucial issue will determine the success of Big Bang'. *Financial Times* 26 March, VI.

Thornhill, John (1999) 'Tough assets emerge from the bunkers'. *Financial Times* 14 May, II.

Tomkins, Richard (1998) 'Justice is blind'. *Financial Times* 17 July, 15.

Truglia, Vincent, Levey, David and Mahoney, Christopher (1995) *Sovereign Risk: Bank Deposits vs. Bonds.* Moody's Investor Service, Special report No. 03871 (October). New York.

Tsatsaronis, Kostas (2000) 'Hedge funds'. *BIS Quarterly Review* November, 61–71.

United Nations Statistical Yearbook 1998, 45th issue. New York.

Vittori, Jean-March (1992) 'Emprunteurs attention, on vous notera tous bientôt Aaa ou BBB...'. *L'Expansion* 2/15 avril, 52–54.

Waller, David (1996) 'International accounting standard wins recruits'. *Corporate Finance* August 40–43.

Waters, Richard (1992) 'Salutary september'. *Financial Times* 8 December, VI.

—— (1996) 'The world according to the US GAAP'. *Financial Times* 1 February, 22.

White, Lawrence J. (2001) 'The credit rating industry: an industrial organization analysis'. Presentation at the Conference on *The Role of Credit Reporting Systems in International Economy.* World Bank, Washington, DC. March.

Williamson, Hugh (2001) 'Now the aim is to be ahead of the pack'. *Financial Times* 15 October, IV.

—— (2002) 'New regime takes root'. *Financial Times* 12 June, II.

Willman, John (2001) 'Cleaning up'. *Financial Times* 21 September, 16.

Wood, Philip R. (1997) *Maps of World Financial Law* 3rd edn. Allen & Overy, London.

Zlotnick, Brian (1996) 'Dutch managers fight back'. *Global Investor* July–August, 28–30.

3 Markets

Adams, Jeremy (1997) 'Meet the U.S. investor on the right level'. *Corporate Finance* June, 28–31.

Adams, Richard (1997) 'Voice-brokers are lapsing into silence'. *Financial Times* 18 April, II.

Anonymous (1989) *Clearing and Settling the Euro-Securities Market: Euro-Clear and Cedel.* March. Federal Reserve Bank of New York.

—— (1992) 'Move over, big brother'. *The Banker* July, 63.

—— (1993) *Cross-Border Clearance, Settlement, and Custody: Beyond the G30 Recommendations.* June. Morgan Guaranty Trust Company, Brussels.

—— (1996) ' "Pfandbriefe". Guide to Germany'. *Euromoney* June, 12–15.

—— (1997a) ' "Equities". Guide to the Russian Financial Markets'. *Euromoney* March, 11.

—— (1997b) ' "Pfandbriefe". The 1997 Guide to Germany'. *Euromoney* June, 6–9.

Authers, John and Burt, Tim (1997) 'Nasdaq turns to Europe for new entries'. *Financial Times* 31 December, 12.

Bank of England (1996) *Practical Issues Arising from the Introduction of the Euro* 2. 16 September.

—— (2001) *Practical Issues Arising from the Introduction of the Euro.* June.

Banque de France (2000) *Annual Report.*

Bartko, Peter (1991) 'BIS plugs the holes in netting'. *Euromoney* May, 101–102.

Bedford, Lucy (1998a) 'The jumbo factor'. *Global Investor* June, 43–46.

—— (1998b) 'One Europe, many benchmarks'. *Global Investor* July–August, 28–33.

Bennet, Rosemary (1993) 'The six men who rule world derivatives'. *Euromoney* August, 45–49.

—— (1994) 'Follow those funds – see the flows'. *Euromoney* January, 49–54.

Benzie, Richard (1992) *The Development of the International Bond Market.* BIS Economic Papers 32, January.

Berton, Lee (1999) 'Countdown to harmonization'. *Institutional Investor* June, 101–103.

Bilefsky, Dan (2000) 'Code-makers flex their muscles'. *Financial Times* 24 October, 17.

Birchler, Urs W. and Rich, George (1994) 'Bank structure in Switzerland'. In: Kaufman, George G. (ed.) *Banking Structures in Major Countries* 2nd edn, 389–427. Kluwer, Dordrecht.

Blanden, Michael (1992) 'Obstacle course'. *The Banker* June, 18–20.

Blitz, James (1993) 'Foreign exchange dealers enter the 21st century'. *Financial Times* 13 September, 17.

Blume, Marshall E., Siegel, Jeremy J. and Rottenberg, Dan (1993) *Revolution on Wall Street, The Rise and Decline of the New York Stock Exchange.* Norton, New York.

Boland, Vincent (2000) 'Deal signals LCH merger with Clearnet'. *Financial Times* 5 April, 32.

Brady, Simon (1991) 'American banks' last stand'. *Euromoney* May, 81–86.

—— (1993) 'Why equities will dominate the 1990s'. *Euromoney* July, 30–40.

Bream, Rebecca (1998) 'Daimler and S&P in head-on collision'. *Euromoney* October, 7.

Breedon, Francis (1996) 'Why do the Liffe and DTB *Bund* futures contracts trade at different prices?'. Working Paper 57 (December), Bank of England.

de Brouwer, Gordon (2001) *Hedge Funds in Emerging Markets.* Cambridge University Press, Cambridge, UK.

Brown, Jonathan (2001) 'Twists and turns on the straight-through route'. *Euromoney* April, 112–118.

Butler, Rick (2001) 'All to play for'. *Euromoney* June, 182–186.

Caplen, Brian (1998) 'Two crises ahead of Asia'. *Euromoney* March, 47–54.

Catán, Thomas (2002) 'Argentines' love of dollar threatens economic fortune'. *Financial Times* 21 February, 3.

Chernow, Ron (1990) *The House of Morgan.* Simon & Schuster, New York.

Chesler-Marsh, Caren (1992) 'The global conundrum'. *Euromoney* January, 69–71.

Clifton, Kieran (1996) 'A vision of the future'. *Euromoney* March, 114–117.

Clow, Robert (2000) 'Bond daze'. *Institutional Investor*, July, 27–32.

Cohen, Benjamin J. (1998) *The Geography of Money.* Cornell University Press, Ithaca, NY.

Committee on the Global Financial System (2001) *The Implications of Electronic Trading in Financial Markets.* January. BIS, Basle.

Cooke, Stephanie (1995) 'Rising hub of global trading'. *Financial Times* 6 June, IV.

—— (1996) 'Will brokers go broke?'. *Euromoney* May, 90–93.

Corrigan, Tracy (1995) 'Funds ready if price is right'. *Financial Times* 14 September, 3.

—— (1997a) 'Pot of money for foreign issuers'. *Financial Times* 2 May, I.

—— (1997b) 'Daunting price but high rewards'. *Financial Times* 2 May, IV.

Corrigan, Tracy and Harverson, Patric (1992) 'Ever more complex'. *Financial Times* 8 December, I.

Corrigan, Tracy and Iskander, Samer (1997) 'Yankees grab the spotlight'. *Financial Times* 2 May, III.

Covill, Laura (1996) 'Telekom rules OK'. *Euromoney* December, 32–36.

—— (1999) 'The quick and dirty way into Emu'. *Euromoney* October, 28–31.

Cowan, David (1996a) ' "Cinderella" sector wins new status'. *Financial Times* 8 October, VI.

—— (1996b) 'Rivals eye each other closely'. *Financial Times* 26 November, VI.

Crabbe, Matthew (1988) 'Oh, to buy in England'. *Euromoney* January, 37–42.

Currie, Anthony (1997) 'Still big, but more sensitive'. *Euromoney* January, 107–110.

—— (2000) 'A true exchange for forex'. *Euromoney* June, 17–26.

Dalla, Ismail, Khatkhate, Deena, Rao, D.C., Kondury, Kali, Jun, Kwang and Chuppe, Terry (1995) *The Emerging Asian Bond Market.* The World Bank, Washington, DC.

Dalla-Costa, Julie (2002) 'When shareholder value conflicts with shareholder utility'. *Euromoney* March, 61–63.

Davis, E.P. (1990) *International Financial Centres – an Industrial Analysis.* Discussion Paper 51, Bank of England.

Dawkins, William (1996) 'A currency for business'. *Financial Times* 28 March, III.

Derrick, Simon (2002) 'Why portfolio flows are important'. The 2002 Guide to Foreign Exchange. *Euromoney* 4–7.

Dickenson, Tim (1999) 'When crunch became crisis'. *ISMA Quarterly Comment* January, 6–7, 33.

van Duyn, Aline (2000) 'Broader horizon for portfolios'. *Financial Times* 12 May, V.

—— (2001a) 'Only the best will survive'. *Financial Times* 28 March, VII.

—— (2001b) 'Spotlight turns on German bond futures'. *Financial Times* 27 April, 31.

Dyer, Geoff (1993) 'Global bonds aim to broaden their scope'. *Euromoney* June, 84–88.

Edwards, Ben (1994) 'Morgan's magic circle'. *Euromoney* August, 35–38.

Featherstone, James (1997) 'Looking after Latin paper'. *Euromoney* 133–138.

Field, Graham (1996) 'New members for the GDR club'. *Euromoney* November, 87–90.

Froud, Jeremy (1996) 'Feeding the capital-hungry corporate'. *Corporate Finance* September, 37–40.

Galati, Gabriele (2001) 'Why has global FX turnover declined? Explaining the 2001 triennial survey'. *BIS Quarterly Review* December, 39–47.

Galati, Gabriele and Tsatsaronis, Kostas (2001) *The Impact of the Euro on Europe's Financial Markets*. BIS Working Paper 100 (July).

Gardener, Edward M. and Molyneux, Philip (1993) *Changes in Western European Banking*. Routledge, London.

Gawith, Philip (1995a) 'The voice of experience is beginning to fade away'. *Financial Times* 6 June, VI.

—— (1995b) 'Market growth startles foreign exchanges'. *Financial Times* 20 September, 4.

—— (1995c) 'Brokers lose voices to the small screen'. *Financial Times* 15 December, 20.

—— (1996a) 'Exotic but not for faint hearts'. *Financial Times* 15 May, 13.

—— (1996b) 'Funny money comes of age'. *Financial Times* 3 July, IV.

Ghaffari, Paul (1998) 'Getting countries right is key for returns'. *International Bond Investor* Spring, 15–16.

Goodhart, Will (2000) 'e-bonds: a revolution in the making'. *Global Investor* May, 40–44.

Gordon-Walker, Rupert (1995) 'Can gilts get glitzier?'. *Euromoney* December, 57–60.

Graham, George (1996) 'Fractional fees bring cheer'. *Financial Times* 26 November, II.

—— (1997) 'Settlement risk has banks in a quandry'. *Financial Times* 18 April, V.

Greenbaum, Stuart I. and Thakor, Anjan V. (1995) *Contemporary Financial Intermediation*. Dryden, Fort Worth, TX.

Guide to Japanese Government Bonds (1999). Ministry of Finance, Tokyo.

Guide to Switzerland (1996). Euromoney Publications, London.

Hagger, Evan (1992a) 'The search for value'. *Euromoney* July, 81–83.

—— (1992b) 'Handle exotics with care'. *Euromoney* October, 71–78.

Haindl, Andreas (1991) *The Euro Money Market*. Haupt, Bern.

Hampton, Mark P. (1996) *The Offshore Interface, Tax Havens in the Global Economy*. Macmillan, London.

Harding, David and Marshall, Tom (2002) 'Sub-sovereign bonds prove slow to catch on in Europe'. *Euromoney* February, 90–92.

Harding, James (1998) 'China passes law to improve stock market regulation'. *Financial Times* 30 December, 1.

Hargreaves, Deborah (1988) 'Chicago struggles towards margin reform'. *Financial Times* 16 November, 35.

Harnischfeger, Uta (2000) 'Corporate Germany's love and loathing of the American way'. *Financial Times* 7 December, 18.

Harverson, Patrick (1992a) 'It's time to know what's going on'. *Financial Times* 8 December, II.

—— (1992b) 'Products before geography'. *Financial Times* 8 December, VIII.

Helleiner, Eric (1995) 'Explaining the globalization of financial markets: bringing states back in'. *Review of International Political Economy* 2 (2), 315–341.

Herges, Udo (2001) 'The European liquid covered bond market'. Opportunities in Global Fixed Income. *Euromoney* February, 24–26.

Higgins, Kieran (1996) 'Ingredients of a successful Asian deal'. *Corporate Finance* September, 32–36.

Hills, Bob and Young, Chris (1998) 'Competition and co-operation: developments in cross-border securities settlement and derivatives clearing'. *Bank of England Quarterly Bulletin* May, 158–165.

Hope, Kerin and Wright, Hope (2001) 'Banks eye Balkans mattress money'. *Financial Times* 12 June, 3.

Horwood, Clive (1997) 'Euro-Asians: a gimmick or good marketing?'. *International Bond Investor* Summer, 3–12.

Howell, Michael (1997) 'A question of balance'. *Euromoney* September, 105–108.

Humphreys, Gary (1992) 'Poised to reveal more'. *Euromoney* August, 77–79.

Industry of Free China (2001). Council for Economic Planning and Development, Executive Yuan, Taipei.

International Financial Statistics (IFS) (2002). March. International Monetary Fund, Washington, DC.

Irvine, Steve (1997) 'A clear loser'. *Euromoney* June, 135–139.

Ito, Takatoshi and Folkerts-Landau, David with others (1996) *International Capital Markets, Developments, Prospects, and Key Policy Issues*. September. International Monetary Fund, Washington, DC.

Jeanneau, S. (1995) 'Interest rate futures: characteristics and market development (Part 1)'. *International Banking and Financial Market Developments* 27–43, November. BIS, Basle.

Kerr, Ian (1995) 'Cedel group charts new course'. *Euroweek* 17 February.

King, Paul (1994) 'Confidence soars as exchanges' business hits fresh peaks'. *Euromoney* June, 180–188.

Klapwijk, Philip *et al.* (2002) *Gold Survey 2002*. Gold Fields Mineral Services Ltd, London.

Kodres, Laura E. (1996) 'Foreign exchange markets: structure and systemic risks'. *Finance & Development* December, 22–25.

Koenig, Peter (1988) 'Big, important – but a divided soul'. *Euromoney* January, 42–50.

Kuper, Simon (1997a) 'Dealers on the spot as margins narrow'. *Financial Times* 18 April, I.

—— (1997b) 'Reuters falls behind rival EBS on electronic broking market'. *Financial Times* 30 June, 19.

Kutler, Jeffrey (2000) 'T-time'. *Institutional Investor* October, 28.

Kynge, James (1997) 'Exotics reach the major league'. *Financial Times* 9 May, III.

Laitner, Sarah (2001) 'Demand for debt puts swaps at the cutting edge'. *Financial Times* 25 September, II.

Lambert, Richard (1987) 'A benchmark for investors'. *Financial Times* 17 March, 21.

Lapper, Richard (1995) 'Spreading the world's wealth'. *Financial Times* 23 January, 13.

408   *Bibliography*

—— (1996) 'A slice of NY's pie'. *Financial Times* 7 June, V.
Large, Jack (1996a) 'Europe moves to real-time gross settlement'. Guide to Technology in Treasury Management. *Corporate Finance* 26–27.
—— (1996b) 'Swift moves into a new era'. *Corporate Finance* November, 13–15.
Laulajainen, Risto (1999) 'Subnational credit ratings – penetrating the cultural haze'. *GeoJournal* 47 (4), 501–510.
Laurie, Samantha (1990) 'Garbage in, garbage out'. *The Banker* July, 46, 49.
—— (1991) 'Sharing and caring?'. *The Banker* October, VI–VII, X.
Lee, Peter (1992) 'How to exorcise your derivatives demons'. *Euromoney* September, 36–48.
—— (1995) 'A question of collateral'. *Euromoney* November, 46–49.
—— (1997a) 'Taking stock of Russian companies'. *Euromoney* January, 63–70.
—— (1997b) 'SEC rules not OK'. *Euromoney* July, 64–68.
—— (1999a) 'The great equity rebalancing act'. *Euromoney* January, 35.
—— (1999b) 'What the euro means to America'. *Euromoney* June, 166–180.
—— (1999c) 'Pots, plots and fair shares'. *Euromoney* August, 37.
Lee, Peter and Irvine, Steven (1996) 'The back-to-back born in the Dorchester'. *Euromoney* September, 24.
Lewis, Julian (1989a) 'Busting the big banks' closed shop'. *Euromoney* August, 73–74.
—— (1989b) 'Can the big players save the game?'. *Euromoney* October, 52–63.
Lowenstein, Jack (1998) 'Tall tales about T-bills'. *Euromoney* September, 26.
Luce, Edward (1997) 'Spreads have a one-way ticket'. *Financial Times* 23 May, II.
—— (1998) 'Mystery of Europe's missing banks'. *Financial Times* 19 November, 27.
—— (1999a) 'Master middleman takes centre stage'. *Financial Times* 10 February, 9.
—— (1999b) 'Bonded to a bright future'. *Financial Times* 14 June, 17.
—— (1999c) 'Bonding together'. *Financial Times* 6 August, 15.
—— (1999d) 'Rules of the game'. *Financial Times* 26 August, 10.
Marshall, Julian (2000) 'Now the real work starts'. *Euromoney* June, 48–51.
Mathias, Alex (1999) 'Deutsche Telekom's bumpy ride'. *Euromoney* August, 26–28.
MB (1996) 'Petronas runs gamut of maturity'. *Corporate Finance* December, 44, 46.
McCauley, Robert N. (2001) 'Benchmark tipping in the money and bond markets'. *BIS Quarterly Review* March, 39–45.
McDonough, William J. (1993) 'The global derivatives market'. *FRBNY Quarterly Review* Autumn, 1–5.
Middelman, Connor (1995) 'Investor appetite still keen'. *Financial Times* 20 February, VI.
Miller, Matt (1999) 'Underground banking'. *Institutional Investor* January, 32–37.
Montagnon, Peter (1998) 'The price of the prize'. *Financial Times* 12 February, 11.
Moore, Philip (1996) 'Can a jumbo give birth to a baby?'. *Euromoney* January, 79–89.
Mooyart, Brian (1998) 'Battle of the benchmarks'. *The Euro* September–October, 6–14.
Moritz, Gundolf (1995) 'Pfandbriefe go for liquidity'. *ISMA Quarterly Comment* July, 14–15, 26.
Morris, Margaret (1996) 'A tale of gallant bond rivals'. *Financial Times* 10 June, VI.
Murphy, Paul (1989) 'The silent approach'. *The Banker* March, 75–76.
Nairn, Geoffrey (2001) 'Rushing to the web'. *Financial Times* 7 February, IX.

Oakley, Tessa (2001) 'Swapnote's flying start'. *Euromoney* May, 12, 14.
—— (2002) 'Continuous linked settlement at last'. *Euromoney* March, 112–113.
OECD (1991, 1994, 1995), *Financial Market Trends* 50, 57, 62, 63.
Ogino, Akira (1992) 'Japanese bond market'. In: *Capital Markets and Financial Services in Japan, Regulation and Practice* 206–214. Japan Securities Research Institute, Tokyo.
Olivier, Charles (1996) 'Breaking out of bondage'. *Euromoney* November, 91–96.
Osborn, Neil (1988) 'Germans march to foreign music'. *Euromoney* November, 137–140.
Ostrovsky, Arkady (1999) 'The odds are good on future growth'. *Financial Times* 20 September, V.
Parsons, Nick (2001) 'Local and regional issuers bring bond market diversity'. *Euromoney* September, 190–199.
Patel, Jyoti (1992) 'Nasdaq narrows the gap'. *Euromoney* June, 44–50.
Peterson, Michael (2000) 'Only the liquid need apply'. *Euromoney* March, 12.
Peyer, Hans Conrad (1996) *Roche, A Company History 1896–1996*. Editions Roche, Basle.
Politi, James (2002) 'Germany's crown starts to slip'. *Financial Times* 11 March, 25.
Porter, Richard D. and Judson, Ruth A. (1996) 'The location of U.S. currency: how much is abroad?' *Federal Reserve Bulletin* October, 883–903.
Pouzin, Gilles (1995) 'Chaos monétaire: il faut changer les règles'. *L'Expansion* 497, 20 mars–2 avril, 14–16.
de Prati, Christian F. (1998) *Chinese Issuers in International Capital Markets*. Haupt, Bern.
Querée, Anne (1997) 'Private and public nets intermesh'. *Corporate Finance* March, 36–37.
RB (1993) 'Banks retaliate in dealing-room war'. *Euromoney* Supplement, May, 87–90.
von Ribbentrop, Barthold (1990) 'Frankfurt throws down the gauntlet'. *Euromoney* October, 42–43.
Riley, Barry (1997) 'Growth on a grand scale'. *Financial Times* 24 April, I.
Rose, Harold (1994) *International Banking Developments and London's Position as an International Banking Centre*. The City Research Project XII, London Business School.
Rutter, James (1999) 'Custody is dead, long live custody'. *Euromoney* May, 79–84.
Salmon, Felix (1996) 'When is a market like treacle?'. *Euromoney* July, 155–156.
Sele, Cyrill (1995) *Standortkonkurrenz zwischen Finanzplätzen unter besonderer Berücksichtigung des Offshore-Geschäfts – der Fall Liechtenstein*. Haupt, Bern.
Shale, Tony (1987) 'Men who call the yen's tune'. *Euromoney* March, 109–116.
—— (1992) 'Forex fiasco forces radical rethink'. *Euromoney* March, 49–53.
Sharpe, Antonia (1995a) 'Ready now for a strong second-half comeback'. *Financial Times* 14 September, 1.
—— (1995b) 'European banks are finally converted to US concept'. *Financial Times* 14 September, 5.
—— (1996) 'Hard work prevails'. *Financial Times* 1 February, 22.
Sharpe, Richard (1998) 'Triple trouble for hackers'. *Banking Technology* May, 56.
Shirreff, David (1996) 'The fear that dares to speak its name'. *Euromoney* September, 66–72.
—— (1998) 'Plotting the death of settlement risk'. *Euromoney* May, 70–72.

sigma (7/2001) *World Financial Centres: New Horizons in Insurance and Banking.* Swiss Reinsurance Company, Zurich.

Simpkin, Guy (1999) 'European fixed-income capital markets: benchmark curves and futures contracts'. The 1999 Guide to Euro-denominated securities. *Euromoney* June, 2–5.

Skorecki, Alex (2002a) 'London Clearing House mulls link with Clearnet'. *Financial Times* 15 February, 22.

—— (2002b) 'Stock exchanges play for a winning position'. *Financial Times* 8 July, 14.

Smalhout, James (1999) 'Freddie and Fannie aren't sovereign'. *Euromoney* July, 125–128.

—— (2001) 'The long goodbye'. *Euromoney* December, 104–108.

Stewart, Tim (1997) 'Finding value in European high yield debt'. *International Bond Investor* Summer, 17–22.

Targett, Simon (2000) 'Giant stocks bring nightmare choice to fund managers'. *Financial Times* 18 February, 22.

Tassell, Tony (1997) 'Culture change on Dalal Street'. *Financial Times* 24 June, XXI.

Terazono, Emiko (1995) 'Haggling delays deregulation'. *Financial Times* 1 June, 23.

Thomas, Dale (1995) 'The foreign exchange market in London'. *Bank of England Quarterly Bulletin* 35 (4), 361–369.

Thornhill, John (1997) 'Strange beast is eye-catching'. *Financial Times* 28 February, VI.

—— (1999) 'Tough assets emerge from the bunkers'. *Financial Times* 14 May, II.

Turner, Philip (1991) *Capital Flows in the 1980s: A Survey of Major Trends.* BIS Economic Papers 30, Basle.

Urry, Maggie (1996) 'Shares perform better than bonds'. *Financial Times* 1 February, 22.

Vogt, Ronny and Symons, Paul (2001) ' "TSN – the Settlement Network". Guide to European Equities'. *Euromoney* 10–11.

Vortmüller, Claudia (2001) *Going Public in China* [in German]. Haupt, Bern.

Walker, Marcus (2000) 'Transparency or skulduggery?' *Euromoney* February, 51–54.

Warf, Barney (2002) 'Tailored for Panama: offshore banking at the crossroads of the Americas'. *Geografiska Annaler* 84B (1), 33–47.

Warms, Mark and Penney, Neill (2001) 'Straight through processing: from promise to reality'. The 2001 Guide to Forex. *Euromoney* September, 8–9.

Warner, Alison (1994a) 'Border meltdown'. *The Banker* September, 56–61.

—— (1994b) 'Under the spotlight'. *The Banker* December, 53–57.

Waters, Richard (1993) 'Reshaping the trading floor'. *Financial Times* 23 February, 8.

—— (1997) 'Demand for foreign investments may grow'. *Financial Times* 2 May, V.

Wendlandt, Astrid (2000) 'Settlement books set to double'. *Financial Times* 14 July, XI.

Wheatley, Jonathan (1997) 'Brazil DR issuers go upmarket'. *Financial Times* 15 January, 20.

Willoughby, Jack (1997) 'Trade secrets'. *Institutional Investor* November, 65–71.

—— (1998) 'House-raising'. *Institutional Investor* August, 88–94.

Wright, Chris (2000) 'Gentz's task'. Global M&A Yearbook. *Corporate Finance* 26–28.
Wooldridge, Philip D. (2001) 'The emergence of new benchmark yield curves'. *BIS Quarterly Review* December, 48–57.
Zimmermann, Heinz (1998) 'Innovationsprozesse im Finanz- und Risikomanagement'. In: Popp, Werner and Zimmermann, Theo (Hrsg) *Strategie und Innovation in Universalbanken* 11–32. Haupt, Bern.

4 Exchanges

Abken, Peter A. (1991) 'Globalization of stock, futures, and options markets'. *Economic Review* July–August, 1–22.
Adams, Jeremy (1997) 'Meet the U.S. investor on the right level'. *Corporate Finance* June, 28–31.
Anonymous (1987) 'Close shave'. *The Banker* December, 20, 22.
—— (1991a) 'Dramas welcome'. *The Banker* November, 31, 34–35.
—— (1991b) 'The bourse for the future'. *Euromoney* Special Supplement, January, 25–32.
—— (1993) 'Lean on the lenders'. *The Banker* June, 34–35.
—— (1997a) *Matcher* 5, 10. Swiss Exchange.
—— (1997b) 'Board approves revision to Rule 500'. *The Exchange* 4, November, 11.
—— (2001) 'Recent developments in exchange-traded equity derivatives'. *BIS Quarterly Review* September, 34–35.
Atkins, Allen B. and Dyl, Edward A. (1997) 'Market structure and reported trading volume: Nasdaq versus the NYSE'. *Journal of Financial Research* 20 (3), 291–304.
Baker, Gerard and Waters, Richard (1995) 'Tokyo exchange hit by departures of US companies'. *Financial Times* 25 March, 1.
Baker, Gordon (2000) 'Is this the end for stock exchanges and brokers?'. *Global Investor* February, 39–41.
Bank of England (2000) *Practical Issues Arising from the Euro.* June.
Barber, Tony (2000) 'Market maestro'. *Financial Times* 22 April, 7.
Blume, Marshall E., Siegel, Jeremy J. and Rottenberg, Dan (1993) *Revolution on Wall Street, The Rise and Decline of the New York Stock Exchange.* Norton, New York.
Boland, Vincent (1999) 'Super bourse takes shape slowly'. *Financial Times* 23 March, II.
—— (2000a) 'Paris exchange seeks to woo new partners'. *Financial Times* 26 April, 15.
—— (2000b) 'Deutsche Börse and LSE overcome merger hurdle'. *Financial Times* 22 April, 1.
—— (2001a) 'D-Day for a stock market migrant'. *Financial Times* 25 June, 10.
—— (2001b) 'A healthy appetite for Liffe'. *Financial Times* 29 September, 9.
—— (2001c) 'Failure to achieve victory puts LSE in the line of fire'. *Financial Times* 31 October, 21.
Boland, Vincent and van Duyn, Alice (2000) 'Hard talking begins in proposed exchange merger'. *Financial Times* 12 May, 32.
Boland, Vincent and Pretzlik, Charles (2001a) 'Euronext set to launch bid for Liffe'. *Financial Times* 3 October, 23.
—— (2001b) 'Euronext wins battle for Liffe exchange'. *Financial Times* 30 October, 1.

Bowe, Christopher (2002) 'Upstarts upset the applecart'. *Financial Times* 6 June, IV.

Brady, Simon (1989) 'Some joy in euroequities at last'. *Euromoney* May, 123–131.

Breedon, Francis (1996) 'Why do the Liffe and DTB *Bund* futures contracts trade at different prices?'. Working Paper 57, December, Bank of England.

Bromhead, Laurence (ed.) (1990) 'Who's where on world markets. How the heavyweights shape up'. *Euromoney* May, 56–68. Correction in August, 34.

Butler, Rick (1999) 'Euro bourses fight back'. *Institutional Broking and Trading Supplement* October, 30–32.

Campbell, Katharine (1989a) 'They may kick the puppy-dog'. *Financial Times* 8 March, I.

—— (1989b) 'Suspicion lingers in the pit'. *Financial Times* 8 March, II.

Campbell, Katharine and Hargreaves, Deborah (1990) 'Frankfurt fights to regain *bunds*'. *Financial Times* 26 November, 21.

Caplen, Brian (2000) 'Death of a stock market'. *Euromoney* March, 64–70.

Carroll, Michael, Lux, Hal and Schack, Justin (2000) 'Trading meets the millennium'. *Institutional Investor* January, 34–49.

Clow, Robert (1998) 'Is there a future for futures?'. *Institutional Investor* June, 101–105.

Cockerill, Chris (2002) 'A very pricey typo'. *Euromoney* January, 9.

Cohen Norma (1994) 'Waiting for the mist to clear'. *Financial Times* 3 August, 12.

—— (1995a) 'A City flea waits to draw blood'. *Financial Times* 4 September, 15.

—— (1995b) 'Bourses bite back at London'. *Financial Times* 6 November, 17.

Commins, Kevin (1987) 'Will Goliath defeat the Davids?'. Special Supplement, *Euromoney* November, 12–13.

Contract Specifications (1996) October. Chicago Board of Options Exchange.

Cooke, Stephanie (1994) 'The threat from cyberspace'. *Euromoney* December, 26–28.

—— (1996) 'Who shot Michael Lawrence?'. *Euromoney* March, 24–27.

Corkish, Jo, Holland, Allison and Vila, Anne Fremault (1997) *The Determinants of Successful Financial Innovation, an Empirical Analysis of Futures Innovation on Liffe.* Bank of England, Working Paper Series No. 70, October.

Corrigan, Tracy (1992) 'A new Liffe together'. *Financial Times* 4 February, 15.

—— (1993) 'Exchanges fight for the future across Europe'. *Financial Times* 15 January, 13.

—— (1997) 'Daunting price but high rewards'. *Financial Times* 2 May, IV.

Corrigan, Tracy and Harverson, Patric (1992) 'Ever more complex'. *Financial Times* 8 December, I.

Corrigan, Tracy and Morse, Laurie (1992) 'A global game for allies and rivals'. *Financial Times* 8 December, III.

Covill, Laura (1996) 'Survival of the fittest'. *Euromoney* August, 60–62.

Currie, Antony (1998) 'Dancing to a new tune...'. *Euromoney* August, 24–27.

—— (2001) 'A new breed of online equity firm'. *Financial Times* January, 65–68.

Dalla-Costa, Julie (2002) 'Pan-European approach starts to pay off for Virt-x'. *Euromoney* May, 46–47.

Davey, Emma (1995) 'Slow but steady convergence'. *Financial Times* 16 November, II.

Davies, Ben (1991) 'Simex keeps its edge'. Sponsored Supplement, *Euromoney* January, 47–48.

Dawkins, William (1996) 'A big bang in slow motion'. *Financial Times* 10 December, 15.

Deutsche Terminbörse (DTB) (1995) *Annual Report*. Frankfurt.

Domowitz, Ian (1993) 'A taxonomy of automated trade execution systems'. *Journal of International Money and Finance* 12, 607–631.

Dudley, Nigel (1997) 'Blue chips are ripe for conversion'. *Financial Times* November, 77–82.

Durr, Barbara (1990) 'Chicago lines up a link with Japan'. *Financial Times* 13 June, 26.

van Duyn, Alice (2000) 'European links push exchange towards US costs'. *Financial Times* 1 September, 8.

—— (2001) 'Hopes for unity are diminished'. *Financial Times* 28 March, V.

Evans, Gary (1988) 'Chicago traders' unnatural pessimism'. *Euromoney* April, 107–114.

Evans, Jules (2001) 'There's Liffe, but not as they knew it'. *Euromoney* January, 22–24.

Evans, Richard (1992) 'The banks that refused to die'. *Euromoney* May, 55–60.

—— (1994) 'Stick-in-the-mud financial centre'. *Euromoney* December, 35–37.

The Exchange (1996, 2002). New York Stock Exchange.

Fisher, Andrew (1997a) 'DTB is preparing to spread its wings'. *Financial Times* 27 June, II.

—— (1997b) 'Frankfurt exchange adds new dimension'. *Financial Times* 28 November, 21.

Gapper, John (1996a) 'Tamer required for lion's den'. *Financial Times* 5 January, 11.

—— (1996b) 'Farewell to mounds of paper'. *Financial Times* 15 July, 15.

Gapper, John and Denton, Nicholas (1996) *All that Glitters, the Fall of Barings*. Hamish Hamilton, London.

Gemmill, Gordon (1998) 'In defence of Sets'. *Financial Times* 28 May, 18.

Gordon-Walker, Rupert (1996) 'A terminal case . . .'. *Euromoney* March, 106, 108.

Gould, John F. and Kleidon, Allan W. (1994) 'Market maker activity on Nasdaq: implications for trading volume'. *Stanford Journal of Law, Business & Finance* 1 (Fall), 11–28.

Graham, George (1996) 'US-owned banks to push for order-driven trading'. *Financial Times* 21 February, 9.

—— (1997a) 'Stock Exchange to cut charges by 60%'. *Financial Times* 10 September, 12.

—— (1997b) 'All change at the exchange'. *Financial Times* 20 October, 17.

—— (1998) 'SEC breakthrough for Tradepoint'. *Financial Times* 3 July, 15.

Grasso, Richard A. (1995) 'New chairman views NYSE's future'. *The Exchange* July, 1–2.

Grinblatt, Mark and Keloharju, Matti (2001) 'How distance, language, and culture influence stockholdings and trades'. *The Journal of Finance* 56 (3), 1053–1073.

Hargreaves, Deborah (1988) 'Chicago struggles towards margin reform'. *Financial Times* 16 November, 35.

—— (1989) 'The new player arrives for work'. *Financial Times* 30 November, 11.

Harnischfeger, Uta and Boland, Vincent (1999) 'Dispute hits London–Frankfurt link'. *Financial Times* 24 February, 17.

Harrington, Henry (1996) 'Behind the remote reality'. *Financial Times* 16 February, IV.

Harverson, Patrick (1992) 'The NYSE begins to show its age'. *Financial Times* 15 May, 27.

Hasbrouck, Joel, Sofianos, George and Sosebee, Deborah (1993) 'New York Stock Exchange systems and trading procedures'. NYSE Working Paper 93-01, April.

Hau, Harald (2001a) 'Location matters: an examination of trading profits'. *The Journal of Finance* 56 (5), 1959–1983.

—— (2001b) 'Geographic patterns of trading profitability in Xetra'. *European Economic Review* 45, 757–769.

Hayes, Samuel L. III and Hubbard, Philip M. (1990) *Investment Banking, A Tale of Three Cities.* Harvard Business School, Boston, MA.

Hennessy, Elizabeth (2001) *Coffee House to Cyber Market.* Ebury Press, London.

Huang, Roger D. and Stoll, Hans R. (1992) 'The design of trading systems: lessons from abroad'. *Financial Analysts Journal* September–October, 49–54.

Iskander, Samer (1996) 'Exchanges square up for a fight'. *Financial Times* 17 December, 2.

—— (1997) 'Fierce battle rages for market share'. *Financial Times* 27 June, I.

Jack, Andrew (1994) 'The Matif success story'. *Financial Times* 14 November, V.

—— (1996a) 'The French revolution'. *Financial Times* 16 February, II.

—— (1996b) 'Matif considers 1998 euro move'. *Financial Times* 21 August, 13.

—— (1997) 'Dreaming of an alliance'. *Financial Times* 28 February, II.

Jack, Andrew, Cohen, Norma, Gapper, John, Urry, Maggie and Hamilton Fazey, Ian (1993) 'Angry City takes stock of the cost'. *Financial Times* 12 March, 32.

Jeanneau, Serge (1995) 'Interest rate futures: characteristics and market development (part 1)'. *BIS International Banking and Financial Market Developments* November, 27–43.

—— (1996) 'Interest rate futures: characteristics and market development (part 2)'. *BIS International Banking and Financial Market Developments* February, 30–45.

—— (2000) 'Global ranking of exchanges'. *BIS Quarterly Review* February, 29–30.

—— (2001) 'Activity on major exchanges in 2000'. *BIS Quarterly Review* March, 37–38.

Khan, Bushra and Ireland, Jenny (1993) *The Use of Technology for Competitive Advantage: A Study of Screen v. Floor Trading.* The City Research Project IV, September. London Business School.

Kuprianov, Anatoli (1993a) 'Money market futures'. In: Cook, Timothy Q. and LaRoche, Robert K. (eds) *Instruments of the Money Market* 7th edn, 188–217. Federal Reserve Bank of Richmond, Richmond, VA.

—— (1993b) 'Options on money market futures.' In: Cook, Timothy Q. and LaRoche, Robert K. (eds) *Instruments of the Money Market* 7th edn, 218–237. Federal Reserve Bank of Richmond, Richmond, VA.

Kynge, James (1997) 'Ingenious new ideas for futures'. *Financial Times* 9 May, II.

Labate, John (2000) 'Tarnished dotcoms hang on to Nasdaq listings by a thread'. *Financial Times* 3 November, 20.

Labate, John and van Duyn, Aline (2001) 'Nasdaq hopes it will be third time lucky in Europe'. *Financial Times* 28 March, 26.

Lambert, Richard (1997) 'NY exchange sees wider'. *Financial Times* 24 September 1997, 7.

Lapper, Richard (1995a) 'Revival for the floor show'. *Financial Times* 27 July, 13.

—— (1995b) 'Strategic global electronic connections'. *Financial Times* 16 November, III.

—— (1996) 'No longer the new kid'. *Financial Times* 21 March, 11.

—— (1997a) 'Brokers need volumes'. *Financial Times* 25 March, IV.

—— (1997b) 'Restrictions set to ease'. *Financial Times* 25 March, V.

Lapper, Richard and Mulligan, Mark (2001) 'Picture continues to darken'. *Financial Times* 28 March, VIII.

Laulajainen, Risto (1998) *Financial Geography*. Departments of Geography Series 93B, Gothenburg School of Economics.

—— (2001) 'End of geography at exchanges?'. *Zeitschrift für Wirtschaftsgeographie* 45 (1), 1–14.

Lee, Peter (1993) 'The fight to gain control of world equities'. *Euromoney* July, 42–48.

—— (1997) 'Goldman shifts oil without a spill'. *Euromoney* June, 14, 16.

Lee, Ruben (1998a) *What is an Exchange?* Oxford University Press, Oxford, UK.

—— (1998b) 'A question of ownership'. *Euromoney* September, 348–349.

Lindemann, Michael (1997) 'Tasty morsels for a ravenous appetite'. *Financial Times* 2 May, II.

Lindsey, Richard R. and Schaede, Ulrike (1992) 'Specialist vs. saitori: market-making in New York and Tokio'. *Financial Analysts Journal* July–August, 48–57.

Littmann, Annette (1991) 'Prozent oder Promille'. *WirtschaftsWoche* 10, 159–162.

London Stock Exchange (LSE) (1996) *Regulatory Guide* December. London.

—— (1997, 2001) *Fact File*. London.

Lucas, Louise (1998) 'Hong Kong pits its wits against Singapore futures'. *Financial Times* 12 November, 20.

Luce, Edward (1997) 'Light touch draws the big league'. *Financial Times* 18 March, 13.

—— (1999a) 'New technology is driving mating dances'. *Financial Times* 23 March, I.

—— (1999b) 'A local's last orders'. *Financial Times* 30 October, 9.

Luce, Edward and Boland, Vincent (1999) 'Nasdaq goes global'. *Financial Times* 6 November, 8.

Luce, Edward and Tait, Nikki (1997) 'Exchanges struggle with costs'. *Financial Times* 5 September, 13.

MacIntyre, Desmond (1991) 'Nasdaq Market Profile'. *Stock Exchange Quarterly with Quality of Markets Review* April–June, 49–52. London Stock Exchange.

—— (1992) 'Institutional transaction costs in major European markets'. *Stock Exchange Quarterly with Quality of Markets Review* Summer, 19–26. London Stock Exchange.

Maguire, Frances (1998) 'Electronic trading versus open outcry'. *ISMA Quarterly Comment* 34, July, 20–21, 25.

—— (1998/1999), 'LSE denies threat from Xetra'. *Banking Technology* December–January, 10.

Market Statistics. Measuring Trade Volumes (1995). Paris Bourse, March.

Massimb, Marcel N. and Phelps, Bruce D. (1994) 'Electronic trading, market structure and liquidity'. *Financial Analysts Journal* January–February, 39–50.

Matif (1995) *Rapport d'activite*. Paris.

McKenzie, Heather (1998/1999) 'Stock questions'. *Banking Technology* December–January, 40–43.

Metzger, Jochen (1994) *US-Börsen*. Institut für Kapitalmarktforschung, Johann Wolfgang Goethe-Universität, Frankfurt am Main.

Minder, Raphael (2001) 'Flirting with the Nasdaq can end in tears'. *Financial Times* 20 February, 12.

Minto, Robert (1997) 'The big fizzle?'. *Euromoney* September, 14.

Moran, Nuala (1996) 'Stock exchange gets fuzzy logic'. *Financial Times* 4 September, VIII.

Morse, Laurie (1992a) 'After-hours Globex has yet to live up to its promise'. *Financial Times* 1 December, 30.

—— (1992b) 'Outcry over exchange expansion'. *Financial Times* 9 December, 17.

—— (1994) 'Shift away from US continues'. *Financial Times* 16 November, II.

—— (1995a) 'CBOT and Liffe link up to trade each other's products'. *Financial Times* 16 March, 17.

—— (1995b) 'Both sides benefit from London–Chicago link'. *Financial Times* 16 March, 26.

—— (1995c) 'Chicago bourses turn volume down'. *Financial Times* 30 December, 6.

—— (1996) 'CME starts to plot strategy for euro contracts'. *Financial Times* 20 August, 18.

—— (1997a) 'Chicago exchange rethinks Liffe link'. *Financial Times* 3 February, 21.

—— (1997b) 'CBOT warming to the computer'. *Financial Times* 6 March, 19.

Nasdaq (1996) *1996 Fact Book*. The Nasdaq Stock Market, Inc., Washington, DC.

New York Stock Exchange (NYSE) (1996, 2002a) *Fact Book for the Year 1995, 2001*. NYSE, New York.

—— (2002b) *New York Stock Exchange, a Guide to the World's Leading Securities Market*. NYSE, New York.

Nickson, Clare (2000) 'Back to the buttonwood tree'. *Euromoney* June, 41–45.

OECD (1995) *Financial Market Trends* 62.

Osborn, Neil (1989) 'Running scared in the Windy City'. *Euromoney* February, 38–45.

Pagano, Marco and Roell, Ailsa (1990) 'Trading systems in European stock exchanges: current performance and policy options'. *Economic Policy* 10, 65–115.

Paris Bourse (1996) *Fact Book*. October.

Peagam, Norman (1993) 'Chicago chases market share in equity derivatives'. *Euromoney* November, 96–99.

Postelnicu, Andrei (2002) 'Invisible trades come under scrutiny'. *Financial Times* 6 June, II.

de Prati, Christian F. (1998) *Chinese Issuers in International Capital Markets*. Haupt, Bern.

Pretzlik, Charles and Boland, Vincent (2001) 'US suitors join race for UK futures exchange'. *Financial Times* 29 September, 1.

Pretzlik, Charles and George, Nicholas (2000) 'Bid battle highlights differing visions of market hub'. *Financial Times* 30 August, 8.

Raybould, Jane (1994) *London's Futures Exchanges*. The City Research Project XVII, September, London Business School.

Regas, Peter (1997) 'Liffe shows it has the strength'. *Financial Times* 13 October, 18.

Rodger, Ian (1994) 'The real time breakthrough'. *Financial Times* 6 December, IV.

Rogge, Peter G. (1997) *The Dynamics of Change, Swiss Bank Corporation 1872–1997.* Friedrich Reinhardt, Basle.

Ross, Katharine D., Shapiro, James E. and Smith, Katherine A. (1996) 'Price improvement of SuperDot market orders on the NYSE'. NYSE Working Paper 96-02, New York.

Sarkissian, Sergei and Schill, Michael J. (2001) 'The overseas listing decision: new evidence of proximity preference'. Unpublished paper, McGill University and University of Virginia, June.

Shale, Tony (1987) 'Crisis in the back office'. *Euromoney* July, 58–66.

—— (1993a) 'City-state loses its glitter'. *Euromoney* January, 42–45.

—— (1993b) 'Foreign banks scramble to win Chinese business'. *Euromoney* August, 38–40.

Shirreff, David (1994) 'MoF clings to the same old levers'. *Euromoney* February, 32–38.

—— (1997a) 'Battle for the euro'. *Euromoney* January, 50–53.

—— (1997b) 'How tough is enough?'. *Euromoney* February, 60–64.

—— (1998a) 'Exchanges – who needs them?'. *Euromoney* July, 33–37.

—— (1998b) 'Sorry Liffe, says DTB'. *Euromoney* May, 10, 12.

sigma (7/2001) *World Financial Centres: New Horizons in Insurance and Banking.* Swiss Reinsurance Company, Zurich.

Sington, Philip (1990) 'Milan's Borsa catches up'. *Euromoney* September, 281–286, 291.

Smith, Katherine and Sofianos, George (1997) 'The impact of a NYSE listing on the global trading of non-U.S. stocks'. NYSE Working Paper 97-02, June.

Sofianos, George and Werner, Ingrid M. (1997) 'The trades of NYSE floor brokers'. NYSE Working Paper 97-04, November.

Sollmann, Kathryn (2001) 'Best of both worlds'. *NYSE Magazine* 3 Winter, 40–45.

Szegö, G.P. and Szegö, V.S. (1992) 'The structure of the Italian financial system'. In: Kaufman, George G. (ed.) *Banking Structures in Major Countries* 293–331. Kluwer Academic, Dordrecht.

Targett, Simon (2001) 'It's the liquidity that matters'. *Financial Times* 28 March, II.

Taylor, Robert (1988) 'Foreigners dissuaded by taxes and stake limits'. *Financial Times* 20 July, 44.

Terazono, Emiko (1996) 'Fighting back after the crash'. *Financial Times* 13 September, III.

Tett, Gillian (1998) 'Tokyo Stock Exchange to close trading floor'. *Financial Times* 18 November, 6.

Tradeus, Trading Across Europe (1994) November. Deutsche Börse and Matif, Frankfurt and Paris.

Tokyo International Financial Futures Exchange (Tiffe) (1996) *Yearbook.*

Tokyo Stock Exchange (TSE) (2001) *Fact Book 2001.* April.

Urry, Maggie (1995) 'Nasdaq operator unveils proposals to calm critics'. *Financial Times* 22 March, 19.

Waller, David (1993) 'Germany takes stock'. *Financial Times* 7 May, 14.

Waters, Richard (1991) 'Delays to Taurus keep costs high'. *Financial Times* 11 November, 22.

—— (1992a) 'An upheaval waiting to happen'. *Financial Times* 30 January, 19.

—— (1992b) 'A tune-up for City traders'. *Financial Times* 9 April, 14.

—— (1993a) 'Reshaping the trading floor'. *Financial Times* 23 February, 8.

—— (1993b) 'Survival through a part-exchange'. *Financial Times* 22 April, 14.
—— (1996) 'Nasdaq dealers come under SEC scrutiny'. *Financial Times* 10 August, 3.
Willoughby, Jack (1998) 'Exchange or die'. *Institutional Investor* November, 107–114.
Wolman, Clive (1988) 'An empty space at the market's heart'. *Financial Times* 22 November, 22.
Zimmermann, Heinz (1998) 'Innovationsprozesse im Finanz- und Risikomanagement'. In: Popp, Werner and Zimmermann, Theo (Hrsg) *Strategie und Innovation in Universalbanken* 11–32. Haupt, Bern.
Zurich Stock Exchange (1995) *Annual Report.*

5 Banking

Abken, Peter A. (1991) 'Globalization of stock, futures, and options markets'. *Economic Review* July–August, 1–22.
Abrahams, Paul (1999) 'Great asset now being derided as liability'. *Financial Times* 17 December, II.
Adams, Richard (1997) 'Voice-brokers are lapsing into silence'. *Financial Times* 18 April, II.
Agnes, Pierre (2000) 'The "end of geography" in financial services? Local embeddedness and territorialization in the interest rate swap industry'. *Economic Geography* 76 (4), 347–366.
AH (2002) 'Pictet takes a stock-picking approach'. *Euromoney* January, 70.
Allen, Robin (1995a) 'Anomalies inhibit growth'. *Financial Times* 20 December, II.
—— (1995b) 'Classified as "pre-emerging"'. *Financial Times* 20 December, III.
Alworth, Julian S. and Andresen, S. (1992) 'The determinants of cross-border non-bank deposits and the competitiveness of financial market centres'. *Money Affairs* 5 (2), 105–133.
Anonymous (1990) 'A question of relationships'. *Euromoney* June, 145–150.
—— (1993) 'The well-kept secret'. *The Banker* October, 33–34.
—— (1995) 'Where are the players?'. *The Banker* December, 35–39.
—— (1996) 'Resist the temptation'. *Euromoney* August, 5.
Aris, Ben (2001) 'Too many banks doing too little'. *Euromoney* January, 44–48.
Authers, John (1996) 'Specialisation brings rewards'. *Financial Times* 26 November, III.
—— (1997) 'Swiss banks on funds offensive'. *Financial Times* 11 November, 8.
Baer, Herbert L. and Mote, Larry R. (1992) 'The United States financial system'. In: Kaufman, George G. (ed.) *Banking Structures in Major Countries* 469–553. Kluwer Academic, Dordrecht.
Baker, Gerard (1995) '"Japan premium" hurts bank profits'. *Financial Times* 27 October, 4.
—— (1996) 'Grasping the bad loans nettle'. *Financial Times* 29 March, 22.
Barber, Tony (1998) 'Breuer aims for the top'. *Financial Times* 26 November, 15.
Barchard, David, Cohen, Norma and Peston, Robert (1992) 'Hongkong raises Midland bid'. *Financial Times* 3 June, 1.
Barrett, Matthew (1988) 'Money managers seek market links'. *Euromoney* March, 152–154.

Bedford, Lucy (1998) 'One Europe, many benchmarks'. *Global Investor* July–August, 28–33.

Betts, Paul and Hargreaves, Deborah (2001) 'No way in'. *Financial Times* 3 May, 12.

Bicker, Lyn (1996) *Private Banking in Europe*. Routledge, London.

Birchler, Urs W. and Rich, Georg (1992) 'Bank structure in Switzerland'. In: Kaufman, George G. (ed.) *Banking Structures in Major Countries* 389–427. Kluwer Academic, Dordrecht.

Bischofberger, Alois (1996) 'The Swiss financial centre and Emu'. *Euromoney* September, 124–126.

Blanden, Michael (1995) 'The walls come down'. *The Banker* June, 22–24.

Blattner, Niklaus, Gratzl, Benedikt and Kaufmann, Tilo (1996) *Das Vermögensverwaltungsgeschäft der Banken in der Schweiz*. Haupt, Bern.

de Boerr, Hilary (1989) 'Indexing catches on'. *Financial Times* 26 October, VII.

Bokhari, Farhan (2000) 'Islam's interest and principles'. *Financial Times* 31 August, 19.

Bowley, Graham (1997) 'Sleeping giant awakens'. *Financial Times* 30 May, VII.

—— (1998) 'Deutsche to spin off $24bn assets'. *Financial Times* 16 December, 1.

Brealey, R.A. and Kaplanis, E. (1994) *The Growth and Structure of International Banking*. City Research Project Report XI. London Business School.

Brown Jr., Robert J. (1994) *Opening Japan's Financial Markets*. Routledge, London.

Buckley, Christine (1995) 'New technology helps improve standards'. *Financial Times* 27 April, VI.

Capon, Andrew (1997) 'When it pays to be different'. *Global Investor* September, 17–20.

—— (1998/1999) 'Goldman Sachs's asset management revolutionaries'. *Global Investor* December–January, 15–19.

Cargill, Thomas F. and Royama, Shoichi (1992) 'The evolution of Japanese banking and finance'. In: Kaufman, George G. (ed.) *Banking Structures in Major Countries* 333–388. Kluwer Academic, Dordrecht.

Cassis, Youssef (1995) 'Le marché finacier et les banques Suisses'. In: Lévy-Leboyer, Maurice (ed.) *Les banques en Europe de l'Ouest de 1920 à nos jours* 177–185. Comité pour l'histoire économique et financière de la France, Paris.

Cave, Andrew (2002) 'Beyond borders'. *NYSE Magazine* January–February, 14–19.

Celarier, Michelle (1996a) 'Cash return or crash and burn?'. *Euromoney* July, 32–36.

—— (1996b) 'Battle of the bulge'. *Euromoney* November, 38–50.

—— (1997) 'Picking the winning combination'. *Euromoney* March, 51–54.

Chernow, Ron (1990) *The House of Morgan*. Simon & Schuster, New York.

Chesler-Marsh, Caren (1991) 'The real issues behind bank reform'. *Euromoney* February, 33–36.

Citicorp (1995) *Annual Report*. New York.

Cockerill, Chris (2000) 'The two faces of Chinese capital'. *Euromoney* December, 46–56.

—— (2001) 'Bad debts just get bigger'. *Euromoney* June, 188–190.

Cohen, Norma (1994) 'The cost of making your voice heard'. *Financial Times* 29 November, X.

—— (1995) 'Shake-up beckons as a sleepy service wakes with vigor'. *Financial Times* 6 April, 15.

Cooke, Stephanie (1995) 'This time we're here to stay – no kidding'. *Euromoney* February, 44–50.

Cooper, Cathy (2002) 'Route to expansion lies in the European market'. *Financial Times* 5 July, II.

Cooper, Wendy (1998) 'They let the bull get away'. *Institutional Investor* February, 16–18.

Corrigan, Tracy (1997) 'Wall Street's Big Bang'. *Financial Times* 25 September, 13.

Covill, Laura (1996a) 'Votes in custody'. *Euromoney* November, 16.

—— (1996b) 'Telekom rules OK'. *Euromoney* December, 32–36.

Cramb, Gordon (1999) 'A boycott too far'. *Financial Times* 30 November, 15.

Crowe, Charles (1995) 'Treasurers put their views on banks'. *Euromoney* May, 65–72.

Dawkins, William (1996) 'A big bang in slow motion'. *Financial Times* 10 December, 15.

Delamaide, Darrell (1990) 'The Deutsche Bank juggernaut will keep on rolling'. *Euromoney* January, 33–44.

Denton, Nicholas (1996) 'Irresistible pull of the poachers'. *Financial Times* 8 June, 13.

Dickson, Martin (2000) 'Complexities will pose challenges'. *Financial Times* 14 July, VI.

Drexhage, Glenn (1998) 'There's money in ethics'. *Global Investor* February, 56.

Dudley, Nigel (2001) 'Islamic banks tap a rich new business'. *Euromoney* December, 92–97.

Dullforce, William (1990) 'Advantages may slip away'. *Financial Times* 9 October, V.

van Duyn, Aline (1994) 'Sub-custodian services survey'. *Euromoney* January, 116–118.

Eade, Philip (1996) 'Jack of all trades'. *Euromoney* April, 46–49.

Edwards, Jeremy and Fischer, Klaus (1994) *Banks, Finance and Investment in Germany*. Cambridge University Press, Cambridge, UK.

Ehlern, Svend (1997) *International Private Banking*. Haupt, Bern.

Evans, Garry (1987) 'Japan's debt and tax anomalies'. *Euromoney* September, 89–91.

—— (1992) 'The banks that refused to die'. *Euromoney* May, 55–60.

Fabre, Thierry, Talbot, Caroline and Rodriguez, George (1996) 'La banque américaine change de ténors'. *L'Expansion* 25 janvier–7 février, 517, 60–62.

Fairlamb, David (1997) 'Succeeding Sir Willie'. *Institutional Investor* June, 65–76.

—— (1998) 'Why Deutsche put its trust in BT'. *Institutional Investor* December, 19–20.

—— (1999) 'Dueling markets'. *Institutional Investor* May, 32–40.

Featherstone, James (1997) 'Looking after Latin Paper'. *Euromoney* May, 133–138.

Fidler, Stephen and Bush, Janet (1988) 'Swallowed by its offspring'. *Financial Times* 11 October, 24.

Fingleton, Eamonn (1987) 'Japanese capital is not what it seems to be'. *Euromoney* September, 57–67.

Fisher, Andrew (1996) 'Cat set among the pigeons'. *Financial Times* 21 October, II.

Fisher, Andrew, Lapper, Richard and Denton, Nicholas (1994) 'Investment banks take stock after telecoms battle'. *Financial Times* 28 November, 15.

Fitzmaurice, Guy (1989) 'The joy of being named correspondent'. *Euromoney* September, 220–227.

—— (1990) 'Strangers in town settle down'. *Euromoney* May, 123–124.

Fleck, Fiona (2001) 'Non-bank sector the new focus of scrutiny'. *Financial Times* 16 November, IV.

Fleming, Stewart (1999) 'Rules, rules'. *Institutional Investor* May, 60–61.

Forsyth, Neil (1991) 'Old questions new answers'. *Euromoney* March, 113–116.

Freeman, Andrew (1990) 'A systems challenge'. *Financial Times* 7 November, III.

Gall, Lothar, Feldman, Gerald D., James, Harold, Holtfrerich, Carl-Ludwig and Büschgen, Hans E. (1995) *Die Deutsche Bank 1870–1995*. Beck, München.

Gapper, John (1994) 'Relatively low risks and stable earnings'. *Financial Times* 29 November, II.

—— (1995) 'Contest to guard the nest-egg'. *Financial Times* 7 February, 17.

—— (1996a) 'Rush for the big league'. *Financial Times* 11 July, 11.

—— (1996b) 'End-game nears for consolidation stage'. *Financial Times* 26 November, I.

—— (1996c) 'Regulators drag their feet'. *Financial Times* 26 November, V.

—— (1997) 'In retreat from the world'. *Financial Times* 4 October, 6.

Gapper, John and Cohen, Norma (1994) 'They've really got a hold on EU'. *Financial Times* 20 April, 13.

Gardener, Edward M. and Molyneux, Philip (1993) *Changes in Western European Banking*. Routledge, London.

Gawith, Philip (1995a) 'When the empire strikes back'. *Financial Times* 3 July, 15.

—— (1995b) 'Forex surge masks maturing market'. *Financial Times* 24 October, 6.

Gehrig, Bruno (1992) 'Im Wandel der Wettbewerbsverhältnisse: Der Finanzplatz Schweiz und das Liechtensteinische Bankwesen unter Anpassungszwang'. *Finanzmarkt und Portfolio Management* 6 (4).

Gibson, Paul (1997) 'London changes the rules'. *Institutional Investor* July, 135–136.

The Global Custody Yearbook (1999). Euromoney Publications, London.

The Global M&A Guide to Advisory Services (1996/1997). Euromoney Publications, London.

Goenfeldt, Tom (2001) 'The road less traveled'. *Institutional Investor* March, 91–93.

Goldberg, Lawrence G. and Johnson, Denise (1990) 'The determinants of US banking activity abroad'. *Journal of International Money and Finance* 9, 123–137.

Goldberg, Lawrence G. and Saunders, Anthony (1980) 'The causes of US bank expansion overseas'. *Journal of Money, Credit, and Banking* 12 (4), 630–643.

—— (1981) 'The determinants of foreign banking activity in the United States'. *Journal of Banking and Finance* 5, 17–32.

Graham, George (1996a) 'Mass caterers woo the few'. *Financial Times* 19 June, I.

—— (1996b) 'Fractional fees bring cheer'. *Financial Times* 26 November, II.

—— (1997) 'Covers come off the wealth business'. *Financial Times* 26 November, I.

Graham, George and Timewell, Stephen (1997) 'City confident of keeping status'. *The Banker* November, 8–10.

Green, Milford B. and Meyer, Stephen (1997) 'International acquisitions: host and home country explanatory characteristics'. *Geografiska Annaler* 79B (2), 97–111.

Grunfeld, Henry (1995) 'Grunfeld welcomes SBC deal'. *Financial Times* 13 May, 6.

Guerrera, Francesco and Mallet, Victor (2002) 'Crédit Mutuel faces order to repay €160m of state aid'. *Financial Times* 15 January, 1.

Haga, Hirobumi (1999) 'Changing networks of Japanese banks among mega-cities in the world'. In: Aguilar, Adrián G. and Escamilla, Irma (eds) *Problems of Megacities: Social Inequalities, Environmental Risk and Urban Governance* 117–129. Universidad Nacional Autónoma de México, Mexico City.

Hagger, Evan (1993) 'Bahrain banks eye the Saudi investor'. *Euromoney* June, 107–111.

Haindl, Andreas (1991) *The Euro Money Market.* Haupt, Bern.

Hall, William (1996) 'Four core businesses in refocused international financial institution'. *Financial Times* 3 July, 15.

—— (1998) 'A center of excellence'. *Financial Times* 13 October, V.

—— (1999) 'Scourge of Swiss banks hopes for war crimes job'. *Financial Times* 9 August, 1.

—— (2002a) 'A clarion call to the "core affluent"' *Financial Times* 26 June, II.

—— (2002b) 'Economies of scale begin to kick in'. *Financial Times* 26 June, II.

Hall, William and Williams, Frances (2002) 'Geneva's oldest private banks to merge'. *Financial Times* 4 June, 15.

Hampton, Mark P. (1996) *The Offshore Interface, Tax Havens in the Global Economy.* Macmillan, London.

Harnischfeger, Uta (1999) 'State guarantees under pressure from EU'. *Financial Times* 28 September, IV.

ter Hart, H.W. and Piersma, J. (1990) 'Direct representation in international financial markets: the case of foreign banks in Amsterdam'. *Tijdschrift voor Economische en Sociaale Geografie* 81 (2), 82–92.

Harverson, Patrick (1992) 'Products before geography'. *Financial Times* 8 December, VIII.

—— (1995) 'Competition intensifies'. *Financial Times* 21 June, II.

Hayes, Samuel L. III and Hubbard, Philip M. (1990) *Investment Banking, A Tale of Three Cities.* Harvard Business School, Boston, MA.

Heinkel, Robert L. and Levi, Maurice, D. (1992) 'The structure of international banking'. *Journal of International Money and Finance* 11, 251–272.

Helk, Anja (2001a) 'Missing a great historical chance?'. *Euromoney* March, 54–64.

—— (2001b) 'Landesbanks face new dawn'. *Euromoney* August, 8.

Helleiner, Eric (1995) 'Explaining the globalization of financial markets: bringing states back in'. *Review of International Political Economy* 2 (2), 315–341.

Higgins, Kieran (1996) 'Emu will bring "18 months of hell"'. *Corporate Finance* September, 23–31.

Horvat, Andrew (1998) 'And then there were three'. *Euromoney* January, 58–61.

HSBC Group: a Brief History (2000). June. London.

HSBC Group: a Profile (2000). August. London.

HSBC Holdings Annual Report and Accounts (2001). London.

Hultman, Charles W. and McGee, L. Randolph (1990) 'The Japanese banking presence in the United States and its regional distribution'. *Growth and Change* 21, 69–79.

Humphreys, Gary (1987) 'Now customers are ringing the changes'. *Euromoney* May, 226–237.

—— (1991) 'Force-feeding makes money'. *Euromoney* May, 23–27.

Hyam, Tim (1997) 'Controlling sub-custody risk'. *Global Investor* May, 38–43.

Ioannou, Lori (1990) 'Custodians tighten their belts'. *Euromoney* July, 125–128.

Iskander, Samer (1996) 'New trends in raising funds'. *Financial Times* 22 May, VI.

Jack, Andrew (1995) 'Distinctive characteristics'. *Financial Times* 1 December, II.
—— (1996) 'Trouble behind the facade'. *Financial Times* 1 March, 19.
Johnston Pozdena, Randall and Alexander, Volbert (1992) 'Bank structure in West Germany'. In: Kaufman, George G. (ed.) *Banking Structures in Major Countries* 555–590. Kluwer Academic, Dordrecht.
Kay, John, Laslett, Robert and Duffy, Niall (1994) *The Competitive Advantage of the Fund Management Industry in the City of London*. February. The City Research Project Report IX. London Business School.
Keslar, Linda (1987) 'At the centre of the web, there's profit'. *Euromoney* December, 29–30.
Khalaf, Roula (1994a) 'The west embraces Islamic banking'. *Financial Times* 7 October, 6.
—— (1994b) 'An inherent contradiction'. *Financial Times* 15 December, 36.
—— (1995) 'Consensus still sought on important issues'. *Financial Times* 28 November, I.
Kibazo, Joel (1990) 'Sleep with a dealing machine by the bed'. *Financial Times* 14 May, VI.
King, Frank H.H. (1991) *The Hongkong Bank in the Period of Development and Nationalism, 1941–1984*, Vol. IV. Cambridge University Press, Cambridge, UK.
Kochan, Nick (1992) 'Service or sophistication?'. *Euromoney* July, 84–86.
—— (1993) 'Guardian seeks fresh role as independent'. *Euromoney* February, 112–114.
—— (1996) 'Shackling the custodians'. *Euromoney* May, 137–138.
Koenig, Peter (1989) 'Can the UBS colonels win the overseas battle?'. *Euromoney* July, 34–48.
Koshci, Sergey and Bagramov, Khristofor (1997) 'Unlocking value in second-tier companies'. Guide to Investment in Russia, *Global Investor* 2–5.
Krayer, Georg F. (1998) 'Die zukünftige Rolle des Privatbanquiers im Private Banking'. In: Basler Bankenvereinigung (Hrsg) *Private Banking – Die Herausforderung für den Finanzplatz Schweiz* 123–135. Haupt, Bern.
Kynge, James (1996) 'Malaysia sees Islamic banking boom'. *Financial Times* 3 October, 7.
—— (2002) 'Chinese banks put up some stiff resistance'. *Financial Times* 7 February, 18.
Lanchner, David (2000) 'Online and upward'. *Institutional Investor* May, 43–48.
Langdale, John (2001) 'Global electronic spaces: Singapore's role in the foreign exchange market in the Asia–Pacific region.' In: Leinbach, Thomas R. and Brunn, Stanley D. (eds) *Worlds of E-Commerce: Economic, Geographical and Social Dimensions* 203–219. Wiley, Chichester.
Lapper, Richard (1996) 'Banks battle for deals of the decade'. *Financial Times* 8 October, I.
Lapper, Richard and Middelman, Conner (1996) 'Risks of a concrete proposal'. *Financial Times* 21 August, 11.
Lebeque, Daniel (1985) 'Modernising the French capital market'. *The Banker* December, 23–29.
Lee, Peter (1993) 'The start of a global bulge bracket'. *Euromoney* April, 28–33.
—— (1996a) 'Developing a taste for equity'. *Euromoney* July, 139–144.
—— (1996b) 'Eat or be eaten'. *Euromoney* August, 28–34.
—— (1997) 'Shopping for the big day'. *Euromoney* September, 130–134.

Lewis, Julian (1990) 'Switzerland's saviour?'. *Euromoney* November, 9–10.
—— (1991) 'Investors flex their muscles'. *Euromoney* February, 57–61.
Lewis, William (1996) 'The fight for rights'. *Financial Times* 11 December, 13.
—— (1997) 'The big get bigger as the sector grows'. *Financial Times* 11 July, I.
Leyshon, Andrew and Thrift, Nigel J. (1992) 'Liberalisation and consolidation: the Single European Market and the remaking of European financial capital'. *Environment and Planning A* 24, 49–81.
Lord, J. Dennis (1992) 'Geographic deregulation of the US banking industry and spatial transfers of corporate control'. *Urban Geography* 13 (1), 25–48.
—— (1996) 'Charlotte's role as a major banking center'. In: Bennett, G. Gordon (ed.) *Proceedings of the 92nd Annual Meeting of the AAG.* Washington, DC.
Lucas, Louise (1996) 'Tactics change as fight gets tougher'. *Financial Times* 19 March, 5.
Maclaren, Andrew (ed.) (2001) *Pension Fund Indicators.* Philips & Drew, London.
Marguerat, Philippe (1995) 'La Banque Nationale Suisse et la position internationale du franc 1914–1970'. In: Lévy-Leboyer, Maurice (ed.) *Les banques en Europe de l'Ouest de 1920 à nos jours* 243–260. Comité pour l'histoire économique et financière de la France, Paris.
McCauley, Robert N., Ruud, Judith, S. and Wooldridge, Philip D. (2002) 'Globalising international banking'. *BIS Quarterly Review* March, 41–51.
Mellow, Craig (1999) 'A new role for tough cop Del Ponte'. *Institutional Investor* October, 13.
Middelman, Conner (1996) 'Fierce fight for market share'. *Financial Times* 29 April, VI.
Mikdashi, Zuhayr (1998) *Les banques à l'ère de la mondialisation.* Economica, Paris.
Moore, Philip (1996) 'The quest for a risorgimento'. *Euromoney* September, 356–360.
Morris, Margaret (1996) 'The art of buying piece of mind'. *Financial Times* 26 November, VII.
Neish, Stephen (1996) 'Boutiques for sale'. *Euromoney* October, 57–61.
Nelson's Directory of Investment Managers (1996) Vols I–II, 9th edn. Nelson Publications, Port Chester, NY.
Oakley, Tessa (2002) 'Top 5 banks take control'. *Euromoney* May, 52ff.
O'Barr, William M. and Conley, John M. (1992) 'Managing relationships: the culture of institutional investing'. *Financial Analysts Journal* September–October, 21–27.
Orlow, Daniel K., Radecki, Lawrence J. and Wenninger, John (1996) *Ongoing Restructuring of Retail Banking.* Research Paper 9634, November, Federal Reserve Bank of New York.
P.A. (2000) 'Country may be entering era of hostile bids'. *Financial Times* 8 May, 4.
Page, Rob (1997) 'Why going overseas still makes sense'. *Global Investor* September, 39–40.
Paneldiskussion (1998) 'Die zukünftige Rolle des Privatbanquiers im Private Banking'. In: Basler Bankenvereinigung (Hrsg) *Private Banking – Die Herausforderung für den Finanzplatz Schweiz* 137–162. Haupt, Bern.
Parsley, Mark (1996) 'Credit derivatives get cracking'. *Euromoney* March, 28–34.
Peston, Robert (1992a) 'Griffins and dragons'. *Financial Times* 18 March, 14.
—— (1992b) 'Lloyds Bank eyes Midland riches'. *Financial Times* 20 April, 19.

Peston, Robert and Holberton, Simon (1992) 'Lloyds Bank launches £3.6bn bid for Midland'. *Financial Times* 29 April, 1.

Pilling, David (2002) 'Japanese banker finds options have changed'. *Financial Times* 8 May, 9.

Plender, John (2001) 'In charge in Japan'. *Financial Times* 1 August, 12.

Plender, John and Fisher, Andrew (1995) 'No end to the wave of buying'. *Financial Times* 16 June, 15.

de Prati, Christian F. (1998) *Chinese Issuers in International Capital Markets.* Haupt, Bern.

Premchand, Sanjeev (2000) *Islamic Banking.* Haupt, Bern.

Pretzlik, Charles (2000) 'HSBC acquires CCF in €11.1bn entente cordiale'. *Financial Times* 3 April, 18.

Putnam, Bluford (1996/1997) 'Asset allocation in 1997'. *Global Investor* December–January, 55–59.

Rafferty, Kevin (2000) 'Big, bold but...'. *Euromoney* December, 30–35.

Rawal, Rakesh (1997) 'Obviously, it's all in the recruitment'. *Financial Times* 25 June, 12.

Riley, Barry (1998) 'Surrender in the City'. *Financial Times* 7 January, 13.

—— (2000) 'Dubious practices are outlawed'. *Financial Times* 12 May, IX.

Rodger, Ian (1994) 'Fund managers stay healthy'. *Financial Times* 6 December, III.

—— (1995a) 'The not-so-secret Swiss bank accounts'. *Financial Times* 3 February, 2.

—— (1995b) 'A discrete welcome'. *Financial Times* 7 February, 17.

—— (1995c) 'Weaknesses beneath the surface'. *Financial Times* 23 March, II.

Roell, Sophie (1996) 'Bank of China's cultural revolution'. *Euromoney* April, 148–150.

Rogge, Peter G. (1997) *The Dynamics of Change, Swiss Bank Corporation 1872–1997.* Friedrich Reinhardt, Basle.

Rose, Harold (1994) *International Banking Developments and London's Position as an International Banking Centre.* City Research Project Report XII. London Business School.

Rudnick, David (1992) 'Praying for profit'. *Euromoney* November, 23–25.

Saunders, Anthony (1994) 'Banking and commerce: an overview of the public policy issues'. *Journal of Banking and Finance* 18, 231–254.

Scheuenstuhl, G. and Spremann, K. (1992) *Banks and Financial Markets in Switzerland.* Hochschule St. Gallen, St. Gallen.

Schierenbeck, Henner (1998) 'Private Banking in der Schweiz – Märkte, Kunden, Geschäftskonzeptionen'. In: Basler Bankenvereinigung (Hrsg) *Private Banking – Die Herausforderung für den Finanzplatz Schweiz* 3–51. Haupt, Bern.

Schwander-Auckenthaler, Katharina (1995) *Missbrauch von Bankgeschäften zu Zwecken der Geldwäscherei.* Haupt, Bern.

Schweizerische Nationalbank (2001) *Die Banken in der Schweiz 2000.* Ressort Statistik, Zürich.

Shapiro, Harvey (1998) 'What's all this talk about global banking?'. *Institutional Investor* March, 137.

Shirreff, David (1995) 'Deutsche's Anglo-Saxon gamble'. *Euromoney* January, 24–29.

Shreeve, Gavin and Timewell, Stephen (1990) 'Summer wishes, winter dreams'. *The Banker* November, 74–76.

Silverman, Gary (2002a) 'Level playing field still elusive'. *Financial Times* 22 February, IV.

—— (2002b) 'Simple virtues'. *Financial Times* 26 July, 12.

Sirius, Jim (1996) 'Have giants had their day?'. *Euromoney* August, 52–57.

Skorecki, Alex (2001) 'Tracker funds forced to stalk a bear market'. *Financial Times* 17 May, II.

Spink, Christopher (1996) 'Jumps in the cycle'. *Euromoney* August, 69–70.

Spong, Kenneth (1994) *Banking Regulation, Its Purpose, Implementation, and Effects* 4th edn. Federal Reserve Bank, Kansas City.

Stewart, Jules (1998) 'More than just champagne and peacocks'. *Euromoney* February, 161–163.

Szegö, G.P. and Szegö, V.S. (1992) 'The structure of the Italian financial system'. In: Kaufman, George G. (ed.) *Banking Structures in Major Countries* 293–331. Kluwer Academic, Dordrecht.

Taeho, Kim (1993) *International Money and Banking.* Routledge, London.

Targett, Simon (2000) 'Riches keep growing for $bn industry'. *Financial Times* 14 July, I.

—— (2001a) 'An industry enjoying life in the fast track'. *Financial Times* 18 July, I.

—— (2001b) 'On track with a goal in mind'. *Financial Times* 18 July, II.

—— (2001c) 'Looking for management of their core portfolios'. *Financial Times* 18 July, IV.

Taylor, Roger (1996) 'Western funds scent rich rewards in Islam'. *Financial Times* 13 February, 17.

Tett, Gillian (1997a) 'Tokyo moves to contain Yamaichi turmoil'. *Financial Times* 24 November, 1.

—— (1997b) 'Scandals and market forces unseat Yamaichi'. *Financial Times* 24 November, 2.

—— (1997c) 'Ready for a dream take-off'. *Financial Times* 26 November, VI.

—— (2000) 'Foreign asset managers start to feel the pinch in Japanese market'. *Financial Times* 27 October, 8.

Thal Larsen, Peter (2002) 'Deal kings lose their crown'. *Financial Times* 10 June, 11.

Thornhill, John (1998) 'Russian banks claim "expropriation"'. *Financial Times* 4 September, 2.

Tickell, Adam (1994) 'Banking on Britain? The changing role and geography of Japanese banks in Britain'. *Regional Studies* 28 (3), 291–304.

Timewell, Stephen (1995) 'Where's the exit?'. *The Banker* May, 53–56.

Tsatsaronis, Kostas (2001) 'Market practice ahead of institutional structures in pricing euro area equities'. *BIS Quarterly Review* March, 13–14.

Vortmüller, Claudia (2001) *Going Public in China* [in German]. Haupt, Bern.

Wallace, Ellen (1987) 'Profiting from privacy'. *Euromoney* August, 60–62, 65.

Warner, Alison (1994) 'Under the spotlight'. *The Banker* December, 53–57.

Waters, Richard, Cohen, Norma and Holberton, Simon (1992) 'Shareholders express preference'. *Financial Times* 29 April, 22.

Whittington, James (1995) 'Moves to standardise the systems'. *Financial Times* 28 November, II.

Williams, Frances (1995) 'Weathering the recession'. *Financial Times* 26 October, VI.

Willman, John (2001) 'No concessions to EU pressure'. *Financial Times* 16 November, V.

World Wealth Report (2001). Merrill Lynch and Cap Gemini Ernst Young.

Yamori, Nobuyoshi (1998) 'A note on the location choice of multinational banks: the case of Japanese financial institutions'. *Journal of Banking & Finance* 22, 109–120.

Zlotnick, Brian (1996) 'Winning ways with insurance companies'. *Global Investor* October, 16–17.

6 Insurance

Adams, Christopher (1997a) 'On track but not out of danger'. *Financial Times* 24 March, II.

—— (1997b) 'Names and numbers'. *Financial Times* 6 June, 17.

—— (1997c) 'Lloyd's A+ rating is lower than rivals'. *Financial Times* 2 October, 11.

Anonymous (1995) 'Nine regional CATs from Chicago'. *The Re Report* 2 October, 4.

Atkins, Ralph (1996a) 'Lloyd's emerges into the daylight'. *Financial Times* 9 September, II.

—— (1996b) 'Revolution on the beach'. *Financial Times* 9 September, VI.

Authers, John (1996) 'Insurers take fresh look at disasters'. *Financial Times* 30 December, 17.

Ballantine, Robert (2001) 'Surplus lines on the rise'. *Reactions* October, 26, 29.

Bolger, Andrew (1999) 'Axa poised to cast its acquisition net wider'. *Financial Times* 29 March, 19.

Caine, Naomi (1994) 'Bermuda is top domicile'. *Financial Times* 28 March, 24.

Captive Insurance Company Directory (1995). Towers Perrin, Stamford, CT.

Carter, Robert L. and Falush, Peter (1994) *The London Insurance Market: Issues and Responses*. Association of British Insurers, London.

Challis, Simon (1996) 'Rush hour'. *Reactions* January, 26–28.

Chichilnisky, Graciela (1996) 'The future of global reinsurance'. *Global Reinsurance* North American Special Issue, 67–71.

Coburn, Andrew (2001/2002) 'Urban catastrophe'. *Global Reinsurance* December–January, 58–63.

Corroon, Willis (1994) '"Third party underwriting". Captives and Captive Locations'. *Reactions* Supplement, 12–17.

Dawkins, William (1997) 'Tokyo gives Lloyd's a licence to sell'. *Financial Times* 10 January, 6.

Day, Roger (1996) 'European captive domiciles: spoiled for choice'. *Global Reinsurance* June–August, 47–49.

Denney, Valerie (1995) 'Rating the future'. *Global Reinsurance* September–November, 145–146.

Dyson, Ben (2002) 'Out with the old, in with the new?'. *Reactions* March, 52–55.

Evans, Nick (2002) 'Bermuda: the new standard setter'. *Euromoney* January, 52.

Feller, Gordon (2001/2002) 'Indian summer'. *Global Reinsurance* December–January, 74–79.

—— (2002) 'Entry of dragon opens hidden potential'. *Global Reinsurance* June, 43–45.

Felstead, Andrea (2001) 'On the road back to profitability'. *Financial Times* 11 September, VI.

Freeman, D.J. (2002) 'True separation?'. *Reactions* May, 76.

Goddard, Sarah (2002) 'Bermuda force'. *Global Reinsurance* May, 4–6.

Goddard, Sarah, Doak, Nick and George, Saffi (2001/2) 'Technobeat'. *Global Reinsurance* December–January, 54–55.

Jack, Andrew (1996) 'A model system'. *Financial Times* 9 September, IV.

Jenkins, Patrick (1997) 'Tame cats hasten diversification moves'. *Financial Times* 5 September, III.

Jenkins, Wyn (2002) 'Made of true Bermudian stuff'. *Reactions* February, 30–32.

Kilgour, Simon and Coull, Gavin (2002) 'Law in progress'. *Global Reinsurance* May, 10–13.

Leonard, Adrian (1998) 'Good reason to be self-assured'. *Financial Times* 29 June, IV.

—— (1999) 'Tapping into the captives'. *Financial Times* 25 June, IV.

—— (2001/2002) 'Mineral rights'. *Global Reinsurance* December–January, 20–23.

Lines, David (2002) 'Market watching'. *Global Reinsurance* May, 20–23.

Luce, Edward (1997) 'A happy business medium'. *Financial Times* 18 March, 14.

Mayer, Martin (1997) 'Return from the dead'. *Institutional Investor* June, 59–62.

Moore, Kim (2002) 'Putting the squeeze on captives'. *Reactions* April, 64–68.

Munich Reinsurance Company (1996, 2001) *Topics, Annual Review of Natural Catastrophes*. München.

Murray, Alan G. and Kritz, John J. (1996) 'US reinsurers: facing consolidation and securitization'. *Global Reinsurance* North American Special Issue, 25–28.

Non-life Insurance in Japan, Fact Book 1993–1994 (1994). The Marine and Fire Insurance Association of Japan, Inc., December.

Osborn, Neil (1988) 'Taking captives by cajolery'. *Euromoney* April, 55–56.

Peagam, Norman (1989) 'Treasure islands'. *Euromoney* Supplement, May.

Pierce, Carol (2001/2002) 'Unknowingly understated'. *Global Reinsurance* December–January, 24–25.

Pomerantz, Frederick J. and Nilsen, Martin J. (1995) 'Harmonising the American system'. *Global Reinsurance* September–November, 97–101.

Rakiya, Ibrahim (ed.) (1999) *Directory of Islamic Insurance*. Institute of Islamic Banking and Insurance, London.

sigma (4/1994), *Der US Property/Casualty Markt aus europäischer Perspektive*. Swiss Reinsurance Company (Swiss Re), Zurich.

—— (1/1995) *The Performance of the Insurance Industry in International Comparison: A Risk-Adjusted Analysis*. Swiss Re, Zurich.

—— (2/1995) *The London Market*. Swiss Re, Zurich.

—— (6/1995) *Non-proportional Reinsurance of Losses due to Natural Disasters in 1995*. Swiss Re, Zurich.

—— (2/1996) *Natural Catastrophes and Major Losses in 1995*. Swiss Re, Zurich.

—— (4/1996) *World Insurance in 1994*. Swiss Re, Zurich.

—— (5/1996) *Insurance Derivatives and Securitization*. Swiss Re, Zurich.

—— (6/1996) *Asia's Insurance Industry on the Rise*. Swiss Re, Zurich.

—— (1/1997) *US: Consolidation Accompanied by Weak Growth – a Business Challenge in Property and Casualty Insurance*. Swiss Re, Zurich.

—— (2/1998) *Health Insurance in the United States*. Swiss Re, Zurich.

—— (9/1998) *The Global Reinsurance Market in the Midst of Consolidation*. Swiss Re, Zurich.

—— (2/1999) *Alternative Risk Transfer (ART) for Corporations.* Swiss Re, Zurich.

—— (4/2000) *Emerging Markets: the Insurance Industry in the Face of Globalisation.* Swiss Re, Zurich.

—— (6/2000) *Asset-liability Management for Insurers.* Swiss Re, Zurich.

—— (8/2000) *Japan's Insurance Markets – a Sea Change.* Swiss Re, Zurich.

—— (2/2001) *Natural Catastrophes and Man-made Disasters in 2000.* Swiss Re, Zurich.

—— (4/2001) *Insurance Markets in Asia.* Swiss Re, Zurich.

—— (6/2001) *World Insurance in 2000.* Swiss Re, Zurich.

—— (3/2002) *The London Market in the Throes of Change.* Swiss Re, Zurich.

Smith, Michael A. (1996) 'Play it again, Sam!' *Global Reinsurance* North American Special Issue, 19–22.

Survey of Current Business (1995–2001). Bureau of Economic Analysis, Washington, DC.

Terazono, Emiko (1995) 'Minimal after shocks'. *Financial Times* 4 September, 4.

Woodman, Jon (1996) 'Global insurance programmes'. *Global Risk Manager,* 170–171.

7 Finance centres

Agnes, Pierre (2000) 'The "end of geography" in financial services? Local embeddedness and territorialization in the interest rate swap industry'. *Economic Geography* 76 (4), 347–366.

Anonymous (1987) 'Banking moves into a new era'. *Euromoney* Sponsored Supplement, December, 7–12.

—— (1992) *Hong Kong: The Facts, Banking.* Government Information Services, October.

—— (1993a) 'Taurus done to death'. *Financial Times* 12 March, 13.

—— (1993b) 'The well-kept secret'. *The Banker* October, 33–34.

—— (1995a) 'Shanghai bid to encourage foreign banks'. *Financial Times* 12 January, 4.

—— (1995b) 'Cowardly custody'. *Euromoney* May, 94.

—— (1995c) 'A solid network for offshore entities'. *Asiamoney* September, 21–23.

—— (1997) 'At the centre of the financial web'. *Financial Times* 23 June, II.

—— (1999) 'A jurisdiction of substance'. *Institutional Investor* September, 8–9.

Authers, John (1997) 'Victim of its own success'. *Financial Times* 22 January, 13.

—— (1998) 'Banking on moving targets'. *Financial Times* 14 April, 13.

Baker, Gerard (1995) 'Still strong but less ambitious'. *Financial Times* 30 March, I.

Baker, Gerard and Urry, Maggie (1995) 'Daiwa's road to financial disaster'. *Financial Times* 30 September, 9.

Ballantine, Robert (1999) 'Germans flourish in Dublin'. *Reactions* March, 78–80.

Bank of England (1995/96) *Banking Act Report.*

—— (2002) *Practical Issues Arising from the Euro.* November.

Barrett, Matthew (1988) 'Feather-footed shuffle in the grand duchy'. *Euromoney* July, 91–94.

Batchelor, Charles, Crooks, Ed and Major, Tony (2002) 'More big money flows into London as Deutsche Bank plans a "leaning tower"'. *Financial Times* 8 February, 8.

Bindemann, Kirsten (1999) *The Future of European Financial Centres.* Routledge, London.

Blanden, Michael (1987) 'Fortress Luxembourg'. *The Banker* November, 33–35.

Blume, Marshall E., Siegel, Jeremy J. and Rottenberg, Dan (1993) *Revolution on Wall Street, The Rise and Decline of the New York Stock Exchange.* Norton, New York.

Boland, Vincent (2000) 'Bolstering its position'. *Financial Times* 27 June, IV.

Bounds, Andrew (2001) 'Flow of hot money dries up'. *Financial Times* 19 December, VI.

Brady, Simon (1991) 'Roll up, roll up'. *Euromoney* April, 65–71.

Brealey, Richard and Ireland, Jenny (1993) 'What makes a successful financial centre?'. *Banking World* June, 23–25.

Brown, Gordon (1997) 'The Chancellor on the City'. *The Banker* November, 1.

Brown Jr., Robert J. (1994) *Opening Japan's Financial Markets.* Routledge, London.

Buckley, Neil (1996) 'Leading role at the centre of the EU'. *Financial Times* 30 May, I.

—— (1998) 'Euro could spark tax dilemma'. *Financial Times* 2 June, 26.

Burns, Tom (1997) 'New venture for the colonial outpost'. *Financial Times* 24 September, II.

Burt, Tim (1995) 'Challenge from Ireland'. *Financial Times* 5 April, 7.

Caplan, Basil (1987) 'Taking its own medicine'. *The Banker* September, 81–85.

Chernow, Ron (1990) *The House of Morgan.* Simon & Schuster, New York.

Choi, Sang-Rim, Park, Daekeun and Tschoegl, Adrian E. (2002) 'Banks and the world's major banking centers, 2000'. Wharton Financial Institutions Center, Working Paper 02-36, mimeo, July. University of Pennsylvania, Philadelphia, PA.

The City Research Project (1995) *Final Report.* March. London Business School.

Cobb, Sharon C. (2001) 'Globalization in a small island context: creating and marketing competitive advantage for offshore financial servives'. *Geografiska Annaler* 83B (4), 161–174.

Cockerill, Chris (2002) 'More questions than answers'. *Euromoney* May, 90–93.

Coggan, Philip (1996) 'Out of proportion to its size'. *Financial Times* 8 February, VI.

Cooke, Kieran (1995a) 'Offshore Labuan hits snags'. *Financial Times* 19 September, 4.

Cooke, Stephanie (1995b) 'This time we're here to stay – no kidding'. *Euromoney* February, 44–50.

Corrigan, Tracey (1994) 'Firms switch staff to Hong Kong'. *Financial Times* 30 March, 35.

—— (1995) 'Funds ready if price is right'. *Financial Times* 14 September, 3.

—— (1997) 'Wall Street's Big Bang'. *Financial Times* 25 September, 13.

Cottrell, Robert (1988) 'Stock exchange recovers – bloody but unbowed'. *Euromoney* June, 142–146.

Courtenay, Adam (1996a) 'Avoidance without evasion'. *Financial Times* 19 June, II.

—— (1996b) 'The lands of the tax-free'. *Financial Times* 19 June, V.

Covill, Laura (1996) 'Playing second fiddle'. *Euromoney* March, 100–104.

—— (1999) 'Making the move to centre stage'. *Euromoney* March, 75–77.

Crisell, Michaela (ed.) (1995) *Offshore Finance Yearbook 1994–95.* Euromoney Publications, Colchester.

—— (2002) *Offshore Finance Yearbook 2002/2003.* Euromoney Publications, Colchester.

Davis, E.P. (1990) *International Financial Centres – An Industry Analysis*. Bank of England Discussion Paper 51, September.

Dudley, Nigel (1996) 'Bahrain's survival instincts'. *Euromoney* May, 124–126.

Dugan, Ann (1989) 'Playing a canny fiscal hand'. *Euromoney* October, 83–84.

Eade, Philip (1996) 'Facing up to harder times'. *Euromoney* May, 132–134.

Ehlern, Svend (1997) *International Private Banking*. Haupt, Bern.

Evans, Garry (1992) 'Bundesbank clings to power'. *Euromoney* April, 55–58.

—— (1996) 'Mitchell on markets'. *Euromoney* September, 91.

Fabre, Thierry and Jacquin, Jean-Baptiste (1996) 'L'argent sale'. *L'Expansion* 22 février–6 mars, 519, 38–61.

Fidler, Stephen (1995) 'Growing role of offshore finance'. *Financial Times* 26 April, 4.

—— (1996) 'Back to a straight and narrow path'. *Financial Times* 7 June, I.

Fisher, Andrew (1996) 'Home away from home for Germany's money'. *Financial Times* March, 3.

Fisher, Andrew and Luce, Edward (1997) 'Finance centres need global view'. *Financial Times* 2 September, 2.

Franck, Nick (1997) 'Financial centralization in Asia'. *Corporate Finance* April, 2–5.

Gapper, John (1994) 'Clouds on banks' horizon', *Financial Times* 27 April, IV.

—— (1996) 'Painful struggle back to centre of world markets'. *Financial Times* 25 October, 8.

Gapper, John and Denton, Nicholas (1996) *All that Glitters, the Fall of Barings*. Hamish Hamilton, London.

Gardener, Edward M. and Molyneux, Philip (1993) *Changes in Western European Banking*. Routledge, London.

Garner, Catherine (1997) 'Not so secret services'. *Euromoney* July, 141–146.

Garton, Robert (1996) 'Duchy is a victim of its own success'. *Financial Times* 30 May, III.

Gift Mullins, Ronald (2002) 'Taxing issues'. *Global Reinsurance* May, 14–18.

Goddard, Sarah (2002) 'Extending the city limits'. *Global Reinsurance* June, 20–22.

Goodstadt, Leo (1988) 'Hong Kong must conserve its talent'. *Euromoney* June, 147–148.

Graham, George (1997) 'Grand Cayman fights off illicit image'. *Financial Times* 10 January, 4.

—— (1998) 'Banking scandals tarnish golden reputation'. *Financial Times* 22 January, 8.

Graham, George and Timewell, Stephen (1997) 'City confident of keeping status'. *The Banker* November, 8–10.

Graves, William (1998) 'The geography of mutual fund assets'. *Professional Geographer* 50 (2), 243–255.

Gray, Simon (1997) 'Shrugging off café chatter'. *Financial Times* 28 May, 10.

Green, Milford B. (1993) 'A geography of institutional stock ownership in the United States'. *Annals of the Association of American Geographers* 83 (1) 66–89.

Green, Milford B. and Meyer, Stephen (1992) 'A temporal, spatial and functional view of investment companies in the United States'. *The East Lakes Geographer* 27, 48–64.

Grote, Michael E., Lo, Vivien and Harrschar-Ehrenburg, Sofia (2002) 'A value chain approach to financial centres – the case of Frankfurt'. *Tijdschrift voor Economische en Sociale Geografie* 93 (4), 412–423.

Grubel, Herbert G. (1989) 'Multinational banking'. In: Peter Enderwick (ed.) *Multinational Service Firms* 61–78. Routledge, London.

Haga, Hirobumi (1997) 'Banking centres and the network of international banks in Pacific Asia'. *Asian Geographer* 16 (1–2), 1–20.

Haindl, Andreas (1991) *The Euro Money Market.* Haupt, Bern.

Hamlin, Kevin (2000) 'Opening Japan's capital markets'. *Institutional Investor* June, 51–56.

Hampton, Mark P. (1994) 'Treasure islands or fool's gold: can and should small island economies copy Jersey?'. *World Development* 22 (2), 237–250.

—— (1996a) *The Offshore Interface, Tax Havens in the Global Economy.* Macmillan, London.

—— (1996b) 'Exploring the offshore interface'. *Crime, Law and Social Change* 24, 293–317.

Handley, Paul (1998) 'Singapore's Big Bang'. *Institutional Investor* September, 157–164.

Harding, James (1997a) 'Mammon comes to Shanghai'. *Financial Times* 18 March, 28.

—— (1997b) 'Shanghai's market ambition takes shape'. *Financial Times* 28 July, 3.

Häuser, Karl, Götz, Ralf-Joachim, Müller, Johannes and Grandjean, Birgitt (1990) *Frankfurts Wettbewerbslage als europäisches Finanzzentrum.* Institut für Kapitalmarktforschung, Johann Wolfgang Goethe-Universität, Frankfurt am Main.

Häusler, Gerd (1994) 'The competitive position of Germany as a financial centre as seen by a central banker'. Speech at the SUERF Colloquium , Dublin, 19 May. Frankfurt, Bundesbank.

Hayes, Samuel L. III and Hubbard, Philip M. (1990) *Investment Banking, A Tale of Three Cities.* Harvard Business School, Boston, MA.

Helleiner, Eric (1993) 'The challenge from the east: Japan's financial rise and the changing global order'. In: Cerny, Philip G. (ed.) *Finance and World Politics* 207–227. Edward Elgar, Aldershot, Hants.

—— (1995) 'Explaining the globalization of financial markets: bringing states back in'. *Review of International Political Economy* 2 (Spring), 315–341.

Holtfrerich, Carl-Ludwig (1999) *Frankfurt as a Financial Centre.* Beck, München.

Hope, Kerin (1995) 'Tax-incentive island'. *Financial Times* 24 October, 7.

Humphreys, Gary (1987) 'Bigger fish in a smaller pond'. *Euromoney* July, 83–92.

—— (1990) 'The Belgian dentist bites back'. *Euromoney* October, 54–60.

Hunt, Jonathan (2002) 'Taxing times for custodians'. *Financial Times* 5 July, VI.

Hutton, Bethan (1995a) 'Exodus to Asia has slowed'. *Financial Times* 30 March, V.

—— (1995b) 'Pessimism may be a ploy to hasten deregulation'. *Financial Times* 30 March, V.

Hyam, Tim (1997) 'Getting the best out of China'. *Global Investor* January, 9–11.

Ibison, David (2001) 'Firm signs that restructuring gathering pace'. *Financial Times* 12 April, I.

International Financial Statistics (IFS) (2002). International Monetary Fund, Washington, DC.

Irvine, Steven (1995) 'Undermining the Grand Duchy'. *Euromoney* May, 87–93.

—— (1997) 'Beijing's war on the stock markets'. *Euromoney* June, 22, 24.

—— (1999) 'Cruel and unusual punishment'. *Euromoney* September, 48–51.

James, Canute (1997) 'Revolution? No, thanks'. *Financial Times* 18 March, 12.

—— (2001) 'Playing on the level, or losing business'. *Financial Times* 19 December, VI.

James, Canute and Fidler, Stephen (1997) 'Caribbean nervous at UK power boost'. *Financial Times* 15 January, 8.

Jeune, Phillip (1997) 'US awards police $1m for foiling drugs deal'. *Financial Times* 4 January, 4.

Johns, R.A. and Le Marchant, C.M. (1993) *Finance Centres, British Isle Offshore Development Since 1979*. Pinter, London.

Kennedy, Sean (1995) 'Beijing sheds some weight'. *The Banker* March, 48–50.

Kindleberger, Charles (1974) *The Formation of Financial Centers: A Study in Comparative Economic History*. Princeton University Press, Princeton, NJ.

—— (1993) *A Financial History of Western Europe* 2nd edn. Oxford University Press, New York.

King, Frank H.H. (1991) *The Hongkong Bank in the Period of Development and Nationalism, 1941–1984*, Vol. IV. Cambridge University Press, Cambridge, UK.

Kochan, Nick (1991) 'Cleaning up by cleaning up'. *Euromoney* April, 73–77.

—— (1992) 'Service or sophistication?'. *Euromoney* July, 84–86.

Kynge, James (1997a) 'Exotics reach the major league'. *Financial Times* 9 May, III.

—— (1997b) 'Battle is on for the hub role'. *Financial Times* 19 May, 27.

Labasse, Jean (1955) *Les capitaux et la région*. Colin, Paris.

Lapper, Richard (1996) 'A tale of two cities'. *Financial Times* 12 June, II.

—— (1997) 'Brokers need volumes'. *Financial Times* 25 March, IV.

Lascelles, David (1989) 'Questions over the City's future'. *Financial Times* 22 December, 13.

—— (1999) 'The future of the City'. *Financial Times* 16 February, 14.

Lascelles, David *et al.* (1991) 'Watchdogs who did not bark'. *Financial Times* 15 November, 8.

Laurie, Samantha (1988) 'The Switzerland of the future?'. *The Banker* November, 42–49.

Lee, Peter (1996) 'Banks scrap over Target'. *Euromoney* September, 18.

Leonard, Adrian (1997) 'Novel legislation is big attraction'. *Financial Times* 24 March, Guernsey Supplement, 8.

Lines, David, (2002) 'Market watching'. *Global Reinsurance* May, 20–23.

Lord, J. Dennis (1987) 'Interstate banking and the relocation of economic control points'. *Urban Geography* 8 (6), 501–519.

—— (1992) 'Geographic deregulation of the US banking industry and spatial transfers of corporate control'. *Urban Geography* 13 (1), 25–48.

—— (1996) 'Charlotte's role as a major banking center'. In: Bennett, G. Gordon (ed.) *Proceedings of the 92nd Annual Meeting of the AAG* 209–213. Association of American Geographers, Washington, DC.

Lowenstein, Jack (1990) 'Ready to join the big league?'. *Euromoney* October, 66–73.

Lucas, Louise (1998) 'Two new indices for Hong Kong shares'. *Financial Times* 20 April, 20.

Luce, Edward (1997) 'Light touch draws the big league'. *Financial Times* 18 March, 13.

Luce, Edward and James, Canute (1997) 'Paradise under pressure'. *Financial Times* 18 March, 11.

Mallet, Victor (2001) 'Firmer stand adopted'. *Financial Times* 23 May, 24.

Mann, Michael (2002a) 'Still big business and still doing rather nicely'. *Financial Times* 6 June, II.

—— (2002b) 'Amazing growth bucks the trend'. *Financial Times* 6 June, II.

—— (2002c) 'Watch out, the rivalry is beginning to hot up'. *Financial Times* 6 June, III.

Marriott, Cherie (1995) 'Mauritius, Offshore Financial Centre'. *Asiamoney* Supplement, July–August.

Marshall, Julian (2002) 'LTCM: a cautionary tale'. *Euromoney* January, 107.

Martin, Ron (1994) 'Stateless monies, global financial integration and national economic autonomy: the end of geography?'. In: Corbridge, Stuart, Martin, Ron and Thrift, Nigel (eds) *Money, Power and Space* 253–278. Blackwell, Oxford.

Martinson, Jane (1998) 'The offshore centers' most valuable asset'. *Financial Times* 22 January, 8.

McGregor, Richard (2000) 'First big step on the long road to reform'. *Financial Times* 13 November, X.

Montagnon, Peter and Walker, Tony (1995) 'Shanghai markets await signals from the north'. *Financial Times* 18 May, 15.

Morris, Marc D. and Walter, John R. (1993) 'Large negotiable certificates of deposit'. In: Cook, Timothy Q. and LaRoche, Robert K. (eds) *Instruments of the Money Market* 7th edn, 34–47. Federal Reserve Bank of Richmond, Richmond, VA.

Murray-Brown, John (1997) 'Dublin's firm base for tax allowances'. *Financial Times* 30 July, 10.

—— (1999) 'Old centres are new havens'. *Financial Times* 4 November, II.

OECD (1998) *Harmful Tax Competition: An Emerging Global Issue.* OECD Taxation 4 (May). Paris.

—— (2001) *The OECD's Project on Harmful Tax Practices: the 2001 Progress Report.* OECD Taxation 19 (May). Paris.

Peagam, Norman (1989) 'Treasure Islands'. *Euromoney* Supplement, May.

Peel, Michael (2000a) 'Making clean work of dirty money'. *Financial Times* 7 July, IX.

—— (2000b) 'Tough questions for a tranquil island'. *Financial Times* 2 October, I.

—— (2000c) 'Good reputation crucial for offshore centers'. *Financial Times* 8 November, III.

—— (2001) 'US "failing to do enough" on financial crime'. *Financial Times* 23 June, 2.

—— (2002) 'Battle to crack down on tax evasion in offshore centres nears milestone'. *Financial Times* 20 February, 20.

Peet, John (1992) 'Financial centres: rise and fall'. *The Economist* 27 June.

Peston, Robert (1992) 'London's trade role faces invisible threat'. *Financial Times* 8 July, 7.

Petzinger Jr., Thomas (1987) *Oil & Honor.* G.P. Putnam & Sons, New York.

Picretti, Patrice (2002) The Impact of Financial Places on the Local Economy, the Case of Luxembourg Financial Center with a Focus on Technological Spillovers. Workshop on the relationship between finance and innovation. Zurich, 3–5 October.

Pouzin, Gilles (1995) 'La riche Europe des paradis fiscaux'. *L'Expansion* 2–15 octobre, 509, 68–72.

de Prati, Christian F. (1998) *Chinese Issuers in International Capital Markets.* Haupt, Bern.

Rafferty, Kevin (2000) 'Playing a whole new ball game'. *Euromoney* August, 32–35.

Rahul, Jacob (2001) 'Territory falls prey to a bout of insecurity'. *Financial Times* 16 October, IX.

Reed, Howard (1981) *The Preeminence of International Financial Centers.* Praeger, New York.

Reid, Margaret (1988) *All-Change in the City.* Macmillan, London.

Rice, Robert (1996) 'Danes challenge island attorney-general'. *Financial Times* 24 December, 6.

Riley, Barry (1991) 'Big three join battle for supremacy'. *Financial Times* 4 July, III.

—— (1995) 'A quiet phase of consolidation'. *Financial Times* 12 April, 8.

—— (1996) 'New mood of expansion'. *Financial Times* 22 May, 4.

—— (1997) 'Baby-boomers look to their old age'. *Financial Times* 9 May, I.

Roberts, Susan M. (1994) 'Fictitious capital, fictitious spaces: the geography of off-shore financial flows'. In: Corbridge, Stuart, Martin, Ron and Thrift, Nigel (eds) *Money, Power and Space* 91–115. Blackwell, Oxford.

—— (1995) 'Small place, big money: the Cayman Islands and the international financial system'. *Economic Geography* 71 (3), 237–256.

Robinson, Gwen (1997a) 'Backward in coming forward'. *Financial Times* 27 June, IV.

—— (1997b) 'Tokyo Exchange to relax rules'. *Financial Times* 18 September, 15.

Rodger, Ian (1993) 'Triple shock for principality'. *Financial Times* 30 April, III.

—— (1994) 'The Swiss are watchful'. *Financial Times* 6 October, 15.

Rogge, Peter G. (1997) *The Dynamics of Change, Swiss Bank Corporation 1872–1997.* Friedrich Reinhardt, Basle.

Rose, Harold (1994a) *International Banking Developments and London's Position as an International Banking Centre.* The City Research Project XII. London Business School.

—— (1994b) *London as an International Financial Centre: A Narrative History.* The City Research Project XIII. London Business School.

Rousset-Deschamps, Marcel (2002) 'La Bourse parisienne, équipement des services de marchés des capitaux producteur d'identité métropolitaine: témoin de l'histore ou point de réseau mondial?'. Speech at the colloquim of Comité National français de Géographie, Toulouse, 6 September.

Russia, Economic and Financial Situation (2002). The Central Bank of the Russian Federation. July.

Rutter, James (1998) 'The slow demise of a capital market'. *Euromoney* May, 87–88.

Saunderson, Allan (1994) 'Eyes off the ball'. *The Banker* March, 31–34.

Scholtens, L.J.R. (1992) 'Centralization in international financial intermediation: theory, practice, and evidence for the European Community'. *Banca Nazionale del Lavoro Quarterly Review* 182 (September).

Schwander-Auckenthaler, Katharina (1995) *Missbrauch von Bankgeschäften zu Zwecken der Geldwäscherei.* Haupt, Bern.

Sele, Cyrill (1995) *Standortkonkurrenz zwischen Finanzplätzen unter besonderer Berücksichtigung des Offshore-Geschäfts – der Fall Liechtenstein.* Haupt, Bern.

Shale, Tony (1993) 'City-state loses its glitter'. *Euromoney* January, 42–45.

Shirreff, David (1995a) 'Richard Hu's rearguard action'. *Euromoney* February, 84–87.

—— (1995b) 'A hub to replace Hongkong?'. *Euromoney* February, 80–82.

—— (1997) 'How tough is enough?'. *Euromoney* February, 60–64.

—— (1999) 'Heroes and villains'. *Euromoney* June, 31–48.

—— (2000) 'Betting on survival'. *Euromoney* June, 128–140.

sigma (7/1996) *Deregulation and Liberalization of Market Access: the European Insurance Industry on the Threshold of a New Era in Competition*. Swiss Reinsurance Company (Swiss Re), Zurich.

—— (7/2001) *World Financial Centres: New Horizons in Insurance and Banking*. Swiss Re, Zurich.

Simon, Pierre (2000) 'Forces et faiblesses de la place de Paris'. *Problèmes économiques* 2.674, 19 juillet, 19–25. La Documentation française.

Slaughter, Joanna (1995) 'Offshore sites shed "palm tree" image'. *Financial Times* 21 June, IV.

Spencer, Michael (1995) 'Securities markets in China'. *Finance & Development* June, 28–31.

Stewart, Jules (1996) 'Cleaning up offshore'. *Euromoney* April, 128–130.

Stuart, Sue (1996) 'Authorities keep pace with changes'. *Financial Times* 22 May, 9.

Taeho, Kim (1993) *International Money and Banking*. Routledge, London.

Tett, Gillian (1997a) 'Chinks in the fortress'. *Financial Times* 25 July, 21.

—— (1997b) 'Shock to the system'. *Financial Times* 31 July, 11.

—— (1998) 'A bang or a whimper?' *Financial Times* 1 April, 15.

—— (1999) 'Lawyers find a way through small print'. *Financial Times* 17 December, VII.

Tett, Gillian and Gowers, Andrew (1996) 'Walking the Emu tightrope'. *Financial Times* 16 September, 15.

Tett, Gillian and Ibison, David (2001) 'Tokyo "may have to support banks"'. *Financial Times* 14 September, 3.

Tett, Gillian and Nusbaum, Alexandra (1999) 'Busting the brokers' cartel'. *Financial Times* 1 October, 17.

Thrift, Nigel (1987) 'The fixers: the urban geography of international commercial capital'. In: Henderson, Jeffrey and Castells, Manuel (eds) *Global Restructuring and Territorial Development* 203–233. Sage, London.

—— (1994) 'On the social and cultural determinants of international financial centres: the case of the City of London'. In: Corbridge, Stuart, Martin, Ron and Thrift, Nigel (eds) *Money, Power and Space* 327–355. Blackwell, Oxford.

Tickell, Adam (1994) 'Banking in Britain? The changing role and geography of Japanese banks in Britain'. *Regional Studies* 28 (3), 291–304.

Timewell, Stephen (1994) 'Shanghai's renaissance'. *The Banker* May, 34–38.

Ungefehr, Friederike (1987) 'Offshore-Zentren (I): Bahamas'. *Die Bank* (10), 562–565.

—— (1988a) 'Offshore-Zentren (II): Cayman Islands'. *Die Bank* (1), 33–34.

—— (1988b) 'Offshore-Zentren (V): Niederländische Antillen'. *Die Bank* (8), 446–449.

—— (1988c) 'Offshore-Zentren (VI): Barbados'. *Die Bank* (11), 629–632.

—— (1989a) 'Offshore-Zentren (VII): Die Kanalinseln'. *Die Bank* (2), 105–109.

—— (1989b) 'Offshore-Zentren (X): Singapur'. *Die Bank* (7), 392–395.

—— (1989c) 'Offshore-Zentren (XI): Hongkong'. *Die Bank* (10), 572–575.

—— (1990a) 'Offshore-Zentren (XIII): International Banking Facilities in den USA'. *Die Bank* (8), 464–468.

—— (1990b) 'Offshore-Zentren (XIV): Japan Offshore Market'. *Die Bank* (11), 635–637.

Vogt, John (1995) *International Target Cities Report.* Technimetrics, New York.

Vortmüller, Claudia (2001) *Going Public in China* [in German]. Haupt, Bern.

Warner, Alison (1994) 'Border meltdown'. *The Banker* September, 56–61.

—— (1997) 'Capital working city'. *The Banker* November, 25–26.

Wells, Kathryn (2002) 'Wide off the mark'. *Reactions* February, 46–49.

Willman, John (2001a) 'Cleaning up'. *Financial Times* 21 September, 16.

—— (2001b) 'Move back onshore may gain momentum'. *Financial Times* 25 September, 3.

Wright, Robert (1998) 'Review met with clear conscience'. *Financial Times* 22 January, 8.

Yassukovich, Stanislas M. (1996) 'Why London will gain'. *Euromoney* December, 31.

Index

442   *Index*

444   *Index*

CPSIA information can be obtained
at www.ICGtesting.com
Printed in the USA
JSHW011455201219
3107JS00006B/126